Public Sector
ECONOMICS

Public Sector
ECONOMICS

C. V. Brown
P. M. Jackson

SECOND EDITION

Martin Robertson · Oxford

© C. V. Brown and P. M. Jackson 1978 and 1982

First published in 1978 by Martin Robertson & Company Ltd.,
108 Cowley Road, Oxford OX4 1JF.
Reprinted with corrections 1980.
Second edition 1982.

British Library Cataloguing in Publication Data

Brown, C. V.
    Public sector economics – 2nd ed.
    1. Finance, Public – Great Britain
    I. Jackson, P. M.
    336.41   HJ1001

    ISBN 0-85520-525-3
    ISBN 0-85520-526-1 Pbk

Typeset by Unicus Graphics, Horsham
Printed and bound in Great Britain by TJ Press, Padstow

Contents

Preface to the First Edition

Public sector economics can mean many things to different people. It is, there-fore, necessary that we make clear to the reader how we interpret our subject matter. Public sector economics examines the relationships between public expenditures, taxation and the behaviour of economic agents such as individuals, households and firms. An examination of all such relationships would be an Herculean task. We need therefore to be selective, and the relationships that we have decided to concentrate upon in this book are those that could usefully be called 'microeconomic'. Thus, little will be said about the macroeconomic functions of the public sector, which are treated at length in specialist textbooks.

When examining the micro-relationships of public sector economics we have chosen to adopt a framework that examines the expenditure side of the govern-ment budget in addition to the tax side. This breaks with the tradition of public 'finance' which has been concerned almost exclusively with taxation and has virtually ignored public expenditure.

The approach adopted in this book also differs from the tradition of public finance in that orthodox public finance textbooks provide elegant theoretical structures with very little indication of the empirical magnitudes that can put flesh on these structures. Wherever possible we provide results from recent research to give the reader some indication of relevant orders of magnitude (e.g. of the public sector), of elasticities (e.g. of labour supply) and of welfare losses from particular taxes (e.g. corporation tax).

This approach is not costless. Because we devote about half the book to public expenditure (without – it must be stressed – being exhaustive), because we have added empirical material as well as trying to be reasonably up to date on the theory, and because we are constrained on the overall length, we have had to be selective. We have said very little about local taxes, little about the inter-national taxation of companies and nothing about tax harmonisation, to name only a few particularly glaring omissions. We justify our decisions as follows. Given a constraint on overall length, the opportunity cost of a fuller treatment of taxes would have been to omit or drastically curtail the discussion of expendi-ture. We think it more important that students know something about expenditure than about some of the omitted topics.

Earlier versions of parts of this text have appeared elsewhere: part of Chapter 5 in 'The Rising Costs of Local Government Services' in *Local Government Finance 1973* Institute for Fiscal Studies (IFS); Chapter 11 in a report to the Commission of the EEC entitled 'The Impact of Government Measures on the Structure of Employment'; parts of Chapters 13 and 14 in 'Survey of the Effects of Taxation on Labour Supply of Low Income Groups' in *Fiscal Policy and Labour Supply* (IFS, 1977). An early draft of the appendix to Chapter 13 was first read to a seminar of the Belgian Institute of Public Finance in Brussels, and has subsequently been read in seminars at Edinburgh, Erasmus and Stirling Universities. In some of these cases others hold the copyright, and we are grateful to them for permission to reuse this material. We are also grateful to the London Office of IFS for permission to draw heavily on the report of the Meade Committee in Chapter 18 and to the Royal Commission on the Distribution of Income and Wealth for permission to draw heavily on their reports in Chapters 12 and 15.

Acknowledgements are particularly difficult with a textbook because our indebtedness is so wide-ranging. We are indebted to our teachers, our colleagues and our students as well as to the profession generally, and it is impossible to express this debt adequately without an inappropriately large array of footnotes. We have added references to the literature for each chapter with the primary intention of encouraging students to read widely, but these references also give at least a partial indication of our debt.

The acknowledgements that follow are limited to people who have provided specific help in the preparation of this text. We are grateful to Martin Robertson for arranging for comments from several referees and to the following individuals all of whom have commented on one or more chapters: A. Baker, J. Bonner, E. B. Butler, R. Clarke, D. Dawson, P. G. Hare, M. Hoskins, J. King, M. A. King, D. Pyle, J. Stanford, D. T. Ulph and A. Young. We are grateful to M. Smith for preparing tables and diagrams and to C. McIntosh, E. Bruce, J. A. Watson and P. A. Greatorex for typing successive drafts. One of the authors is especially grateful to those secretaries who had to cope with his handwriting which is almost illegible, while the other is grateful to his secretary who neglected her family duties so that the final manuscript was produced by the deadline.

While we both accept the blame for all of the remaining errors, those who are acquainted with our interests will not be surprised to learn that P.M.J. has drafted the expenditure chapters and C.V.B. the tax chapters.

C. V. Brown   *P. M. Jackson*
Department of Economics   *Public Sector Economics Research Centre*
University of Stirling   *University of Leicester*

February 1978

Preface to the Second Edition

The object of this book, as of the 1978 edition, is to introduce students to the concepts and applications of public sector economics. Emphasis is placed on analysis and the interpretation of data resulting from empirical work.

In this second edition we have incorporated new analysis and brought up to date the statistics and data which describe the public sector. When a subject is in the process of rapid analytical development and when its character is changing statistically this forces choices to be made when it comes to updating a textbook. We are confident that our choices have been correct and in doing so we have been guided by a large number of people who read our first edition.

A new chapter (Chapter 9) on Fiscal Federalism has been added which recognises that modern governments are stratified. This gives rise to a complex set of intergovernmental financial relationships which are analysed. Additions to the public expenditure chapters include, the theory of clubs, impure public goods, preference revelation mechanisms, majority voting with two public goods and the political theory of the business cycle. Empirical estimates of the determinants of public expenditure are also incorporated into this new edition along with new estimates of the distributional impacts of public-spending programmes. Most of the tax chapters have been thoroughly revised to include some sixty new tables and figures. In addition many figures have been redrawn for additional clarity. New analytical and empirical material has been included on income distribution, tax incidence, negative income taxes, labour supply and corporate taxation.

The revisions to this new edition have been made easier by the help and guidance which we have received from our students and from those who have sent us comments. It would be impossible to name them all but we would like to single out for special mention, Keith Hartley, Wallace Oates, Masazo Ohkawa and Terry Wanless.

We would also like to thank individuals and organisations who have provided us with data and other reading materials which we have freely incorporated into this new edition. They include the Cabinet Office, the Inland Revenue, Bob Inman, Ned Gramlich, Julian Le Grand, the OECD, HMSO and HM Treasury. The economics profession generally are also given our thanks for producing the material which forms the substance of public sector economics.

The burden of producing a new edition falls not only on the authors but on those who help with its production. We would like to thank Pat Greatorex, Shirley Hewitt and Catherine McIntosh plus the technical staff of Martin Robertson who have coped with a difficult task.

C. V. Brown
P. M. Jackson
February 1982

CHAPTER 1

Introduction to the Scope of Public Sector Economics

In every developed society there is some form of government organisation, which may or may not represent the members of the society collectively, but certainly has the co-ercive authority over them individually. As a rule the government organisation is broken up into a central government with large powers and a number of local government authorities with limited powers. The governing authority, whether central or local, is endowed with functions and duties, the detailed nature of which varies in different places. These duties involve the expenditure and, consequently, require also the raising of revenue.

A. C. Pigou, *Public Finance*

Since Pigou wrote his celebrated book *Public Finance* in 1928, the form of government organisation has changed. It has grown in absolute terms and, more especially, it has increased in size and scope relative to other sectors of the economy. Some of the specific functions and duties of government known to Pigou have disappeared, but the majority remain and have been added to on such a scale that today's functions of government bear but a slight relationship to those of 1928.

The 'mixed economy' has emerged and grown during the twentieth century. As the name suggests, a mixed economy is one that has a mixture of different means of allocating society's scarce resources among competing alternative ends. There is the social institution of the market which, through the 'invisible' guiding forces of competition, uses prices to allocate land, labour, capital and enterprise to the production of final consumption goods. Alongside the market there exist, in mixed economies, other means of allocating resources. These other allocative systems can be referred to generally as non-market allocative processes. One such non-market system for allocating resources is the public sector or the 'government organisation', as Pigou called it. Non-market allocative processes allocate resources among competing uses by means of 'allocative rules'. Such rules may or may not allocate resources in the same pattern as the market would; such rules may or may not attempt to mimic the market. One interesting

1

line of inquiry in the study of the public sector is, therefore, to examine these allocative processes and to compare them with those that would have been produced by the market.

The emergence of the UK mixed economy is shown in Table 1.1. The total expenditure of the UK government relative to the total amount of economic activity is shown for the period 1932–76. While there are a number of points that have to be taken into consideration when interpreting such statistics (see Chapter 6), the trend of the UK towards that of a mixed economy is clear. Other countries have displayed similar trends. In the United States, for example, public expenditure as a proportion of GNP increased from 21.0 per cent in 1940 to just over 40.0 per cent in 1976, whereas in Canada the ratio increased from 15.4 per cent in 1926 to 42.1 per cent in 1976.

Table 1.1   The Growth of the Mixed Economy (UK) 1932–80

	1932	*1951*	*1970*	*1976*	*1980*
Public expenditure as a percentage of GNP (at factor cost)	29.0%	40.2%	44.8%	51.4%	53.4%

The trend towards a mixed economy has come about from the expansion of government activities and from an increase in the scope of government. Thus the UK, along with Australia, New Zealand, Western European and North American countries, have expanded the socioeconomic functions of government, e.g. education, health and welfare services, social insurance, and also the protective services, e.g. police, fire and the administration of justice. Government has also expanded its scope, taking over some functions that were previously performed by the private or market sector of the economy; e.g. the public corporation/nationalised industry sector of government in the UK includes transportation, coal, gas, electricity, airports, steel, etc. At the time at which Pigou wrote his treatise these activities were in the private sector. Indeed, it is instructive to note that, of the 268 pages that Pigou devoted to his study of public finance, only 14 pages were devoted to public expenditure.

The growth of public expenditure obviously implies that taxation has also increased. Taxation in the UK as a percentage of GNP rose from 33.5 per cent in 1955 to 47.7 per cent in 1980. One of the major topics for study in public sector economics is the financing of public expenditures and the effects that alternative means of financing have upon economic behaviour. In other words, we are interested to know the effects that the public sector has upon the allocation of resources in the private or market sector and upon the distribution of welfare throughout the whole economy.

Public sector economics is, therefore, the study of the effects of public expenditures and taxes upon the economy. What functions should be performed by government? Does the financing of public expenditures through taxation reduce the growth potential of the economy by increasing inefficiency? How should an economy decide upon how much public expenditure to undertake? What causes public expenditure to grow? Do public expenditures and taxation destroy incentives? Does government action make people better off or worse off? Whom does it make better off and whom does it make worse off? What happens to market economic behaviour when one tax is substituted for another tax with equal yield? Does the public sector allocate resources efficiently between public sector activities?

These are just a selection of questions that are representative of those asked in public sector economics. This book will serve as an introduction to these problems and will, if its function is fulfilled, take the reader some considerable way down the path to answering them.

The plan of the book

Following this chapter, the next eight chapters concentrate upon the expenditure side of the government's budget. Up until now we have taken the existence of government and what it does as given. We all know that the public sector exists. Most of us in the UK were born in public sector hospitals, are tended by public sector doctors, were educated in public sector schools, colleges and universities, play in public sector parks, are protected by the public sector, will end up in public sector hospitals when we are old and will be buried in public sector graveyards; and, if our survivors require it, a death grant will be paid to help with the cost of disposing of our remains! The public sector is ubiquitous and we know it, especially when we pay taxes!

But why does the public sector exist? Why does the government perform the functions and produce the activities that it does? Is there a logical and well articulated argument that can be presented to explain the socioeconomic rationale of the state, or are the state's functions to be explained by referring to ideology? This is the question that is set out and answered in Chapter 2.

Questions of the rationale of the state can be reduced in many instances to an examination of private sector collective action v. public sector collective action. In considering the logic of choosing certain topics for inclusion in this book, it is useful to look at a simple example of collective action. This example will serve to highlight some of the problems that public sector economics analyses.

Private *v*. public collective action

Imagine that a local community is plagued by mosquitoes or wasps. These insects carry disease and are a health hazard. Individuals, therefore, are strongly motivated to reduce the unwanted effects of mosquitoes/wasps. There are a number of alternative technologies that are available to the individual to deal with the problem. Each technology differs with respect to its effectiveness and also with respect to its unit cost. These alternatives along with a description of their cost and effectiveness are listed as follows.

(1) Reduce the amount of time spent out of doors, thereby reducing the probability of coming into contact with the mosquitoes/wasps. This is effective only if no wasps enter the house. It is cheap in terms of there being no direct outlay cost but there is an opportunity cost of giving up outdoor activities. For the purposes of example we note the opportunity cost element but assign a zero price (cost) to this alternative; £0.

(2) It would be possible to stay indoors but to install air conditioning, thereby eliminating the need to have windows open and thus reducing the probability of mosquitoes/wasps entering the house. The direct outlay cost is £100.

(3) The individual might decide that his freedom to enjoy outdoor activities is too important and therefore would choose to use anti-mosquito creams and sprays which are applied to his person at regular intervals in order to keep the mosquitoes at bay. The cost of such creams is £1.

(4) It may be possible for the individual to carry out a private spraying campaign in his garden in an attempt to keep the mosquitoes away from the vicinity of his house. This would cost £20.

(5) Finally, if an aircraft were chartered and the breeding grounds of the mosquitoes/wasps were sprayed with chemicals, then the problem would be eradicated at source. The cost of this alternative is £5000.

Now it is clear that each of these technologies differs in its effectiveness to deal with the problem. The technologies are not mutually exclusive but we will assume that the individual will choose one of them. Acting on his own, the individual's choice is very much dependent upon the prices of the alternatives in relation to his budget constraint. Thus, for most individuals, while alternative (5) may be desired on grounds of its effectiveness, it will not be budget-feasible. The remaining four options will be chosen by individuals in accordance with their incomes.

A set of different solutions, therefore, emerges for individuals acting on their own. These solutions will, on 99 per cent of occasions, be distributed over the first four options because, in addition to its cost, the fifth option suffers from another problem. If some rich member of the community decided that he would charter an aircraft etc. then everyone else in the local community would benefit as a result of his action. Everyone would be free of the health hazard that the mosquitoes bring and could, therefore, throw away their sprays and creams and reduce their own costs. In other words, such individuals would get a 'free ride' following from the actions of a single individual. They would be able to enjoy the benefits without paying the costs.

This notion of the *free-rider* will occupy our attention in Chapter 2 and throughout many other parts of the book. We will see that it is difficult to extract payment from the free-rider. Thus the rich man in the community may not feel so benevolent as to give everyone else a free ride and will therefore not choose alternative (5). (The reader should try to work out under what conditions he would choose alternative (5) irrespective of the free-riders.)

Under these conditions, the most effective alternative is unlikely to prevail. But there is another means by which individuals may arrange their consumption. While alternative (5) may be too expensive for each individual, and while no individual may feel inclined to bear the full cost and allow everyone else a free ride, it is, however, possible that individuals would join together as a group or as a consumers' co-operative and charter the aircraft collectively. That is, suppose there are 1000 people in the local community; if each paid an equal share of the total cost of £5000, then each person could enjoy the benefits of the most effective technology at a price of £5. Collective action would make alternative (5) budget-feasible.

Individuals will join a group or a collective if the benefits they gain are greater than the costs of joining. There are many examples of collective action and, indeed, individuals are more likely to act in groups than as isolated individuals. Consider the family, sports clubs, trades unions, professional associations, work groups, research teams, firms, political parties, pressure groups, etc. - all are examples of everyday collectives. In each case there are advantages of joint action. There may be economies of scale or a synergy effect in performing some task, or advantages in spreading the very high fixed costs of some indivisible consumption good (like a golf course) between many individuals.

The public sector is also clearly a form of collective action. Individuals join together to provide goods and services for their common consumption and to spread the costs. Let us now use this notion of collective action to set out some of the themes in the chapters that follow.

(1) Why are some activities organised through private collective action (i.e. the market etc.) whereas other activities are organised through public collective action? This is the focus of attention in Chapter 2.

(2) How should we decide upon how much of the collective good to produce? How should resources be allocated? This is discussed in Chapters 3 and 7.

(3) How should we allocate the costs of providing the collective good among the members of the collectivity? This is introduced in the appendix to Chapter 3 and developed in more detail in Chapter 21.

(4) In contrast to the normative questions of (2) and (3), we ask how *are* collective decisions made? How do individuals express their demands within a group setting? How are these individual demands 'added up' in coming to a group decision? What are the problems of organising large groups? i.e. if we are not going to make cardinal interpersonal comparisons between individuals,

then how will a collection of individuals arrive at a collective decision? This is discussed in Chapter 4 and elaborated in Chapter 8.

(5) Does everyone enjoy the benefits of the collective good equally? How are the benefits and costs distributed? Who benefits and who pays? This kind of question runs throughout the book but is dealt with in some detail in Chapters 13, 15, 20 and 21.

Given that it is the public sector and public collective action that we are studying, then on the expenditure side we ask what factors have contributed to the growth of the public sector (Chapter 5) and what the changing trends and patterns of public expenditure and taxation look like in the UK and other countries (Chapter 6). The costs of collective public action are met from tax revenues. What tax revenues does the government have at its disposal and what are the effects of different taxes on the behaviour of the individual? How do taxes affect his decisions to spend, to save, to work, to take risks, etc.? These questions of taxation are discussed in Chapters 11, 12, 14, 15, 17, 18 and 19.

Incomes are unequally distributed. The meaning and the measurement of inequality and its underlying causes are examined in Chapter 13, while Chapter 14 considers alternative means by which members of a collectivity such as the state can, through a system of transfer payments and taxation, reduce income inequality and poverty. Wealth taxation is examined in Chapter 16.

Members of a sports club or a professional association or any other private collectivity must observe the rules of group membership or run the risk of expulsion and hence the loss of benefits from that group. Having left one group they may be able to join another, but while they hold membership of any group, they surrender an amount of their own personal freedom and liberty to pursue their own self-interest, and instead 'contract' to serve the collective interests of other members in the group. Likewise with public collectivities. In the beginning, individuals implicitly make a social contract to agree to the 'constitution', i.e. the basic rules of the group, including rules about how group decisions will be made. However, in the case of a group like the state, if an individual doesn't like the rules of the group then it becomes more difficult to move to another group because this implies moving to another country. The state also has a number of sanctions embodied in its system of laws to deal with those who do not conform. This is particularly true in the case of taxation. Whereas the free-rider could exist under private voluntary arrangements, it is more difficult for him to escape payment of his subscription/membership dues (taxes) for public collective action. Because the state has the power to coerce individuals to pay taxes, to modify their behaviour, to allocate and distribute resources in a particular way, then actions that would not be feasible under voluntary arrangements become possible under the organisation of the state.[1]

These are the problems that will occupy our attention in the chapters that follow. As is seen, the approach that is adopted is microeconomic. The remainder of this chapter will place modern public finance in an historical context and this will be followed by a review of some basic microeconomics which are used throughout the text.

Public finance in the history of economic thought[2]

Public sector economics is one of the fastest growing fields of theoretical and applied microeconomics. Many of the most difficult theoretical problems in economics are found in this branch of the subject, along with the most tricky empirical questions. Like other fields in economics, especially international trade, developments in public sector economics were constrained by the extent of our knowledge of microeconomic theory. Developments in microeconomic theory, especially general equilibrium analysis, during the 1950s provided a quantum jump for public sector economics. Now theoretical developments in public sector economics contribute directly to microeconomic theory.

In the majority of colleges and universities, public sector economics is still taught under the heading of 'public finance'. However, in the history of the subject public finance is considered to be a much narrower field of study which concentrates upon the taxation side of the budget. Public sector economics is more general and recognises the transition that has taken place from public finance to the theory of 'public choice' which incorporates both sides of the budget, public expenditure and taxation.

Although this name is normally associated with the theory of markets, Adam Smith clearly had a theory of the state and a theory of public finance.[3] In a very famous passage, Smith sets out the functions of the state as he saw them to be:

> According to the system of natural liberty, the sovereign has only three duties to attend to; three duties of great importance, indeed, but plain and intelligible to common understanding; first, the duty of protecting the society from the violence and invasion of other independent societies; second, the duty of protecting, as far as possible, every member of society from the injustice or oppression of every other member of it, or the duty of establishing an exact administration of justice; and third, the duty of erecting and maintaining certain public works and certain public institutions, which it can never be for the interest of any individual, or small number of individuals, to erect and maintain because the profit could never repay the expense of any individual or small number of individuals, though it may frequently do much more than repay it to a great society.[4,5]

For Alfred Marshall, public finance was confined to theories of tax shifting and tax incidence. Marshall used tax shifting in the context of a partial equilibrium analysis to illustrate the principles of price theory:

> there is scarcely any economic principle which cannot be aptly illustrated by a discussion of the shifting of the effects of some tax.[6]

Marshall's comparative static analysis provided a positive theory for analysing the relative price and output effects of alternative taxes on individuals and firms (see Chapter 12 below, which is in part within the Marshallian tradition). As Buchanan points out,[7] this part of public sector economics is essentially applied price theory. As price theory (microeconomics) has developed sophisticated techniques, so too has tax incidence analysis, so that the partial equilibrium analysis is now accommodated in a general equilibrium framework (see Chapter 13 below).

In addition to Marshall's positive theory of tax incidence, the period up until the 1950s also had a normative theory of taxation based on Pigou's[8] utilitarian approach to the question of how the tax burden should be allocated between individuals (see appendix to Chapter 3 below and Chapter 21).

The Marshallian–Pigovian traditions in public finance were characteristic of the treatment of the subject in Britain and North America until about the mid-1950s. There were two important omissions from the subject at that time: first, the public expenditure side of the budget was not discussed, and second, the process of collective decision-making was completely ignored. Those gaps in the Anglo-Saxon tradition of public finance should be compared with the traditions that existed in parallel in Scandinavian and other European countries.

In the 1880s the continental economists Wicksell, Mazzola, Panteleoni, Sax and De Viti De Marco had started to analyse the public economy in an exchange framework.[9] These economists were the originators of the ideas and models that are presented in their modern form in Chapters 3, 4 and 5.

Wicksell's work is worthy of particular attention since his analysis has probably done more to inspire the current 'public choice' school, which is characterised by the work of James Buchanan and his colleagues at the Centre of Public Choice at the Virginia Polytechnic Institute. Wicksell brought together the expenditure and the tax side of the accounts and clearly saw public sector decision-making as an exercise in political and collective choice. Wicksell's work, once it had been translated into English,[10] provided the basis upon which some of the future empirical and theoretical developments were to be made. The public-choice school focuses upon government behavioural postulates of the economist's paradigm, i.e. individuals are self interested and rational utility maximisers. Moreover, it is the behaviour of the principal agents in political decision-making which is of interest. The interaction of voters, politicians and bureaucrats who together produce final outcomes in terms of the levels and mixes of public outputs and taxes. Is the voter sovereign or is the bureaucrat all powerful? It is the behaviour of individual economic agents and not some corporate entity such as 'the government' or 'the nation state' which is analysed. In this respect the public-choice school is firmly rooted in the tradition established by Wicksell who rejected anthropomorphism or the re-ification of the state. By examining the behaviour of bureaucrats in addition to that of voters the public-choice school has opened up the 'black box' of public sector decision-making and has brought together both the demand and the supply sides of the public sector equation. Whilst the public-choice school has become well established in the US this approach is comparatively new in the UK. Buchanan

(1979) suggests that the UK economist's lack of proper regard to the problems raised in the public-choice literature is due to the dominance of the standard equilibrium public-finance literature. Buchanan remarks: 'In Britain, you surely held on longer than most people to the romantic notion that government seeks to do good in some hazily defined Benthamite sense, and furthermore, to the hypothesis that government could, in fact, accomplish most of what it set out to do.'

In Sweden, Erik Lindahl,[11] in 1919, generalised Wicksell's analysis by looking more closely at the relationship between standard efficiency norms and the political bargaining process. Indeed, modern general equilibrium theorists have generalised Lindahl's analysis further in an attempt to examine the properties of a public sector equilibrium or 'Lindahl equilibrium' – see Chapter 3 below where this is discussed in greater detail.

The paradigmatic shift in the Anglo-Saxon tradition of public finance was not sudden and dramatic. It did not emerge from a rediscovery of the European theory of the public economy – these earlier studies were translated into English after the change had taken place. Instead, the change occurred gradually over the period from the late 1930s to the mid-1950s. The pathway was cleared and the foundations for change were laid in a series of articles which, when taken together, gathered momentum.

The first person to present the central ideas of the 'voluntary exchange' theory of the public economy was Richard A. Musgrave[12] in 1938. This was followed up in 1943 by Howard Bowen's celebrated work on the theory of the demand for public goods and voting[13] and in 1949 by Buchanan's[14] critique of Pigou's normative analysis employing a Wicksellian framework to do so.

Developments during the 1950s and 1960s accelerated. Since these developments constitute the basis of the chapters that follow, we do nothing other than signpost them here. The theory of the demand for public goods was set down by Samuelson[15] in 1954. The earlier work of Bowen into voting problems was generalised by Black[16] in 1948, and Arrow[17] in 1950 examined the logical problems of collective choice and the social welfare function. Collective choice, decision-making rules and voting procedures were combined into a theory of public choice by Buchanan and Tullock[18] in 1962, while the microeconomic behaviour of political parties was presented by Downs[19] in 1957 and the theory of bureaucracy by Tullock[20] in 1965 and by Niskanen[21] in 1971.

The synthesis of the expenditure and tax sides of the public sector budget has been made but is certainly not complete.

Modern public sector economics is an exciting and challenging branch of economics in which many problems remain to be solved. The developments in the subject, which are outlined above, are only a selection of the principal landmarks. Other major developments will be presented in much greater detail throughout the book.

An examination of the development of the ideas of a subject is instructive. It serves to place current theories in perspective and helps to give a fuller

appreciation of the problems that these theories are designed to solve. One of
the tragedies of the way in which modern economics is taught is that by
omitting the historical perspective, the purpose of modern economics is often
obscured. Wherever possible, the reader should take a look back; unlike the case
of Lot's wife, it will pay dividends.

Review of some basic microeconomics[22]

This book is about the microeconomics of the public sector. The purpose of
this section is to review the basic microeconomic concepts that are used in
subsequent chapters.

We saw above that the allocation of society's scarce resources may take place
through the market or alternatively through some non-market allocative device
such as the public sector. In either case, the allocative system integrates the
separate goal-seeking activities of individuals. Microeconomics is concerned
about the behaviour of individual economic agents; individuals in their capacity
of consumer, producer, voter, politicians, bureaucrat, etc. Microeconomics
postulates that individual behaviour can be analysed by identifying the objective
that the individual seeks to satisfy and the constraints that force him to choose
one means of achieving that objective, rather than another. Objectives, incentives
and constraints, therefore, play a central role in microeconomic analysis.

Frequently economic analysis is criticised because it is considered to be un-
realistic in its choice of objective function and, therefore, in its explanation of
economic behaviour. While such criticisms may, on some occasions, be justified,
they generally stem from a mistaken view of the purpose of economic theory
and economic analysis. Reality is complex, and in order to deal with such
complexity any discipline, including economics, has to abstract from reality;
in so doing assumptions are made which simplify the analysis, thereby making
it tractable. By assuming that consumers and voters seek to maximise their
utility or that producers attempt to maximise their profits while bureaucrats
maximise their budgets, economic analysis is an approximation to reality. Having
made the approximation, it is then possible to apply the techniques of optimisation theory (i.e. maximising an objective function subject to a constraint(s)) in
order to see how changing certain variables such as prices, incomes or taxes may
affect behaviour. Economic theory, therefore, predicts how individuals might
behave under alternative conditions. These predictions constitute testable
hypotheses which, if the theory is any good, will conform to the general pattern
of observed regularities as they appear in reality. Such theories do not state that
individuals *do* behave in accordance with the description of the abstract model;
instead, they state that individuals behave 'as if' they maximised a particular
objective function subject to constraints. The distinction may be subtle but it is
nevertheless important. Any reader who is not convinced should accept the
following challenge – take a theory whose assumptions you don't like because

of their lack of reality; replace them by those assumptions you prefer; but do not stop there – now proceed to perform the analysis. If you succeed in getting through the analysis, congratulations – write up your results and publish them! If you don't, then at least you might appreciate why we make simplifying assumptions!

The type of economic analysis described above should be contrasted with that of behavioural theory. Behavioural theories are much more descriptive. They outline in detail the institutional and organisational constraints that face economic actors in specific situations. They are extremely important and useful for explaining behaviour, in particular organisational settings, but because they are specific they lose a great deal of generality, and therefore their predictions cannot be used with any certainty in other situations. The abstract theories and the behavioural theories have their own specific uses which should always be borne in mind.

Another source of confusion about economic theories lies in the distinction between normative and positive analysis. Positive economics answers the question, 'What is reality like?' Normative economics is concerned with policy issues that attempt to answer the question, 'What *should/ought* to be done?' In order to answer the 'ought' question, a social or policy objective is set up and economic analysis then proceeds to seek out efficient means of attaining the desired end.

Finally, the economist may use partial or general equilibrium analysis. In partial equilibrium analysis the relationship between two variables such as price and quantity are examined, as in the case of the standard demand and supply analysis. Other variables such as incomes and other relative prices are held constant (i.e. *ceteris paribus*). Feedback effects resulting from changes in prices and quantities on, say, factor incomes are omitted from the analysis, and further simplifications such as linear approximations of demand and supply curves are frequently made. On the other hand, general equilibrium analysis starts off from a set of axioms and allows all variables in the system to interact with one another as the equilibrium (if it exists and if it is unique) is established. Partial equilibrium is, therefore, used to estimate the impact of a change on the economy, e.g. a tax change, when the complete solution of a general equilibrium system is not required.[23]

Given the above remarks, let us now summarise the main results in welfare economics and price theory.

(1) Welfare economics and pricing; summary notes

Let X and Y be any two goods, K and L be any two factors, and 1 and 2 any two consumers. Let p_x, p_y, p_k and p_l be prices of X, Y, K and L respectively.

(a) *Definitions.* MRS_{xy} = marginal rate of substitution *of* X *for* Y, = amount of Y that a consumer must surrender to compensate for the gain of one

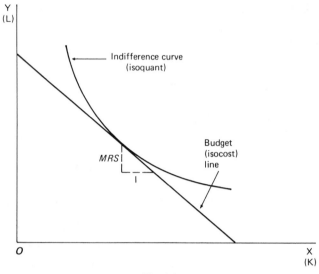

Fig. 1.1

(marginal) unit of X (substituting X for Y) in order that he remain on the same indifference curve. A simple geometrical argument (see Figure 1.1) shows that MRS_{xy} is the numerical value of the slope of the indifference curve along which the consumer is moving, evaluated at the point from which he starts (here X is on the horizontal and Y on the vertical axis).

MRS_{kl} = marginal rate of substitution *of* K *for* L, = amount of L that a producer must surrender to compensate for the gain of one (marginal) unit of K in order that he remain on the same isoquant (equal product curve). MRS_{kl} is the slope of the isoquant (where the isoquant map is drawn with K on the horizontal and L on the vertical axis). Note that since $MP_l \cdot MRS_{kl}$ is the marginal product of the amount of L surrendered, while MP_k is the marginal product of the (one) unit of K gained, in order that output remain constant we must have $MP_l \cdot MRS_{kl} = MP_k$, or $MRS_{kl} = MP_k/MP_l$.

MRT_{xy} = marginal rate of transformation *of* Y *into* X, = amount of Y that must be given up in order to produce one more (marginal) unit of X, assuming efficient reallocation of factors. MRT_{yx} is the slope of the production possibility frontier (transformation curve). Note that, since $MC_y \cdot MRT_{yx}$ is the marginal cost of the amount of Y given up, while MC_x is the marginal cost of the (one) marginal unit of X gained, efficient allocation must require $MC_y \cdot MRT_{yx} = MC_x$, or $MRT_{yx} = MC_x/MC_y$. We can call MRT_{yx} the opportunity cost of X in terms of Y.

If we think geometrically of the consumer seeking the highest indifference curve allowed by his given budget line, we see that his equilibrium position is at the point of tangency between the budget line and an indifference curve (see

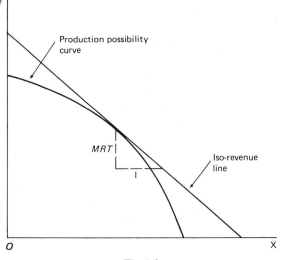

Fig. 1.2

Figure 1.1). At this point the slope of the budget line (ratio of commodity prices p_x/p_y) equals the slope of the indifference curve (MRS_{xy}). Similarly, the producer's 'minimise cost for given output' or 'maximise output at given cost' problem requires tangency of isocost line and isoquant (in equilibrium), and thus equality between factor price ratio p_k/p_1 and MRS_{k1}. Finally, maximum value of output will be attained at the point of tangency between the production possibility frontier and the highest isorevenue line that still touches it; and at this point, MRT_{yx} will equal p_x/p_y, (see Figure 1.2). Thus under perfect competition (which ensures that prices are *given* for any individual), for the consumer $MRS_{xy} = p_x/p_y$, while for the producer

$$\frac{p_k}{p_1} = MRS_{k1} = \frac{MP_k}{MP_1}$$

and

$$\frac{p_x}{p_y} = MRT_{yx} = \frac{MC_x}{MC_y}.$$

(*b*) *The Paretian marginal conditions for an economic 'optimum'*. ('Pareto optimum', 'efficient allocation of resources'): a Pareto optimum is an allocation of resources such that no member of the community can be made better off ₊without some other individual being made worse off. The necessary conditions for such an allocation are the following.

(1) $MRS^1_{xy} = MRS^2_{xy}$. The marginal rate of substitution between *any* given pair of goods should be the same for *all* consumers who consume both goods. For suppose this condition were violated – say, for example, $MRS^1_{xy} = 2$ and $MRS^2_{xy} = 3$. Then at the margin, for consumer 1, one unit of X will substitute for two of Y, while for consumer 2, one unit of X will substitute for three of Y. Then consumer 1 could swap with 2, giving up one unit of X, for which 2 would be willing to relinquish three of Y; but 1 requires only two of Y in compensation, so that this swap could leave both 1 and 2 as well off as before, while releasing a unit of Y to be allocated as desired between them, thereby finally raising at least one of them to a higher indifference curve. Thus the original allocation must have been inefficient – it was in fact possible to make one better off without making the other worse off.

(2) $MRS^x_{kl} = MRS^y_{kl}$. The marginal rate of substitution between any given pair of factors should be the same in the production of *all* goods for which both factors are used. By an argument exactly analogous to that above, we see that if this condition were violated, the output of one of the commodities could be increased without decreasing the output of the other (while using the same amounts of both factors).

(3) $MRS_{xy} = MRT_{yx}$. The marginal rate of substitution between *any* given pair of goods for any consumer (since, by (1), these MRS_{xy}'s are the same for all consumers in an optimum, we take one to do for all) should be the same as the marginal rate of transformation between those two goods in production. Thus the rate at which any consumer is willing to substitute X for Y (the amount of Y he will give up to get a marginal unit of X) should equal the rate at which Y can be 'transformed into' X (the amount of Y that must be given up to produce a marginal unit of X). If this condition were violated, we could make someone better off while making no one else worse off, merely by reallocating production as between X and Y.

Under perfect competition, these three conditions would be satisfied (in the absence of any of the qualifications we shall introduce below). For p_x and p_y would be the same to all consumers, each of whom would equate MRS_{xy} to their ratio; so that all MRS_{xy}'s would be equal, and (1) would hold. Similarly p_k and p_l would be the same to all producers, so that all MRS_{kl}'s would be equal, satisfying (2). Finally, all MRS_{xy}'s, being equal to p_x/p_y, would therefore equal any MRS_{yx}, which any producer who produced both would also equate to p_x/p_y (as would any pair of producers, one producing X and the other Y). Thus a Pereto optimum could be sustained by a competitive equilibrium.

Geometrically, the first condition can be represented by an Edgeworth–Bowley 'box diagram', the axes of which represent given quantities of X and Y to be allocated between 1 and 2 (whose indifference maps are drawn with the origins at the south-west and north-east corners of the box, respectively) (see Figure 1.3). The '*contract curve*' (the locus of points of tangency between indifference curves) represents the (infinite) set of possible 'efficient' allocations

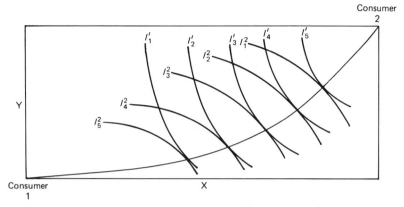

Fig. 1.3 Exactly the same box diagram illustrates efficient allocation of factors between producers: the isoquants of the producer of X originate from the south-west corner, those of the producer of Y from the north-east corner; the horizontal axis measures the quantity of capital available to allocate between the producers, the vertical axis the quantity of labour.

(in the sense of condition (1)); at each such point,

$$MRS^1_{xy} = \frac{p_x}{p_y} = MRS^2_{xy};$$

but each point represents a different *distribution* of X and Y between 1 and 2. This curve is the 'exchange efficiency' locus. Similarly, condition (2) is represented by a box diagram whose axes measure given quantities of K and L to be allocated between producers of X and Y; X-isoquants are drawn from the south-west origin and Y-isoquants from the north-east, and the contract curve which is the locus of their points of tangency is also the locus of efficient allocations of K and L in the sense of (2), i.e. at each point $MRS^x_{Kl} = MRS^y_{Kl}$. But each point on this contract curve represents a different efficient allocation of production between X and Y. Thus if we 'transfer' this contract curve to another diagram with X- and Y-axes, we get the production possibility curve, each point of which shows the maximum amount of Y that could be produced given that a certain amount of X were to be produced (assuming that the amounts of K and L to be used were the same as those shown on the axes of the original box diagram.

Now if we pick a point on the production possibility curve (i.e. a point representing levels of production of X and Y, with efficient allocation of K and L), this will define axes for a box diagram of the first kind (see Figure 1.4). This box diagram will generate a contract curve, each point of which will have

$$MRS^1_{xy} = \frac{p_x}{p_y} = MRS^2_{xy}.$$

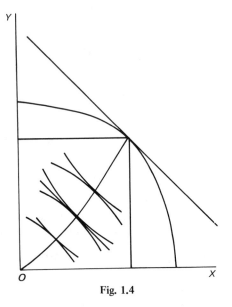

Fig. 1.4

Pick *that point* on this contract curve for which

$$MRS_{xy} = \frac{p_x}{p_y} = MRT_{yx},$$

where MRT_{yx} is the slope of the production possibility curve at the point we chose originally. The point now arrived at will represent certain levels of 'utility' for 1 and 2. Transfer it to a final diagram whose axes measure the levels of utility attained by 1 and 2 (see Figure 1.5). Each point on the production possibility curve will determine such a point on our 'utility diagram'; call the locus of all such points the 'utility possibility curve' (or 'welfare frontier'). Then *any* and *every* point on this curve represents a Pareto optimum which satisfies *all three* of our marginal conditions; they are all efficient points, and as Pareto optima they differ only in the distribution of income between individuals 1 and 2.

Why is this so? Let us recapitulate the argument used to derive this curve. We start with given supplies of K and L; their efficient allocation yields a production possibility curve, at each point of which $MRS_{Kl}^x = MRS_{Kl}^y$. Now allocating efficiently between 1 and 2 and X and Y represented by any *given* point on the production possibility curve, we get a contract curve on which $MRS_{xy}^1 = MRS_{xy}^2$; at some point on this contract curve, $MRS_{xy} = MRT_{xy}$. Hence each such point satisfies $MRS_{Kl}^x = MRS_{Kl}^y$, $MRS_{xy}^1 = MRS_{xy}^2 = MRT_{yx}$. Putting it in yet another way, each point on the utility possibility frontier tells us the maximum level of utility that one of the individuals can attain given that the other individual is at the level of (his) utility corresponding to the point.

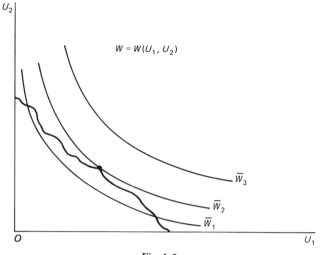

Fig. 1.5

So each point on the utility possibility curve represents a Pareto optimum, *the choice between which can be made only on distributional grounds.* That choice can be represented by a 'social welfare function', which can be thought of as a 'social' utility function whose arguments are the levels of utility attained by individuals 1 and 2. If we draw the contours ('indifference curves') of this function on the same diagram as our utility possibility curve, and pick that point on the latter that touches the highest such contour, we have the 'welfare optimum'. The social welfare function, representing a preference map that gives distributional weights to 1 and 2, allows us to choose a point on the utility possibility curve - and thus a particular allocation of K and L, particular levels of production of X and Y, and a particular distribution of this X and Y between 1 and 2. But *classical* (Paretian) welfare economics - and the 'marginal conditions' - do not allow us to go beyond the derivation of the utility possibility curve to pick a particular point on it; that choice is no longer one of 'efficiency', but is rather an 'ethical' or 'value' judgement embodying our relative preferences between individuals 1 and 2. Note that each point on the utility possibility curve corresponds (in general) to a distinct allocation of factors and outputs. Thus any move *along* the curve involves not merely a redistribution of income among individuals, but also a complete reallocation of factors and outputs.

(c) The 'marginal cost pricing' rule. This follows as a simple corollary of our (necessary) condition (3) for efficient allocation, $MRS_{xy} = MRT_{yx}$. We know that consumers maximising utility will set $MRS_{xy} = p_x/p_y$, the price ratio given them in the market; but $MRT_{yx} = MC_x/MC_y$; so that if price ratios equal marginal cost ratios, i.e. $p_x/p_y = MC_x/MC_y$, then our marginal condition

$MRS_{xy} = MRT_{yx}$ will be satisfied. This is the essential justification for marginal cost pricing.

There are many qualifications and criticisms of the 'marginal conditions', and *a fortiori* these become qualifications of the $MC = P$ rule. We list some of the most important.

(1) Assumption of a Pareto-type criterion for 'welfare' requires that our 'social welfare function' be such that a change that makes someone better off while making no one else worse off, each according to *his own* preferences, is to be desired. But we may feel that there are cases in which the society should disregard or overrule individual preferences.

(2) Our argument has been conducted under static assumptions. Introducing a time dimension requires that we treat the 'same' commodities as 'different' if they are produced or consumed in different periods; this complication is theoretically trivial but is overwhelming in practical applications. And the extension of the analysis into more than a single period also requires that we make distribution ('value') judgements *over time*; what time horizon should we choose to delimit the group of individuals with whom we are concerned? How shall we provide (if we should) for those who will live beyond the horizon – i.e. what 'terminal capital stock' should be left for the use of future generations? And how should consumption – and 'welfare' – be distributed over the time period before the horizon? In other words, satisfaction of the marginal conditions does not guarantee that the rate of investment is appropriate.

(3) We have taken factor supplies as given (inelastically supplied) and assumed that all factors are fully employed. The argument justifying the marginal conditions can be modified to allow for price-elastic factor supply (although the geometrical presentation then fails). But price flexibility or government action must be sufficient to maintain full employment. And if the analysis is to apply over time, we must suppose that factors are perfectly mobile and non-specific, so that it is possible to reallocate them without waste.

(4) Both inputs and outputs must be perfectly divisible. Indivisibilities raise the question, 'What is marginal cost?' – e.g. of the marginal passenger on a train.

(5) We must assume the absence of risk and uncertainty, with regard to both technology and tastes.

(6) We must assume either that external effects are absent or that they are compensated by a suitable system of taxes and subsidies. External economies or diseconomies in production or consumption are by definition 'external' to the price mechanism; they are not reflected in market prices. Since private costs and returns are calculated from market prices, external effects create divergences between private and social costs and returns, and thus between private and social *MRS*'s and *MRT*'s. Our analysis has implicitly assumed that

the MRS's and MRT's are society's rates of substitution and transformation; but it is individuals, not society, who react to market prices and decide to produce and consume certain quantities of goods.

(7) The marginal conditions are *necessary* but *not sufficient* conditions for a Pareto optimum. Certain 'second-order' conditions are required for sufficiency. For example, suppose that there were increasing returns in the production of a particular good, i.e. a falling average cost curve. Falling AC implies $MC < AC$, so under marginal cost pricing, where $P = MC$, we would have $P < AC$, so the producer would make a loss. In order to enforce marginal cost pricing, the government would have to pay such producers subsidies. In terms of our original argument, a production possibility curve showing increasing returns would be convex rather than concave to the origin, so that the highest iso-revenue line touching it would be one intersecting it at one of the intercepts: we would have a 'corner maximum', and the normal tangency would be a *minimum* revenue position.

(8) Even if the marginal conditions do lead us to a point on the utility possibility curve, this is only one of an infinite number of possible Pareto optima. Only our distributional judgements can tell us whether the one we arrive at is preferable to the others, *or indeed whether it is preferable to any of the non-'optimum' positions*; for an efficient allocation of resources with a bad income distribution may be vastly inferior to an inefficient allocation with a good distribution, depending on the 'social welfare function' of the individual comparing the two. Efficiency is hardly a sufficient criterion to evaluate alternative resource allocations. In this sense, welfare economies can never yield prescriptions that do not involve 'value judgements' about income distribution.

(9) The marginal conditions are jointly necessary for a Pareto optimum. If any one cannot be satisfied, there is no presumption that a move in the direction of satisfying one of the others will be beneficial. This is a rather over-simplified version of the *'second-best'* argument, which says roughly the following: if some given constraint in the economy prevents the attainment of one of the conditions for a Pareto optimum, then the conditions characterising the best position that *can* be attained *given* this constraint (the 'second-best optimum', in contrast to the 'first-best' Pareto optimum attainable without the constraint) may involve violating any or all of the Pareto conditions (our (1), (2) and (3)). Thus with regard to marginal cost pricing, the rule must be universally applied: if price does not equal marginal cost in one sector, there is no presumption that it 'should' in any other. Taken strictly, this point would make the entire discussion of the marginal conditions totally irrelevant to economic policy. For it is clear that in practice they can never all be satisfied – and if this is so, the argument says that we cannot in any particular case recommend that any given one should be approached. But we may still allow some scope for 'piecemeal welfare economics', since the second-best argument seems to have greatest practical

relevance to cases in which the sectors (industries) under consideration are significantly interdependent. As with externalities, in such cases we should consider the interdependent sectors together, as a whole; and we may then be justified in neglecting the second-order effects arising from their relations with other sectors.

(*d*) *Distributive justice.* Incomes and welfares were distributed in the model according to the distributional weights applied to each individual's utility in the social welfare function. The choice of distributional weights is a controversial topic. For example, a utilitarian may argue for equality of incomes. If each individual had an identical cardinal utility function characterised by diminishing marginal utility, then the total social aggregate of utility would be maximised by dividing income equally. Clearly this approach requires strong assumptions including that of interpersonal comparisons.

The distribution of income that is thought to be socially just is an ethical question. Recently the philosopher John Rawls[24] has advocated a strongly egalitarian criterion of 'social justice' which is based on his concept of 'the difference principle'. According to this principle, inequality in a society is justified only to the extent that it benefits the least advantaged. For Rawls, the ethical principle that should be used is to choose that social structure which will produce the distribution that maximises the benefit of those individuals receiving least benefit. This notion can be summarised in Rawls 'maximin' criterion. That is, if we imagine a number of alternative social states, each state generating a different distribution of welfares, then we choose that social state which maximises the welfare of the worst-off person in society. It should be noted that the maximin conception of social justice does not generally result in equality of incomes.

This principle is demonstrated in Figure 1.6. The incomes of two individuals Y^1 and Y^2 are shown on the axes. A social opportunity cost frontier of alternative income distributions II_1, is shown along with the 45° line. All distributions lying along the 45° represent income equality. The distribution S is the Rawlsian maximin distribution. The income of the least well-off (i.e. Y^2) is maximised at this point. More that individual 2 is better off at S than at F, which is the distribution corresponding to the equality of incomes.

The Rawlsian theory of distributive justice is contractarian in the sense that rational individuals would, in some pristine state of the world, agree to a particular income distribution (the maximin one). In this initial state each individual faces a veil of ignorance since (s)he does not know where (s)he will end up in the final distribution. Since life is a lottery with each individual facing an uncertain future those who are risk averse are likely to contract to minimise income disparities.

Alternative specifications of the social welfare function are of importance when it comes to theoretical discussions such as the analysis of optimal income taxes. In many theoretical exercises the results obtained are heavily dependent

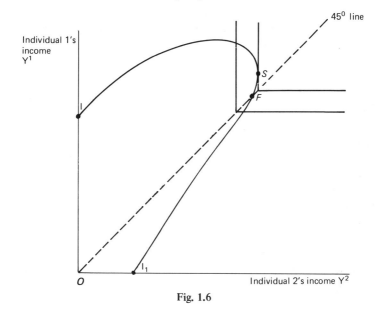

Fig. 1.6

upon the form of the social welfare function which is used. Moreover, when it comes to the design of social policies an understanding of the underlying ethical properties of alternative concepts of distributive justice will assist in the clarification of the objectives of these policies. As Frank Hahn has so aptly put it, the purpose of abstract theorising is to ensure that we get the grammar of the arguments of policy correct.

CHAPTER 2

The Economic Rationale of the Modern State

In the previous chapter it was seen that modern economies are 'mixed economies' with a large proportion of their gross national products originating in the public sector. Correspondingly, a significant percentage of their GNPs are collected in taxation in order to finance these public outputs. Moreover, these percentages have been growing over time. Modern governments provide a variety of services via the budget including housing, education, police and fire services, defence, the system of justice and laws, and pensions.

The extent to which governments get involved in providing goods and services via the budget and the kinds of services actually provided varies from country to country and has also varied across time. This prompts us to ask two different kinds of questions. The first is, why do governments provide the specific types of goods and services that they do? Is there anything particular about these goods and services such that they be allocated via the public sector's budget rather than through the market mechanism? The second is, which activities should the government allocate via the budget? Clearly, these questions are not unrelated. The first is an example of the type of question asked in positive economics, whereas the second is a normative question. What government actually does, however, may or may not be at variance with what it should do. As we shall see, the positive question is relatively more straightforward to answer than is the normative question.

The extent to which the state has involved itself in economic activities has varied over time. The period from the sixteenth to the eighteenth century was a time of nationalism and consolidation; small provinces joined together to form larger countries. Consolidation implied the unification of laws of contract, the establishment of a common currency and system of tariffs, and a co-ordinated infrastructure (i.e. communications, water supply, etc.). These periods were also accompanied by mercantilism, i.e. the state regulation of production, commerce and trade. In contrast, the eighteenth and nineteenth centuries were periods of liberalism and saw the removal of many mercantilist regulations. In the 1920s, however, the world depression brought about many changes in international relations and increased government intervention into domestic economic relations. In the postwar period of the 1940s onwards there has been a departure from the liberal economic policies of previous ages. Governments now intervene in economic affairs on an unprecedented scale and provide social services, etc., on a scale unknown and unthought of in earlier periods. Why is this the case? This question along with those already posed above will be answered in this chapter.

The problem that we set ourselves in this chapter is to provide a framework which will assist us to understand the rationale that underlies government intervention in economic and social affairs. Rather than record the historical development of government activities, we would prefer to understand the logic of such developments. Also, rather than assume that the existence of any particular set of government activities reflects some particular ideology, we want to inquire if there are technical as well as ideological reasons for government's existence and the form that it takes.

What we will show is that there is no single economic explanation for the rationale of government. Instead, governments exist to deal with a large number of different problems and in doing so they perform a number of different roles, which are often quite separate from one another and which frequently conflict. Nor will our approach be fully comprehensive in the sense that it will explain the rationale for all government actions. Our main concern is to explain the role that government plays in economic affairs and in providing social goods and services.

Market failure

In the previous chapter the voluntary exchange model of the perfectly competitive model was set out. The outputs of the goods and services of the economy and the set of prices for these outputs were determined competitively in the market place in accordance with consumer's preferences and incomes. The market outcome was assumed to be Pareto-efficient in the sense that, given the set of factor prices, a reallocation of factor inputs could not increase total output and, given the initial distribution of incomes, it was not possible, by reallocating final output between individuals, to make one person better off without making another worse off. These results depended upon the usual assumptions of perfectly competitive markets.

Market failure refers to those situations in which the conditions necessary to achieve the market efficient solution fail to exist or are contravened in one way or another. Market failure is an extremely important feature of observed markets. Left to itself, the market system of any economy is unlikely to operate efficiently. There will be a tendency for it to produce too much of some goods and an insufficient amount of others. In the extreme case of complete market failure the market will fail to exist, so that certain goods will not be produced at all.

Factors that bring about the failure of markets to achieve efficient outcomes includes: (a) the existence of public goods and externalities; (b) the presence of decreasing costs/increasing returns to scale as in the case of monopoly and other forms of imperfect competition; (c) incomplete information; (d) uncertainty. In most of these cases the origin of the market failure is to be found in the notion of transactions costs. Exchange transactions, including market exchanges, are not costless to perform. It might, for example, be costly for consumers and producers to be informed about the quality of the final products and factor inputs that they purchase. The acquisition of forecasting information about the likely course of events over an uncertain future is also costly. Setting up futures markets in contingent claims is usually so expensive that these markets fail to exist.

Given the presence of market failure, one possible role for government would be to intervene in the allocative function of the market and thus correct the market failure or introduce policies that would compensate its effects. This has been identified by Musgrave as the allocative role of government.

There is another sense in which the market might fail. This time we are not so much concerned about the efficiency of the market solution; instead we would wish to question the equity or the social justice of the distribution of incomes and welfare, which the market system produces. The market might fail to produce a just distribution of welfares, and government could therefore intervene bringing the distribution of incomes into line with that distribution which is considered to be just and fair. Musgrave refers to this as the distributive role of government.

There are another two roles assigned to government, which are also of interest to us. First, there is the stabilisation role. Economies periodically suffer from inflation, unemployment, lack of real growth, balance of payments problems, etc. A stabilisation role exists for government to intervene in the economy, using monetary and fiscal policies to reduce inflation and unemployment and thereby to improve the welfare of the members of society. Second, there is a regulatory role that governments play. As part of its allocative role, government enacts and enforces laws of contract, etc. This ensures that market trades and private exchanges take place smoothly. But government also administers the more general system of law and justice which regulates individual behaviour. As we will see, the regulatory role of government has expanded in the postwar period and has been a source of concern for those who see increased government intervention in the economy as meaning a reduction in individual freedom and liberty.

The allocative role of government

Underlying the model of competitive markets there is a theory of property rights. Property rights give an individual the right of ownership over some commodity (property) and thus the right to exclude others from enjoying the benefits that the commodity provides. The origin of the actual distribution of property rights would be an interesting inquiry to pursue, but for our present purposes we take the distribution as given. At any moment in time a set of property rights exists, which is codified and embodied in the society's structure of laws.

The erection of fences, the planting of 'no trespassing' signs, the branding of cattle and the legal machinery to enforce contracts are all examples of devices designed to establish and to signal the existence of property rights. When individuals exchange goods and services, either in a market or a non-market trade, they are in fact exchanging property rights, the legal claims to the benefits of the commodity. The definition of property rights, their enforcement and their exchange is not a costless operation. The more complex or ambiguously defined property rights are, the higher enforcement costs are likely to be. Any ambiguity in the set of property rights associated with a commodity will reduce its market-ability and the price at which it can be exchanged. Thus stolen goods require a special set of 'underground' or black-market exchanges. Also, the exchange of property rights is defined within the constraints of the law. While property rights might be well defined, their exchange can be severely constrained as in the case of dangerous drugs. Once again, illegal exchanges take place in an irregular way.

For some commodities property rights cannot be assigned to any single individual. An example of such a commodity is that of 'common property'. In the case of common property a group of individuals has an unrestricted right to all the benefits of the asset. Because the benefits of the property are made equally available to all members of the group, no single individual is able to sell his right to the benefits of the property to another member of the group. What kind of economic behaviour is likely to result from this situation? This is the question that was asked by David Hume in the eighteenth century, and his analysis of the problem has come to be known as the 'tragedy of the commons'.

In Hume's example, a number of neighbours have access to a meadow. The meadow is common property in the sense that each individual has the right to graze his cattle on it but no single individual has the right to sell the meadow. Since everyone has free access to the good there is no way in which any single person will be able to sell his grazing rights to another. Logically such an exchange cannot exist.

Since the good is free (i.e. available at zero user price) individuals will tend to over-use the meadow. The result is that the property rapidly deteriorates and the unregulated self-interest behaviour of each individual produces a less-than-optimal solution for the group as a whole. If, for example, it was demonstrated that the introduction of a drainage system or some other maintenance scheme would improve the productivity of the land, then which member of the group would institute such a scheme? If one person decides to incur the cost of the drainage scheme then all others will benefit without contributing to the cost, since they have the right to enjoy the benefit of the common property.

The problem arises first because of the indivisibility of the common property, and second because of the size of the group that consumes the service. In the case of a small group of two or three consumers some kind of agreement about the intensity of use of the common resource, the introduction of maintenance programmes and the sharing of the costs of using the resource could be reached. However, when the group is large, e.g. hundreds or thousands of members, achieving agreement is extremely difficult and extremely costly. In other words, the transactions or decision costs are high and would have to be incurred by a few members of the group without hope of recovery. Hume puts it this way:

> it is very difficult, and indeed impossible, that a thousand persons should agree on any [collective] action; it being difficult for them to concert in so complicated a design, and still more difficult for them to execute it — while each seeks a pretext to free himself of the trouble and expense, and would lay the whole burden on others.[1]

In Hume's example there is an obvious conflict between the maximisation of the individual's utility in the short-term and the maximisation of his utility in the long-term. Moreover, the extent to which one individual makes use of the common resource in pursuing the maximisation of his own welfare, will constrain the amount of the resource available to others. In the absence of regulated use, the self-interests of each individual come into conflict.

The example also serves to illustrate the concept of the 'free-rider'. The free-rider is an individual who misrepresents his preferences on the expectation that he can enjoy the benefits of a collective common property resource without paying for them. From the point of view of each individual member of the group, it is rational to be a free-rider. However, if all members of the group play the game of the free-rider, the final outcome is to no single member's benefit. The free-rider must, therefore, assume that all other members of the group are not playing the same game, or he must be unaware of the final outcome.

The tragedy of the commons is that the unregulated behaviour of self-interest utility-maximising individuals will result in a deterioration in the quality of the common resource. Hume saw that it was government's role to regulate individual behaviour, thereby reducing the tragedy of the commons. Government's role is, therefore, to allocate the use of the resource both between individuals and inter-temporally, thereby maximising the common interest of all members of the group.

There are many modern examples in which governments pursue such an allocative objective. Take, for example, resources such as water supplies, fishing reserves, or, in the UK context, North Sea oil reserves. In each case the property rights to a large proportion of these resources are communally owned rather than privately owned. For each resource government allocates the right to use that resource so as to serve the common interests of the members of the group.

(1) Public goods

Another source of market failure arises from the existence of pure public goods. Following in the Italian tradition of public finance Samuelson, in his seminal article, defined the concept of a pure public good as follows: 'each individual's consumption of such a good leads to no subtraction from any other individual's consumption of that good'.[2]

Pure public goods of the Samuelson type are different from the common property resources of the previous section. Any single individual's consumption of the good does not subtract from any other individual's consumption of a pure public good. Common property resources are not, therefore, Samuelson pure public goods. To see the differences, we will make use of the two concepts, non-excludability and non-rivalness. The differences between pure private goods and pure public goods can be summarised as follows:

(i) For a pure private good.

$$X_j = \sum_{i=1}^{n} X_j^i$$

In this case the total amount of good X_j is the sum of the amounts consumed (owned) by each ith consumer (X_j^i).   That is the private good is wholly divisible amongst individuals.

(ii) For a pure public good.

$$X_{n+j} = X_{n+j}^i.$$

That is each of the i individuals have at their disposal for consumption purposes the total amount of the public good X_{n+j}. The public good is indivisible over the set of individuals.

(a) *Non-excludability.* In the case of a pure private good the set of property rights defines the ownership of the good. The individual who possesses the property right has the sole claim to enjoy the benefits of the good and can, therefore, exclude others from doing so. In the case of a pure public good the technical features of excludability begin to break down. First, it might not be technically feasible to exclude beneficiaries. National defence is often quoted as an example of pure public good. If some geographical area, e.g. a country, is provided with defence services it is extremely difficult to exclude anyone who lives within that country from being defended. The exclusion principle does not apply to a pure public good. Not only are pure public goods non-excludable; they are also non-rejectable. Thus a pacifist living within a country is defended whether he likes it or not. He would be able to reject the services of defence only by moving to an area that is undefended. However, while he remains within the defended area, he cannot reject the service by selling his 'share' of defence. Another example of a pure public good is that of the light from a lighthouse. No ship within the vicinity of the light can be excluded. A similar example is found in street lighting. However, lighthouses are not in practice provided or financed publicly. Instead they are paid for out of voluntary subscriptions from ship owners. The degree of exclusion depends upon the technical characteristics of the commodity and the resources available to producers to prevent non-buyers from consuming his product. In general, however, there is no perfect exclusion. The optimal (or actual) amount of exclusion is a decision made by the producer.

In the above examples, it was not technically feasible to exclude individuals from consuming the good. The second way in which the exclusion principle breaks down is that, while it may be technically feasible to exclude, the application of an exclusion device may be very expensive. That is, the cost of exclusion can outweigh any advantages obtained from its application. A pure public good, therefore, is a good for which exclusion is either technically not feasible or, if technically feasible, expensive to apply.

(*b*) *Non-rivalness in consumption* (also called 'jointness in supply'). A good is said to be non-rival in consumption when the marginal cost of adding another person to consume the good is zero. Examples of non-rivalness include a non-crowded bridge, a less-than-full railway compartment or an under-utilised computer. Non-rivalness arises from the indivisibility of the product. Adding one or more person (up to a capacity constraint) does not add to the variable costs of producing the non-rival good and so does not add to marginal costs.

The definition of a pure public good implies that it is non-rival in consumption since the addition of one more consumer will not lead to the subtraction from any other individual's consumption of that good. Non-rival goods are not necessarily non-excludable. In the case of the railway compartment or the bridge these goods are non-rival (up to a capacity constraint); but simple exclusion devices, such as a toll gate, can be applied which make them excludable.

It can now be seen that the common property resource of the previous section is an example of a non-excludable good which is, however, rival in consumption. One individual's cows grazing on the meadow are in competition (rivalness) with those belonging to other individuals. The feature of non-excludability in this instance arises from the law of common property rather than from the nature of the meadow.

The above discussion is summarised in Figure 2.1.

(2) *Public goods, externalities and mixed goods*

We now need to consider how the characteristics of pure public goods relate to the concept of market failure. If a pure public good is to be available for consumption then it must be provided collectively either through private voluntary arrangements or publicly via the budget. Given the characteristic of non-excludability, there is no incentive for a profit-maximising producer to supply the public good because once he produces it he cannot exclude individuals from consuming it and hence he is unable to charge a price. Individuals wishing to consume the benefits of a pure public good could, however, form a private co-operative. They could agree to contribute to the cost of supplying the public good. Such an arrangement might be feasible for a small group of individuals,

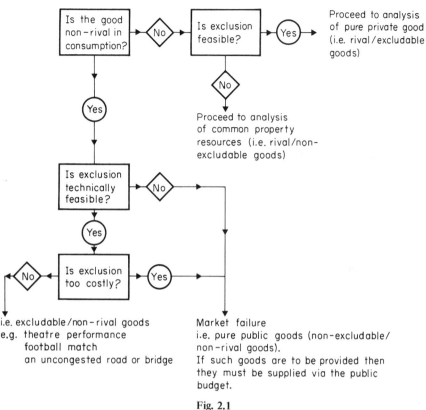

Fig. 2.1

but as the group grows in size the possibility of individuals becoming free-riders increases and the private voluntary arrangement fails.

For a large group pure public goods are supplied via the public sector budget. Provision via the budget, however, does not imply public production. The public sector could sub-contract the production of the good to a private producer. Whether or not the public sector decides to produce the good directly or to sub-contract its production depends upon a number of factors. For example, the public sector might wish to maintain a strict control over the quality of the service or it might, in other instances, consider it undesirable to leave the production of the good to the private sector as in the case of defence and the administration of the legal system.

If the allocative role of government was confined to the provision of pure public goods then the public sector would not feature as a major provider of goods and services because examples of pure public goods are extremely rare. We know, however, that the government is a major provider and supplier of goods and services and so we need to look for other arguments.

In practice, the market economy is not characterised by the prevalence of pure private goods but instead by 'mixed goods' which, while they have a private good component, also produce externalities or spill-over effects. The existence of these externalities influences the decisions of producers and consumers resulting in an allocation of resources that differs from that which the perfectly competitive market would have produced in the absence of externalities. Externalities, therefore, generate market failures, which government could correct.

An externality arises when the production or consumption activities of one party enters directly as an argument into the production or utility function of another party. The smokey chimney serves as an example of a production–consumption externality. The particular technology used in the production of a private good produces smoke as a by-product (i.e. the externality or spill-over) which is involuntarily consumed by third parties such as consumers. If the utility of the third party increases as a result of the externality, then an external benefit or economy is said to exist, whereas if the utility of the third party falls then an external cost, or diseconomy, exists.

In order to avoid subsequent confusion two distinct notions of externality are used. First there are 'technological externalities'. This is the meaning of externality used above; i.e., the consumption and production activities of one agent or group of agents affect the levels of production and consumption of other agents. Second there is the class of externalities referred to as 'pecuniary externalities'. In this case the behaviour of producers and/or consumers influences the set of prices in the economy; and hence, through changes in the budget constraints, the welfare of other producers and/or consumers is affected. A pecuniary external diseconomy could arise when an expansion in the output of one industry causes an increase in the price of one or more of the inputs used by other industries. (A pecuniary external economy would operate in the opposite direction.) Pecuniary externalities show up as changes in prices and profits but do not alter the technical possibilities of production or consumption.

Clearly there is a strong analytical relationship between the concepts of public goods and externalities, but it is useful to keep the concepts distinct and separate. The externality has public good characteristics. Like public goods externalities are non-excludable and non-rival in consumption.

If individuals wish to reduce the detrimental effects of external diseconomies they are required to allocate their own resources to deal with the spill-over effects. This gives rise to the notion of 'social costs'. In the example of the smokey chimney the 'social costs' of production are the sum of the costs to the producer of hiring inputs (i.e. the private costs) plus the costs due to the externality, which are borne by the third party (i.e. external costs). By a similar argument 'social benefits' are defined. Since well-defined property rights to the air, the sea and rivers often do not exist, individuals dump their effluent into these natural recepticals free of charge, i.e. free of private cost. If an individual is inoculated against some disease, then he receives a private benefit, but an external benefit is granted to his neighbours, who run less risk of catching the disease from him (note, however, that the external benefit is not a perfect substitute for an actual inoculation). The individual would, however, find it extremely difficult to trade that external benefit to his neighbours. In both of these examples, because property rights are not well defined and because the externality is non-excludable, individuals are unable to internalise the effects of the externality through private trades. For reasons already discussed the transactions costs of organising such trades would be too high, especially if the number of persons involved is large. External effects, therefore, influence the behaviour of individuals. An external diseconomy will result in the over-production of the good associated with the diseconomy, while an external benefit will result in under-consumption. These allocations differ from those that would have been produced by perfectly competitive markets.

Externalities provide an allocative role for government. The problem is to allocate the external effect optimally. For example, if the problem is one of pollution of the environment, the government could arrange to sell property rights to individuals who wish to use the environment for that purpose. This additional cost, reflecting society's evaluation of the environment, would be borne by the polluter, thereby forcing him to modify his production decisions by reducing the level of output and hence the level of pollution. Since an optimal level of externality is usually not zero, the revenue raised from the sale of the property rights could then be used to reduce that damage which is actually done to the environment. Other policies used by government include pollution taxes and emission standards.

In the case of external diseconomies, the government attempts to counteract the market failure by reducing the volume of output of those goods that are over-produced. However, in the case of external economies the government may choose to correct the allocative inefficiency by encouraging the production of those goods that are under-produced. It can do this either by directly producing the service (e.g. education and health services) or by providing consumption or production subsidies. It has, therefore, been shown that government also has an allocative role to play when market failure arises owing to the existence of mixed goods, which are private goods with production or consumption externalities associated with them.

The allocative role of government and decreasing cost industries. The efficient allocation of resources brought about by the market system assumes the existence of perfectly competitive markets. In practice, however, a large number of goods are supplied by decreasing cost industries (i.e. industries with increasing returns to scale in their production functions).

The decreasing cost industry's cost and demand curves are shown in Figure 2.2. It is seen that average costs continually fall over the whole range of output. The pricing rule, which will produce an efficient allocation of resources, is that which equates price with marginal costs. For the decreasing cost industry the marginal cost price (OP_2) will not cover costs. Instead, the profit-maximising

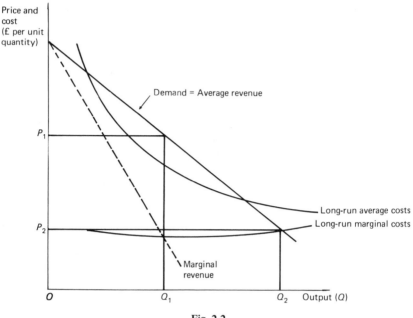

Fig. 2.2

producer will charge a price of OP_1 and produce OQ_1 units of output. The profit-maximising price, therefore, differs from the efficient price by an amount equal to P_1P_2 and the efficient level of output differs from the profit-maximising output by Q_1Q_2. If a marginal cost price is to be charged, so that society enjoys the benefit of a larger volume of output (Q_2 compared with Q_1) and a lower price (P_2 compared with P_1), then government must intervene in the market. The government could instruct the private industry to charge a marginal cost price, subsidising the loss out of tax revenues. As an alternative course of action, the government could take over the entire production operation (i.e. nationalisation) produce the output and charge a marginal cost price; again subsidising the loss from general taxation. The problem of decreasing costs, therefore, establishes an allocative role for government.

Examples of decreasing cost industries include the public utilities gas, electricity, water and sewerage. In each case decreasing costs arise because of indivisibilities. The uncrowded bridge and the half-empty railway compartment are also examples of indivisible outputs. In both these cases the marginal cost of adding another consumer (up to a capacity constraint) is zero. Charging a positive non-zero price for these products will result in an allocative inefficiency, since price should be set equal to marginal cost which is zero in this example.

The perceptive reader will have already recognised that the way in which we finance the loss made by marginal cost pricing/decreasing cost industries or the way in which we levy pollution taxes is of importance. Since most taxes influence relative prices, they will introduce a distortion and hence another inefficiency. Ideally, lump sum taxes which leave relative prices unchanged should be used. However, lump sum taxes are generally not available, and so other taxes must be used in practise. The design of optimal government policies is, therefore, one of weighing up the distortions and inefficiencies introduced by government compared with the inefficiencies that the policies are supposed to reduce. Clearly the design of optimal government policies is an exercise in the theory of the second-best.

We have seen that the allocative role of government arises because of the failure of markets and voluntary agreements/exchanges to produce an efficient solution. These market failures were brought about because of indivisibilities, pure public goods, and externalities. The different elements of the allocative role of government are summarised in Figure 2.3. The vertical axis represents economies of scale in service provision and is shown as the ratio of the marginal cost of one more user to the average cost of one more user (MC/AC) holding service quality fixed. The horizontal axis represents the degree of option a user may have in consuming the good. The reader should try providing his own examples of services that fit into Figure 2.3.

The distributive role of government

In addition to being concerned with the allocative efficiency of markets, economists are also concerned with the distribution of income and welfare between

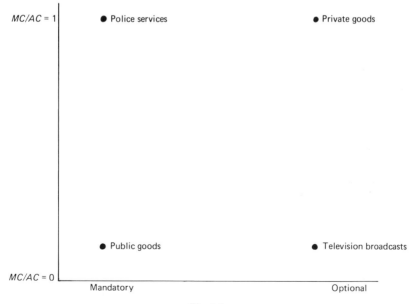

Fig. 2.3

individuals and households, etc. It will be recalled from the analysis of the market that underlying each Pareto-efficient allocation there is a particular distribution of initial endowments (i.e. property rights and skills, etc.). Thus the distribution of wealth depends upon the distribution of rights to inherited wealth and the accumulation of wealth over the individual's lifetime, and the distribution of earnings will depend upon the initial distribution of skills, subsequent training and the market price of these skills.

The resulting distribution of income, wealth and welfare may not be in accordance with what society considers to be just. The source of this injustice might lie in the original distribution of endowments, or it might be due to the way in which the prices at which the endowments are valued are established. Factor endowments may be priced in perfectly competitive markets or in imperfect markets. In either case the resultant distribution of income might not be acceptable.

The problem that faces society is to decide which particular distribution of incomes and welfare it prefers and then to consider alternative measures which will take it from its existing distribution to its most preferred. Establishing the most preferred distribution is obviously a complex problem, and one that has been intensively debated and discussed by welfare economists and moral philosophers down through the ages. For our present purposes the optimal distribution of income is not of immediate concern. What we want to know is whether or not there is a role for government in bringing about the most preferred distribution of income.

For example, why would it not be possible to redistribute incomes and welfare by means of a system of private redistributions made voluntarily through charities? One argument is that such redistribution would not exist on a sufficiently large scale. Moreover, many individuals could easily opt out and become free-riders. While a system of private charities would be able to make redistributions, it would be unable to tackle the problems at source. Finally, in the absence of a co-ordinated policy the actions of one charity might compete with those of another.

Government is in a better position to pursue a co-ordinated and comprehensive redistribution policy, and because it has the resources of compulsory taxation it is better placed to redistribute incomes on a large scale. Moreover, government can correct problems of income distribution that arise from imperfections in the factor markets, e.g. monopoly pricing of factors of production.

Government redistributes incomes and welfare by using progressive taxes to finance cash benefits, subsidies and also publicly provided goods and services. Public education, health services, welfare services and housing are examples of goods and services provided through the budget for redistributive purposes.

These goods are either provided and financed completely out of taxation or are provided at a subsidised price. It is never clear whether government's role should be to provide such goods directly or whether, for distributional purposes, the government would be better providing income supplements to individuals, thereby leaving them to purchase from the market the quantity and quality of services that satisfies their preferences. Two arguments that are frequently given against the income supplement idea are, first, that individuals, if given the freedom, are unlikely to choose the most appropriate amount of, say, education or health care. Second, government would prefer to have some direct control over the quality and price of these services because they are so important to general welfare. These two arguments constitute the case that Musgrave made out for the government providing 'merit goods' via the budget. However, the reader should be aware that the debate between the direct provision of 'merit type' goods *v.* the provision of income supplements is by no means settled and constitutes an interesting problem in the formation of an optimal social policy (see Figure 14.2 and the accompanying text).

The regulatory role of government

The regulatory role of government was touched upon when we considered government's allocative role. It was seen that government could attempt to regulate the decisions of producers and consumers, thereby reducing monopoly elements and externalities. But there are other instances in which it can be thought to be appropriate for government to regulate behaviour. For example, governments regulate the behaviour of producers in order to protect consumers. But why can't consumers protect themselves; why do we have governments performing this task? The immediate answer is that there are, for the individual consumer, high costs of obtaining and interpreting information relating to product safety and design. Thus government sets up a system of regulation and control which will produce such information either directly or indirectly. Other answers to the question suggest that the individual might not be capable of protecting himself in the sense that he does not have the resources at his disposal to establish and to police minimum standards.

Controls and restrictions are designed to increase the welfare of certain groups within society by protecting their interests. Government, therefore, intervenes and regulates the allocative process of the market by legislating against monopolies, controlling trading arrangements such as those of the stock exchange, and introducing legislation to protect the consumer from fraud, to prevent the consumers' health being damaged, to control the design of goods for the purpose of safety, and to control working conditions.

Moreover, the government regulates the money supply; regulates the prices of utilities and nationalised industries; and through prices and incomes policies it regulates many of the allocative decisions in the economy. Recent experience in the US and the UK has been against the regulatory role of government on the grounds that such controls constrain personal freedoms and efficient market choices. In addition their implementation imposes costs on the economy. Apart from the bureaucratic costs of administering the system consumers and producers incur costs when conforming to regulatory controls. Estimates for the US economy suggest that in 1970 federal outlays or regulatory activities amounted to $0.9b. This had increased to $6.5b in 1980 ($3.3b at 1970 prices). The benefits of regulation have been compared to the costs which, apart from the direct administrative and implementation costs, include increases in uncertainty and the delays in investment decisions. The result has been an increased demand for deregulation especially in the areas of airlines, automobile safety standards and environmental controls.

The stabilisation role of government

The market failures that have been examined up until now have all referred to imperfections in the structure of markets. For a number of technical reasons detailed above, markets failed to produce a Pareto-efficient outcome or an ethically acceptable distribution of welfare. That kind of discussion is very much the subject matter of microeconomics. It is, however, also possible to consider 'macroeconomics' within the context of the general notion of market failure. The central idea in macroeconomics is the existence of self-regulatory capabilities of a system of markets. In other words, are there automatic forces and mechanisms within a market system which will move the economy to a state in which all market excess demands and supplies are zero? Does there exist a system whereby economic activities are perfectly co-ordinated?

It is well known in macroeconomics that if economic activities are not sufficiently well co-ordinated the result is a general disequilibrium, which can show up in a number of possible ways, each having an undesirable effect, e.g. the under-employment of capital and labour, a rise in the general price level, or an imbalance on the country's external trading account. The market failure in this case is frequently a failure of communication between different economic agents operating in different markets within the economic system. The inequality between *ex ante* savings and investment is a case in point.

The failure of the market system to co-ordinate all activities and to come into equilibrium provides the focal point for macroeconomic policy. Government pursues a stabilisation objective by using the instruments of monetary and fiscal policy in an attempt to aid the restoration of equilibrium. This is not to suppose that the government has the ability to 'fine-tune' the economy. Friedman has clearly demonstrated that fine-tuning is not a feasible objective, and an examination of postwar economies supports this view. Government can, however, by pursuing money supply targets, adjusting tariffs or exchange rates, and changing public expenditures, taxes and interest rates, provide some of the conditions that are required to bring the system into stability.

In addition to the short-term demand management policies, outlined above, governments also co-ordinate the economic decisions of the various groups in the private sector, in an attempt to create the conditions necessary for sustained long-term economic growth. Thus we have the five-year plans produced by the French Government and the recent introduction of planning agreements between industry and government in the UK. These are examples of a situation in which all members of the group may benefit as a result of the co-ordination of decisions, but for which there is no incentive for any single individual to incur the costs of co-ordination.

Governments and insurance

Finally, governments can provide an insurance function. Examples include unemployment insurance, health insurance, and insurance against being unable to work when you are old (pension). In each case the individual is interested in purchasing insurance against the outcome of some future contingency. In most cases what is being sought is an income guarantee in the event that the individual loses his job through ill health, old age or being unemployed. It is possible to purchase insurance against these contingencies from the private market, but such markets are usually imperfect and can discriminate against those in greatest need, e.g. those who are already sick, aged or infirm. Moreover, many individuals would be unable to pay the price for such insurance. Government, therefore, supplies 'social insurance' (at a price) partly as a means of overcoming the allocative inefficiency of the market failure and also partly as a redistributive measure. As an exercise the reader should consider how welfare is redistributed through the 'social insurance' system.

The modern-day apostles of *laissez-faire*

The discussion in the previous section has demonstrated that there are technical as well as ideological reasons for the provision of goods and services through the public sector budget rather than through the market system and, moreover, that there are logical grounds for government regulation and control of market activities. Government attempts to adjust the overall allocation and distribution of resources in the economy because various imperfections cause the market system to fail.

However, government intervention does not bring about a perfect allocation of resources, either. The policy instruments used by government introduce other inefficiencies and distortions into the economy. The theory of the second-best demonstrates that government intervention might make the situation worse off rather than better off. In designing optimal government policies it becomes necessary to weigh up the allocative and distributional inefficiencies of the market with the allocative and distributional inefficiencies created by government intervention. Tullock puts the point this way:[3]

> The injuries that externalities may inflict on individuals if everything is left to the market and the injuries that government may inflict on individuals through the inherent nature of its decision process are the two basic factors in selecting the proper institutions to deal with any given problem. We must always weigh the specific advantages and disadvantages of these two imperfect instrumentalities.

To assume that government can improve upon *all* market inefficiencies is a naive position to adopt. Stigler[4] likens such a position to the example of the Roman emperor who judged a musical competition between two players and gave the prize to the second player having only heard the first.

Some economists, along with some social philosophers, are concerned about dimensions of the effects of government other than the allocative inefficiencies that it might introduce. Thus Friedman, for example, focuses attention upon the effect of government on personal freedom and liberty. It is instructive to weigh up the functions of government that we considered earlier alongside Friedman's views, which are clearly to limit the sphere of government activity:[5]

> Every act of government intervention limits the area of individual freedom directly and threatens the preservation of freedom indirectly. . . . The widespread use of the market reduces the strain on the social fabric by rendering conformity unnecessary with respect to any activities it encompasses. The wider the range of activities covered by the market, the fewer are the issues on which it is necessary to achieve agreement. In turn, the fewer the issues on which agreement is necessary, the greater is the likelihood of getting agreement while maintaining a free society. . . . A government which maintained law and order, defined property rights, served as a means whereby we could modify property rights and other rules of the economic game, adjudicated disputes about the interpretation of the rules, enforced contracts, promoted competition, provided a monetary framework, engaged in activities to counter technical monopolies and to overcome neighborhood effects widely regarded as sufficiently important to justify government intervention, and which supplemented private charity and the private family in protecting the irresponsible whether madman or child — such a government would clearly have important functions to perform. The consistent liberal is not an anarchist.

The above quotation from Friedman has been used to demonstrate that discussions of the balance between private sector and public sector activities in the economy are complex and are unlikely to be resolved by simply appealing to 'the facts'. The facts are open to subjective interpretation. The relative allocative and distributional inefficiencies of the market and the public sector can to a limited extent be quantified. This is to a large measure part of the subject matter of public sector economics. But for those areas that cannot be measured, e.g. the erosion of personal freedom and liberty, the debate is highly subjective.

The 1970s have witnessed an increased reaction against the activities of government and the expansion of the public sector. In the UK and the US governments were elected upon tickets which advocated massive reductions in public spending, taxation and the regulatory sphere of government. There have been local taxpayers' revolts such as that of Proposition 13. Reactions to high tax rates include an increase in the growth of the underground economy (or the black economy) in which transactions are made in cash so as to avoid paying taxes. Some estimates have put this at between 10 and 20 per cent of GNP for the US economy with such transactions growing at about 30 per cent per annum. The growth in the underground economy also means that policy-makers who formulate macro policy on the basis of the estimates of the 'observed' economy will be producing policies which have an inflationary bias. In this way taxation policy spills over into macrostabilisation policy-making in an unexpected way.

Other reactions against government are a belief that welfare payments are made to scroungers and a realisation that many of the social policies of government have not realised their goals. Traditional fiscal policies have been challenged on the grounds that they are ineffective. Instead of stabilising output and bringing the economy closer towards full employment some economists, in the monetarist tradition, have claimed that the budget deficits of fiscal policies promote inflation, raise interest rates and 'crowd out' private expenditures.

There can be no doubt that 'political failure' is just as real a phenomenon as is 'market failure'. Public sector bureaucracies do not operate frictionlessly and without cost. Inefficiency, malfunction and bureaucratic inertia do exist. The public sector is frequently asked to perform tasks which in complex, uncertain and rapidly changing environments are impossible to achieve. What is necessary is to discover the limits of government action and to define more clearly the comparative advantage of the public sector in a mixed economy.

CHAPTER 3

The Economic Analysis of Public Goods

In Chapter 2 the concept of a pure public good was defined as a commodity that had certain characteristics such that its consumption by any one economic agent does not reduce the amount available for others. Thus, making the commodity available to any single individual makes it possible to provide it for everyone without additional cost. The benefits of a private good are consumed exclusively, whereas a public good may be consumed jointly or concurrently by many individuals; i.e. public goods are non-excludable and non-rival.

Having introduced the concept of a pure public good, the purpose of this chapter is to follow through the implications of integrating pure public goods into economic analysis. A number of questions require to be answered. How many public goods 'should' be produced; i.e. what is the socially optimal mix between public and private goods? Following from this there is the complementary question of what is the optimal allocation of inputs between the public and the private sectors of an economy? Assuming that public goods are financed completely from taxes, how should the tax payments be distributed between the different members of society? Can a set of perfectly competitive markets satisfy the optimality conditions for public goods, and what are the necessary and sufficient conditions to establish a general equilibrium from an economy that has both public and private goods? These are just a selection of the many problems of 'public choice'. Some of them will be considered directly in this chapter, while others will be developed in greater detail throughout the remainder of the book.

This chapter will concentrate upon the optimality conditions for the allocation of society's resources to the provision of public goods. That is to say, using the framework of modern welfare economics, the necessary marginal conditions for allocative efficiency in the provision of public goods will be defined. This approach is abstract and belongs in the tradition of equilibrium economics. The questions to be answered are, therefore, does a set of equilibrium prices exist for an economy with pure public goods and what does that set of prices look like? There are, therefore, no institutional details of how the political decision-making process actually determines the levels of public outputs produced. This question is considered in a subsequent chapter. Abstraction is a necessary first step if the problem is to be well defined.

The chapter will begin with a brief examination of Pigou's approach to the question, which will be followed up by a more detailed treatment of the partial and general equilibrium models that have been used in the literature on this topic.

The Pigovian approach

Pigou's analysis of the optimal allocation of resources to public and private goods is contained in his discussion of the normative principles of taxation.[1] Using a utilitarian approach, Pigou assumed that each individual received benefit (utility) from the consumption of public goods. At the same time the payment of taxes to finance these public goods resulted in a disutility for the individual. The disutility of tax payment is defined as the opportunity cost of forgone private good consumption.

For each individual the optimal supply of public goods occurs at the point at which the marginal utility of public goods is equal to the marginal disutility of tax payments. Applying the general equi-marginal principle will result in an optimal allocation of the individual's budget between all private and public goods.

Pigou's analysis suffered from a number of pertinent problems. First, it was based upon the concept of cardinal utility. Second, although each individual might allocate his budget optimally between public and private goods, there was no mechanism by which these individual optima could be aggregated. If the whole of society was to be treated 'as if' it behaved like an individual,[2] then the analysis could proceed by balancing the marginal social utility against the marginal social disutility of tax payments. An optimal level of output for the public good(s) is determined where marginal social utility equals marginal social disutility of tax payments. But for that level of public good each individual may or may not equate *his* marginal utility from the public good with the marginal utility of his tax payments. Thus, while 'society' might be in equilibrium, in the Pigovian sense, each individual is unlikely to be.

Despite its obvious deficiencies, the Pigovian analysis is instructive, since it throws into relief many of the questions that a theory of public choice has to answer. How are individual preferences for public and private goods aggregated and a collective preference determined? How should the marginal utilities and disutilities be distributed among individuals in the society?

For Pigou the answer to the question of the distribution of the tax burden was that it should be based upon an individual's ability to pay. Unequals should be treated unequally and as a principle it gives government a role to redistribute welfare. But this is not the sole principle of social justice as the appendix to this chapter and as subsequent chapters show.

Optimal provision of a public good – partial equilibrium analysis

Proceeding on the basis of a number of restrictive assumptions partial equilibrium analysis establishes the demand and supply conditions that will produce the equilibrium price and output for a single commodity. It is assumed that the consumer's tastes and incomes and the prices of other goods are determined elsewhere in the system and are, therefore, taken as given for the purposes of the analysis.

The partial equilibrium analysis of a pure private good is presented first and then this is followed by the analysis of a pure public good. The essential differences between the analysis of pure private and pure public goods are then drawn.

Figure 3.1 sets out the analysis of a private good. The curves D_A and D_B represent the demand curves of individual A and individual B. The differences in the individual's demand curves reflect differences in their incomes and/or their tastes. To derive the market demand curve, DD, the individual demand curves are added *horizontally*; i.e. market demand $D = D_A + D_B$. Any point on the individual's demand curve shows how much of the commodity he is willing to consume at a certain price (*ceteris paribus*). The market demand curves shows how much all individuals would be willing to consume if they all faced the same price for the commodity. Therefore, by varying price and adding up across output, the market demand curve is derived; this is equivalent to saying that individual demand curves are added horizontally. Given the market supply curve SS, the equilibrium price, OP, is set where demand equals supply. Since we assume that markets are perfectly competitive, each individual is a 'price-taker'.

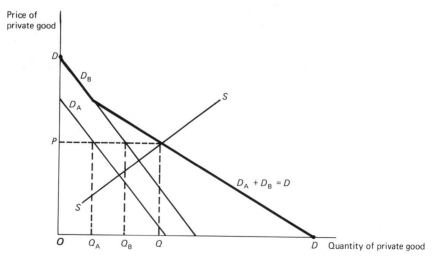

Fig. 3.1

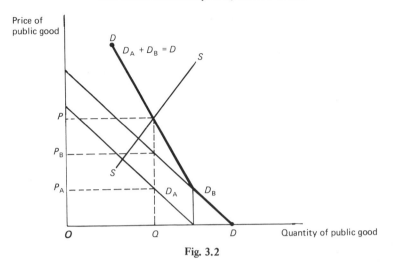

Fig. 3.2

Thus, given the equilibrium market price OP, individual A will demand OQ_A and individual B will demand OQ_B such that $OQ = OQ_A + OQ_B$.

Figure 3.2 sets out a similar analysis for a public good, however, with a number of significant differences. Again D_A and D_B represent the demand curves of individuals A and B, this time for the public good. Samuelson has, however, referred to these demand curves as 'pseudo-demand curves' because to draw them we must assume that each person accurately reveals his willingness to pay for the output of the public good. In other words, no one is a free-rider or a strategist in this analysis of public goods. Given that once the public good is made available it is made equally available to everyone, the total willingness to pay for the public good is found by adding the individual demand curves *vertically*; i.e. the total demand for the public good is the vertical sum of the individual demands. This is shown as DD in Figure 3.2,[3] and the supply curve is given by SS; the equilibrium level of public output is found from the intersection of the total demand curve and the supply curve, i.e. at OQ. Given this equilibrium level of output and the assumption that everyone will accurately reveal their willingness to pay, the total equilibrium willingness to pay for OQ is OP, and $OP = OP_A + OP_B$. At the equilibrium the total revenue received is equal to the total cost of supplying the good.

The difference between the analysis of private goods and the analysis of public goods follows from differences in the characteristics of these goods. In the analysis of private goods each individual is a price taker and a quantity-adjuster, whereas, for a public good each person is a quantity-taker and adjusts price, i.e. his willingness to pay. A private good equilibrium is found when an equilibrium market price is established such that the total quantity demanded is equal to the total amount that is willing to be supplied at that price. A public good equilibrium is established when the total willingness to pay for the public good output is equal to the price at which a producer is willing to supply that level of output.

In this analysis the price that an individual is willing to pay for the output of a public good is directly proportional to the marginal consumption benefits received from the good. If the price of a public good is thought of as a 'tax', then this partial equilibrium analysis assumes the use of benefit taxes for the financing of pure public goods. The benefit principle of taxation is explored further in the appendix to this chapter.

In order to see that OQ is an equilibrium level of output for the public good the following simple conceptual experiment can be performed. Take some level of output that lies to the left of OQ. For that level of output the total willingness to pay would exceed the supply price of providing it (i.e. total revenue $>$ total cost). It would, therefore, be in everyone's interests to expand output. Total willingness to pay for output levels beyond OQ, to the right, are less than the supply price. Hence, there is an incentive to reduce output. The equilibrium level of output is, therefore, OQ.

If we assume that the supply curves in Figures 3.1 and 3.2 are the marginal costs of supplying additional units of output, then the efficient pricing rules for private goods and public goods can be stated as follows.

(1) Private goods:

$$OP^A = OP^B = OP = MC.$$

Each individual faces an identical market price, for some level of output of the private good, and that market price is equal to the marginal cost. The efficient pricing rule for a private good is, therefore, that price equal marginal cost.

(2) Public goods:

$$OP^A + OP^B = OP = MC.$$

Each individual is willing to pay a different price for some level of public good output. The efficient pricing rule for a pure public good is that the sum of the individual prices equal marginal cost. These individual prices are often called 'individualised' prices or 'personalised' prices for public goods.

Given this efficient pricing rule for public goods, we can return to a question that was asked in the previous chapter: can the achievement of this efficiency condition be achieved by market prices? Take, for example, a commodity such as television, for which a coded message is broadcast which can only be interpreted by means of an unscrambling device. This is an example of an excludable non-rival good (i.e. an exclusion technology is feasible and cheap to operate). If a private producer supplied this good efficiently then he would need to charge each individual a different price such that the price charged to each person equalled that person's marginal valuation of the output supplied.

This is similar to the example of the discriminating monopolist who segments his market in such a way (assuming resale of the commodity between consumers is impossible, as it is in this case) that he charges different prices to each consumer. A profit-maximising monopolist would not, however, find any incentive in providing a non-rival excludable good at a set of prices such that $\Sigma p_i = MC$ (where p_i is the price individual i is willing to pay for the good). Since he maximises profit where $MC = MR$ the monopolist chooses a level of output that is smaller than that required by the efficiency condition (i.e. $\Sigma MR_i = MC$, but since each individual's marginal revenue curve lies below his demand (average revenue curve) then $\Sigma MR_i \neq \Sigma p_i$). The market, therefore, fails to implement the efficient pricing rule for such goods.

The efficiency conditions for excludable non-rival goods and for pure public goods (non-excludable, non-rival goods) require price discrimination in addition to the condition that the sum of the individual prices for the good be equal to marginal costs. However, as we saw in Chapter 2, there is every incentive for the consumer to conceal his preferences and thereby not reveal his willingness to pay for the public good. Therefore, even if a perfectly discriminating monopolist were to charge an efficient marginal cost price for the public good, the free-rider would still cause the market to fail.

(1) The derivation of the demand curve for public goods

In the above analysis the demand curve for a pure public good, as in Figure 3.2, was assumed to show the individual's willingness to pay for quantities of the public good. The reader will, however, when consulting the literature on pure public goods encounter similar analysis using demand curves, marginal rate of substitution curves or marginal valuation curves. This section will set out the similarities between these approaches along with their differences.

The downward-sloping 'pseudo-demand' curves in Figure 3.2 reveal each individual's diminishing marginal utility for public goods. The demand curve for a public good can be derived from a set of indifference curves in exactly the same way as the demand curves for private goods. Each individual is faced with a constant money income, a given set of preferences and a given set of prices for private goods and other public goods. The prices of the public goods are then varied and the price consumption curve (i.e. the locus of the points of tangency between the individual's budget constraint and his indifference curves) is generated. It is then a simple exercise in demand analysis to translate the price consumption curve into a demand curve.

However, when deriving the demand curve from a set of indifference curves, a choice has to be made as to whether it is real or money income that is held constant. The final choice depends upon the use to which the demand curves are to be put. In the public finance literature Musgrave[4] favours holding money income constant (thereby following Hicks), whereas Bowen[5] (following Samuelson) prefers to hold real incomes constant. Indeed, instead of talking about demand curves for public goods both Bowen and Samuelson[6] employ the use of 'marginal rate of substitution curves' which are analogous to demand curves but are derived by keeping real incomes constant and finding the marginal price for the quantity of the public good that will keep utility unchanged.

Yet another way of analysing the optimal supply of a public good is to follow Buchanan[7] and to construct the 'marginal valuation curve'. This curve is derived by plotting the slope of successive indifference curves (i.e. the marginal rates of substitution) as they intersect the budget line for a given price ratio. The marginal valuation curve, thus derived, is, however, only unique for a single price ratio. A change in the price ratio will produce a different marginal valuation curve. Thus, while the marginal valuation curve can be used to examine the properties of the partial equilibrium, it cannot be used to derive that equilibrium since the equilibrium price ratio has to be known before the appropriate marginal valuation curve can be derived.

Although these approaches to the problem differ, in terms of the interpretation placed on the demand curve, they are all similar in the final result that they produce; in other words, the efficient supply of a public good requires that the cost of providing the public good be distributed so that the sum of the individual marginal prices equals marginal cost; i.e.

(1) Musgrave: Σ individual prices = marginal cost.
(2) Bowen/Samuelson: Σ marginal rates of substitution = marginal cost.
(3) Buchanan: Σ marginal valuations = marginal cost.

Optimal provision of a public good – general equilibrium analysis

The partial equilibrium analysis of the previous section was limited to the case of a single public good. General equilibrium analysis relaxes the *certeris paribus* assumptions and extends the problem to a situation in which there are many public goods and many private goods.

To derive the conditions for the Pareto-efficient provision of private and public goods the standard geometrical construction of a two-person, two-commodity economy will be used. This is the geometric analysis which was first used by Samuelson in his seminal article on public goods.[8] The following simplifying assumptions are made:

(1) there are two commodities available for final consumption: a private good X and a pure public good G;
(2) the production possibility set is given;
(3) the tastes of the two consumers are given.

The problem that is to be solved is to establish the weakest possible set of conditions necessary to ensure the existence of a Pareto-efficient allocation of resources for the economy described above; that is, to solve the system for a set of efficient relative prices and outputs for the two commodities X and G.

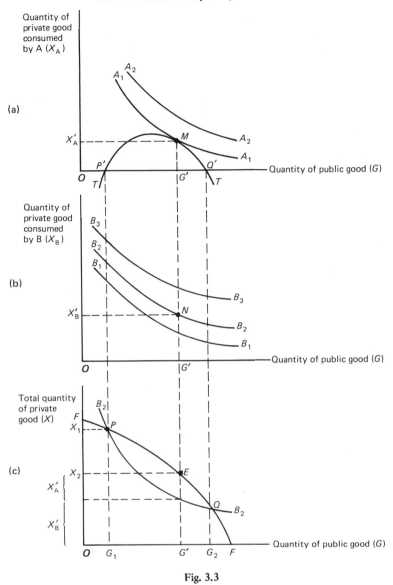

Fig. 3.3

The problem, therefore, is no different in principle from the standard general equilibrium problem, which has been extensively treated elsewhere and summarised by Bator.[9] The interest, however, now lies in the fact that one of the commodities is a pure public good.

Consider Figure 3.3, which is divided into three sections. The two individuals are labelled A and B. Individual A's indifference map for commodities X and G is shown in Figure 3.3(a) and individual B's indifference map is shown in Figure 3.3(b). Individual A's consumption of the private good X is labelled as X_A while that of B is labelled X_B. Figure 3.3(c) shows the production possibility curve for the economy.

To start the analysis choose a given level of utility for individual B, for example, represented by indifference curve B_2B_2. Given this level of utility for individual B what is the highest indifference curve that can be achieved by individual A? To answer this question superimpose indifference curve B_2B_2 on to the production possibility curve in Figure 3.3(c). It is now possible to define the set of public and private goods available to individual A assuming that individual B is to be maintained on indifference curve B_2B_2. The set of public and private goods available to A is represented by A's consumption possibility curve which is shown as TT in Figure 3.3(a).

The consumption possibility curve (TT) is derived by vertically subtracting B_2B_2 from FF in Figure 3.3(c). At the point P in Figure 3.3(c) individual B consumes G_1 units of the public good and OX_1 units of the private good. Since B is consuming all the available units of the private good there is no private good available for individual A's consumption and since the public good G_1 is available to both A and B this defines the point P' on TT in Figure 3.3(a). At P' individual A consumes zero units of the private good and G_1 units of the public good. The point Q' is derived in a similar way. Moving down the curve B_2B_2 in Figure 3.3(c) and vertically subtracting B_2B_2 from FF over the range G_1G_2 generates a series of combinations of public and private goods that are available for A's consumption. The consumption possibility curve TT is thus the locus of these combinations of public and private goods available for A's consumption once B's consumption has been satisfied.

The combination of X and G that will maximise A's utility function, given that individual B must remain on indifference curve B_2B_2, is given by the tangency between A's indifference map and the consumption possibility curve TT. Note, however, that it is not given by the maximum of TT.

At the point M in Figure 3.3(a) individual A will consume X'_A units of the private good and G' units of the public good. By definition individual B will also consume G' units of the public good whereas he will consume X'_B units of the private good (point N in Figure 3.3(b)). At the point M in Figure 3.3(a) it is impossible for individual A to move to a higher indifference curve without making individual B worse off. Thus the combination of outputs represented by points M in Figure 3.3(a) and N in 3.3(b) must be a Pareto-optimal combination of the public and private goods.

At any value of G, the slope of the TT curve (in Figure 3.3(a)) equals the scope of the production possibility curve FF (in Figure 3.3(c)) minus the slope of B_2B_2. At a Pareto optimum, the slope of the TT curve equals the slope of A_1A_1. Thus at a Pareto optimum we have the following condition: slope of production possibility curve = slope of B_2B_2 + slope of A_1A_1. This can be written equivalently in more formal terms as:

$$MRT = MRS^A + MRS^B$$

where MRT is the marginal rate of transformation between X and G and MRS^A and MRS^B are the marginal rates of substitution between X and G for individuals A and B respectively.

The reader will recall that the corresponding Pareto optimality of an economy with two private goods is:

$$MRT = MRS^A = MRS^B.$$

The above construction defines one particular Pareto optimum. A series of Pareto optima could be generated by choosing other indifference curves for individual B, thereby deriving a family of consumption possibility curves for individual A. This is shown in Figure 3.4. The locus LL represents the points of tangency between A's consumption possibility curves and his indifference curves. For each point on LL, giving a location on individual A's ordinal utility index, there is a corresponding point on B's ordinal utility index. Thus it is possible to translate these points of correspondence in A's and B's ordinal utility indices into utility space and thereby to derive the utility possibility locus of all Pareto-optimal points. This is given in Figure 3.5, where UU is the utility possibility locus and U^A and U^B measure A's and B's utilities respectively on an ordinal scale.

To determine the most preferred social state or the 'bliss point' B in Figure 3.5, a social welfare function $W_0 W_0$, of the Samuelson-Bergson type, is introduced which reflects society's ethical preferences by ranking the alternative Pareto-optimal allocations. This most preferred state of the world, B, i.e. the

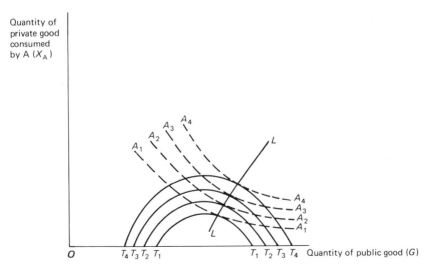

Fig. 3.4

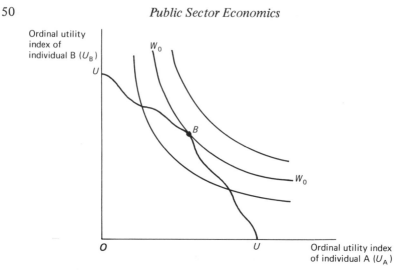

Fig. 3.5

tangency between W_0W_0 and UU, now feeds back into the model and defines the optimal mix of public and private goods and the distribution of private goods between individuals A and B. It furthermore defines the set of efficient prices both for the public and private goods and for the factors of production, and thus the distribution of welfare between individuals A and B.

In the general case for any economy characterised by the existence of public goods, private goods and many individuals, the condition for the optimal supply of public goods is, therefore, that the sum of the marginal rates of substitution must equal the marginal rate of transformation

$$\sum_{i=1}^{n} MRS_i^{jk} = MRT^{jk} \qquad i = 1 \ldots n \text{ (the number of individual consumers)}$$

$$\text{and } j, k = 1 \ldots m \text{ (the number of commodities)}$$

In other words, if the marginal rate of substitution reflects the marginal benefit that the individual receives from a marginal increase in the quantity of the public good (taking the private good as *numeraire*), then because everyone consumes the public good the marginal benefits must be summed over all individuals. The increase in total benefit resulting from a marginal increase in the quantity of a public good is the sum of the individual marginal benefits.

By taking the private good as *numeraire* it is possible to express the optimality conditions for the supply of public goods in terms of efficiency prices. By definition $MRS_{GX}^A = P_G^A/P_X^A$ and $MRS_{GX}^B = P_G^B/P_X^B$; furthermore,

$MRT_{GX} = MC_G/MC_X$. Thus:

$$P_G^A/P_X^A + P_G^B/P_X^B = MC_G/MC_X = MRT$$

since
$$P_X^A \equiv P_X^B \equiv P_X$$

i.e.
$$\frac{P_G^A + P_G^B}{P_X} = \frac{MC_G}{MC_X} = MRT.$$

Set $P_X = 1$. Then:

$$P_G^A + P_G^B = MC_G.$$

That is, the Pareto-optimal supply of a public good requires a set of individualised (or personalised) prices for each consumer adding to marginal cost. This is the same result that was derived and discussed in the partial equilibrium analysis section.

Samuelson's model for the optimum supply of a pure public good is a general equilibrium model and is concerned to demonstrate the internal logical consistency of the analysis which will determine the existence, uniqueness and stability of the set of equilibrium prices for public and private goods. As such it rests upon a number of restrictive assumptions each of which is highly instructive when considering the problems that any fiscal organisation will face when trying to supply the optimal level and mix of public goods in the real world.

First, the model assumes the existence of some omniscient planner who knows the set of prices that each individual would be willing to pay for public goods. These prices are then fed into the general plan which computes for the economy as a whole the set of public and private good quantities. To be able to solve for the distribution of welfare within the economy, the omniscient planner would require a complete specification of the utility functions of all individuals.

Clearly, it is impossible for any central planning authority to have this detail of information and Samuelson is not foolishly suggesting that a government should rush out and start collecting it. But what is clear from the analysis is that a Pareto-optimal supply of public goods would require this kind of information.

The failure of the planning authority to secure information on the set of prices that each individual would be willing to pay for the public good is related to the second restrictive assumption on which the model is based. It assumes that each individual would be willing accurately to reveal his preferences for public goods. This assumption, it will be recalled, we also made in the partial equilibrium analysis of public goods.

The fact that individuals will find it to their advantage not to reveal their preferences for public goods accounts for the failure of the planning authority to compute a set of prices for public goods, and as we have seen also accounts for the failure of decentralised markets to do the same. Since non-exclusion implies that individuals can enjoy the benefits of the public good (once it is produced) without contributing to the cost of providing it there is every incentive for an individual to act as a 'free-rider', i.e. not reveal his preferences.

It is of interest to note, however, that the non-revelation of preferences or the less extreme case of distortion of preferences is part of the more general problem of specifying the conditions and incentives necessary for the correct revelation of preferences both for public *and* private goods. The key to understanding the issue is to consider the number of participants involved in the economic exchange.

In a pure exchange economy with a small number of participants and with only private goods, the demand registered by any single agent is likely to be a significant proportion of the aggregate demand. If an agent was to distort his preferences, thereby altering his offers to buy and sell at values that depart from their competitive values, then he could by this action influence the final prices at which trade takes place. Whether or not the individual will engage in such behaviour depends upon the incentive to do so, i.e. the expected utility gain. The expected gains to the individual from distorting his preferences are clearly greater the smaller the number of agents in the economy. As the size of the group increases the individual's demand relative to total demand becomes increasingly smaller and his ability to influence prices diminishes, thereby reducing any potential gains from deviant behaviour.

For an economy with public goods and a small number of consumers, each individual's share of the total cost of producing the public good is likely to be substantial. In this small group there is a strong incentive for the individual to reveal his preferences accurately, because if he did not the supply of the public good would be significantly reduced. As the size of the group increases, each individual's contribution to the total cost becomes much smaller, so that his failure to contribute will not lead to a reduction in the supply of the public good. In this case there is a very weak incentive for the individual to reveal his true preferences. The result of the combined actions of all individuals who take this position is that the public good will not be supplied through a set of decentralised markets – a result that we have already noted.

Thus, in the case of private goods, when the group size is small the incentives for individuals to distort their preferences are greater than in the large-group case; whereas in the case of public goods the converse is true.

It also seems unlikely, even in the small-group case, that voluntary agreements will enable a Pareto-efficient supply of public goods to be achieved. Each individual within the group has an incentive to minimise his contribution to total cost and is thus likely to engage in strategic behaviour which will involve preference distortion (but not the extreme case of preference non-revelation).

In general, neither a set of decentralised markets, nor a central planning system, nor a set of voluntary agreements is likely to produce a Pareto-efficient supply of public goods, without the strong assumption of true revelation of preferences.

Finally, it should be noted that public goods in the Samuelson model must be financed by a set of benefit taxes while distributional objectives be taken care of by means of a set of lump sum taxes. Lump sum taxes will be non-distortionary; i.e. the effects of lump sum taxes are pure income effects leaving relative prices unchanged. Since the set of relative prices is not affected, the imposition of lump sum taxes will not influence the consumer's relative demands for public and private goods. The neutrality of alternative taxes is taken up and developed in more detail later, especially in Chapter 19.

Wicksell and Lindahl's model of public good provision

One of the conclusions of the previous section was that, while Samuelson had established the conditions for the optimal provision of public goods, there did remain a number of questions about how his analysis related to actual economies. Samuelson's model, however, is a neoclassical generalisation of the earlier models of Wicksell[10] and Lindahl.[11] These earlier studies made use of the voluntary exchange approach of the benefit principle of taxation. Moreover, in contrast to Samuelson's more abstract approach, they attempted to relate their analysis to the decision-making processes that are found in actual democracies.

Both Wicksell's and Lindahl's models are normative. They seek to determine the principles and decision-making rules that democracies should adopt when choosing 'just' levels of output for public goods and when deciding upon a 'just' distribution of the tax burden between individuals. But prescription and description get badly mixed up in their models, which makes reading the original works extremely difficult.

It is, however, instructive to consider the Wicksell/Lindahl model since it brings out clearly a number of analytical problems that democracies face when providing public goods and determining tax rates.

Lindahl's model[12] can be thought of as describing a pseudo-equilibrating process for providing public goods. In the model there are two individuals A and B; they can also be thought of as two political parties representing the homogeneous preferences of two groups of the electorate. The problem is then to find out the conditions that will guarantee a set of equilibrium tax shares and public good outputs and to examine the properties of that equilibrium further in terms of its uniqueness and stability.

The model is set out in Figure 3.6. The vertical axis (h) represents individual A's share of the total cost of providing the public good. If individual A's tax share is h then individual B's must, by definition, be equal to $(1-h)$. These tax shares are, for the purpose of the analysis, regarded as 'tax prices'. The horizontal axis (G) represents the quantity of public goods provided. It could also represent the volume of public expenditures. The two curves AA and BB represent the public good demand curves of individuals A and B respectively. The curve AA is drawn with respect to origin O_A and BB with respect to origin O_B.

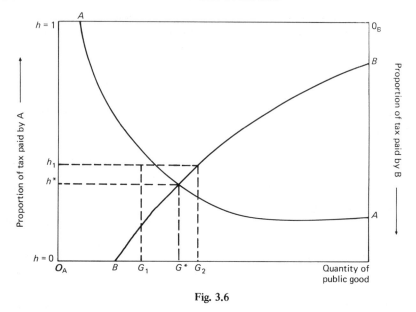

Fig. 3.6

The problem can be set out in general terms as follows. Each individual has a utility function U with public goods (G) and private goods (X) as arguments:

$$U_A = \phi_A(X^A, G)$$

$$U_B = \phi_B(X^B, G)$$

where X^A and X^B are the vectors of private goods consumed by A and B and G is the vector of public goods.

Both A and B wish to maximise their utilities subject to their budget constraints:

$$Y^A \geqq pX^A + hG$$

$$Y^B \geqq pX^B + (1-h)G$$

where Y^A and Y^B are individual A's and B's income respectively, and p is the vector of private good prices.

By varying h, and keeping all other variables constant, individual A's demand curve is generated; likewise so is B's. Given the two demand curves AA and BB in Figure 3.6, the next step is to establish an equilibrium tax share for A (h^*) and an equilibrium level of output (G^*). Take some arbitrary tax share h_1. Individual A would prefer, given h_1 a level of public goods equal to G_1, whereas individual B would prefer G_2. There is a disagreement between the two parties, and in such a situation the more powerful party would win. This is the normal outcome of all bilateral monopoly situations. The final solution is, therefore, *a priori* indeterminate and dependent upon the relative power of the two parties. In order to overcome this indeterminacy Wicksell and Lindahl proposed that the power of the two parties be equalised. Thus an alternative tax share is suggested and the outputs of G demanded by A and B are again compared. It can be seen that this process of tatonnment will continue until tax share h^* is reached. At h^* both A and B agree on the single level of public good output G^*. The combination h^*G^* is referred to in the literature as the '*Lindahl equilibrium*'.

This geometrical presentation of the Lindahl equilibrium used partial equilibrium analysis. Recently a number of economists have examined both the existence and other properties of the Lindahl equilibrium in a general equilibrium context; see Foley,[13] Milleron[14] and Roberts.[15] Each takes a slightly different approach in proving the existence of the equilibrium. Foley replaces each public good in the analysis by a 'personalised' private good. Each good has its own price and each person must be constrained to choose the same quantity. Milleron's approach uses duality theory, in which the indirect utility function is used to choose prices. Roberts uses a mixture of Walrasian analysis (price adjustment) and Marshallian analysis (quantity adjustment). In Roberts' model, public good prices adjust for a given price. Private good prices are common to all, while public good quantities are common to all. The advantage of Roberts' approach over the others is that it is not necessary to make artificial constructions as in Foley's model nor is it necessary to consider an associated economy such as the dual as in Milleron's. The above outline can give the student nothing other than a taste of the flavour of the analysis which is representative of modern general equilibrium analysis' treatment of public goods, and a useful starting point to such analysis is found in Roberts.

The welfare significance of the Lindahl equilibrium has been demonstrated by Johansen,[16] who shows that the Lindahl equilibrium is Pareto-optimal. Given that Wicksell and Lindahl's main emphasis was to establish a solution to the public goods problem which would produce a set of 'just' tax shares and public good outputs, it is now possible to see that their view of social justice was limited to that which produced a Pareto-optimal outcome. The story told by Wicksell and Lindahl was, however, more complex than this. They saw the budgetary process as two stages. The first stage adjusted the distribution of welfares within society according to some principle of social justice. Having established a just distribution of welfare, the next stage was to determine a just set of public expenditures and tax shares. Such an outcome was to be established in a democracy by employing the 'unanimity principle' whereby only those tax and expenditure proposals that receive 100 per cent of the votes were to be accepted. Anyone who would be made worse off under any other set of proposals had a veto which he had the right to express.

While the Wicksell/Lindahl model attempted to present a realistic discussion of how decisions should be taken in a democracy, the assumptions upon which it is based reveal the problems that tax and expenditure decision-making in actual democracies face. Again the process of voluntary exchange between the two parties is based upon the benefit principle of taxation and individuals are assumed to reveal their preferences accurately. The unanimity principle (as will be shown later in Chapter 4) is expensive to operate. The time taken to search out the unanimous solution would be considerable and in the mean time the benefits of the public programme would be lost.

Wicksell and Lindahl's description of the adjustment process towards an equilibrium is also not convincing. When the system is, for example, out of equilibrium, who adjusts the tax shares to bring it back into equilibrium? This question is of particular relevance if the equal power assumption is dropped and if the individuals engage in strategic behaviour. Individual A, for example, could search out the maximum tax share individual B would be willing to pay rather than not have the public good produced. A would then adjust his voting for tax shares accordingly. But bargaining takes time and can delay (as in the case of unanimity) the introduction of public programmes.

Mixed goods

A mixed good is one which possesses both public- and private-good character-istics. For example, education and health services have in general a private consumption benefit element which the individual consumer enjoys and at the same time a public consumption benefit or externality which other members of the community enjoy. If an individual receives an injection to reduce the effects of malaria or smallpox he receives a private benefit whilst at the same time his neighbours receive a benefit through the reduction in the probability of them catching the disease. These goods are analysed in Figure 3.7.

In Figure 3.7(a) the demand curves D_p^1 and D_p^2 of individuals 1 and 2 for the private good X are shown. The total demand curve D_p^{1+2} is derived from *horizontally summing* the individual demand curves. There is, however, a non-excludable element or externality in the sense that individual 1 benefits from individual 2's consumption and vice versa. In Figure 3.7(b) individual 1's and 2's marginal valuation of this public-good element are shown by D_E^1 and D_E^2 and the total marginal valuation is the *vertical summation* of the two individual marginal valuation curves and is shown as D_E^{1+2}. The overall demand curve is derived in (c) by vertically adding D_p^{1+2} and D_E^{1+2}. Given the marginal cost curve *MC* the optimal output is $\bar{X}$. The overall price $(p + r)$ is made up of a market price element (p) and the social valuation of the externality (r).

Impure public goods and the theory of clubs

In practice there are few cases of pure public goods. Instead, the characteristics of goods place them either towards the pure private good end of the spectrum or

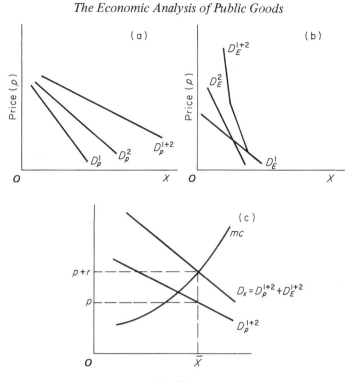

Fig. 3.7

towards the pure public good end. There are many goods which are indivisible and which many individuals could consume simultaneously up to the capacity constraint, thereafter the good becomes congested. There usually exists, however, some exclusion technology which makes it possible to charge individuals prices for the use of the commodity. Examples of such cases include swimming pools, golf courses, and bridges. These cases have come to be analysed in the context of the general theory of clubs following the seminal work of James Buchanan (1965), although earlier writers such as Jack Wiseman (1957) had already set out the basic notion. The purpose of a club is to exploit economies of scale, to share the costs of providing an indivisible commodity or to satisfy a taste for association with other individuals who have similar preference orderings. In their survey article on the theory of clubs Sandler and Tschirhart (1980) define a club as 'a voluntary group deriving mutual benefit from sharing one or more of the following: production costs, the members characteristics or a good characterised by excludable benefits'.

  The theory of clubs has been put to a number of uses including the analysis of congestion and the establishment of an optimal set of congestion taxes, the determination of optimal group size in the cases of alliances, cooperatives, communities and cities.

Buchanan model of clubs

The assumptions underlying Buchanan's model are, a club can costlessly exclude non-members, there is no discrimination against its members by other members of the club, and the benefits and costs are shared equally amongst the membership. A Buchanan club is a voluntary association of individuals and the analysis is carried out by examining the behaviour of the representative individual member of the club denoted by i. Assume that the individual's utility function is given by:

$$\text{Max } U^i(y^i, X, s)$$

where $y^i = i$th individuals consumption of private goods
$\quad\ X$ = an impure public good
$\quad\ s$ = the size of the group

The analytical problems are to, (a) determine the optimality conditions for the club good, (b) determine the quantity of the good to be provided, and (c) determine the optimal size of the club. The optimality conditions are as for the mixed good case (*op. cit.*). Both (b) and (c) have to be determined simultaneously and this is illustrated, following Sandler and Tschirhart (1980), by graphical means in Figure 3.8.

In the first quadrant are shown the benefit and cost curves of providing the shared commodity to three different sized groups, s_1, s_2 and s_3. The shape of the benefit curves shows diminishing returns to consumption whilst the cost curve shows constant returns to scale. Take some given membership such as s, the optimal level of X is at X_1 where the marginal benefit (i.e. the slope of the B curve) is equal to marginal cost (the slope of the C curve). For a facility of a given quantity X as the size of the consuming group increases from s_1 to s_2 the benefit curve moves down because of the negative effects of congestion, whereas the cost per person falls as membership size increases because there are more people over which to spread the total cost. In quadrant I a set of optimal combinations of club size and output are established (i.e. $\{s^*, X^*\}$, $\{s_1, X_1\}$, $\{s_2, X_2\}$). These are then plotted in quadrant IV as the locus X_{opt}.

A similar exercise is carried out in quadrant II. In this case the optimal membership size for given facility sizes X_1, X_2 and X^*. The shape of the benefit curve shows the increasing benefits of a number of people associating with one another and then the costs of congestion. The falling cost curve shows the advantages of sharing the fixed costs of the facility over increasingly larger groups. Because equal cost sharing is assumed the cost curves are rectangular hyperbolas. Optimal membership exists where the slopes of the benefit and cost curves are equal. Thus, s is the optimal club size for X_1; s_2 for X_2 and s^* for X^*. These optima are translated to the locus S_{opt} in quadrant IV.

The overall optimum exists where the S_{opt} curve and the X_{opt} curve intersect in quadrant IV. The reader should carry out the following exercise. Starting

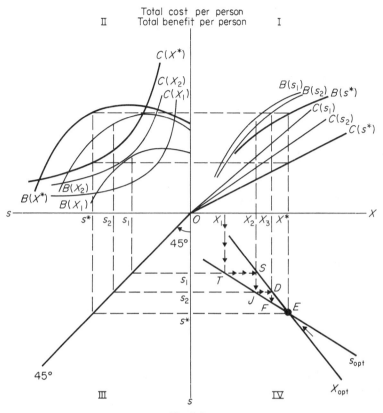

Fig. 3.8

[Source: T. Sandler and J. T. Tschirhart, 'The Theory of Clubs: A Survey', *Journal of Economic Literature*, Vol. XVIII (December 1980), page 1486]

at public good provision X_1 show that by following the path *TSJDFE* an equilibrium is established.

Mechanisms for preference revelation

Throughout this chapter the 'tax price' approach has been used in the analytical treatment of pure public goods. But given the nature of pure public goods there are problems of getting the consumer to reveal both his preferences for public goods and how much he would be willing to pay for them. The consumer has no incentive to reveal his true preferences and rational individuals will tend to understate their preferences. This problem has led to a number of economists studying, at an abstract level, possible mechanisms for the revelation of preferences.

At the simplest level it is possible to think of asking a representative from the group which consumes the public good to state his marginal willingness to pay. Suppose that there are N people in the population and that the representative consumer's marginal willingness to pay is t. At the optimum the marginal cost will be Nt and the public good will be supplied up to that point. The total cost of providing the public good will be collected via taxes. In this case if the representative is truely representative he will accurately reveal information about preferences since to do otherwise will result in the wrong quantity of the public good being provided. But to the truly representative this individual needs to be fully informed and that is a costly exercise when the consuming group is large. Furthermore, it runs into a number of collective choice problems which are discussed in Chapter 4.

An alternative suggestion was made by the economist, Charles Tiebout. In his formulation Tiebout imagined an economy which was characterised by local public goods, i.e. public goods, the benefits of which are confined to a specific region.[17] Individuals are then assumed to 'vote with their feet', allocating themselves between neighbourhoods or regions according to their preferences for public goods and the associated tax rates. The Tiebout hypothesis (which is discussed again in Chapter 9) gives an apparent mechanism for individuals to reveal their preferences and a solution to the public goods optimality problem. The solution is not, however, without its problems. First, there would need to be a very large number of potential neighbourhoods for individuals to move to. Second, there are important economies of association to be gained when a number of persons share the financing of an uncongested public good. This non-convexity creates problems for the optimality conditions.

Recently a group of economists working in game theory have examined exchange relationships in which truth telling by each party to the exchange is necessarily the dominant strategy. In particular the work of Clarke, Groves and Ledyard is of interest and Tideman and Tullock have provided an interesting graphical analysis. The flavour of this kind of analysis can be obtained from the following example. Suppose that there are two choices facing three individual consumers (A, B and C) of a public good. They can either choose an amount of the good L or an amount of S. Each consumer is asked to assign his 'money votes' for each of the alternatives L and S, equivalent to the marginal benefit received. These are recorded in Table 3.1.

It is seen that individual A is £30 better off if L is chosen over S; individual B is £40 better off if S is chosen and individual C is £20 better off if L is chosen. Assume that S is the status quo. The following rule is chosen to decide upon which alternative wins. Add up the benefits associated with each alternative: that with the most benefits wins. In this case it is L. The next problem is to ensure that each individual will reveal his true preferences and this is the focus of the analysis. Each individual will be charged a tax which will be calculated in the following way. Add up the 'money votes' of all individuals except the ith one and find out the outcome. Now add in the money votes of the ith individual

Table 3.1.

Individual	Alternative		Tax
	L	S	
A	30		20
B		40	0
C	20		10
Totals	50	40	30

and determine whether or not this changes the outcome. If it does not then he pays no tax. If it does he pays a tax equal to the *net* gains expected from the victory of the other alternative in the absence of his vote. Under this rule the individual only pays a tax if his vote is decisive in changing the outcome. In terms of Table 3.1 these rules can be illustrated as follows. The tax column shows the taxes paid by each individual. If A does not vote alternative L has 20 votes and S has 40 votes; thus A is decisive for the determination of the outcome by 20 votes. Hence he pays a tax of 20. Individual B's vote is not decisive and so he pays no tax whereas C's vote is since without it L would receive 30 votes and S 40. Therefore C pays a tax of 10.

In this process each individual has an incentive to reveal his true preferences since if A declared benefits less than 20 alternative S would win and if he declared benefits more than 20 it would make no difference to the final outcome. There is no incentive to understate one's preferences since this runs the risk of losing and there is no incentive to overstate them since this runs the risk of being the decisive vote and hence a tax payment is incurred. It should be realised that these tax payments are over and above the 'tax prices' used to finance the public-goods provision. Rather the taxes in this example are part of the incentive system used to get individuals to reveal their true preferences.

The above example is only one (a very simple one) of a large number of mechanisms and proposals which have been recently analysed. They are very much conceptual exercises with little real-world application, but they do serve to illustrate the problems which are posed in the real world and the elaborate mechanisms and enormous amount of information which are required. The student who wishes to follow up this literature should consult Mueller's book *Public Choice* (pp. 72-84) which contains an excellent survey.

Conclusion

This chapter has concentrated upon the question of efficiency in the provision of public goods. Using partial and general equilibrium analysis we have shown the conditions that must be satisfied if public goods are to be allocated according to the requirements of Pareto efficiency. Clearly the approach has been abstract, but it has shown us the nature of the problems that actual fiscal institutions have to deal with. The economic behaviour and allocative processes used by fiscal institutions can now be considered against the background of the results provided by this chapter.

Appendix: The benefit principle and the ability-to-pay approach to taxation

Taxes finance the activities of government; they are, therefore, used to finance public expenditures. However, taxes are also the instruments through which governments redistribute income and wealth and, moreover, they are an integral part of government's fiscal policy, being used to stabilise aggregate demands. Clearly, taxes, as policy instruments, have a number of functions to perform and objectives to satisfy, and it is not too surprising, therefore, that the tax system is strained when the policy objectives come into conflict. Whether or not government activity improves social welfare will partially depend upon whether or not the government has a 'good' tax system. To answer this question we need to know something about the principles of taxation and what is meant by 'good'. The purpose of this appendix is to set out two alternative principles of taxation that have emerged from the literature on taxation during the past 200 years. These are the benefit principle of taxation and the ability-to-pay approach. Since the benefit principle is implicitly used in public good optimisation models it is useful to explain these terms at this point. Some of the other terms used in this appendix are defined in the glossary in Chapter 9.

(1) The benefit principle

The benefit principle of taxation has its roots firmly established in the voluntary exchange or price theory of public finance and examines the costs and benefits of public sector activities that face individual citizen/voters. Individuals are assumed to adjust their consumption of any good (public or private) until the marginal benefit from consumption is equated to the marginal cost. The prescriptions that follow from this are that each individual's tax contributions should be based upon the benefit received from consuming public goods. Thus the benefit principle for the public sector is analogous to the market approach used to study the private sector.

While the benefit principle is a useful first approximation which can be used to simplify optimisation analysis, it obviously has a number of drawbacks from the point of view of discussions of the equity and justice properties of tax systems.

By thinking of taxes as voluntary payments for publicly provided goods, the principle does not conform to a reality in which taxes are coercive. If taxes were voluntary and based upon the marginal valuation of each individual, then this offers scope for everyone to under-record the benefits that they, in fact, receive. In other words, the benefit principle suffers from the strategic behaviour of the 'free-rider'. Moreover, the benefit principle ignores completely the redistribution of income aims of government by concentrating purely on the efficient allocation of resources to public and private sector activities.

(2) The ability-to-pay principle

The nineteenth- and early twentieth-century public finance economists were concerned with the design of tax systems. They believed in minimising the individual sacrifice of taxation and to achieve this end were more concerned to reduce public spending. They also required that the tax system be 'just'.

Rather than basing an individual's tax liabilities on how much benefit the individual received from public spending the ability-to-pay principle preferred to levy taxes on how much the individual could afford to pay. Unequals, according to the principle, should be treated unequally while equals were to be treated equally. This 'equity principle of taxation' was based upon a particular notion of justice, namely that equality in tax payments implied equality in sacrifice.

The ability-to-pay approach has its foundations in the writings of both Adam Smith and John Stuart Mill. In the *Wealth of Nations*, Smith pointed out that:

> The subjects of every state ought to contribute toward the support of the government, as nearly as possible, in proportion to their respective abilities; that is, in proportion to the revenue which they respectively enjoy under the protection of the state. The expense of government to the individuals of a great nation is like the expense of management to the joint tenants of a great estate who are all obliged to contribute in proportion to their respective interest in the state. In the observation or neglect of this maxim consists what is called the equality or inequality of taxation.[19]

He further points out:

> It is not very unreasonable that the rich should contribute to the public expense, not only in proportion to their revenue but something more than that proportion.[20]

John Stuart Mill also subscribed to the ability-to-pay approach to taxation. Mill founded the debate firmly on questions of justice and fairness as can be seen in the following extract from his *Principles of Political Economy*:

> Government must be regarded as so pre-eminently a concern of all, that to determine who are the most interested in it is of no real importance.... As in a case of voluntary subscription for a purpose in which all are interested, all are thought to have done their part fairly when each has contributed according to his means, that is, has made an equal sacrifice for the common object....[21]

It can be seen, however, from his opening sentence that Smith was not consistent, since he also seemed to believe in the benefit principle.

Mill rejected the benefit principle because he believed it would result in regressive taxation since the poor were more in need of the services of the state than were the rich. For Mill the tax system based on the benefit principle was not 'just'. Instead, all individuals should be treated equally under the law. 'For what reason ought equality be the rule in matters of taxation? For the reason that it ought to be so in all affairs of government'.[22]

Mill's interpretation of the ability-to-pay principle led him to propose a system of proportional taxation. He made no attempt to prove his case but merely asserted it. As a utilitarian he assumed that the absolute loss in income to the rich man would represent a smaller welfare loss than it would to a poorer man.

But what is meant by the deceptively simple and appealing notion of 'equality of sacrifice'? There are three distinct interpretations:

(1) equal absolute sacrifice; i.e. each individual experiences the same loss in total utility;
(2) equal proportional sacrifice; i.e. for each individual the ratio of the utility lost to total utility should be equal;
(3) equal marginal sacrifice; i.e. for each individual taxation will reduce income to the point that the marginal utility of income is equal for all.

Consider each of these cases in turn.

(*a*) *Equal absolute sacrifice.* Assume that each individual has identical preferences. Given this assumption the same utility function can be used for each individual. This utility function is shown in Figure A3.1. It shows that as income rises total utility rises but at a decreasing rate (i.e. declining marginal utility of income). There are two individuals A and B. Individual A's original income is shown as OY_A^1 and that of B as OY_B^1. If individuals are taxed so that both experience an equal absolute sacrifice, then $AB = CD$:

(1) tax paid by individual A = (pretax income − post-tax income)
$$= (OY_A^1 - OY_A^2)$$
(2) tax paid by individual B $= (OY_B^1 - OY_B^2)$

i.e. the total utility lost by each individual is equal as a result of the imposition of the tax.

(*b*) *Equal proportional sacrifice.* Under this rule, and making the same assumptions as in the equal absolute sacrifice rule, then for two individuals A and B;

$$OU_A^1/OU_A^2 = OU_B^1/OU_B^2.$$

This is shown in Figure A3.2.

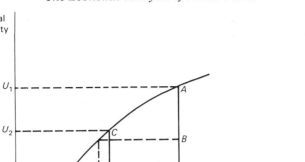

Fig. A3.1

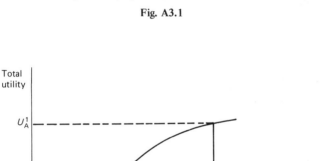

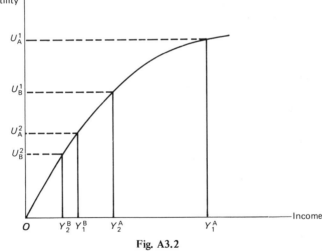

Fig. A3.2

(c) *Equal marginal sacrifice.* The slope of the total utility curve is the marginal utility at that point. In Figure A3.3 the slope of the total utility curve at point X is given by the slope of the tangent to X, i.e. TT. If Y_A and Y_B are individual A and B's pretax incomes respectively, then the equal marginal sacrifice principle

Public Sector Economics

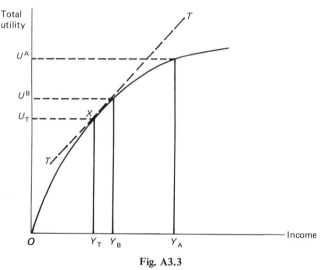

Fig. A3.3

will reduce A and B's incomes post-tax to the point at which they are equal. This is a point such as X where incomes post-tax are equated to Y_T.

Let us now use these three alternative interpretations of 'equal sacrifice' to consider their implications for the structure of tax rates. In the case of equal absolute sacrifice and a declining marginal utility of income function, nothing conclusive can be said about whether or not the tax will be progressive. This will depend upon the rate of decline in the marginal utility of income (i.e. it depends upon the value of the elasticity of the marginal utility – MU – of income). Therefore, the tax may be proportional, progressive, or regressive depending upon the rate of decline in the MU of income.

In the case of equal proportional sacrifice a falling straight line MU of income function requires progressive taxation. However, if the MU of income function is not a straight line the result is inconclusive and will depend upon the level and the rate of change in the MU function in addition to the amount of tax revenue that has to be raised and the initial distribution of income.

Finally, in the case of equal marginal sacrifice, the arguments for progressive taxation are unambiguous. Thus, top incomes are reduced until the amount of the tax revenue is achieved. If the tax is used to redistribute incomes, to the point of making incomes equal, then this would call for maximum progression. If, however, the objective of the tax is to finance public expenditures, then the degree of progression will depend upon how much revenue is to be raised.

It is, therefore, seen from this brief discussion that the ability-to-pay rule is ambiguous and inconclusive with respect to whether or not progressive taxes are required. The result will depend upon the precise definition of 'equal sacrifice' chosen and the properties of the utility function which is used, i.e. the shape of the MU of income function.

(*d*) *Critique of ability-to-pay approach.* First examine the assumptions:

(1) income is assumed to be the main determinant of utility;

(2) marginal utility of income is assumed to be known and to decline as income increases;

(3) individual relative utilities are assumed to be measured by differences in their incomes;

(4) interpersonal comparisons of utility are allowed.

Clearly, income is not the only determinant of utility. It is an extremely difficult exercise to move from a total income schedule to a total utility schedule. The rules of the transformation are not at all clear. Very rich people can be miserable! Nor is it at all clear that the law of diminishing marginal utility applies equally to income as it does to commodities. It is assumed that as an individual's utility of each successive unit of the commodity will fall. But why should this be so for incomes?

Interpersonal comparisons of utility, which are assumed in the ability-to-pay approach, rely on the assumption of cardinal measures of utility. However, as the 'new welfare economics' of Robbins, Hicks and Kaldor have emphasised, it is better to consider ordinal measures of utility, and if that is done interpersonal comparisons are not possible.

There are, therefore, problems with both the benefit principle and the ability-to-pay approach. In the case of the benefit principle it was seen that as a principle of justice it was found wanting and that by implicitly assuming a market-type mechanism it therefore assumed that the exclusion principle applied to public goods; whereas the difficulties with the ability-to-pay approach are the restrictive assumptions placed on the utility function.

Questions of equity and justice in the design of tax systems are complex and will be dealt with more fully in Chapter 19. The answers to such questions will vary with the particular notion of justice that is chosen. This appendix has done nothing more than to introduce the problem. In the meantime, Robbins is given the last word:

> I do not believe and have never believed that in fact men are necessarily equal or should always be judged as such. But I do believe that in most cases, political calculations which do not treat them as if they were equal are morally revolting.[23]

CHAPTER 4

Social Choice

Each day governments make decisions that will influence the lives of most citizens of the state. Economic decisions are taken on particular policy variables such as the minimum lending rate of the central bank, the rate of change in the money supply, incomes policies, tax rates and the size and composition of public expenditures. Social policy decisions are taken on who will and who will not receive the benefits of specific welfare programmes while decisions in the field of international relations establish the basis for future exchanges (economic and non-economic) between the citizens of different nation states.

In each of these examples a group of individuals, referred to as 'the government', make decisions that commit the members/citizens of the state to certain actions. Social choice (or collective choice) is concerned with the relationships between the preferences of the individual members of the state (or society) and the collective choices made by government. There is a large number of possible relationships that might exist between the individual and the agency of collective choice. For example, in the case of liberal democracy, individuals, through a voting procedure, elect persons to *represent* their views. The group of elected representatives then makes decisions and choices on behalf of the wider group that has elected it. In the case of a dictatorship, the relationship between the individual's preferences and that of the ruling group is simple. The dictator's preferences are supreme and will overrule or dominate all other competing preferences.

For the purposes of this chapter we will be interested primarily in the problems that liberal democracy poses for social choice, first, because of the prevalence of liberal democracy in one form or another in many countries and second because it is implicitly such a theory that underlies most of our analysis of social choice. It is the social institution of liberal democracy that poses the most interesting and most difficult analytical problems in social choice. This should not, however, be thought to imply that the moral and ethical questions of collective choice are unimportant. Such considerations as we shall see are of extreme importance.

The approach that will be adopted in this chapter is, first, to consider the ageless debate between economists and political scientists on how we should approach the problem. This tends to be a complex methodological debate but one that should be encountered, if only briefly, in order to clear away some of the confusion caused by the vocabulary used. Second, we will consider a number of normative questions in social choice theory. The problem of defining the characteristics of a 'good' rule which will enable us to aggregate individual preferences into a social or collective preference will be examined. Third, some of the recent developments in the positive theory of collective choice will be reviewed, especially the economic theory of politics and voter behaviour. However, before embarking on the study of these problems let us now define the social choice problem more clearly.

The problem of social choice defined

In the previous chapter a Pareto-efficient level of public outputs was determined by assuming that each individual had a demand curve for public goods and that these individual demand curves were vertically aggregated to produce a total demand curve. The interaction of the total demand curve and the supply curve established the set of marginal conditions that are required for a Pareto-efficient allocation of resources to public goods (i.e. $\Sigma MRS = MRT$). Each individual was assumed to pay a price or a tax for the public output, which was directly proportional to the benefits received from consumption of the public good.

That particular model had a specific purpose. It abstracted from reality in an attempt to establish the necessary conditions for an optimum. At no point was it even thought of as a description of reality. Indeed, Samuelson, the architect of the model, throughout his writings has stressed that very point. Samuelson has pointed out that what the model demonstrates is the amount of information a perfectly discriminating monopolist would require in order to establish Pareto efficiency. As we have seen, a set of decentralised markets will fail to perform this task and so too would the public sector. The transactions costs of collecting the information on individual preferences, quite apart from the costs of dealing with the free-rider problem, would be quite enormous.

The problem of deciding upon the optimal distribution of welfare over the individuals in society was solved in the Samuelson public goods model in the standard fashion. That is, a Bergson social welfare function was used. Such a social welfare function assumes that non-economic influences on the individual's wellbeing are exogenous (they can affect economic variables but are not influenced by them). Furthermore, social welfare depends upon individual utilities. The Bergson social welfare function can be written as:

$$W = W(U_1\{X_1; V_1\} \ldots U_i\{\cdot\} \ldots U^s\{X_s; V_s\})$$

where: $X_i \equiv$ the vector of goods and services (public and private) that enter individual i's ordinal utility function $U\{\cdot\}$

$V_i \equiv$ the vector of factors of production supplied by individual i.

The Bergson social welfare function is a heuristic device for considering the role of distribution in economics; however, it does not provide an analysis of how society does in fact formulate and express collective value judgements.

These observations of the neoclassical public goods model serve to highlight two problems in social choice theory:

(*1*) *the collective decision*: a group, a committee, a cooperative or some other kind of collectivity has to choose among alternative proposals for action. Each member of the group has his own preferences over the set of alternatives. How do we go about aggregating these diverse individual preferences into a 'group' decision or collective outcome?

(2) *the social welfare judgement*: this problem is related to the first. How does a group of individuals decide upon the objectives that the members of the group should collectively pursue? In other words, where does the society's objective function or social welfare function originate?

Once the economist knows the aggregation rule, and once he knows what function is to be maximised, then he can apply his standard tools for the optimisation of social choices.

There are other questions that will interest us. We will be especially interested in the properties of the process or rule that enables us to move from a set of diverse individual preferences to a social preference. Since social choice rules and social welfare functions belong to the same family, it will be useful to speak more generally in terms of social or collective choice rules. This generally means that we will be able to think of the problem of social/collective choice as applying to collective choices made by society (i.e. the social welfare function approach) and equally to all collective choices irrespective of the size or the nature of the group, e.g. committees, boards, senates, sports clubs, etc. When dealing with social/collective choice rules we will regard them as representing society's constitution. A constitution is a set of legal rules that guides and constrains the way in which social/collective choices may or may not be made. The constitution, therefore, in practice embodies the social/collective choice rules. To ask if a constitution is good or bad is to ask whether or not the social/ collective choice rule is good/bad. In order to consider this question we need to have information about the properties of the social/collective choice rules and also a set of criteria against which they might be judged.

These questions are not too dissimilar from those that economists ask about the allocative and distributional efficiencies of alternative market structures. Given that social/collective choices refer to non-market decision-making, and, further, given that alternative social/collective choice rules will produce different allocations of goods and distributions of welfare, then what we are asking is, which constitutions are Pareto-efficient and maximise social welfare and which are not?

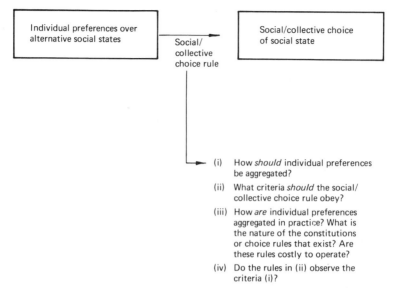

Fig. 4.1 *Notes:* (a) When considering the choices of committees etc. we think of choices being made over alternative actions. (b) When considering social choice it is useful to think of government making choices over alternative 'social states' where a social state is defined as: 'a description of the amount of each type of commodity in the hands of each individual, the amount of labour supplied by each individual, the amount of productive resource invested in each type of productive activity, such as municipal services, diplomacy, and its continuation by other means, and the erection of statues to famous men' (K. A. Arrow, *Social Choice and Individual Values*, p. 17).

The discussion so far can be summarised as in Figure 4.1. When choosing between alternative social/choice rules three questions are generally considered:

(1) is the rule ethically acceptable?
(2) is the rule technically feasible to operate?
(3) is the rule costly to use in practice?

Answers to these questions will be considered in the remainder of this chapter. Thus, we consider the set of possible social/collective choice rules and evaluate them, first, against a set of independently established ethical postulates in order to judge their normative properties and, second, against a set of technical criteria in order to judge their allocative efficiency.

The public interest *v.* the self-interest approaches

Economists and political scientists approach the problem of social/collective choice from the standpoint of different methodologies. Generally speaking, political scientists use the public interest approach while economists apply the self-interest approach.

(1) The public interest approach

This is set out in the works of Wildavky, Lindblom and Lindblom, and Dahl.
For political scientists, concepts of social welfare are embodied in theories of
the state and the social contract. In the public interest approach the individual,
in the analysis of collective choice, plays a subservient role to the set of social
organisations that makes social choices. The subject of analysis is the behaviour
of groups or organisations that are assumed to exist in order to serve the public
interest. Thus there is a tendency in the public interest approach to treat groups
'as if' they behaved like individuals. Groups are thought to have preferences and
the state is frequently referred to as if it existed independently of the persons
who make it up.

As far as this approach is concerned, the public interest is not a simple
aggregation of the individual's private self-interest. Thus, decisions made by the
collectivity will not necessarily be related in any precise way to the preferences
of the individuals who comprise the collectivity.

An immediate and interesting question that arises is: Where does the public
interest originate? Within this approach there is no single answer to the question.
First, there is a group who might be called the 'rationalists', who take the
existence of the public interest, or as they prefer to call it 'the common good',
as given. The common good is assumed to be expressed through the popular or
common will of the people, and it is the function of political and social
organisations to interpret this common will. Second, there are 'the idealists',
who regard the public interest to reside within the natural law. Since natural law
is axiomatic the public interest is as given. Third, there is that group of analysts
that regards the public interest as emerging from a process of continual conflict.
Policy is designed to produce agreement, to establish consensus and to minimise
instability. Such policies are regarded as serving the public interest. Furthermore,
instead of taking individual preferences as given, the political process is seen as
one that is designed to change preferences so as to bring about consensus.

(2) The self-interest approach

In contrast to the public interest approach, this uses the individual as the unit of
analysis and therefore studies the behaviour of the individual. This work is
usually associated with the work of Downs, Buchanan and Tullock, and
McKean. Individuals have a set of preferences and are assumed to behave in such
a way as to maximise their objective (i.e. utility), subject to a number of
constraints, which will include a resource constraint, legal and organisational
constraints, imperfect knowledge and imperfect foresight, etc. Thus the arguments of the individual's objective function and the set of incentives and constraints that he faces are the points of interest to the economist.

The self-interest approach can be used to explain a good deal of political
behaviour. By postulating that the individual behaves 'as if' he maximises utility

(note, there is nothing in the theory that requires that the individual must maximise utility in practice), a set of testable hypotheses can be generated. Judged as a methodology, the self-interest approach is more scientific in the Popperian sense since its hypotheses are at least capable of falsification by recourse to empirical investigation. That is, unlike the public interest approach, it does not depend upon the notion of some external set of circumstances generating the public interest. The public interest is the aggregation of individual self-interests.

Individual interests are satisfied through a complex set of voluntary exchanges. Agreement and stability between individuals will occur when there are no further gains to be made from exchanges. Thus individuals will agree to observe the rules of group membership (i.e. will accept the 'social contract') if the net benefits of doing so outweigh the costs (i.e. in terms of paying a price for the benefits of the collective output and also the cost of surrendering an amount of one's liberty and freedom).

Groups and collectives are seen to make decisions, but this is very different from saying that the group acts as if it were an individual. Thus the self-interest approach does not require the adoption of concepts such as the 'group mind', the 'group will' or 'collective rationality'.

The self-interest approach should not, however, be considered dogmatically individualistic. It is possible to use this approach and yet still recognise that individuals acting in a group may act differently from the way they would act as separate persons. In this case the self-interest approach identifies a synergy or an interdependence that has to be explained rather than taken as given. Likewise, it is possible in this framework to maintain the separation of the 'public interest' and 'self-interest'. Individuals can consider what is in the public interest and what would be in their own self-interest. The former takes into account the existence of others in the group whereas the latter does not. In Hume's tragedy of the commons the unregulated pursuit of self-interest was clearly identified from actions that were in the interest of the group as a whole. Finally, individuals may be willing to enter into a social contract only if certain others do so also.

Criteria for social choice rules

The economist's approach to the examination of social/collective choice rules is firmly based on the two pillars of individualism and ordinal preferences. In this section we will address ourselves to considering the following problem: What are the minimum conditions we would require a social choice rule (i.e. a constitution) to conform to for it to be ethically acceptable? This is the problem that Kenneth Arrow considered and his results have provided a much deeper understanding of the foundations of social choice.

Arrow's analysis proceeds by making the following set of assumptions.

(1) Rationality assumptions

For any given set of individual preferences the social choice rule must produce a social ordering that is complete and transitive where:

(1) completeness is defined as: for each pair of alternative social states either one is preferred to the other or the relationship between the two is indifference.

(2) transitivity: if social state x is preferred to social state y and social state y is preferred to social state z then x is preferred to z.

(2) Independence of irrelevant alternatives

Social choice over a set of alternative social states only depends upon the orderings of individuals over these alternatives and not on anything else. Thus if the choice is between x and y and if the relationship between x and w changes then this change is irrelevant to the ordering of x and y. Likewise, if the relationship between alternatives w and z changes then this does not affect the ordering of x and y.

Thus Arrow is placing a strong insistence upon the social ordering being derived from individual ordering; i.e. if the set of feasible alternative social states remains unaltered and if the option chosen by society from that set changes, then the change must have come about from a change in some individual's preferences.

(3) Pareto principle

If every individual in society strictly prefers x to y then the social ordering must show that x is preferred to y. If at least one person in society prefers x to y and if everyone else is indifferent between x and y then the social ordering must show that x is preferred to y.

(4) Unrestricted domain

The social ordering must be produced in such a way that the domain from which it is derived includes all logically possible individual orderings. That is, we do not wish to generate a social ordering by restricting the domain of individual orderings.

(5) Non-dictatorship

There does not exist an individual 'i' such that, for all alternatives x and y, if 'i' strictly prefers x to y then society will strictly prefer x to y regardless of other individual's preferences.

These conditions define the ethical requirements that need to be satisfied by any rule or procedure used to translate individual orderings into a social/collective ordering such that the social ordering determines the social/collective choice. Moreover, these conditions are necessary to ensure the internal logical consistency of constitutions. Moreover, since they are based on individual ordinal preferences, collective decision-making by making interpersonal comparisons of utilities is ruled out.

Majority voting

In a democracy one of the most prevalent social/collective choice rules is that of majority voting. The majority rule requires that at least the first whole integer above $n/2$ support an issue before it can be adopted (where n = number of votes). We can think of two distinct forms of majority decision-making and their distinction will be useful later. First, there is direct democracy, whereby social choices are determined *directly* by citizens on a major voting rule. Second, in comparison there is representative democracy, in which individuals are elected (via a majority voting procedure) to represent the interests of those who elected them to office. The representatives then vote on issues to make social choices. Either interpretation can be used in the examples that follow.

Does the majority decision rule conform to Arrow's conditions as outlined in the previous section; i.e. is the majority decision rule a good rule? Consider the following example. There are three voters labelled 1, 2 and 3, and there are three alternatives labelled A, B and C. The three alternatives could be thought of as three different policies or three different budgets, a high budget, a medium budget and a low budget. Each individual's preference ordering is revealed in his ranking of the three alternatives as shown below. Given these individual preference orderings over the three alternatives, and given the social/

	1st choice	*2nd choice*	*3rd choice*
Individual 1	A	B	C
Individual 2	B	C	A
Individual 3	C	A	B

collective choice rule of majority voting, let us now examine what will happen when we attempt to translate those individual preferences into a decision for the group. To find out which alternative is the majority outcome make a pairwise comparison between the alternatives:

(1) Compare alternatives A and B; since individuals 1 and 3 prefer A to B, A will win over B, two votes for and one against.
(2) Now compare A with C; individuals 2 and 3 prefer C to A, therefore, C wins over A.

The overall winner is C. But if C is compared with B individuals 1 and 2 prefer B to C, hence B wins over C! In other words, the outcome of this voting process is intransitive. The majority decision rule does not, therefore, conform to all of Arrow's conditions.

Arrow's analysis goes much further than the observation that the majority decision rule produces an intransitive social ordering. After all, this voting paradox was well known following the work of Condorcet in the eighteenth century. What Arrow established was that there does not exist a social choice rule that will satisfy all of his conditions. This is known as Arrow's possibility theorem and was stated by him as follows:

> If we exclude the possibility of interpersonal comparisons of utility, then the only methods of passing from individual tastes to social preferences which will be defined for a wide range of sets of individual orderings are either imposed of dictatorial.[1]

That an ethically satisfactory social choice rule is barred on formal logical grounds is an important result for the analysis of non-market decision-making and government decision-making in particular. It was also an important result for welfare economics since it hit at the foundations of the social welfare function. Since Arrow produced his results, a number of developments have taken place. Some individuals have attacked Arrow's conditions. The condition that has come under the most severe criticism is that of the independence of irrelevant alternatives.[2] Others have examined the properties of alternative aggregation procedures in relation to Arrow's criteria. Rather than regarding Arrow's postulates and his results as a stumbling block, a more useful way of proceeding is to regard them as a datum against which social/collective choice rules can be compared; in much the same way as perfectly competitive markets are used to make welfare judgements of alternative market structures.

(1) Single-peaked preferences

One means of proceeding from Arrow's results is to consider relaxing some of his assumptions.[3] It has been suggested by Duncan Black[4] that, by suitably restricting individual preferences to conform to a specific pattern, a transitive outcome to majority decision-making can be produced. The particular pattern imposed on individual preferences by Black was that they be single-peaked. This

	1st choice	2nd choice	3rd choice
Individual 1	A	B	C
Individual 2	C	B	A
Individual 3	B	C	A

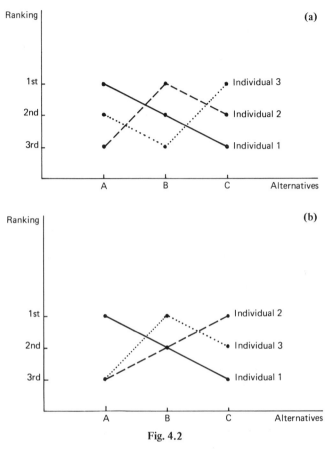

Fig. 4.2

can be demonstrated as follows. Assume as in the previous example that there are three individuals, 1, 2 and 3, and three alternatives, A, B and C. The individual's preferences are now given as shown below. Making pairwise comparisons between A and B, B wins over A and comparing B and C, B wins over C. Similarly C wins over A. Thus, in this example, given the particular configuration of individual preferences, the outcome of the majority decision rule is transitive. The configuration of individual preferences in the two examples chosen so far are set out in Diagram 4.2. The top panel shows that configuration of individual preferences which will produce an intransitive social ordering whereas the bottom panel results in a transitive ordering. The difference is that in the second case all individual preferences are 'single peaked'. The idea of single peakedness can be seen by looking at the configuration of individual 3's preferences in Figure 4.2(a). It is seen that this individual's preference ordering has two peaks; i.e. the line goes down and then up.

Some remarks about this result are in order. First, the outcome of the majority decision rule is now stable. In the previous example, which produced an intransitive social ordering, majorities 'cycled'. That is to say, the outcome depended upon the order in which alternatives were considered (the reader should prove this for himself). Single-peaked preferences break the cycle and thus produce a stable result. Second, while single-peakedness overcomes the voting paradox it violates Arrow's condition of the 'unrestricted domain'; i.e. Black's result depends upon restricting the set of individual preferences to those that are single-peaked. Third, is single-peakedness likely to exist in practice? Black thought that in most cases individual preferences would be single-peaked. There is good reason for holding this belief. Consider the first example in which individual 3's preference ordering was not single-peaked. In this case, if alternative A represents a small budget, B a medium-sized budget and C a large budget then on probabilistic grounds individual 3's preference ordering is not likely to occur; i.e. most individuals would not prefer a large budget to a small budget but prefer a small budget to a medium-sized budget! Furthermore, it has been demonstrated by Meyer and Plott[5] that for the case of three alternatives the probability that a unique majority outcome exists tends towards 91 per cent as the number of voters becomes very large. An associate piece of analysis has been carried out by Tullock and Campbell.[6] If n represents the number of individual optima (i.e. the number of outcomes that each individual considers to be optimal) and if m represents the number of alternative social states, then the probability of there being no majority winner is given by $A(m, n)$, which is an increasing function of m and n. As m increases or as n increases (or as both increase), the probability of majority decision-making resulting in ties increases. For highly homogeneous communities, however, in which there is a degree of consensus (i.e. common preferences), n will decline and therefore the probability of a majority outcome existing increases.

Tullock[7] has also argued that in the real world, where there are many more voters than there are alternative issues to be voted on, the probability of the voting paradox occurring is 'so small that it makes no practical difference'. The chances of concurrence will, therefore, be high while the costs of advocating alternatives and seeking agreement on them will invariably be greater than the benefits. If the actual outcomes of majority voting are indeed those that are close to the middle ground, then the outcomes can be considered to be acceptable. The validity of Tullock's analysis is clearly an empirical question.

It is fair to say that Tullock's analysis is better suited to some of the American voting procedures, in which individuals are asked to vote more frequently, on a larger number of issues and at different levels of government. In the UK system of representative democracy, where voting takes place less frequently, the number of 'voters' is essentially reduced to the three major parties, Conservative, Labour and Liberal-SDP Alliance, with the other parties (e.g. Scottish National Party) lining up with the 'big three' on specific issues. This, therefore, reduces to the case of a small number of voters for which concurrence is difficult to achieve. The difficulty of securing concurrence is seen in the problems of finding the basis of a coalition between any of the major parties. In looking for a coalition programme the number of available options increases. A coalition programme that will gain support over all others probably does not exist, which means that coalitions that are formed are in practice usually unstable.

Two additional features of simple majority voting models that should be noted are, first, that the majority decision rule will not produce a Pareto-optimal solution and, second, that it is impossible to express an intensity of preference for alternatives.

The majority decision rule will produce a Pareto-optimal outcome only in the trivial case for which all individuals have identical preference orderings. In other cases the rule does not take into account the changes in the utilities of losers and gainers. The decision is based on the number who gain as compared with the number who lose. Majority voting cannot be Pareto-optimal since a vote registered against an alternative implies that the marginal loss for that individual resulting from adoption of that alternative exceeds any marginal gain which that alternative might give to that individual. Majority voting outcomes will clearly have implications for the distribution of welfare in society and this result is regarded by many as the 'tyranny of the majority'.

(2) *Intensity of preferences*

In simple majority decision models it is not possible for the individual to express his intensity of preference for one alternative compared with another. The individual has a single vote, which is cast in favour of one of the alternatives. This should be compared to consumer decision-making in the market place, where intensity of preference can be registered by showing a willingness to pay a higher price for the commodity (up to the limit of the budget constraint). There are a number of ways round this problem of majority decision-making. For example, it may be possible to devise a majority voting procedure which mimics the market place. This is done in the 'point voting system' shown below. Each voter is assigned 100 points and allocates them to each alternative policy (A, B or C) depending on the extent to which he prefers one alternative relative to

	Policy A	*Policy B*	*Policy C*
Individual 1	70	15	15
Individual 2	10	50	40
Individual 3	45	45	10
	125	110	65

another. Thus, in this example individual 1 is indifferent between policies B and C but feels strongly about policy A. The number of points assigned to each policy are added up and the policy with the greatest number of points wins. Another advantage of the point voting system is that its outcomes will be transitive; however, the probability of ties increases (the reader should prove these two results by considering alternative examples). The point voting system does not, however, conform to the requirements of Arrow's system since individual preferences are now regarded as being cardinal rather than ordinal. Furthermore, the point voting system is more complex and costly to administer than the simple majority voting system; a feature of voting systems that we will return to later.

(3) Vote trading (log-rolling)

Another way in which intensity of preference may be registered is through the process of vote trading (also frequently referred to as 'log-rolling'). We have already seen that the sum of the value of benefits to the majority brought about by the introduction of the majority outcome may be less than the value of the costs to the minority. In such a situation the minority might be willing to trade votes in order to prevent that situation occurring. Consider the following example. The Member of Parliament representing constituency X wishes to reduce unemployment in his region by ensuring that a large government contract be approved and placed with factories in his constituency. The MP for constituency Y is indifferent about whether or not the contract be approved, let alone to which company it is granted. He is more concerned to see that his amendment to a new education bill be approved. It is found, however, that the MP for constituency X is indifferent about whether or not the education bill's amendment is passed. Clearly in this situation there is scope for trading of votes.[8] The MP for constituency X could offer to the MP for constituency Y his agreement to vote in favour of the education bill amendment provided that in return the MP for constituency Y agreed to vote for the government contract. The voluntary exchange of votes in this way is the basis of politics, which can be thought of as the means of searching out agreement in situations where preferences are diverse.[9]

Vote trading is a logical extension of the economist's rational self-interest maximising model. It is a means by which the majority voting process is assisted in moving towards a position of social welfare maximisation. Buchanan and Tullock[10] have demonstrated that vote trading makes majority voting more efficient both in terms of the allocation of resources and in the distribution of welfares. By enabling individuals to exchange their votes a more acceptable outcome is established. Outcomes that, on welfare distribution grounds, are considered to be better have a greater probability of being adopted than those that are not.

Majority voting and two public goods

It is now possible to draw together some of the earlier material discussed in this chapter whilst at the same time extending the analysis to a consideration of more than one public good. In the simple majority voting model the analysis was confined to individuals making choices about different amounts of a single public good or publicly supplied programme. Now consider three individuals A, B and C making choices about their most preferred quantities of two publicly supplied goods, e.g. health services and education. It is assumed that the decisions are made independently of one another. The most preferred positions of each individual are shown in Figure 4.3 by the points A, B and C. These most preferred positions are defined as the peaks of each individual's ordinal utility surface. Moreover, as shown, the preferences are single peaked.

Given the information contained in Figure 4.3 and assuming that the median voter's preferences (see below for a full discussion) dominate then individual C's most preferred level of health service spending dominates and individual B's most preferred level of education spending dominates. In other words, since the decisions on each level of spending are taken independently the median voters,

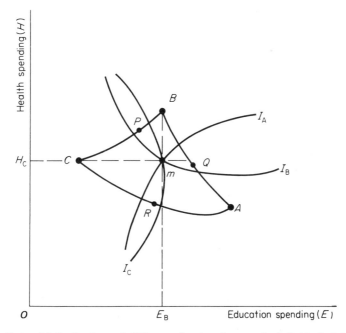

Fig. 4.3 *Notes:* (a) I_A, I_B, I_C are indifference (contours) curves for individuals A, B and C. (b) Points A, B and C are the maxima (most preferred positions) of each individual's respective ordinal utility function. The preference functions are obviously single peaked.

in this example B and C, can differ. The final outcome is the combination of health service and education expenditures given by the point *M*.

In the single public good case it was demonstrated that single-peaked preferences broke up the cyclical majority problem and provided for the existence of a unique and stable outcome. When the analysis is extended to more than one public good this result breaks down. This is demonstrated in Figure 4.3. Individuals B and C might collude via vote trading, or some other kind of political exchange, and move to a position such as *P*. This is closer to both B and C's most preferred positions than is *M*. Since this will make A worse off it will force A to make a deal with either C or B which is an improvement, from their point of view, on the point *P*. Such positions are represented by *R* and *Q*. It is, therefore, seen that the final outcome becomes unstable once again.

Finally, the solution *M* is Pareto optimal since it lies within the set of all Pareto-optimal combinations which is the set *ABC*, including all points on its boundary. Any movement from one point in that set will make someone worse off and a movement from any point outside the set to a point within it will make at least one person better off. Whilst there might be cycles of the voting outcome and whilst such cycles involve the transactions costs of forming coalitions there is no loss of economic efficiency in a Paretian sense. Movements from one point of the set to another can only be judged on grounds of distributive justice.

Transactions costs and non-market decision-making

The world is not characterised by zero transactions costs. It was seen in Chapter 2 that market failures may arise because of the costs of voluntary exchanges. Likewise, in the case of voting systems and other processes of non-market decision-making, transactions costs are of importance when many persons must agree on single outcomes. There is a large number of possible variants of the majority voting rule. Two have already been examined, i.e. the simple majority decision model and the point voting model. In addition there are plurality voting systems, proportional representation models, and, of course, the unanimity rule, which requires 100 per cent consensus before a policy is adopted. Each social/collective choice rule has associated costs. According to Buchanan and Tullock the adoption of a social/collective choice rule should be regarded as a cost-minimising exercise. In their analysis the costs of the voting system are comprehensively defined so that, in addition to the costs of administering the system, the costs of participating in the decision-making process are considered along with the efficiency and distributional costs of the outcome.

The nineteenth-century economist Knut Wicksell pointed out that the decision-making rule of unanimity was required before the political process would produce budgets that are Pareto-optimal. Assuming that the distribution of welfare was optimal prior to the introduction of the public sector budget, he required that taxes and expenditures be considered together and voted on simultaneously. If the sum of the individual marginal costs of a tax/expenditure proposal exceeded the sum of the individual marginal benefits, then at least one individual would be paying a tax price that exceeded his marginal benefits for the service. That individual would vote against such a proposal,[11] which would, therefore, be rejected under a decision rule of unanimity. Because it is only those proposals that make at least one person better off and no one worse off that survive the test of the unanimity rule, such a decision-making process must produce Pareto-efficient outcomes.

While the extent of allocative inefficiencies are reduced as the number of persons required for agreement approaches 100 per cent, the decision-making costs increase as unanimity is reached.[12] These decision-making costs include the bargaining costs of attempting to get the members of the group to agree to the adoption of a particular tax/expenditure package. In addition there are the opportunity costs of the benefits that are lost if action to implement the expenditure plan is delayed while agreement is being sought. As the size of the group increases there is greater scope for an individual to become a 'free-rider'. Additional decision-making resources are, therefore, required to ensure that individuals reveal their preferences accurately.

These costs are shown in Figure 4.4. The vertical axis shows the costs associated with inefficient budget allocations (E) along with the decision-making costs (D). The distance ON_{max} shows the number of persons (N) in the group.

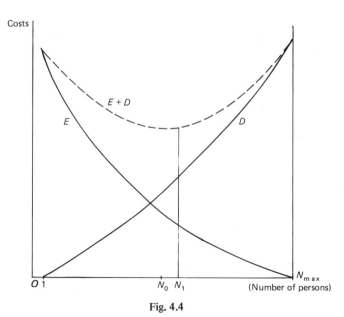

Fig. 4.4

As the voting rule becomes more inclusive (i.e. requires more persons to agree to the outcome) the inefficiency costs fall and become zero when unanimity is required, i.e. at N_{max}. Decision costs, however, rise with increasingly more inclusive decision rules. The efficient voting rule can be derived by minimising the total costs $(E + D)$. At the minimum of $(E + D)$ the fall in the marginal inefficiency costs will just be equal to the rise in the marginal decision. The efficient decision-making rule (i.e. that which minimises costs) would therefore require that N_1/N_{max} per cent of the group agreed before any proposal is adopted.

This demonstrates clearly that there is no reason to believe that simple majority voting is an efficient decision-making rule. In this example N_0/N_{max} is the proportion of the group that is required for a majority, and as can be readily seen this does not correspond to the efficient decision rule N_1/N_{max}. This has led to arguments in favour of a modified majority decision-making rule, thereby reducing the inefficiencies of majority decisions by breaking the 'tyranny of the majority'. But the tyranny of the majority may in these cases be replaced by the tyranny of the minority. In the case of unanimity the veto of the minority places it in a powerful position. Baumol has identified the problem as follows: [13]

> The obverse of a unanimity rule is the veto power which it gives to any one person if an arrangement is not initially optimal.... A unanimity rule is the ideal instrument for the preservation of externalities and inequities which are already extant.

Baumol's observation is a forceful reminder that Buchanan and Tullock's analysis was conducted in terms of establishing an *efficient* collective decision-making rule. This is not the same as establishing an *optimal* collective decision-making rule. Buchanan and Tullock following the tradition of Wicksell assume that the initial distribution of incomes (and welfares) was optimal. Their decision rule will be optimal only if, following the introduction of the tax/ expenditure package of the budget, the distribution of incomes remains unchanged. If the budget upsets this initially optimal distribution of income or if the initial distribution of income was not optimal, then the search for an optimal social choice rule becomes an extremely complex task.

Buchanan and Tullock's framework also has the advantage that it reminds us that fiscal institutions and organisations are not costless to operate. Real resources are consumed in the allocative processes of the market and the non-market modes of social organisation. These transactions costs had until recently been ignored and did not feature as an integral part of economic analysis. It is now generally recognised that the social institution of monetised exchange is a development that minimises the costs of exchange. Similarly, market exchange reduces transactions costs when compared with other forms of exchange such as barter. However, the presence of high transactions costs can cause markets to fail to allocate resources efficiently. As we saw in Chapter 2, these market failures provide a role for government. But as we have just demonstrated (and will expand upon in Chapter 7), there are also transactions costs in operating fiscal institutions. The public sector, using the majority decision rule, will introduce another set of inefficiencies into the system. This means that government's role of correcting the inefficiencies of the market can be ambiguous because what might happen in practice is that one set of inefficiencies will be replaced by another. High on the agenda for fiscal economists is the need to examine more closely the design of optimal government policies, which will minimise the allocative inefficiencies of government intervention. To assume that the public sector should intervene to correct every form of market failure is to deny the existence of the costs of the fiscal system.

An economic theory of politics

The previous sections to this chapter have concentrated upon the normative properties of the social choice rule. One feature of political life in a representative democracy is the existence of political parties, which represent the views of those who elect them into office. A partial explanation for the existence of political parties can be given in terms of the costs of participating in the process of political exchange. In the absence of elected representatives, as in a direct democracy, each individual who wishes to be informed about the relative costs and benefits of each alternative policy would be required to spend time and resources acquiring information. These information costs are fixed costs which means that there are gains, in the form of resource savings, to be obtained if individuals join together and share the costs. Moreover, as we have seen there are decision-making costs incurred by individuals who participate in collective choice. If individuals have identical preferences there are resource savings to be gained if one of them represents the preferences of the rest. For these reasons elected representatives (political parties and politicians) exist in order to reduce the costs of collective decision-making.

Both Wicksell and Lindahl introduced political parties into their analysis but they did so in an uninteresting way. Theirs was a model of a *pure* representative democracy in which political parties accurately reflected the preferences of their electorate. Anthony Downs introduced into economics an economic theory of politics based upon the assumptions that voters are utility-maximisers and that political parties are vote-maximisers. The theory is stated by Downs as follows:[14]

> The political parties in our model are not interested *per se* in making society's allocation of resources efficient: each seeks only to get re-elected by maximising the number of votes it receives. Therefore, even if the government has the ability to move society to a Paretian optimum it will do so only if forced by competition from other parties. ... Thus the crucial issue is whether interparty competition always forces the government to a Paretian optimum.

In a Downsian world, therefore, the behaviour of political parties and elected representatives is guided by self-interest rather than the idealised goal of 'the public interest'. Politicians may, and indeed many do, seek to serve the wider national interest by introducing sweeping social reforms. But they will never be able to do so unless they get elected to office, and to get elected to office it is necessary to adopt those policies that will win votes. Vote maximisation is, therefore, a reasonable view of politicians' behaviour.[15] The Downsian approach also recognises that an individual may be motivated to seek election to political office for reasons other than representing the views of his electorate. For example, the benefits of political office, e.g. power, prestige, perquisites, etc., may be important arguments in the politician's utility function.[16]

The preferences of the median voter play a central role in the Downsian model of competition between political parties. This can be seen from the *'median voter theorem'*, which states that in a majority decision model for which preferences are single-peaked it is the policy that is most preferred by the median voter that will win, since it is the median voters' preferences that produce the minimum welfare loss for the whole group. The median voter theorem can be illustrated with the aid of Figure 4.5. Assume that there are three individuals whose demand curves for the public output, e.g. police protection, are shown as D_1, D_2 and D_3. Each individual faces a price of OP for the public output. Given a price of OP, individual 1's most preferred output is OQ_1 while individual 2's is OQ_2 and individual 3's is OQ_3. In order to determine which level of police protection will be publicly supplied, individuals vote on the three alternatives OQ_1, OQ_2 and OQ_3. Individuals 2 and 3 both prefer outcomes that lie to the right of OQ_1, which means that output levels OQ_2 and OQ_3 will win over OQ_1. Individuals 1 and 2 prefer levels of output that lie to the left of OQ_3, which means that OQ_2 and OQ_1 will win over OQ_3. Taking these outcomes

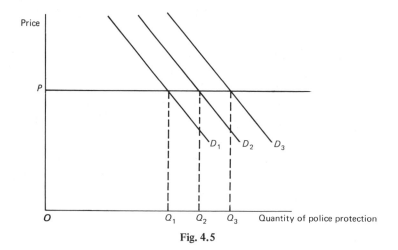

Fig. 4.5

together it is seen that the preference of the median voter (individual 2) will be chosen, i.e. output level OQ_2.[17]

The implications of the median voter theorem for vote-maximising politicians and political parties is clear. In order to secure the majority of the votes the preferences of the median voter must be identified. It also implies that political competition, between the major parties, will produce consensus politics. Each party has the same objective, i.e. to get elected to office, and will therefore introduce similar policies in order to woo the median voter.

Clearly, the median voter model is a naive behavioural specification of politics. Similarly, the profit-maximising model of the firm is a naive specification of business behaviour. Both models, however, have their uses. Each, in its own particular context, is useful for optimisation analysis and for assisting the investigator to make a complex reality more tractable.

The features of reality are, however, that voters and politicians are imperfectly informed. Voters are ill-informed about the process of representative government, about the effects of alternative budget proposals on their welfare, and they frequently feel alienated. Politicians are not fully informed about voters' demands and do not know who the median voter is. Therefore, instead of relying completely upon Downsian-type models it would be useful to consider the problem in the context of oligopoly bargaining models. This, however, remains on the agenda of current research and so all that can be done is to sketch out the kind of models that are currently being considered.[18]

The principal agents in political decision-making (i.e. social/collective choice) are voters, politicians and bureaucrats. The role of the bureaucrat will be examined in detail in Chapter 7. Voters act individually when they cast their vote in an election but between elections many of them form pressure groups and lobby politicians on specific issues. Another feature of voter behaviour is that there is usually less than full voter participation at elections.[19] This can partly be explained by non-economic factors such as the weather or competing interests such as popular television programmes. Economic factors that influence voter participation include the costs of voting, i.e. the opportunity cost of the time and effort required to turn out to vote; also, because political activity has 'public good' characteristics, individuals can free-ride. Voter participation limits the median voter model since we now need to know the probability of the median citizen participating in the voting process. The uncertainties caused by incomplete voter participation account for many of the activities carried out by the central office of political parties, e.g. collecting information on the socio-economic characteristics of those who vote and those who do not vote.

The argument outlined above can be made more precise. When there are costs associated with voting the benefits which the individual voter expects to receive as a consequence of casting his vote must outweigh these costs, i.e.

$$E(B) - C \geqslant 0$$

where $E(B) = pB$ which is the expected value of the benefits B arising from voting where p is the probability of these benefits occurring and C are the voting costs.

If the individual finds one political party to be diametrically opposed to all he believes in and also realises that the election is a foregone conclusion (i.e. his vote does not count) then he is unlikely to vote because $E(B)$ will be very small. Moreover, if the two parties' platforms are very close to one another then the voter might be indifferent between either. This will make voting not worth-while for him.

The Downsian model does not (and does not claim to) explain all aspects of voter behaviour. It does, however, give a formal account of the probable factors which will explain voter apathy and low voter turnout. The outcome of the voting process is a public good and is, therefore, vulnerable to free-riding. The model does, however, leave a number of interesting questions unanswered, though it does force them into the open. For example, what determines voters' expectations of benefits and what determines the voters' subjective perception of voting costs? The Downsian model is similar to the Hotelling model of spatial bilateral competition. In the case of political parties politicians offer policies in order to maximise votes, i.e. they offer that set of policies which will satisfy the preferences of the median voter. If both parties are engaged in competing for the median voter (i.e. the middle ground, depending on the shape of the distribution of voter's preferences) then the most likely result will be consensus politics.

The Downsian model is open to a number of criticisms. First, it is not necessary to assume vote maximisation. All that a political party is required to do is to gain sufficient votes to enable it to obtain a majority. Vote maximisa-tion is too strong an assumption. Satisficing assumptions of the kind suggested by Herbert Simon would give similar results. Second, multi-party systems are more complex to study than two-party systems of the Downsian model. However, a full analysis of multi-party systems requires a game-theoretic approach and has still to be developed.

One means that politicians have of gaining information about the views and the demands of the electorate is to examine the arguments presented to them by *pressure groups*. The formation of pressure groups by individuals with similar or identical preferences enables them to share information costs and transactions costs. In the UK a variety of pressure groups exist which cover a wide range of topics of social and economic concern. At the national level of government the Confederation of British Industry and the Trades Union Congress are two important economic pressure groups which, although each serves the interests of a different group in the production process, are concerned to make sure that govern-ments operate full employment policies. Consumer pressure groups are more interested in government regulation and legislation directed towards consumer safety and in policies that will keep down the prices of key commodities such as food, fuel and housing. At the local level of government local taxpayers' associations and chambers of commerce pressure politicians on local matters.

Politicians are frequently unable to ignore the demands made by pressure groups. Their political survival may depend upon whether or not such demands are met. This can, however, lead to an expansion in public expenditures. Since the preferences of the median voters are ill-defined, and since their participation in the voting process is uncertain, political parties will attempt to maximise their votes in the next election by responding to a large number of the pressure groups' demands. Public expenditure will, therefore, expand and is likely to be larger than it would be if the median voters' preferences were satisfied.

The political business cycle

The Downsian vote-maximising model of government has been put to a number of uses in the public-choice literature. It has been used to explain the over expansion of public expenditure programmes (*op. cit.*) and more recently in the literature on the political business cycle it has been used to provide a partial explanation of macroeconomic cycles in prices, output and employment. This literature is associated with work of Nordhaus, Frey and Schneider, and Lindbeck. An earlier consideration of these issues is to be found in the work of Kalecki and more recently it is paralleled in Marxian economists' approaches to the business cycle.

The essential ideas which underlie the political theory of the business cycle is that a government's behaviour is determined by a set of ideological or value judgement/political considerations and by its desire to produce policies which will ensure the enhancement of its popularity, and thus the maximisation of its votes in the next election. But the analysis goes further than this. Instead of being a passive or exogeneous factor in economic affairs responding to changes in the business cycle the actions of vote-maximising governments, it is hypothesised, will generate cycles in prices, output and employment. In other words a government's actions become endogenous because vote maximisation will influence, (a) the policy goals it decides to pursue (i.e. reduction in inflation or reduction in unemployment, promotion of growth, and income distribution objectives), (b) the mix of policy goals where there is a trade off as in the case of inflation and unemployment, and (c) the choice of policy instruments, since these have distributional consequences.

The difference between this new public choice approach and the traditional macro-economic approach can be illustrated by means of the following example. In Figure 4.6 the standard short-run Phillips curve *PP* is shown along with a welfare function W_0 showing increases in welfare as a movement from W_0 to W_1 (i.e. lower levels of inflation and unemployment are preferred). The Theil/ Tinbergen approach to economic policy would choose that point on the Phillips trade-off which maximises social welfare, i.e. point 6. If, however, we consider a group of seven individuals each with a different inflation/unemployment preference then the vote maximising outcome is that which satisfies the

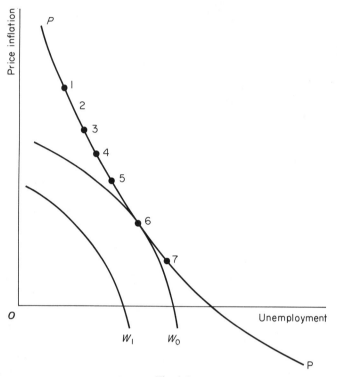

Fig. 4.6

preferences of the median voter and is given by point 4. Thus, the public-choice vote-maximising outcome differs from the neo-classical social welfare maximising outcome.

This does not, however, provide an explanation of how government *reactions* to the general macro-economic climate will generate cycles in unemployment and inflation. Suppose a government realises that its popularity will be damaged more by high levels of unemployment than by inflation. A rational vote-maximising government would, therefore, ensure that just prior to an election unemployment is low. It will, therefore, activate policies to ensure that this outcome is brought about but in doing so will relax its control on inflation which will rise. Cycles in unemployment and inflation will thus be set up and the periodicity of these cycles will centre around election dates. This is shown in Figure 4.7. Once the election is over the government can clamp down on inflation by introducing deflationary policies and thereby allow unemployment to rise.

A number of attempts have been made to test this hypothesis particularly by Frey and Schneider. They proceed by estimating a vote function (or popularity

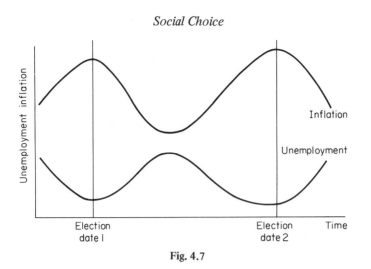

Fig. 4.7

function) which measures the support given to a government by the electorate. These are typically measured through Gallup-type opinion polls. The three main macro-economic indicators which have had a significant effect on vote outcome and government popularity are, the rate of unemployment, the rate of inflation, and the growth rate of real disposable income.

Table 4.1 summarises the main econometric results of Frey and Schneider's analysis, which shows the size of the influence of these three macro-economic variables upon government popularity. For this table it is seen that in the UK an increase in the rate of unemployment of one percentage point leads on average to a decline in the government's popularity of 6 per cent. An increase in

Table 4.1 Economic variables and government popularity

Economic variable	USA (1953-75)	UK (1959-74)	West Germany (1951-75)
Rate of unemployment	−4.2	−6.0	−0.9
Rate of inflation	−1.0	−0.6	−0.7
Growth rate of real disposable income	+0.4	+0.8	+0.4

the inflation rate has a smaller impact which gives some indication of the electorate's preferences for alternative points on the unemployment/inflation trade off.

The Frey and Schneider results have not been accepted without criticism (see Chrystal and Alt). The main thrust of these criticisms is over problems of model specification and estimation. They do not destroy the theory of the political business cycle but temper the results. For example, how accurately can government popularity be defined and measured; how stable are the estimates of the parameters; and how should ideological differences between political parties be modelled and incorporated into the analysis?

The theory of the political business cycle is an exciting and interesting development in public choice theory and demonstrates clearly the interface between economic analysis and political science which has for too long been ignored by both disciplines.

CHAPTER 5

Theoretical and Empirical Analysis of Public Expenditure Growth

Public expenditure reflects the policy choices of governments. Once governments have decided upon which goods and services to provide and the quantity and quality in which they will be produced, public expenditures represent the costs of carrying out these policies. This definition is sufficiently broad to enable us to make two distinctions. First, there are the costs of providing goods and services through the public sector budget. This is the usual interpretation of public expenditures, i.e. the amount that appears in the public sector accounts. Second, most rules, regulations and laws introduced by government result in private sector expenditure. For example, the passing of a law that requires an hotel to install minimum fire precautions will result in the hotel owner spending money. Some economists would count such expenditure along with other public expenditures since these private sector expenditures were caused by public sector decisions. This wider definition of public expenditure is of interest when discussing the 'costs of government actions'. However, for most purposes, including those of this chapter, the narrower definition of public expenditure is used.

In this chapter we want to draw together some of the concepts and discussions of previous chapters. The activities of the government arise from ideological reasons but also from government's attempts to deal with allocative and distributional inefficiencies brought about by market failure. Government, therefore, provides public and quasi-public goods along with transfer payments in response to the collective demands of the electorate. What we want to consider now is the growth of government.

There are a number of alternative ways of approaching the question of the growth of government. For example, we could look at the growth in the absolute size of public expenditure. Thus public expenditure[1] in the UK grew from £280.8m in 1900 to £103,720m in 1980. This startling increase in public expenditure must, however, be seen in relation to increases in other economic magnitudes such as the rise in the general price level, the growth in GNP, and population changes. For example, between 1900 and 1980 public expenditure (at current prices) increased at an annual compound rate of 7.3 per cent p.a. while GNP (also at current prices) grew at 5.3 per cent p.a. Examining the 'relative' increase in public expenditures (i.e. public expenditures relative to some other economic magnitude) does, therefore, place the problem in a different perspective. The absolute level of public expenditure and changes in that level have to be explained and accounted for, but evaluations of the changes are best made in relation to other quantities.   *Caution in the G/Y ratio use*

Public expenditures, as they appear in the national income accounts, are represented by two broad categories of government activity. First, there are exhaustive public expenditures. These expenditures correspond to the government's purchases of current goods and services (i.e. labour, consumables, etc.) and capital goods and services (i.e. public sector investment in roads, schools, hospitals, etc.). Exhaustive public expenditures are, therefore, purchases of *inputs* by the public sector and are calculated by multiplying the volume of inputs by the input prices.

Moreover, exhaustive public expenditures are claims on the resources of the economy. Use of these resources by the public sector precludes use by other sectors. The absorption of resources by the public sector means that the opportunity cost of these public expenditures is the forgone output of the other sectors. It is opportunity cost arguments of this kind that underlie the arguments of those who disapprove of the size of the public sector and that also form the basis of many of the techniques used to measure public sector efficiency (see Chapter 8). These arguments underlie the recent 'crowding-out' debate. Keynes argued that crowding out will only take place at full employment. A £1 increase in exhaustive public expenditures must, by definition, be at the expense of £1 spent in the non-public sector, which includes the overseas sector for an open economy. At less than full employment an increase in public expenditure if it is bond financed will, *ceteris paribus*, cause interest rates to rise. If it is assumed that private sector expenditures, such as investment, are interest elastic then a bond-financed increase in public expenditure will crowd out private sector activities via its impact on capital markets. It should, however, be emphasised that this is an *a priori* argument. Whether or not crowding out does occur depends upon whether or not the *ceteris paribus* assumptions hold and on the values of the interest elasticities. This is a controversial area in current macro-economics.

Care must, however, be taken when interpreting public expenditure data, as we will see again in the next chapter. Consumer expenditure in the national income accounts refers to consumers' expenditure on *final output*. Part of government expenditure, as we have indicated above, is expenditure on inputs. This means that an increase in government expenditure does not necessarily imply an increase in public output; neither does it always imply a reduction in efficiency, which makes efficiency calculations using national income data tricky!

The second category of public expenditures is transfer expenditures, i.e. public expenditures on pensions, subsidies, debt interest, unemployment benefits, etc. These expenditures do not represent a claim on the society's resources by the public sector as in the case of exhaustive public expenditures. Instead, transfers are a redistribution of resources between individuals in society, with the resources flowing through the public sector as intermediary. Indeed, many items that are generally regarded as transfers come within the social insurance function of government and, while they may have a transfer element in them, they cannot be distinguished conceptually from the payouts made by a private insurance company to those members who claim benefits, having already paid their premiums in the past.

When it comes to examining the growth of public expenditure it is useful to keep these two categories of public expenditure (exhaustive and transfer expenditures) separate. Factors that affect the growth of one category may not apply with equal force to the other. What we want to know, therefore, is what factors influence the growth in the absolute level of public expenditures, and the size of the public sector relative to other sectors of the economy.

In order to answer these questions and to give a meaningful interpretation of empirical data, it is necessary to construct an analytical model that will bring together the economic, political and social forces that, when taken together, determine public expenditures. Two classes of model are discussed in this chapter. The first can be described as 'macro-models'. These models begin with data on public expenditures and proceed to explain the time pattern of public expenditures in terms of broad aggregate variables such as GNP or the rate of inflation. The second class of models can be labelled as 'microeconomic' or 'decision process' models of public choice. These micro-models seek to explain the underlying microeconomic foundations of the decision processes that ultimately give rise to public expenditures.[2]

Macro-models of public expenditure

The macro-models that we will consider in this section differ from short-run macroeconomic forecasting models in their treatment of public expenditure, in so far as the latter take government expenditure as exogenously determined. The macro-models that interest us seek to explain how government expenditure has behaved over the long term; i.e. they analyse the 'time pattern' of public expenditure.

Three models that categorise this class will be examined. First, there are what can be conveniently labelled the 'development models of public expenditure growth'; second, Wagner's 'law of expanding state activity' will be examined, and third, Peacock and Wiseman's classic study of public expenditure growth will be reviewed.

(1) Development models of public expenditure growth

This approach to the problem is best represented by the works of Musgrave[3] and Rostow.[4] In the early stages of economic growth and development, public sector investment as a proportion of the total investment of the economy is found to be high. The public sector is, therefore, seen to provide social infrastructure overheads such as roads, transportation systems, sanitation systems, law and order, health and education and other investments in human capital. This public sector investment, it is argued, is necessary to gear up the economy for 'take-off' into the middle stages of economic and social development. In the middle stages of growth the government continues to supply investment goods but this time public investment is complementary to the growth in private investment. During all the stages of development, market failures exist which can frustrate the push towards maturity; hence the increase in government involvement in order to deal with these market failures.

Musgrave argues that over the development period, as total investment as a proportion of GNP rises, the share of public sector investment to GNP falls. Rostow's claims are that once the economy reaches the maturity stage the mix of public expenditures will shift from expenditures on infrastructure to increasing expenditures on education, health and welfare services. In the 'mass consumption' stage income maintenance programmes, and policies designed to redistribute welfare, will grow significantly relative to other items of public expenditure and also relative to GNP.

It should be realised that both Musgrave's and Rostow's models are broad sweeping views of the development process. Their views are generalisations gleaned from the examination of a large number of different case histories of developing economies. However, the data that each assembles to support his case certainly give the impression of changes in the relative share of government expenditures and variations in the mix of public services over the development cycle, which are much in accord with the summary views presented above.

(2) Wagner's law

The nineteenth-century German economist, Adolf Wagner, was concerned to explain the share of GNP taken up by the public sector. This has been formalised in what is now referred to as 'Wagner's law'. Wagner did not state his ideas in the form of a law – this was done by later commentators.[5] It is not clear if Wagner was referring to the growth in the ratio of government expenditure to GNP, i.e. the relative growth in the public sector, or if it was the absolute size of the public sector that Wagner was thinking of. We will follow Musgrave's[6] interpretation and refer to Wagner's law as an expression of the growth of the relative size of the public sector. We can now state Wagner's law in the following terms: as *per capita* incomes in an economy grow, the relative size of the public sector will grow also.

The basis of Wagner's statement was empirical. He had observed the growth of the public sectors of a number of European countries plus the United States and Japan during the nineteenth century. The forces determining those movements in the ratio of public expenditure to GNP were explained in terms of political factors and economic factors. Wagner's explanation of the expansion of the 'scale of the states' activities' reveals a great deal of insight. As early as the nineteenth century he had a primitive explanation of the modern idea of market failure and externality. Wagner recognised that as an economy became industrialised the nature of the relationships between the expanding markets and the agents in these markets would become more complex. This complexity of market interaction would result in a need for commercial laws and contracts, which would require the establishment of a system of justice to administer such laws. Urbanisation and high density living would result in externalities and congestion requiring public sector intervention and regulation.

Wagner therefore explained *why* he had observed the emergence of public sector services such as legal services, police services and banking services. Banking services, provided by state banks, had been geared towards linking the suppliers of surplus funds with those who had the best investment opportunities.

The growth of public expenditures on education, recreation and culture, and health and welfare services were explained by Wagner in terms of their income elasticity of demand. For Wagner these services represented superior or income-elastic wants. Thus as real incomes in the economy rose (i.e. as GNP increased) public expenditures on these services would rise more than in proportion, which would account for the rising ratio of government expenditure to GNP.

Wagner's model, while containing many insights, suffered from the drawback that it did not contain a well articulated theory of public choice. Indeed, Wagner assumed away the problems of public choice by employing an 'organic theory of the state'. Thus the state was assumed to behave as if it were an individual existing and making decisions independently of the members of society.[7]

(3) Peacock and Wiseman's analysis

Peacock and Wiseman's study[8] is probably one of the best-known analyses of the 'time pattern' of public expenditures. They founded their analysis upon a political theory of public expenditure determination, namely that 'governments like to spend more money, that citizens do not like to pay more taxes, and that governments need to pay some attention to the wishes of their citizens'. Thus they opened up public expenditure to the influence of the ballot box.

Peacock and Wiseman viewed the voter as an individual who enjoyed the benefits of public goods and services but who disliked paying taxes. Thus the government, when deciding upon the expenditure side of its budget, keeps a close watch on the electorates' reactions to the implied taxation. They assume that there is some 'tolerable level of taxation' which acts as a constraint on

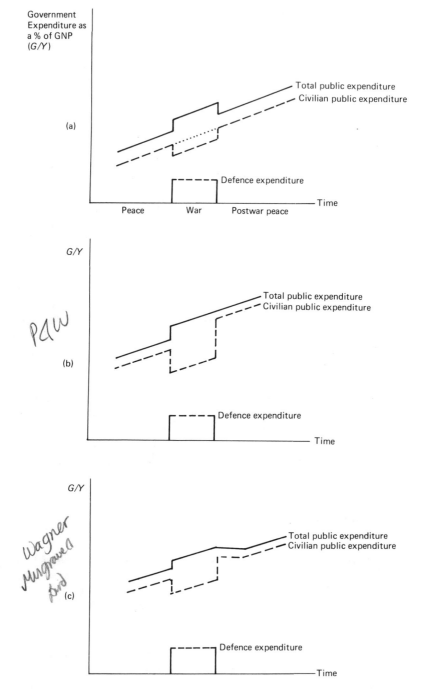

Fig. 5.1

government behaviour. This is a variant on Clark's 'catastrophic school' of taxation.[9]

While not explicitly subscribing to Clark's view, Peacock and Wiseman saw taxation as setting a constraint on government expenditures. As the economy and thus incomes grew, tax revenue, at constant tax rates, would rise, thereby enabling public expenditure to grow in line with GNP. In normal times, therefore, public expenditure would show a gradual upward trend, even although within the economy there might be a divergence between what people regarded as being a desirable level of public expenditure and a desirable level of taxation. During periods of social upheaval, however, this gradual upward trend in public expenditure would be disturbed. These periods would coincide with war, famine or some large-scale social disaster which would require a rapid increase in public expenditures. In order to finance the increase in public expenditures the government would be forced to raise taxation levels. This raising of taxation levels would, however, be regarded as acceptable to the electorate during periods of crisis.

Peacock and Wiseman referred to this as the 'displacement effect'. Public expenditure is displaced upwards and for the period of the crisis displaces private expenditures for public expenditures. The process represents an upward shift in the trend line of public expenditure. Following the period of crisis public expenditure does not, however, fall to its original level. A war is not fully paid for from taxation; no nation has such a large taxable capacity. Countries therefore borrow and debt charges have to be met after the event.

Another effect that they thought might operate was the 'inspection effect'. This they suggested arises from voters' keener awareness of social problems during the period of upheaval. The government therefore expands its scope of services to improve these social conditions, and because the electorate's perception of tolerable levels of taxation does not return to its former level the government is able to finance these higher levels of expenditure originating in the expanded scope of government and debt charges.

Peacock and Wiseman's theory has not gone without criticism.[10] Figure 5.1 shows three possible patterns of the influence of war expenditures on government expenditures. The increase in war-related expenditures, we assume, displaces both other public and private civilian expenditures. This means that, while total public expenditures rise dramatically, the increase is, however, less than the increase in war-related expenditure. This displacement is shown in all three diagrams.

What happens to expenditure in the postwar period? It is the alternative answers to this question that have formed the basis of the disagreement between Peacock and Wiseman and their critics.

Figure 5.1(a) shows that case in which civilian public expenditures in the postwar period return to their original growth path; whereas Figure 5.1(b) represents the case in which the trend in total public expenditure experienced during the war period continues into the postwar period along with an upward

If you concur with the message then this advice
you must heed :-
Tvr nav petpab llepfa Brnpl d'sat vtpribls
100   *Public Sector Economics*

shift in the level of civilian public expenditures. In the final example, Figure 5.1(c), there is an increase in postwar civilian public expenditures. This, however, is only a temporary phenomenon until the old trend line is reached. The long-term trends shown in cases 5.1(a) and 5.1(c) are thus similar and show that there is no long-run displacement effect as demonstrated in case 5.1(b), where there has been a permanent displacement of private by civilian public expenditures.

The question of which of the three alternative cases accurately reflects the UK's 1939–45 postwar experience is in dispute. Peacock and Wiseman's interpretation would favour case 5.1(b), whereas Musgrave and Bird would support the time pattern of Figure 5.1(c). Despite this disagreement over the interpretation of the immediate postwar trend in expenditures, Peacock and Wiseman's remains a mammoth and pioneering study of the secular trends of public expenditure in the UK up to the period 1958.[11]

This concludes our examination of the macro-models of public expenditure growth. In the development models of Musgrave and Rostow it was seen that public expenditure growth reflected the government's role in the process of development as a supplier of infrastructure capital and social investment and in its attempts to overcome market failures, especially where markets failed to exist. Wagner on the other hand concentrated more on the income elasticity of demand for public outputs and again recognised the market failure type arguments that have been used since. Peacock and Wiseman's approach was to look at the underlying politics of the fiscal system in an attempt to account for the time pattern of public expenditures that they had observed. They concentrated especially on the shift points in the relative scale of public expenditure which coincided with periods of catastrophe such as wars.

None of the macro-theories can be used to account for the details of the public expenditure process. Indeed, few of the lessons that have been learned so far can usefully be employed to explain the growth that has taken place in the public sectors of most countries during the post-1950 period. For example, over the period 1955–80 total public expenditure in the UK rose from 41.1 per cent of GNP to 53.6 per cent of GNP.[12] To account for these changes we need to look deeper into the processes that give rise to the formation of public expenditures; i.e., we need to examine the micro-foundations of public expenditure.

A microeconomic model of public expenditure

The purposes of a microeconomic model of public expenditure growth are to set out the forces that generate demands for public outputs (i.e. publicly supplied goods and services) and to examine the influences on the supply of public services. The interaction of the demand and supply for public services determines the levels of publicly provided services that will be supplied via the public budget, which in turn generates a derived demand for outputs. It will be recalled that it is expenditure on these inputs to the public sector 'production'[13] of budget activities that is accounted for as 'exhaustive public expenditures'. Therefore, to account for increases in exhaustive public expenditures we need to account for increases in the volume of inputs employed along with changes in the prices paid to these inputs.

The purpose of the micro-model of public expenditure growth is, therefore, to give an explanation of changes in the derived demand for public sector inputs. In providing such an explanation we will have recourse to make use of economic variables; however, political and social variables will be shown to have a role to play also. A number of initial remarks about the nature of the model that will be used are in order.

First, it is a positive model of the time pattern of public expenditure. As such it seeks to explain the growth path of public expenditure in terms of the factors that generate it. The model says very little about whether or not observed public expenditure corresponds to an 'equilibrium budget'. Second, the model is not designed to show the efficiency of public output supply. Normative questions such as how much output 'should' be supplied via the public sector budget and what set of efficient tax prices should be charged were discussed in the context of Samuelson's model in Chapter 3. Third, as a positive model it is also behavioural, but some of behavioural propositions as will be seen, are naive. This is recognised, but it should be pointed out that more complex behavioural propositions would make the model less tractible and less useful as an explanatory aid.[14] Fourth, in its present form as a pedagogic teaching device the model is a comparative static one. Additional limitations to the model will be considered subsequently.

The first thing that we have to consider is the output of the public sector. It was seen in Chapter 2 that the major part of public sector exhaustive expenditures refer to quasi-public goods or mixed goods rather than pure public goods. For the purposes of this exercise we take as given[15] those activities that are organised through public collective action rather than private collective action. Thus, given that certain activities are organised in the public sector, why do these activities, over some period of time, rise in absolute terms and relative to private sector activities?

The outputs of the public sector are extremely difficult to measure because in most instances they are intangible. This means that at the conceptual level we must be clear about the nature of the output of the public sector. Clarity at this level will safeguard against drawing incorrect or ambiguous inferences when empirical analysis is carried out. The good that we refer to as 'education' serves a number of purposes. It is an investment in human capital and will influence the individual's earning potential. But there are aspects of education that make it a current consumption good and there are still others that characterise it as a durable consumption good. Individuals have a demand for knowlege for knowledge's sake, or 'to be educated' which is independent of their demand for the future earnings that education may provide. Other goods and services such as police services, fire services, sanitation services or health services are also multi-dimensional goods which serve to satisfy a number of different demands.[16] Despite the 'multi-product' nature of each service provided by the public sector, in order to simplify the analysis we will talk about a 'level' of education or a 'level' of police protection or a 'level' of health care. This enables us to consider individuals demanding different amounts or quantities of services (i.e. different levels of service) and to talk about the public sector supplying different levels of service.

The problems of identifying the output of the public sector should not, however, be exaggerated. These problems are common to all products, especially 'services', whether public or private, and are indeed common to private goods. For example, tangible private goods are really intermediate consumption goods. That is, it is the intangible flow of benefits from tangible consumption goods that the consumer is really interested in. Thus, the automobile is an intermediate consumption good. It is hours of travel rather than the automobile *per se* that the consumer demands.[17] What happens with many public sector services is that the acts of production and consumption of the benefits of the service are simultaneous; i.e., there is not an intermediate consumption good produced. Thus, while the doctor or the nurse is producing health care the patient (consumer) is simultaneously consuming it.[18] This is especially true of services that require a high labour input and an intense client–personnel relationship for the consumption of the service. These ideas can be summarised in Figure 5.2. It is, therefore, the consumption benefits of both public and private sector goods that interest the consumer. Let us summarise this as follows:

$$U^i = \Phi^i(G, P)$$

where

G = vector of public sector *final* outputs
P = vector of private sector *final* outputs
i = ith individual; $i = 1 \ldots i \ldots n$
U = utility function.

An individual will, therefore demand some level of G_k (i.e. the kth publicly provided good) subject to a budget constraint. Let G_{ik} represent some level of the kth publicly provided good demanded by individual i.

In order to produce some level of G_k the public sector organises a number of production activities; e.g., if we are thinking of providing some level of police protection then the police department will choose to provide a set of activities — such as the number of streets patrolled, the frequency at which they are patrolled, whether they are patrolled by policemen on foot or by car, and the amount of crime prevention — that are necessary to produce that level of police protection. There may not be a single mix of activities for any single level of output. It might be possible to produce the same level of output using different activity mixes. In other words, different production functions can be used to

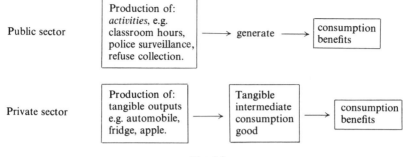

Fig. 5.2

produce the same level of output. However, while the level of output may be the same (using different production functions), the quality and the cost of producing the output is likely to change with the production function. The relationship between public sector final outputs and the set of public sector activities used to produce them is summarised formally as

$$X_i = \phi(L_i, M_i)$$

$$G_i = g_i(X_i, N)$$

where: G_i = final output of the ith public service
X_i = intermediate activities used to produce G_i
L_i = labour inputs used in production of G_i
M_i = materials used to produce G_i
N = population size.

Taking all the points of the discussion together we can now see what is required to provide the ingredients of a positive model of public expenditure growth. Public expenditure can be explained in terms of:

(1) changes in the demand for public sector final outputs;
(2) changes in the set of production activities used to produce public sector outputs and thus changes in the mix of inputs used in the production process;
(3) changes in the quality of public sector outputs;
(4) changes in input prices.

(1) Determination of the level of output

In Chapters 3 and 4 the demand for public sector output was discussed. The Samuelson 'pseudo-demand' curves of Chapter 3 along with the Wicksellian and Lindahl models of expenditure and tax determination were supplemented by a theory of fiscal politics in Chapter 4. Consumers/voters were seen to express their demands for public sector goods and services in a number of ways — through the ballot box, by lobbying, and/or by forming pressure groups. In order to simplify the analysis and without too much loss of realism we will use the median voter theorem of Chapter 4 along with the Downsian vote-maximising politician to provide the basis of the theory of the determination of levels of output for public sector goods and services.

This approach is not at variance with many of the facts, as can be seen from the following statement provided by Patrick J. Lucey, who was a US state governor:

> As an elected public official and the chief executive of a State, a governor must be concerned with both the quality of services the State provides and the cost of these services. If he is a good politician, he knows that in order to be re-elected he must walk a narrow line between those who want government to do more and those who want to pay less for whatever it is that government does. If he is a good administrator, he may be able to widen that line — by improving the efficiency and productivity of government.[19]

A politician has to seek out the preferences of his electorate with respect to their attitudes to taxation and public expenditure programmes. If he wishes to be elected he must be sensitive to what they regard as being 'the tolerable burden of taxation'[20] while at the same time trying to satisfy a diversity of demands for public sector goods and services.

For the purposes of economic modelling, the median voter theorem, set out in Chapter 4, is a useful means of capturing these items. Thus, the vote-maximising politician will attempt to introduce those tax and expenditure programmes that satisfy the median voter.

Having set out the basic behavioural assumption let us now turn to other assumptions of the model.

(1) The analysis is based upon methodological individualism; i.e., the individual is the best judge of his own welfare. This automatically discounts the anthropomorphic concept of the state as an organic entity which is independent of the citizens that make it up. It also discounts the paternalistic role of the state.

(2) The institutional structure is one of representative democracy; i.e., individual citizens elect, through a voting procedure, a representative who will present their views to an assembly.

(3) A constitution exists which defines the voting rights of individuals, the scope of the authority of elected representatives, the legislative and executive function of the government, and the method and procedure of voting.

(4) Majority voting is the decision role employed.

(5) Voters are well informed about the impact of alternative policies offered to them. They are informed about the costs and benefits of government spending.

(6) Citizens vote for policies, not for the personality of the politician.

(7) A multi-party system exists; one party is in power while the remainder are in opposition.

(8) A bureaucracy exists which services the political system and 'produces' the public sector goods and services. The bureaucracy is assumed to be neutral; i.e., it does not enter directly into decisions about how much public output to produce, etc.

(9) Public sector agencies or departments are assumed to be cost-minimising, non-profit-making bodies. This means that there is no slack or X-inefficiency in the system and that any level of output is produced at the least cost for the current state of technical knowledge. This assumption conforms to the neutral bureaucracy assumption.

(10) Politicians choose to produce that vector of goods, services, policies and taxes which will satisfy the preferences of the median voter and hence ensure their election to office. Politicians wish to be elected in order to enjoy the benefits associated with the role of politician, which might include personal status and financial reward; i.e., the politician's utility function could be summarised as:

$$U^p = \Phi(P, G, S)$$

where:

$U^p =$ the utility function of the pth politician
$S =$ private gain or benefit from holding political office
$P =$ vector of private sector goods
$G =$ vector of publicly supplied goods/services

(11) The individual household has a set of preferences over private goods and publicly supplied goods. The household attempts to maximise its utility function subject to its budget constraint. If the vector of public outputs and taxes that is *actually* provided for the household is at variance with that which is *desired* by the household, then the household will engage in some form of political action provided that the costs of such action are less than the expected benefits to be gained.

(12) The public sector budget is assumed to balance.

These assumptions can now be used to construct a rudimentary micro-economic model which will outline the process by which the level of public outputs are determined. Consider the demand side first.

The median voter is assumed to maximise the following utility function.

$$\text{Max } U^i = \Phi^i(P, G)$$

subject to the budget constraint

$$pP + tB_i \leqslant M_i$$

where

i = the median voter and P and G are vectors of private and public goods respectively

p = vector of relative prices for private sector goods

M_i = income of median voter

t = tax rate

B_i = tax base of median voter

ΣB_i = total tax base of the economy

e_k = unit cost of producing the kth publicly supplied good

T_i = total tax bill paid by the median voter, i.e. $T_i = tB_i$

To keep the model simple, assume that there is only a single tax base in the economy and that there is only a single tax rate for all individuals. Then by definition:

$$t \equiv \frac{eG}{\Sigma B_i}$$

where e is the vector of public sector unit costs for all public outputs; i.e., $e = \{e_1 \ldots e_k \ldots e_m\}$.

The median voter's demand curve is derived as a two-stage process. First, assume that he is a public output-taker and a tax rate-taker. Thus, values of t and G are fed into his utility-maximising calculation. These values of t and G, given his income and the prices of private sector goods and services, might not be the best for him. In other words, given p and M_i, adjustments in t and G could make him better-off. Demands for alternative values of t and G are, therefore, made by the median voter through the political process. The vote-maximising politician responds to these demands and moves t and G closer to the values required by the median voter. The extent to which the politician is able to respond to these demands is constrained by the need to balance the public sector budget.

This iterative process between median voter and politician captures many of the essential features of the process of fiscal politics. Assuming that the median voter now maximises his utility function, subject to the constraints outlined above, we can now define his demand function for *total* public output (D_G^i) as follows:

$$D_G^i = \Phi_G^i(p, B_i, M_i, t, \Sigma B_i).$$

The demand curve for public output, as set out above, has a great deal of intuitive appeal since it gathers together all the variables that might be thought, *a priori*, to be relevant. However, rather than think in terms of the demand curve for total public output it is more realistic to consider the demand function for a single public service such as education, or fire protection service. In that case the single service demand function is derived from the individual's utility function by making the usual *ceteris paribus* assumptions, including keeping the 'prices' of other public sector services constant.

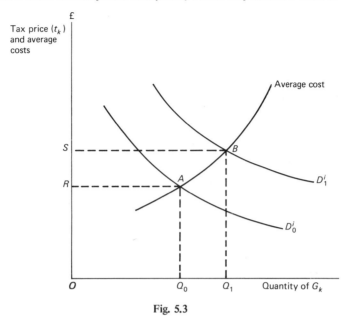

Fig. 5.3

Figure 5.3 shows a graphical representation of the median voter's demand function D_0^i for the kth public sector good (G_k). In this case the 'price' of the kth public good t_k can be thought of as being the median voter's share of the unit costs of providing the good. The prices of all other goods, including the public goods, are represented by the vector p. The signs of the demand relationship in Figure 5.3 are:

(1) quantity increases (i.e. an outward shift of the demand curve) if the median voter's tax base B_i decreases (*ceteris paribus*);
(2) quantity increases if the median voter's income M_i increases (*ceteris paribus*);
(3) quantity increases if ΣB_i the total tax base increases (*ceteris paribus*);
(4) the effect of a change in the relative price of another good on the quantity demanded depends upon the nature of the relationship between the two goods, i.e., it depends upon whether they are complements or substitutes.

In order to close the model the average cost function of supplying different levels of G_k is shown in Figure 5.3. The equilibrium level of G_k is shown as OQ_0. It is an equilibrium in the sense that the tax price that the median voter is willing to pay for OQ_0 is equal to the unit cost at which the government is willing to provide that level of the good.

Figure 5.3 can now be used to show how changes in public expenditure are brought about. Assume that the median voter's real income increases. The demand curve, therefore, shifts out to the right from D_0^i to D_1^i and the equilibrium level of output of G_k rises from Q_0 to Q_1. Assuming no other changes, then total costs (i.e. public expenditures on k) will rise from OQ_0AR to OQ_1BS.[21]

What assumptions can be made about the price and income elasticities of demand for public goods? Certain publicly supplied goods are closely associated with private sector goods. Thus, for example, motorcars and motorways are complementary, so that when there is an increase in the demand for motorcars so too will there be an increased demand for the services that public motorways provide. In this way it would be possible to derive price and income elasticities of demand for publicly supplied goods. Not all public sector goods have derived demands in this way. It is, however, generally believed that publicly supplied goods have a high income elasticity of demand. Inferior goods are just as rare in the public sector as they are in the private sector. It is also generally assumed that the price elasticity of demand for public sector goods is low.

But empirical studies of price and income elasticities of demand for public sector goods and services run into many problems. Given that public sector outputs cannot be measured, empirical studies of price and income elasticities of demand are reduced to measuring public *expenditure* elasticities with respect to changes in income. These expenditure elasticities are ambiguous since it is not possible to identify whether the income change affects the demand function or the cost function or both.

Assume that the median voter's income increased, as in the previous example. The demand curve shifts out to the right. But, if the median voter's income increase was part of a general increase in incomes throughout the economy, the average cost curve will also shift up and to the left, because labour costs will rise following the general income increase. Therefore, the final effect of the income change upon public expenditure will depend upon the shift in the demand curve relative to the shift in the average cost curve. Expenditure elasticities cannot, therefore, be used to infer unambiguously the *values* of demand elasticities for public outputs.

If the public expenditure elasticity with respect to income is greater than one then it follows that the income elasticity of demand for such goods is also greater than one but not equal to the value of the expenditure elasticity. Moreover, the public expenditure on such goods will rise relative to increases in GNP over time.

(2) Service environment

Another important determinant of public expenditure is the set of production activities used to produce public services. The mix of activities employed will vary with the 'environment' within which the service has to be provided; i.e., the concept of environment used here refers to the set of socioeconomic and topographic variables that influence the resources required to produce a certain *level* of output.

Take, for example, the case of police services. At any moment the median voter has a demand for some *level* of police protection. Assume that it is an equilibrium level that is being provided. The police activities used to produce that level of police protection are geared up for a specific environment defined by the amount of 'swag' in the area, the probability of arrest, and the general social and demographic profile of the area.[22] If any of these factors changes then the set of police activities currently used may not be appropriate to continue to provide *that level* of police protection. Consider an increase in the amount of 'swag'. This will attract more criminals, which means that more policemen will be drafted, in an attempt to maintain the previous level of protection.

This can be shown in Figure 5.4. The median voters' demand curve is shown along with the average cost of providing levels of police protection (i.e. the output of the police service). The initial equilibrium is at OQ_0. The average cost function AC_0 is defined for a particular service environment (H_0). If the service environment deteriorates to H_1 then the costs of providing that level of police protection will rise to $AC_1(H_1)$. To maintain equilibrium either the level of police protection will fall to OQ_1 or real income increases will allow an outward shift in the demand curve from D_0^i to D_1^i and a maintenance of the original level of police protection.

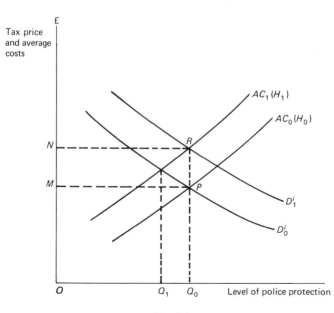

Fig. 5.4

In this example, total public expenditure on police protection could increase from OQ_0PM to OQ_0RN *without* a change in the level of police protection. This is an extremely important observation because what it implies is that increases in public expenditures without increases in the level of service provision do not necessarily imply inefficiency in service provision. The service is supplied efficiently, but what has happened is that service conditions have deteriorated. Indeed, public expenditure could rise and service levels could fall and this would still not be proof of the existence of inefficiency. The casual use of public expenditure data to examine the efficiency of the provision of public sector services is fraught with difficulties.

(3) The impact of population change on public expenditure

The growth of population has frequently been cited as a factor that contributes to the growth of public expenditures. Changes in the general population might affect some services, such as defence, police protection or fire protection, whereas in other cases it is a specific section of the population that is of importance to the provision of the service, for example the school-age population in the case of education.

Population size and other population characteristics such as age structure and population density can be thought of as a subset of the environmental variables discussed above. Intuitively it would be expected that as population increases, then the level of activity produced by the public sector would have to expand in order to serve the larger population. Thus, for example, as the number of children of school age expands, the number of teachers and other inputs in the education process increase also if existing class sizes and other service conditions are to be maintained with the now larger population. This increase in the derived demand for total inputs is reflected as an increase in total expenditure in the public sector budget. The intuitive answer is, however, only a first approximation, and a more careful modelling of the relationship between population size and the rate of change of total public expenditure is necessary.

The nature of the relationship between population size and the public expenditure size depends upon the nature of the good or service that is being supplied. Thus, in the case of a pure public good the marginal social cost of an additional member to the population is by definition zero. There is therefore no reason to expect, in the case of a pure public good, that an increase in population will result in an increase in expenditure.

Different goods are, however, characterised by differing degrees of publicness. It could, therefore, be expected *a priori* that if population increased, and furthermore if the *level* of output consumed by each member of the group was to remain constant, then for those goods that are 'near public goods' an increase in population would result in a less-than-proportional increase in expenditure.

For those services that have surplus capacity, a population change, which simply takes up the slack in the system, will result in a less-than-proportional increase in expenditure. Consider the example of an old people's home which is only 50 per cent occupied. Changes in the number of old people entering the home will only result in changes in certain variable costs, such as food costs.

Population changes have, until now, been considered in the context of assuming that the level and quantity of the service remains constant before and after the population change. These assumptions are now examined.

In the case of pure public goods a population increase will result in a zero increase in public expenditures. Since, however, total public expenditure is now to be allocated over a large group, each member of the group's share of expenditure will fall. This is equivalent to a price change, which will cause the demand for the *level* of the service to increase. This result could be generalised to the case of any public sector good for which a change in population leads to a less-than-proportional increase in expenditure. In that more general case, expenditure *per capita* declines and a price effect would result. These population influences on public spending are summarised in a *crowding function* given by

$$A_i = \frac{X_i}{N^\alpha}$$

where A_i = utility services of ith public good (G_i)
$\quad\quad X_i$ = activities (facilities) used to produce G_i
$\quad\quad N$ = size of population
$\quad\quad \alpha$ = crowding parameter: for a pure public good $\alpha = 0$; for a private good $\alpha = 1$, i.e. adding more consumers reduces utility; for quasi public goods $0 < \alpha < 1$.

Population increases can, however, place strains upon service conditions in addition to the direct impacts discussed above.[23] As population increases population density may also increase with the result that social costs of congestion will arise. These congestion costs influence in a negative way the individual's utility such that additional resources would have to be expended upon the service in order to make each individual just as 'well off' after the change in population as he was before the change. Given the existence of external costs of congestion, an increase in population will result in a more-than-proportional increase in expenditure, assuming that the *level* of output and quality of the service remains constant. On this occasion the price effect discussed above will operate in the opposite direction.

(4) The quality of publicly supplied goods

This section considers the effect of quality changes upon public expenditures. Throughout the foregoing analysis it has been implicitly assumed that the median voter has demanded a level of public sector output of a *given* quality. The quality dimension has always been assumed to remain constant. Indeed, much of the behaviour that was outlined above could be interpreted as the public sector's attempt to maintain the quality of its output. Thus a congested service (i.e. one for which the level of output provided is insufficient for the size of the population) could be thought of as a public sector good of an inferior quality to one that was less congested. Quality is a difficult magnitude to define clearly, but a useful approximation to what is implied by the use of the word is that a good that requires the efficient use of more inputs in its production (*ceteris paribus*) is of a superior quality to one that requires less. For example, hand-tailored garments are regarded to be of a higher quality than those that are machine-stitched. A Rolls-Royce embodies more manhours of labour than an assembly-line car. Thus, especially in the public sector, a good that requires more labour input is assumed to be of a higher quality than one that requires less. However, note that the rate of increase in quality may slow down with successive increases in inputs.

An education system that has a lower pupil–teacher ratio is generally assumed superior to one that has a high pupil–teacher ratio. An education system that provides the most modern equipped classrooms is considered superior to one that has no equipment. A hospital fully equipped with capital equipment and with a low patient–personnel ratio is considered superior to one that has little in the way of equipment or personnel.

Products possessing different qualities are, however, different products, and this is where the problem lies. Public expenditures will therefore rise if the median voter demands a more expensive product which is of a higher quality. Public expenditures therefore may change as a result of changes in the product. In order to integrate quality changes into the model it should be appreciated that an increase in demand has two meanings. There is the interpretation, frequently used in economics and everyday speech, which is that an increase in demand is an increase in the willingness to purchase more of the output *at the same price*. But there is a second interpretation of an increase in demand which is usually forgotten, and that is a willingness to pay a higher price for the current *level* of output. It is the latter interpretation that is important when discussing quality differences. Because individuals are willing to pay more for a modified product, this provides an incentive for producers to supply the new product.

The median voter now has a complicated choice to make. Originally he had to choose the *levels* of public outputs that would maximise his utility function subject to his budget constraint. Now his choice is over a set of different levels of public outputs *and* different qualities of these outputs. There are many more products to choose from.

The quality dimension is part of a wider class of problems, which could be labelled '*product differences*'. In all public expenditure analyses the most obvious first question to ask is, are there differences in the product that is being produced? Thus variations in public expenditures cross-sectionally and inter-temporally could be explained in terms of product differences. Is the education provided by the government in country X the same as that provided in country Y; or is the education that was produced in 1940 the same as that produced in

1970? These fundamental questions, however, are extremely difficult to answer empirically because of the immense problems involved in measuring outputs and defining the characteristics of the goods produced. They are nevertheless questions that cannot be ignored.

(5) *The price of public sector inputs and public expenditure*

It has been demonstrated that public expenditure rises as a result of an expansion in the activities provided by the public sector. The level of public sector production activities is determined by the level of public sector output demanded by the median voter, the size of the population, the quality of the product and the nature of the service environment within which the public sector has to operate.

Increases in public expenditure also result from rises in the prices of the inputs used in the public sector production functions. This section will show that the public sector shares, with other sectors of the economy, especially the services sector, the problem of not being able fully to offset increases in its costs against the advantages of productivity increases, economies of scale and technological change. This problem was formally analysed by Baumol[24] and helps to account for the persistent and cumulative rising costs of producing an economy's 'personal services', of which the services provided by governments are a large part.

In his model Baumol divides the economy into two sectors, which he labels as the progressive and non-progressive sectors. The progressive sector is characterised by cumulative increases in productivity per manhour, which arise from economies of scale and technological change. In the non-progressive sector labour productivity advances at a slower rate than that experienced in the progressive sector. Baumol's results depend upon there being a productivity differential between the two sectors. It does not imply, as some have incorrectly thought, that there are always zero productivity increases in the non-progressive sector.

One reason for the existence of a productivity differential is the key role that is played by labour inputs in the production of the non-progressive sector's goods. In the progressive sector labour is 'primarily an instrument, an incidental requisite for the attainment of final product'.[25] This contrasts with the non-progressive sector, for which 'labour is itself the end product'. This means that in the case of the progressive sector capital can be substituted for labour without affecting the nature of the product. In the non-progressive sector, however, since labour services are themselves part of the product that is being consumed, a reduction of the labour content would change the product that is being produced.

The non-progressive sector generally includes the service industries; for example central and local government services, restaurants, craft industries and the performing arts, that is, services that are labour intensive in their production. Productivity increases are not impossible in these services. They do, in fact, frequently occur, but they take place either sporadically or at a very slow rate. Thus, changes in fire-fighting technology and the technology used to combat crime are obvious examples of technological changes that have resulted in improved efficiency, quality and productivity in the delivery of these public services.

The essence of the problem of introducing technological changes into the services sector is highlighted in the following remarks made by Peacock and Baumol and Oates:

> Removing Judge Bouch from the case of Hedda Gabler would certainly reduce labour input to Ibsen's masterpiece but it would also destroy the product. Nor could one increase the productivity of the cast by performing the play at twice the speed. Anyone doubting this proposition should try playing modern long-playing discs at 78 revolutions per minute.[26]

> A Schubert trio scored for a half hour performance simply requires one and a half man-hours of labour in its public presentation and that is all that there is to the matter.[27]

Therefore, as long as consumers expect a 'certain degree' of labour content in the production of non-progressive sector goods, then the scope that technological change offers for improving the labour productivity in these activities is limited.

Consider now the behaviour of the progressive sector of the economy. In that sector it is assumed that improvements in labour productivity are matched by equal increases in hourly wage rates. It follows that unit costs in the progressive sector will remain constant over time.

In order to prevent labour moving from the non-progressive to the progressive sector of the economy, in search of higher hourly wage rates, the non-progressive sector has to match the hourly wage rate increases given by the progressive sector. If, as it is assumed, the productivity increase in the non-progressive sector is less than that in the progressive sector, then unit costs in the non-progressive sector will rise. This means that in the next time-period the opportunity cost of the non-progressive sector's output relative to that in the progressive sector will have increased. The consumer's reaction to this change in the relative prices of the outputs depends upon a number of other factors. For example, it can be demonstrated[28] that the level of output (of the non-progressive sector) demanded by the consumer will not fall, provided that the income elasticity of demand is greater than the price elasticity of demand. If output does not fall and if unit costs rise, the total costs of the non-progressive sector will rise also. Baumol's model, therefore, provides a possible explanation of public expenditure increase. If the public sector is one for which productivity increases are less than those in other sectors of the economy, and if the wages of public sector employees move in line with wages in other sectors of the economy, then *ceteris paribus* public expenditure will rise. In other words, it will cost the public sector more just to stand still.

The Baumol hypothesis of unbalanced productivity growth as an explanation of the relative expansion of the public sector can be stated more formally in the following terms. The output of the non-progressive public sector (X_1) is produced only by labour inputs (L_1) which have a constant productivity level. In the progressive private sector labour productivity grows at an exponential rate r; this produces an exponential growth in the output (X_2) of that sector. These simple production functions can be written as

$$X_{1t} = a_1 L_{1t} \tag{1}$$

$$X_{2t} = (a_2 e^{rt}) L_{2t} \tag{2}$$

where L_2 = labour force in the private sector
  t = time index
  a_1 and a_2 are constants.

From equations (1) and (2) we derive,

$$\frac{X_{1t}}{X_{1t} + X_{2t}} = \frac{a_1 L_{1t}}{a_1 L_{1t} + (a_2 e^{rt}) L_{2t}} \tag{3}$$

Equation (3) gives the ratio of government *output* to total output. Assume that wage rates are equal between the sectors and that they increase in line with productivity in the private sector. Then

$$w_t = w_0 e^{rt} \tag{4}$$

where w_t is the wage rate in period t and w_0 is a constant.
  We can now derive the unit cost in the public sector (c_{1t})

$$C_{1t} = \frac{(w_0 e^{rt}) L_{1t}}{a_1 L_{1t}} = \frac{w_0 e^{rt}}{a_1}. \tag{5}$$

The unit costs in the private sector (C_{2t}) are

$$C_{wt} = \frac{(w_0 e^{rt}) L_{2t}}{(a_2 e^{rt}) L_{2t}} = \frac{w_0}{a_2}. \tag{6}$$

Hence the unit costs in the public sector will steadily increase with the rate of productivity increase in the private sector whereas private sector unit costs will remain constant. A number of observations follow from this model. First, if the ratio of public sector output to private sector output is to remain constant then labour resources must be transferred from the private to the public sector. Such a movement is indeed observed in the major industrialised economies. Second, it follows that public sector exhaustive expenditure of which a large proportion is spent on wages and salaries will rise faster than private sector expenditure.

  Before concluding this section it should be made clear that in this formulation of the relative price effect model the productivity differential does not arise because labour in the public sector is working inefficiently: this was ruled out earlier when it was assumed that there was no X-inefficiency in the system.

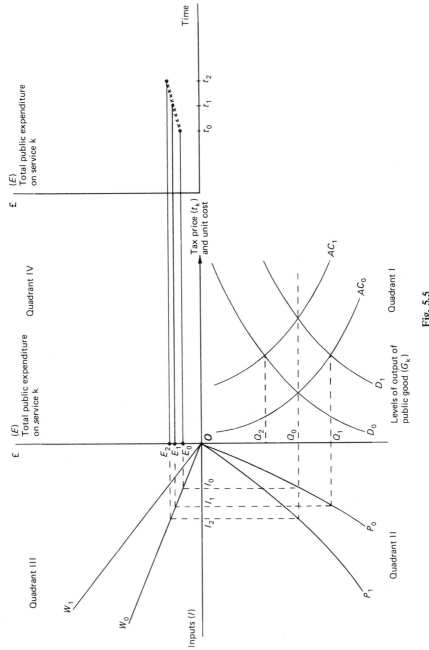

Fig. 5.5

(6) The combined model

The elements of a microeconomic model of public expenditure have been presented in the previous sections. This section draws these elements together combining them into a general model of public expenditure determination. It will be recalled from earlier remarks made above that the purpose of this model is to sort out the factors that determine the level of public expenditure, the relative size of the public sector and the time pattern of public expenditure. Moreover, it is the secular long-run trend in public expenditures that interest us, although, as we will show, short-run deviations about the longer-run trend can also be explained by the model.

Another reason why we are interested in the foundations of public expenditure can now be readily appreciated from our earlier discussions. Public output and the quality of that output are extremely difficult to quantify, which means that just about the only data that describe the size and composition of public sector activities and which are readily available are public expenditure data. In order to ensure that appropriate inferences are drawn from these data it is essential that the interaction of the forces that determine public expenditures is appreciated. This is the purpose of the combined micro-model, which is now set out.

The combined model is set out as a quadrant diagram in Figure 5.5. Quadrant I shows the demand curve for the median voter and the average cost curve for publicly supplied good k. The horizontal axis represents the tax price facing the median voter and the average cost of supplying a unit of good k.

The underlying production function for the publicly supplied good k is given in quadrant II. It shows the vector of inputs (I) used in the production of G_k. The production function is drawn for parametric values of technology, population size and the service environment. The significance of changes in these parameters will be made apparent in the example below.

Quadrant III makes use of the input unit cost line OW_0 to cost the service. If, for example, a single input such as labour was used in the production of G_k then the slope of OW_0 could be thought of as the wage rate, which when multiplied by the total volume of labour inputs used would result in a value for total cost or total expenditure.

The final quadrant, quadrant IV, is offset from the others. It displays the data that are frequently observed in practice. Along the vertical axis we measure total expenditure and we plot intervals of time along the horizontal axis. This is *not* a functional relationship that is shown in quadrant IV. Instead we wish to show how changes in total public expenditure over time on service k can originate in the behaviour of the functions in quadrants I, II, III. That is its time pattern.

To show how the diagram operates, let us take a simple example. We take as given the demand curve of the median voter and the production function and input prices of quadrants II and III which give substance to the average cost curve in quadrant I. Start with D_0 and AC_0. The equilibrium level of output G_k is OQ_0. Given the production function OP_0 the derived demand for inputs is

OI_0 which, when we have an input price of OW_0, gives a total expenditure of OE_0 in period t_0.

A change in total expenditure can then be explained either by a change in the demand function or by a change in the average cost function.

Let us first examine a change in demand. If there is a change in the underlying parameters of the demand functions this will cause a shift in the demand function to take place. Thus, if the real income of the median voter increases *ceteris paribus* the demand curve will move from D_0 to D_1. A new equilibrium is established at an output level of OQ_1 which results in an increase in the derived demand for the inputs to OI_1 and thus total expenditure rises to OE_1 in period t_1. (Note that the *ceteris paribus* assumption implies that the voter's income alone increases and civil servants' incomes do not increase — what would happen if civil servants' incomes *did* increase?).

Changes in expenditure that originate on the supply side are more complex to explain. In order to inject the greatest degree of realism as is possible into the analysis, we shall present the argument in the form of a disequilibrium adjustment towards an equilibrium. The average cost function will shift if the input unit cost line OW_0 shifts owing to increases in the real wage rate *or* the money wage rate. Moreover, if the underlying parameters of the production function OP_0 change, then the average cost function will shift also (e.g. OP_0 to OP_1 then for OQ_0 units of output OI_2 inputs are now required and for OW_0 expenditure is now OE_2 in period t_2).

Assume that the real wages paid to public sector labour causes the line OW_0 to move to OW_1. The average cost curve will move to AC_1. For the original demand curve D_0 this would result in a new output level of OQ_2. However, an adjustment to the equilibrium OQ_2 would be very much a partial equilibrium analysis of the problem. If real wages have increased for public sector workers, then given the nature of wages rounds that exist in practice we can assume that a general real wage increase has occurred throughout the entire economy and will be picked up by the median voter. The result of this reasoning is that the shift from OW_0 to OW_1 and AC_0 to AC_1 is accompanied by a shift in the demand curve from D_0 to D_1 owing to the general rise in real wages.[29]

These simple examples serve to illustrate the mechanics of the model. The reader should try to trace out the following changes for himself:

(1) a change in technology which substitutes capital for labour;
(2) a deterioration in the service conditions environment;
(3) an increase in *money* wage rates throughout the whole economy;
(4) an expansion in the total tax base of the economy;
(5) an increase in population and/or population density;
(6) a combination of the above.

In addition to the effects of changes in the absolute price level (i.e. inflation) upon the money value of public expenditures (or public expenditure measured at current prices), relative price changes also have important effects. There are two possible *'relative price effects'* that can be identified. First, as was shown in the Baumol differential productivity model, the prices of public sector ouputs relative to private sector outputs will rise over time. However, there is a second relative price effect that can be identified and this is the meaning that is usually adopted by national income accountants.[30] In this case the relative prices of public sector *inputs* rise faster than the prices of private sector final outputs. Therefore, the ratio of public exhaustive expenditures to GNP will rise if GNP is measured at market prices. These statistical ratios are discussed further in the next chapter; however, in the meantime it can be seen that the relative price effect is an important cause of the increase in the relative size of the public sector.

Public expenditures on transfer payments

The above discussion has concentrated upon public sector exhaustive expenditures. What we want to do now is to apply a similar logic to transfer payments.

Transfer payments refer to items of public expenditure that depend upon some particular state of nature occurring. Thus they are contingent upon some particular set of events faced by individuals. Given the precise formulation of the law, an individual will usually qualify for a transfer payment if a number of conditions are fulfilled; e.g. if the person is sick, infirm, unemployed, over the age of sixty-five, widowed etc. In the case of subsidies, a subsidy will be paid if the individual's income (legally defined) falls below a certain level, if prices rise above a certain rate, or if local tax rates or rents paid on housing lie above a certain proportion of disposable income.

Given the formulation of transfer payments and subsidies, money public expenditure on these items will depend upon the number of persons who qualify for receipt (i.e. who satisfy the conditions for payment), the number of persons who actually claim transfers and the basic money value of transfer paid. However, as it stands the answer to the question, 'Why do public expenditures on transfers increase?' is incomplete. The first questions that have to be asked are: What are the qualifying conditions for receipt of transfers, and how are the money values of the transfers determined?

These questions once again can be answered only by reference to fiscal politics. Different individuals, pressure groups and other associations let their demands for transfers be known. The vote-maximising politician will choose those transfer payments policies that will ensure him votes.

Empirical analysis of public expenditure

The previous sections of this chapter have set out at considerable length the underlying *a priori* model of public expenditure determination. It is important to do so because the interpretation of public expenditure data is extremely tricky and unscrupulous debaters can gloss over the more substantive issues. As it stands the model gives a picture of the likely contenders as influences on public spending. To separate out the relative contribution of each in practice requires empirical estimates of the elasticities of each variable with respect to public spending. In particular it would be of interest to know the price elasticity of demand for particular public services (expenditures) and the income elasticity (Wagner's Law).

Empirical research into estimating public expenditure functions has principally been carried out in the USA. During the 1950s and 1960s there was a massive outpouring of what has come to be known as *'determinant studies'*. These studies, carried out on a cross-section basis, sought to explain variations in spending levels between states, local governments, cities, school districts and other jurisdictions. A few time-series studies were also conducted. The general approach was to estimate the parameters of a general reduced-form equation of the kind;

$$E = \alpha_0 + \alpha_1 I + \alpha_2 A + \alpha_3 X + u$$

where E = total absolute spending for the level of government; or in some studies per capita spending and in other studies per capita spending on particular services

I = per capita incomes of the jurisdiction

A = per capita grants in aid

X = vector of socio-economic characteristics of the jurisdiction, e.g. unemployment, population density, age structure of the population, proportion of the population non-white and urbanisation.

Given the variety of levels of government, cross section years, and different services to be studied the number of determinant studies on record are close to 1000! Because of data availability problems few such studies were carried out in the UK. The more interesting UK studies are recorded in the Appendices of evidence to the Layfield Committee (Cmnd 6453, 1976).

The estimates of α_1 in the above reduced form equation range from 0.01 to 0.09, i.e. a £1 increase in per capita income caused a 1 per cent to 9 per cent rise in local public spending. Estimates of α_2 were found to vary widely but were generally greater than unity suggesting that on average federal grants-in-aid stimulated lower levels of government to spend more.

Those early determinant studies were crude. They were *ad hoc*, lacked theoretical rigour, the variables were chosen because they were plausible and they ignored the many econometric problems inherent in them (see Gramlich and Jackson). For example the expected sign on the income variable was ambiguous. A positive sign was to be associated with the idea that in higher income states there was a greater ability to pay for higher levels of public spending. But it could equally be argued that low levels of income are associated with a need to spend more on welfare services. The inclusion of the grants-in-aid variable was clumsy. Since a large proportion of expenditures were financed out of grants the reduced form implied that an identity was being estimated. Finally, the approach implicitly assumed that all local governments used identical production functions and that there was no X-inefficiency. Whilst there were many draw-backs with these studies they were nevertheless suggestive and gave a lead into more substantive studies based upon careful modelling.

The basic model used in these studies is similar in essence to that set out earlier in this chapter. Those models were used for formal modelling of the budgetary process and for hypothesis testing and proceeded on the assumption that local governments behaved 'as if' they maximised the preferences of the median voter subject to a budget constraint, which was to be specified as part of the analysis. From this approach a set of demand equations for public services could be derived and which could then be estimated. This approach is summarised as

Preference function (P)

$$P = (G, Y) \tag{7}$$

where G = vector of public services
Y = after tax income

$$X_i = \phi_i(L_i, M_i) \tag{8}$$

where X_i = public facility i which is an intermediate good used to produce public service G_i
L_i = labour inputs
M_i = other material inputs

$$G_i = g_i(X_i, N) \tag{9}$$

where G_i = ith public service
N = size of consuming group

$$C_i = c_i(w_i, s_i) \cdot X_i(L_i, M_i) \tag{10}$$

where w_i = wage rate
s_i = prices of materials.

These are exogenously determined. Equation (10) is the total cost function for producing G_i. The average cost function is given by

$$\frac{C_i}{X_i} = c_i(w_i, s_i) \tag{11}$$

The budget constraint is

$$T + Z + m_i \sum_i c_i X_i = \sum_i c_i X_i \tag{12}$$

i.e.

$$T + Z = \sum_i (1 - m_i) c_i X_i$$

where T = tax revenues, Z = lump sum grants-in-aid and m_i is the matching rate for matching grants-in-aid.

The set of equations above are at the level of the local authority. They can be also set out at the individual level

$$G_i = \frac{X_i}{N} \qquad (13)$$

i.e. per capita service benefits.

$$Y = I - tb\pi \qquad (14)$$

where Y = after tax
  I = gross income
  t = effective tax rate
  b = tax base
  π = a factor which adjusts for tax credits etc.
assume

$$t = \frac{T}{BN}$$

where B = total tax base per resident.

From the above it is possible to derive the individual's budget constraint

$$I + \tau z = \sum_i \tau c_i (1 - m_i) G_i + Y \qquad (15)$$

where τ = individuals net share of per capita taxes $(b/B) \pi$
  z = lump sum and per capita = Z/N.

The individual's preference function $P(\cdot)$ given in equation (7) is then maximised subject to the budget constraint (15). This gives a set of public service demand equations

$$G_i = f_i(p_1 \ldots p_n; 1; \tau z + I) \qquad i = 1 \ldots n \qquad (16)$$

where $p_i = \tau c_i (1 - m_i)$, i.e. the 'taxprice' of service i. 1 is the price of current private income.

The above model is illustrative of the general approach and each empirical study obviously has its own variants and embellishments. In Table 5.1 the more interesting recent empirical literature is summarised. The elasticities of $G (= X/N)$ with respect to each independent variable are listed by services. For the income and lump-sum aid variables the table gives the marginal increase in own expenditures following a \$1 increase in I or z. Four alternative price variables are used and shown. In summary

(1) All public services are price inelastic.
(2) Income elasticities are generally less than unity. Those greater than unity are housing and urban renewal (1.1) parks and recreation (1.0) and welfare (1.2).
(3) Grants-in-aid elasticities are low lying between 0.0 and 0.4.

Embellishments to the micro-model

The micro-model of public expenditure growth rested upon a number of simplifying assumptions. While the results of the model do not rest or fall upon the reality of these assumptions, they probably constrain the model to a degree such that it does not fully account for all the factors that contribute to the observed rate of growth in public expenditures.

Thus, to conclude this chapter we will draw attention to some of the features of reality that are not captured by the model but that will nevertheless form the basis of further discussion and development in subsequent chapters. Bureaucrats were assumed to be neutral and X-inefficiency was assumed not to exist. While bureaucratic behaviour and the presence of X-inefficiency are both related and are likely to cause an upward shift in the average cost curve, neither is likely to be a powerful explanation of the secular growth in public expenditures.

The median voter was assumed to be fully informed. Again, this is unlikely. Politicians often act as political entrepreneurs. In an attempt to gain votes they create expectations in the mind of the electorate which are difficult to fulfil. By over-emphasising the benefits of public expenditure programmes and playing down their costs, politicians, when electioneering, provide the ill-informed consumer with biased information.[31]

However, Downs[32] has also argued that the budget may be too small in a democracy. The full benefits of many public expenditure programmes are not felt immediately but are instead spread out into the future. On the other hand, the taxes levied to pay for these public expenditures weigh heavily in the present. Thus, the consumer/voter's myopia may result in his favouring small budgets because of the lower taxes. Downs's views must, however, be weighed up against the budget expansionary forces of the political entrepreneur.

Buchanan and Tullock also argue that there is likely to be an over-expansion of public expenditures. The benefits of public expenditures are enjoyed by particular groups, whereas taxation is general and public sector borrowing can push the costs of current programmes on to future taxpayers. Vote-maximising politicians who are lobbied by minority groups will attempt to satisfy their demands. This leads to an expansion in public expenditures in excess of that

Table 5.1 Demand for local services

Service	Price elasticities with price measured as:				Income elasticity $\epsilon_1\,(d\mathrm{Exp}/dI)$	Exogenous aid elasticity $\epsilon_2\,(d\mathrm{Exp}/dz)$
	$b/B = (\tau)$	B	$(1-m)$	c		
Education						
Bradford-Oates (1974)[d]	−0.36				0.65	
Ehrenberg (1973)[a]		0.1 to 0.36	−1 to −1.6	−0.57 to −0.09	0.54	
Feldstein (1971)					0.47	0.21, federal aid 0.06, state aid
Gramlich-Galper (1973)			0		(0.02)	(0.1, revenue sharing aid) (0.6, for exogenous education aid)
Inman (1971a, b)			−0.20		0.56 (0.005)	(0.69)
Inman (1978)	−0.37 to −0.51				0.6 to 0.75	0.71
Ladd (1975)[b]	−0.31				0.46	0.23 to 0.40
Lovell (1977)	−0.14 to −0.16		−0.48		0.24 to 0.39 (0.041)	0.03
Olsen (1972)						(0.27)
Pack-Pack (1975)	−0.07				0.34	
Peterson (1975)	−0.25 to −0.70				0.85 to 1.35 (0.001)	
Weicher (1972)						(0.41 to 0.58)
Health and Hospitals						
Ehrenberg (1973)[a]				−0.51 to −0.26	0.43 to 0.51	0.12 to 0.15
Gramlich-Galper (1973)			−0.74		~0	(0.1, for revenue sharing) (0.6, for exogenous health aid)
Inman (1971a, b)			−0.34		0.52 to 1.31 (0.004)	0 (0)
Jackson (1972)					1.1 (0.001)	0 (0 to 0.02)
Housing and Urban Renewal						
Gramlich-Galper (1973)			−0.74		~0	(0.1, for revenue sharing) (0.6, for exogenous housing aid)
Inman (1971a, b)			−0.10		1.1 (0.001)	0 (0)
Jackson (1972)						0 (0. to 0.01)
Parks and Recreation						
Bergstrom-Goodman (1973)	−0.19				1.32	0.06
Ehrenberg (1973)[a]				−0.60 to −0.39	0.21	
Gramlich-Galper (1973)			−0.92		0.99 (0.01)	0.34
Inman (1971a, b)			−0.50		(0.003)	(~0)
Jackson (1972)					1.01	(0.10)
Pack-Pack (1975)	−0.23					(0.02)

Protection (Police and Fire)

Study			c	Income		Aid	
Bergstrom-Goodman (1973)	−0.25			0.71	(0.01)	0.16	(−0.06)
Ehrenberg (1973)[a]			−0.35 to −0.01	0.60	(0.01)	0	(0)
Gramlich-Galper (1973)		−0.71		0.61			(0.04 to 0.10)
Inman (1971a, b)		−1.00					
Jackson (1972)							
Pack-Pack (1975)	−0.19						
Weicher (1972)				0.52	(0.001)		(0.05 to 0.07)

Public Works

Study			c	Income		Aid	
Ehrenberg (1973)[a]			−0.64 to −0.40	0.33 to 0.45	(0.01)	0.10 to 0.13	(~0)
Gramlich-Galper (1973)		−0.92		0.79	(0.01)	0.13 to 0.28	(0.14)
Inman (1971a, b)		−1.00			(0.001)		(0 to 0.02)
Jackson (1972)							(0.03 to 0.10)
Weicher (1972)							

Welfare

Study			c	Income		Aid	
Ehrenberg (1973)[a]			−1.13 to −1.33	1.2	(0)	0.34	(0.04)
Inman (1971a, b)		−0.04		0		0.30	

Investment

Study			c	Income		Aid	
Gramlich-Galper (1973)				1.12	(0.07)		(~0)
Inman (1971a, b)		−0.04			(0.01)	0	(~0)

Total Expenditures

Study			c	Income		Aid	
Bergstrom-Goodman (1973)	−0.23			0.64			(0.25 to 0.43)
Ehrenberg (1973)[a]				0.75	(0.05 to 0.095)		(1.0)
Gramlich-Galper (1973)		−0.68			(0.04)	0.22	(0.2)
Inman (1971a, b)							
Jackson (1972)							
Ladd (1976)	−0.31 to −0.56			0.34 to 0.89			

Notes: Income and exogenous aid elasticities are reported without parentheses. The marginal effects of income and aid are reported within parentheses.

[a] Ehrenberg's results give the elasticity of labour employed with respect to the corresponding wage (under column c), income, and exogenous aid variables.
[b] Based on Ladd's results in table 1, equation 1.
[c] Real total expenditures in the Ehrenberg study is total employment.
[d] Strictly speaking, Bradford and Oates use the ratio 'school children to population' as a measure of the relative tax price for education.

Source: Inman (1978).

which we would expect if politicians satisfied the preferences of the median voter.

The behaviour of politicians and bureaucrats in the process of budget-making is explored further in Chapter 7. In the next chapter we examine the growth in the absolute and the relative size of public expenditure in the UK. When reading that chapter the lessons learned in this one should be kept in mind.

Public Expenditure and Taxation in the UK

The measurement of government activity, public expenditure[1] and taxation is essential to most policy analysis. Considerable political attention frequently focuses upon the relative size of the public sector,[2] the size of the public sector deficit or surplus, and the amount of taxation raised. These indicators are commonly used as measures of the degree of government intervention in the economy. Though a government's activity is measured in each instance by the flow of transactions that pass between it and the rest of the economy, a number of preliminary questions need to be answered. What is government; i.e., what set of transactions is to be considered as being that of the public sector? Is the measurement of such transactions an adequate measure of the scope of government activity? For example, government might intervene in private sector activity by providing goods and services directly or by redistributing incomes. Both of these public sector activities will show up in the budget as increases in government expenditure, but each may have different consequences for economic behaviour.

The government does, with almost every law passed, regulate private sector activities. In this case, if government expenditure is used as the measure, the degree of government intervention would appear to be relatively low since regulatory activities do not appear as increases in public expenditure (of course there will be a small increase in expenditure on bureaucratic activity).

There exist, therefore, even from the outset, problems of measuring government activity. But many additional problems also exist. Any measure of the size of government is arbitrary. The use of statistics must be made with the greatest of care and requires the user to be acutely aware of their logical basis.

In this chapter measurement of the relative and absolute size of government will be considered along with the problems involved. Changes in the composition of public expenditure along with explanations of these changes are analysed as are changes in taxation and other means of financing public spending. The chapter also places the UK in an international context comparing the UK's public expenditure and taxation with those of other countries.

What is public expenditure?

Total public expenditure is the sum of the expenditure on current and capital account of the public sector and is by definition equal to the sum of consolidated public sector receipts. This is the UK national income accounting definition and assumes that government is defined to include the current and capital account activities of central and local government. Since 1976, however, it excludes the appropriation and capital account activities of the public corporations. In defining total public expenditure transactions within the public sector, such as grants paid by central government to local governments, have been eliminated, thereby avoiding double counting.

The public expenditure total is made up of the following components:

(1) *public sector consumption*: i.e. current expenditure on goods and services at market prices by central government and local authorities. This includes the wages, salaries, NHS contributions of public sector employees, and expenditures on all items required in the production of public output. In 1980 expenditure on wages and salaries and employers' contributions accounted for 64 per cent of public sector consumption;

(2) *public sector investment*: i.e. expenditure on fixed assets (land and buildings, vehicles, plant and machinery etc.) by central government and local authorities, less sales of fixed assets, plus the increase in book value of stocks and work in progress of central government and public corporations;

(3) *subsidies*: i.e. unrequited payments on current account by central government and local authorities to enterprises both in the private and public sectors;

(4) *current grants*: i.e. grants to the personal sector, principally national insurance benefits such as unemployment benefits and pensions; grants paid abroad; e.g. development aid, are also included in current grants;

(5) *capital transfers*: i.e. unrequited payments on capital account by central and local government to the private sector and abroad, e.g. investment grants and local government mortgages;

(6) *debt interest*: total payments of interest by public sector less all identified payments to other parts of the public sector;

(7) *net lending to the private sector and overseas*: i.e. net lending to the private sector and overseas governments drawing from UK subscriptions to international lending bodies, other net lending and investment abroad, and cash (net) expenditure on company securities.

The above catalogue of the elements that go to make up total UK public expenditure testifies clearly to the fact that total expenditure is a varied quantity. Public sector consumption and investment represent the public sector's claim on the real resources of the economy, whereas subsidies, current grants and capital transfers represent transfer payments from one group in the economy to another. As far as transfer payments are concerned, the government acts as an intermediary transferring rather than consuming resources. Debt interest also represents a transfer payment. Net lending to the private sector and overseas refers to the net expenditure of government's transactions in financial assets reflecting its limited role as a financial intermediary in providing loans to industry.

A number of points are worth noting. Since 1976 the nationalised industries are not included in the definition of public expenditure. Prior to that year the nationalised industries had been included in the definition of public expenditure in a limited way by including their gross capital formation in the definition of public investment. However, central government subsidies to the nationalised industries are included in the definition of public expenditure.

The absolute size of public expenditure can also reflect the method used to execute policies. Thus investment grants will show up as an increase in capital transfers, and therefore total public expenditures, whereas an increase in investment allowances will be recorded as a reduction in tax revenue. While both fiscal instruments have the same intended effect, they have different impacts on the size of public expenditure.

The composition of public expenditure for the years 1966, 1976 and 1980 is shown in Table 6.1. It is seen that subsidies and transfer payments have been the fastest growing elements of public expenditure. We will discuss these changes in the composition of public expenditure in more detail later in this chapter.

Table 6.1   Composition of UK total public expenditure, 1966–80

Item	1966		1976		1980	
	£m	%	£m	%	£m	%
Public sector consumption	6308	43.7	25742	44.0	46562	44.9
Public sector investment	1873	13.0	6202	10.6	7575	7.3
Subsidies	559	3.9	3463	5.9	5215	5.0
Current grants	3005	20.8	13614	23.3	27308	26.3
Capital transfers	189	1.3	1421	2.4	2282	2.2
Debt Interest	1465	10.1	5446	9.3	11285	10.9
Net lending	1024	7.2	2579	4.5	3493	3.4
TOTAL	14,448	100.0	58,506	100.0	103,720	100.0

Note: All magnitudes are at current prices.
Source: *National Income and Expenditure* (London: HMSO, various editions).

Measuring the size of government

The absolute size of public expenditure is a meaningless concept until it is seen alongside other magnitudes such as the size of the whole economy. While total public expenditure may have been increasing, other items in the economy such as personal incomes, prices, population and total output will have been increasing also. The interest lies in the relative rates of increase in these magnitudes rather than their absolute increase. The relative size of the public sector is usually measured by comparing public expenditure with some national income aggregate.

There are, however, a number of alternative national income aggregates that public expenditure could be related to. Table 6.2 presents a variety of measures. The differences between the ratios depend upon whether it is national or domestic product that is used in the denominator and whether the denominator is measured at market prices, factor cost, gross or net of capital consumption. Since the difference between domestic product and national product is equal to net property income from abroad there will only be a slight difference between ratios (1) and (3). Market prices, by definition, exceed factor costs by an amount equal to the net difference between indirect taxes and subsidies. Thus ratio (2) is smaller than ratio (1) because indirect taxes exceed subsidies. Finally, by using 'national income', which is defined as net national product at factor cost, the denominator is made as small as possible. It follows, therefore, that ratio (4) is the largest.

Table 6.2   UK public expenditure ratios, 1980

		%
(1)	Public expenditure as a proportion of GDP (factor cost)	53.6
(2)	Public expenditure as a proportion of GDP (market prices)	50.0
(3)	Public expenditure as a proportion of GNP (factor cost)	53.4
(4)	Public expenditure as a proportion of national income, i.e. net national product (factor cost)	62.3

Source: *National Income and Expenditure* (London: HMSO, 1981).

A comparison of the ratios in Table 6.2 and an appreciation of the basis of their variation is instructive. Frequently political points are made using such ratios. Ratio (4) will obviously be that chosen by those who wish to argue that the public sector is too large. But what is the 'true' relative size of the public sector: is it about 60 per cent or 50 per cent? The answer is that the relative size of the public sector is an arbitrary measure. No single measure is the true one but one measure can be more useful than another for particular purposes. Political arguments that rest upon the value of these ratios must likewise be arbitrary.

Are there any strong arguments for using one ratio as compared to another? The arguments against using the 'national income' measure (ratio (4)) is that the errors in estimating capital consumption are likely to be greater than the errors in the measurement of gross product, so that variations in the ratio, either over time or when making inter-country comparisons, will be sensitive to the precise method used to calculate capital consumption. A similar argument can be used to decide upon the choice between market price and factor cost measures. Variations in the ratio will be sensitive to variations in the mix of direct taxes, indirect taxes and subsidies. This means that if ratio (2) is to be used to show changes in the relative size of the public sector over time or to compare the sizes of the public sectors in different countries, the conclusions that can be drawn are clouded because the ratio will not only be an indicator of the relative size of the public sector; it will also reflect variations in the structure of public sector revenues. The following example illustrates the point:

Example: two countries A and B each spend 100 units on public expenditure. Country A and country B each have gross domestic products, measured at factor cost, equal to 200 units.

Country A finances its public expenditure from the following mix of taxes:

10 units from direct taxes

90 units from indirect taxes

Country B finances its public expenditures from the following mix of taxes:

90 units from direct taxes

10 units from indirect taxes.

Subsidies in country A = 20 units and in country B = 30 units.

For country A,

GDP (market prices) = GDP (factor cost) + indirect taxes − subsidies

$$= 200 + 90 - 20$$

$$= 270.$$

For country B,

GDP (market prices) = 200 + 10 − 30

$$= 180$$

In Table 6.3 the alternative measures of the public sector in the two countries are shown. While the absolute sizes of the public sector in this example are identical, and while their relative sizes are identical when using the factor cost measure of GDP, their relative sizes differ when using the market price measure. The difference arises, in this case, from variations in the tax structure and not because of variations on the public expenditure side.

Table 6.3 **Alternative measures of the public sector**

	Country A	Country B
	%	%
(1) *Public expenditure*		
GDP (factor cost)	50	50
(2) *Public expenditure*		
GDP (market prices)	37	56

The reader should note that this example depends upon a number of assumptions about the incidence of indirect taxes. Once the taxation chapters have been read the reader should return to this example and work out what the implicit incidence assumptions are.

It would, therefore, seem that GDP measured at factor cost is the most appropriate ratio. But this measure has its problems also. As a national income accounting concept the factor cost measure of GDP makes extremely strong assumptions about the degree of shifting of indirect taxes and subsidies. GDP, measured at factor cost, is calculated by subtracting indirect taxes and adding subsidies from GDP, measured at market prices. Thus the standard national income accounting procedure assumes complete forward shifting of indirect taxes and subsidies. This is an extremely strong assumption, and in so far as it does not hold in practice or varies from time to time and from country to country, the factor cost measure of GDP will be biased and measures of the relative size of the public sector will be subject to error.

In summarising this section on the measurement of the size of government, the lessons that should be drawn are that such measures are tricky, that the appropriate use of any measure requires an understanding of the conceptual basis of the data as well as its source, and that there is no such thing as a 'true' measure of the size of government. Instead, indicators vary in their degree of usefulness. But before any measurements are made, the first thing that must be done is to define statistically what the public sector is. This can be the most difficult problem of all. Variations in the size of the public sector can vary from one country to another because some include public corporations, nationalised industries and other quasi-government organisations while other countries do not. It is for this reason that organisations such as the OECD use a standard set of national income definitions when making international comparisons.

Composition of public expenditure

Public expenditure is divided among broad categories such as claims on resources, transfer payments, debt interest and net lending. This is shown in Table 6.4. The public sector makes claims on resources in two ways: first, on current account, which covers expenditure on wages and salaries and other consumables necessary in the production of public goods; second, on capital account, that is expenditure on schools, hospitals, roads and other plant and machinery. Taking the current and capital accounts together represents in very broad terms a major part of the allocative function of government. This is not a precise counterpart to the definition of the allocative role of government since it ignores taxes and some transfers. Some items such as education and housing might be considered to have redistributive elements associated with them and many capital programmes in the public sector are designed to serve in the pursuit of governments' stabilisation objective for the management of the economy.

The transfers of resources are obviously associated with government's redistribution objective. These transfers are divided between current grants to the personal sector, subsidies, grants abroad and capital transfers. All of these terms have already been defined in this chapter.

Table 6.4 Composition of total public expenditure by level of government, 1966-80

	1966	1970	1976	1980
	%	%	%	%
A Claims on resources (= (a) + (b))	(56.7)	(55.0)	(54.3)	(52.2)
(a) total current expenditure	(43.7)	(42.0)	(43.8)	(44.9)
(i) by central government	28.0	25.8	26.4	27.6
(ii) by local government	15.7	16.2	17.4	17.3
(b) total capital expenditure	(13.0)	(13.0)	(10.5)	(7.3)
(i) by central government	2.7	3.1	2.8	2.0
(ii) by local government	10.3	9.9	7.7	5.3
B Transfers of resources (= (c) + (d) + (e) + (f))	(25.8)	(29.6)	(36.4)	(37.0)
(c) current grants to the personal sector				
(i) by central government	18.8	20.1	21.0	23.5
(ii) by local government	0.7	0.7	1.0	1.1
(d) subsidies				
(i) by central government	3.3	3.7	5.0	4.1
(ii) by local government	0.5	0.5	0.8	0.9
(e) current grants abroad	1.2	0.8	1.4	1.8
(f) capital transfers				
(i) by central government	1.2	3.7	2.6	1.6
(ii) by local government	0.1	0.1	0.2	0.6
C Net lending	7.1	5.1	4.4	3.4
D Debt interest	(10.2)	(9.8)	(9.3)	(10.8)
(i) by central government	7.2	6.3	6.2	8.3
(ii) by local government	3.0	3.5	3.1	2.5
TOTAL = (A + B + C + D)	100.0	100.0	100.0	100.0

Source: *National Income and Expenditure* (London: HMSO), various editions.

The other feature of Table 6.4 is that these categories of public expenditure are distributed between central and local government. This is a point that will be returned to. In the meantime it can be seen that in 1980 just over 30 per cent of total public expenditure was carried out by local government. Whether or not local government has autonomy to make decisions on 30 per cent of public expenditure is another matter that will be considered later.

The general picture that emerges from Table 6.4 is that the rate of increase in the public sector's claim on real resources has been much slower than the rate of increase of transfer payments. Net lending and debt interest have not increased as fast as transfer payments.

Within the total of resource claims, current expenditure has maintained a steady proportion of total public expenditure while capital expenditure's relative share has declined since 1970. This has in part been due to the methods used to control public expenditures during the 1970s. Public expenditure cutbacks generally fall, in the first instance, on capital programmes. Some planned capital expenditures are not given approval to start, and those that are already in the pipeline are frequently modified. This follows from having a no-redundancies policy, or a reluctance, on political grounds, to sack people in the public sector in order to reduce the size of planned public expenditure. Another reason for the relative decline in capital expenditure's share is that in some services there has been a slowing down in capital building. Thus, school building has slowed down in response to the changes in the number of children of school age.

Table 6.4 also shows that local government's current expenditure has increased faster than that of central government. This is in large measure due to the absolute decline in defence expenditure, which is a central government function. However, local government does administer a greater proportion of the faster-growing services such as housing, education and the personal social services.

Expenditures on transfers have shown the fastest rate of growth of all the public expenditure components. Within this total, central government subsidies are by far the fastest growing element and have increased remarkably since 1970. Increases in price subsidies have been part of the government's anti-inflation policy and are clearly indicated here.

The allocation of public expenditures to various functions or services is shown in Table 6.5. The decline in defence expenditures' share of public expenditure is shown clearly. This relative decline in defence has released resources that have been used by the faster growing services such as housing, education, the national health service, personal social services and social security benefits.

Table 6.5 Functional composition of total public expenditure, 1953–80

Service	1953	1965	1970	1980
	%	%	%	%
Defence	24.5	14.9	11.9	11.0
External relations	1.3	1.9	1.6	2.0
Roads, transport, communications	4.4	5.8	6.2	3.4
Industry, trade and employment services	5.0	6.0	7.6	5.6
Research	0.3	1.0	1.0	0.8
Agriculture, fishing, forestry and food	4.7	2.4	1.9	1.5
Housing	8.5	6.8	6.3	6.9
Environmental services	3.4	4.3	4.1	3.7
Libraries, museums and arts	0.2	0.4	0.4	0.6
Law and order and protective services	3.0	2.4	2.9	3.6
Education	6.9	11.2	12.2	11.5
National Health Service	7.8	9.0	9.6	11.1
Personal social services	0.5	0.7	1.2	2.1
School meals, milk and welfare foods	1.2	0.9	0.8	0.5
Social security benefits	13.3	17.0	18.9	21.0
Other public services	3.1	4.9	3.6	3.8
Debt interest	12.0	10.4	9.8	10.9
TOTAL	100.0	100.0	100.0	100.0

Source: *National Income and Expenditure* (London: HMSO), various editions.

Long-term trends in public expenditure

Attention has been drawn to some of the changes that have occurred within the composition of public expenditure. This section will examine long-term changes in the relative size of the public sector and the causes of these developments. One of the principal difficulties with an analysis of this kind is that definitions of public expenditure change over time; this is quite separate from changes in the scope of government activities. In order to make a long-term comparison of the ratio of public expenditure to GNP for the period 1790–1980 we define public expenditure to be essentially the sum of all public expenditures excluding any expenditures by or on the nationalised industries and excluding net lending by all governments. This definition of public expenditure to GNP for the period 1790–1980 is shown in Table 6.6. The relative size of the public sector has increased dramatically since 1890. The first notable expansion took place in the period after 1932, and the second period of rapid expansion was post-1966. The definition of public expenditure that has been used makes all elements of the series compatible with one another. Rather than place any special significance on any one of these ratios (recall that all such ratios are arbitrary), the simple point to note is the upward rising trend in the relative size of the public sector. The scope and the degree of government intervention in the economy and in society has increased.

Table 6.6   Long-term growth in the relative size of the UK public sector: government expenditure as a percentage of GNP (at factor cost), 1790–1980

	1790	1840	1890	1910	1932	1951	1961	1966	1970	1976	1980
	%	%	%	%	%	%	%	%	%	%	%
G/GNP × 100	12.0	11.0	8.0	12.0	29.0	40.2	37.7	40.2	44.8	51.4	53.4

Sources:
(a) 1790–1951 J. Veverka, 'The Growth of Government Expenditure in the United Kingdom since 1790' *Scottish Journal of Political Economy* 1963.
(b) 1961 *National Income and Expenditure 1966* (London: HMSO, 1967).
(c) 1966–1976 *National Income and Expenditure 1966–1976* (London: HMSO, 1977).

In Table 6.7 the growth of the elements of public expenditure are shown in greater detail for the period 1955–80. In this case the elements of public expenditure correspond to their formal national income accounting definitions. The interpretation of public expenditure to GNP ratios can be extremely tricky and the following points should be borne in mind.

(1) The ratio will rise if the absolute size of public expenditure remains constant but the denominator falls. For the years 1974 and 1975 GNP at constant prices fell by 2.25 per cent between 1973 and 1975. In 1974 and 1975 the public expenditure ratio increased rapidly.

Table 6.7 The relative size of the UK public sector 1955–80

	1955	1960	1965	1970	1971	1972	1973	1974	1975	1980
	%	%	%	%	%	%	%	%	%	%
(1) Current expenditure on goods and services	19.0	18.6	19.1	20.7	20.8	21.2	20.6	22.1	24.4	24.1
(2) Investment	4.1	3.6	4.8	5.9	5.8	5.4	5.9	6.4	6.1	3.9
TOTAL (1) + (2)	23.1	22.2	23.9	26.6	26.6	26.6	26.5	28.5	30.5	28.0
(3) Subsidies	2.1	2.2	1.8	2.0	1.9	2.1	2.3	4.0	4.1	2.7
(4) Current grants	6.5	7.3	8.8	10.3	10.0	10.9	10.5	10.9	11.3	14.1
(5) Capital transfers and net lending	0.8	0.6	1.6	2.3	1.8	2.3	3.1	3.0	2.9	3.0
(6) Debt interest	5.3	5.1	4.6	4.9	4.5	4.4	4.6	5.1	4.8	5.8
TOTAL (3) + (4) + (5) + (6)	14.7	15.2	16.8	19.5	18.2	19.7	20.5	23.0	23.1	25.6
(7) Total (1) + (2) + (3) + (4) + (5) + (6)	37.8	37.4	40.7	46.1	44.8	46.3	47.0	51.5	53.6	53.6
(8) Investment by the nationalised industries	3.3	3.5	4.1	3.8	3.7	3.1	3.2	3.7	4.1	3.7
(9) TOTAL (7) + (8)	41.1	40.9	44.8	49.9	48.5	49.4	50.2	55.2	57.7	57.3

Note: Each item is shown at current prices and as a percentage of GNP at factor cost.
Source: *Economic Trends Annual Supplement 1976* (London: HMSO 1976).
      National Income and Expenditure (London: HMSO), various editions.

(2) The ratio is made up of a numerator and denominator which are both measured in current prices. If the absolute sizes of both the numerator and the denominator measured at constant prices remain constant but the prices of the numerator rise faster relative to the denominator, then the ratio will rise. Between 1970 and 1976 the implied price deflator on government final consumption rose by 140 per cent compared with an increase of 120 per cent in the GDP deflator. This is the essence of the 'relative price effect' that was discussed in the previous Chapter.

(3) Items included in the numerator are not included in the denominator. The denominator does not incorporate transfer payments and therefore does not include subsidies, current grants, capital transfers, debt interest or net lending. This means that for 1976 more than half of the definition of public expenditure was not included in the denominator. This means, first, that there is no logical reason why the ratio could not exceed 100 per cent, second that when examining the growth in the relative size of government care should be taken to distinguish between growth owing to increases in the public sector's claim on the economy's resources and growth owing to increases in transfer payments.

The information contained in Table 6.7 confirms the earlier observation that a major source of the growth in public expenditure is due to the increase in transfer payments.

The previous chapter set out an abstract model which explained the interaction of various elements upon the growth of public expenditures on goods and services. Peacock and Wiseman's thesis explained the expansion of the relative size of the public sector during wartime. It did not, however, explain the expansion of the post-1960s. This has been a period of expansion in the social services and increases in transfer payments.

The origin of the growth in the social services can be found in changing social and political attitudes during the late nineteenth and early twentieth centuries. The recommendations of the 1905 'Royal Commission on the Poor Law' resulted in the introduction, in 1908, of non-contributory pensions for those over seventy years of age. During the interwar years, 1918–39, there was a general extension of state benefits with the introduction of unemployment insurance and national health insurance.

The formation of social policy in the post-1945 period was influenced in great measure by the 1942 Beveridge Report on 'Social Insurance and Allied Services'. One of the major pieces of social legislation that was introduced following the recommendations of the Beveridge Report was the comprehensive national insurance scheme financed by compulsory contributions from employers and employees and also from the Treasury. Under this system a wide range of benefits was provided, e.g. unemployment benefits, retirement pensions, widows' and orphans' pensions, sickness benefits, maternity benefits and death grants.

Table 6.8 Public expenditure on goods and services (at 1970 prices) as a percentage of GNP (factor cost)

	1966	1970	1971	1972	1973	1974	1975	1976	1980
	%	%	%	%	%	%	%	%	%
(1) Total public expenditure on goods and services[a] (at 1970 prices) as a percentage of GNP (factor cost)	26.5	26.0	25.9	26.2	25.5	26.0	27.5	27.1	27.0
(2) Public sector current expenditure on goods and services (at 1970 prices) as a percentage of GNP (factor cost)	21.4	20.4	20.5	21.0	20.3	20.9	22.5	22.6	24.1
(3) Public sector capital expenditure (at 1970 prices) as a percentage of GNP (factor cost)	5.1	5.6	5.4	5.2	5.2	5.1	5.0	4.5	3.0
(4) Current expenditure on goods and services (at 1970 prices)[b] as a percentage of GNP at factor cost									
(a) Defence	7.2	5.5	5.4	5.4	4.9	4.9	5.1	5.0	5.4
(b) National Health Service	4.2	4.2	4.2	4.3	4.1	4.3	4.8	4.8	5.4
(c) Education	3.7	4.0	4.1	4.3	4.2	4.4	4.7	4.8	5.2
(d) Other	6.3	6.7	6.8	7.0	7.1	7.3	7.9	8.0	8.1
	(1965–66)	(1969–70)	(1970–71)	(1971–72)	(1972–73)	(1973–74)	(1974–75)	(1975–76)	(1975–80)
(5) Annual increases in GNP (at 1970 prices)	2.0	2.3	2.4	1.6	7.6	−1.1	−2.2	2.8	1.2
(6) Annual increases in public expenditure on goods and services (at 1970 prices)	2.8	1.5	2.0	2.7	4.6	1.0	3.3	1.4	−0.5

Notes: [a] row (1) = row (2) + row (3).
[b] Public expenditure is deflated by the implied public sector goods and services deflator and GNP is deflated by the GNP deflator.
For details see *National Income and Expenditure 1966–76* (London: HMSO, 1977).
Source: *National Income and Expenditure* (London: HMSO), various editions.

The 1944 Butler 'Education Act' was instrumental in extending the coverage of secondary education for all, raising the compulsory minimum school-leaving age to fifteen. It was again raised, this time to sixteen, in 1972–73. A host of Royal Commissions which examined the health services, nursery schools, the probation and prison services, and the social services, etc., also made recommendations that resulted in expansions in these services and, therefore, in increases in public expenditures.

(1) Growth of public expenditure on goods and services

The growth of public expenditure on goods and services reflects the public sector's increasing demands on the resources of the community, i.e. on labour, capital, goods and services. In order to see clearly what has been happening to the growth in the public sector's demand on real resources it is necessary to abstract from price changes. Table 6.8 shows the composition of total final expenditure for the economy as a whole.

When price increases have been adjusted for, as in Table 6.8, it is seen that the growth in the public sector's claims on the resources of the economy has been modest, over the period 1966–80. As the annual changes of the magnitudes show, the increase in the public sector's share of the nation's resources in the 1970s was due to the low rates of growth in the economy, especially over the period 1973–75 when real GNP actually declined in absolute terms. The decline in the relative size of defence is also seen in Table 6.8, along with a very modest growth in the National Health Service and a slightly faster growth in education.

It was seen in the previous chapter that public expenditure on goods and services can respond to changes in the general population, to changes in specific client groups, to changes in the general environment and so on. This is not an automatic response but one due to the existence of legislation that enables public sector executives to vary services as these other factors change. Table 6.9 gives a selection of indicators that have affected public expenditures on education.

(2) Growth of public expenditure on transfer payments

While factors such as population changes and legislative changes have affected the long-term trend in public expenditure, other factors of a short-term nature have also had an influence. This is especially true of transfer payment expenditures during the 1970s. The rapid increase of transfer payments has already been noted. In large measure this was due to the short-term influences of the general economic climate as transfers were used as an integral part of the stabilisation policies chosen by government to deal with the situation. Moreover, the nominal values of transfers such as pensions were raised in order to increase their real values during a period of rapid inflation.

The first half of the 1970s was characterised by rapid inflation, high unemployment, low industrial output, a quadrupling of the world price of oil

Table 6.9   Selected indicators of factors that affect public education expenditure (UK)

I *Pupil numbers UK*	*1961*	*1976*	*1980*
Thousands of boys and girls in January each year aged:[a]			
2–4	255	576	804
5–10	4550	5453	4959
11–14	3484	4609	4684
15	282		
16[b]	172	432	266
17	87	175	160
18 and over	29	56	19
Total all ages	8859	11,301	10,892

Notes: [a] Part-time pupils counted as 1.
       [b] The statutory school-leaving age was raised to 16 in the educational year 1972–73.
Source: *Social Trends* No. 8 (HMSO, 1977), Table 4.4 and No. 12, Table 3.4.

II *Further education UK*	*1966*	*1975*
Thousands of students in public sector and assisted establishments:		
(i) Major establishments:[a]		
Full-time	207	481
Sandwich	23	52
Day-release	693	616
Other part-time day	92	214
Evening only	854	847
Total	1868	2210
(ii) Evening institutes	1436	2030

Notes: [a] i.e. including former colleges of education in England and Wales, universities, colleges of advanced technology, colleges of education in Scotland and Northern Ireland and colleges of music etc.
Source: *Social Trends* No. 8 (HMSO, 1977), Table 4.12.

III *Public–teacher ratios*	*1961*	*1976*	*1980*
Public sector schools (UK)			
Nursery schools	22.7	22.6	19.7
Primary schools	28.9	23.8	22.7
Secondary schools	20.0	16.8	16.6
Special schools	12.5	8.9	7.7

Source: *Social Trends* No. 8 (HMSO, 1977), Table 4.17 and No. 12, Table 3.26.

and a general economic depression of world trade. These factors were obviously all related to one another. The reduction in the expansion of world trade, following the rise in oil prices, fed back into the UK domestic economy and contributed to the rise in unemployment. Rises in prices of key raw materials such as basic foods and energy, which were in part due to changes in world markets and also to the deterioration of the UK exchange rate against other major world currencies, resulted in substantial increases in the consumer price index (i.e. 'the rate of inflation').

In addition to introducing a prices and incomes policy, the government, over the period 1974–77, also chose to increase price subsidies on essential items such as food, gas, electricity, coal, and local authority rates and rents. These increases in price subsidies were an attempt to keep down the rate of increase in inflation. Subsidies as a share of total public expenditure and as a share of GNP, therefore, rose.

Increases in unemployment benefits were due to increases in the real and nominal level of benefits paid and also to the increase in the numbers unemployed. Unemployment benefits for a single person rose from £2.50 per week in 1960 to £9.80 in 1975 (for a married person the corresponding figures were £4.00 and £15.90). The numbers unemployed in 1960 were 345,800 and in 1975 were 599,700 (clearly the unemployed figures fluctuate from year to year). In real terms (i.e. at 1970 prices) unemployment benefit per person unemployed averaged £268 in 1960 and £462 in 1975. By 1982 the numbers unemployed topped the 3 million mark and unemployment benefit per person averaged £1404 p.a. The cost to the Exchequer of unemployment arising from all benefits and subsidies paid along with the loss of tax revenues was about £5500 per unemployed person p.a.

Old age pensions, a major component of grants to the personal sector, have also increased for reasons that are similar to those that caused the increase in total unemployment benefits. The number of persons aged sixty years and above increased from 7.9 million in 1951 to 11.0 million in 1975. The increase in transfer payments is part of the reason for the trends in the distribution of income discussed in Chapter 13.

Public sector receipts

Public expenditures are financed principally from taxes, but also from user charges, rents and borrowing. National insurance benefits in 1976 were financed 51 per cent from employers' contributions, 34 per cent from insured persons' contributions and 15 per cent from a grant paid by central government into the national insurance fund. As the ratio of public expenditure to GNP has increased over time, so too has the ratio of tax revenue to GNP. In 1955 total tax revenue (defined as the revenue from all direct and indirect taxes plus national insurance contributions) as a percentage of GNP (factor cost) equalled 33.5 per cent. By 1976 this magnitude had increased to 40.4 per cent. Other items of public sector revenue that are not included in the tax ratio are gross trading surpluses, interests and dividends, rents and miscellaneous user charges. These non-tax elements of public sector revenue accounted for 11 per cent of public sector current account receipts in 1976.

The structure of the UK tax system is treated in much greater detail in the chapters on taxation that follow. In the meantime it is interesting to examine an item that has in recent years come to be regarded as an important economic indicator. This is the public sector borrowing requirement (PSBR). Tax revenues and other miscellaneous revenues are generally insufficient to finance total public expenditure, i.e. total current account expenditure plus total capital account expenditure plus the public sector's net acquisition of financial assets. The deficit is the PSBR and is defined as:

$$\text{PSBR} = \frac{\text{Tax}}{\text{revenue}} - \frac{\text{Total government}}{\text{spending}} - \frac{\text{Net lending of}}{\text{the public sector}}$$

For 1976 the PSBR was made up as follows:

Public sector current receipts exceed current expenditure by	+ £39m
Capital taxes	+ £ 885m
Public investment and stock appreciation	− £6842m
Financial deficit	− £5918m
Net lending to the private sector and abroad	− £2003m
PSBR	− £7921m

Readers wishing to obtain more details of the PSBR, its composition and its financing should consult Bain (1981).

The PSBR as a percentage of GNP (at factor cost) is shown in Table 6.10. During the 1970s the percentage increased because of the very rapid increase in the absolute size of the PSBR relative to GNP. The PSBR increased in absolute terms because public expenditures (at current prices) grew very much faster than tax receipts. This was due to the following factors.

Table 6.10   Public sector borrowing requirement (PSBR) as a percentage of GNP (factor cost)

	1966	1970	1971	1972	1973	1974	1975	1976	1980
	%	%	%	%	%	%	%	%	%
PSBR	−2.9	+0.3	−2.6	−3.8	−5.7	−7.5	−10.7	−7.2	−6.3

Note: A negative indicates a deficit and a positive (as in 1970) represents a surplus.
Source: *National Income and Expenditure* (London: HMSO), various editions.

(1) There was a decline in the relative yields of indirect taxes. If indirect taxes had in 1975, when the PSBR was at a maximum, financed the same proportion of total spending as they had in 1970, then they would have been 12 per cent higher. This decline in the relative yields of indirect taxes was in

part due to the Chancellor of the Exchequer's reluctance to increase the nominal rates of indirect taxes. If the rates of indirect taxation had increased, then this would have increased the rate of inflation since such a change would have caused the post-tax prices of goods and services to rise, which would have been recorded as an increase in the retail price index (this issue is further discussed in Chapter 16).

(2) The Chancellor resisted large increases in nominal rates of income taxes. Such an increase would have aggravated taxpayers since their real disposable incomes were being eroded by inflation. The Chancellor also needed to secure the co-operation of labour to adhere to an incomes policy, and one means of gaining this co-operation was to promise that nominal rates of income tax would not rise; nevertheless, income tax receipts increased as a share of GNP (see Chapter 13).

(3) During periods of high unemployment and economic recession, tax yields were lower and public expenditure higher than they would have been under full employment.

(4) While there were factors holding back the rate of increase in tax revenues, other factors were causing public expenditures at current prices to rise; e.g. governments tried to spend their way out of the recession, and subsidies and other transfers increased rapidly in response to the inflation.

The combined effects of these influences on public revenues and expenditures was that the PSBR increased rapidly.[3] Since 1979 it has been an explicit element of government policy to reduce the PSBR in an attempt to reduce the rate growth in the money supply and to reduce the pressure on interest rates.

Central government–local government relations in the UK

In this section the financial relationships between central government and local government are examined. Local government in the UK is a creature of statute. That is to say, it does not have any autonomous powers to spend money or to raise finance independent of central government. Local government operates within the structure of central government laws so as to serve the interests of its local population. Many functions of government are, therefore, acted out through local government who administer central government policies (see Chapter 9 for a more complete discussion).

The relationship between central and local government is partially seen through their financial arrangements. Local government's principal source of finance on current account is the grants that it receives from central government. The other major source of finance is that raised through a local tax, based on the assessed rental value of property. This local tax is referred to as the 'local rate' or the 'rates'. Local governments have discretion to vary their local rate which serves to give them a degree of independence from central government and thus to provide a quality or level of service that differs from that expected by central government. While local government's access to an independent source of finance, such as the local rate, means that it can interpret legislation in such a way that will serve local preferences, it is not free to use this source of finance in the provision services outwith those that it has statutory powers to provide.

Local government faces other central government controls. Before a local government can proceed with any item of capital expenditure it must first of all receive the approval of central government that the capital programme proposed conforms to specific standards. If the programme passes these tests the local government is granted an approval to start, but at the same time it must be granted a permission to borrow to finance the programme.

The sources of local government revenue are shown in Table 6.11. It is seen that central government grants have increased in relative importance. This is especially true of the Rate Support Grant, which is designed to finance the provision of minimum levels of services, to equalise the taxable resources between different local governments, and to relieve the domestic (as opposed to the commercial) ratepayer of the local tax burden. In 1981/82 the RSG was replaced by a unitary or block grant.

Table 6.11 Sources of local government revenue, UK

		1966	1970	1976	1980
		%	%	%	%
(1)	Current grants from central government:				
	(a) Rate support grant	32.7	41.7	46.0	39.0
	(b) Specific grants	8.8	3.9	9.0	11.0
	(c) Total: (a) + (b)	41.5	45.6	55.0	50.0
(2)	Rates	38.5	34.0	26.7	31.3
(3)	Trading surplus	2.5	2.2	0.5	0.5
(4)	Rent	11.3	12.5	11.0	14.1
(5)	Interest	2.4	2.0	3.6	14.1
(6)	Other	3.8	3.7	3.2	4.1
		100.0	100.0	100.0	100.0

Source: *National Income and Expenditure* (London: HMSO), various editions.

International comparison of public expenditures and taxes

It is useful to place the data on UK public expenditure and taxation into perspective by seeing how they compare with public expenditure and taxes in other countries. There is no single comparison that will provide an overall picture and, indeed, it is possible with a selective presentation to 'prove' a variety of points (e.g. UK taxes are 'too high' or 'too low', etc.). As with all international comparisons, there is the problem that detailed national accounting definitions (of income, for example) are likely to vary from country to country. Fortunately the Taxation Division of the OECD has published a careful comparison of tax systems. Furthermore, it is possible to use the national accounts of countries published by OECD to make a comparison of public expenditures.

A number of words of caution are in order at this point. First, the information presented here is an extremely condensed summary so that readers wishing to make detailed comparisons are advised to consult the original sources. Second, the data on the UK that are presented in this section of the chapter are not directly comparable with the UK data of earlier sections. This is because, in common with all other countries, the UK's national accounts have been related on a consistent set of definitions so that comparisons between countries might be made. What is of interest in the tables that follow is the rank order of the UK.

Figure 6.1 shows taxes as a proportion of GNP in the OECD countries for the years 1965-79. It can be seen that in 1975 the percentage ranged from a high of

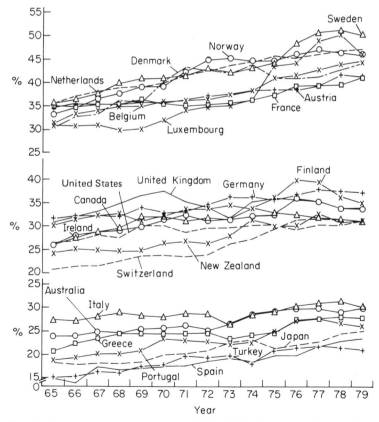

Fig. 6.1 Total tax revenue as percentage of GDP, 1965–79. Source: *Revenue Statistics of OECD Member Countries 1965-79* (Paris: OECD), Table 3.

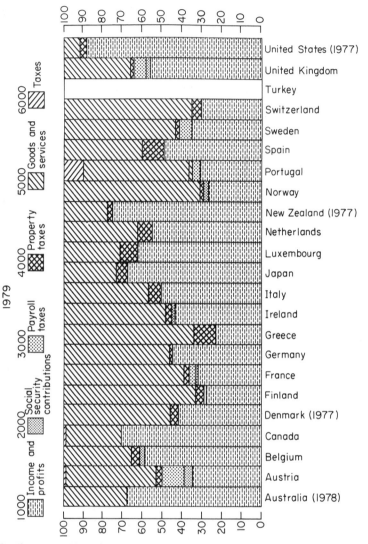

Fig. 6.2 The composition of central government tax receipts (1). Source: *Revenue Statistics of OECD Member Countries 1965–79* (Paris: OECD).

Note. 1. This refers to only those taxes which are classified as central government taxes. Social security contributions paid to social security funds are excluded.

50.0 per cent in Sweden to a low of 20.4 per cent in Turkey, with the UK somewhere in the middle at 38.2 per cent (the reader's attention is drawn to the discontinuities in the vertical scale). On the criteria of tax as a proportion of GNP the UK is not, therefore, a relatively heavily taxed country. But this is only one of a number of criteria.

Figure 6.2 shows the importance of various broad groups of taxes relative to total tax revenue in 1979. The differences in the structure of taxation between different countries and for different periods in time will be examined in more detail in subsequent chapters on taxation.

A comparison of the public expenditures of OECD countries is shown in Table 6.12. The picture of the UK in relation to other countries varies when we compare the ratios of public expenditures to GDP. Table 6.12 shows the UK coming sixth out of the eleven countries compared. However, the general picture that emerges is that the UK's public expenditures relative to GDP are not wildly out of line with those of other European and Scandinavian countries.

Table 6.12 Public expenditures as a percentage of GDP (market prices) in a selection of OECD countries

	Current expenditure on goods/services	Capital	Transfers	Total public spending
	%	%	%	%
Netherlands (1978)	18.4	3.3	33.0	54.7
Sweden (1979)	28.7	3.3	27.7	57.7
United Kingdom (1979)	20.3	2.7	15.8	38.8
Italy (1979)	15.7	3.2	23.6	42.4
Germany (1978)	19.9	3.2	21.9	45.0
France (1979)	14.8	3.0	26.2	44.1
USA (1979)	18.0	1.6	11.2	30.8
Australia (1978)	16.5	3.8	7.9	28.2
Japan (1979)	10.0	6.4	12.9	29.4
Finland (1979)	18.3	3.7	15.6	37.7
Portugal (1976)	14.1	3.0	17.4	34.6

Note: 'Transfers' are defined as subsidies, social security benefits, social assistance grants, unfunded employee welfare benefits and capital transfers.
Source: *National Accounts of OECD Countries 1950–1979* (Paris: OECD, 1981).

The ratios of total public expenditure to GDP are ranked in Table 6.12. It can be readily seen that the ranking does, however, vary slightly when total public expenditure is disaggregated into its components. For example, the UK is ranked tenth when we examine capital expenditures, following Japan, which occupies first position in the ranking. Countries such as the Netherlands and Germany spend more on transfers than they do on current expenditures on goods and services. The UK's ranking on transfer payments is comparatively low.

The public expenditure and taxation comparisons that have been made are at a very high level of aggregation. In order to uderstand the substantive variations between countries a more detailed comparison is necessary. What we can say, however, is that the UK, like all other countries we have compared, is a 'mixed economy', having a large public sector allocating and distributing resources alongside the market system.

CHAPTER 7

Public Budgets and Efficiency

The budget, which is presented each year to Parliament by the Chancellor of the Exchequer, as in the case of the UK, or to Congress by the President in the United States, contains an implicit expression or statement of the objectives and aspirations of the political party in power. It contains a package of public expenditure plans and tax legislation for the next year, or until the next budget if that should come sooner. While Parliament and Congress give birth to the budget in a legal or formal sense, the process of establishing a budget prior to its presentation is an extremely complex and, to outsiders, a bewildering procedure.

The budget that emerges results from a number of political exchanges. It has already been seen that political parties seeking election to office may attempt to ensure that they adopt that menu of fiscal and social programmes that will win them the majority of votes. Within a political party, programme and policy priorities are likely to be established as the result of vote trading among members of the Cabinet.[1] Pressure groups and other interest groups also bring a number of pressures to bear in their attempt to influence the end result.

But voters and politicians are not the only agents in the drama of budget preparation; bureaucrats (or civil servants) are also key members of the cast. The bureaucrat can be thought to serve his political masters, first, by ensuring that the executive branch of government provides information for ministers to make decisions and, second, by administering previous legislation and making sure that public sector goods and services are delivered efficiently to the voter/consumer. This view of the bureaucrat is, however, now somewhat out of date. It is more useful to assume that, like the voter and the politician, the bureaucrat also has self-interests and, therefore, seeks to maximise his own utility. The bureaucrat then becomes an actor in the drama of budget preparation rather than a stage manager. An interesting question is: What are the consequences of a utility-maximising bureaucrat upon the budget?[2]

In this chapter we will examine, (1) the economic behaviour of bureaucrats, (2) the process of budget decision-making, and (3) budget planning and control in the UK. Each of these topics is concerned with a different dimension of the efficient allocation of public sector goods and services. Taken together as a group, they form a much wider and comparatively new topic in economics, which can be usefully labelled 'the design of government'.

148

Using the rational efficiency model of the economist, the objective of the study of the design of government is to create a set of institutions that will ensure that resources are allocated and distributed in accordance with the preferences of the electorate. We have already seen in Chapter 4 that, when dealing with collective choice, it is difficult to interpret statements of this kind. However, given the demand for public sector output, we can ask if the organisation that produces that output responds to demand by providing outputs, first, in accordance with the consumers'/voters' tastes and, second, at minimum cost.

This means that we will look closely at the behaviour of bureaucrats and the nature of the organisational/institutional framework in which they work. Are there, for example, incentives and an appropriate structure of rewards that will encourage bureaucrats to search for and institute efficient methods of producing and delivering public sector goods and services? What are the organisational constraints placed upon the behaviour of the utility-maximising bureaucrat? Thus, when looking at the process of budget-making we will examine the relationship between the bureaucrat and the politician. Who has the ultimate effect on decisions: the politician or the bureaucrat?

Having examined the relationships between the bureaucrat and the politician, we then proceed to look at the relationship between the voter and the decision-making system, made up of politicians and bureaucrats. What are the relative advantages and disadvantages of centralised and decentralised forms of government? A highly centralised form of government would have most decision-making centralised in a limited number of institutions, whereas a decentralised system would consist of a number of smaller local governments, each making decisions on behalf of the voters in their jurisdiction. In a centralised system voters can become alienated because of the remoteness of government, so that a demand for decentralised government is generated. But the demand for decentralisation must be weighed up against the advantages of centralisation, especially in the general areas of stabilisation policy and the redistribution of welfare.

The relative growth of the public sector means that more appropriate control systems are sought to contain the growth of public expenditure and ensure that it is allocated efficiently. Simple control systems are usually centralised, which conflicts with demands for decentralisation. Reform of the institutions of government is, therefore, high on the agenda in most countries, especially as modern governments face new problems. Institutional change in the private sector, such as the birth of the multi-national corporations, means that the public sector has to adapt its organisations to deal with the problems that the multi-nationals create.

But the optimal design of government and the decision of institutional change is not the prerogative of the economist. The economist contributes to the debate through considerations of the demands placed upon the *fiscal* institutions of government. Through this topic economics and politics come very close together. It is worth while reminding ourselves of the primacy of politics in public sector decision-making. The rational decision-making models of the economist, such as cost–benefit analysis (which is examined in the next chapter), are designed to answer specific questions and to aid decision-making by providing information. But the actual decision-making rules followed by politicians can often be found to be at variance with the prescriptions of the economist's model. Decisions are made within organisations that have specific incentive structures; therefore, to understand actual decision-making behaviour it is necessary to understand the organisations in which these decisions are made. In the meantime it is worth while bearing in mind the words of one budget decision-maker:

> Political values permeate every aspect of the decision-making process in the majority of federal domestic programmes. There is no simple division of labour in which the politicians achieve consensus on an agreed set of objectives while the 'analysts' design and evaluate – from efficiency and effectiveness criteria – alternative means of achieving those objectives.[3]

Before proceeding further it is necessary to give a precise meaning to the word efficiency. To the economist there are two aspects to efficiency

(a) *allocative efficiency*, i.e. have resources been allocated according to the preferences and budget constraints of the consumers of final products? This produces the familiar Pareto conditions for private and public goods which were examined in earlier chapters. In a pragmatic sense allocative efficiency refers to the following questions; does the public sector produce the level and mix of services (public expenditures) which the electorate demands? Is the voter sovereign in the 'political market place'? Whose preferences count?

(b) X-*efficiency*, this refers to the supply side. Irrespective of whether or not the public sector does produce the optimal level and mix of public services are these services produced at minimum cost? Is there over-manning? Are the best practices and most efficient technologies used? To the extent that they are not, there is said to exist X-efficiency in the system. In other words, the public sector is not operating on its efficiency frontier whereas in the case of allocative efficiency it is operating at the wrong point on its efficiency frontier.

Given earlier discussions of the median voter it should be clear that since each individual is a public service quantity and quality taker everyone except the group of median voters will prefer an alternative level and mix of public services. The more articulate, resourceful and better organised pressure groups will make these allocative inefficiencies known. But such signals are insufficient to prove inefficiency – they could simply record one group's dissatisfaction with the median solution. Moreover, it is likely that competing signals originating from a number of different groups will be registered. The business of politics is balancing up these different signals and deciding how to respond to them. Thus, it is not straightforward to discuss public sector inefficiency. It is a tricky concept that must be handled with a great deal of care and attention.

The economic analysis of bureaucracy

It has already been argued that the performance of any economic system depends upon its institutional framework. When dealing with the public sector one of the institutions that is of significance is that of the bureaucracy. Bureaucracy can be defined as a set of bureaus, i.e. the departments responsible for the services provided by government. Each bureau is treated as a non-profit-making organisation that is financed mainly from a lump sum grant rather than from the sale of its output. Thus, alternative institutional structures can be defined in terms of alternative relationships existing between bureaus. Some bureaus may co-operate with one another and be complementary in their activities while others will compete with each other for scarce resources. While the structure of bureaus will influence bureaucratic behaviour by establishing a specific set of constraints and incentives, any analysis of the behaviour of the bureau and its bureaucrats and their roles in resources allocation must pay specific attention to the motives and objectives of the bureaucrat. What is it that motivates bureaucrats?

The bureaucrat (i.e. senior decision-maker) is seldom found to be an administrative eunuch, who dispassionately observes the established set of administrative rules and carries them out unquestioningly. This was the prescriptive view of the rational bureaucrat that Weber had in mind in the nineteenth century, but it has been subsequently modified by economists like Niskanen and Breton.

Niskanen suggests that the bureaucrat, in common with all other individuals, acts as a utility-maximiser. Employing a 'managerial utility function approach', Niskanen proposes that the arguments of the bureaucrat's utility function include his salary, the size of the staff working for him and their salaries, his public reputation, his perquisites and his power or status. Since many of the items that appear in the bureaucrat's utility function are directly related to the size of the budget, it follows that bureaucrats, who are utility-maximisers, will also be budget-maximisers. The utility-maximising or budget-maximising bureaucrat is, therefore, not a neutral agent in the budget decision-making process.

Using this model of bureaucratic behaviour, we now consider the output decision of the bureaucrat. Like non-profit-making private sector organisations and monopolists, the bureaucracy is insulated from competitive forces. However, there do exist a number of interesting differences between the behaviour of bureaus and the behaviour of these other organisations. Whereas the monopolist chooses a level of output that, when sold on the market, will maximise his profit, the bureaucrat receives a lump sum grant from a higher authority (referred to as the sponsor), such as the Treasury or Office of the Budget, and promises to provide a certain amount of total output in exchange for a budget. The precise nature of the relationship between the bureaucrat and the agency providing the budget will be returned to later. In the meantime it is assumed that the sponsoring agency is acting on behalf of the taxpayer.

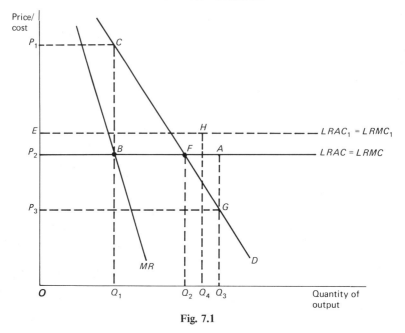

Fig. 7.1

A comparison of the output decisions of the private sector monopolist, the private sector non-profit-making organisation and the public sector bureau are shown in Figure 7.1. Each organisation faces the same demand function and production function and the same prices of factors of production. Thus each 'firm' is confronted with the same long-run average cost curve ($LRAC$). It is furthermore assumed that constant returns to scale exist; therefore $LRAC = LRMC$. The demand curve is shown as D and the marginal revenue curve as MR. For the purposes of this exercise we will assume that D represents the market demand curve and also the median voter's demand curve.

The monopolist will choose output level OQ_1 and charge a price of OP_1, his monopoly profit being represented by P_1CBP_2. The non-profit-making private sector firm will choose output level OQ_2 and will charge a price of OP_2. In this example, it is assumed that the bureaucrat is offered a budget equal to OP_2AQ_3. The size of this budget is determined by the political process (see next section to this chapter). Given the production relationships and, therefore, the cost function, the bureaucrat could produce OQ_3 units of output.

If, having been offered a budget equal to OP_2AQ_3, the bureau employs the production relationship, which is represented by $LRAC$, then he will provide OQ_3 units of output. In that case the bureau's level of output is greater than that produced by the monopolist and the non-profit-making firm. Moreover, the bureau is providing more output than the median consumer/voter is willing to consume if faced with a price of OP_2. Therefore, given that OP_2 is the long-run

Pareto-efficient price, the monopolist will under-supply the good while the bureaucrat will, given his budget, over-supply. In both cases there is a welfare loss. In the case of monopoly the welfare loss to the consumer is equal to CBF, whereas in the bureaucracy case it is FAG. The reader should note that throughout this example it has been assumed that the monopolist and the bureaucrat both face the same production function and the same set of input prices.

The outcome for the bureaucracy partially depends upon the size of the budget that is provided. If, instead of receiving a budget equal to OP_2AQ_3 the sponsoring authority had only provided a budget of OP_2FQ_2, then (*ceteris paribus*) the output for the bureau would have been the same as that for the non-profit-making firm. On the other hand, if the budget provided was less than OQ_2FP_2 but greater than OP_2BQ_1, then the output level would lie between that of the monopolist and that of the non-profit-making firm. In the latter case the sponsoring authority would be placed under great pressure by the consumer/voter to increase the size of the budget in order to satisfy demand, whereas in the original case of a budget equal to OP_3AP_2 the consumer/voter would prefer a reduction in the size of the budget.

Interest, therefore, centres upon the process of budget determination. Will the actual budget be more than or less than optimal? The utility-maximising bureaucrat will find it in his interest to maximise the size of his budget whereas the sponsoring authority, whom we assume to be the politicians responsible to the consumer/voter, will be keen to ensure that the budget will be large enough to satisfy the voters' demand but not too large to upset the voter.

The relationship between the bureaucrat and the sponsoring agent is similar to one of bilateral monopoly, in which the final outcome depends upon the distribution of power and influence between the two parties in the exchange. While the sponsoring agents may have legislative power and authority in a formal sense, they are often, in practice, heavily dependent upon the bureaucracy for information relating to service provision. It is ministers (politicians) who formally make a request for a budget; however, their request is heavily dependent upon the information provided by the bureau. It is, therefore, the bureau that is seeking a budget request, through the formal office of their political head. The bureaucrats rather than the minister in charge of a department have the detailed information relating to service provision, the prices of inputs, trends in the demand for the service, etc. In the absence of external expert advice the minister is unable to challenge this information and so the sponsoring authority is in an insufficiently well-informed position to question the bureau's budget request.

The sponsor is interested in granting a budget that will maximise the quantity of output supplied for a given level of quality of service. On the other hand, the bureaucrat wishes to maximise the size of his budget since that provides him with the resources to maximise his utility. A number of alternative arguments might enter into the bureaucrat's utility function. For example, there is the traditional stereotype bureaucrat occupying an expensively furnished office, enjoying expense account activities while unproductively sending pieces of 'red tape' memos around the bureaucratic machine. While most bureaucrats would deny the reality of this stereotype, many people nevertheless believe it to be an accurate description. Another way in which the bureaucrat might increase his utility would be to 'empire-build' by increasing the number of public sector employees who are responsible to him. Or, in order to gain the favour and respect of his employees he may ensure that their wages and perquisites are maximised. In each of these cases a part of the bureau's budget is allocated to furnishings, expense accounts, overmanning or rents enjoyed by public sector employees, rather than to the production of output. There is, therefore, a welfare loss to the consumers of the service and a gain to the producers of the service.

This is another way of saying that the costs of providing public sector outputs are greater than they might otherwise be, i.e. if there were fewer public sector employees each of whom were paid less. In this case the bureau produces its output inefficiently. Instead of facing long-run average cost curve $LRAC$ in Figure 7.1 it faces $LRAC_1$. The sponsor grants a budget of OP_2AQ_3 on the assumption that costs are $LRAC$ and on the expectation that the bureau will deliver OQ_3 units of the good. The bureaucrat, however, trades off the 'fat' in the budget against output of the good. Facing $LRAC_1$ the bureau will produce OQ_4 units of output, where $OP_2AQ_3 = OEHQ_4$.

This graphical example has been presented purely for illustrative purposes. The extent to which the bureaucrat is able to trade off public output for economic rents in his budget depends upon the degree of knowledge that the sponsor has with respect to the production function and the costs of production. Such knowledge, while necessary, is not by itself sufficient for the control of the bureau. A set of institutions of checks and balances must exist to police and control the system. But this can create a problem in public administration because who is to regulate the regulators?

This description of bureaucratic behaviour lies within the precinct of 'allocative efficiency'. To the extent that the system allows the bureaucrat sufficient freedom and discretion to pursue his own objectives resources will only by accident be allocated according to the preferences of the median voter. In other words, how *accountable* is the bureaucratic organisation to the democratic political process – a great deal is written about this topic in the public administration literature. Generally speaking it is found that whilst accountability and control exist *de jure*, *de facto* they are weak. This is especially true when it comes to the *implementation* of policies. Policies are implemented and services are delivered by lower levels of the organisation. At each stage of the implementation process someone has to interpret some piece of legislation, which is usually formulated in a vague and imprecise way. Successive interpretation can result in cumulative deviations from the intentions of the original legislation. Thus, the services which are delivered are not exactly those planned.

Furthermore, not only might bureaucrats and the implementation process promote allocative inefficiencies there is also the role of the professional to be taken into consideration. Professionals abound within the public sector (teachers, doctors, planners, lawyers etc.). Each group has its own particular set of professional norms and standards which it sets in relation to the planning and delivery of services. The question to be asked is where do the preferences and interests of the consumer or client fit into this? Is it the case that because of their training and knowledge that professionals 'know best'? In what sense do professional interests and the public interest come into conflict? These are the kinds of questions which require answers if the public sector is to be accountable to those whom it serves. To test this case, ask yourself how it might apply to a local planning enquiry to redevelop a central city site or how it might apply to the doctor/patient relationship or the teacher/pupil (parent) relationship. The power and discretion of the professional, especially within the public sector, is an area which requires more investigation.

It would be a mistake to conclude that it is only public sector bureaucracies for which actual costs lie above the costs of the most efficient and feasible production function, i.e. $LRAC$ as compared with $LRAC_1$. This is an example of a more general phenomenon which is commonly referred to as X-inefficiency.

The notion of X-inefficiency can be illustrated by referring once again to the previous example. The problem of the bureau's output decision contains two quite separate concepts of efficiency. First, there is the allocative inefficiency which arises because the shadow price that the consumer/voter is willing to pay for OQ_3 units of the good is less than the implicit price charged, i.e. OP_3 compared with OP_2. Put another way, the consumer voter would be willing to pay OP_2 for OQ_2 units of output but would not be willing to pay OP_2 for OQ_3. The inefficiency arises because the actual allocation of resources does not correspond to the allocations that would satisfy the consumers'/voters' preferences.

Second, there is the inefficiency that arises because of technical inefficiency in producing the output. This is referred to as X-inefficiency.[4] In the above example the bureau did not use the least-cost technology represented by $LRAC$. Instead it used a more expensive one represented by $LRAC_1$. The presence of X-inefficiency is another way of saying that the bureau is not operating on its production possibility frontier but is instead at some point within the frontier.

X-inefficiency arises because of imperfectly specified contracts and because, even although contracts may be unambiguously specified, it is nevertheless technically difficult to ensure that the terms of the contract are being fulfilled. The policing and enforcement of contracts might, therefore, be technically non-feasible or, if feasible, so costly that the benefits are less than the costs of enforcement.[5] The existence of X-inefficiency is, therefore, an example of market failure brought about by high transactions costs. In the case of the bureaucracy, X-inefficiency arises because, although a formal contractual arrangement may exist between the bureau and its sponsor, it is nevertheless costly to enforce and to police such contracts. If the contract is poorly specified this gives the utility-maximising bureaucrat additional degrees of freedom to maximise the size of his budget since he will be less constrained.

Imperfectly specified contracts and/or the costs of enforcing contracts give rise to X-inefficiency. Costs lie above the level that would exist if X-inefficiency were absent. The degree of X-inefficiency that exists depends upon the nature of the competitive environment in which the organisation finds itself. That is, it depends on whether there are incentives to eliminate the waste and inefficiency. The presence of competition and the fear of possible take-over are important factors which may force firms to eliminate waste. When these competitive forces are weakened, as in the case of imperfect competition and non-market bureaucracies, the pressures for eliminating inefficiency are weakened and agents within the organisation can then adjust their behaviour to maximise their own utility. In the case of monopoly, X-inefficiency is passed on to the consumer as higher prices and reduced output and to the shareholders as reduced dividends. For public enterprises and public sector bureaucracies, X-inefficiency is passed on to the taxpayer in higher taxes, and/or lower levels of public service output.

It has been repeatedly emphasised throughout this chapter that the extent of the existence of both allocative and X-inefficiency depends upon the precise nature of the incentives that exist to eliminate such waste. One possibility would be to increase the amount of competition between bureaus in an attempt to simulate the competitive forces of the market and thus to force reductions in bureaus' costs. It might be possible to do this if the total public sector budget was fixed and if bureaus had to bid against one another for budget shares.[6] The problem with this suggestion is that such competitive forces are unlikely to be sufficiently great to produce a perfectly competitive solution. Moreover, bureaus may find it to their mutual advantage to collude if the benefits of collusion exceed the costs. The competitive solution is, therefore, likely to be only partial. Even if a perfectly competitive solution were simulated by competing bureaus, the solution is not guaranteed to be welfare-maximising; that is, while the outcome might be allocatively efficient, in the sense that the bureau is operating on its production frontier, nevertheless a redistribution of resources between bureaus could increase welfare. This is the familiar problem of choosing that particular Pareto-efficient allocation that maximises welfare.

The approach adopted in this chapter to study bureaucratic behaviour is not intended to be cynical. To assume that bureaucrats are self-interested and concerned to maximise their own utility functions subject to budget and institutional constraints is merely a logical extension to the public sector of Williamson's 'managerial discretion' model, which was developed for the private sector firm.[7] Interest lies in considering the consequences for resource allocation of the existence of such a bureaucrat. Whether or not bureaucrats have scope for the pursuit of their own self-interest depends upon the institutional constraints that they face. However, it is clear that, in the absence of competitive forces from the market, if X-inefficiency and allocative inefficiency are to be eliminated or at least reduced, public administration has to consider what combination of organisations will provide incentives to reduce waste, control the allocation of resources between bureaus and act as a watchdog to ensure that the implicit contracts made between bureau and sponsor are observed.

An interesting case study of bureaucratic behaviour is to be found in Hartley (1980).

The process of budget decision-making

Bureaucrats attempt to maximise their budgets subject to the institutional constraints that confront them. The sponsoring authority will seek to grant a budget to the bureau of a size that is sufficient to satisfy the median voter and hence the politician's utility function. This characterisation of budget determination, as a process of exchange between bureaucrats and politicians, is devoid of any details of the decision-making process. How do bureaus go about making requests for budgets, and by what means are these requests considered by the legislative branch of government?

A behavioural analysis of the process of budgeting has been advanced by the political scientist Aaron Wildavsky. According to Wildavsky, 'the largest determining factor of the size and content of this year's budget is last year's budget'.[8] To the economist, who is accustomed to thinking of decision-making as if it were the result of a calculation that weighs up the benefits against the opportunity costs of one budget as compared with another, this statement might at first thought seem a bit strange. This is because implicit in the economist's approach is an assumption that the decision-making process is one of simultaneous determination of all factors. That is certainly the kind of model that was presented in the earlier chapters, which dealt with the analysis of public goods.

In general equilibrium and partial equilibrium models of public good output determination, voters expressed their demands for public goods. There was an adjustment towards an equilibrium which, when established, simultaneously determined (1) the total level of public expenditure relative to private expenditures, (2) the relative sizes of the public expenditure programmes, (3) the size of the tax bill and (4) its distribution among taxpayers. Moreover, in arriving at a decision it was assumed in these partial and general equilibrium models that everyone acts rationally, that everyone is fully informed and that bureaucrats are perfectly neutral. The standard economic model tells a strange tale about decision-making. But that is mainly because it is not intended to be a model of actual decision-making.

The standard neoclassical maximising model is concerned with following through the behaviour of individuals 'as if' they maximised some objective function, such as a utility function. Given a set of exogenous changes it is possible, using these models, to consider the consequences of these changes for individual behaviour and hence for the allocation and distribution of resources. While these models might be considered to be behaviourally naive, they do nevertheless have a significant role to play in the analysis of optimisation. Behavioural models, in contrast, have a different role to play. While they may be more descriptive, the price that is paid for this added realism is a loss of generality.

The model of decision-making that Wildavsky has in mind is one made up of sequential or iterative procedures. The outcome of a sequential decision-making model depends upon the order in which events are decided upon. Thus the outcomes of earlier decisions may enter as binding constraints on current decisions. Placing this model in the context of budget decision-making implies that a decision made about this year's budget must take into account the decisions made about the last year's budget and the one the year before that and so on. A decision to build a school, or a motorway, or to install a programme of public sector education or health care is not a commitment to allocate resources to these activities for the next year only. Instead, these resources are committed until a decision is taken to alter the level or quality of service provision. Thus, last year's budget in large measure determines this year's budget because of the large commitment of resources that is carried forward into the present from the past. Budget decision-making is, therefore, described more accurately by sequential models than by simultaneous models.

Another feature of budget decision-making is that the size of the volume of resources upon which current decisions are made is a relatively small percentage of the total. The reason for this is that the decision-maker does not start with a clear sheet but instead carries forward a commitment of resources from previous decisions. Wildavsky refers to this as 'incrementalism'. Current decisions are limited to accepting previous decisions, considering marginal adjustments to earlier decisions, and evaluating new programmes that are to be included in the budget.

Incrementalism also describes the way in which decision-makers deal with the complexities and the costs of decision-making in practice. Decision-makers have a limited amount of time to prepare their budgets. To start each budget cycle with a clean sheet and consider the balance of resources between sub-programmes and the interrelationships between different parts of the implicit production function would be an immense task requiring a large volume of computational resources. Such decision-making would be expensive. Wildavsky, in common with many decision-making theorists, assumes that the decision-maker has a limited personal computational faculty. Incrementalism is cheaper on decision-making resources and presents the decision-maker with a limited number of alternative options on which he has to make a decision.[9] Moreover, if the decision-maker did not proceed via a piecemeal incrementalist approach, there is always the possibility that programmes would run the risk of being completely reorganised each year. Large changes are not only impractical and expensive, but they also create uncertainty for those who manage and plan the services and for those who consume the output.[10]

While incrementalism has its advantages, it also has its costs or disadvantages. The system may not be quick to change or to adapt. This means that reform of the social services and the fiscal system is likely to proceed via piecemeal changes. The problem with piecemeal adaptation is that, unless each marginal adjustment is considered in relation to the whole system and in relation to the overall objective function, change can result in a reduction of welfare rather than an increase. This problem is the familiar one of the 'second-best'.[11] A related problem of incrementalism is that errors can be compounded. If an incorrect decision is continually carried forward without an adjustment being made (perhaps because the errors have not been noticed), then the errors of the decision will accumulate.

Empirical studies have been carried out to test whether or not incrementalism is a reasonable description of the decision-making process. The best-known study was that carried out by Davis, Dempster and Wildavsky. Their study, which used time-series data for the period 1948–63, examined the implicit budgeting rule observed by fifty-six non-defence agencies (i.e. spending departments) of the US federal government.

Each year an agency makes a request for an appropriation (i.e. a budget request). This request is considered by a congressional committee which grants the agency its budget. The process of request and appropriation was modelled by Davis, Dempster and Wildavsky according to the following simple statistical decision rules:

(1) Agency decision rule:

$$X_{it} = \beta_i Y_{it-1} + \xi_{it}$$

where: X_{it} = the requested appropriation of agency i in period t
Y_{it-1} = the actual budget granted to agency i in the previous period $(t-1)$
β_i = a constant; such that $\beta_i > 1$
ξ_{it} = a randomly distributed variable with mean equal to zero.

That is, an agency makes a request for an appropriation that is a mark-up on its previous budget. If $\beta_i = 1.12$ then the agency makes a request that is 12 per cent greater than it was granted the previous year.

(2) Committee decision rule:

$$Y_{it} = \alpha_i X_{it} + \epsilon_{it}$$

where: α_i = constant; such that $\alpha_i < 1$
ϵ_{it} = a randomly distributed variable with mean equal to zero.

That is, the actual budget granted by the Committee is equal to some proportion (less than one) of the actual amount requested.

Combining the two decision rules by substituting the agency's decision rule into the committee's decision rule produces the following simple rule:

$$Y_{it} = \alpha_i \beta_i Y_{it-1} + (\xi_t + \epsilon_t).$$

That is, this year's budget is a function of last year's budget, which is the decision rule of incrementalism. The randomly distributed variables in each rule reminds us that these are statistical decision rules. In other words, the actual outcome is dependent on the actual budget granted plus random events that occur during the year, such as unforeseen contingencies that were not budgeted for and for which supplementary appropriations are required.

On testing this simple decision rule Davis, Dempster and Wildavsky found that incrementalism proved to be a reasonable empirical description of what happened in thirty-six out of fifty-six non-defence agencies examined. More complicated decision rules, which were also tested, turned out not to work as well as explaining actual budgetary behaviour when compared with the simple rules.

While Davis, Dempster and Wildavsky's study gives support to the belief in incrementalism and sequential decision-making models, there does remain a good deal to explain. This can be explained by incorporating into this analysis the earlier analysis of the behaviour of politicians and voters. If the demand for some services grows faster than that of others, politicians, seeking to satisfy their own utility function and that of their voters, will be keen to ensure that those agencies with the fastest growing service demands get an appropriate share of the budget's resources. Hence, the α and β coefficients for such agencies will be greater than those of agencies whose service demand is static or slow-growing.

How does such behaviour fit into this model? While it is formally the political 'bosses' of each agency who make the agency's request and it is the politicians in Congress who grant the request, they are at all points served and advised by the bureaucracy. It is the bureaucrats who make the forecasts of the underlying technical relationships on which the budget is founded; it is the bureaucrats who cost the options; and, therefore, it is the bureaucrats who, through their intimate knowledge of the day-to-day operation of the system of service production and delivery, can make adjustments that will satisfy bureaucrat's utility function.

Budget planning and control in the UK

Budgetary planning and control refers to the system by which governments plan their public expenditure programmes, monitor and control these programmes and relate their expenditure plans to policies of finance and taxation. This section will examine first the system of expenditure planning, second the system of taxation planning, and third a critical evaluation of the system as a whole.

(1) Public expenditure planning

The UK system of public expenditure planning and control has developed since 1960, first in recognition of the deficiencies of the earlier system of planning and second in response to the relative growth in the share of resources absorbed by the public sector. It is impossible, in this chapter, to go into much detail of the planning system. The interested reader should consult Jackson (1979 and 1982), Wright (1977 and 1980) and Clarke (1978).

During the 1950s there was increasing dissatisfaction in the Treasury, among the spending departments and from Members of Parliament that the information relating to public expenditure was fragmented and that the planning horizon was too short. The supply estimates (civil and defence) that were presented to Parliament for approval presented estimates of public expenditure only for the following twelve months. The likely buildup of new public expenditure programmes was never clearly shown, since it was only the tip of the iceberg that was ever presented. Ministers, by approving these estimates, were therefore committing themselves to an unknown rate of resource absorption by the public sector in the future. This dissatisfaction with the system brought about a Treasury inquiry into the whole system of public expenditure planning, which was eventually presented in July 1961 as the Plowden Committee Report, *The Control of Public Expenditure* (Cmnd 1432). The Plowden Committee Report was a significant landmark in the development of public expenditure planning in the UK. The present system of planning and control has its origins in the Committee's recommendations. The two key recommendations of the Committee were:

> that decisions involving substantial future expenditure should always be taken in the light of surveys of public expenditure as a whole, over a period of years, and in relation to the prospective resources.... [para. 7]

> Public expenditure decisions, whether they be in defence or education or overseas aid or agriculture or pensions or anything else, should never be taken without consideration of (a) what the country can offer over the period (b) the relative importance of one kind of expenditure against another. [para. 7]

In other words, the Committee recommended that a rational and coherent system be set up within which public expenditure decisions might be taken. The report furthermore emphasised that total public expenditure had to be planned; i.e. the expenditure of central government (and, *a fortiori*, not only that part of central government expenditure that happened to be authorised annually by the House of Commons through the supply estimates), all expenditures by local authorities, however financed, the gross expenditure of the National Insurance funds, and the whole of the investment of the nationalised industries and other public corporations. By placing public expenditure in the context of the assessment of the real resources likely to be available to meet these demands (i.e. not only the effects on taxation), the report succeeded in drawing attention to the opportunity cost of the public sector in terms of the other claims on GNP, i.e. from private sector investment and consumption and from exports.

The procedures adopted in drawing up the public expenditure plan follow the standard 'budget cycle' that is, in outline if not in detail, common to almost all systems. Expenditure is planned by function (i.e. education, police, defence, health, etc.) and by economic category (i.e. current expenditure and capital expenditure); an analysis of public sector gross domestic fixed capital formation by type of asset is obtained; and new construction is also analysed by region. In addition, information is obtained about manpower implications of the expenditure forecasts. The timetable or cycle is roughly as follows.

(1) Instructions on the conduct of the coming year's public expenditure survey are issued by the Treasury.

(2) Spending departments submit their expenditure plans for the next five years to the Treasury.

(3) Discussions take place between the Treasury and the spending departments in order to reach an agreement on the figures and the underlying policy and statistical assumptions. Agreement here means no more than an identity of view on what present policies are and on the probable costs of continuing them.

(4) Work is started on preparing a medium-term assessment of the trends in the whole economy, i.e. GNP investment, exports, etc.

(5) A draft report is drawn up by the Treasury and is considered by the Public Expenditure Survey Committee (PESC).

(6) The medium-term economic assessment report is agreed upon in the appropriate official interdepartmental committee; the medium-term assessment committee (MTAC).

(7) Both the PESC and the MTAC reports are submitted to ministers.

(8) Decisions are taken on the aggregate of public expenditure and its broad allocation to the major functional heads.

The Treasury undertakes the task of collating all of the material required for the annual Public Expenditure Survey and also drafts the PESC report. The PESC is a large committee chaired by the third secretary to the Treasury, and is composed of the principal finance officers of the major spending departments in Whitehall. The PESC does not try to agree upon any particular level of public expenditure to be recommended to ministers or upon its allocation. It instead confines itself to the task of agreeing a factual report showing where present policies, if they remain changed, are likely to lead in terms of public expenditure at constant prices and what would be implied by a range of possible alternative policies. The main purpose of the exercise, therefore, is to enable ministers to see where persistence in present policies will take them so that, when considering this in conjunction with the medium-term assessment of economic prospects (also in constant prices), they may decide whether the forecast demand upon resources by the public sector can be increased, decreased, or left unchanged. Moreover, they can view whether the allocation of public expenditure among the spending departments, both now and over the next five-year period, is what is desired in terms of their own political priorities.

Thus public expenditure decisions are taken in the light of the forecast of the effects of alternative policies over a number of years into the future and in relation to the public sector's claims on the resources that are made available to the economy generally.

(2) *Taxation planning*

The previous section concentrated upon public expenditure planning. However, while public expenditure is planned and controlled by making forward estimates for a number of years in advance, taxation is not treated in the same way. There is not the same well informed debate several years in advance about the policy implications of financing the projected public expenditure by alternative mixes of taxation, contributions, borrowing and user charges.

Taxation serves a number of functions which include the financing of public spending, control of the level of aggregate demand for economic stabilisation purposes, redistribution of wealth and/or earnings, provision of selective incentives in an attempt to modify economic behaviour (as in the cases of the Selective Employment Tax), investment incentives and the regulation of imports. In attempting to satisfy this diversity of functions a single set of fiscal instruments such as taxes may be insufficient both in number and in scope to deal with the demands placed upon them. Thus, their efficiency can be impaired, and moreover they can have perverse effects on the rest of the economy by creating disincentive effects on work effort, on savings and on capital accumulation (these points are dealt with more fully in the chapters on taxation). Whether or not these consequences of taxation are desirable depends on the value placed upon the benefits gained from public expenditure. Parliamentary debate is one means of deciding where upon the trade-off one should be. Moreover, it has now become a matter for discussion whether or not the public sector borrowing requirement should be treated as a residual, especially given the effects of public sector borrowing on the money supply. Thus it has become desirable to consider – and therefore for Parliament to debate – the level of the borrowing requirement. If this is the case for borrowing then why is not taxation treated in a similar way?

Finally, taking up the point raised earlier about the disincentive effects of taxation, these effects could be minimised by choosing an appropriate structure of taxation. There has been a good deal of informal debate both inside and out-side government on this question of the structure of taxation; for example, whether or not the emphasis should lie towards taxes on incomes as compared with taxes on goods and services, or whether or not some variant of the negative income tax would be a more appropriate means of redistributing income. But any rational discussion of the whole tax system has to recognise that the present tax system is administratively complex and displays all the evidence of proliferation and piecemeal evolution. The rationalisation of the present tax system and discussion of its reform by Parliament means that Parliament must first of all equip itself with the institutions that will serve it in this task. That is, the system of financing public expenditure needs to be debated and scrutinised by Parliament in ways similar to those used to debate and to scrutinise public expenditure itself.

While discussions about the structure of taxation do take place in Parliament, Mackintosh has pointed out that the majority of members of the House of Commons are ill-equipped to discuss the effects of new taxes as they are introduced. Thus it is argued that the introduction of the Selective Employment Tax and the Value Added Tax into the UK's fiscal menu were not discussed in very much detail but were instead accepted in ignorance. The same can also be said about the long-run fiscal implications of the UK joining the European Economic Community with the possibility of tax harmonisation existing at some point in the future. Discussions about such matters tend to be made out with the normal business of Parliament and are left to royal commissions and departmental committees.

With regard to the discussion of the tax implications of public expenditure plans, it has always been the Treasury's reply that the presentation and discussion of such information would limit the flexibility of the tax system, thereby reducing the scope for future tax changes as demands for stabilisation policy arise. This unfortunately misses the point. Just as public expenditure plans are drawn up on the assumption of present policies continuing into the future, and just as the medium-term assessment is likewise based on a number of assumptions, so also could the tax implications of financing the public expenditure plan be based upon a number of assumptions.

One means of proceeding would be to calculate the tax revenue implications of public expenditure plans on the basis of various assumptions about the rate of economic growth, the level of unemployment, the rate of inflation and so on. An increase in planned expenditure could then be said either to require an increase in planned revenues or to mean forgoing tax cuts. Such a method has been proposed by two Cambridge economists, Nield and Ward,[12] who use the concept of the 'full employment budget' (FEB). The FEB is a fiscal concept used in the Netherlands, West Germany and the United States. It indicates what tax revenues and public expenditures would be consistent with a constant pressure of demand as measured by the level of unemployment. Thus it is technically possible to discuss the tax side of the budget over a longer planning horizon than one year. What is required is the political will to do so.

(3) A critique of the system of planning and control

While the post-Plowden system of budgetary planning and control represented a major step forward, it was not without its own inherent difficulties. The weaknesses in the system, some of which were recognised earlier, did not become practical problems until the 'stagflation' of the 1970s. Some of these problems are related to the separation of the tax and expenditure sides of the budget but others are not.

First, there was the fact that public expenditures were forecast at constant prices. Since the actual financing of public expenditure is at current prices rather than constant prices, no view could be taken with respect to the public sector's share of GNP at future current prices. Concentration on the public sector's absorption of real resources diverted attention from the problems of financing planned expenditure. Once public expenditure programmes are approved and initiated it is extremely difficult to cut them. Public expenditure tends to be flexible upwards but sticky downwards. This means that during a rapid inflation, in the 1970s, public expenditure at current prices relative to GNP at current prices will shoot up rapidly. This is due partly to the difficulty of being unable to cut back public expenditure in real terms over the short term; partly to the fact that public sector input prices tend to rise faster than the GDP deflator; and partly to the fact that some items of public expenditure such as food and rent subsidies are directly related to the rate of inflation, so that items in the numerator have a tendency to rise faster than the denominator.

During an inflation, therefore, not only does the ratio of public expenditure to GDP rise (at current prices), but so also will the ratio of tax revenue to GDP – unless of course it is decided to finance most of the increase out of borrowing. The question that then arises is, Would the public expenditure pro-grammes in real terms have been approved if the financing implications had been known? This is an academic question since the system does not allow such discussions to be held. Inflation rates, especially if caused by unforeseen factors such as the quadrupling of world oil prices, cannot be forecast. But the produc-tion of simulated results, showing the sensitivity of the public expenditure plans to changes in the assumptions of the forecasting model, such as the rate of inflation, is possible. A comparison of expenditure plans and tax revenue plans, shown in relation to different assumptions, would provide much more information than is readily available now.

Second, the rate at which public expenditure in real terms is allowed to grow depends upon the rate of growth in real resources in the economy generally. Thus, the projected public expenditure growth rate is sensitive to the projections of the medium-term assessment, since that gives political decision-makers a measure of the real resource costs of the expenditure plan. If, however, the medium-term assessment is wrong and the rate of growth in real GDP is not realised, then public expenditure as a proportion of GDP at constant prices will rise. That is what happened in 1965–68 and again 1974–75. In the first case, public expenditure was planned to grow in real terms at 4.25 per cent p.a. on the expectation that GDP would grow at 3.8 per cent p.a. In actual fact, GDP grew at only 2.2 per cent p.a. For the period 1974–75 real GDP fell by about 1.8 per cent p.a. In both cases the relative size of the public sector increased because, while the public expenditure plans were fulfilled, the GDP forecasts were not.

If the economy is both stagnating and inflating (the UK during the 1970s) then shortcomings of public expenditure planning described above will compound one another and the ratio of public expenditure to GDP at current prices will rise rapidly. In other words, in addition to failing to take account of the financing of public expenditure plans, the post-Plowden system was at its weakest during periods of uncertainty, high inflation and low growth. Under these conditions the Public Expenditure Survey System needed to be supplemented.

The supplementary controls on public expenditure came in April 1976 with the introduction of the White Paper on *Cash Limits*. Since then the major part of public expenditure has been planned one year ahead in cash terms and three years ahead in real terms. Thus, in order to deal with the uncertainty caused by low growth and high inflation, the public expenditure planning horizon was shortened so that the government does not commit itself to a buildup of expenditure programmes in the future.

The introduction of the Conservative Government of 1979 brought with it stricter controls on public expenditure. It was the view of that government that public expenditure had, during the 1970s, been out of control and had played a major role in reducing the overall performance of the economy. Not only were the public expenditure targets of the previous Labour administration drastically revised downwards, a new tighter system of cash control was introduced. Financial planning of public expenditure pushed out real resource planning. These changes must be seen in the context of the government's overall view of how the economy operates (see Jackson, 1980 and 1981). Monetary policy replaced fiscal policy as the principal set of instruments. The main target was the rate of growth in the money supply and all other variables such as the PSBR had to be compatible with it. Moreover, in order to restore incentives to the economy it was the government's aim to reduce the level of taxation and to effect a switch from direct to indirect taxes.

Given these objectives of a reduction in the PSBR and a reduction in taxation it is clear that public-spending programmes had to be squeezed. But the problem was made more difficult because some programmes such as defence and law and order were to expand. This meant that the incidence of the cuts fell most heavily on social services, housing and education programmes (see Else and Marshall, 1981).

Since it was local government which administered these programmes it was necessary to ensure that changes in the system of central local government financial relations would make the cuts effective. This was carried out through the *Local Government Planning and Land Bill* (No. 2) which gave central government greater control over the spending decisions of local governments. In particular it gave central government the power to with-hold grant-in-aid from a local government if it thought it was overspending. Moreover, central government for the first time began to set spending limits for individual local authorities. This was challenged by many at the time to be a threat to local democracy.

A cash limit system places public sector wages at the centre of a political storm. Since wages and salaries are such a large proportion of current-account public expenditure whether or not the cash limit is met will depend upon the level at which wages in the public sector are settled. If too high a level of settlement is made then, assuming the cash limit is binding, savings must be made in non-wage costs or redundancies will follow. By setting the cash limits in such a way that assumes a low wage settlement the government can exercise a hidden public sector incomes policy.

Public expenditure planning in the UK is clearly incremental with the major proportion of expenditure comprised of the on-going programmes of previous years. The bureaucracy also plays a dominant role. It produces the expenditure forecasts and the medium-term forecasts of the state of the economy, and through the PESC it collates and presents the full complexity of public expenditure information to ministers. But ministers do not act as a check or a balance on overspending. Larger rather than smaller budget forecasts are welcomed by ministers, who in Cabinet argue for increases in their share of the overall budget. After all, every public expenditure programme is a deserving case and any single minister's programme is more deserving than the rest. These political forces are, therefore, unlikely to check any demands from the bureau to expand their budgets; on the contrary, they will reinforce them.

Parliament itself does not check the growth in public spending. As Mackintosh indicates, the turnout to discuss the public expenditure White Papers is low and the debates on the Finance Bill, which contains the chancellor's tax proposals and overall budget strategy, are limited to a small number of ministers who have a special interest and competence in such matters. Moreover, Parliament is never presented with a set of 'costed' alternative policies to discuss and debate. Some would question if government is either.

The problems of public expenditure planning and control should not, however, be dismissed. Given that most public sector output is not marketed, and given that a large proportion of the benefits of public sector goods and services are intangible, simple efficiency calculations such as relating inputs to outputs cannot be made. In this respect the public sector is similar to the services sector of the economy (see Chapter 5). However, despite difficulties of this kind there remains a good deal of scope for improving the planning of public expenditures, especially in the following ways:

(1) relating public expenditure plans to the means of financing them;

(2) improvements in the medium-term planning of the economy;

(3) improving the efficiency of allocating public sector resources and the elimination of waste (see Chapter 8);

(4) improving the information that relates public expenditure and taxation projections to changes in inflation and economic growth, etc.;

(5) ensuring that plans are monitored and that outcomes are kept within the limits of the plan;

(6) costing alternative policies and discussing these costs.

Conclusion

The design of government to achieve efficiency is a complex process of weighing up the costs and benefits of alternative organisation structures. Allocative, stabilisation and distributional efficiencies are all served by differing degrees of decentralisation, so that some point on the trade off between these objectives must be chosen. Within any given structure of government the achievement of allocative efficiency will be frustrated if X-inefficiency exists. The elimination or reduction of X-inefficiency requires the introduction of an appropriate set of incentives such that those who produce public output are encouraged to serve the public interest while at the same time fulfilling their own objectives.

CHAPTER 8

Cost-Benefit Analysis

The most general use of the phrase 'cost-benefit analysis' (CBA) is that it is an attempt to measure the costs and the gains that would result from alternative courses of action. All rational choices involve the weighing up of benefits and costs. Cost–benefit analysis has, however, a more specific meaning in economics. It is a means of setting out and comparing the factors that need to be taken into account when making choices between alternative public sector policies. The particular group of public policies to which CBA has been most frequently applied are those that involve public sector investments in capital projects, such as building a motorway, constructing a new reservoir, urban renewal, land reclamation, siting a new airport or building a nuclear-powered electricity generating station.

Cost–benefit analysis is a set of techniques that are designed to ensure that scarce resources are allocated efficiently, first between competing private sector and public sector uses, and second between alternative public sector projects. In the UK during 1976 public sector investment accounted for 44 per cent of total investment in the economy, of which 24 per cent was undertaken by central government and local government and 20 per cent by nationalised industries. As a set of decision-making techniques designed to contribute towards the global efficiency of the economy, CBA seeks to establish criteria that will aid the realisation of this efficiency objective.

This chapter will review the analytical foundations of CBA. Since the decisions produced by a cost–benefit exercise can have significant and lasting effects upon the efficiency and the distribution of welfare of the economy, a fundamental question that has to be answered is, How robust are the foundations and premises upon which the analysis is based? Rather than consider how decisions in the public sector are made (this was the content of the previous chapter), we now want to know how they *should be* made.

The general efficiency framework

Any capital investment project, whether undertaken in the public or the private sector, generates a stream of consumption benefits. Subtracting the capital and operating costs of the project gives a value of the net consumption benefits of the project. In order to make the diverse variety of benefits and costs commensurate with one another, for the purpose of comparison, it is necessary that they be converted to a common dimension or scale. The measuring rod of money is used and benefits and costs are converted to monetary units by evaluating them at a set of market prices.

The stream of net benefits, generated by the investment, is distributed over successive periods of time. To find the total value of the stream of net benefits it is necessary to convert the net benefit in each time period to its present value. This is done by discounting. The total value of the project's *net* benefits is, therefore, the algebraic sum of the present values of the benefits and costs in each time period.

When confronted by a number of alternative investment projects and asked to choose one of them, a rational utility-maximising individual will choose that project that possesses the largest present value of net benefits, provided, of course, that his budget constraint is satisfied. This simple result follows from the assumptions necessary for utility maximisation. The opportunity cost of employing the scarce resources embodied in one investment project is the present value of the forgone net benefits associated with the next best alternative use of those resources. In other words, in choosing one project rather than another, the benefits of one consumption stream are compared with those of another.

Weighing up the present value of the benefits and costs of each alternative and choosing that level of activity for which marginal benefit equals marginal cost (i.e. the utility-maximising requirement) is the economist's standard approach to the efficient allocation of resources. In the perfectly competitive market economy, given an initial endowment of resources, voluntary exchange takes place until a set of equilibrium prices is established. At that equilibrium resources are efficiently allocated, in the sense that no individual can make himself better off without making another individual worse off; i.e. a Pareto-efficient allocation exists.

Public sector outputs are not allocated via markets. They are instead provided via the budget. What CBA attempts to establish is a set of pragmatic administrative rules, which will mimic the functions of the market, so that public sector outputs might be allocated Pareto-efficiently. CBA is, therefore, a means of moving the economy towards its efficiency frontier.

The CBA framework in detail

Stated most simply and most clearly, cost benefit analysis is:

> a practical way of assessing the desirability of projects, where it is important to take a long view (in the sense of looking at repercussions in the further, as well as nearer, future) and a wide view (in the sense of allowing for side-

effects of many kinds on many persons, industries, regions etc.), i.e. it implies the numeration and evaluation of all the relevant costs and benefits.[1]

Given a set of investment projects, labelled $1 \ldots i \ldots n$, cost–benefit analysis structures the problem of choosing between the alternative projects in the following way:

$$B_i(x_i) = \sum_{t=0}^{n} \frac{b_i(t) - c_i(t)}{(1+r)^t} - K_i$$

where:

$B_i(x_i)$ = the net benefit received from spending £x on project i
$b_i(t)$ = the consumption benefits received from the project in year t
$c_i(t)$ = the costs of the project in year t
$\dfrac{1}{(1+r)}$ = the discount factor at rate of interest r
n = the lifetime of the project
K_i = the initial capital outlay (cost) of the project i

Since the net benefits of a project, defined as

$$\sum_{t=0}^{n} [b_i(t) - c_i(t)] - K_i$$

extend over the lifetime of the project (i.e. Prest and Turvey's 'long view'), the value of the net benefit stream must be discounted, thereby obtaining a measure of the 'present value' of the net benefits of each project (i.e. $B_i(x_i)$).

The problems that face the cost–benefit analyst can now be stated as follows: (1) Which costs and benefits are to be included? (2) How are they to be valued? and (3) At what interest rate are they to be discounted? However, before we proceed to a detailed consideration of these questions, there is an issue that is worth while dispensing with immediately: that is, the problem of the appropriate investment criterion to use.

(1) Investment criteria

In the general analysis of investment appraisal the analyst has two alternative decision rules that could be used. These are (1) the internal rate of return method and (2) the present value method.

(a) *The internal rate of return method.* This method solves for that rate of interest which will make the present value of the net benefits of the project zero. That rate of interest, called the internal rate of return (*IRR*), is then compared with an appropriate market rate of return r_m (see below for a discussion of the appropriate market rate). If $IRR > r_m$, then the resources that are invested in the project will give the investor a better return than he would have received by investing them elsewhere. Thus on opportunity cost grounds it is worth while proceeding with the investment, since determining a project's admissibility requires comparing its annual net benefit stream with the time pattern of consumption that would have occurred if the resources had not been used in that project. If $IRR < r_m$, then by the same argument the opportunity cost of investing in the project is the forgone net benefits from investing elsewhere, which in this case are greater than the net benefits received from the project. In that case it would not be worth while investing resources in the public sector project. When $IRR = r_m$ the decision-maker is indifferent as to whether he invests in the project or not. When there are many mutually exclusive projects to choose from, the projects are ranked in terms of their internal rates of return and that project with the highest IRR is chosen, provided that its $IRR > r_m$.

(*b*) *The present value method.* In this case a rate of interest is chosen, e.g. the market rate of interest, and the present value of the net benefits of each project is then calculated for that rate of interest. If the present value of net benefits is positive this implies that the resources that are employed in the project produce a greater net benefit stream than any other project in the market whose rate of return is r_m. If the present value of the net benefits is zero then the decision-marker is indifferent as to whether he invests in the public sector project or on the market. In the case of a single project, the answer to the question, Should resources be invested in this project?, is yes, provided that the present value of the net benefits of the project is positive. When there is more than one mutually exclusive project to choose from, the projects are ranked, in terms of their present values of net benefits, and that project with the largest present value is chosen, provided, of course that its present value is positive.

The internal rate of return method has a number of disadvantages. First, there might be no unique internal rate of return. Since we are solving some polynomial of degree *n* there might be more than one solution and hence more than one internal rate of return to choose from. Second, if the two projects have different time profiles of net benefits, then the internal rate of return method will not rank mutually exclusive projects in an unambiguous way. Hence we prefer the net present value method over the internal rate of return method. Moreover, as we will see below, choosing the appropriate rate of interest for the discount factor is an extremely tricky problem.

Another decision rule, which is referred to widely in the CBA literature and which warrants particular attention, is that which advocates the maximisation of the benefit–cost ratio. The benefit–cost (B–C) ratio approach requires that those projects whose present-value B–C ratio exceeds one should be undertaken. When there are a number of alternative projects the projects are ranked according to the value of the B-C ratio. The project with the largest B-C ratio is assumed to be the most preferred. The B-C ratios of three mutually exclusive projects X, Y and Z are shown in Table 8.1. It is seen that project X has the greatest B-C ratio and so would, on the basis of this decision-making rule, be

Table 8.1 Comparison of present value and benefit cost ratio methods

	(1) Present value of costs	(2) Present value of benefits	(3) Benefit–cost ratio (2) ÷ (1)	(4) Present value of net benefits (2) − (1)
Project X	200	450	2.25:1	250
Project Y	400	800	2.00:1	400
Project Z	600	900	1.50:1	300

chosen as the most preferred of the three projects. In the same table, however, the present values of the net benefits of each of the three projects are also shown. Applying the present value decision rule would result in the choice of project Y, and project X would be ranked bottom in the list.

Figure 8.1 illustrates the source of the ambiguity. The vertical axis measures the present value of the benefits and the costs of the project and the horizontal axis measures the scale of the project. The two projects produce the same output; what differs between them is the scale of the activity. An efficient allocation of resources would require that investment be carried on until the marginal benefit of investment equals marginal cost. At this point (Q_1 in Figure 8.1) the present value of net benefit is a maximum. This is compatible with the present value decision rule. The maximisation of the B–C ratio, however, occurs at a lower scale of activity, i.e. at Q_2. Clearly this is not an optimum since $MB > MC$. At this scale of activity $B_2/C_2 > B_1/C_1$, and so applying the benefit-cost ratio decision rule would result in scale Q_2 being chosen in preference to Q_1.

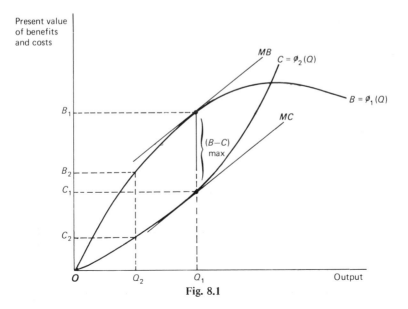

Fig. 8.1

(2) Which benefits and costs are to be included?

It will be recalled from Prest and Turvey's definition of CBA that a 'wide view' is taken when enumerating the benefits and the costs of the project. This reveals one of the principal distinctions between project selection in the public and private sectors. The private sector profit-maximising producer selects projects according to the degree to which they contribute to total profits at the margin. When calculating his profits the private sector decision-maker is concerned only with private costs and private benefits.

On the other hand, the public sector decision-maker's objective function is the maximisation of social welfare (the reader is referred back to Chapter 3 for the meaning and limitations of this statement). Because it is the interests of all the members of society that are being considered when public sector decisions are taken, we need to examine the relevance of externalities generated by the public sector projects in addition to the direct benefits and costs.

Externalities were defined in Chapter 2 where they were classified into technological and pecuniary externalities. Since CBA is concerned with the allocative or efficiency aspects of project appraisal, technological external benefits and costs are included in the calculation of total benefits and costs, whereas pecuniary externalities are excluded. This can be illustrated by means of a simple example.

Consider the benefits and costs of constructing a new motorway. The direct benefits to road-users may include the savings due to a reduction in travel to work time, the increased potential leisure time, and reduction in accident costs. The direct costs are the construction costs, the road maintenance costs, and other costs such as motorway police costs. Technological external benefits include the benefits to non-road-users such as pedestrians and property-owners who were adversely affected by the external costs of the traffic before it was diverted onto the motorway. These external benefits are of importance for allocative efficiency because they influence production and consumption decisions by entering as arguments into the individual's production function or utility function.

There are, however, other benefits and costs associated with the new motorway. For example, the absolute level of the profits of garages, shops, and restaurants along the motorway will have increased as a result of the increase in the flow of traffic. These are examples of pecuniary externalities and should not be included in efficiency calculations for two reasons. First, they represent a redistribution of income from one group in society to another, i.e. from non-motorway to motorway garages. The total welfare of society does not increase: it is merely redistributed. Second, in so far as these pecuniary external benefits reflect the benefits of more journeys being undertaken, including them in the calculation would amount to double counting.

It should not be concluded from this discussion that it is, in practice, easy to distinguish clearly between technological and pecuniary externalities. It is not, and a great deal of the 'art' of CBA lies in being able to make appropriate judgements on this question. Moreover, externalities can be quite widespread in their effects, which gives rise to another problem, namely, At what point should we stop measuring benefits and costs? Once again there are no clear-cut rules that can be applied to answer this question, and a judgement has to be made as to where the relevant boundary lies.

(3) *The valuation of benefits and costs*

Having identified the relevant benefits and costs, the next problem is to determine an appropriate set of prices at which they will be valued. Since the CBA investment decision rule is based upon the efficiency criteria of the perfect competition model, the ideal set of prices would be Pareto-efficient equilibrium prices. These prices are frequently referred to as 'accounting prices'. If it is believed that market prices are Pareto-efficient, then market prices should be used to compute the value of the net benefits. However, if market prices are not Pareto-efficient, or if market prices do not exist, as is the case for a large proportion of public sector output, then 'shadow prices' must be computed from the market price information such that they reflect the Pareto-efficient accounting prices.

Because of wide-spread market failures and imperfections, market prices are seldom Pareto-efficient and must, therefore, be adjusted before they are used in CBA calculations. Monopoly elements in product and factor markets generate divergences between final product market prices and their accounting prices. The prices of factors of production frequently include some rental element raising them above their marginal opportunity costs. It has already been seen in Chapter 2 that the market price of the output of decreasing cost industries exceeds its long-run marginal cost price.

Taxes will also cause market prices to diverge from their accounting prices, as too will the use of tariffs, import controls and subsidies. Because relative prices are influenced by taxes and public sector borrowing, the means by which the project is financed is an important consideration. This is considered in more detail below. However, it should be clear that only lump sum taxes will leave relative prices unchanged.

In the case of pure public goods the market failure is complete. For Pareto-efficiency we would require a set of personalised equilibrium prices for the public good with each price reflecting each individual consumer's income and preference for the public good. This efficiency result, which was demonstrated in Chapter 3, means that, given the problem of the free-rider, market prices for pure public goods do not exist.

There are also the problems that arise when the economy is in a state of less-than-full employment. When there is an excess supply of any input at the current market price, then that price overstates the social cost of employing that input. Thus, if unemployed labour, for example, is employed on a public sector capital project, its social cost will be less than its market price. After having taken unemployment benefits into account, the social opportunity cost of employing an unemployed person is zero since there is no real output forgone by diverting the labour input from an alternative use.

Finally, market prices may be transitional or temporary equilibrium prices and not long-run equilibrium prices. In all of the instances of market failure considered, the market price diverges from its accounting price. This means that shadow prices, which reflect social opportunity costs, must be calculated either from the available market price information or, if that does not exist, from other means.

When market prices do not exist (as in the case for public goods, externalities and intangibles such as a scenic view), information can be obtained by means of questionnaires. In the case of the benefits of the project, what the questionnaire seeks to elicit is the consumer's willingness to pay for the benefit. If the costs of the project are being measured by this means, the objective is to ascertain how much compensation the consumer would require in order to make him indifferent to the costs of the project, as they affect him. There are clearly problems with using this method. First, the person answering the questionnaire may adopt a strategic position and misrepresent his preferences in order to influence the result (i.e. like the free-rider). The precise nature of the game played will depend upon whether or not the individual answering the questionnaire knows what benefits he will receive and what his costs will be. (The reader should as an exercise consider when it would be advantageous for the consumer to overstate and understate his preferences and what information he will require to do so.) Whether or not this will influence the final result will depend upon the size of the gain and the extent to which others play similar games. Second, having got information on prices from a wide range of individuals differing in tastes and incomes, the analyst then has to average them. The problem is which averaging procedure to choose. Should the mean be used, or should prices be weighted by incomes?

The calculation of the relevant prices with which to evaluate the benefits and costs of a project is, therefore, clearly a complex business and one that demands skill of the analyst. Moreover, when calculating shadow prices it may, in some instances, be necessary to know how the economy will react following the marginal adjustment to the public sector investment.

If, for example, a monopolist supplying inputs for the project increases his output in order to accommodate the change, then we would use the marginal cost of the additional units of output rather than their market price. This follows because the market price overstates the social value of the output. On the other hand, if the monopolist did not increase his output then we would use the market price since this reflects the value of the inputs in their alternative use. If the public sector investment takes resources away from the monopolist, the market value of the inputs understates the value of the lost production.

A similar argument applies to products (inputs) that are subject to indirect taxes. The producer's supply price (i.e. marginal cost) is used if output changes, and the market price is used if output does not change. The costs of the resources (inputs) taken away, by the government, from private sector uses is greater in the case of taxed goods than what the government actually pays.

While the reaction of the economy following the public sector investment is clearly of importance, nevertheless it should be remembered that CBA is a partial equilibrium approach to the problem. Therefore, when an investment project is so large that it alters the set of relative input and output prices in an economy, the technique of CBA is inappropriate and a general equilibrium approach is required. Examples of this arise in small developing economies when large projects such as the construction of a hydroelectric system are introduced.

(4) The choice of discount rate

The choice of a suitable rate of interest, with which future net benefits are to be discounted, has occupied a major part of the discussions on CBA. Choosing a suitable interest rate is of vital importance for a number of reasons. First, if too low a rate of interest is chosen, socially inefficient projects will be undertaken. Conversely, if too high an interest rate is chosen efficient projects will fail to clear the hurdle of acceptability. Second, what is at stake in the choice of a discount rate is not just the acceptance or rejection of specific projects, but also the allocation of resources between the public and the private sectors of the economy.

In a neoclassical world of perfect capital markets a single rate of interest equates the marginal rate of time preference (MRTP)[2] of savers with the marginal productivity of capital.[3] The welfare significance of this rate is that it is Pareto-efficient. In equilibrium this rate equates the volume of funds that surplus units are willing to lend and deficit units are willing to borrow. In a perfect capital market such as this, each individual will have the same MRTP and so the social rate of time preference (SRTP) equals the individual rate.

The intertemporal optimisation of a general equilibrium model assumes knowledge of future savings, which depends upon future incomes, which in turn depend on previous investment decisions. Investors are required to know the marginal efficiency of their investments, and if certainty is not assumed the existence of markets for contingencies is required. The amount of information required for perfect capital markets is great, so much so that perfect capital markets clearly do not exist in practice. Thus, there is no single market rate of interest and, therefore, no single discount rate which can be taken as a measure of both the rate of time preference and the marginal productivity of capital. A wedge, owing to market imperfections, has been driven between the two rates.

In the face of this imperfection in the capital market how should the choice of discount rate for public sector investments be made? What factors should influence its choice? To answer these questions it is necessary to inquire more closely into the functions that the discount rate performs.

There are essentially two schools of thought on the choice of discount rate for public sector investments, and they can be divided as follows:

(1) the social opportunity cost of capital (SOCC) school, who wish to obtain some measure of the marginal cost of capital used in public sector projects. This school is characterised by the work of Harberger, Hirschliefer and McKean;

(2) the social rate of time preference (SRTP) school, who wish to obtain an explicit measure of the social rate of time preference. Those who have contributed to this thinking are Feldstein, Marglin and Steiner.

The social opportunity cost of capital is a measure to society of the next best alternative use to which the resources employed in the public project might otherwise have been put. The social opportunity cost of a project in the public sector depends upon whether or not the resources used are diverted from private consumption or investment. Thus, assuming an absolute savings constraint, £x spent on a public sector project might displace £x of private sector investment. However, the cost of these resources is greater than £x since the private sector investment would have yielded a consumption benefit valued, in present value terms, in excess of £x. It is the consumption stream of the private sector investment, which is the forgone benefit. If however, the public sector investment, £x displaced private sector consumption then the cost of the resources would be £x.

The social rate of time preference assigns current values to future consumption reflecting society's evaluation of the relative desirability of consumption at different periods of time. A social time preference function will reflect social ethics and judgements about future economic conditions.

There are two distinct problems that each school is dealing with:

(1) the determination of a shadow price to reflect the value of the resources transferred from the private sector (i.e. the social opportunity cost school);

(2) the price of future consumption valued from the point of view of society as a whole (the social rate of time preference school).

Where the conflict or difference of opinion arises between the two schools is that each wants to use a single price, namely the discount rate, to solve its problem. The SOC school wishes to use the discount rate to measure the value of the resources transferred from the private sector (the social opportunity cost rate), whereas the SRTP school wishes to use the discount rate to reflect society's valuation of future consumption.

Using a single rate of discount to perform these two separate functions is asking a great deal. As Prest and Turvey have eloquently put it, 'the truth of the matter is that, whatever one does, one is trying to unscramble an omelette, and no-one has yet invented a uniquely superior way of dealing with this'.

The above discussion has identified the problem but has not given pragmatic advice on which rate of discount to choose. Should the 'market rate of interest' or a weighted average of marketed rates be used to calculate the discount rate? There are a large number of problems in using the market rate of interest.

(1) It has been argued for some time that individuals have a tendency to discount the future incorrectly. This idea can be found in Pigou, who claimed that individuals had a 'defective telescopic faculty', being myopic with regard to the future. Being more concerned with immediate consumption benefits, individuals would fail to take an appropriate view of future benefits and costs. Thus the private rate of time preference (market rate of interest) that individuals used to discount private sector investments should be adjusted, thereby bringing the rate (and the composition) of private sector investment (and savings) closer to the social optimum.

(2) Individuals' myopia with regard to the future can present a problem (externality) for future generations. Consumption decisions of the current generation, which require technologies with a high propensity to pollute the environment, will build up a stock of pollutant that will be inherited by future generations. A rapid depletion of non-renewable natural resources in order to satisfy the consumption plans of the current generation will influence (constrain) the consumption plans of future generations.

This then leads to the question of how the preferences of future generations are to be taken into account, especially for those projects (such as found in transport, housing or energy sectors) that produce benefits and costs well into the future. Even if current generations did have a preference to transfer present consumption to future generations, there is no simple market mechanism through which such a preference can be expressed; i.e. markets in such transactions fail to exist. Moreover, there is the additional problem of Sen's 'isolation paradox'. Left to himself, an individual might not be willing to save for future generations or take into account the preferences of future generations. If, however, the individual knows that all others are willing to make provisions in current decisions for future generations then he is more likely to do so also. Once again, such sentiments must be made known and there is no readily available means of doing so.

In summary, substantial increases in shadow prices attached to distant events are required before they play a significant part in current decision-making. This requires that a view be taken on the relative preferences for current and future consumption of present generations and the welfare of future generations. Since markets fail to deal with this kind of transaction the choice of appropriate discount rate must be a political act.

(3) The financing of government expenditures (investment) can also influence private sector investment. Taxation and also the retirement of public sector

debt are important sources of the divergence between market rates of return. Moreover, the rates of interest faced by households and firms will then differ. This means that the way in which the public sector project is financed is an important factor in determining the correct discount rate.

Tax finance usually reduces private consumption and loan finance usually reduces private investment. The opportunity cost of a £1 of public investment that displaces a £1 of private consumption is less than a £1 of public investment that displaces private investment. The distortionary effects of tax finance becomes a problem in the 'second-best' and optimal taxation. Given that most taxation is distortionary in practice the relevant question is: If we must have distortions, what is the best set of distortions to have?

Moreover, there is the question of the complementarity and substitutability of public and private goods, and therefore the effect on tax revenue. If increased government expenditure leads to a greater consumption of taxed private goods, this reduces the revenue that has to be raised and hence increases the benefit measure.

Baumol has shown that the existence of a corporation tax will affect the market rate of return on private sector investment. He argues that if, for example, the corporation tax is 50 per cent then the social rate of discount is approximately twice the market price. If the gross rate of return is 20 per cent, then for a 50 per cent profits tax the net return to the shareholder is 10 per cent and 10 per cent goes to the taxpayer. The Baumol rule is complicated by the existence of investment grants and subsidies, which are assumed not to prevail in this simple example, and also by the tax treatment of individuals through the personal tax system. The corporation tax therefore, has the effect of lowering the return received by shareholders, but, since the taxpayer is also receiving a return from the investment, the social opportunity cost of not undertaking the investment will exceed the private return. Baumol's rule, however, is not sufficiently general, since not all public sector investment replaces private sector investment. The problem that Baumol refers to, however, again leads us to question the appropriateness of using market rates of interest to discount public sector investments.

(4) A high rate of return on private sector investments could be due mainly to the existence of monopoly pricing. Also, the market rate of time preference may, as does any price in the standard neoclassical model, depend upon the initial distribution of income. These two additional factors cast doubts upon using the market rate in public sector investment decision-making.

(5) Finally, there is the question of the risk premium contained within any market rate of interest. Private sector investments carry with them varying amounts of risk. Hence market rates of interest have a risk premium. Investments in the public sector are often assumed to be less risky. But this statement is in need of some clarification. On a project-by-project basis the public

The real vowels are found from b, F, j, P, v
hence b = a etc. Not all b's are as some are bj.
Decode message l turn to 100

Cost–Benefit Analysis   181

sector does not necessarily engage in projects that are below the average risk of private sector projects. On the contrary, many public sector projects are extremely risky. But because of the absolute number of projects, in addition to the diversity of risks in the portfolio of public sector investments, a loss in one project will be cancelled by a gain in another. Indeed, because it can spread risks on such a scale there is a good argument to be made for the public sector engaging in high-risk projects, which normal capital markets would fail to support. Thus, assuming that the returns to different public sector projects are uncorrelated, the probability of a net loss to total public investment is small (tending to zero as the number of projects increase).

Another argument on the same topic has been advanced by Arrow and Lind. They also demonstrate the disappearance of a social risk premium in public sector investments which comes about because of the spreading of risks across a large number of people (taxpayers and investors). Thus the government reduces the overall cost of bearing risk to zero in the limit. Risk aversion arises because of diminishing marginal utility of income. As the scale of a risky project (gamble) increases, then the difference between the utility of the potential income gain and the loss increases also. In other words, the average cost of the risk will (assuming risk aversion) rise with the scale of the gamble. The scale effect on risk costs provides the advantages of risk-spreading.

Therefore, because the public sector enjoys the advantages of diversification and risk-pooling,[4] the risk premium on government investments is lower than that on market rates of interest.

The normative significance of the market rate of discount for public policy decisions has, therefore, been criticised on a number of counts. The argument has been that the private market generally results in a rate of consumption that is too high, makes too little provision for the future, does not adjust for the risk-spreading capabilities of the public sector and does not adequately reflect social benefits and costs which are of importance when maximising social welfare. If the objective of the exercise is to reduce current consumption and to make greater provision for the future throughout the economy, then government's monetary policy should be directed towards reducing the market rate of interest in the expectation of an expansion in investment (public and private).

While the choice of discount rate remains to be resolved at the theoretical level, the practitioner has to use some method of making public sector investment choices. A reasonable way of proceeding would be to calculate a shadow price for the social opportunity cost of funds used in public sector investment and to include this in the calculations. In this way both public and private sector investment projects would be compared in a standard accounting framework. This would leave the discount rate free to reflect the social rate of time preference. It is also possible to vary the rate of interest, thereby discovering how sensitive the decision of whether or not to invest in the project is to changes in the rate of discount.

(5) *Risk and uncertainty*

Until now it has been assumed that future benefits and costs are known with complete certainty. This, however, is clearly at variance with reality. The future is not known. The effect of insecticides on the ecology is largely unknown. The impact of radioactive waste produced by nuclear power stations is not known; neither is the magnitude or the timing of the income and employment multipliers of public investments.

There are two broadly defined categories of situations that we distinguish between. First, there are risky situations in which the future time-pattern of benefits and costs is not known with certainty but where the decision-maker, nevertheless, is able to assign probabilities to future outcomes.[5] That is, all possible outcomes could be listed and a probability of occurrence assigned to each one. Second, there are uncertain outcomes for which absolutely no probabilities for the occurrence of the outcomes are available. There are also situations in which the outcomes themselves may be unknown. In this section we will discuss different means of incorporating risky and uncertain situations into public sector investment decisions.[6]

One method of incorporating risk into the analysis is to calculate the *expected value* of the outcome. For example, if the value of benefits in year 1 of the project can take one of the values b_1^1, b_2^1, b_3^1, b_4^1, b_5^1 with probabilities p_1, p_2, p_3, p_4, p_5 then the expected value of benefits in year 1 $E(b^1)$ is given by:

$$E(b^1) \equiv p_1 b_1^1 + p_2 b_2^1 + p_3 b_3^1 + p_4 b_4^1 + p_5 b_5^1$$

$$\equiv \sum p_i b_i^1 \qquad \left(\sum p_i = 1 \right).$$

Thus, each possible outcome is weighted by the probability of its occurrence. The expected value of the project's benefits is the sum of the weighted outcomes. Working through the analysis, the decision-maker is left with an expected value of the present value of net benefits for each project. These expected values are ranked as in the case of complete certainty.

A less ambitious means of proceeding is to carry out a sensitivity analysis. In situations where little is known about the possible outcomes or the limits to the range of outcomes, or about the values of their probabilities, the analyst might proceed by calculating the present value of the net benefits based upon the most pessimistic values of the outcomes, the most optimistic, and some middle-road. The ranking of the projects and their acceptability are then examined for their sensitivity to variations in the values of the assumptions and the parameters of the system.

However, carrying out sensitivity analysis and calculating expected values are only elements to the decision process. The decision-maker, when considering each uncertain outcome, must take into account his attitude towards risk. His risk preference might be to go for a big pay-off, even although the risk is great (risk-loving attitudes). On the other hand, the risk-averse decision-maker would prefer a smaller and more certain outcome.

When faced with complete uncertainty the results of decision theory[7] are appropriate for CBA. It is the properties of some of the more common decision rules that are of interest here rather than the derivation of the rules themselves. The simplest rule is described as 'Bayes criterion'. In this case when the probabilities of future events are unknown equal probabilities are assigned to each possible event. For example, assume that there are three projects, I, II, and III, and that three possible present values of net benefits (NPVs) are assigned to each project. These values are given below in the matrix.

		NPVs	
Project	N_1	N_2	N_3
I	200	180	120
II	350	100	200
III	180	240	150

Assigning equal probabilities of one-third to each possible event gives expected pay-offs for the three projects as:

$$\text{I} \quad (1/3 \times 200) + (1/3 \times 180) + (1/3 \times 120) = 166\tfrac{2}{3}$$

$$\text{II} \quad (1/3 \times 350) + (1/3 \times 100) + (1/3 \times 200) = 216\tfrac{2}{3}$$

$$\text{III} \quad (1/3 \times 180) + (1/3 \times 240) + (1/3 \times 150) = 190$$

On the basis of Bayes criterion project II would be chosen. The problem with Bayes criterion is that the outcome will depend upon the number of possible events that are considered.

Two further well-known decision rules are those of maximin and minimax regret. The maximin criterion assumes risk aversion on the part of the decision-taker so that he will always assume that the worst of all possible worlds will occur. Applying the maximin rule, the decision-maker lists the worst possible pay-off for each project. In the previous example these were for project I, 120; for project II, 100 and for project III, 150. He then chooses that project that possesses the maximum of the minimum pay-offs ('maximin'), i.e. in this case project III. By concentrating upon the worst outcomes the decision-taker is blind to all the other pay-offs and so is really ultra-conservative in his attitudes to uncertainty.

The minimax regret criterion is based upon a slightly more complex reasoning. What this decision rule tries to do is to give penalty points for making wrong

Public Sector Economics

decisions. Thus, if project I is chosen and if assumption N_2 turns out to be the correct assumption, then the opportunity cost of this decision is the forgone additional pay-off of the best outcome given assumption N_2; in this case it would have been better to choose project III, thereby gaining 60 more units of pay-off. The difference between the best pay-off and the pay-off for each project under each assumption is calculated and set out in a regret matrix as below:

| | | NPVs | | |
Project	N_1	N_2	N_3	Row sum
I	150	60	80	290
II	0	140	0	140
III	170	0	50	220

Since each element of the regret matrix is the cost (penalty) incurred of making an incorrect choice, the decision-maker will choose that project with the lowest maximum regret. In this example project II has the lowest row sum.

This brief summary of some of the more common decision-making rules demonstrates that there is no simple solution to the problem of making decisions under conditions of complete uncertainty. However, in a stochastic world of uncertainty and ignorance, and when decision-making is sequential, the decision-taker need not decide today that which can be put off until tomorrow. This delay gives a chance for searching out data, learning about the situation and updating existing information so that more informed decisions might be taken.

Other considerations

The previous discussion of CBA has concentrated on the economic efficiency aspects of the decision. The objective of the exercise has been to move the economy closer towards its Pareto-efficiency frontier. Thus attention has been focused upon the maximisation of the present value of net benefits and nothing has been said about the distribution of benefits and costs across socioeconomic groups of individuals. All public policies have distributional consequences, and in so far as the public sector decision-maker has a distributional objective, the effect of the project on the distribution of welfare will act as a constraint. In other words, the actual choice of public sector project will now depend upon the trade-off between efficiency and distributional objectives. The problems of measuring the distribution of net benefits is considered in detail in Chapter 21.

Another important set of constraints that influence the choice of project are the political constraints. The discussion of CBA has so far concentrated upon the technical aspects of the problem. But CBA is only a decision-making technique.

It generates information that the decision-maker may or may not take into account in reaching his final decision. It was shown in Chapter 4 that social choice is frequently a complex set of trades between different interest groups in society. These trades are usually aimed at ensuring that the party in power is returned at the next election. Again, this means that who benefits as a result of the project can be of crucial importance. Such considerations can influence the choice of projects, their timing and their location.

It is not only political decision-makers who influence the choice of project. Bureaucrats can do so also. If there is a particular project that is favoured by the bureaucrat, then his preferences can influence the analysis of data and the information that is finally produced. For example, bureaucrats may choose the rate of discount.

Bureaucratic influences can be of significance when decisions are made in highly uncertain environments. A bureaucrat wishing to minimise the adverse consequences of a risky situation could, if he is highly risk averse, choose that project which provides the maximum amount of safety. Whether or not bureaucrats are willing to take risks will depend upon the set of incentives which they face.

Finally, there is the problem of sub-optimisation or the problem of the second-best. In an economy characterised by market failures and imperfections, optimisation in one sector may lead the economy further away from a global optimum rather than bringing it closer. Thus, although shadow prices are calculated to measure benefits and costs, the implementation of the final decision may, in a second-best world, take the economy further away from its efficiency frontier. Such considerations tend to focus upon the general equilibrium features of the problem, but it should be recalled that CBA is a partial equilibrium decision rule. At all times the design of optimal government decisions requires that we balance up the distortions of the market economy against the distortions that are introduced by government action.

Cost–benefit analysis as a decision-making tool is as useful as the framework within which the calculations are made. There is no pretence that the technique will accurately measure benefits and costs, or that all the disputes about the choice of an appropriate framework have been resolved. The CBA framework can reveal to the decision-maker his areas of ignorance. Used appropriately and with caution, it can assist decision-making by providing a more informed body of knowledge about the detailed implications of particular decisions. Used blindly and unquestioningly, it can delude.

PPBS, ZBB, PAR and all that

Cost benefit analysis is only one member of a set of management techniques which are used to give more rationality into public sector resource allocation decisions. Others include Programme Planning and Budgeting Systems (PPBS) and Zero Based Budgeting (ZBB). These are essentially management accounting systems which attempt to relate the costs of inputs to the outputs or activities performed by the public sector. Thus, by identifying how much certain functions cost, decisions can be made about whether or not more or less resources should be allocated to them. In the UK the PPBS approach has been called 'Output Budgeting' or 'Functional Budgeting' and has been applied on a limited scale in the Departments of Education and Science, Health and Social Services and the Home Office.

Traditionally governments account for expenditure in terms of who does the spending (i.e. which department) and what they spend on (i.e. wages and salaries, equipment, buildings etc.). This is called input budgeting. In a PPB system expenditure is classified by programmes. These programmes are as closely identified with policy objectives as is possible. As such they can cut across departmental boundaries. Within the programme budget a variety of information can be arranged with the objective of seeking to clarify the following questions.

(1) Defining the *objectives* of the programmes.

(2) Providing information on how resources are being currently used.

(3) Evaluating the *effectiveness* of current programmes in relation to the stated objectives.

(4) Assessing *alternative* means of achieving the stated objectives (i.e. using CBA etc.).

(5) Systematic periodic review of plans and programmes in the light of new situations, new evaluations and new analysis.

The PPB approach can be illustrated by comparing two fictitious sets of accounts for the defence department.

Account A	*Input Budget*	*£m*
1.	Pay and Allowances (Navy)	111
2.	Pay and Allowances (Army)	208
3.	Pay and Allowances (RAF)	153
4.	Pensions	125
5.	Administration, stores, supplies	304
6.	Pay of civilians	384
7.	Defence equipment	625
8.	Royal Ordinance Factory	4
9.	Ministry of Technology defence spending	187
10.	Ministry of Public Works defence spending	181
	Total	2280

Account B	*£m*
1. Nuclear Strategic Forces	32
2. European Theatre Ground Forces	211
3. General Purpose Combat Forces	
(a) Navy	295
(b) Army	143
(c) Airforce	365
4. Air Mobility	105
5. Reserve and Auxiliary Formations	27
6. Research and Development	222
7. Training	222
8. Production and repairs	189
9. War and Contingency Stocks	25
10. Other support functions	420
11. Special materials	24
Total	2280

In Account A defence expenditure is set out in the traditional way whereas in Account B it is broken down according to the functions performed. The first set of accounts will satisfy the legal requirements of auditors whose task it is to ensure that funds have not been misappropriated. The second set of accounts provides more relevant information to those who manage the service and have to ensure that resources are being allocated in the most efficient way.

A limited number of detailed micro-level reviews of specific programmes have been carried out in the UK over the 1970s. Referred to as PAR exercises (Programme Analysis and Review) these make an attempt to reorganise services. In a similar way the Central Policy Review Staff (CPRS) or 'Think Tank' has also scrutinised specific programmes. Finally, the Public Accounts Committee (PAC) will each year produce a detailed report on the activities of those departments which are referred to them by the Comptroller and Auditor General's office.

Attempts by economists and management scientists to inject a greater degree of rationality into public expenditure decision-making have run up against practical difficulties and criticisms from political scientists. The pursuit of efficiency in decision-making is not costless. The programme planning and budgeting systems (PPBS) that were introduced by McNamara to the US Defense Department during the Johnson administration attempted to relate inputs to outputs. Rather than concentrating only upon the inputs (i.e. public expenditures), it was considered to be more appropriate to look at outputs also. Moreover, it was the outputs that met broad policy objectives that were examined rather than the narrowly defined outputs of single departments. Thus, if the outputs of two different departments contributed to the same policy objectives, these two departments would be considered jointly.

Given that it is extremely difficult to measure the outputs of the public sector (a point we have noted on several other occasions), an elaborate system such as PPB was confronted by a larger number of measurement problems. Attempts to quantify input–output relationships, therefore, proved to be an expensive exercise. The second point is that the objectives of policies are frequently not clearly defined. This has certainly been the experience of UK attempts to introduce 'PPB-type' exercises on a very modest scale. A system of output budgeting was introduced by the Departments of Health and Education and Science in the 1970s. Both these departments have been constrained in pursuing the output budgeting system on a large scale, partly because of information costs and partly because outputs are not clearly defined.

A third point is that large-scale efficiency systems such as PPB cut across departmental boundaries within the bureaucracy. They are a means of centralising hitherto decentralised decision-making. This implies that the system also cuts across the vested department interests of competing bureaus. To the extent that bureaus can in the end frustrate the smooth operation of a PPBS in an attempt to maintain their decision-making autonomy, the budgeting system is likely to fail.

Political scientists such as Wildavsky and Self have made a spirited attack upon the techniques of rational budget decision-making. Much of this literature whilst entertaining is muddled and confused. First, it is often argued that the economists' model of budget decision-making as portrayed in CBA, PPBS etc. is not a description of reality and that decision-makers are not rational. The response to this is straightforward. The rational model is not intended to be a description of how decisions *are* made. It is a normative or prescriptive model which makes recommendations about how resource allocation decisions could be improved on. Second, politics is left out of the economist's picture. This is also true. Political decisions are about who benefits and who pays the cost. Such judgements are left out of the economist's model. It is always possible to make incidence measurements but decisions about who will and who will not benefit are left to the political process. Third, decision-making is not rational it is incremental. It does not take much argument to suggest that incrementalism might be a rational response by decision-makers who face highly complex, unstable and uncertain environments.

The efficiency model of the economist is straightforward. Objectives are defined, alternative means of achieving the objective(s) are identified, and their relative costs and benefits calculated and compared. Decision criteria are applied and the answer is derived. Simple? As set out it is a simple prescription, but a chain is as strong as its weakest link and as we have seen the above chain of reasoning has a number of weak links when applied to the public sector.

CHAPTER 9

Fiscal Federalism

The public sector in most countries is not organised as a unitary or centralised system. It is instead stratified into a number of levels of government with each having its own particular set of functions and tax-raising powers. For example, in a federal country such as the USA or Australia there is the top tier of government, the federal government, and below that the state governments, and then the local governments, municipalities and special function districts. Even in a less federated country such as the United Kingdom a tier of local government exist.

Stratified systems of government give rise to an interesting set of fiscal problems frequently referred to as 'fiscal federalism' or 'central/local government relations'. For example, which level of government should perform which function? This is the 'assignment problem'. Why does local government exist? What is the nature of the financial relationships between the different levels of government? Which taxes should be allocated to which level of government? Should central government use grants-in-aid to redistribute resources between local governments? What is the impact of grants-in-aid on local government behaviour? These are a selection of the questions which are considered under the general umbrella of fiscal federalism. Moreover, many of the interesting social problems exist at the level of local government. The central cities of the world contain problems of social hardship, poverty and a decline in the quality of the stock of public sector housing. These give pressures for increases in local public spending. It is, however, often the case that local government tax bases are inelastic. The growth in expenditures is not matched by a growth in local tax revenues. This gives rise to a growing fiscal gap which can end up like the New York crisis in which a local or city government borrows to finance its expenditure growth. The nature of the fiscal crisis of local governments depends upon the structure of its finances. Clearly the fiscal gap could be filled (as in the UK) by central government grants.

In this chapter the rationale for local government, the decentralization theorem and the assignment problem will be considered. This is then followed by a discussion of the basic principles of fiscal federalism and an examination of local government revenue sources (especially grants-in-aid) and their impacts.

The rationale for local government

Why should there be a system of local governments rather than a centralised unitary state? This is the converse to the question, why should government be decentralised and how much decentralisation is optimal? The economic case for federalism or decentralisation is based upon the limited geographic extent of the benefits of public goods and the costs of decision-making if everything is centralised. There are non-economic arguments which must also be taken into consideration. A fundamental question in the federalist literature is, 'how shall Man so organise his political and economic institutions so as to limit the power of one individual over another?' This recognises the inherent political dangers of centralisation. Limiting power concentration through decentralisation implies fragmentation and diversity in the structure of government.

Not all public goods are national in scope. In practice *local public goods* exist whose benefits have a limited geographic scope. As the size of the local population increases these local public goods become congested. Since the geographic scope of different local public goods differ local governments can be thought of as a set of spatially differentiated service clubs. Local public goods which are subject to crowding and congestion are treated in exactly the same way as club goods were in Chapter 3 above. The problem is to determine simultaneously the optimal quantity of the impure public good and also the optimal population of the local government, which consumes the good. Impure local public goods can be characterised by a simple crowding function,

$$Z_i^* = \alpha^{-1} Z$$

where: $Z_i^* \equiv$ the output of the public good actually consumed by the ith person
$Z \equiv$ the output of the public good produced
$\alpha \equiv$ a crowding parameter which is an increasing function of population (n).

In Figure 9.1 after n^* is reached (i.e. the capacity constraint) α increases. For a pure public good $\alpha = 1$.

Local governments exist because the spatial incidence of the benefits of these goods differ from one service to another. This produces a problem for the design of jurisdictions since economic efficiency considerations would require different but over-lapping jurisdictions for each service. A person living in one location would be a member of a number of different service clubs. For some services he would join with 100 people for others 10,000 depending upon the geographical incidence of the benefits. This whole system would be extremely complex and far too costly to administer. The boundaries of jurisdictions such as state and local governments are historically given and are not drawn up on the basis of fiscal rationality so that they co-incide with benefit areas. Because local government boundaries are imperfect in this sense spillovers of benefits and costs exist at the boundaries between different local governments.

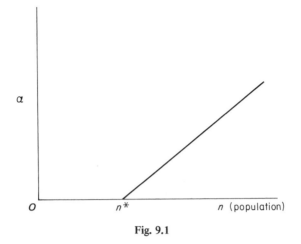

Fig. 9.1

The assignment problem or the 'layer cake' model of government

One of the issues in the optimal design of government structures in a federal system is to decide which functions should be carried out (assigned to) which level? Is it possible to appeal to logical analysis to answer this question or is it the outcome of political debate? The Tiebout–Musgrave 'layer-cake' model of the public sector maintains that the stabilisation and distribution functions of the public sector should be discharged by the central government and that state and local governments should engage in allocation activities. Lower levels of government are regarded as more efficient in the allocation of resources since · they provide that mix of outputs which best reflects individual tastes. Assuming that private households are extremely mobile, Tiebout sets out an analysis in which each individual selects his residential location so as to optimize his individual consumption of public services provided by regional governments. Through this mechanism a pseudo market solution is found for the efficient provision of public goods (see below).

The arguments in favour of central government being assigned the stabilisation role are clear enough. Suppose a single local government attempted to use its budget by way of a fiscal policy to stimulate demand in the local economy. It would increase its public spending and reduce its taxes. A number of problems follow from such actions. First, it is likely that the budget deficit so created would be difficult to finance. There is no guarantee that the deficit would be self-financing from the increased incomes and savings generated locally by the expansion in economic activity. Most of the local debt would be held by individuals living outside of the region and would represent a 'burden' in the same sense as foreign-owned national debt does. Second, the import leakages from a locally initiated stimulatory fiscal policy are likely to be so high as to reduce the value of the fiscal multipliers close to zero. Locally determined fiscal policies tend, therefore, to be impotent. Moreover, other local governments will probably pursue similar policies in competition with one another. Since no local government can control the money supply, or interest rates, or prices and incomes or imports, the availability of instruments for macroeconomic control is severely constrained. Those instruments are, however, available to central government which is in a much better position to effect a fiscal policy and coordinate it with other policies such as monetary policy.

Local governments are also severely restrained in their abilities to effect an income redistribution policy. Such a policy requires transfers to be made to lower income groups in the form of public expenditures on pensions, unemployment benefits, subsidies, housing, education etc. These are financed from progressive taxation. A local government with a high concentration of poor would be required to levy very high taxes relative to more prosperous regional governments. Wide variations in local taxes would promote a fiscal migration of middle to high income groups from the poor to the low-taxed rich regions. This would result in pronounced variations in regional per capita income and wealth and the poor regions would be constrained in the amount of redistribution that they could carry out. It therefore, requires a central government to redistribute between individuals (and, therefore, between regions) to give maximum effectiveness to income redistribution policies.

Whilst central government is assigned responsibility for macro-economic stabilisation and income redistribution this does not deny that the allocative decisions of local governments have implications for macro-economic policy and income distribution. Clearly they do and the reader should consider for himself some of these effects.

The Tiebout model

The theory of local public goods has been used recently as a partial explanation for the distribution of a nation's population among different fiscal jurisdictions (i.e. local governments). Individuals are assumed to select that community which best satisfies their private preferences. It will be recalled from Chapter 3 that individuals are public good quantity takers and in the absence of benefit taxes they face a schedule of taxes based upon some interpretation of their ability to pay. Moreover, Samuelson recognised that when there are a large number of consumers inefficiencies would result from decentralised choice for public goods arising from the non-revelation of preferences. The economist Charles Tiebout countered some of these problems by providing a model of local public goods which showed the efficiency of decentralised choice for public goods and also provided some primitive mechanism for the revelation of preferences.

Tiebout suggested that if there were a sufficiently large number of local communities or jurisdictions, and if each community offered a different menu of public goods (expenditures), then each individual could be thought to select that local community to live in which provides a level of public good output corresponding to his preferences. By 'voting with their feet', individuals simultaneously reveal their preferences and promote an efficient allocation of resources in the public sector. Furthermore, since all of those who choose to live in the same community will have similar tastes, there is no voting problem (see Chapter 4 for an elaboration of the majority voting problem). The allocation of resources will, therefore, be Pareto-optimal, Tiebout considered that this formulation of the problem provided an allocative process for public good provision which mimicked that of the market:

> Just as the consumer may be visualized as walking to a private market place to buy his goods, the prices of which are set, we place him in the position of walking to a community where the prices (taxes) of community services are set. Both trips take the consumer to market. There is no way in which the consumer can avoid revealing his preferences in a spatial economy. Spatial mobility provides the local public goods counterpart to the private market's shopping trip. (p. 422)

For an equilibrium to exist in the Tiebout model, it is necessary to make a number of very restrictive assumptions. First, consumers are perfectly mobile and live only on divided income; i.e. individuals are not constrained to living in a specific local community because of friendship or family ties or because of employment prospects. Second, the model does not explicitly contain a local tax variable. Third, if there are diverse preferences for public goods then the number of local communities required to produce an equilibrium would be extremely large. This could also result in a single person living in a community. This last point ignores the likely existence of economies of scale in the production of public goods and the benefits of cost sharing. Consider the case of two public goods and one hundred members in a community. Given 100 different levels of output of each public good then there are 1,000,000 potential one-man communities. Finally, the outcome of voting with one's feet may not be considered to be desirable on grounds of distributive justice. That is, the rich may live in their 'ghettos' and the poor will live in theirs; poverty and affluence will be segregated and concentrated in local communities.

What evidence exists to suggest that the real world behaves in a Tiebout way? Do individuals respond to variations in fiscal variables when they make their location decisions? Planners in some countries such as the USA do make use of zoning laws. These laws restrict community size. Oates (1969) in a now classic study carried out a cross-section analysis on 1960 data of fifty-three communities in the New York metropolitan region. His study showed that fiscal variables do play a role in individuals' location decisions although other factors obviously play a role too. This gives rise to non-homogeneous communities as individuals trade-off different community attributes against fiscal variables. Oates' study was based upon the following set of arguments. Assuming that property is fixed, as people move into an area, to enjoy the benefits of superior public services, they will drive up the price of property in the area. Thus, part or all of the benefits of public services become *capitalised* in house values. The amount of capitalisation depends upon, (a) the degree of mobility of the population, and (b) the elasticity of supply of houses. Local taxes will have the opposite effect upon property values. Oates found that capital values were significantly inversely related to the tax rate but significantly directly correlated with current expenditure per pupil. What is the net effect of these two opposing effects? Oates' study showed that they just about offset one another.

The 1969 Oates study was updated in Oates (1973) and has been the subject of criticism and much debate: Edel and Sclar (1974), Hamilton (1976) and Linneman (1978). The main criticism is the specification of the model plus the presence of non-tax financing of local public spending. Since Oates set out to find out whether or not a Tiebout equilibrium existed he has been criticised by Edel and Sclar on the grounds that capitalisation only takes place because a full Tiebout equilibrium has not emerged. Capitalisation is part of the process of adjustment to an equilibrium and, therefore, describes a disequilibrium situation. It is also difficult to interpret the tax effects on property values since higher taxes finance higher levels of public spending. Whether or not individuals do respond to fiscal differentials as Tiebout suggested and whether or not local public spending is capitalised in property values remain controversial issues in local public finance.

The optimality of the Tiebout equilibrium has also been subjected to some penetrating criticism; Buchanan and Wagner, 1970 and Buchanan and Goetz, 1972. A Tiebout equilibrium is said to exist when no individual could improve his utility by changing communities. But this is not so. As individuals migrate externalities are imposed on others. Also, if the local public good is impure then congestion costs are imposed on the accepting region. Consider two regions X and Y. Suppose that there is more land in region X. As individuals move from Y to X there is an increase in the returns to land in X. In equilibrium incomes are equalised and migration ceases. Such a move is optimal since individuals are being made better off and no-one is being made worse off. But *total* incomes in X are now higher. The tax base in region X has increased whilst that in Y has fallen. There are also more people in region X to share the cost of providing the public goods than there are in Y. Thus, the 'tax prices' differ between X and Y and this is not optimal.

In practice we live in *non-Tiebout worlds*. A Tiebout first-best world is unlikely to exist because without a Tiebout-type selection process there is no guarantee that the number of communities is optimal; hence the outcome will be second best in practice with a small number of communities. Moreover, the Tiebout equilibrium could be highly unstable if all factors are free to move. A stable equilibrium will only exist if there are strong disincentives to move such as high set-up costs and adjustment costs. The model implicitly assumes homogeneous labour, which is mobile, and land which is fixed. Thus, homogeneous communities emerge because of differences in taxes. But mixed communities exist in practice. The Tiebout model does not explain this. In its defence the Tiebout model is only designed to give an indication of the economic factors that play a role in migration decisions. A complete model would also include, distribution of skills, geography, topography, transport costs, climate, density, and the distribution of natural resources.

Centralisation *v.* decentralisation

Earlier discussions in this chapter have referred to decision-making that takes place within a particular structure of government. Systems or structures of government do, however, differ in their degree of decentralisation. A decentralised government is one for which a number of small autonomous governments join together to form a federation of states or governments. A central or federal government usually exists to co-ordinate the activities of the smaller local governments. The local governments, however, have autonomy to determine their own levels of public outputs and their own mix of taxes and tax rates. The degree of centralisation varies with the amount of autonomy that local governments have over expenditure and tax decisions. For example, in the UK about 60 per cent of local government expenditure is financed from grants-in-aid received from the central government. Moreover, local governments in the UK are creatures of statute, whose functions and powers originate from central government. They require central government approval to proceed with capital expenditure programmes and permission from central government to borrow funds. Thus, while there is some degree of decentralised decision-making given to local governments in the UK, it is not as great as that enjoyed by the USA. In the USA state and local governments have greater freedom to allocate resources, levy a variety of taxes and pursue their own independent policies. It is a federal system of government, with the federal (central) government playing a coordinating role and providing services whose benefits serve the national rather than the local interest.

What are the advantages and disadvantages of varying degrees of decentralisation, and which level of government is most appropriate to perform which function? These are the questions that have to be answered by those interested in the 'design of government'. It is these questions that are central to the devolution debate in the UK and which were considered at the time of the reorganisation of local government in the UK during the early 1970s.

One of the arguments that is frequently advanced in favour of decentralised government is that it offers a greater choice between different amounts of public goods. Since individuals differ in their preferences for levels of public good provision, the capacity of decentralised government to diversify public outputs, in accordance with local preferences, will improve resource allocation in the public sector. This is the essence of the Tiebout model which was explored above.

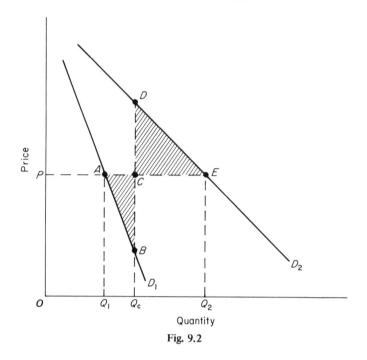

Fig. 9.2

The welfare gains from decentralised public choice are shown in Figure 9.2. In this simple illustrative example the population is divided into two groups. For ease of exposition assume that the demand curve for the public good is identical for all individuals in each of the groups but that demand differs between the two groups. Thus, all individuals in group 1 possess demand curve D_1 and all persons in group 2 have demand curve D_2 Assume that the public service is supplied at a constant cost per head. The preferred level of output for people in group 1 is Q_1 and for group 2 is Q_2.

In a system of centralised government a single uniform level of public service would be provided, say Q_c. Given this level of output the welfare loss to group 1 individuals is shown as the shaded area *ABC*. This represents the excess costs to each individual over his valuation of the excessive units of consumption (Q_1Q_c). The welfare loss to group 2 individuals is given as the area *CDE*. This is the essence of Oates' 'decentralisation theorem'.

There are, however, a number of qualifications that have to be made to the simple model described above. First, the extent of the welfare loss depends upon the degree of homogeneity of individual preferences. Highly heterogeneous groups will suffer welfare losses from a centralised solution. Second, the size of the loss in consumer surplus varies inversely with the price elasticity of demand, i.e. as the demand curve becomes relatively steeper the shaded area becomes larger. Third, if there are economics of scale in the production of the good then the unit cost to larger communities will be lower than for smaller ones. Thus the extent of the welfare loss depends upon the distribution of preferences throughout the community, the elasticity of demand and the existence of economies of scale. The net position in practice will depend upon the empirical estimates of these magnitudes. However, given the nature of publicly provided goods these magnitudes are extremely difficult to measure in practice and remain generally unknown.

While efficiency gains may be made by decentralisation of the allocative functions of government, there seems to be general agreement that the macroeconomic stabilisation function and the redistribution of income and wealth policies of government are best carried out by central governments. Local governments, since they cannot control the money supply or influence interest rates, are unable to pursue an active regional monetary policy. Moreover, they are severely constrained in the extent to which they can have a fiscal policy. The openness of their local economies implies that the effects of fiscal stimuli leak out into other regions which dampens the intended effects on local income and employment. Given the size of these leakages out of the region, local government would be required to run a massive budget deficit in order to stimulate the local economy. Clearly it is unable to do so.

Local government is also severely limited in the extent to which it is able to pursue an independent welfare policy of redistributing income and wealth from rich to poor. If it did attempt such a policy then those in the upper income and wealth groups would migrate to fiscally more favourable localities taking the tax base of the local government with them and thereby making the local region worse off.

Since central or federal level governments are in a better position to internalise these effects of stabilisation and redistribution policies they, rather than local governments, pursue these policies. Clearly the spending and taxing activities of local governments will have effects upon central government's stabilisation and distributional policies. This often means that, in attempting to control the state of the economy at the macro-level, central government must control the spending and taxing powers of lower levels of governments also. Such controls are a frequent source of discontent for local governments, who are constrained in the pursuit of their own policies; i.e. there is a conflict between national and local interests.

Financing local government

The Tiebout–Musgrave layer-cake model of the public sector stressed decentralisation and limited the regional provision of public goods to those which could be easily internalised for a region. Moreover, in a decentralised system efficiency is achieved if, 'expenditure decisions are tied more closely to real resource costs' (Oates, 1972; p. 13). This approach gives a strong theoretical presumption in favour of financing state and local functions primarily with benefit taxes. In addition each individual should be able to associate the benefits and costs of state local-spending programmes. This is also an argument for earmarked benefit taxes (see Buchanan, 1967; Ch. 6). These kinds of taxes are assumed to be neutral (minimizing excess burden, *vis* Chapter 11) whilst at the same time they are assumed to be horizontally equitable since regional rate differentials will induce locational shifts. McLure (1971) has summarised this approach as

> the division of functions and tax bases amongst the various levels of sub-national government would depend upon the geographic extent of benefits, economies of scale in production and administration, decision making cost, the mobility of tax payers and recipients of benefits of public services, and the advantages of vote trading in expressing intensity of feeling. (p. 462)

Federal economies do not adhere to this model of federal financing. State and local taxes in practice cannot be described as pure regional benefit taxes, also, state and local taxes contribute only a part of the expenditures of subnational governments. The difference is made up from federal government grants-in-aid to state and local governments. In the sections which follow we shall examine the economics of the property tax which is the most prevalent used tax by sub-national governments. This is then followed by a study of grants-in-aid. Table 9.1 shows the composition of UK local government revenues for 1970 and 1980. Rates in the UK are paid by individuals on domestic properties and also by the company sector on commercial and manufacturing properties etc. (referred to as

Table 9.1 Composition of UK local government revenues

	1970 (%)	1980 (%)
Current receipts		
Non-specific grants	41.7	39.7
Specific grants	8.6	10.3
Total grants	50.3	50.0
Rates	34.0	31.3
Rents	12.5	11.5
Miscellaneous	3.2	7.2
	100.0	100.0
Capital receipts		
Current surplus	74.8	77.0
Capital grants	25.2	20.5
Miscellaneous	–	2.5
	100.0	100.0

Source: *National Income and Expenditure*, 1981 edition (HMSO).

non-domestic rates). In 1969 business interests lost their vote. The share of local government spending met from domestic rates fell from 30 per cent in 1938 to 8 per cent in 1981. There is, therefore, a weak link between voter's consumption of the benefits of local public services and what they are asked to pay locally. There is, therefore, some justification for believing that such a state of affairs could result in an over expansion in this sector of government. Reform would require that the cost of service provision be made more obvious to the local voter.

The economics of the property tax

In most countries the property tax is an important source of government revenue, especially for state and local governments. The importance of the property tax as a proportion of total tax revenues for a number of OECD countries is shown in Table 9.2. A comparison for 1960 and 1977 indicates the changes which have taken place in the structure of taxation: see especially USA.

In the UK the property tax is the second highest yielding tax, next to the income tax. The base of the property tax and the means of valuing the base differs from country to country. Generally speaking, it is a tax on immovable property, both domestic and non-domestic (i.e. manufacturing, commercial and agricultural). The base can either be valued by taking the capital value of the property (as in the USA) or by imputing the rental value of the property (as in the UK). In all systems there are exemptions, concessions and reliefs. For

Table 9.2 **The property tax in OECD countries**

	Taxes on immovable property as a percentage of total tax revenue		Taxes on immovable property as a percentage of GDP	
	1960	*1977*	*1960*	*1977*
Australia	6.55	5.15	1.54	1.53
Canada	12.80	9.36	3.09	2.97
France	–	1.61	–	0.64
Germany	1.72	1.16	0.54	0.44
Ireland	15.73	5.90	3.47	2.08
Japan	6.31	5.66	1.15	1.26
Netherlands	1.02	1.23	0.31	0.57
New Zealand	6.60	5.78	2.12	1.91
Spain	–	0.24	–	0.05
Switzerland	0.50	0.61	0.11	0.19
Turkey	–	0.85	–	0.21
UK	–	10.37	–	3.70
USA	12.42	0.47	3.30	0.12

Source: Unpublished OECD (Paris) material.

example, in most countries charities, non-profit organisations and religious organisations, do not pay the property tax on their buildings and in the UK the agricultural sector is exempt. In some federated countries there are wide variations between local jurisdictions both in the tax base and also in tax rates. This is in contrast with a country such as the UK in which the property tax base is common to all local governments and valuation of the base is centrally determined.

One important issue about the property tax is its buoyancy or yield. It has long been argued that the yield from the property tax does not keep pace with changes in income and wealth. Thus, for constant tax rates the yield from the property tax will lag behind that of the personal income tax. Tax rates do not, however, remain constant but there are strong incentives on the part of politicians to moderate their increases. There is, therefore, a strong *a priori* reason to believe that the property tax share of total tax revenue will decline. This was demonstrated in Table 9.2. The lack of buoyancy is due to the way in which the tax base is valued. In most countries property tax valuations (be they of the capital or the rental value of the property) are infrequent; every five or ten years. This means that the yield will not keep in line with price and income increases. The result of this lack of buoyancy can be quite devastating for local government finances. The pressures on local government spending increases have been discussed in Chapter 5. If local public spending is rising rapidly in line with price and income increases but local property tax revenues are static then strong upward pressures are placed on local property tax rates. To the extent that local governments do not wish to increase property tax rates they will rely more on central government grants-in-aid (*viz*) and have recourse to borrowing. The cumulative effects can be to bring about a 'tax payer's revolt' as in the case of the famous *Californian Proposition 13* case or to promote a fiscal crisis as in the New York case (see Gramlich, 1976).

Another important issue relating to the property tax is the question of its incidence or who bears the burden of the tax. Is the property tax progressive or regressive? This question has provoked a great deal of controversy in recent years. In asking this question we are interested in a number of related questions; who actually pays the property tax; how does the property tax affect the behaviour of property and land owners; if the property tax was to be replaced in part or in whole by another set of taxes (e.g. a local income tax and/or a local sales tax) what would be the overall impact upon the progressivity of the whole fiscal system (this is the question of differential incidence)?

There are two approaches in the literature which have been used to answer these questions. They can be set down as the 'old view' and the 'new view'. In summary, according to the old view, the property tax is a tax on land and structures (buildings). An increase in the tax causes an increase in the price of the land and the structures and an increase in the price of the goods and services produced by these factors of production. The property tax is, therefore, assumed to be passed on and in so far as rents are paid, predominantly by the poor, the tax is regressive. The old view of the property tax employs the tools of partial equilibrium analysis and is reasonable for analysing the tax within a given locality. When the analysis is extended to the nation as a whole, the results change. A general equilibrium analysis treats the property tax as a tax on capital. All capital goods are not taxed at the same rate. Thus, high tax items will, in the long run, move to low tax items. This migration of capital affects the price of all capital goods and, therefore, all owners of capital will, in the long run, share the burden of the tax. Since capital ownership is concentrated amongst high income groups then it follows that the tax is progressive. Aaron who has provided the most comprehensive analysis of the property tax concludes that 'most of the available evidence supports the new view and suggests, therefore, that many current proposals for changes in the property tax rest upon misconceptions about its impact on the distribution of income' (p. 20). It is instructive to look at these arguments in greater detail.

Old view

In all incidence studies we distinguish between the *formal incidence* of the tax (i.e. who is logically obliged to pay it) and its *actual incidence* (i.e. who actually pays it). As far as domestic owner-occupiers are concerned there is no ambiguity. An owner-occupier pays the full amount of the property tax. There is no scope for shifting the tax to anyone else. This element of the tax is regressive since rich owner-occupiers are likely to pay a smaller percentage of their incomes on the tax than poor owner-occupiers, such as the young and the aged. Owners who have rented out their property can, however, pass on the property tax in higher rents, whilst those who own or rent commercial properties can pass the tax on in higher commodity prices. To the extent that low income groups rent property then the property tax is again regressive.

In the long run the increase in rents will force some tenants out. This will cause an increase in the supply of rented property and rents will be forced down. It might, therefore, be thought that the tax will eventually fall on property owners. However, once the useful life of the buildings has ceased at low rents owners would wish to invest in low-taxed assets. The stock of buildings would fall and rents would again rise.

What about the impact of the tax on the land component? Since land is essentially in fixed supply land owners cannot vary its stock to force up prices. Therefore, the tax cannot be shifted forward in higher land prices. Also, the tax on land is capitalised in lower land values. Post tax land prices fall and the incidence is borne by the owner of the land at the time the tax is introduced (or if the tax rate is changed). This element of the property tax is, therefore, progressive since land ownership is concentrated in higher income groups.

New view

This approach employs the Herberger general equilibrium analysis which is set out in detail below in Chapter 14. The property tax is viewed as a tax on capital and land, the stocks of which are assumed to be fixed. This fixed supply assumption is crucial for the new view. The property tax is, therefore, fully capitalised. Capital (property) and land values fall and the incidence of the tax is borne by owners. If they try to increase prices or rents, markets will not clear and there will be a downward pressure on prices. (After reading the Harberger analysis in Chapter 14 the reader should try to formulate the property tax in the context of that analysis.)

What is the empirical evidence about the incidence of the property tax? Aaron in his survey of the US property tax found that on balance the 'new view' prevailed as a reasonable description of the real world. In the UK the Layfield Committee (1976; Ch. 10) examined the relationship between rate bills and incomes. When they examined the incidence of 'gross rates' (i.e. domestic rate bills minus the domestic element of the Rate Support Grant) their conclusion was similar to that of the earlier Allen Committee namely that domestic rates were regressive. However, when 'net rates' were considered (i.e. gross rates minus rate rebates and rates paid through supplementary benefits) then rates became more progressive in the lower half of the income distribution, proportional in the middle and regressive in the higher half of the income distribution. This is illustrated in Figure 9.3.

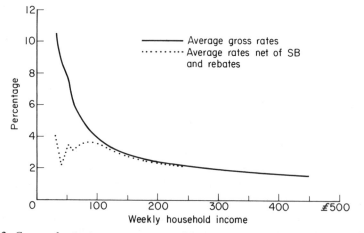

Fig. 9.3 Gross and net rates as a percentage of income. Source: Cmnd 8449. *Alternatives to Domestic Rates* (HMSO, 1981); FES. Family Expenditure Survey.

The economics of grants-in-aid

In all economies local government rely to differing degrees upon central government transfers through grants-in-aid as a source of revenue. In the UK 50 per cent of current revenues came from this source. These grants are financed from central government tax revenues, in particular the personal income taxes, which are more buoyant than the property tax. In some countries such as Germany, Australia, Canada and America there exist revenue-sharing or tax-sharing arrangements. Under these arrangements a fixed proportion, say 1 or 2 per cent, of the federal income tax is assigned to local government and is distributed as a block grant, according to some predetermined formula, amongst the state and local governments.

The immediate question which is asked is: 'Why grants-in-aid?' First, there are few regional public finance functions for which the benefits are captured entirely within the boundaries of the region. Benefits spill over across boundaries to non-residents. If local voter/taxpayers are taxed only according to the benefits they receive then this will result in an allocation of resources to collective consumption which is below the optimum if all benefits were taken into account. One theoretical solution to this problem would be to provide a set of specific optimising grants which would be designed to encourage the activities which produce the spillovers. Such grants would be matching and open ended (see below). Second, grants can be used to satisfy a horizontal equity objective. That is, an individual located in one region with income $£Y$ should not receive less local public goods than an individual in another (assuming identical tastes/ preferences) region whose income is $£Y$. This could arise if the tax base of one region was much lower than the other, i.e. varying fiscal or taxable capacities between regions. In this context horizontal equity requires the equal treatment of equals with respect to local public spending and taxation. Also, the individual in the region with low tax capacity could face a higher tax bill because of higher spending 'needs' in that region compared to the other. For example, there could be a high concentration of school children and elderly residents in that region and it is these population groups who tend to generate demands for local public services and, therefore, increase local public expenditure. Inequities arise, therefore, between regions because of differences in taxable capacities and spending needs. Grants-in-aid attempt to partially rectify these inequities. For example, the objective of the Rate Support Grant (RSG) in the UK (which was modified in 1981 to a block grant) is to supplement a local authority's own finances so that different authorities can provide similar standards of services for a similar tax rate (i.e. 'rate' in the pound in the UK) despite differences in spending needs and rateable values (i.e. tax base capacity). Prior to 1981 the RSG did this through two elements or grant components with one compensating for variations in needs (the 'needs element') and the other compensating for differences in taxable resources (i.e. the 'resource element'). Whilst the details of the UK grants-in-aid system are explored in greater depth below the RSG serves to illustrate how central government grants to lower tier levels of government serve to satisfy the objective of horizontal equity.

A third reason for the existence of grants-in-aid is that they help to keep down local tax rate increases. Given that the property tax is not buoyant in times of rapid inflation local tax rates would rocket. By using the revenues of the more elastic personal income tax to finance local public goods and distributing them via grants the increase in local tax rates can be moderated. If a central government is concerned about local reactions to inflation and if the payment of local taxes is perceived to be a politically sensitive area, which it tends to be, then political capital can be gained by a judicious use of grants-in-aid policies.

Given that there is a rationale for intergovernmental transfers through grants what form do they take? Grants-in-aid can be classified into three broad categories.

1 *Open ended matching grants:* in this system the higher level government pays some proportion of the cost of the local public services thereby effectively reducing their price. Since the grant is open ended the lower level of government is at liberty to use as much of this grant money as it wishes at the new price ratio.
2 *Closed-end lump-sum transfers:* the higher level of government transfers a fixed amount of money to a lower government without restrictions on its use or any change in the relative prices of the local public goods. The revenue sharing programmes in the US fall into this category as too does the UK block grant.
3 *Closed-end categorical grants:* (also referred to as specific grants) a fixed amount of grant is transferred from higher to lower level governments to be used on specific programmes. Capital grant allocations for specific programmes in the UK fall into this category.

As with all taxonomies they tend to be simple and the difficulty arises when real world grant systems are mixtures of these simple types. However, the taxonomy is extremely useful for sorting out the basic properties of different grant structures so that we can then proceed to analyse the differential impacts of these alternative grants on local government spending.

Impact of grants on local government spending decisions

Having classified grants-in-aid and established the rationale for their existence we now want to examine their impact on local government spending decisions. In particular we want to know which grants might stimulate local public spending and by how much. This question is of importance to the more general issues of central government control of local public spending and the design of grant systems. Throughout this analysis we are interested in marginal changes and not absolute levels of local public spending.

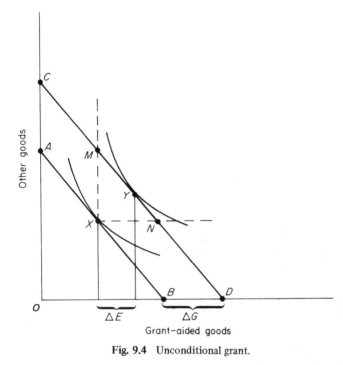

Fig. 9.4 Unconditional grant.

Unconditional grants

These are block grants which can be used by local governments at their own discretion. They represent, therefore, a lump sum transfer from central to local government which can be used either for general purposes, as in the case of a close-end lump sum transfer (*op. cit.*), or for specific programmes, as in the case of a closed-end categorical grant (*op. cit.*). The impact of an unconditional grant on local spending decisions can be illustrated by the use of Figure 9.4.

Assume that the local public grant-aided good and all other goods are normal goods. The grant-in-aid increases by an amount ΔG and is shown by an outward shift in the budget constraint AB to CD. The point X shows the initial equilibrium combination of the local public good and the vector of all other goods (this equilibrium could be thought of as that of the median voter). The new equilibrium is shown by Y and the increase in local public good production and consumption (and hence implicitly expenditure) is shown by ΔE. It is readily seen from the simple geometric construction in Figure 9.4 that the $\Delta E < \Delta G$ (as long as Y lies in the bounds MN). Thus, an unconditional grant will increase local public spending but by less than the amount of the grant, i.e. $0 < dE/dG < 1$. An unconditional grant reduces taxes and allows individuals to spend more on private goods. To the extent that grants-in-aid substitute for own local government revenues (i.e. local taxes) Y will lie closer to M.

Matching grants

These grants alter the slope of the local government budget line by lowering the relative price of the grant-aided local public good (see Figure 9.5). This change stimulates a movement along an existing indifferent curve as well as a movement to a new one (i.e. substitution and income effects of the change). Assume an open-ended matching grant. Thus, we move along the price consumption curve from *A* to *C*. This is compared to the solution for the same total of unconditional grants, the point *B*. Comparing points *B* and *C* it can be seen that *C* implies a greater increase in expenditure on grant-aided local public goods but that *C* is on a lower indifference curve. Also, for both *B* and *C* $dE/dG < 1$, i.e. local public spending increases but by less than the amount of the grant. The points *A* and *C* are drawn such that demand for the local public good is inelastic. If we had been on the elastic portion of the price consumption curve and had lowered the price ratio from point *D* to *F* then $dE/dG > 1$ and the grant would be stimulatory.

Grants do not, in practice, fall into these simple and neat categories of unconditional or matching. Instead grant structures are extremely complex and combine the characteristics of the simple categories. In some instances grants can complement other local spending programmes which will result in an increase in overall spending.

A great deal of empirical work has been carried out in the USA to determine the impact of grants-in-aid programmes or state and local government spending.

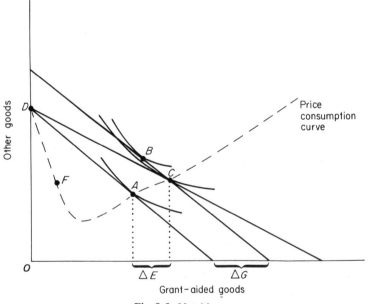

Fig. 9.5 Matching grant.

These studies essentially use a reduced form equation of the kind:

$$E = \alpha_0 = \beta_1 x_1 + \ldots \beta_n x_n + \gamma G$$

where E = total local or state spending (in some studies per capita spending is used)

$x_1 \ldots x_n$ = the factors which determine local public spending, e.g. population, per capita incomes etc.

G = grants-in-aid.

Most studies have used cross-section data and set out to measure dE/dG. A number of problems arise from these studies. First, strong assumptions are required such that each local government in the cross section study is using an identical production function for the production of identical local public goods. Second, since the grants-in-aid variable G is a large component of total spending E it is essentially an identity which is being estimated, hence the results record a statistically good fit. Third, there is the strong possibility of simultaneous equation bias. Since grants are recorded when the money is spent and this is the same time when expenditures are made then this will give dE/dG an upward bias. No-one, however, agrees how severe the bias might be.

Most empirical studies of the impact of matching grants have used simple cross section procedures and have ignored the problems of simultaneous equation bias. In all cases dE/dG is found to be greater than unity but as commentators such as Pogue and Sgontz (1968) have remarked these high estimates represent nothing more than simultaneous equation bias. Moreover, the cross-section estimates are not stable and vary widely depending upon the year chosen. Pogue and Sgontz found that in this type of study dE/dG varied between 1.31 and 2.04 depending upon the cross-section year chosen. In one study (Orr, 1976) of public assistance grants across states which did make adjustments for bias, the price elasticity of demand for public assistance was estimated to be -0.23. This implied that welfare grants stimulate a very small amount of state and local expenditures. With this elasticity the implied value of dE/dG is 0.15 for 1970. Other recent studies show that for matching grants values of dE/dG lie between zero and unity. Gramlich and Galper (1973) found values around 0.8 in a pooled cross-sectional sample of ten cities for the categories of urban support, social services and public safety.

For close ended unconditional grants the estimates of dE/dG are lower than that for matching grants as expected from *a priori* theory (see Gramlich, 1977). The results for close-ended conditional grants are given in Table 9.3. The estimated values of dE/dG range from 2.45 to 0.32, with the mean estimated effect equating 1.40. The values of the early cross-sectional estimates, which did not make adjustments for simultaneous equation bias, tend to be much higher than those studies which used time series or pooled cross-sectional methods to adjust for the bias.

Table 9.3 Econometric results, effects of federal grants on state and local expenditures

Author	Sample	Date	Dep. Var.	Ind. Var.	Result dE/dG	Sign. Diff. from 1
A. Cross-section studies						
Adams (1)	1249 less developed counties	1959	County taxes	Fed. grants	0.96[1]	Yes, −
Bahl-Saunders (2)	48 states	Change between 1957 and 1960	State-loc. exp.	Fed. grants	1.36	Not given
Bahl-Saunders (3)	48 states	1942 1962	State-loc. current exp.	Fed. grants	2.00 (1942) 0.50 (1962)	Yes, + Yes, −
Brazer (6)	462 cities	1951	City general operating exp.	Fed. + state grants	1.74	Yes, +
Campbell-Sacks (7)	48 states	1962	State-loc. exp.	Fed. grants	1.56	Yes, +
Harlow (17)	48 states	1957	State exp.	Fed. grants	1.80	No, +
Henderson (20)	100 metrop. counties 2980 nonmet. counties	1957	County exp.	Fed. + state grants	1.42 (met.) 1.04 (nonmet.)	Yes, + No, +
Kurnow (23)	48 states	1957	State-loc. exp.	Fed. grants	2.45[2]	Yes, +
Osman (29)	48 states	1960	State-loc. exp.	Fed. grants	1.94	Yes, +
Petersen (31)	50 states	Pooled obs. 1962 and 1963	State-loc. exp.	Fed. grants for capital and curr. exp.	0.54[3] (cap. grants) 1.70 (curr. grants)	Yes, − Yes, +
Pidot (33)	81 large met. areas	1962	Met. exp.	Fed. grants	2.35	No, +
Pogue-Sgontz (34)	50 states	1958–64	State-loc. exp.	Fed. grants	1.90 (1958)[4] 2.04 (1959) 2.00 (1960) 1.69 (1961) 1.31 (1962) 1.91 (1963) 1.80 (1964)	No, + No, + Yes, + No, + No, + Yes, + Yes, +

Study	Year	Sample	Dependent variable	Independent variable	Coefficient	
Sacks-Harris (35)	1960	48 states	State-loc. exp.	Fed. grants	1.76[5] 1.55	Yes, + No, +
Sharkansky (37)	1960	48 states	State exp.	Fed. grants	0	Yes, –
Smith (38)	1965	50 states	State-loc. exp.	Fed. grants	1.66[6] 0.67	Yes, + No, –
B. Time series studies						
Bolton (5)	1954–63	Quarterly	State-loc. exp.	Fed. grants	0.32	Yes, –
Chalmers (8)	1952–66	Quarterly	State-loc. const. exp.	Fed. grants	0.49[7]	
de Leauw-Gramlich (10)	1954–67	Quarterly	State-loc. exp.	Fed. grants	1.12	No, +
Gramlich (14)	1954–65	Quarterly	State-loc. exp.	Fed. grants	1.12	No, +
Phelps (32)	1951–66	Annual	State-loc. highway const. exp.	Fed. highway grant authorisations	0.45	Yes, –

Notes:

[1] Using the assumption that the partial derivatives of county own-financed expenditures with respect to county own-financed taxes is unity and that the partial derivative of total county expenditures with respect to Federal grants is one plus or minus the derived partial of own-financed expenditure with respect to grants.

[2] Estimated in elasticity form and converted to partial derivatives using aggregate expenditures and Federal grants for 1957.

[3] Table 7.3 is solved to include effects of lagged construction expenditures. Weighted average of coefficients is 1.09.

[4] Average of coefficients is 1.81, standard derivation is 0.23.

[5] 1.76 is in regression without state aid, 1.55 is in regression with state aid. Latter is presumably preferred.

[6] 1.66 is estimated from linear regression, 0.67 in elasticity form. The latter is converted into partial derivative using aggregate own-expenditures and Federal grants for 1965.

[7] 0.49 is the response of construction expenditures to total Federal grants.

Source: Gramlich (1969).

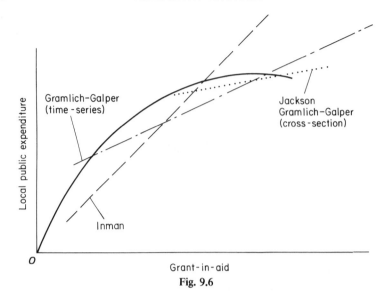

Fig. 9.6

Gramlich and Galper (1973) estimated dE/dG to be between 0.50 and 0.75 which predicts a range for tax relief of between $0.50 and $0.75 per dollar of aid received. Jackson's work (1972) estimates that $0.80 per dollar of aid goes into tax reductions whilst Inman's (1975) study predicts no tax relief. These results are charted in Figure 9.6. Inman resolves these differences in the estimates by suggesting that the three studies estimated different segments of a non-linear relationship between expenditure and aid (see Figure 9.6).

This whole area of grant evaluation is an on going research agenda. The earlier studies have provided some initial insights but much work remains to be done.

Principles of fiscal federalism

The previous discussion can now be brought together and summarised as the principles of federalism:

1 *The principle of diversity:* the federal system should provide scope for variety and differences in fiscal arrangements pertaining to different states and localities. Communities may differ in their preferences for public services and should not be forced into a uniform pattern.
2 *The principle of equivalence:* the spatial scope of various public services differ. The benefits of some are nation-wide (e.g. defence) those of others are region-wide (e.g. roads and flood control) those of others are local (e.g. city police or street lighting). For fiscal arrangements to be truly efficient each type of service would be voted on and paid for by the residents in the area which benefits.

3 *The principle of centralised redistribution:* the redistributive function of fiscal policy (i.e. progressive taxation and transfers) should be centralised at the federal level. Otherwise, redistribution becomes ineffective and location decisions are distorted.

4 *The principle of locational neutrality:* regional fiscal differences tend to interfere with the location of economic activity. Some degree of interference is an inevitable cost of fiscal federalism, but it should be minimised. Differential taxes, which distort location decisions, should be avoided.

5 *The principle of centralised stabilisation:* the use of the fiscal instrument for purposes of macro (stabilisation, growth) policy has to be at the national level. Local governments do not have the policy instruments to make stabilisation policy on their own.

6 *Correction for spillovers:* benefit spillovers between jurisdictions lead to inefficient expenditure decisions. This calls for correction by higher-level government.

7 *Minimum provision of essential public services:* the national government should assure each citizen, that no matter which state/local area he resides in, he will be provided with a minimum level of certain essential public services such as safety, health, welfare and education.

8 *Equalization of fiscal position:* while redistribution is primarily an inter-individual matter, the existence of sharp regional differences in the balance between fiscal capacity and need among local governments cannot be disregarded entirely. Some degree of fiscal equalisation among local governments is called for so that minimum service levels can be secured with more or less comparable tax efforts.

These principles are very difficult to adhere to, some of them conflict and they might have economic costs associated with them. Existing jurisdictions do not correspond to benefit areas and spillovers between jurisdictions exist. The principle of diversity could conflict with the principle of locational neutrality whilst the equalisation of fiscal position in an attempt to establish horizontal equity could reduce labour mobility and hence overall productivity.

Fiscal federalism in the UK

Local government in the UK has always been viewed as an agent of central government which decides upon the framework of the major spending areas such as education, personal social services, housing etc., leaving the implementation of local government. Whilst local government might have few discretionary powers *de jure* it could, in fact, through its control over the implementation process have considerable power *de facto*. The web of central/local government relations in the UK are extremely complex and are the focus of much current research by economists and political scientists. In this section a brief description of the UK grant-in-aid relationship is provided.

Prior to 1981 the main Exchequer Grant to local authorities was the Rate Support Grant (RSG) which provided UK local governments with about 40 per cent of their current income. The RSG, which was the principal grant form throughout the 1970s, was a closed-ended unconditional grant. In addition to the RSG local governments also received income from specific grants particularly for housing, police, fire services and capital projects. These specific grants tend to be matching grants and are paid in relation to estimates of expenditure or policy plans.

The RSG was made up of three elements, (a) a *needs element* which compensated, through grant, those local authorities whose per capita spending levels were relatively high because of local pressures on spending arising from the socio-economic composition of the local population, e.g. number of school children, number of old people, population density, (b) a *resources element* which partially compensated those local governments which had a taxable capacity (rateable value) below an arbitrary 'standard' rateable value per head, and (c) a *domestic element* which is essentially a subsidy on the rates of domestic property.

The basic objective of the needs and resources elements of the RSG was to enable local authorities to levy similar rates for services of a similar standard. The needs element was distributed in England and Wales on the basis of an assessment of needs derived from a regression analysis of those factors which were supposed to influence needs. The resources element was paid on the basis of a local authority's rate poundage multiplied by the amount which its rateable value fell short of the national standard rateable value per head. Finally, the domestic element is paid on a uniform basis as a fixed amount on the domestic rateable value of the local government.

Following much debate about the RSG, mainly that it promoted an increase in local government spending, did not allow sufficient central control over local spending decisions, and was unfair in its distribution of the needs element, a new system was introduced with effect from 1 April 1981. Under the new arrangements the main form of assistance from central to local government will be through a *block grant*. This replaces the former needs and resources elements of RSG. A domestic rate relief grant replaces the former domestic element in name only. The purpose of the block grant is two-fold. First, it has an equalisation objective which will enable different local governments to levy similar rate poundages for similar standards of service. Under the previous RSG local authorities, through the resources element, could only be brought up to the national standard. Those authorities above the national standard could not be levelled down. Hence, redistribution was incomplete. The new block grant makes provision for levelling down subject to the constraint that no authority can receive a negative grant.

The second objective is to give central government a means of controlling the spending of each individual local authority. This is effected through a 'tapering' of grant for those authorities who spend above a predetermined level. These levels are set by central government and differ from authority to authority.

The total of grants to local authorities is close ended; a cash limit is set. Total relevant expenditure is established and total grant is derived as a percentage of this. Out of this total of grant supplementary and specific grants are allocated along with domestic rate relief. The remainder is left for block grant. Since block grant is by far the largest component of total exchequer grants to local authorities we will spend time analysing how block grant is determined. The basic accounting identity which is central to the discussion is:

$$B_i = E_i - \{GRP_i \cdot RV_i\}$$

where B_i = block grant received by the ith local authority

E_i = relevant expenditure of the ith authority (grant-related expenditure)

GRP_i = the grant-related poundage

RV_i = the rateable value of the ith authority.

Grant will increase if local relevant expenditures increase and will decline if the grant-related poundage or the rateable value increases.

The grant-related expenditure is calculated centrally for each local authority according to an assessment of its expenditure needs. This assessment is made by taking into account cost factors, levels of service provision, demographic factors and socio-economic influences. The grant-related expenditures will be unequal across local authorities but they are supposed to reflect the costs of providing comparable levels of service of similar quality for all local governments.

The grant-related poundage schedule is calculated from the GRE and is based on the proposition that different local authorities producing the same services should face the same rate poundage. Since different types of local authorities (e.g. shire counties and district councils) produce different combinations of services each class of authority will have its own GRE schedule. This relationship between GRE and GRP is shown in Figure 9.7. The line AB shows the grant-related poundage that would have to be levied in order that a local authority be able to spend a particular level of GRE. At the point B a threshold is reached at which the schedule tapers – the slope of BC exceeds that of AB. Thus if a local authority overspends in the sense that it actually spends more than its centrally determined/assessed GRE then it will receive less grant. Beyond C total block grant will increase but at a decreasing rate as expenditure increases (in some cases total grant might fall).

The tapering of the GRP schedule gives central government an instrument of control over the local authorities. By making the schedule steeper (e.g. BC compared to AB) more of the additional spending is paid by the local tax payer through an increase in local taxes (rates). It is hoped that the political response to this local fiscal change will be to bring local government spending under control. The central government can, through the block grant, effect greater control over local public spending. This it can do by, (a) moving the schedule ABC vertically up or down, (b) shifting the position of the threshold, i.e. the point B, or (c) changing the slopes of the schedule, e.g. making BC steeper.

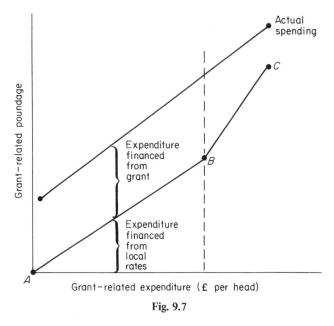

Fig. 9.7

It is too early to report upon the effects of the new grant system. This awaits a period of time after the block grant has been in operation. However, a few remarks are possible. First, the new system introduces a great deal of uncertainty into local government decision-making. This uncertainty arises because the actual amount of block grant which a local government will receive is not known for about two years after the expenditure has been incurred. The grant is paid on the basis of actual expenditure and this is not known until the local authority accounts have been audited, which can take eighteen months to two years. Moreover, the total block grant is cash limited. If all claims for grant entitlement exceed the total available then each claim will be scaled down proportionately. Second, the amount of grant which a local authority receives will depend in part upon the decisions of other local authorities. For example, if some authorities overspend and as a result have grant withheld from them as a penalty then this leaves more grant to be paid out of the rest. The same applies to underspenders.

CHAPTER 10

Taxation: An Introduction

Taxes are a portion of the produce of the land and labour of a country placed at the disposal of the government.
David Ricardo, *Principles of Political Economy and Taxation*

Taxes are collected by governments not only to finance their expenditure but also for purposes of stabilisation, distribution and allocation. (These roles were discussed more fully in Chapter 3.) The overall level of taxes may be chosen in an attempt to stabilise the level of employment, prices or the balance of payments. Governments also try to influence the distribution of income and wealth by varying the tax structure. In addition, taxes may be selected for their allocative effects. Almost all taxes have some effects on resource allocation and they generally impose certain costs on society. Thus an objective of taxation is to minimise these costs and perhaps to encourage particular activities like savings or investment or to discourage other activities like the consumption of cigarettes. Our concern will be primarily with the distributive and allocative effects of taxes.

We saw in Chapter 6 that tax structures vary between countries (see also section on international comparisons below) and that only part of government expenditure in the UK (and in other countries) is financed by taxes. The reason is that taxation is not the only way of financing government expenditure. Expenditure can also be financed by charges to the public (e.g. for admission to a swimming pool) by the surplus (profits) of nationalised industries, and by borrowing (the public sector borrowing requirement). These various non-tax sources of revenue all have important economic implications, even when the revenue they raise is small. Some of the questions of principle raised by these non-tax items are:

(1) What services provided by the public sector should be charged directly to users?
(2) Should any charges be based on average cost? Marginal cost? Historical cost? Replacement cost?
(3) Should the charge be the same for all, or should some (e.g. the poor, or the aged) pay less?

(All of the above relate both to services provided directly by the government (e.g. health, education, housing) and to those provided by public corporations).

(4) How much should be raised by borrowing when the economy is fully employed?

(5) When there is unemployment?

(6) Should a given amount of borrowing be raised with a constant money supply or with an expanded money supply?

(7) What are the costs of government borrowing in terms of its effect on interest rates? How will changes in interest rates affect savings investment and growth in the economy?

(8) Does it matter if the money is borrowed domestically or abroad?

Clearly, these important and wide-ranging questions raise a number of issues in fields such as the economics of nationalised industries, stabilisation economics and monetary economics. Space limitations make it impossible for us to deal with these questions, but it is important to remember that our decision to concentrate exclusively on certain taxes does mean that many important issues are neglected. This is particularly important when the gap between expenditure and the revenue can amount to as much as 11 per cent of GNP at factor cost as it did in 1975 (see Table 6.10 above).

Principles of taxation

Taxes are supposed to be 'fair'. While it might prove easy to find general agreement to this proposition, it is less easy to find agreement as to what 'fair' means. It is possible to identify two separate concepts of fairness: horizontal equity and vertical equity. Horizontal equity means that people with equivalent circumstances should be treated fairly, while vertical equity is concerned with fairness between people with differing circumstances. The circumstances we have in mind include income (a flow) and wealth (a stock), but there is not general agreement as to how income and wealth should be defined for tax purposes (see Chapters 14 and 16). Horizontal equity then is concerned with fairness between persons with the same income and wealth. It does not necessarily mean that two people with identical income and wealth should pay identical amounts of tax (we may for example wish cigarette smokers to pay more tax). Vertical equity is generally taken to mean that those with large amounts of income and/or wealth should pay more tax than those with less income and/or wealth. Some of the reasons that have been advanced for taxing those with high income/wealth more heavily were discussed in the appendix to Chapter 3, where we examined both the benefit and ability-to-pay arguments for taxes, and we return to the issue again in Chapter 20. The other basic principles of taxation can be briefly stated. Taxes should be sufficiently simple so that those affected can understand them. Costs of collection (both government and taxpayer) should be as low as possible consistent with other objectives. Finally, taxes should be designed to minimise harmful distortions caused by the tax. Much of the rest of this book is concerned with explaining the meaning of this last sentence.

Classification of taxes

Direct v. indirect taxes

Taxes are commonly classified into direct and indirect taxes. Broadly, direct taxes are taxes levied (directly) on individuals, households, firms, etc. Indirect taxes are, broadly, taxes levied on goods and services and hence paid for only indirectly. Thus the distinction depends in part on who ultimately pays the tax. As we will see, this is a complex question and the direct–indirect dichotomy can be misleading because it is based on the assumption that we know the answer before we start. An example may help. Is an employer's social security (national insurance) tax a direct or an indirect tax? One view is that the employee will be better off (when unemployed or retired) because of national insurance, and that as a result he accepts a lower wage because of his employer's national insurance contribution. Thus the employer's contribution is a direct tax. This was the view at one time adopted by the Central Statistical Office (CSO) in Britain. Another view is that wages are not affected by employers' social security contributions and that these taxes are passed on to the consumer in the form of higher prices. Thus the employer's contribution is an indirect tax. The CSO has now adopted this view. While it does little harm to speak loosely of income tax as a direct tax or VAT as an indirect tax, our preference is to avoid the use of the terms except in the most clear-cut cases, because the direct–indirect terminology implies that we know who pays the tax when in fact this is one of the things we have to find out.

Another reason for avoiding the direct–indirect terminology is that it led to a long – largely fruitless – debate in the literature that turned out in the end to revolve largely around a misunderstanding of terms. (Those interested in following this debate are referred to an excellent summary by Walker).

The OECD list

In our view it is preferable to avoid classification systems (such as direct or indirect) that prejudge important questions. We therefore have a general preference for classifications that are descriptive, not prescriptive. It is also obviously convenient to have a classification system that is used as widely as possible. For these reasons we see much to commend the OECD classification of taxes and we reproduce it in Table 10.1.

While preferring the OECD list to many classifications, any scheme must have arbitrary features. For example, the OECD counts dog licences and motor

Table 10.1   The OECD list of taxes

1000	*Taxes on income, profits and capital gains*
 1100 Individual taxes on income, profits and capital gains
   1110 On income and profits
   1120 On capital gains
 1200 Corporate taxes on profits and capital gains
   1210 On profits
   1220 On capital gains
 1300 Unallocable as between 1100 and 1200
2000	*Social security contributions*
 2100 Employees
 2200 Employers
 2300 Self-employed or non-employed
3000	*Employers' payroll or manpower taxes*
4000	*Taxes on property*
 4100 Recurrent taxes on immovable property
   4110 Households
   4120 Other
 4200 Recurrent taxes on net wealth
   4210 Individual
   4220 Corporate
 4300 Estate, inheritance and gift taxes
   4310 Estate and inheritances
   4320 Gifts
 4400 Taxes on financial and capital transactions
 4500 Non-recurrent taxes
   4510 On net wealth
   4520 Other non-recurrent
 4600 Other
5000	*Taxes on goods and services*
 5100 Taxes on production, sale, transfer, leasing and delivery of goods and rendering of services
   5110 General taxes
     5111 Value added taxes
     5112 Sales taxes
     5113 Other
   5120 Taxes on specific goods and services
     5121 Excises
     5122 Profits of fiscal monopolies
     5123 Customs and imports duties
     5124 Taxes on exports
     5125 Taxes on investment goods
     5126 Taxes on specific services
     5127 Other international taxes
     5128 Other taxes
 5200 Taxes on use of, or permission to use, goods or to perform activities in connection with specified goods
   5210 Recurrent taxes
     5211 Paid by households in respect of motor vehicles
     5212 Paid by others in respect of motor vehicles
     5213 Paid in respect of other goods
   5220 Non-recurrent taxes
6000	*Other taxes*
 6100 Paid solely by business
 6200 Other

Source: *Revenue Statistics of OECD Member Countries 1965–1980* (Paris: OECD, 1981), pp. 35–6.

vehicle licences as taxes (on goods and services), but TV licences as non-taxes. The scheme also omits cash transfers from the government (e.g. family allowances), although it is possible to think of such transfers as negative taxes.

The OECD classification differs from the classification of taxes used in Britain in some respects; for example, capital gains tax is treated as a wealth tax in the British accounts and as a tax on income in the OECD list (see Chapter 14 for further discussion of this point). In Britain stamp duties, which are levied on the transfer of assets, are treated as an expenditure tax, and in the OECD list as a property tax.

One of the major advantages of the OECD list is that the OECD has undertaken a major exercise – which is updated annually – comparing the tax structures of all OECD countries using a single consistent set of definitions. We will make considerable use of these comparisons below and in subsequent chapters. One difficulty with these comparisons is that OECD shows taxes as a proportion of GDP at market prices. For reasons we explained in Chapter 6 we would have preferred the comparison to be made using GDP at factor cost, but this is an issue on which reasonable people can differ and the most important consideration is that we know what basis we are using.

The structure of UK taxation

The ways in which the British Government has raised its tax revenue in the period 1965-80 is shown in Table 10.2. In the decade to 1975 there was a very sharp increase in the importance of taxes on individual incomes (Code 1110). As we will see in Chapter 14, this is to be expected in an inflationary period. There was a correspondingly sharp fall in the proportion of revenue raised from taxing commodities (Code 5000) which fell from one-third to one-quarter of tax receipts. The fall was particularly severe in the revenue from specific commodity taxes (Code 5120) or unit taxes as we prefer to call them. The revenue from these taxes fell from about one-quarter of all revenue to about one-seventh. Unit or specific taxes such as much of the tax on beer, spirits and tobacco are taxes that are levied as pounds sterling per unit. As the price of the unit increases in an inflationary period the tax stays constant, which means that the tax, which is fixed in money terms, declines as a proportion of the price unless deliberate action is taken to raise the nominal amount of the tax. *Ad valorem* taxes, called general taxes in the OECD list, are expressed in percentage terms. With VAT, for example, the amount of tax due increases as the price rises and it can be seen that these taxes have increased their share of revenue. These changes were particularly or wholly reversed between 1975 and 1980. The proportion of tax raised by income tax reverted to its 1965 level. While unit taxes continued to decline in importance, VAT was increased sharply (in 1979) raising the overall proportion of commodity taxes. The employers national insurance surcharge (Code 3000) formed an important new source of revenue. These issues are considered further in Chapter 17.

Table 10.2 The structure of UK taxation 1965–80

OECD code	Taxes	1965		1975		1980[c]	
		£m	%[b]	£m	%[b]	£m	%[b]
1100	Individual income, profits + gains	3264	29.8	14,368	38.2	23,796	29.5
1200	Corporate profits + gains	763	6.9	2330	6.2	6855	8.5
	Total 1000[a]	4027	36.8	16,698	44.4	30,651	37.9
2100	Employees' social security	785	7.2	2477	6.6	8188	10.1
2200	Employers' social security	831	7.6	3868	10.3	5171	6.4
	Total 2000[a]	1685	15.4	6540	17.4	13,676	16.9
3000	Employers' payroll or manpower tax	0	0.0	0	0.0	3426	4.2
4100	Rates	1228	11.2	4178	11.1	8624	10.7
4300	Estate, inheritance, gift	287	2.6	307	0.8	447	0.6
4400	Stamp duties	76	0.7	266	0.7	631	0.8
	Total 4000[a]	1591	14.5	4753	12.7	9733	12.0
5110	General commodity	648	5.9	3299	8.8	11,133	13.8
5120	Specific Commodity	2728	24.9	5541	14.7	10,761	13.3
	Total 5000[a]	3611	33.0	9537	25.4	23,158	28.7
	Total Tax Revenue[a]	10,944	100.0	37,572	100.0	80,784	100.0

Notes: [a] Totals are generally greater than the sum of individual items shown as some small items have been omitted.
[b] Of total tax revenue.
[c] Provisional.

Source: *Revenue Statistics of OECD Member Countries 1965–1980* (Paris: OECD, 1981), pp. 140, 173.

International comparison of taxes

A useful means of finding a perspective on an individual country's taxes is to see how they compare with taxes in other countries. There is no single comparison that will provide an overall picture, and indeed, it is possible with a selective presentation of statistics to 'prove' a variety of points (e.g. British taxes are 'too high', 'too low'); for example the country with the highest rate(s) of income tax will not necessarily collect the highest proportion of personal income or of national income in income tax. A further problem is that detailed definitions (of income, for example) are likely to vary from country to country. Fortunately, the Taxation Division of the OECD has published a careful comparison of tax systems that we have drawn upon freely.

Table 10.3 shows estimates of taxation as a proportion of GDP at market prices for OECD countries for the period 1965-80. It can be seen that in every country total tax including social security was higher in 1980 than in 1965. Some countries such as Sweden and The Netherlands have consistently been countries with a high ratio of tax revenue to GDP. Other countries such as

Table 10.3 Total tax revenue in OECD countries as percentage of GDP at market prices

	1965	*1970*	*1975*	*1980*[a]
Australia	23.78	25.49	29.14	25.82[b]
Austria	34.64	35.66	38.54	41.54
Belgium	31.21	35.96	41.07	42.49
Canada	25.94	32.00	32.93	32.81
Denmark	30.05	40.23	41.05	45.14
Finland	30.13	32.18	36.15	34.46
France	34.97	35.58	37.44	42.51
Germany	31.59	32.80	35.68	37.23
Greece	20.58	24.30	24.64	27.69[b]
Ireland	26.02	31.23	32.49	37.54
Italy	27.25	27.91	28.98	30.09[b]
Japan	18.05	19.72	21.10	25.85
Luxembourg	30.83	31.94	43.57	47.56
Netherlands	35.48	39.89	45.80	46.19
New Zealand	24.32	26.39	30.04	31.18[b]
Norway	33.22	39.19	44.82	47.36
Portugal	18.57	23.21	24.82	29.78
Spain	14.73	17.22	15.60	23.16
Sweden	35.60	40.89	44.24	49.87
Switzerland	20.71	23.81	25.61	30.74
Turkey	14.93	17.63	20.67	20.84[b]
United Kingdom	30.80	37.51	36.08	35.91
United States	26.51	30.10	30.18	30.69
Range	15-36	17-41	16-46	21-50

Notes: [a] 1980 figures provisional.
   [b] 1979.

Source: *Revenue Statistics of OECD Member Countries 1965-1980* (Paris: OECD, 1981) pp. 79, 174.

Turkey and Spain have tended to remain relatively low tax countries. Britain remained in the middle with a rank of eleventh in 1980 compared with a rank of ninth in 1965.

Table 10.4 contains provisional 1980 figures for the importance of various broad groups of taxes relative to tax revenue. Greece (16 per cent) and France (18 per cent) put the lowest reliance on taxes on income and profits, while Australia (55 per cent), Denmark (55 per cent) and New Zealand (62 per cent) put the greatest reliance on these taxes. The UK (38 per cent) was fourteenth out of the twenty-three countries. Australia and New Zealand (both nil) put least reliance on social security taxes while France (43 per cent) and Spain (45 per cent) put most emphasis on social security taxes. The UK (17 per cent) was thirteenth. The UK (12 per cent) and the US (10 per cent) were the countries with the most reliance on property taxes with Sweden and Portugal (both 1 per cent) giving least weight to these taxes. Greece (45 per cent) and Ireland (44 per cent) placed most emphasis on taxes on commodities with the US (17 per cent) and Luxembourg (10 per cent) giving least emphasis to these taxes.

Table 10.4 Percentage shares of tax revenues, OECD countries 1980[a]

Country	Type of tax: OECD code:	Income and Profits 1000	Social Security 2000	Payroll 3000	Property 4000	Goods and Services 5000	Other 6000
Australia[b]		54.63	–	5.09	8.57	31.71	–
Austria		26.68	31.48	6.98	2.77	31.25	0.84
Belgium		42.35	30.74	–	2.99	23.92	–
Canada		45.97	10.65	–	9.27	32.63	1.48
Denmark		54.63	1.79	–	5.93	37.52	0.13
Finland		48.47	8.64	–	1.97	40.92	–
France		18.17	43.12	2.15	3.38	30.14	3.04
Germany		35.44	34.10	0.16	2.63	26.99	0.68
Greece[b]		15.56	30.32	1.29	7.72	45.07	–
Ireland		36.67	14.30	–	5.20	43.70	0.13
Italy[b]		31.49	36.74	–	4.28	27.49	–
Japan		40.79	30.10	–	8.05	16.21	4.85
Luxembourg		44.87	28.95	0.67	5.80	19.71	–
Netherlands		32.45	38.52	–	3.94	24.82	0.27
New Zealand[b]		68.49	–	–	8.57	22.94	–
Norway		47.24	15.17	–	1.57	35.39	0.62
Portugal		22.27	27.09	2.27	1.46	40.33	6.59
Spain		26.20	44.97	–	5.58	23.03	0.23
Sweden		43.35	28.68	2.72	0.94	24.31	–
Switzerland		41.50	30.82	–	7.24	20.45	–
Turkey[b]		54.56	6.34	–	5.92	33.18	–
United Kingdom		37.94	16.93	4.24	12.05	28.72	0.12
United States		46.98	26.34	–	10.06	16.62	–

Notes: [a] 1980 figures provisional.
       [b] 1979.

Source: *Revenue Statistics of OECD Member Countries 1965–1980* (Paris: OECD, 1981), pp. 80, 175.

For our final comparison we report a special OECD study of the position of a taxpayer with the average earnings for production workers. Each (male) worker is assumed to have average earnings from employment and no other income. Figure 10.1 shows the position for each country after the deduction of income and social security payments and after the addition of cash transfers. The figures should be treated cautiously for they make no allowance for

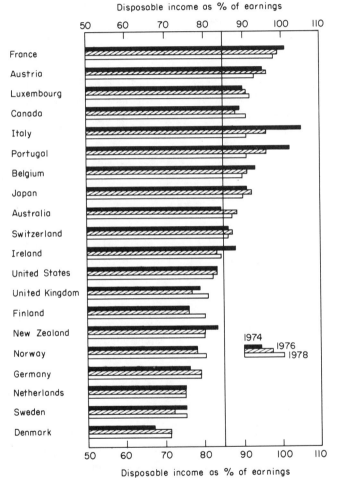

Figure 10.1 Disposable income as percentage of gross earnings. (One-earner families at APWs[a] wage level[b],[c] 1974–78.)

Notes: [a] Average production worker.

[b] Disposable income equals gross earnings minus income tax and employees' social security contributions paid plus cash transfers received.

[c] Countries are ranked by the percentages relating to 1978.

Source: *The Tax Benefit Position of Selected Income Groups in OECD Member Countries* (Paris; OECD, 1980), p. 42.

differences in government services in different countries, and as only income and social security taxes are deducted, the comparison will be affected by the relative importance of these taxes. It should also be noted that the average production worker is nearer the top of the income distribution in some countries than in others. For the single worker disposable income as a percentage of gross earnings in 1978 was lowest in Denmark and highest in France, with the UK somewhat below the average of 85 per cent.

In the light of the frequent references to the high levels of taxation in Britain the data in this section may have come as something of a surprise, for in general it does not suggest that Britain is a particularly highly taxed country. Two points should, however, be borne in mind. British taxes would clearly be very much higher if government expenditure were kept at the same level and if there were no public sector borrowing requirement (PSBR). The PSBR amounted to 10 per cent of GDP at market prices in 1975. This means that the tax–GDP ratio is not a good measure of the size of the government sector and if other countries had smaller deficits than Britain then Britain would rank higher in a ranking of countries by size of the public sector. Second, when people think of high British taxes they often think particularly of income taxes. We have seen that the importance of income taxation grew in the UK during the 1970s (see Table 10.2), and a more detailed international comparison of income taxes in Chapter 14 does lend some support to the view that British income taxes were relatively heavy, particularly for those with either very high or very low taxable incomes. The international comparison of production workers above puts the British worker at the bottom of the top third in 1978. However, in 1979 there was a considerable switch from income taxation to VAT. Given this general evidence that Britain is not especially highly taxed, it is impossible to be sure why so many people in Britain believe British taxes are particularly high, but a possible explanation is that marginal tax rates (see glossary below) were (until 1979) *very* high (up to 98 per cent on an earned income) for a *very* few people. Continual reference to these very high rates may create an impression that is not justified by the overall picture.

Glossary of tax terminology

To avoid scattered and/or repeated definitions, we define below some of the terms we will most frequently employ. Italicized terms in the definitions are defined elsewhere in the Glossary. See also table of income definitions (Table 14.2).

Ability-to-pay principles Shorthand for the view that the taxes should be heaviest on those with the highest incomes and/or wealth. See appendix to Chapter 3 for a fuller discussion.

Average rate of tax Amount of tax paid per period divided by income in that period. Synonymous with *effective rate of tax*.

Avoidance   Legal rearrangement of one's affairs so as to minimise one's tax liability.

Basic rate of tax   The rate of tax payable on the first £11,250 (1981-82) of taxable income in the UK.

Benefit principle   Shorthand for the view that taxes should be levied in accordance with the benefits arising from the government services financed by the taxes. See appendix to Chapter 3 for a fuller discussion.

Burden   See *excess burden* and *incidence.*

Cumulative basis   A system of withholding tax on wages and salaries at source by adding (or when appropriate subtracting) this pay period's *taxable income* to the cumulated total (i.e. cumulated gross income less cumulated allowances and deductions).

Deadweight loss   Synonymous with *excess burden.*

Deductions   Income in the UK that is free of tax if used for certain specified purposes such as the payment of retirement annuity premiums and allowable interest payments.

Direct taxes   Taxes on persons (which can be varied in the light of personal circumstances).

Effective rate of tax   Synonymous with *average rate of tax.*

Evasion   Illegal rearrangement of one's affairs so as to minimise one's tax liability.

Excess burden   The net welfare loss from a tax which is total loss of welfare from a tax less the welfare loss caused by raising the same revenue in a way that does not disturb economic activity.

Exemptions   Synonymous with *personal allowances.*

Final income   *Original income* plus all benefits allocated by the UK Central Statistical Office (CSO) less all taxes allocated by the CSO.

Gross income   *Original income* plus state pensions and cash benefits.

Gross taxable income   The sum of all sources of income that are subject to tax.

Higher rates of tax   Rates of tax charged in the UK on *taxable incomes* over £11,250 (1981-82).

Horizontal equity   Equal treatment of persons with equivalent circumstances.

Incidence   The final resting place of a tax. Thus the incidence of a tax is on the person who, in the end, pays the tax.

Indirect taxes   Taxes on goods (which cannot be varied in the light of individual circumstances).

Investment income   Interest, dividends and rent. Synonymous with *unearned income.*

Investment income surcharge   An extra tax on investment income in the UK imposed in addition to income tax from the early 1970s.

Marginal rate of tax   The rate of tax charged on a small increase in income.

Neutral taxes   Taxes that have no *excess burden.*

Original income   Term used in the UK by the CSO for *gross taxable income* plus imputed rent.

PAYE (Pay-as-You-Earn)   The name for the UK system of withholding tax from wages and salaries on a *cumulative basis.*

Personal allowances   Income free of income tax or more precisely the difference between *total net income* and *taxable income.*

Progressive tax.   A tax with an *average rate of tax* that rises as income rises. (It may be noted that if negative taxes (transfers) are included the *average tax* may be negative with a progressive tax/transfer system. If there are no negative taxes the *marginal rate* must lie above the *average* rate. With transfers a progressive tax may have the *marginal rate* below the average rate. It may also be noted that some authors define progressive to mean rising *marginal rates of tax.*)

Proportional tax   A tax with an average *rate of tax* that remains constant as income rises. (It may be noted that the *marginal rate of tax* will equal the *average rate of tax* with a proportional tax.)

Regressive tax   A tax with an *average rate of tax* that falls as income rises.

Surtax   Predecessor to *higher rates of tax.*

Taxable income   *Total net income* less *personal allowances.*

Total deductions   Retirement annuity payments, alimony, allowable interest and other annual payments.

Total earned income   *Gross earned income* less employee's superannuation contributions, employment expenses, losses, capital allowance, and stock relief.

Total income   *Total earned income* plus *total investment income.*

Total investment income   Gross investment income (see Table 14.2) less allowances against rent.

Total net income   *Total income* less *total deductions.*

Unearned income   Synonymous with *investment income.*

Vertical equity   The desirable degree of unequal treatment of persons with unequal incomes and/or wealth.

CHAPTER 11

Partial Equilibrium Analysis of Taxation

Taxes may have a great variety of effects. They may cause some goods to become more expensive relative to others and so cause a change in the pattern of consumption. They may fall more heavily on some households than others, thus altering the distribution of net income. They may affect people's willingness to work and to save, and to take risks; that is, they may affect the total *supply* of resources available to the economy. They reduce the taxpayer's purchasing power over goods produced in the private sector. Unless the government purchases precisely the same total amount of each good as previously purchased by the private sector there will be a change in the pattern of demand. It is also likely that a change in taxes will alter the level of demand and hence the level of employment, and so on.

In order to keep the overall length of this book within manageable limits we are excluding, so far as possible, any discussion of the role of taxes in stabilising the economy. This is not always easy to do. We might say we would restrict ourselves to tax changes that left total government revenue unchanged. This would create little difficulty if we were considering substituting a tax on apples for a tax on bananas; but if we were considering raising taxes paid by 'rich' households and reducing taxes paid by 'poor' households, a change that left government revenue unchanged would increase the level of aggregate demand if the marginal propensity to consume of the 'rich' is lower than the marginal propensity to consume of the 'poor'. Even if we are considering a tax change that leaves total demand unaffected, the balance between supply and demand will be affected if the tax changes affect total supply (e.g. by affecting the amount of work people do).

The limitations imposed by our assumptions should become clear in the next chapter, but for the meantime the reader is simply asked to note that the analysis in this chapter basically assumes the stabilisation problem away. This is not a very serious problem for small tax changes on, for example, small industries, but is a more serious problem for large changes on large industries or groups of industries.

Our concern then will for the most part be with the allocative and distributive effect of taxes. The present chapter contains a partial equilibrium analysis of taxes and the next chapter a general equilibrium analysis. An example can clarify both this distinction between partial and general equilibrium and the equally important distinction between the legal incidence of a tax and its economic incidence. Suppose we are considering putting a new tax on corporate profits. The law would require corporations to pay the tax. Thus the *legal* incidence of the tax is on the corporation. But a corporation is only a legal entity – not a real person. Some real persons or households in the economy must be made worse off by the tax. It might be that the corporation would reduce its dividends to shareholders by the amount of the tax, in which case *economic* incidence of the tax would be on shareholders. It might be that the corporation would attempt to reduce wages by the amount of the tax; if it succeeded the economic incidence of the tax would be on the workers. A third possibility is that the corporation would raise consumer prices by the amount of the tax, which makes the economic incidence of the tax fall on the consumers.

If analysis stops at finding which of these possibilities occurs (or more realistically in what combination they occur) our analysis would be a partial equilibrium analysis. But the final repercussions of the tax will not stop there. For example, if shareholders tend to come from high-income households and workers from low-income households, then the incidence of the tax affects the distribution of income. If high-income households tend to purchase different goods from those purchased by low-income households, there will be further effects on the pattern of demand. Suppose high-income households have a high income elasticity of demand for travel and low-income households have a low income elasticity of demand for travel. In that case, if the incidence of tax were on shareholders the demand for travel would fall by a greater amount than it would fall if the incidence were on low-income households. If the demand for travel were to change, then the demand for factors used in producing travel goods (airline pilots, automotive assembly workers, etc.) would fall, producing a fall in income of those concerned. To trace through the full effects of a tax change is thus very complex and requires a general equilibrium analysis. One example of a general equilibrium approach is the subject matter of the next chapter. The present chapter contains a partial equilibrium approach to taxes, and it should be clear to the reader that this approach is inevitably incomplete. The reader is also asked to note that some of the partial equilibrium results are called into question by developments in optimal taxation (see Chapter 20).

Taxes on the output of single industries

(1) Competitive industries

We begin our partial equilibrium analysis of taxes by considering the effects of taxes on goods and factors that are traded in perfectly competitive markets.

The formal analysis is the same whether we are considering a product market or a factor market, but for convenience of exposition we will refer to product markets for the most part.

(*a*) *Unit taxes*. The tax may be expressed in one of two ways: a tax per unit of output or a tax as a proportion of the selling price. A tax per unit of output is called a unit tax (or sometimes a specific commodity tax). In Britain a substantial proportion of the tax on cigarettes, alcoholic beverages and petrol is a unit tax (see Chapter 16 for detail). The taxes are expressed as £x per pound of tobacco, £x per gallon of spirit of a specified alcoholic content, or £x per gallon of petrol.[1] Taxes expressed as a percentage of the price are called *ad valorem* taxes. Value added tax (VAT) is an *ad valorem* tax (as was the purchase tax that it replaced in 1973).

We will look at the effects of unit taxes first. Figure 11.1(a) will aid the exposition. Prior to the introduction of the tax there is an original demand curve D_0 and an original supply curve S_0 leading to equilibrium price and quantity of P_0 and Q_0 respectively. A tax of t per unit of output is then levied. We can think of the tax as *either* raising the supply curve *or* lowering the demand curve by t. Let us first consider it as raising the supply price. Prior to the introduction of the tax, firms were willing to supply Q_0 units at the price P_0. But after the tax they will require a price of $P_0 + t$ in order to be willing to supply Q_0 units. The supply curve will thus shift vertically upwards by the amount of the tax to S_G. This gives us two supply curves. There is the tax-inclusive supply curve or gross supply S_G (which represents the supply on offer to the consumer), and a net or tax-exclusive supply curve S_N. The difference between S_G and S_N is t: the amount received by the government for each unit sold. As consumers are faced with S_G they will demand Q_1 units for which they will pay a gross (tax-inclusive) price of P_G. Producers will receive $P_N = P_G - t$. The effect of the tax is thus to raise the price paid by the consumer from P_0 to P_G, reduce the price received by the producer from P_0 to P_N, reduce the industry output by $Q_0 - Q_1$, and bring in revenue of $P_N P_G BD$ to the government.

Any final understanding of the effects of the tax will depend on an understanding of what the government does with the revenue. Clearly the economic effects of (1) reducing the national debt, (2) building a hospital or (3) giving the money back in the form of a lump sum handout are likely to differ. For the moment we ignore these effects.

Prior to the introduction of the tax, consumers' surplus was $P_0 AE$ and producers' surplus was $FP_0 E$. After the introduction of the tax, consumers' surplus falls to $P_G AB$ and producers' surplus to $FP_N D$. There is thus a *gross* loss from the tax of $P_N P_G BED$ ($P_0 P_G BE$ from the consumer and $P_N P_0 ED$ from the producer). However, it seems reasonable to assume that the tax revenue will be used to provide something useful. If what is provided by the tax revenue is of equal value to the revenue that pays for it, then we subtract the revenue raised from the tax from the gross loss to find the net loss. The triangle BDE then represents the *net* loss to the society from the imposition of the tax. This

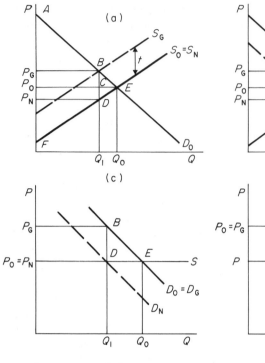

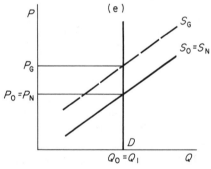

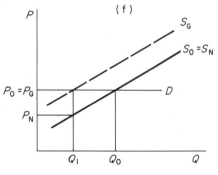

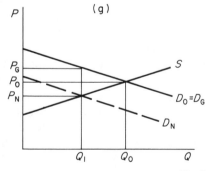

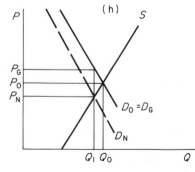

Fig. 11.1

net loss is variously referred to as the 'deadweight loss' of the tax and the 'excess burden' of the tax. If the government services provided from the tax revenue are worth more to the public, i.e. if there is consumers' surplus, there need be no net loss to society from the combined effects of the taxation and the resulting expenditure.

We have looked at the tax as adding to the supply price of the taxed good. Alternatively we may regard it as a reduction in the price of the good that the producer receives. Figure 11.1(b) shows the same pretax equilibrium as Figure 11.1(a). A unit tax t is introduced, which means that the amount available to the producer falls by t at every level of output, which gives a new net of tax demand curve $D_N(= D_G - t)$. The reader should verify that this alternative method of presentation gives identical results. Frequently, as will be seen, this alternative presentation is more convenient; for example if the supply curve is completely inelastic. Shifting the supply curve is perhaps more intuitively appealing if we think of the legislation as saying the tax is paid by the producer, while shifting the demand curve is more appealing if the legislation says the tax is paid by the consumer. The fact that two approaches yield identical results reinforces the distinction between the legal and economic incidences of the tax.

It can be seen from Figure 11.1(c) that if the supply curve is perfectly elastic the price paid by the consumer rises by just the amount of the tax. Thus the burden of the tax – *BED* – and the loss of consumers' surplus are identical (there is no producers' surplus). The situation in which prices rise by just the amount of the tax is an interesting case for two rather different reasons. First, under certain assumptions competitive industries can be expected to have perfectly elastic long-run supply curves. Second, official calculations of tax incidence in the UK assume that prices will rise by the amount of the tax (see Chapter 17). This prompts the question, 'Is it reasonable to assume that most or all of British industry is both perfectly competitive and in long-run equilibrium?' If not, is there an alternative theory that could account for the prices rising by exactly the amount of the tax? We discuss the questions further below, but in the meantime the reader should note that the same effect on price will occur if demand is totally inelastic (see Figure 11.1(e)).

More generally, we find that both the incidence and the excess burden of the tax depend on supply and demand elasticities. In Figure 11.1(d) the supply curve is perfectly inelastic and it is clear from the figure that in this case the price paid by the consumer will be unaffected by the introduction of the tax $(P_0 = P_G)$, so that incidence of the tax is entirely on the producer. Note also that perfectly inelastic supply means that quantity is also unaffected by the introduction of the tax and there is no excess burden from the tax. A tax with no excess burden is particularly attractive to economists and has led to proposals for a tax on land as a particularly good tax on the assumption that the total supply of land is fixed.[2]

Figures 11.1(e) and 11.1(f) show the effects of totally inelastic and perfectly elastic demand respectively. With zero elastic demand price rises by just the amount of the tax (as with perfectly elastic supply) and there is no excess burden (as with zero elastic supply). Perfectly elastic demand on the other hand (11.1(f)) means no increase in price (as with zero elastic supply).

For most goods supply and demand elasticities are both likely to lie between zero and infinity (elasticity may be negative, but this is more likely with factors such as labour than with goods). In these cases the extent of the rise in price, the incidence and the excess burden all depend on these elasticities. For example, Figures 11.1(g) and 11.1(h) show that when elasticities are high tax receipts tend to be lower and excess burden higher than when elasticities are low. This suggests that unit taxes should tend to be concentrated on goods with low demand and/or supply elasticities. The high unit tax on cigarettes in Britain seems to meet with criterion very well as demand elasticity for cigarettes is generally assumed to be very low. This is perhaps paradoxical, because the government's intention is to reduce cigarette consumption – presumably on the argument that the external effects of cigarette smoking mean that the demand curve does not in this case measure – even in the roughest way – the net *social* benefits from consumption.

(*b*) Ad valorem *taxes.* It is a simple matter to extend the analysis to *ad valorem* taxes, which are expressed in percentage terms. Diagrammatically the only difference is that we now shift the demand (or supply) curve by a constant *percentage* amount rather than by a constant absolute amount. Figure 11.2(a) shows the effect of introducing an *ad valorem* tax where the rate equals EF/EQ_0. Price rises from P_0 to P_G, revenue of BD per unit ($P_N P_G BD$ in total) is collected, the producer receives P_N, quantity falls from Q_0 to Q_1 and the excess burden is BED.

We should draw the British reader's attention to the potential dangers in applying this analysis to VAT. While VAT is an *ad valorem* tax, it is so broadly based that partial equilibrium analysis is not generally appropriate. It would on the other hand be appropriate to use partial equilibrium analysis to examine minor changes in the coverage of VAT. For example, grape juice used by home wine-makers was originally exempted from VAT (as a food), but subsequently VAT was levied on it.

(*c*) *Comparison of unit and* ad valorem *taxes.* To raise the same amount of revenue a unit tax has to be set at a higher percentage of the original price than an *ad valorem* tax, as can be verified from Figure 11.2(b). The *ad valorem* tax of EF/FQ_0 raises $P_N P_G BD$ in revenue. To raise the same revenue a unit tax of $BD = EG$ would be needed. EG is a larger proportion of the original price than is EF.

(*d*) *Taxes on goods and inflation.* We now wish to drop the assumption that taxes are the only cause of price changes. Because discussion of the causes of inflation is beyond the scope of this book we will simply assume that inflation

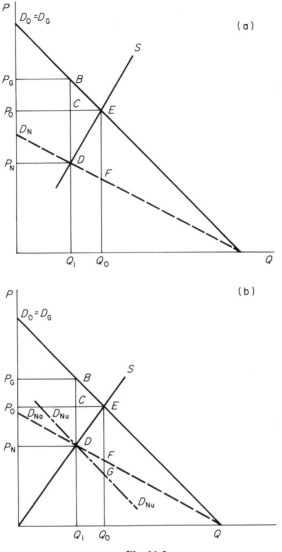

Fig. 11.2

is occurring and ask how this effects our analysis. A great deal is written in standard macroeconomic textbooks about the ways in which taxation may affect the rate of inflation. Our present question is quite different: we want to examine how inflation affects taxation, and we intend to ignore feedback effects on inflation. More specifically, we will assume that in the absence of tax all prices will rise exogenously at the same rate. It is obviously restrictive to assume that (before tax) all prices rise at the same rate. If, in fact, some prices rise faster than others we have a standard and familiar problem of changing relative prices as well as general inflation. We also assume that taxes are not automatically adjusted for inflation. We show that frequently the effect of inflation is to change real tax rates even though nominal rates of taxes have not been altered by Parliament (see Chapter 17 for a discussion of what has happened in the UK).

It is convenient to use a two-period model. Nominal pretax prices in period 2 thus equal nominal pretax prices in period 1 times $1 + r$ where r is the rate of inflation. Thus while nominal prices rise, real prices are constant before tax (but not after tax, as we will see).

In a period of inflation goods that are subject to unit taxes will tend to rise less in price than goods subject to *ad valorem* taxes – assuming no change in tax rates. An *ad valorem* tax will continue to collect the same proportion of price before tax as that price rises. Because a unit tax is a fixed nominal amount per unit, the real tax per unit will fall as prices rise (a tax of 30p on a 20p packet of cigarettes is 150 per cent of the pretax price but the same tax of 30p is 'only' 75 per cent if the price of the cigarettes rises to 40p).

We can compare the two types of taxes with the aid of Figure 11.3. Note the vertical axis measures prices in units of constant real purchasing power. In the first period the figure shows the same prices and quantity with either a unit tax of BD or an *ad valorem* tax of BD/DQ_0^a. In the second period prices have risen by r per cent. This reduces the real value of the unit tax from BD to

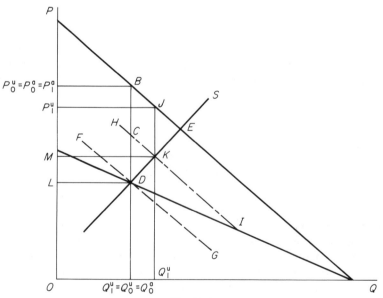

Fig. 11.3

$BC[=BD/(1+r)]$. The net of tax demand curve thus shifts up from *FG* to *HI*. Thus in the second period price (at P_1^u) is lower and output (Q_1^u) higher than with an *ad valorem* tax.

This change in relative prices can be expected to alter the pattern of demand away from goods with *ad valorem* taxes and towards goods with unit taxes. Such a change in the pattern of demand might be thought to be undesirable in some cases. If unit taxes tend to be levied on 'bads' such as tobacco and spirits, and *ad valorem* taxes tend to be levied on 'goods', these relative price changes could tend to increase consumption of cigarettes, etc., over time.

In an inflationary period tax receipts from a unit tax will *probably* fall relative to tax receipts from *ad valorem* tax. In the first period tax receipts from both taxes are equal at $LP_0^u BD$ in Figure 11.3. In the second period the real revenue from the *ad valorem* tax remains unchanged but the revenue from the unit tax changes to $MP_1^u JK$. We want to answer the question, 'Will the tax revenue from the unit tax in the second period be greater or less than the revenue from the *ad valorem* tax in the second period?' As the second period *ad valorem* tax revenue is the same as the first period unit tax revenue we can rephrase this question as 'Will the unit tax revenue in the second period be greater or less than the unit tax revenue in the first period?' If the unit tax revenue in the first period were maximised,[3] clearly tax receipts would fall in the second period with a lower real rate of tax. Likewise if the unit tax rate in the first period were too low to achieve maximum revenue a further reduction in the rate would reduce revenue. Only if the first period unit tax rate were so high that revenue was not being maximised in that period would there be a possibility that tax receipts would rise in the second period. It seems unlikely that a government would knowingly set tax rates so high that receipts fell (unless possibly to discourage consumption of, say, cigarettes), so it appears likely that the normal case is that real tax receipts would fall in the second period. Returning to the *ad valorem* - unit tax comparison, it thus seems likely that real tax receipts will be lower with a unit tax than with *ad valorem* tax. This means that *ad valorem* taxes provide greater built-in flexibility.

Unit and *ad valorem* taxes under monopoly

In analysing the effects of commodity taxes under profit-maximising monopoly, the only additional complication is caused by needing to take account of the divergence between average and marginal revenue.

The effects of the introduction of a unit tax is shown in Figure 11.4(a), where for convenience the case of constant marginal cost is considered.[4] A unit tax of *AB* shifts both average and marginal revenue curves down by the amount of the tax. The gross price will rise to P_G. Tax revenue will be $P_N P_G CE$ and the deadweight loss will be *CDF*. Before tax the monopolist's profit is *AHG* and after tax is *BIH*, so that the monopolist's loss of profit is *BAGI*.

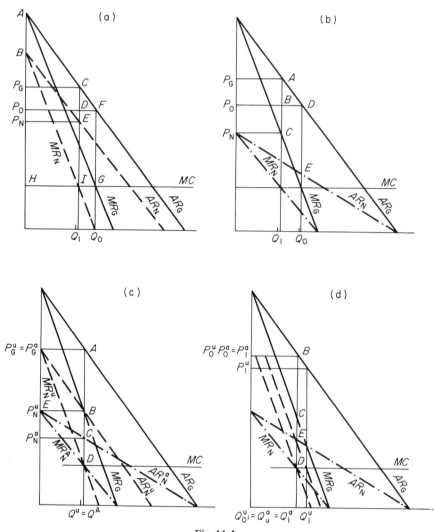

Fig. 11.4

An *ad valorem* tax of DE/EQ_0 will result in the average and marginal revenue curves swinging down to AR_N and MR_N in Figure 11.4(b). The price rises to P_G and revenue from the tax is $P_N P_G AC$. Note that with both unit and *ad valorem* taxes the price rises by less than the tax.

Under monopoly a unit tax will raise less revenue than an *ad valorem* tax for a given effect on price and output. The argument can be illustrated with reference to Figure 11.4(c). With a unit tax of AB, price is P_G^u and output Q^u. If an *ad valorem* tax is to have the same effect on price and output, the marginal revenue curve net of *ad valorem* tax (MR_N^a) must pass through point D. The unit tax raises $P_N^u P_G^u AB$ in revenue and the *ad valorem* tax $P_N^a P_G^a AC$ in revenue. It is evident that $P_N^a P_G^a AC$ exceeds $P_N^u P_G^u AB$ as the former area includes the latter. It should be noted that extra government revenue from the *ad valorem* tax is just matched by a reduction in monopoly profits.

In periods of inflation, prices of goods subject to unit taxes will tend to fall in price relative to goods subject to *ad valorem* taxes. The argument is very similar to the one made above for perfect competition. Inflation reduces the real amount of the unit tax. In Figure 11.4(d) both taxes have the same effects on price and output in the first period. In the second period the real value of the unit tax falls from CD to $CE [= CD/(1 + r)]$, so that with a unit tax the real price is lower in the second period $(P_1^u < P_0^u)$ for the unit tax while the real price would not change with the *ad valorem* tax.

Taxes in imperfect competition

The analysis thus far has been restricted to the polar extremes of perfect competition and monopoly. There are a variety of models of imperfect competition that could be used as a basis for analysing the effects of taxes, and we now turn to an examination of two of these.

(1) Mark-up pricing

If firms set their prices by adding some mark-up to either variable costs or total unit costs, then if taxes are thought of as a cost, the price will rise by more than the tax. Thus if prices were set at twice variable costs (including taxes in factor cost), then if factor taxes were raised prices would rise by twice the tax increase. Clearly this is very different from the predictions of the profit-maximising model and would result in prices above the profit-maximising level. This in turn would lead to a larger fall in quantity and a larger loss of consumer surplus.

(2) Sales maximisation

If firms try to maximise sales rather than profits the results of commodity taxes may be rather different. In the absence of tax a strict sales-maximising company will produce when $MR = 0$, that is to say it will produce at Q_0 in Figure 11.5(a) with price at P_0. A unit tax would shift the AR and MR curves vertically downwards thus reducing the level of output where $MR = 0$ and raising price. However, an *ad valorem* tax would have no effects on output or price and marginal revenue would still be equal to zero at Q_0. But this surprising prediction disappears if, as is usually assumed, sales maximisation is subject to a profit constraint. Suppose the minimum required profit is π_{min} in Figure 11.5(b). Prior to the tax the profit constraint is not binding and output and price are

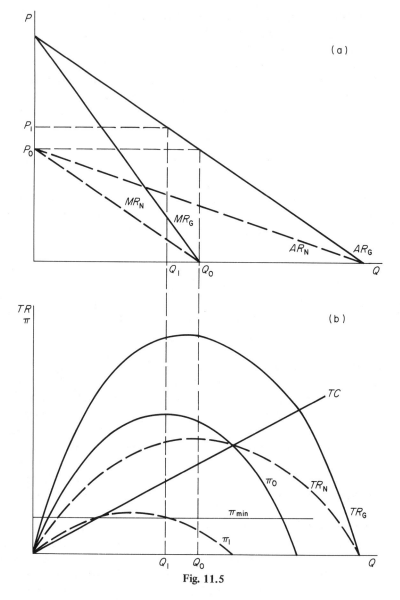

Fig. 11.5

again Q_0 and P_0. The introduction of the tax now reduces profitability from π_0 to π_1 and the profit constraint now becomes operative. As a result the company reduces output to Q_1 where π_1 is equal to π_{min} and thus raises price to P_1.

Taxes on profits in single industries

An alternative to taxing the goods that companies make is to tax the profits that they earn. Under profit-maximising assumptions it can be shown that taxes on profits are lump-sum taxes with no deadweight losses. However, under other circumstances taxes on profits change the output and price of firms, thus introducing a deadweight loss. An example of the latter is a revenue-maximising monopolist.

(1) Profit taxes on profit-maximising monopoly

We have seen that both *ad valorem* and unit taxes reduce the output and raise the prices charged by a profit-maximising monopoly. If instead we tax monopoly profit, then under static profit-maximising assumptions there is no effect on either price or output. The reason is that the tax affects neither marginal cost nor marginal revenue. This means that there is no change in the profit-maximising output or price. The incidence of the tax is thus entirely on the monopolist, and there is no deadweight loss. The argument is illustrated in Figure 11.6. Prior to the tax output and price are Q^π and P^π. The profits tax reduces the profits function from π_0 to π_1 but profit maximisation is unaffected.

(2) Profit taxes on revenue-maximising monopoly

In the absence of tax and with a non-binding profits constraint, a revenue-maximising monopolist would produce Q_0^R and sell this at P_0^R in Figure 11.6(a). A profits tax would shift the after-tax profit to π_1 in this Figure 11.6. As the figure is drawn the profits constraint now becomes operative and quantity is reduced to Q_1^R (where $\pi_1 = \pi_{\min}$) and price is raised to P_1^R. Thus in contrast to the profit-maximising case part of the incidence of the tax is on the consumer.

We return to this question in the next chapter on general equilibrium analysis, and in Chapter 18 we discuss studies of the incidence of the corporate income tax.

The reader should bear in mind the partial equilibrium nature of the results. For example, when we say the burden of the tax is on the producer, this leaves open the question of whether the tax is paid out of labour income or out of profits. In either case we ignore any secondary effects of reduced incomes on demand just as we have ignored the question of what the government does with the money that has been collected. To the extent that the tax in question is at a low rate on a small industry these effects *may* be small enough so that they can be safely ignored. However, if we are considering a broadly based tax these neglected factors are likely to be too important to safely ignore. This qualification is important because taxes on goods are often broadly based – VAT, for example. We look at a general equilibrium treatment of taxes in the next chapter.

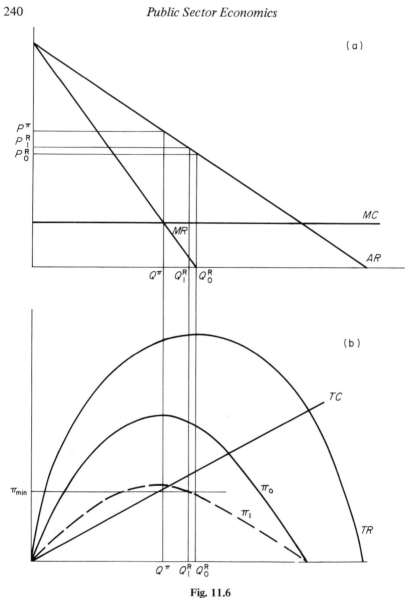

Fig. 11.6

General taxes and selective taxes

In the last section we examined the effect of a tax on a single industry and we now want to raise the question, 'Does it matter if a tax is levied on one or two industries rather than on all industries?' The answer is that it does matter, and that under very restrictive assumptions there is a presumption in favour of taxes that fall on all goods rather than one only (see also Chapter 20). The argument is presented first in terms of consumption goods excluding leisure and is then extended to include leisure and the choice between present and future income.

In the analysis that follows we employ a number of restrictive assumptions which enable us to study a *very* simplified version of the general or selective tax controversy. The conclusions from this simplified analysis *cannot* in general be assumed to apply in more complex circumstances. In the analysis we assume competitive markets and well-behaved preferences. We assume the economy is initially in a position of Pareto optimum and ignore problems of second-best (see Chapter 1). We also assume, until the section on inflation in this chapter, that prices change only as the result of taxes. This comparison of general and selective taxes is valid only in the two-good case, and we discuss the comparison between two ordinary present goods and the choice between ordinary goods and leisure. The effect of taxes on the choice between present and future goods is considered in Chapter 16.

(1) The choice between two present goods

Suppose there are only two consumption goods, which we call food and clothing, and that we want to compare the effects on resource allocation of a tax on clothing alone with the effects of a tax on both food and clothing using Figure 11.7 as an aid. In the absence of tax the consumer has an income with which he can purchase either OA units of food or OB units of clothing. In Figure 11.7 the individual's budget constraint is BA and in the absence of tax he will be in equilibrium at E_0. If a general consumption tax $BD = AE$ is introduced the new equilibrium will be at E^G. Tax revenue measured in units of food is AE and measured in units of clothing is BD. To raise the same revenue with a tax on clothing alone would require a tax rate of BC/BO (as E^S must lie on the line DE), which means the new equilibrium will be at E^S. The equilibrium E^S, with the selective tax on clothing alone, must lie in a lower indifference curve than E^G, the equilibrium with the general tax on both goods. The excess burden from the selective tax is thus the difference between the two indifference curves $(I^G + I^S)$. As the curves are drawn this represents EG units of food. The excess burden of the selective tax arises because with the selective tax the marginal rate of substitution (MRS) is no longer equal to the marginal rate of transformation (MRT).

We have assumed a Paretian optimum before the introduction of tax. In such a world the MRT of food into clothing would be equal to the MRS between food and clothing. A general tax on both food and clothing is neutral in that it leaves the MRT equal to the MRS. A selective tax on the other hand drives a wedge between the MRT and the MRS. We should note that this result depends on assuming either that the supply of labour is inelastic or that leisure is not an argument in the utility function (see Chapter 20).

(2) The choice between goods and leisure

The argument may be repeated for general taxes that include leisure and for selective taxes that tax goods other than leisure. If there is only one good other than leisure, which for convenience we can refer to as current income, then we can compare the effects of a tax that includes leisure with one that does not. Figure 11.7 can be used again, relabelling the vertical axis 'income' and the horizontal axis 'leisure'. In the absence of tax the individual can have OA units of leisure (if he does not need to eat) or OB units of income (if he does not need to sleep). His budget constraint is again BA and the pretax equilibrium is again E_0.

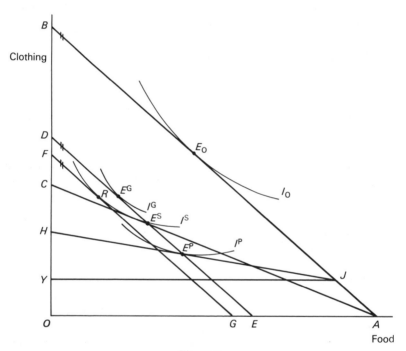

Fig. 11.7

The introduction of a head tax or poll tax of the fixed sum of $BD = AE$ units of income would result in a new equilibrium at E^G. Thus a poll tax has no excess burden. The reason is that it is a general tax on all goods including leisure and as such does not disturb the marginal qualities. An income tax – which is a selective tax on income *excluding* leisure – will destroy the marginal equalities and introduce an excess burden.

In examining the leisure-income choice it is convenient to begin by comparing a proportional income tax with a head tax. A proportional income tax that raised $BD = AE$ in revenue would require a tax rate of BC/CO and would lead to a new equilibrium at E^S. Once again the marginal equalities would be broken and an excess burden introduced.

It may be noted that a proportional income tax will increase the demand for leisure relative to a poll tax that raises the same amount of revenue. (Diagrammatically E^S must lie to the right of E^G.) Hours spent at work may be defined as total hours less hours of leisure (work on the diagram can be measured as moving to the left from point A), so that a proportional tax on the individual will reduce work relative to a head tax raising the same revenue.

It can also be shown for a single individual that a progressive tax normally reduces work relative to a proportional tax that raises the same revenue. It is convenient to illustrate this argument using a proportional tax with an exemption. Such a tax is progressive because the exemption excludes a larger proportion of low incomes from tax. (This is the form of progression used in the UK for basic rate taxpayers – see Chapter 14). If the tax exempts the first OY units of income then the tax rate required to raise BD units of revenue is BH/BY. Equilibrium will be at E^P where leisure is greater (work less) than at E^S. Note also that the excess burden of the tax has risen still further (I^P is a lower indifference curve than I^S) because a larger wedge has been driven between the MRT and MRS of leisure into income.

It would be wrong to jump from the above analysis to the conclusion that income tax systems should be regressive. The arguments for progressive income taxes are considered in the appendix to Chapter 3 and in Chapter 20. Clearly, progressive income taxes makes income redistribution very much easier because they place a higher tax burden on those with high incomes. This suggests a conflict between the excess burden of taxation and equalising after-tax income.

(a) *Effects of changes in taxes.* The effects of changes in taxes on income and leisure depend on the precise tax changes that are to be considered and we consider three changes here. We look first at the effects of a change in the rate of proportional income tax. This is an instructive case, because it causes the individual to move along his supply curve, but not a realistic one. We then look at the two most common types of tax changes in the UK: a change in allowances and a change in the basic rate. Both these changes cause the supply curve to shift: the former in the direction of less work and the latter in the direction of more work.

If we had an existing proportional income tax an individual's net wage would be his gross wage times $1 - t$. In Figure 11.8(a) the slope of the line AB measures this net wage and the individual is in equilibrium at E_0. If the proportional tax rate is then cut, the net wage rises, say, to AC and the new equilibrium is at E_1. This is absolutely standard application of price theory, which will be familiar to readers of any standard microeconomics textbook. The movement from E_0 to E_1 is a pure price effect; that is to say, it is a movement along the price consumption curve, *which is also called the supply curve of*

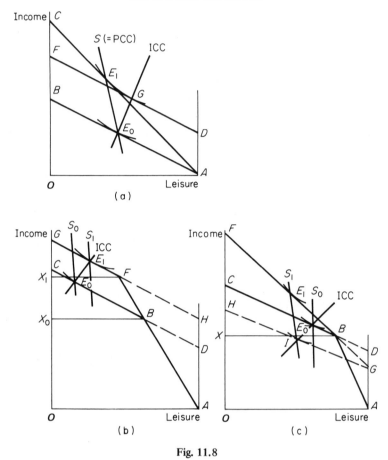

Fig. 11.8

labour (S). The important distinguishing feature in this case is that the price effect involves a change in the slope of the budget constraint only. The price effect can as usual be decomposed into an income effect (E_0 to G), which will increase leisure (decrease work), and a substitution effect, which will decrease leisure (increase work). The balance of these two effects is indeterminate *a priori*.

If the British chancellor of the exchequer decides to cut taxes it is almost impossible for him to do anything that will amount to a pure price effect. For basic rate-payers he has two choices: to put up allowances or to cut the basic rate. We take the increase in allowances first. Suppose the present level of allowances exempts the OX_0 income from tax (see Figure 11.8(b)). Equilibrium is at E_0. The allowance is then raised to OX_1 and the budget constraint shifts from ABC to AFG. Equilibrium is now at E_1. There are two important points to note: first, the movement from E_0 to E_1 is a pure income effect *for people remaining in the basic rate band.*[5] Note that *CBD* is parallel to *GFH*; that is to say, the slope of the budget constraint has not changed. Second, note that E_1 is on a new supply curve, S_1, which is to the right of S_0. People are better off because of the additional allowances, and their marginal return to a lost hour's leisure is unchanged so they will work less.

If instead of increasing allowances the chancellor had cut the basic rate of tax, the supply curve would shift in the opposite direction. As before we start from E_0 (in Figure 11.8(c)). The basic rate of tax that is applied to incomes above *OX* is then cut, so that the budget constraint shifts from *ABC* to *ABF* and the individual moves to a new equilibrium at E_1; and the supply curve has shifted to the left which is the direction of more work. To see this, note that E_0 is on the linearised budget constraint *CBD* and E_1 is on *FBG*. We now construct *HG* parallel to *CBD*. We can think of the movement from E_0 to E_1 as being composed of two movements. First, there is a pure income effect; down the ICC from E_0 to *I*. Second, it may be noted that the movement from *I* to E_1 is a pure price effect as only the slope of the budget line has changed. The reader should note that we have said that S_1 in Figure 11.8(c) lies to the left of S_0. We have *not* said that E_1 *necessarily* lies to the left of E_0 in this figure. It might or it might not, and the question can be resolved only by empirical investigation. What we can say is that for a given loss of revenue people will wish to work more with a cut in the basic rate than they would with an increase in allowances that will have the same effect on total receipts.

We return to these issues in Chapter 14, where we discuss the empirical evidence (which tends to show income effects predominating price effects) and in the appendix to Chapter 14, where we discuss the macroeconomic implications of this analysis.

(*b*) *Effects of inflation.* We now examine the effects of inflation and taxation on the choice between two goods. As before (see the discussion of indirect taxation and inflation), we assume that pretax prices of all goods as well as wages and other factor prices are rising at the same rate. The argument is made in respect of the taxes that affect the leisure–income choice but similar arguments apply to other choices between general and selective taxes.

Given our assumptions, inflation reduces the real rate of a head tax and leaves the excess burden at zero. With a proportional income tax the real tax rate is unchanged and the excess burden unchanged. With progressive taxes the real tax system changes and in some instances the excess burden will rise. We show with the aid of Figure 11.9 the change in the real budget constraints with various types of tax that can affect the leisure–income trade-off. In each case income is on the vertical axis and leisure on the horizontal axis; the pretax budget constraint is *AB*; the pretax equilibrium is at a position such as E_0 where the indifference curve (not shown) is tangent to the budget constraint. A poll tax of *AC* would give a first-period budget constraint of *CD* in Figure 11.9(a). In the second period the real amount of the poll tax would fall if the tax is fixed in money terms. Thus in period 2 the poll tax would be $AE[= AC/(1 + r)]$ and the new equilibrium would be at a point such as E_2. Note that, given the assumption that leisure and income are both normal goods, E_2 must lie to the north-east of E_1. Disposable income rises, tax receipts fall, and work falls (leisure rises).

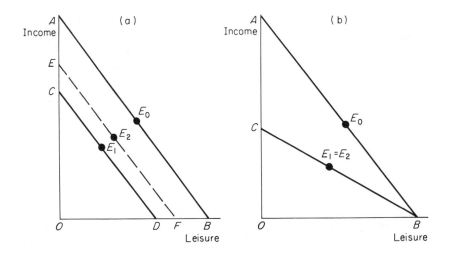

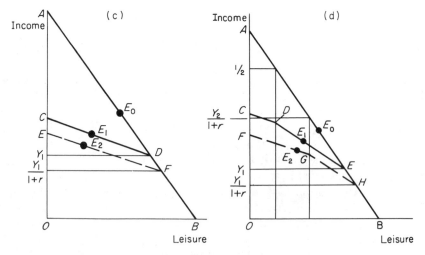

Fig. 11.9

A proportional income tax of AC/AO would give a first-period budget constraint of CB in Figure 11.9(b) and equilibrium at a point such as E_1. Inflation would have no effect on this budget constraint so that equilibrium in the second period, E_2, will be the same as first-period equilibrium. The reason for this is that all the relevant magnitudes (gross wage rate, gross income, tax net wage and net income) change by the same percentage (i.e. the rate of inflation), thus leaving the real magnitudes unaffected. (The argument thus far has very exact analogies with taxes that affect other choices. For example, Figure 11.9(a) could be used to show the effect of inflation on goods both subject to unit taxes.)

With a proportional income tax with an exemption, however, there is again a change in the real tax rate as a result of inflation (see Figure 11.9(c)). In the first period OY_1 income is exempted, and income above the exemption level is taxed at AC/CY_1 and equilibrium is at point such E_1. The effect of inflation is to reduce the purchasing power of the exemption to $Y_1/(1 + r)$. The budget constraint becomes EFB. As the tax rate is unchanged EF is parallel to CD so that E_2 must lie to the south-west of E_1. Thus we see that inflation can have opposite effects – on, for example, work effort – depending on the type of tax. With a poll tax, work will fall (leisure rise) because inflation reduces the tax. However, with a proportional tax with an exemption work will rise because inflation has reduced the value of the exemption from the tax (not the tax itself).

With income taxes with several rate bands the position becomes more complex because inflation will shrink real tax bands. The essentials are evident if there are two positive rates of tax as in Figure 11.9(d). In period 1 OY_1 is exempted from tax, income in the range $Y_1 Y_2$ is taxed at a low rate and income above Y_2 is taxed at a higher rate. The budget constraint is $CDEB$ and equilibrium is at a point such as E_1 (which may be either to the left or right of E_0). In period 2 both tax bands are compressed. The exemption level falls to $Y_1/(1 + r)$ and the starting point of the higher band is reduced to $Y_2/(1 + r)$. This reduces the period 2 budget constraint to $FGHB$. As the diagram is drawn E_2 is in a higher tax band than E_1, but the person might remain in the same band, in which case we would again have a pure income effect (as in Figure 11.9(c)). If, as shown, the person does move into a higher band the new equilibrium may involve either more leisure (as shown) or less.

We have assumed that nominal tax rates are not adjusted for inflation. Of course, if the tax system were indexed so that nominal tax rates were adjusted to leave real tax rates unchanged (as happens in some countries), then none of this analysis would apply. Indeed, this is an argument for indexing the tax system. Clearly, the changes in real tax rates caused by inflation can have very complex effects. It is hard to imagine how Parliament could possibly foresee – let alone approve – all of these changes, even if it could forecast the rate of inflation accurately. If the tax system were indexed, real tax rates would of course be altered from time to time but such changes require parliamentary approval and would not depend on the degree of failure of attempts to control inflation. The question of indexing income taxes is further discussed in Chapter 14.

(3) Multiple choices

We have seen that with single choices there is a clear presumption in favour of general rather than selective taxes. The argument in favour of general taxes does not necessarily hold when we are considering multiple choices. For example, a general tax on both food and clothing will cause less distortion than one on clothing alone but we can not be sure what effect such a general tax would have on the choice between present and future goods (i.e. on saving) or on the choice between food and clothing together on the one hand and leisure on the other hand. The outcome in these more complex cases will depend on the different elasticities of demand for the various goods. We showed a general presumption in favour of taxes in commodities at uniform rates. However, it has been shown by Atkinson that this result may not hold unless the supply of labour is fixed. When labour supply is not fixed it may be necessary to have differentiated tax rates in order to minimise the excess burden (see Chapter 20).

Summary and conclusions

We have shown that the predicted partial equilibrium effects of taxes vary widely depending whether or not firms are competitive, whether they attempt to maximise profits, etc. Table 11.1 summarises the predicted effects of unit taxes on the prices paid by consumers. It can be seen that there is a wide variation in the predicted results. As the reader can see, the result of price

Table 11.1 Predicted effects of a unit tax on price

Perfect competition		Expected increase in price (P) paid by consumer relative to the tax (t) imposed
Elasticity of		
Demand	*Supply*	
$E = 0$	$0 < E < \infty$	$\Delta P = t$
$0 < E < \infty$	$0 < E < \infty$	$\Delta P < t$
$E = \infty$	$0 < E < \infty$	$\Delta P = 0$
$0 < E < \infty$	$E = 0$	$\Delta P = t$
Profit Maximising Monopoly		$\Delta P < t$
Revenue Maximising Monopoly		$\Delta P < t$
Mark-up model		$\Delta P > t$

increasing by just the amount of the tax (which as we will see in Chapter 17 is an assumption often made in studies of tax incidence) is relatively infrequent and requires relatively implausible assumptions. The reader may wish to compile a similar table for *ad valorem* taxes and for profits taxes as a review exercise.

CHAPTER 12

General Equilibrium Analysis of Taxation

In this chapter we consider the allocative and distributive effects of taxation in a general equilibrium context. General equilibrium analysis has the advantage of allowing us to see the full effects of tax changes on the goods market and on the factor market, as well as on the distribution of income. General equilibrium analysis is, of course, complex, particularly if one wants to actually estimate the effect of particular tax changes, which means that certain simplifying assumptions are usually employed. Perhaps the best known general equilibrium model in public sector economics is the two-sector general equilibrium model developed by Arnold Harberger, and the bulk of this chapter will be devoted to the exposition of a version of the Harberger model.

The main simplifying assumptions in the Harberger model are that there are only two goods (or two sectors) in the economy, that there are only two factors of production, that these factors of production are supplied in a fixed quantity, that markets are competitive and that we start from a position of Paretian optimum in the absence of taxation.

The version of the Harberger model that is employed here[1] contains a further simplifying assumption that both the production and consumption patterns in the economy are Cobb–Douglas. Cobb–Douglas production (and consumption) functions have two special properties: they exhibit constant returns to scale, and they have a unitary elasticity of substitution. Elasticity of substitution is a measure of the shape of an isoquant (or of an indifference curve). It may be defined as the percentage change in the ratio of labour to capital divided by the percentage change in the marginal rate of substitution between the inputs. If the elasticity of substitution were zero the isoquants would be L-shaped and factor substitution would be impossible, and if the elasticity were infinity isoquants would be straight lines and the factors would be perfect substitutes. The case of unitary elasticity of substitution has the interesting property that at any place on an isoquant the total payment to both labour and capital remains the same. Suppose that the price of labour is rising relative to the price of capital. As firms substitute the relatively cheap capital for the relatively dear labour, there are two opposing forces operating on total factor incomes. Labour income will fall because less labour is employed and will rise because each unit used is paid more. Similar arguments apply to capital, and when the elasticity of substitution is unity these forces just cancel each other out leaving the totals unaffected.

To appreciate the significance of these assumptions, let us spell them out in terms of two industries which we can call, for convenience, the food industry and the clothing industry, and the two factors of production, which, again for convenience, we can label labour and capital. Both the food industry and the clothing industry will exhibit constant returns to scale. Both industries will have a unitary elasticity of substitution, but the factor intensities in the two industries need not be identical. The share of labour, and of capital, in both industries will be constant and hence the share of labour and capital will be constant in the economy as a whole. The reason for this is that with unitary elasticity of substitution any change in the relative price of labour and capital will cause an offsetting change in their quantity, such that the total income paid will remain constant. If the value of output in each industry is held constant, this means that the demand for factors of production will have unitary elasticity.

The same relationships hold on the consumption side. The preferences of labourers, and of capitalists, are such that they will always want to spend a constant proportion of their income on food and on clothing, and if their money income is constant this means that the expenditure on food and clothing will also be constant. While labourers and capitalists may spend different proportions of their income on food and clothing, the overall proportion of income spent on food and clothing will be constant. The reason for this is that the share of labour and of capital is constant, and if each group spends a constant proportion of its income on each commodity, then the overall proportion will remain the same. If income is held constant, then the demand functions for both products will have unitary elasticity.

Because we wish to concentrate on the distributive and allocative effects of taxes rather than on the effects of aggregate demand, it is assumed that the government spends all of its revenue from taxation. This ensures that the money level of aggregate demand is constant. To remain within the framework of a two-good model, the government must spend this tax revenue on some combination of the two goods. It is highly convenient to assume that the government in fact spends the money on goods in the proportion that the private sector would have spent in the absence of taxation. This assumption, together with our earlier assumptions about Cobb–Douglas consumption and production functions, ensures that the money expenditure on food and clothing is held constant.

The general equilibrium model: graphical exposition

We now turn to a graphical representation of this model. One of the highly convenient results of assuming particular production and consumption relationships is that we can draw out fairly simply a complete general equilibrium system, and this is done in Figure 12.1. We start by taking an overview of the system. Part (e) shows the constant money demand for clothing and part (f) shows the constant money demand for food. The associated desired demands for capital for both industries is shown in part (a) and the desired demand for labour for both industries is shown in part (g). This factor demand together with the fixed factor supply determines factor prices and the distribution of factors between the two industries. Factor prices and quantities also determine factor incomes, which when combined with preferences determine the demand for the goods in parts (e) and (f). Parts (b) and (c) show the production functions for the clothing and food industries. Knowing factor prices and quantities from parts (a) and (g), we determine the level of output of the industry. Having thus determined the output of each industry in parts (b) and (c), we find the prices of food and clothing from parts (e) and (f). Knowing the demand of labourers and of capitalists for food and clothing we can also find the amounts of both goods that will be consumed by both labourers and capitalists. When the economy is in overall equilibrium all of the markets will be cleared; i.e., we will have consistent sets of supply and demand curves in both goods and factor markets. The solid lines in Fig. 12.1 show such a position of general equilibrium. We have described the equilibrating process as a sequential one, but the reader should bear in mind that with static analysis we can say nothing about the process of reaching equilibrium.

Turning now to a more detailed examination of the model, it is convenient to begin with part (a), which shows the market for capital. It will be remembered that it is assumed that the supply of capital is totally fixed and fully employed. This fixed amount of capital can be represented by the length of the horizontal line from O_C^K to O_F^K. We measure the amount of capital employed in the clothing industry to the right from O_C^K and the amount of capital employed in the food industry to the left from O_F^K. The price of capital in the clothing industry is measured on the left-hand vertical axis, and the price of capital in the food industry is measured on the right-hand vertical axis. By our assumptions the demand for capital in both industries has unitary elasticity, and in fact can be represented by D_{F0}^K and D_{C0}^K. Equilibrium in the capital market will occur where total demand is equal to supply; and, of course, if there are no barriers to the movement of capital, then capital will flow until the price is equal in the two markets. Thus the equilibrium in the capital market will occur where the two demand curves intersect. It can be seen that the price of capital will be P_0^K and that the division of the stock of capital between the two industries is given by Q_0^K.

The labour market is shown in part (g) of the figure where, for convenience, the fixed quantity of labour is measured by the vertical distance O_F^L to O_C^L. On this diagram the price of labour is measured horizontally, and the equilibrium price of labour is P_0^L and the division of labour between the two industries is given by Q_0^L.

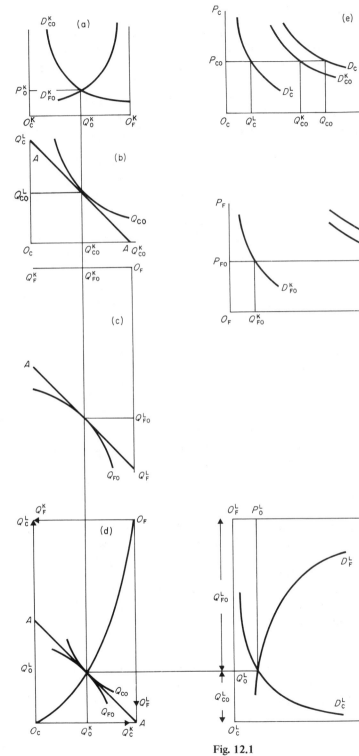
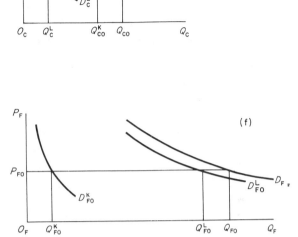

Fig. 12.1

The production functions for the two industries are shown separately in parts (b) and (c) of the figure. Part (b) shows the production function for the clothing industry. Having found the amount of capital that will be employed in the clothing industry from part (a) (Q_{Co}^K) and the amount of labour that will be employed from part (g) (Q_{Co}^L), we can then read off the total amount of clothing that will be produced (Q_{Co}). We can also find the price of labour and capital from parts (a) and (g) and use these prices to construct an isocost curve AA in part (b).

The production function for the food industry is shown in part (c) of the figure where the origin is in the top right-hand corner. The amount of capital is measured to the left along the horizontal axis, and the amount of labour is measured downwards along the vertical axis. Once again, the isoquants show the Cobb–Douglas production function and, knowing the equilibrium quantities of capital and labour (Q_{Co}^K, Q_{Co}^L) we can find the total amount of food that is produced (Q_{Fo}) and we can again show the same price ratio AA. Figures 12.1(b) and 12.1(c) are combined into Figure 12.1(d), which is a familiar Edgeworth box diagram. The equilibrium position is seen to be on the contract curve ($O_C O_F$) where the two isoquants (Q_{Co}, Q_{Fo}) are at tangent to each other and to the price line (AA).

The demand for the output of the two industries is shown in parts (e) and (f) of the figure. It will be remembered that we are holding money national income constant and that the share of labour and of capital in that income is also constant. Labourers and capitalists also spend a constant proportion of their income on each of the two goods. We can thus indicate in part (e), which shows the demand for clothing, the separate demands of labourers for clothing and of capitalists for clothing. It will be remembered that these demand curves will be of unitary elasticity and thus the combined demand curve of capitalists and labourers will also have unitary elasticity. As we know both the total demand for clothing (D_C) in part (e) and the total output of clothing from part (b) (Q_{Co}), we can find the price of clothing by transferring the equilibrium amount of clothing from part (b) to part (e) and reading off the appropriate price (P_{Co}).

Finally, part (f) of the diagram shows the food market. The construction of the demand curves is in principle the same as for the clothing market, and we can show the separate demand curves of capitalists for food (D_{Fo}^K) and of labourers for food (D_{Fo}^L), and the total demand for food (D_F). Knowing the demand curve for food and, for part (c), the quantity of food, we can find the equilibrium price of food (P_{Fo}).

The effects of a tax on one factor in one industry

(1) Long-run effects

One of the earliest uses of the Harberger model was to investigate the general equilibrium implications of a corporation tax. It is possible to think of a corporation tax as a tax on capital in the incorporated sector. Thus, one could carry through the analysis using as the two sectors an incorporated sector and and unincorporated sector, and as the two factors capital and labour. Of course the formal analysis is the same irrespective of what labels we attach to the factors or to the sectors and for our example we will take the effect of a tax on capital in the clothing industry (if one likes, one can think of the clothing industry as being incorporated and the food industry as being unincorporated). It will be remembered from Chapter 11 that we can think of a tax as shifting the demand curve down to the left, which means that a 50 per cent tax on capital in the clothing industry would shift the demand curve for capital in the clothing industry halfway from its original level to the origin. Thus the demand curve shifts from D_{C0}^K to D_{C1}^K (note that in Figure 12.2 all of the original equilibrium positions are shown with solid lines, and where the curve shifts these are shown with dashed lines). The effect of the tax is, of course, to reduce the net return to capital in the clothing industry. In the first instance it will be below the net return to capital in the food industry. If capital is free to move, it will naturally wish to leave the clothing industry and move towards the food industry where the return is now higher. This movement of capital from the taxed clothing industry to the untaxed food industry will continue until the net return is again equal in both industries. This occurs where the distribution of capital between the two industries is at Q_1^K. It may be noted that the net return to capital is then NP_{C1}^K, and that the gross return to capital in the clothing industry is now GP_{C1}^K. It should be noted that, while the net price of capital is the same in both industries, the gross price of capital now differs between the two industries. In particular, the gross price of capital is higher in the taxed clothing industry than in the untaxed food industry (given our assumption of a 50 per cent tax, it will be exactly twice as high). It may also be noted that the total return to capital in the food industry is exactly the same as before the tax, given our assumption that the demand curve has unitary elasticity. The total net return to capital in the clothing industry is just half of what it was prior to the tax, and of course government revenue is also just equal to half of the pretax income of capitalists in the clothing industry. Thus the basic effect of a tax on a factor in one industry is to cause some of that factor to leave the taxed industry.

With the aid of the rest of Figure 12.2 we can trace the effects of this change on the rest of the system. We can see from part (a) of the figure that the amount of capital in the clothing industry has fallen from Q_0^K to Q_1^K and that the price of capital has risen from P_0^K to GP_{C1}^K. In part (b) the isocost curve shifts from AA to AB, and with the new lower quantity of capital employed, output falls to Q_{C1}. It is worth noting that exactly the same quantity of labour will be employed both before and after the tax. The reason for this is our special assumption that we have a unitary demand for factors of production (the expenditure on labour can be represented by the distance AQ_C^L. If the elasticity of demand is unity, total expenditure will be constant and hence the vertical distance will be constant).

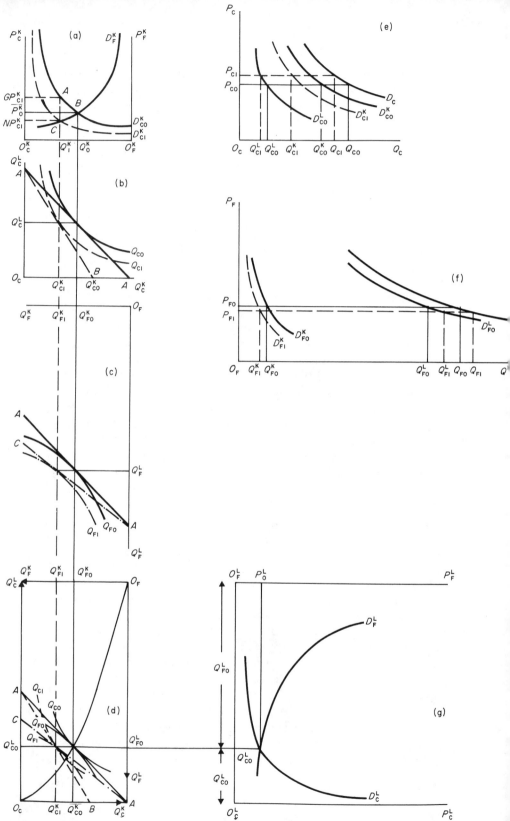

Fig. 12.2

Part (c) of the figure shows the position in the food industry. In this instance we have a fall in the gross price of capital, represented by the price line changing from AA to CA, and the output of the food industry rises from Q_{F0} to Q_{F1}. Note once again that the amount of labour employed is the same both before and after tax.

Parts (b) and (c) are once again combined in part (d) of the figure. It can be seen that the new after-tax price ratios (CA and AB) differ in the two industries and, hence, that the isoquants intersect. The new equilibrium position is thus not on the contract curve.

Before turning to the food and clothing markets, it is worth noting again that this tax has no effect whatsoever on the labour market given our Cobb–Douglas assumptions. This means that total labour income is unaffected. We have also seen that the income from capital in the food industry is not affected by the tax, and that the income from capital in the clothing industry has fallen by 50 per cent. However, it will be remembered that government tax receipts will be just equal to this fall in capitalists' income and if the government spends the tax receipts in the same proportion as was previously spent by the capitalists, then the total demand for the outputs of the two industries will be unaffected in money terms.

Thus in parts (e) and (f) of the figure the total demand for clothing and for food will be unaffected. We know from part (b) that the total output of clothing has fallen from Q_{C0} to Q_{C1}, so we can read off from part (e) that the price of clothing will have to rise from P_{C0} to P_{C1}. Similarly, in the food industry the increase in output from Q_{F0} to Q_{F1} will cause a fall in price from P_{F0} to P_{F1}.

We now know the new prices of both factors in both industries, the new levels of output and the new prices in both industries, and we also know factor income. All that remains is for us to see what happens to the consumption of food and clothing by labourers, and by capitalists. We begin by looking at the consumption of clothing with the assistance of part (e) of the figure. The increased price of clothing will cause the consumption of clothing by labourers to fall from Q_{C0}^L to Q_{C1}^L. The position for capitalists is slightly more complicated because we must remember that there is a reduction in capitalist income as a result of the tax. The new, after-tax, demand curve of capitalists for clothing is represented by the dashed demand curve D_{C1}^K and it can be seen that capitalists' consumption of clothing will have fallen from Q_{C0}^K to Q_{C1}^K.

In the food industry, the consumption of food by labourers will have risen from Q_{F0}^L to Q_{F1}^L as a result of the fall in price. The consumption of food by capitalists will have fallen from Q_{F0}^K to Q_{F1}^K. The reason that the consumption of food falls is that the reduction in capitalist income more than offsets the fall in the price of food in this example.

It is clear that the effect of taxation in this example is to reduce the real income of capitalists because their consumption of both food and clothing falls. What can we say of the real income of labourers, whose consumption of clothing has fallen and whose consumption of food has risen, and of national income as a whole? Clearly, in order to do this we will have to weight the changes in the amounts of food and clothing by some set of prices. There seem to be two basic alternatives open. We could value the output at the pretax prices, or at the post-tax prices. This is the familiar index number problem and gives rise to a Laspèyres index if we use the pretax prices, or a Paasche index if we use the post-tax prices.

The example has been carefully constructed so that the money value of national income stays the same. However, this does not imply that the real national income stays the same or that there are no welfare losses from the tax. Calculation of the Laspèyres or Paasche indices would provide one approach to the measurement of real income changes. Two other methods are readily available to us, given our diagrammatic tools. In part (d) of the figure we saw that the new equilibrium position is not on the contract curve, and the difference between the actual output levels and the position on the contract curve represents a fall in real income. Alternatively, we can think of the new level of output of food and of clothing as lying within the original food–clothing production possibility frontier. Finally, we can measure the fall in welfare with reference to part (a) of the figure where the loss of welfare is equal to the roughly triangular area ABC. To see why this is so, we must remember that the area under the demand curve represents the value of capital in each industry. Thus the reduction of capital in the clothing industry results in a loss of welfare equal to the area $Q_1^K ABQ_0^K$. The increase in capital in the food industry on the other hand results in an increase in welfare corresponding to the area $Q_1^K CBQ_0^K$. The difference between these two areas, the area ABC, is thus the net welfare loss. Harberger's estimates of the welfare loss from the corporation tax are discussed in Chapter 18.

It is perhaps worth pausing to list some of the alternative applications of this model. It is, of course, possible to tax labour differently in different sectors or industries. For example, in the United Kingdom such a tax was the Selective Employment Tax, which was a tax on labour employed in certain, broadly service, industries; and one could predict the effects of such a tax by dividing the economy into a sector that had to pay the tax and a sector that did not. Another tax which is in effect a tax on some uses of labour is the ordinary income tax. Domestic production, or do-it-yourself work, is normally not subjected to income taxation. Once again, one could apply the Harberger model and obtain the obvious prediction that an income tax will create an incentive to switch labour out of the taxed, that is the market, sector and into the un-taxed, that is the non-market or do-it-yourself, sector. Such a study is discussed in Chapter 14.

The model could also be used to examine a subsidy to labour by industry or by region, for example the regional employment premium. Subsidies to capital by industry or by region, such as special incentives to development areas, could be studied. The motive for such incentives is often to reduce unemployment in certain regions. The reader may note that with our Cobb–Douglas assumptions employment would be totally unaffected by a subsidy to capital. Should this be taken to imply a criticism of the model or of regional policy?

(2) *Short-run effects*

It has been assumed that factors are in fact completely free to move from one industry to another in response to tax-induced price changes. However, this may not be the case. By definition, capital is not free to move from one industry to another in the short run, which means that it may be interesting to look at the case where factors are not free to move. This can quite easily be done. Referring again to Figure 12.1, the post-tax employment of capital between the two industries will, by assumption, be the same as prior to the imposition of the tax, namely at Q_0^K. This means that there is no change in the employment of factors or in post-tax incomes. Consequently, the output of both industries will remain the same and so the prices will remain the same. The only effect is to reduce the income of capitalists by the amount of the tax and to replace the capitalist's demand for food and clothing by government demand for these products.

A tax on all uses of a factor

We now look at the general equilibrium effects of a tax on all uses of a factor. Suppose we consider the effect of a 50 per cent tax on capital in both the food and the clothing industries. In part (a) of Figure 12.1 the tax could be represented by a shifting of both demand curves halfway to the origin. As both demand curves go down by the same amount, the equilibrium quantity of capital employed in each industry will remain the same, although of course the net price will have fallen by half. Because the employment of capital in both industries is the same, and because the labour market is not affected, then the output of clothing in part (b) of the figure and the output of food in part (c) are unchanged, which means that there are no changes in the Edgeworth box diagram of part (d). In parts (e) and (f) the total demand for both products is unaffected because government demand will precisely replace the demand of capitalists and as output of both products does not change the price of both products is unaffected as well. This means that the tax has no effect on the consumption of food or of clothing by labour. The demand of capitalists for both food and clothing will, however, fall by just half because their income will fall by just half as a result of the 50 per cent tax. We thus have a result that is entirely consistent with the partial equilibrium prediction (see Chapter 11) of a tax on a factor that is totally inelastic in supply. We can see with our assumptions that the price of that factor falls by the amount of the tax and that the tax is borne entirely by that factor. There are no welfare losses from the tax. To test his understanding of this paragraph the student is advised to pencil in the changes on Figure 12.1.

It is not easy to think of actual examples of non-selective taxes on factors. The property tax or rates are a fairly general tax on property, but typically they are levied at different rates in different localities. Perhaps a better example would be a general payroll tax on labour, although there would again be selectivity between the market and non-market sectors.

We have thus seen that a general tax on a factor of production in all its uses is to be preferred on the grounds of allocative efficiency to one that is on only some of the uses of that factor. When we turn to taxes on goods, we will also find that general taxes are preferable on allocative grounds to selective taxes. In this rather important conclusion, partial and general equilibrium analyses are in agreement. This does not necessarily mean that in all circumstances general taxes are to be preferred to selective taxes, as we will see in Chapter 20.

A tax on one good

We now turn to an exposition of the general equilibrium effects of a tax on one good. Given the assumptions of our model, and in particular the absence of personal or corporate savings, a tax on the output of one industry is, in effect, a tax on the factors used in making the output in that industry. Thus, in our model a tax on clothing is identical in its effects to a tax on capital and on labour employed in the clothing industry. As it turns out, it is more convenient to handle the tax as a tax on factors, than as a tax on output, and that is the procedure we follow in this section. In part (a) of Figure 12.3 we show the effect of a tax on capital in the clothing industry and in part (g) we show the effect of a tax on labour in the clothing industry. Clearly the tax will cause both labour and capital to leave the clothing industry. Thus both factors will leave the clothing industry and will be employed in the food industry. If both industries are equally capital-intensive, then factors will be released from the clothing industry in the same ratio that they will be demanded in the food industry and, in that event, there will be no change in relative factor prices. However, more generally, it will not be the case that the two industries use factors in the same proportion. It can be seen from a comparison of parts (b) and (c) of the figure that in the present example the clothing industry is relatively capital-intensive and the food industry relatively labour-intensive. This means that the ratio of units of capital to units of labour released by the clothing industry will be higher than the ratio of units of capital to units of labour demanded by the food industry. There will thus be a relative surplus of capital and a relative shortage of labour. To restore equilibrium and to maintain full employment, this means that the price of capital will have to fall relative to the price of labour. Close inspection of parts (b) and (c) of Figure 12.3 will show that the new price line *BC* is not parallel to the original price line *AA*. (In the numerical example that lies behind the figure the line *AA* represents the price of capital of one and the price of labour of one. In the initial equilibrium the clothing industry uses one unit of capital to one unit of labour, whereas the food industry uses one unit of capital to three units of labour. A 50 per cent tax changed the ratio of the price of capital to the price of labour to about 0.86 : 1.)

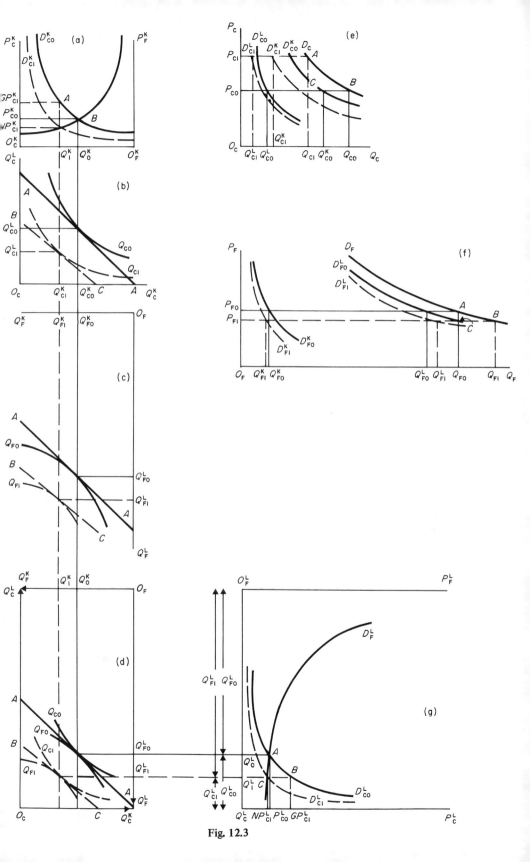

Fig. 12.3

The movement of factors of production out of the taxed clothing industry and into the untaxed food industry will cause the output of clothing to fall and the output of food to rise. The change in relative factor prices will mean that *both* industries will become more capital-intensive, as may be verified by constructing a line from the origin to the positions of equilibrium in parts (b) and (c).

Despite the rather complex changes in relative factor prices and in methods of production, our Cobb–Douglas assumptions mean that the gross, i.e. tax-inclusive, income of both labourers and capitalists will be unaffected. Net incomes will fall by exactly the amount of the tax. Maintaining our assumption that the government spends its tax revenue, this again means that the total demand of food and of clothing is unaltered.

We can see from part (e) of Figure 12.3 that the fall in the output of clothing causes an increase in the price of clothing from P_{C0} to P_{C1}. Because both labour and capital have a reduction in their net income, both will demand less clothing. The combined effect of the leftward shift in the demand curve and the increase in price is a reduction in the consumption of clothing to Q_{C1}^K for capitalists and to Q_{C1}^L for labourers.

In the food industry the increase in output to Q_{F1} causes the price of food to fall to P_{F1}. Lower incomes of labourers and capitalists shift the demand curve down to the left. The leftward shift in the demand curve will on its own cause the consumption of food to rise. What actually happens is of course determined by the combined effect of these offsetting forces. As the diagram is drawn, labourers increase their consumption of food slightly to Q_{F1}^L and capitalists decrease their consumption of food slightly to Q_{F1}^K.

We can represent the welfare loss of this tax as the sum of the roughly triangular area *ABC* in part (a) and the roughly triangular area *ABC* in part (g), or as the difference between the roughly triangular area *ABC* in part (e) and the roughly triangular area *ABC* in part (f).

Appraisal of the Harberger model

The great virtue of the Harberger model is its simplicity. For pedagogic purposes this is a great advantage in bringing out what is involved in a general equilibrium analysis of taxes. While the virtues of simplicity are considerable, they are achieved at a certain cost and we would now like to examine this cost. It will be remembered that the Harberger model is restricted to two sectors. This prevents an analysis of both intermediate and final goods, or of a public good as well as two private goods, or of internationally traded goods as well as two domestic goods. Because of the restriction to two sectors the model can usefully deal with only a single tax at a time, which means that it is not useful for the analysis of alternative tax bundles.

The model is also restricted to inelastic factor supplies. If total factor supplies in fact respond to price changes (see Chapter 14 for empirical evidence on the elasticity of the supply of labour), then this is an important limitation on the model. Both factors of production are also assumed to be homogeneous. Thus there is no distinction between groups of workers with different skills. Workers from one industry or region are assumed to be able to move to another industry or region. Capital is also treated as a homogeneous entity with no distinction between financial assets and fixed assets, or between firms and their owners. Thus there is no distinction in the model between a general tax on wealth and a tax on profits. The homogeneous capital stock is assumed to be able to move from one industry/region to another and there is no discussion of any difficulties that might arise in practice.

Clearly then the Harberger model is most suited to the analysis of the long-run effects of tax changes, because in the long run it seems reasonable to suppose that factor mobility is higher than in the short run (the reader will nevertheless remember that it is possible to assume complete factor immobility). The model is thus best suited to comparisons of alternative long-run equilibria corresponding to alternative tax rates.

The model also assumes competitive markets where prices move up *or down* as required to ensure full employment. If, say, because of monopolistic influences or government interference with goods or factor prices, markets are not free to clear, then once again the analysis is vulnerable.

Thus far the limitations we have mentioned apply to the Harberger model generally. In addition, the version employed in this chapter has additional restrictions imposed by the Cobb–Douglas assumptions we have employed. These additional restrictions are important primarily in terms of the incidence predictions that arise from the model. For example, the prediction that the incidence of the corporate income tax is entirely on the capital depends on the assumption of unitary elasticity of substitution. We return to this question in Chapter 18, where we examine some empirical work on the incidence of the corporation tax. Table 18.4 shows that Harberger's results depend on the assumptions about elasticities of substitution.

Other general equilibrium models

Recently a less restrictive general equilibrium system has been developed by Scarf, Shoven and Whalley. Like the Harberger approach this approach assumes flexible prices and is thus within the neoclassical tradition. This approach is based on some exceptionally powerful mathematical techniques which make it possible to compute equilibria with more than two sectors. In their approach the economy is very carefully stimulated and all taxes are converted to *ad valorem* equivalents. This method represents a significant step forward because it is possible to compare the likely economic effects of complex alternative tax packages. The approach has the disadvantages of very heavy information require- ments; also, the results are applicable only to the specific situations that are studied, and the work-leisure choice is not adequately considered.

In addition to these neoclassical models in which it is assumed that agents respond to price changes, there is an approach in which the basic assumption is that the structure of the economy is fixed. In this approach - input-output analysis - the structural relationships of the economy can be explored for a very large number of sectors. The basic structure of the economy is set out in a way that shows the relationships between different sectors. Thus sector A may purchase components from sectors B, C and F and sell its output to D, E, F and G. An input-output table summarises all of these relationships and the basic assumption is that there are fixed technical relationships among factors and between factors and products. So long as these relationships remain fixed it is possible to estimate how a change of policy affecting one group of sectors will affect other sectors. The principle weaknesses are the heavy data requirements and the assumption of fixed coefficients. As coefficients may change over time, either because of changes in relative prices or because of technical progress, an input-output table dates relatively quickly.

We thus have two alternative approaches. As the neoclassical approach emphasises price changes, and as input-output analysis is based on quantity changes, the two approaches are complementary.

CHAPTER 13

The Distribution of Income in the UK

One of the major considerations in the design of tax systems in the modern welfare state is their effect on the distribution of income. In part this concern is with factor shares, as we saw in the last chapter, but even greater interest attaches to the distribution as between high- and low-income individuals or households. The subject is sufficiently complex and controversial so that in the UK a standing Royal Commission on The Distribution of Income and Wealth was established in 1974 to provide 'a thorough and comprehensive enquiry into the . . . distributions of income and wealth', both past and present. Unfortunately the Commission was disbanded in 1980.

The purpose of the chapter is to introduce the reader to various measures of inequality, to provide the factual background about the UK distribution of income and to indicate the deficiencies in the statistics. Subsequent chapters will discuss ways in which various taxes can influence income distribution and in the final two chapters of the book we will discuss the question of what the distribution of income should be. There is, however, one caveat arising from that discussion which requires emphasis at this stage: the distribution of income and the distribution of welfare are not the same thing. There are three sets of reasons for this. First, the definition of income that is used for statistical distributions is derived from the definition of income for tax purposes, and as we will see in the next chapter some sorts of income are not taxed. Second, one reason for inequality of income is that some people work longer than others. Welfare, which includes leisure, is thus a more comprehensive concept than income, which excludes leisure. Finally, welfare may give a broader interpretation altogether including things such as health and happiness.

Measures of inequality

(1) The Lorenz curve and the Gini coefficient

One of the best-known measures of inequality is the Lorenz curve such as those for 1978–79 plotted in Figure 13.1. Households are ordered by income, and it

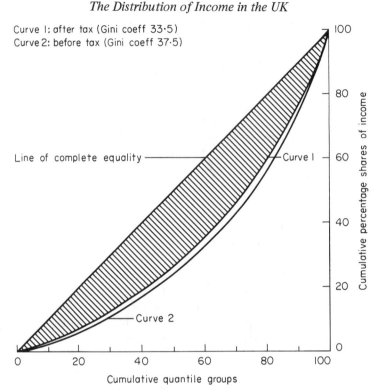

Fig. 13.1
Source: *Economic Trends*, February 1981.

can be seen that the figure has the percentage of the population on the
horizontal axis and the percentage of total personal income on the vertical axis.
The Lorenz curve thus shows the cumulative proportions of income owned by
various proportions of the population. If one person had all of the income with
the rest having none, the Lorenz curve would conform to the two axes, while
if income were equally distributed the Lorenz curve would be a 45° line. Thus,
the nearer the Lorenz curve lies to the 45° degree line of complete equality the
more equal is the distribution of income. A natural measure of inequality, which
is termed the Gini coefficient, is the ratio of the shaded area of the diagram to
the total area under the line of complete equality. Theoretically the coefficient
can vary from 0 (complete equality) to 100 per cent (complete inequality). The
coefficient for pretax income in Figure 13.1 is 37.5 per cent and for post-tax
income is 33.5 per cent. The Gini coefficient is an incomplete measure of
inequality, as can be seen from Figure 13.2. The two Lorenz curves shown have
rather different distributions of income but have the same Gini coefficient.

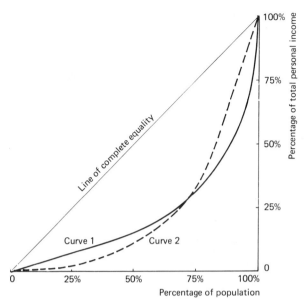

Fig. 13.2 Hypothetical income distributions with identical Gini coefficients. Source: *Royal Commission Report No. 1.*

(2) *The Atkinson coefficient*

Because Gini coefficients are a single summary statistic of inequality they cannot be used to compare inequality in different parts of the income distribution. For example it is obvious from an inspection of Figure 13.3 that the UK has less inequality than West Germany as measured by the Gini coefficient. It is also clear from inspection that West Germany has *less* inequality than the UK at low incomes and *more* inequality at high incomes. Atkinson has developed a measure which he called the 'equally distributed equivalent measure' to compare such distributions. Atkinson proceeds in two stages. He first calculates E. E is society's valuation of the loss it would be willing to occur to transfer £1 to someone with half the income. A low figure of E implies a low concern with inequality. For example if E is 1 we would take £1 from the rich person to give £0.50 to the poor while if E were 2 we would take £1 from the rich in order to give only £0.25 to the poor man. Atkinson then constructs his coefficient which shows how much total income we would be prepared to sacrifice for greater equality. This coefficient the 'equally distributed equivalent measure' shows how much total income society would be willing to sacrifice to achieve equality of incomes. If the Atkinson measure were 0.3 it would mean that equality of incomes would be equally valued to an increase in national income of 30 per cent. Atkinson has found that where E is less than 3.0 and the Atkinson

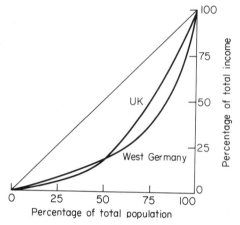

Fig. 13.3 Lorenz curves for UK and West Germany. Source: A. B. Atkinson 'On the Measurements of Inequality' in A. B. Atkinson (ed) *Wealth, Income and Inequality* (Oxford): Oxford University Press, 1980), p. 41.

coefficient is less than about 0.55 the UK has less inequality than West Germany. It will be remembered that the Gini coefficient for the UK implies less inequality than in West Germany. If society thought that equality would be equivalent to a 55 per cent of greater increase in national income then the reverse would hold and West Germany would be judged the more equal society.

(3) The Ulph measure

It has been pointed out by D. T. Ulph (reference in further reading) that the Atkinson measure implicitly assumes that all individuals face the same wage rates and prices. If this condition holds, the redistribution implicit in the Atkinson measure can be achieved without efficiency loss by lump-sum taxes and transfers. However, when, for example, wage rates differ, attempts to redistribute income with an income tax will cause efficiency losses and under fairly realistic assumptions this efficiency loss may exceed the redistribution gain so that society becomes worse off.

   The important lesson is that it is a mistake to assume that one can redistribute the national cake without changing its size. When, for the rest of this chapter we examine income distributions, we should bear this in mind.

The distribution of income in the UK

For our purposes the most useful way of presenting information on inequality is by showing income distribution by percentiles. In this way we can readily see the share of any group – perhaps the top 1 per cent or the bottom 10 per cent and how it changes. Table 13.1 shows the distribution of personal incomes in the UK on this basis. The first column shows both the distribution of income before tax in the UK in 1978-79 and the lower limit of income in each range. It can be seen for example that an income of £5510 was sufficient to bring one into the top quarter of units. The table also shows how the sources of income change at various income levels. Within the top 1 per cent, half of income is employment income while most of the remainder is self-employment income and investment income. For the bottom 25 per cent on the other hand only one-fifth of income is employment income and for this group two-thirds of income is retirement and other state benefits.

The distribution of income before tax

We begin our detailed discussion of income distribution with an examination of the distribution of incomes before tax. It is important to bear in mind throughout this discussion that the existing distribution of pretax incomes is not necessarily what that distribution would be if there were no government. There are a number of ways in which governments may influence the distribution of gross incomes. With a proportional income tax and no overtime, gross earnings would be the gross wage per hour times the number of hours. Even in this simple world a change in the tax rate could (1) cause the number of hours worked to rise or fall (see Chapter 11) thus changing gross incomes. (2) A rise in the tax rate might lead at least some workers to attempt and possibly succeed in raising their gross wage in order to protect their standard of living. (3) Government incomes policy may well lead to changes in gross wage rates which differ from the changes that would occur in the absence of government. (4) The definition of income for tax purposes can have two distinct effects on the distribution of income. Suppose that capital gains are taxed separately from income and at a lower rate. If the distribution of income is based on statistics provided by the tax authorities, the first effect is that capital gains do not appear in the definition of income and hence not in income distribution. Second, if the lower rate of tax on capital gains causes people to reorder their affairs so that they receive gains rather than taxable income, then government will have influenced the statistical distribution of gross incomes still further.

It should be clear from the preceding paragraph that the figures that appear in any distribution of income will depend on the definition of income adopted. In the next chapter we discuss the most appropriate definition of income for tax purposes and in the present chapter we confine our attention to the definition of income currently used in UK official statistics. Income is defined to include taxable income from employment, self-employment, investments and pensions (see Table 14.2) plus non-taxable social security benefits (e.g. supplementary benefit, sickness benefit and unemployment benefit plus current

Table 13.1 Distribution of pre-tax income, 1978/79, by source

					Percentages				
				Sources of pre-tax income					
Quantile group and quantiles	Employ-ment	Self-employ-ment	Investment	Occu-pational pensions and annuities	NIRP[a]	Non-taxable benefits	Other	Total	Income tax as a percentage of pre-tax income
Top 1 per cent (over £14,630)	49.4	28.2	18.5	2.0	0.6	1.3	–	100.0	40.0
Top 25 per cent (over £5510)	81.6	8.0	4.2	2.1	0.5	3.6	–	100.0	22.1
Next 25 per cent (£3370–£5510)	77.5	5.2	4.2	3.4	2.8	6.8	0.1	100.0	15.6
Next 25 per cent (£1850–£3370)	57.6	4.0	5.6	6.1	13.8	12.8	0.1	100.0	10.2
Bottom 25 per cent (up to £1850)	21.0	2.3	5.9	4.3	42.2	24.1	0.2	100.0	2.1
All tax-units	71.9	6.2	4.5	3.3	6.5	7.5	0.1	100.0	16.9
Total amounts (£ million)	85,990	7370	5430	3920	7380	9000	70	119,610	20,210

Note: [a] National insurance retirement pensions.

Source: *Economic Trends*, February 1981, p. 84.

grants (e.g. scholarships) and some income in kind. This definition excludes capital gains, gifts received and the imputed rent of owner-occupied housing.

The most important sources of information are the *Survey of Personal Incomes* (*SPI*), which is based on income tax returns, the *Family Expenditure Survey* (*FES*), which is a survey of a sample of households. Aside from the deficiencies in the definition of income, the main problems with these sources are, first, that there may be under-reporting of income, which is illegal to the Inland Revenue but not to the *FES*. Second, the basic unit for the *SPI* is the tax unit, that is an individual or married couple who may or may not have children. This definition creates problems if we wish to look at the distribution of individual incomes. It also creates problems if an individual is a tax unit for only part of the year. Thus a child leaving school part-way through the year becomes a tax unit, while a single woman marrying part-way through the year ceases to be a tax unit as does someone that dies. If people in any of these categories are earning at the rate of £4000 a year for six months they will appear in the statistics as if they earned £2000 for the whole year. Third, the *Survey of Personal Incomes* omits incomes below the tax threshold, which means that this information has to come largely from the *FES*. Fourth, the *FES* is a voluntary survey with a response rate of about 70 per cent, which makes it possible that there is non-response bias. Indeed, there is some evidence that high-income people are under-represented.

Table 13.2 and Figure 13.4 show the resulting distributions of income by percentile shares for selected years from 1949 to 1978-79. In 1978-79 the top decile had just over one-quarter of the income and the bottom half just under one-quarter of the income. It may be noted that an income of £5510 was sufficient to bring persons into the top 25 per cent of the units. It should, however, be remembered that many tax units will consist of retired persons, whose after-tax income is largely in the form of state benefits (see below), and that other tax units will exist for only part of the year. Thus people who earn for the whole year are unrepresentative of the population as a whole. It may also be seen from Table 13.2 and Figure 13.4 that the share of the bottom half has changed very little between 1949 and 1978-79. However, there has been a considerable fall in the share of the top 1 per cent and to a lesser extent of the next 4 per cent. It can also be seen that the Gini coefficient fell somewhat during the fifties and sixties.

We now report briefly on some exercises undertaken by the CSO and the Royal Commission to study the sensitivity of the estimates to the definitions of income and of tax units. Excluding part-year tax units makes a noticeable difference as can be seen from a comparison of the final two columns of Table 13.2. Excluding the part-year units raises the share of the bottom 20 per cent from 5.9 per cent to 6.6 per cent, reduces the share of the top 20 per cent from 42.6 per cent to 41.4 per cent and decreases the Gini coefficient from 37.5 to 35.5. A similar exercise on the inclusion of imputed income from owner occupation made little difference to the estimates. In the late 1970s the definition of

Table 13.2 Distribution of Personal Income before tax; Selected years 1949 to 1978–79 (percentage shares of total personal income received by given quantile groups of tax units)

United Kingdom quantile group	1949	1959	1968–69	1974–75	1978–79[a]	Excluding part-time units 1978–79
	%	%	%	%	%	%
Top 1 per cent	11.2	8.4	7.1	6.2	5.3	5.2
2–5 per cent	12.6	11.5	10.7	10.6	10.7	10.4
6–10 per cent	9.4	9.5	9.3	9.8	10.1	9.8
Top 10 per cent	33.2	29.4	27.1	26.6	26.2	25.4
11–20 per cent	14.1	15.1	15.4	15.8	16.3	16.0
21–30 per cent	11.2	12.6	12.9	13.1	13.4	13.2
31–40 per cent	9.6	10.7	11.0	11.0	11.0	11.2
41–50 per cent	8.2	9.1	9.4	9.3	9.1	9.2
51–60 per cent		7.5	7.6	7.6	7.3	7.5
61–70 per cent		5.9	6.2	5.8	5.9	6.0
71–80 per cent	23.7	4.4	4.7	4.6	4.6	4.8
81–90 per cent		5.3	3.4	3.6	3.6	3.7
91–100 per cent			2.3	2.6	2.5	2.9
Median £pa	259	514	909	1913	3370	3590
Gini coefficient	41.1%	39.8%	37.4%	37.1%	37.5%	35.5%

Note: [a] The figures for 1978–79 include mortgage interest paid in the definition of income. This is excluded for earlier years. The inclusion of mortgage interest somewhat increases the share of the top 20 per cent. This column and all earlier columns include part-year units.

Sources: *Royal Commission Report No. 5* (London: HMSO, 1977), Tables 5 and D1; pp. 21, 236 and *Economic Trends*, February 1981, p. 82.

income was changed to include mortgage interest paid. As high-income people tend to spend a higher proportion of their income on mortgage interest this change has increased the apparent inequality somewhat.

The distribution of income after income tax

We show the distribution of income after income tax in Table 13.3. As we would expect, the distribution after income tax is more equal than before tax. This is reflected in the fall in the Gini coefficient for 1978–79 from 37.5 to 35.5 per cent. The reduction in after-tax inequality from 1949 to 1974–75 can be seen in the fall in the share of the top 1 per cent, which is down from 6.4 to 4 per cent; in the fall in the share of the top decile, down from 27.1 to 23.2 per cent; and in the small rise in the share of the bottom half from 26.5 to 27.0 per cent; and in the fall in the Gini coefficient from 35.5 to 32.4 per cent. Between 1974–75 and 1978–79 inequality increased. The share of the bottom half has

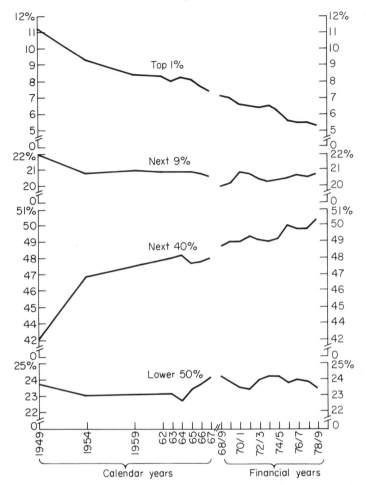

Fig. 13.4 Distribution of income: 1949 to 1978/79 Income shares of selected quantile groups (pre-tax income). Source: *Economic Trends*, February 1981, p. 83.

fallen from 27.0 per cent to 26.2 per cent and much of the increase went to the second decile. The Gini coefficient has increased from 32.4 per cent to 33.5 per cent.

The distribution of income after other taxes and benefits

The government influences the distribution of incomes other than through income taxes in a wide variety of ways. We know from the last chapter that taxes on goods not only reduce our spending power but also may influence the pattern of goods that we buy. Payments to the retired, to the unemployed, to

Table 13.3 Distribution of personal income after tax - selected years 1949 to 1978-79 (percentage shares of total personal income received by given quantile groups of tax units, 1949 to 1974-75)

Quantile group	1949	1959	1968-69	1974-75	1978-79
Top 1 per cent	6.4	5.3	4.6	4.0	3.9
2-5 per cent	11.3	10.5	9.8	9.7	9.8
6-10 per cent	9.4	9.4	9.2	9.5	9.7
Top 10 per cent	27.1	25.2	23.6	23.2	23.4
11-20 per cent	14.5	15.7	15.5	15.8	16.3
21-30 per cent	11.9	12.9	13.1	13.2	13.5
31-40 per cent	10.5	11.2	11.5	11.4	11.3
41-50 per cent	9.5	9.9	9.7	9.4	9.3
51-60 per cent		7.2	8.1	7.8	7.7
61-70 per cent		6.6	6.6	6.4	6.4
71-80 per cent	26.5	5.2	6.3	5.3	5.1
81-90 per cent		6.0	6.6	4.4	4.1
91-100 per cent				3.1	2.9
Median (£pa)	£250	£477	£819	£1604	£2890
Gini coefficient	35.5%	36.0%	33.2%	32.4%	35.5%

Note: Income unit: tax unit.
Source: *Royal Commission Report No. 5* (London: HMSO, 1977), Tables 5, D3 pp. 22, 238.

households with children, to disabled persons, etc., also influence income distributions directly as well as influencing patterns of demand. Expenditure on services such as health and education influence income distribution in rather obvious ways, and even expenditure on things such as defence must influence income distribution at least in a very wide sense because defence services, as a public good, are freely available to all. Clearly a full study of the effects of government spending on income distribution would be an immensely complex task requiring a sophisticated general equilibrium approach. We discuss these issues further in Chapter 21. Until such a study becomes available we have to rely on less satisfactory approaches, and in the UK the best-known attempt to estimate the redistributive effects of government taxation and expenditure is an exercise undertaken by the Central Statistical Office (CSO) and which has also been used by the Royal Commission. The starting point for this exercise is the data set collected for the *FES*, and as we have seen it cannot be assumed to be fully representative of the population. In its incidence calculations the CSO allocates to households certain taxes and certain benefits. The allocated taxes and benefits are shown in the right-hand side of Table 13.4. It can readily be seen that some taxes such as corporation tax and capital gains tax are omitted, as are certain types of government expenditure such as roads and defence. The criteria for inclusion is whether in the CSO's judgement it is possible to assign particular taxes or benefits to individual households. It happens that the CSO

Table 13.4 Definitions of income in CSO study of incidence

Original income	= Employment income plus self employment income plus investment income plus pension income
+	
cash benefits	= Child benefits; retirement and old person's pensions, widow's benefit; sickness, war, invalidity, industrial injury benefits and allowances; unemployment benefit, family income supplement, supplementary benefits, electricity discounts, rent rebates and student maintenance awards; death, maternity and other cash benefits
=	
gross income	
−	
direct taxes	= Income tax plus employ*ees'* and self employed national insurance contributions
=	
disposable income	
−	
indirect taxes	= Rates less rebates; dutes on beer, wine, spirits, tobacco, oil, betting etc.; VAT; car tax, motor-vehicle duties and driving licences; TV licences; protective duties; stamp duties; employ*ers* national insurance contributions including the surcharge
+	
benefits in kind	= Health service; state education including school meals etc.; housing and rail subsidies; option mortage expenditure; life assurance premium relief
=	
final income	

Source: *Economic Trends* (February, 1981), pp. 115–16.

allocate a higher proportion of taxes (59 per cent of total receipts in 1979) than of expenditure (45 per cent), which means that households on average *appear* to pay more in tax than they receive in benefits.

In order to undertake this exercise the CSO has to make certain assumptions about tax incidence. The assumptions that they make are that direct taxes are not shifted and that indirect taxes are shifted 100 per cent to the final consumer. (This question is discussed further in Chapter 17.) Thus it is assumed for example that labour supply is unaffected by tax and that the prices of goods change by just the amount of any tax. It can easily be shown that with competitive markets these assumptions are logically inconsistent. Taxes on goods will be passed on fully to consumers only if supply is totally elastic (see Figure 11.1(c)) or demand totally inelastic. Taxes on factors will not be passed on only if the supply of factors is inelastic (Figure 11.1(d)) or if demand for the product is perfectly elastic (Figure 11.1(f)). The reader should verify for himself that any combinations of these assumptions is illogical. The reader should also remember from the discussion of non-competitive markets in Chapter 11 that prices rising by just the amount of the tax is unusual except with a markup model. Partly for this reason the CSO emphasises that their figures should not be used to estimate the likely effects of large changes in taxes, and of course it would be even worse,

Table 13.5 Summary of CSO estimates of the effects of taxes and benefits, UK, 1979

Average per household (£ per year)	Decile groups of households ranked by original income										Average over all households
	Bottom	2nd	3rd	4th	5th	6th	7th	8th	9th	Top	
Original income	10	270	1390	3160	4380	5430	6460	7670	9360	14040	5220
plus cash benefits	1720	1630	1430	820	530	500	430	370	380	380	820
Gross income	1730	1900	2830	3980	4910	5930	6880	8040	9740	14420	6040
less direct taxes	–	20	170	550	850	1080	1330	1570	1990	3250	1080
Disposable income	1730	1890	2660	3430	4050	4850	5560	6470	7750	11170	4960
less indirect taxes	380	440	670	880	1060	1200	1340	1550	1770	2320	1160
plus benefits in kind	780	680	740	870	960	980	960	960	970	1010	890
Final income	2120	2130	2730	3420	3950	4630	5190	5880	6960	9860	4690
Direct taxes as a percentage of gross income	–	1	6	14	17	18	19	20	20	23	18
Indirect taxes as a percentage of disposable income[a]	18–22	22–23	25	26	26	25	24	24	23	21	23
Benefits in kind as a percentage of final income	37	32	27	25	24	21	19	16	14	10	19
Local authority tenants as a percentage of all householders	60	42	35	38	38	29	27	24	19	18	33
Average per household (number)											
Children	0.3	0.1	0.3	0.7	1.0	1.1	1.0	0.9	0.8	0.8	0.7
Adults	1.3	1.5	1.6	1.8	1.9	2.0	2.1	2.3	2.5	3.0	2.0
Retired people	1.0	1.2	0.8	0.3	0.2	0.1	0.1	0.1	0.1	0.1	0.4
Workers	0.1	0.1	0.6	1.1	1.4	1.6	1.7	2.0	2.1	2.6	1.3

Note: [a] The ranges reflect different possible treatments of rates for households receiving Supplementary Benefit (SB) as SB will include rates paid.
Source: *Economic Trends*, January 1981, p. 105.

as we stressed at the start of this chapter, to use the figures to estimate what income distribution would look like in the absence of government.

As is shown in the left-hand side of Table 13.4 the CSO's estimates are made in three stages and involve four concepts of income. They start with (1) original income and add direct (cash) benefits to obtain (2) gross income. Direct taxes are subtracted to give (3) disposable income. The CSO then subtract indirect taxes and add indirect benefits to reach (4) final income. Table 13.5 shows a summary of results for 1979. It can be seen that in the bottom four deciles that both disposable income *and* final income *exceed* original income given the taxes and benefits actually allocated. From the fifth decile upwards disposable income and final income both fall as a proportion of original income. Clearly the picture that emerges is one of a progressive tax-transfer system.

One of the merits of the CSO data is that they are available by household composition. It can be seen from the bottom part of Table 13.5 that household composition is rather different at different income ranges. Households with higher original income tend to be larger with more non-retired adults and more workers. The bottom three deciles are smaller with fewer non-retired adults, fewer workers, fewer children but a much higher proportion of retired people. This is important when we remember that the object of redistribution may not be only to redistribute from those with high original money incomes to those with low money incomes, but also to redistribute among people with similar money incomes according to household composition and needs. For example we may wish to redistribute from single-adult households to households with large numbers of children. Some indication of the extent to which this happens can be seen from Table 13.6, which shows the CSO's estimates by household type. Each row of the table represents a different household type and each column a decile of original household income. Each cell in the table contains five numbers. The top number, N, is the number of households in that cell. In general, the larger is N the more reliable the information in that cell should be, and when N is less than 10 the CSO does not provide any further information as its reliability is thought to be too doubtful. The second number in the cell, OY, is original income followed by gross income (GY), disposable income (DY) and final income (FY). Looking along any row, it can be seen that for the lowest incomes FY is larger than OY while for the highest incomes the reverse is true. Indeed, it can be seen that FY is over 350 times OY for the single-adult non-retired household in the lowest income range.

Perhaps the most interesting use for Table 13.6 is to see the way in which the state redistributes income by household type. This can be seen by looking down the columns in the table. For example, in decile 6 all household types have original income between £5344 and £5521, while their final income varies from £3256 to £6101. It can be seen that retired households benefit relative to non-retired households; that households with children benefit relative to those without; and, that large households benefit relative to small households. Tables such as those earlier in this chapter which lump all tax units together make it easy to lose sight of this important point.

Table 13.6   The distribution of income by household type: UK 1979

1979	Deciles of original income			
	1	2	3	4
One adult retired				
Number of households (N)	389	306	132	27
Original income (OY)	7	257	1179	2996
Gross income (GY)	1425	1495	2243	3967
Disposable income (DY)	1425	1468	2051	3174
Final income (FY)	1711	1649	1975	2927
One adult non-retired				
Number of households (N)	45	32	124	149
Original income (OY)	4	270	1470	3155
Gross income (GY)	1178	1309	2140	3357
Disposable income (DY)	1176	1308	1925	2646
Final income (FY)	1420	1204	1802	2232
Two adults retired				
Number of households (N)	138	261	181	42
Original income (OY)	8	272	1206	2990
Gross income (GY)	2144	2262	3062	4604
Disposable income (DY)	2140	2249	2911	4002
Final income (FY)	2475	2506	2824	3706
Two adults non-retired				
Number of households (N)	17	20	109	163
Original income (OY)	3	405	1575	3192
Gross income (GY)	1932	2298	3219	3953
Disposable income (DY)	1932	2237	3059	3417
Final income (FY)	1857	2127	2859	3024
Two adults with one child				
Number of households (N)	8	8	26	75
Original income (OY)			1639	3206
Gross income (GY)			3229	3864
Disposable income (DY)			3082	3421
Final income (FY)			3437	3543
Two adults with two children				
Number of households (N)	7	5	23	76
Original income (OY)			1782	3207
Gross income (GY)			3560	3912
Disposable income (DY)			3459	3430
Final income (FY)			4000	3717
Two adults with three or more children				
Number of households (N)	22	6	11	37
Original income (OY)	–		1509	3242
Gross income (GY)	3218		3211	4385
Disposable income (DY)	3218		3147	3968
Final income (FY)	5212		4599	5631

	Deciles of original income						£pa All households
5	*6*	*7*	*8*	*9*	*10*		*households*
9	4	3	2	1	–		873
							484
							1764
							1665
							1827
116	65	49	16	14	11		621
4272	5344	6397	7499	9337	14674		3591
4384	5418	6385	7502	9337	14779		3949
3381	4120	4905	5563	7161	10364		3110
2726	3256	4133	4024	5853	8643		2625
14	15	8	2	3	4		668
4465	5521						1058
5946	6791						2985
4732	5465						2774
4479	4836						2868
154	159	211	245	202	141		1421
4389	5442	6468	7705	9317	13200		6500
4859	5761	6714	7847	9404	13298		6933
3963	4696	5373	6216	7338	10125		5554
3361	4015	4390	5076	5934	8517		4647
114	120	99	66	58	30		604
4396	5420	6417	7630	9273	14412		5874
4740	5795	6680	7926	9547	14633		6329
3920	4783	5400	6294	7649	11441		5183
3576	4372	4954	5555	6917	10171		4786
134	144	138	142	107	77		853
4409	5433	6445	7648	9284	15169		6795
4884	5908	6905	8071	9716	15569		7327
4117	4831	5613	6508	7795	12076		5953
4344	4875	5576	6209	7462	11009		5849
57	82	55	30	32	32		364
4356	5471	6467	7609	9461	14247		5983
5154	6212	7144	8274	10127	14889		6952
4304	5204	5908	6731	8192	11477		5766
5560	6049	6442	7245	8507	11397		6653

Table 13.6 *(Continued)*

1979	Deciles of original income			
	1	*2*	*3*	*4*
Three adults				
Number of households (*N*)	9	11	20	40
Original income (*OY*)		288	1778	3090
Gross income (*GY*)		3393	4480	4909
Disposable income (*DY*)		3378	4232	4392
Final income (*FY*)		4499	5119	4317
Three adults with children				
Number of households (*N*)	2	1	14	31
Original income (*OY*)			1707	3243
Gross income (*GY*)			4189	5207
Disposable income (*DY*)			4105	4791
Final income (*FY*)			5218	5710
One adult with children				
Number of households (*N*)	41	27	38	38
Original income (*OY*)	5	255	1488	3089
Gross income (*GY*)	1910	2057	2609	3631
Disposable income (*DY*)	1910	2054	2516	3303
Final income (*FY*)	2915	2881	3513	3789
All households				
Number of households (*N*)	678	677	678	678
Original income (*OY*)	6	270	1384	3160
Gross income (*GY*)	1707	1889	2825	3968
Disposable income (*DY*)	1706	1871	2658	3420
Final income (*FY*)	2102	2116	2725	3408

Source: Table prepared by the Central Statistical Office.

Another way of looking at the way in which household composition influences redistribution is to weight household composition using equivalence scales. The CSO has done this using weights proposed by the Royal Commission. The weights are: married couple 1.00; single adult 0.67; child 0.27. Table 13.7 shows the comparison of the adjusted and unadjusted redistributions. The adjusted – per equivalent adult – calculations in the lower part of the table show considerably more redistribution than those in the upper part of the table. It can be seen that the differences are largely attributable to cash benefits and to benefits in kind rather than to taxes.

Recently a study has been published based on 1971 FES data which uses similar methods to those of the CSO but which allocates a much higher proportion of taxes and expenditure than the CSO allocates. O'Higgins and Ruggles have allocated all 'relevant' expenditure. The main items excluded from relevant expenditure are debt interest and net lending by the government. Relevant expenditure includes 'unallocatable' expenditure which is, despite the term,

		Deciles of original income				£pa All households
5	*6*	*7*	*8*	*9*	*10*	*households*
35	40	49	71	130	235	640
4387	5450	6459	7656	9476	14042	9259
5818	6330	7437	8208	9992	14400	10060
5148	5192	6015	6741	7938	11183	8042
5662	4574	5681	5840	6767	9572	7131
28	40	59	101	126	147	549
4534	5456	6543	7717	9494	14123	8918
5788	6539	7330	8389	10043	14736	9777
5107	5535	6126	6974	8160	11630	7990
5791	6101	6600	7314	8059	10603	7972
16	9	7	3	4	1	184
4355						2269
4866						3404
4327						3178
4719						3841
677	678	678	678	677	678	6777
4378	5431	6456	7672	9365	14039	5217
4907	5925	6891	8040	9745	14414	6031
4054	4845	5563	6470	7758	11168	4951
3949	4620	5183	5863	6960	9839	4677

allocated on various arbitrary bases including population. On the taxation side all tax revenue from residents including capital taxes and corporation tax are allocated (the basis for this allocation is discussed further in Chapters 16 and 18). Table 13.8 shows their comparison of their results for 1971 with those of the CSO. O'Higgins and Ruggles estimates of the allocation of expenditures are much more equal than those of the CSO. This can be seen by looking at the upper row of bracketed figures in Table 13.8, which show percentages of original income. This is because they assume that most of the extra expenditure they allocate accrues equally on a population basis. Their treatment of the distribution of expenditure is discussed further in Chapter 21. Their treatment of taxation makes much less difference in comparison with the CSO's. If taxes are expressed as a percentage of gross income (not shown in the table) the calculations of O'Higgins and Ruggles appear a little less progressive than those of the CSO.

Table 13.7 Redistribution of income between households; unadjusted and adjusted to a per equivalent adult basis, 1979

Average per household (£ per year)	Quintile groups of households ranked by original income					Average over all households
	Bottom fifth	Next fifth	Middle fifth	Next fifth	Top fifth	
Unadjusted						
Original income	140	2280	4900	7060	11700	5220
Cash benefits	1680	1120	510	400	380	820
Gross income	1820	3400	5420	7460	12080	6040
Direct taxes	10	360	970	1450	2620	1080
Disposable income	1810	3040	4450	6010	9460	4960
Indirect taxes	410	770	1130	1440	2040	1160
Benefits in kind	730	800	970	960	990	890
Final income	2130	3080	4290	5530	8410	4690
Direct taxes as a percentage of gross income	*1*	*11*	*18*	*19*	*22*	*18*
Indirect taxes as a percentage of disposable income[a]	*20–23*	*25*	*25*	*24*	*22*	*23*
Benefits in kind as a percentage of final income	*34*	*26*	*23*	*17*	*12*	*19*
Adjusted to a per equivalent adult basis						
Original income	170	1980	3760	5460	9130	4100
Cash benefits	2080	1050	420	320	190	810
Gross income	2250	3030	4180	5770	9320	4910
Direct taxes	10	300	730	1140	2110	860
Disposable income	2240	2740	3450	4630	7210	4050
Indirect taxes	500	690	870	1090	1590	950
Benefits in kind	880	820	710	570	450	670
Final income	2610	2870	3290	4110	6080	3790
Direct taxes as a percentage of gross income	*–*	*10*	*17*	*20*	*23*	*17*
Indirect taxes as a percentage of disposable income[a]	*20–22*	*25*	*25*	*24*	*22*	*23*
Benefits in kind as a percentage of final income	*34*	*29*	*22*	*14*	*7*	*18*

Note: [a] The range reflects the different possible treatments of rates for households receiving Supplementary Benefits (SB) as SB will include rates.
Source: *Economic Trends*, January 1981, p. 113.

The causes of inequality

A complete discussion of the causes of inequality is beyond the scope of this book but a brief introduction may be helpful, as people's views about the desirable degree of inequality may well turn on the causes of that inequality.

If labour markets were competitive, gross wage rates would equal the marginal product of labour. People who had either substantial inherited ability or who raised their marginal product by education and training would then have higher wage rates. Some people would argue that inequality rooted in inherited differences is undesirable but would approve of inequality arising from individuals' improving their qualifications, which could well reduce their incomes during their period of education or training.

Of course income inequality comes not only from differences in wage rates but also from differences in the amounts of work done. In part this variation will be because some individuals work longer than others. The 1971 Stirling study showed that mean hours worked by weekly paid married male workers was forty-five with a standard deviation of eleven. Thus a person with hours one standard deviation above the mean would have an income of 165 per cent of a person with hours one standard deviation below the mean if both had the same wage rate. While this will account for some of the variation in individual income, variations in household income can also be explained in part by variation in the number of workers. Most obviously we should distinguish between retired and non-retired households. One indication of the difference in income distribution that this makes is given in Table 13.6, where for example it may be seen that the average original income of two-adult retired households was £1058 in 1979 whereas for non-retired two-adult households it was £6500.

Inequality will also arise from non-earned income (see Table 13.1). This may be income from past savings or from inherited wealth or from capital gains, and attitudes towards inequality may depend on the relative importance of these sources of income. We return to this issue in Chapter 16 on the taxation of wealth.

Inequality may also arise because of market imperfections of various sorts. High wages may be determined by whom you know or by monopsonistic or monopolistic labour market practices rather than by workers' marginal products. Households' ability to vary their labour supply may be limited by standard working weeks, unemployment, conventions about retirement, laws requiring compulsory education until a certain age is reached, etc. These special features appear particularly important when one concentrates on the causes of poverty, which is particularly prevalent among the aged, the disabled, one-parent families and the unemployed.

We have not been able to quantify precisely how much inequality can be attributed to each of the factors we have mentioned. Nevertheless three factors stand out as obviously important: life-cycle factors, especially the proportion retired; the amount of work done by economically active households; the

Table 13.8 Distribution of net benefits by decile of original income, UK 1971

Decile	Lowest	2nd	3rd	4th	5th	6th	7th	8th	9th	Highest	All households
Decile Point (original income)	99	482	1029	1367	1685	1967	2274	2698	3410		
No. of households	723	724	725	723	724	724	724	724	724	724	7239
Av. original income	23	257	776	1195	1530	1827	2115	2471	3015	4813	1802
	(0.1)	*(1.4)*	*(4.3)*	*(6.6)*	*(8.5)*	*(10.1)*	*(11.7)*	*(13.7)*	*(16.7)*	*(26.7)*	*(100)*
Av. gross income	505	679	1043	1364	1645	1930	2211	2560	3093	4887	1992
	(2191.3)	*(264.1)*	*(134.4)*	*(114.1)*	*(107.5)*	*(105.7)*	*(104.6)*	*(103.6)*	*(102.6)*	*(101.5)*	*(110.5)*
	(2.5)	*(3.4)*	*(5.2)*	*(6.8)*	*(8.3)*	*(9.7)*	*(11.1)*	*(12.9)*	*(15.5)*	*(24.5)*	*(100)*
Total allocations Expenditures	948	940	883	910	892	920	957	976	956	1059	944
	(4117.2)	*(365.3)*	*(113.7)*	*(76.1)*	*(58.3)*	*(50.4)*	*(45.2)*	*(39.5)*	*(31.7)*	*(22.0)*	*(52.4)*
	(10.0)	*(10.0)*	*(9.4)*	*(9.6)*	*(9.4)*	*(9.7)*	*(10.1)*	*(10.3)*	*(10.1)*	*(11.2)*	*(100)*
Taxes	148	263	449	575	715	816	936	1042	1319	2161	842
	(643.4)	*(102.2)*	*(57.8)*	*(48.1)*	*(46.7)*	*(44.7)*	*(44.3)*	*(42.1)*	*(43.7)*	*(44.9)*	*(46.7)*
	(1.8)	*(3.1)*	*(5.3)*	*(6.8)*	*(8.5)*	*(9.7)*	*(11.1)*	*(12.4)*	*(15.7)*	*(25.7)*	*(100)*
Net benefits	800	677	433	335	177	104	21	−66	−362	−1102	102
	(3473.8)	*(263.1)*	*(55.8)*	*(28.0)*	*(11.6)*	*(5.7)*	*(1.0)*	*(−2.7)*	*(−12.0)*	*(−22.9)*	*(5.7)*

CSO allocations											
CSO expenditures	650	610	475	406	356	364	372	377	345	363	432
	(2821.6)	(237.3)	(61.1)	(34.0)	(23.3)	(19.9)	(17.6)	(15.3)	(11.5)	(7.5)	(24.0)
	(15.0)	*(14.1)*	*(11.0)*	*(9.4)*	*(8.2)*	*(8.4)*	*(8.6)*	*(8.7)*	*(8.0)*	*(8.4)*	*(100)*
CSO taxes	116	177	330	473	598	696	794	891	1128	1786	699
	(506.0)	(68.9)	(42.5)	(39.6)	(39.1)	(38.1)	(37.5)	(36.1)	(37.4)	(37.1)	(38.8)
	(1.7)	*(2.5)*	*(4.7)*	*(6.8)*	*(8.6)*	*(10.0)*	*(11.4)*	*(12.8)*	*(16.1)*	*(25.6)*	*(100)*
CSO net benefits	533	433	145	−67	−242	−332	−422	−514	−783	−1423	−267
	(2315.6)	(168.4)	(18.6)	(−5.6)	(−15.8)	(−18.2)	(−20.0)	(−20.8)	(−26.0)	(−29.6)	(−14.8)

Notes: (1) The first entry in each cell is the average value in pounds per year of the income, expenditure or tax to households in each decile; the bracketed entry expresses this figure as a percentage of decile original income and the italicised figure indicates the percentage of the income, expenditure or tax received in each decile.

(2) Original income is total household income before the addition of any cash transfers or the subtraction of any taxes; gross income is original income plus cash transfers.

(3) The expenditure and net benefit figures in the total allocations are calculated with unallocatable expenditures distributed on the population basis. For an examination of the effects of allocating these expenditures on an alternative basis, see Table 4.

Source: Michael O'Higgins and Patricia Ruggles 'The distribution of public expenditures and taxes among households in the United Kingdom', *The Review of Income and Wealth*, 1981, p. 304.

inequality of investment income. These factors are themselves likely to be interrelated; for example, the retired are more likely to have a high proportion of investment income especially if when younger they worked and saved large amounts.

International comparison of income distributions

One standard of comparison for judging the inequality of income is to compare the distribution of income in the UK with the distribution in other countries. This is in fact an exceedingly difficult task, for countries collect data for different purposes, have differing definitions of income and differing units. For these reasons it is very difficult to compare like with like.

Table 13.9 **Trends in the distribution of taxable income of inner families: Gini coefficients for available years, 1950–73**

Year	USA	UK[c] SPI	UK CSO	Germany (FR)	Republic of Ireland
1950	42.5	36.4[a]	41.1[d]	–	–
1951	–	–	–	–	–
1952	–	–	–	–	–
1953	–	–	–	–	–
1954	–	34.2[b]	40.3	–	33.7[c]
1955	43.5	–	–	–	–
1956	42.3	–	–	–	–
1957	41.9	–	–	–	–
1958	42.9	–	–	–	–
1959	43.4	33.4	39.8	–	–
1960	44.3	–	–	–	–
1961	43.8	–	38.8	–	–
1962	43.9	–	39.7	–	–
1963	44.0	–	39.5	–	–
1964	44.4	33.0	39.9	–	–
1965	45.1	33.5	39.0	–	–
1966	46.4	32.8	38.6	–	–
1967	45.7	32.8	38.2	–	–
1968	46.2	33.1	–	35.8	–
1969	46.0	32.6	–	–	–
1970	44.5	32.2	–	35.7	–
1971	44.7	32.5	–	–	–
1972	46.1	30.5	37.4[e]	–	–
1973	–	–	37.0[e]	–	30.4

Notes:

   [a] 1949–50.
   [b] 1954–55.
   [c] Fiscal year data.
   [d] 1949.
   [e] Fiscal year.

Source: *Royal Commission Report No. 5* (London: HMSO, 1977), Table 56, p. 125.

Table 13.10 Distribution of pretax total personal income of households: Percentage shares of pretax total personal insurance received by given quintiles, deciles and percentiles together with Gini coefficients

Country	Year	Source	Top 1%	Top 5%	Top 20%	21-40%	41-60%	61-80%	81-100%	Gini coefficient
Australia	1966-67	SCEF	–	14.2	38.9	23.3	17.9	13.6	6.3	32.1
France	1965	INSEE	–	–	50.5	22.0	15.4	8.9	3.6	47.0
France	1970	INSEE	–	–	47.0	23.0	15.8	9.9	4.3	41.6(44.0)
Japan	1965	Wada	–	–	44.2	22.8	16.4	11.4	5.4	37.7
Japan	1971	Wada	–	–	46.2	22.8	16.3	10.9	3.8	40.7
Republic of Ireland[a]	1966-67	HBI	5.0	15.9	42.3	23.5	16.9	12.0	5.4	36.0
Republic of Ireland[a]	1973	HBI	5.5	16.5	42.5	23.5	17.1	12.2	4.7	36.7
Republic of Ireland[a]	1973	HBI	5.9	17.5	44.5	23.8	16.6	11.1	4.1	39.5
United Kingdom	1965-66	FES	–	–	39.1	23.6	18.0	13.0	6.5	32.5
United Kingdom	1967	FES	–	–	38.8	23.5	17.8	13.1	6.6	32.2
United Kingdom	1970	FES	–	–	39.9	23.9	18.1	12.5	5.8	33.9
United Kingdom	1971	FES	–	–	39.4	24.3	18.1	12.4	5.8	33.7
United Kingdom	1973	FES	–	–	40.3	24.1	18.1	12.0	5.5	35.0
United Kingdom	1974	FES	–	–	40.1	24.4	18.1	11.9	5.5	34.8
United States	1967	CPS	5.2	16.6	43.7	24.1	17.5	11.0	3.7	39.5
United States	1970	CPS	5.5	17.0	44.6	24.2	17.0	10.3	3.9	40.4
United States	1973	CPS	6.7	18.7	45.5	24.2	16.4	10.1	3.8	41.2
United States	1974	CPS	7.5	19.9	46.4	23.7	16.1	10.0	3.8	41.2

Note: [a] Urban households only.

Sources: Australia: N. Podder, 'Distribution of Household Income in Australia', *Economic Record* (June 1972).

France: M. Sawyer, 'Income Distribution in OECD Countries', *OECD Economic Outlook*, Occasional Studies (July 1973).

Japan: R. O. Wada, Changes in the Size Distribution of Income in Post-war Japan, *World Employment Programme Research*, (Geneva: ILO, October 1974).

Republic of Ireland: Central Statistica Office, *Household Budget Inquiry 1965-66 and Household Budget Survey*, Vol. Summary results (1976).

USA: Bureau of the Census, Department of Commerce, *Current Population Reports, Consumer Income, Household Money Income and Selected Social and Economic Characteristics of Households*.

UK: *Royal Commission, Reports Nos 1 and 4*.

Source: *Royal Commission Report No. 5* (London: HMSO, 1977), Table 62, p. 133.

A painstaking attempt to provide comparable data has been made by Stark for the Royal Commission and is summarised here. It will be remembered that the basic British data relate to tax units and Stark was able to find roughly comparable data for taxable incomes for the USA, Germany (Federal Republic) and the Republic of Ireland. These data are summarised in Table 13.9, where it can be seen that Britain and Ireland have somewhat more equal distributions than Germany and much more equal distributions than the United States. It can also be seen that, while there has been a clear trend to greater equality in the UK, the reverse has been true in the USA.

Somewhat less comparable data are available for pretax personal incomes of households (which may include non-related individuals who eat together) for a total of six countries and these are given in Table 13.10. It can be seen that household income is much more equally distributed in Australia and the UK than it is in France, Germany, Ireland or the United States.

Conclusion

This chapter has tried to provide the factual background necessary for an informed discussion of taxation and income distribution. While it is clear that there is no uniquely correct way of defining either income or units, it does seem reasonable to conclude both that inequality in the UK is decreasing over time and that it is lower than in some of her most obvious competitors. This background should be helpful when we consider the redistributive effects of particular taxes in Chapters 14-18 and when we consider the effects of optimal taxation and of government expenditure on the optimal distribution of income in the final two chapters.

CHAPTER 14

Income Taxation

Income taxation raises a great deal of controversy, which is probably desirable, given that in the UK over £1 in £10 of our GDP (at market prices) was levied in income tax in 1980 and that the proportion is over 1 in 5 in some countries. Income taxation may affect our savings, our work and our attitudes towards risk-taking. It will certainly affect the distribution of incomes after tax and will probably affect the distribution of incomes before tax as well. It is impossible within the limits of this book to discuss all of these issues fully. We have put the major emphasis in this chapter on the effect of income taxation on the supply of work. We have done this for several reasons: the topic interests us; there is now a lot of empirical evidence on the topic; and labour supply response is central to the redistributive effects of taxation and hence to the design of optimal tax systems. This emphasis means, for example, that we have ignored the effects of taxation on risk-taking, and that our discussion of the effects of income taxation on savings is confined to Chapter 16.

We begin this chapter with a discussion of the meaning of income, then describe the UK income tax system and compare it with income taxes in other countries. We then examine the extent to which the tax system is understood. Following the discussion of taxation on labour supply, we end with a look at some current areas of controversy about income taxation. Does income taxation encourage the do-it-yourself industry? Does it encourage tax evasion? Should the UK abolish the present PAYE system in favour of a cheaper system of self-assessment? Was the 1977 decision to accept partial indexation of income taxes a wise decision?

Definition of income

As Lord McNaughton put it, 'Income Tax is a tax on income'.[1] Naturally, this raises the question, 'What is income?', which has been answered in another legal judgment in which Lord Wrenbury said: 'the word income ... means such income as is within the Act taxable under the Act'.[2] While this may sound nearer to a music hall act than to an economist's definition, it is a not unfair statement of the legal position. Furthermore, it may well be the sensible legal approach.

Table 14.1   Types of income liable for income tax in the UK

Schedule	
A	Rent and other receipts from land and buildings.
B	Income from the occupation or use of woodlands managed on a commercial basis.
C	Interest on certain government securities.
D (6 cases)	
I	Profits of trade
II	Profits of a profession or vocation
III	Interest and annual payments
IV and V	All income, other than employment income, arising abroad
VI	Other income including income from furnished lettings and occasional profits.
E	Income from offices, employments and pensions.

Source: *Inland Revenue Statistics 1980* (London: HMSO, 1980), pp. 29–30.

Broadly, there are two approaches to defining income. In one approach (that adopted in Britain and many other countries the law lists a variety of types of receipts (e.g. wages, dividends, etc.) that are defined as income and are subject to tax. Sources of income are listed in five schedules which are summarised in Table 14.1. The best known is Schedule E which covers wages and salaries. Any class of receipt not listed is thus legally not income and as such escapes tax. In Britain some of the receipts that are not classed as income and hence not taxed *as income* (some are taxed in other ways), include some interest paid by banks, gifts from relatives, pools winnings, gambling winnings, capital gains, and social security payments. The complex relationships between these schedules of income and taxable income (what is actually taxed) are explained in Table 14.2.

The other approach, which tends to appeal more to academic economists than to legal draughtsmen, starts from a logical definition of income and then tries to frame the legal definition as near as possible to the logical definition. Probably the best known definition of income is Henry Simon's comprehensive definition of income:

> Personal income may be defined as the algebraic sum of (a) the market value of rights exercised in consumption and (b) the change in the value of the store of property rights between the beginning and end of the period in question. In other words, it is merely the result obtained by adding consumption during the period to 'wealth' at the end of the period and then subtracting 'wealth' at the beginning.[3]

Thus income in the year 1983 can be defined as wealth on December 31 1983 *plus* consumption during 1983 less wealth on December 31 1982. This comprehensive definition of income includes gifts received, real capital gains, pools winnings, etc. Clearly, if I neither save or dissave, my income will equal my consumption which is a moderately good measure of how much use I make of society's scarce resources and a moderately bad measure of my welfare (see Chapters 19 and 20).

Table 14.2 Table of income definitions

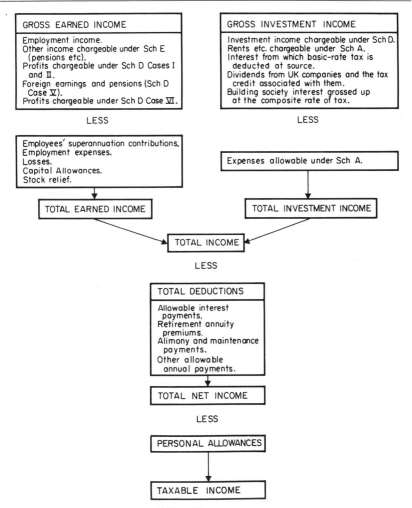

Source: *Inland Revenue Statistics 1980* p. 32.

While this definition of income is conceptually attractive, it does present certain problems. Logically the value of home-grown vegetables should be included in income, but home-grown flowers are a less clear-cut case. Simons considers a problem first posed by Kleinwächter:

> We are asked to measure the relative incomes of an ordinary officer serving with his troops and a Flügeladjutant to the sovereign. Both receive the same nominal pay; but the latter receives quarters in the palace, food at the royal table, servants, and horses for sport. He accompanies the prince to theatre

)pera, and, in general, lives royally at no expense to himself and is able
ve generously from his salary. But suppose, as one possible complication,
the Flügeladjutant detests opera and hunting.
ıhe problem is clearly hopeless.[4]

The Meade Committee point to another difficulty with this definition of income.
Suppose the rate of interest is 10 per cent. A man with wealth of £1,000,000
could have a perpetual annual income of £100,000. However if some year the
interest rate were to rise from 10 to $11\frac{1}{9}$ per cent the stock of wealth would fall
in value to £900,000. With Simons's definition quoted above, the man's income
in that year is nil! An alternative would be to define income as the amount that
could be consumed and still leave future income prospects unaffected. By this
alternative definition income would remain at £100,000 in the year that interest
rates rose, but only at the cost of adopting a subjective definition of income
which, if adopted for practical purposes, would require everyone to agree with
his tax inspector on his future income. We are thus faced with a choice between
Simon's definition with its attendant problems of flowers and flügeladjutants, or
with the UK system of defining certain classes of receipts as income for tax
purposes. If we accept that we want to work towards a comprehensive definition
as far as is practical, then we can attempt to broaden the definition of income to
include things such as imputed rents of owner-occupied housing, real capital
gains, pools winnings, etc. Another possibility is to make consumption rather
than income the tax base. This possibility is discussed in Chapter 19.

Income tax in Britain

(1) British income tax allowances and rates

In principle the British income tax system is very simple for most taxpayers
because of the very wide basic rate band (in 1981–82 the first £11,250 of taxable
income was taxed at the basic rate of 30 per cent). Except for the small minority
who pay higher rates of tax, the British income tax is a proportional tax with an
allowance or exemption. Were it not for the allowances, all basic-rate taxpayers
would pay the basic rate on all income and the tax would be a proportional tax.
However, taxpayers receive a single or married allowance and, where appropriate,
allowances for special circumstances such as age. The main allowances for
1981–82 are shown in Table 14.3.

In much of what follows we will analyse the UK income tax as if it were a
proportional tax on income with allowances. This is at best a simplification as
some income such as pension contributions and some expenditure such as
mortgage interest are excluded from total net income (see Table 14.2) while
other expenditure such as life assurance premiums is partially exempted from
the income tax base. (The tax base is discussed further in Chapter 19.)

With a proportional tax, the marginal and average rates of tax are equal, but
the effect of the exemptions just described is to drive a wedge between the

Table 14.3 Main UK income tax allowances 1981–82

	1981/82 allowance	*Number of single allowances*
Single people	£	
No children	1375	1.0
Children	2145	1.6
Two single people	2750	2.0
Married couples[a]		
Husband and wife both earning	3520	2.6[a] (or 2.0)
Husband working, wife no earned income	2145	1.6
Wife working, husband no earned income	3520	2.6

Note: [a] Assuming no wife's earnings election. Higher income people can sometimes benefit from the wife's earnings election in which case they receive two single allowances but are then taxed on their *earned* income as if they were single.
Source: Inland Revenue.

marginal and average (or effective) rate of tax. This can be seen from Figure 14.1 where the average rate of tax is rising fairly sharply even during the basic rate band of 30 per cent, because the exemption declines as a proportion of income. The figure also shows the net income elasticity which is the percentage increase in post-tax income for a small percentage increase in pre-tax income. It is equal to (1 − marginal rate of tax) divided by (1 − average rate of tax). It will be seen that where the marginal rate of tax is constant the net income elasticity steadily rises.

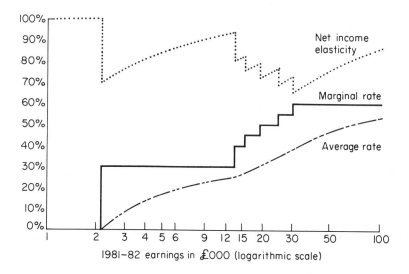

Fig. 14.1 Income tax structure, 1981–82: married man. Source: Inland Revenue.

ncomes above £11,250 higher rates of tax are payable, and these
aximum of 60 per cent on *earned* taxable income over £27,750.
bands for 1981–82 are shown in Figure 14.1 which shows the
married person assuming no relief for mortgage interest, retire-
here all income is earned. For over fifty years British income tax
has undifferentiated between earned income and investment income. At present
this is done by placing a surcharge of 15 per cent on investment income in excess
of £5500. This means that the top marginal rate of tax on investment income is
now 75 per cent (until 1979/80 it was 98 per cent).

(2) *The tax unit*

In recent years there has been increasing criticism of the British definition of the
tax unit. The tax unit is basically a single person (with or without children) or a
married couple (again with or without children). Legally a husband is responsible
for declaring and paying tax on his wife's income. The system has been criticised
as being discriminatory both for cosmetic reasons (e.g. the Inland Revenue
tended until recently to correspond with the husband about the wife's tax
affairs) and also for more fundamental reasons such as the system of allowances
which is shown in Table 14.3. It can be seen from the table that if people are not
legally married their entitlement to allowances depends on whether or not they
have children but does *not* depend on whether or not they work. On the other
hand if they are legally married the allowances depend on whether husband or
wife or both work and *not* on the presence of children.

In 1980 the Government published a Green Paper *The Taxation of Husband
and Wife* which considered various alternative ways of taxing the family. An
obvious alternative would be to change the definition of the tax unit from the
family to the individual. Clearly this would redistribute the tax burden amongst
different types of households with the amount of distribution depending on how
the change was accomplished. One can think of any actual change as consisting
of two steps. In the first step all allowances would be reduced to the present
single allowance. This would produce a great deal of extra revenue which could
be used to give larger allowances for all or it could be used to help families with
children by increasing child benefit, or the extra revenue could be used for some
other purpose altogether.

The choice between these alternatives is not easy. One has to decide on complex issues of fairness, simplicity, ease of evasion, sex discrimination and the
incentive to work. The latter is a more difficult question than any posed either
in Chapter 11 or later in this chapter because we have only considered individual
models of labour supply whereas the essence of the tax unit problems is labour
supply in a household context. That in turn requires us to have both data and
a model which allows for interactions between household members. Work on
this issue is being undertaken at Stirling University using a national data set
especially collected for the project.

In the remainder of this chapter the income tax system is analysed as if individuals were independent units.

(3) Revenue from income tax

The total amounts collected in income taxation in the UK have risen very sharply, as Table 14.4 shows. By most of the measures shown the importance of income tax fell until 1965 or 1970, rose sharply in the mid seventies and then fell again by 1980. In 1980 income tax took about the same proportions of GDP and of personal income as in 1955 but raised a substantially smaller proportion of government revenue. There are a number of reasons for these trends.

Table 14.4   Receipts from UK income taxation 1955–80

	(1)	(2)	(3)	(4)	(5)	(6)
	Income tax[a] + surtax[b]	(1) as % of GDP at factor cost	(1) as % of personal income	(1) as % of total public sector current revenue	(1) as % of government expenditure	(1) as % of central government current receipts
	£m	%	%	%	%	%
1955	2096	12.4	13.6	31.9	29.7	38.4
1960	2463	10.9	11.7	28.8	26.2	36.4
1965	3558	11.4	11.8	28.1	25.2	35.0
1970	5752	13.2	13.2	28.0	27.5	32.1
1975	14448	15.3	15.1	34.3	28.0	39.5
1980	24332	12.6	12.1	26.7	23.5	30.7

Notes: [a] The figures for 1965 and earlier years are not strictly comparable with later years.
[b] Surtax was abolished when the unified tax system was introduced and by 1980 receipts had fallen to £6m.
Source: *National Income and Expenditure 1981 Edition* (and earlier years).

If tax rates and tax bands had remained fixed for the period, then tax receipts would have risen as real or money incomes rose, and this accounts for much of the rise in revenue that has occurred in the mid seventies. But of course allowances and tax bands have not remained unaltered. Successive Chancellors altered allowances and bands almost every year and allowances were altered three times in 1977–78 alone. There have been a variety of reasons for these discretionary changes; for example stabilisation of the economy, altering the distribution of income and altering the balance of taxation. We have seen that if no discretionary changes are made unit taxes fall in real terms and income tax rises in real terms. This would lead us to expect that Chancellors would use their discretion to increase rates of specific taxes and to reduce income tax by increasing allowances and widening bands. Indeed this happened to some extent (see also section on indexation below and Chapter 17).

International comparison of income taxes

It seems almost an article of faith among some people to assume that British income taxes are higher than in her main competitor countries. Many would then go on to suggest that this alleged high British taxation is one of the main causes of Britain's relatively poor economic performance. A test of the second proposition would be an exceptionally difficult exercise well beyond the scope of this book, but we can examine the first by looking at a variety of possible measures of the burden of income taxation.

It can be seen from Table 14.5 that Britain was above the OECD average in 1975 measuring income tax both as a proportion of GDP (at market prices) and of total taxation but was below average by both measures in 1979. In compari-

Table 14.5 **Taxes on personal incomes in OECD countries**

| | Taxes on personal incomes (OECD Code 1100): | | | | | |
| | As a percentage of GDP (at market prices) | | | As a percentage of total taxation | | |
	1965	1975	1979	1965	1975	1979
Australia	8.11	12.67	13.21	34.11	43.48	44.32
Austria	7.01	8.38	9.53	20.23	21.74	23.05
Belgium	6.40	13.11	15.80	20.51	31.92	35.35
Canada	5.98	10.85	10.25	23.05	32.95	33.06
Denmark	12.44	22.95	22.19	41.40	55.91	50.33
Finland	10.81	17.42	15.19	35.89	48.18	43.36
France	3.71	4.56	5.14	10.62	12.18	12.49
Germany	8.20	10.72	10.80	25.95	30.19	28.92
Greece	1.50	2.27	3.29	7.31	9.21	11.89
Ireland	4.34	8.18	10.18	16.67	25.19	30.09
Italy	2.98	4.40	8.95	10.95	15.17	23.09
Japan	3.97	4.99	5.84	22.00	23.64	23.56
Luxembourg	7.61	11.96	12.60	24.68	27.46	27.30
Netherlands	9.78	12.41	12.61	27.56	27.09	26.60
New Zealand	9.67	15.80	17.70	39.77	52.57	56.77
Norway	13.19	17.00	17.08	39.72	37.93	37.09
Portugal	n.a.	n.a.	n.a.	n.a.	n.a.	n.a.
Spain	2.11	2.84	4.30	14.32	14.50	18.49
Sweden	17.19	20.37	21.32	48.29	48.05	42.41
Switzerland	6.45	10.69	10.97	31.16	36.10	35.24
Turkey	3.71	6.82	5.39	24.82	32.98	45.08
United Kingdom	9.19	13.80	10.66	29.82	38.24	31.32
United States	8.10	9.95	11.42	30.53	32.99	36.46
Unweighted/average						
Total OECD	7.38	11.01	11.66	26.33	31.61	32.56
North America	7.04	10.40	10.84	26.79	32.97	34.76
OECD Europe	7.45	11.05	11.65	25.29	29.99	30.71
EEC	7.18	11.34	11.88	23.13	29.24	29.50

Source: *Revenue Statistics of OECD Member Countries 1965–1980* (Paris: OECD, 1981), pp. 81, 82.

son with the EEC Britain has been above average on all the measures shown except for income tax as a proportion of GDP in 1979. While the UK has placed heavier reliance on income tax than many OECD countries, some, particularly the Scandinavian ones have substantial heavier income taxes by the measures shown.

It may be argued that in making the work-leisure choice people react to national insurance deductions in the same way they react to income taxes. In the partial equilibrium analysis of incidence (see Chapter 11) the incidence of both the employees' and the employers' contribution depends on the price elasticity of the supply and demand for labour. We will see below that the price elasticity of labour supply is low (in fact it appears to be negative), which

Table 14.6 Social security contributions in OECD countries

	Social security contributions (OECD code 2000).					
	As a percentage of GDP (at market prices)			As a percentage of total taxation		
	1965	1975	1979	1965	1975	1979
Australia	–	–	–	–	–	–
Austria	8.65	10.70	12.73	24.97	27.75	30.78
Belgium	9.81	13.09	13.18	31.42	31.87	29.48
Canada	1.47	3.32	3.42	5.68	10.09	11.02
Denmark	1.64	0.54	0.67	5.44	1.33	1.53
Finland	2.47	3.89	3.31	8.21	10.77	9.44
France	11.94	15.28	17.60	34.15	40.82	42.77
Germany	8.46	12.17	12.72	26.79	34.10	34.07
Greece	5.54	6.70	8.41	26.91	27.18	30.37
Ireland	1.69	4.48	4.85	6.50	13.79	14.34
Italy	9.31	13.29	11.06	34.17	45.87	36.74
Japan	3.45	6.19	7.25	19.11	29.33	29.27
Luxembourg	9.92	13.15	13.66	32.19	30.18	29.58
Netherlands	10.86	17.61	18.06	30.62	38.44	38.08
New Zealand	–	–	–	–	–	–
Norway	3.97	8.28	7.88	11.96	18.48	17.10
Portugal	3.62	7.76	6.95	19.51	31.28	26.91
Spain	4.16	9.31	11.68	28.26	47.49	50.19
Sweden	4.28	8.61	13.63	12.01	19.46	27.11
Switzerland	4.66	8.64	5.66	22.49	29.17	31.03
Turkey	0.86	1.91	1.32	5.77	9.24	6.34
United Kingdom	4.74	6.28	5.90	15.40	17.41	17.35[a]
United States	4.35	7.39	7.95	16.40	24.48	25.39
Unweighted average						
Total OECD	5.04	7.76	8.34	18.17	23.41	23.43
North America	2.91	5.35	5.69	11.04	17.28	18.21
OECD Europe	5.92	8.98	9.62	20.93	26.37	26.29
EEC	7.60	10.65	10.86	24.07	28.20	27.10

Note: [a] Excludes national insurance surcharge (OECD code 3000).
Source: *Revenue Statistics of OECD Member Countries 1965-1980* (Paris: OECD, 1981), p. 83.

suggests that labour would bear most of the burden unless the demand for labour is very elastic. A general equilibrium analysis by Feldstein shows that the analysis depends not only on the elasticity of the supply of labour but also on the elasticity of the supply of capital and on the elasticity of substitution between the factors. He has shown that under plausible assumptions labour will bear about 80 per cent of the burden of both employees' and employers' social security burdens.

Table 14.6 shows total amounts of social security taxes in OECD countries. It can be seen that the UK is consistently below the OECD average and substantially below the EEC average both as a proportion of GDP (at market prices) and as a proportion of all taxes. Table 14.7 shows income tax plus both employees' and

Table 14.7   Income tax plus social security contributions in OECD countries

	Personal income tax plus social security contributions in OECD countries					
	As a percentage of GDP (at market prices)			As a percentage of total taxation		
	1965	1975	1979	1965	1975	1979
Australia	8.11	12.67	13.21	34.11	43.48	44.32
Austria	15.66	19.08	22.26	45.2	49.49	58.83
Belgium	16.21	26.20	28.98	51.93	63.79	64.83
Canada	7.45	14.17	13.67	28.73	43.04	44.08
Denmark	14.08	22.99	22.86	46.84	57.24	51.86
Finland	13.28	21.31	18.50	44.10	58.95	52.80
France	15.65	19.84	22.74	44.77	53.00	55.26
Germany	16.66	22.89	23.52	52.74	64.24	62.99
Greece	7.04	8.97	11.70	34.22	36.39	42.26
Ireland	6.03	12.66	15.03	23.17	38.98	44.43
Italy	12.29	17.69	20.01	45.12	61.04	59.83
Japan	7.42	11.18	13.09	41.11	52.97	52.83
Luxembourg	17.53	25.11	26.26	56.87	57.64	56.88
Netherlands	20.64	30.02	30.67	58.18	65.53	64.68
New Zealand	9.67	15.80	17.70	39.77	52.57	56.77
Norway	17.16	25.28	24.96	51.68	56.41	54.19
Portugal	3.62	7.76	6.95	19.51	31.28	26.91
Spain	6.27	12.15	15.98	42.58	61.99	68.68
Sweden	21.47	28.98	34.95	60.30	67.51	69.52
Switzerland	11.11	19.33	16.63	53.65	65.27	66.27
Turkey	4.57	8.73	6.71	30.59	42.22	51.42
United Kingdom	13.93	20.08	16.56	45.22	55.65	48.67[a]
United States	12.45	17.34	19.37	46.93	57.47	61.85
Unweighted average						
Total OECD	12.42	18.77	20.00	44.50	55.02	55.99
North America	9.95	15.75	16.53	37.83	50.25	52.97
OECD Europe	13.37	20.03	21.27	46.22	56.36	57.00
EEC	14.78	21.99	22.74	47.20	57.44	56.60

Note: [a] Excludes National Insurance Surcharge (OECD Code 3000).
Source: *Revenue Statistics of OECD Member Countries 1965-1980* (Paris: OECD, 1981), pp. 81–3.

employers' social security contributions. The UK was above the OECD average in 1965 and 1975 by both the GDP and total tax measures but in 1979 was below the OECD average on both measures and has consistently been below the EEC average in both measures. It should be noted however that the UK figures in Tables 14.6 and 14.7 exclude the National Insurance Surcharge which was introduced in 1977. The OECD classify this tax as employers' payroll tax (code 3000) rather than as a social security contribution (code 2000). As it accounted for over 4 per cent of tax revenue in 1980 (see Table 10.2) its *in*clusion would have affected the results for 1979.

By measures that exclude social security contributions the burden of income tax in Britain is higher than average but it is certainly not the world's highest. However, what people sometimes have in mind when they think of high British income taxes is more the structure of tax rates than the overall burden of income tax, and it is certainly true that prior to 1979 Britain did have unusually (but not uniquely) high marginal tax rates on the highest *taxable* incomes. In 1979 the top rates of income tax were reduced from 83 to 60 per cent (for earned income) and from 98 to 75 per cent (for unearned income). While we have no systematic evidence it is our impression that the UK basic rate of 30 per cent is unusually high for the lowest rate of income tax.

There is nothing in this brief international comparison to suggest that the British income tax system is seriously out of line with that in other OECD countries.

Understanding of the income tax system

As part of a survey designed to find out what effect income taxation has on labour supply, economists at Stirling University designed a survey in which over 2000 weekly paid workers were interviewed. One of the subsidiary objects of the survey was to discover how well people understood the tax system.

At the time of the survey (1971) the standard rate of tax (the predecessor of the basic rate) was 38.75 per cent (7s. 9d.). While this was the single most important fact about the income tax system, it was not well understood. As might be expected, those who were not regular taxpayers were particularly badly informed (only 5 per cent were able to identify the standard rate as lying in the range 36-40 per cent). Table 14.8 shows the answers for those who pay tax every week. It can be seen that over half said they did not know the standard rate, and less than one in five placed the standard rate in the correct band.

In the 1971 budget, the standard rate was reduced from 41.25 per cent (8s. 3d.) to 38.75 per cent (7s. 9d.), and in our survey (in the autumn) we asked if the standard rate had been raised or lowered. Less than half knew the rate had fallen (and only 23 per cent knew by about how much). Despite the enormous publicity given to tax changes by the media, 16 per cent of the sample thought the standard rate had risen!

Table 14.8 Knowledge of present standard rate

Present standard rate	Pay tax every week					
	Men		Women		Total	
	N	%	N	%	N	%
0–20p	28	2	10	2	38	2
21–30p	46	4	11	2	57	3
31–35p	123	10	17	3	140	8
36–40p	267	22	49	10	316	18
41–50p	208	17	62	12	270	15
51p+	9	1	0	0	9	1
Total	681	55	149	29	830	48
NA/DK	558	45	357	71	915	52
GRAND TOTAL	1239	100	506	100	1745	100

Source: Stirling survey.

In one or two instances people were quite well informed about reliefs. For example, 85 per cent of men who paid tax regularly knew that relief was given for life assurance premiums. On the other hand, nearly two-thirds of married women did not know approximately how much a married woman could earn before paying tax. Not only were there gaps in factual information about the tax system, but many did not recognise the progressive nature of the system. When asked, 'Out of each pound of income, do rich people pay more or less of it in income tax, or do all taxpayers pay the same?' 40 per cent did not know the correct answer.

Clearly, then, there is widespread ignorance and misinformation about basic features of the tax system. There are three reasons why this low level of knowledge may be undesirable. At a general level a well-informed electorate is important in a democracy and, given the importance of economic matters in elections, knowledge about tax may be particularly important. One shudders to think of a closely fought election being decided by a minority who voted against the incumbents for putting up taxes, when in fact taxes had been lowered. Second, there is the more general problem of the applicability of our basic theory. When we talk about predicting the effects of the tax changes, we assume – usually implicitly – that people understand their budget constraints. Yet our evidence suggests that people do not understand their budget constraints. If people misperceive the world, their actions are presumably determined by their misconceptions rather than by the world as it is. This suggests that to understand a tax change fully we need to understand how the actual alteration in tax changed the world people perceived (if at all) and then how the change in perceptions affected behaviour (if at all). Finally, there is the awkward possibility that the behaviour of people who *mis*understand the tax system is socially preferable to the behaviour of people who do understand the system. Although we have not found very much evidence of misconceptions altering behaviour thus far, the reader should remember in what follows that the tax system is badly understood.

Income taxation and labour supply: the empirical evidence

The starting point for empirical analysis of the effect of income taxation on labour supply is a model such as the one presented in Chapter 11. Even when a relatively simple model is employed, deriving estimates of labour supply can be difficult. This section discusses some of the difficulties and presents some estimates from recent studies. Two broad approaches have been used in estimating the effects of income taxation on labour supply in the UK.[5] In the interview approach the analysis starts from questions in which respondents are asked how their behaviour has been affected by taxation. Various tests are then applied which are designed to eliminate implausible answers. In the other approach people's statements about the effects of taxation are ignored and behaviour is examined directly.

(1) Interview studies – low-income groups

There have been two large-scale British surveys of low-income groups using the interview approach. In the early 1950s the British Royal Commission on the Taxation of Profit and Incomes (1954) commissioned a survey by the Government Social Survey. The sample included industrial workers and supervisors in England and Wales who were able to vary their labour supply either because they could work overtime or because they were paid piece rates. In all, 1203 men and 226 women were interviewed and these were thought to be representative of about half of the total labour force. It was argued in the report that:

> Behaviour may be related (a) to accurate knowledge of the factors or (b) to incorrect information which is believed to be true or (c) it may reflect attitudes which are not directly associated with any specific facts at all.[6]

Under (a) the report concluded that there was no evidence that productive effort was inhibited by the income tax. This conclusion came from studying a subsample of workers who claimed to know all of the following: whether or not they paid tax, the tax rate that they paid (including zero), and about how much more they would earn before paying tax at a higher rate. This sub-sample were then asked, 'Would it be worth your while to earn more if it meant going on to a higher rate of tax?'[7] Unfortunately, this key question could not produce meaningful answers. If people are free to choose how long they wish to work they will move to a position of equilibrium with the budget constraint determined by their present tax rate. Clearly someone in equilibrium will not find it worth while to move. The report found under (b) and (c) that opinions about tax had a slight but statistically significant association with work but that knowledge of facts (whether or not tax is paid) was not significantly associated with variation in hours.

Some twenty years later Brown and Levin collected and analysed data from over 2000 weekly paid workers in Britain. After a large number of factual and attitudinal questions about work, in which tax was *not* mentioned by the interviewer, respondents were asked if tax had made them work 'more overtime', 'less overtime', or 'doesn't apply/neither'. The replies for men are shown in section I of Table 14.9, where it can be seen that about 74 per cent claimed no effect, 15 per cent claimed tax had made them work more and 11 per cent claimed tax had made them work less.

Table 14.9 Claimed effects of tax on overtime hours and actual mean overtime hours worked

Demog. group	Claim	I *All claims*			II *High plausible*			III *High plausible and unconstrained*		
		N	$\%^c$	Mean over-time hours	N	$\%^c$	Mean over-time hours	N	$\%^c$	Mean over-time hours
All men	Less	149	11	3.5	88	7	3.4	61	9	2.8[b]
	Neither	987	74	4.2	987	79	4.2	470	69	6.2
	More	205	15	9.0[b]	173	14	10.6[b]	151	22	10.6[b]
Single men	Less	44	13	2.5	25	8	2.8	19	12	2.3
	Neither	259	77	2.2	259	84	2.2	123	75	3.5
	More	32	10	3.1	24	8	3.3[a]	23	14	4.0
Married men without children	Less	54	12	3.8	33	8	4.1	22	10	3.1
	Neither	339	73	4.3	339	78	4.3	153	68	5.9
	More	69	15	9.9[b]	60	14	11.3[b]	51	23	11.2[b]
Married men with children	Less	45	9	3.8	26	6	2.3[a]	17	6	1.8[b]
	Neither	353	72	5.6	353	77	5.6	182	68	8.6
	More	94	19	9.5[b]	80	17	11.2[b]	69	26	11.1[a]

Notes: [a] Significant at 5 per cent.
   [b] Significant at 1 per cent.
   [c] Percentages are of the demographic group in the relevant column. Thus in the high plausible column the 173 men claiming 'more' at 14 per cent of all high plausible men, but only 13 per cent of all men.
Source: C. V. Brown and E. Levin, 'The Effects of Income Taxation on Overtime', *Economic Journal* (December 1974).

Brown and Levin then decided whether or not these claims were plausible using the general rule that an employee's claim was plausible unless demonstrably inconsistent with earlier statements. For example, people who claimed 'less overtime' were judged implausible if they would not work more overtime at a higher overtime rate than they were currently being paid. Those judged to be plausible are shown in section II of the table, where it can be seen that a larger proportion of men claiming 'more' were judged to be plausible (173 out of 205) than of men claiming 'less' (88 out of 199). In practice, employees may not be free to choose the amount of overtime that they would like to work, for a variety of reasons. Perhaps the clearest and most common form of constraint is that an employee may be required by his employer to work longer or shorter hours than he wishes to work, as a condition of employment: 30 per cent of men were constrained by this definition. In addition to this situation, which was called a 'work' constraint, there are two other classes that may be considered constrained as well. One of these is termed the 'pay' constraint. If a person's total pay does not change because of the number of hours he works, then the tax system cannot really be making him work more or less overtime. With one exception, Brown and Levin treated all workers not paid extra for overtime as being constrained (the exception is where people who are not paid extra for overtime said they chose the job because it did not have any overtime): 9 per cent of men had a pay constraint. The final type of constraint used is a constraint termed 'personal'. An employee may wish to work overtime but for reasons of health or family commitments (e.g. a married woman with a young child) may not be able to. They are constrained by personal factors: 6 per cent of men had a personal constraint.

The results are given in section III of the table. The most dramatic change from excluding the constrained comes in the number of overtime hours worked by married men with children claiming to be unaffected by tax. Brown and Levin concluded:

the number of hours overtime worked 'last week' by those claiming tax had made them work more overtime is consistently greater than the number of overtime hours worked by those claiming that tax had made them work less overtime, and in all cases those claiming 'more' work more overtime than those claiming 'neither'. In most cases those claiming 'less' work less overtime than those claiming 'neither'.

The evidence clearly suggests, therefore, that the aggregate effect of tax on overtime is small; it may perhaps add about 1% to the total hours worked, since on balance tax has made people work more rather than less overtime.[8]

(2) Interview studies – high-income groups

There have been three studies in Britain of high-income individuals the first two of which are particularly interesting because both studied the same professions. A survey of British solicitors and accountants conducted by George F. Break in 1956 found a small but significant number of persons experiencing net tax effects; but he did not find the disincentive effect (13.1 per cent of the sample) to be significantly greater than the incentive effect (10.1 per cent of the sample). He concluded that the net effect 'be it disincentive or incentive, is not large enough to be of great economic or sociological significance'.

In 1969 D. B. Fields and W. T. Stanbury repeated Break's study. They found 18.9 per cent of the sample experienced disincentive effects and 11.2 per cent experienced incentive effects. Unlike Break's findings, the difference in these proportions was statistically significant. Furthermore, the difference in the proportions experiencing a disincentive effect over the twelve-year period between the two surveys (from 13.1 to 18.9 per cent) was statistically significant. Thus Fields and Stanbury's results suggest that, if there is a net tax effect, it is likely to be in the direction of a disincentive, and also that the disincentive effect is growing stronger over time.

This would have been a reasonable conclusion were it not for problems of comparability between these two studies. Fields and Stanbury claim to have repeated Break's study but there were important differences.

(1) In Break's study the interviewer, without mentioning taxation, asked the respondent his reasons for doing the amount of work he was doing, then asked questions about tax influences on his work, and then questioned the respondent about this marginal rate of tax and his income. Fields and Stanbury reversed the order of these questions and asked the respondents about their marginal tax rate and income *before* asking questions about tax influences on work, thereby sensitising their respondents to tax effects in a way that Break had not done.

(2) Fields and Stanbury inserted questions about Capital Gains Tax, the Special Charge and Selective Employment Tax just before asking the respondents about the effect of tax on their work, whereas Break's interviewers had not even mentioned the word 'taxation' in any of their questions before asking about the influence of tax on their work.

(3) Fields and Stanbury asked questions 'relating to the incentive or disincentive effects on work effort of high marginal rates of income tax', whereas Break had asked questions about 'tax influences' on work effort. A subtle point, but one wonders how the results would have been affected if Fields and Stanbury had substituted the word 'average' for 'marginal' or better still just left it out altogether. The words used imply bias because high *marginal* tax rates are relevant to disincentive effects while the *average* rate of tax is relevant to the incentive effect.

We believe that any one of these three criticisms would cast doubt on the validity of a comparison between the two studies; and the three criticisms together make us unwilling to accept Fields and Stanbury's conclusions from the evidence they have represented. This, of course, does not rule out the possibility that their conclusions are broadly correct despite our criticisms of their approach.

Most recently Fiegehen and Reddaway have reported on an Institute for Fiscal Studies study of the incentives of senior managers. An approach was made to 108, mostly large, companies through introductions arranged by IFS and a further sixty-eight smaller companies were approached with the cooperation of the CBI. In all interviews were held in ninety-four companies (53 per cent of those approached) during 1978. What is unusual methodologically about the study is that inferences have been drawn about the behaviour of people *not* interviewed. On each company one interview, lasting over an hour was taken. The interview was with a senior manager — usually at least of Board level — and questions were asked about all senior staff (roughly defined as those earning more than £10,000 a year in early 1978). Table 14.10 shows the reported changes in senior

Table 14.10 Changes in senior staff work behaviour. Analysis of the assessments by company representatives of changes in aspects of senior staff behaviour in the previous 5 years

Aspect of senior staff work behaviour	Change reported	Companies which said senior staff motivation in the previous 5 years had:	
		declined[a]	not declined[b]
Hours worked	Decrease	11	0
	Increase	4	7
	No change	4	29
	No reply or don't know	15	24
Pride in (or dedication to) the company	Decrease	4	2
	Increase	3	3
	No change	5	20
	No reply or don't know	22	35
Standard of work expected from subordinates	Decrease	5	5
	Increase	1	6
	No change	6	18
	No reply or don't know	22	31
Willingness to take responsibility for decision making	Decrease	5	4
	Increase	1	4
	No change	9	19
	No reply or don't know	19	33
Time spent at work on personal financial matters	Increase	6	9
	Decrease	0	1
	No change	8	20
	No reply or don't know	20	30
Complaints about personal financial position	Increase	9	18
	Decrease	0	1
	No change	2	10
	No reply or don't know	23	31

Notes: [a] A total of 34 companies.
[b] A total of 60 companies, including those which gave no reply to this question.
Source: G. C. Fiegehen with W. B. Reddaway *Companies, Incentives and Senior Managers*. (London: Oxford University Press for The Institute for Fiscal Studies, 1981), p. 134.

staff work behaviour. The authors concluded (on p. 101, see further reading for full reference),

> Although a study of this type does not enable precise relative weights to be attached to the various effects of incomes and tax policies, it is clear that in total any disincentive effects that operated on senior managers had a minimal impact on the activities of British industry.

They attached a number of caveats to their findings including the fact that as senior people were studied potential effects on possibly more-mobile junior managers are omitted, and the difficulty in measuring the work effort of managers. In addition we would wish to add a caveat relating to their methodology. There are great difficulties in finding out how tax effects the behaviour of a person when interviewed directly. We found in the 1971 Stirling study that information obtained from one household member about another tended to be very unreliable. Fiegehen and Reddaway had a much more formidable task. They wished to find out about all senior staff from a single interview. Given that many of the companies had over 100 senior staff it seems unlikely, (a) that all would react the same way, and (b) that any one manager would know how all staff had behaved. Even when numbers of senior staff are lower one wonders how well informed managing directors, personnel managers or board members would be – all of whom might be involved in promotion decisions. If for purposes of argument it is assumed that taxes did have disincentive effects on senior staff it seems hard to believe that they would tell their bosses they were slacking off.

In addition to these British studies there have been several American studies of high-income-earners. These studies, which have been surveyed by Holland, show little evidence of taxation reducing or increasing productive work, but rather more evidence of taxation causing businessmen to devote time to minimising their corporate and personal tax liabilities. It would thus seem fair to conclude that there is little hard evidence of tax disincentives from the interview approach but there are three reasons why this conclusion could be wrong. First, despite our criticisms of their method, Fields and Stanbury may have been right in finding a move over time towards a disincentive effect. Second, this move might well have gathered pace as inflation has changed the real tax system (see Chapter 11 and section on indexation below). Finally, the samples of high-income people may all be biased against the finding of disincentives. If there were disincentives from tax some people would be expected to leave countries with high rates and others would be expected to choose less demanding occupations with lower incomes. Neither of these groups would appear in the specially selected high-income samples.

The interview technique has a number of disadvantages. When an emotive subject like taxation is being studied there are a number of potential pitfalls. Respondents may try to mislead the interviewers; their replies may reflect popular prejudices or misconceptions about taxation rather than their own genuine beliefs. While these dangers can be minimised by careful construction of the interview schedule, there remains the possibility that people may not understand how tax affects them. Minimising one set of problems may create another. Brown and Levin (like many others) started their interview schedule with factual questions to provide a check on the later questions about the effects of tax. This meant they were restricted to one interview a household because interviewees after the first might learn that the interviews were about taxation. Multiple interviews would have provided better factual data for household labour supply models.

Most interview studies have reported the proportion of the sample having net incentive and disincentive effects. This has the advantage of making it clear that tax effects may differ for different people, but it has the disadvantage of not providing separate estimates of income and substitution effects. This may however be more a criticism of particular studies than of the method, for Holland estimated substitution effects separately. It does however seem unlikely that one can expect to find accurate estimates of elasticities using this method. A further difficulty is that the relatively small proportion reporting tax effects means that a very large sample may be required to produce enough data for sophisticated analysis.

Given these difficulties with the interview technique, it is not surprising that other methods have received most attention recently. It will be interesting to see if there is a revival of interest in the interview method as the drawbacks of the alternative methods become clearer.

(3) Econometric studies

In the last decade the most common method of estimating the effects of taxation on labour supply have been econometric studies on cross-section data. It is assumed that the effect of taxation (or social security benefits) is to alter the budget constraint (i.e. in most studies it is assumed that attitudes towards taxes have no separate effect on work effort). Because different individuals have different gross wage rates and different amounts of non-employment income, they have different budget constraints. If differences in preferences are adequately controlled for it is possible to derive labour supply estimates from the cross-section data which can then be used as a basis for estimating the effects of taxation.

(i) *Type I studies*. Space limitations prevent separate reference to all of the many studies that have appeared, and it will be necessary to concentrate on studies of male workers. We follow Brown's (1980)[9] classification of these studies into three types of increasing sophistication. We first represent the Type I studies by Kosters (1969) pioneering study.

Kosters employed a model very similar to that outlined in Chapter 11. He used a change in the wage rate to give a price effect ($P = \partial H/\partial w$ where P is the price effect, H is hours worked and w is the wage rate), and a change in non-employment income he gave an income effect ($Y = \partial H/\partial NEY$ where Y is the income effect and NEY is non-employment income). The substitution effect (S) is found in the usual way ($S = P - YH$).

Kosters's estimates of point elasticities are probably far less important in retrospect than the signs he found. He found a negative price elasticity, but in many of his regressions the income elasticity was positive, which is counter to the theoretical prediction if income and leisure are normal goods. In addition many of his substitution effects are negative which is contrary to the theoretical prediction.

Following Kosters's findings of 'wrong' signs, a number of developments have taken place, some of which may be briefly mentioned. Kosters it will be remembered, obtained his income effect, and, by subtraction, his substitution effect, from changes in non-employment income. There are very considerable theoretical and practical problems in defining and measuring non-employment income, particularly among low-income people who are likely to have little rental, interest or dividend income. State transfer income is often means-tested and thus it is not independent of the amount of time worked. The labour supply decisions of all household members may be taken jointly, which means that the employment income of other household members is not likely to be true non-employment income. This has led to an alternative device for measuring the income effect (see below).

Kosters's price effect was $P = \partial H/\partial w$, and, not surprisingly, it has been found since that the definition and measurement of the wage rate is very important. Kosters defined the wage rate, w, as gross labour income divided by hours (this was probably unavoidable given his data source: the US Census). There are a number of problems with this definition of the wage rate (which results in the independent variable, H, appearing on both sides of the regression).

These problems plus the absence of a market wage for non-workers have led a number of authors to use a two-stage procedure with an imputed wage rate. In the first stage the average wage rate is estimated from demographic characteristics such as age and education. This gives a predicted wage which is independent of hours and which is used in the second stage in the labour supply regression. Killingsworth (1973, p. 77) has summed up the difficulties of this procedure as follows:

> the sort of regression used in most studies to obtain the 'predicted' wage in fact accounts for rather little of the total variation in wages, so that the use of the 'imputed' wage not only suppresses a good deal of the variation observed in actual wages but also in effect assigns the same wage to all persons with the same values for the 'predictor' variables (even though they may have very different values for variables which influences wages – hours of work, experience, quality of education, etc. – but are not used as 'predictors'). In addition, it is possible that 'predictors' such as age and education affect supply not only via the wage but also in other, more direct, ways, by, for example, altering (or in effect measuring) tastes, nonpecuniary factors, etc.

There remains the problem that the wage rate is an average wage rate when what should be used is a marginal wage rate. This may lead to severe theoretical problems. Suppose that an individual faces the budget constraint *ABCD* in Figure 14.2. If an average wage rate were used it would be assumed that his budget constraint was *AE*. Clearly S_1 is not the equilibrium position with such a linear budget constraint. More importantly, there are in fact many equilibrium positions consistent with an average wage given by the slope of the line *AE*. For example, an individual with a lower gross wage rate but the same tax threshold and overtime premium could have a budget constraint such as $AB'C'D'$ and be in equilibrium S_2. Thus the average wage rate and non-employment income do not uniquely determine hours worked.

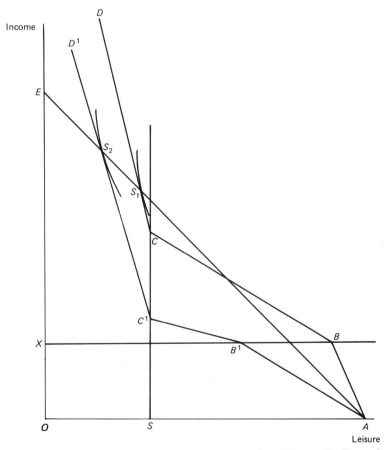

Fig. 14.2 OX = exemption level; AS = length of standard working week; Slope of AB = gross wage rate; Slope of BC = net wage rate without overtime; Slope of CD = net wage rate with overtime; Slope of AE = average wage rate.

The practical importance of this theoretical problem may well depend on the extent to which average and marginal wages differ, that is on the prevalence of overtime and on the structure of the tax system. We have shown that, at least in the case of British male workers (who often work overtime), this problem may be considerable. Estimates of price, income and substitution effects using both the average wage rate procedure and a marginal wage rate procedure (which also employed an intercept – see below) are given in Table 14.11 (in non-elasticity

Table 14.11   Labour supply estimates: comparison of Type I and Type II

	Models	
	Type I	*Type II*
Price effect[a]	−28.3	−15.6
Income effect[a]	−0.3	−0.4
Substitution effect[a]	−15.8	+2.3

Note: [a] All at means of the 'independent' variables.
Source: C. V. Brown, 'Survey of the Effects of Taxation on Labour Supply of Low Income Groups' in *Fiscal Policy and Labour Supply* (IFS, 1977).

form), where it can be seen that the sign of the substitution effect is correct with the marginal procedure and wrong with the average procedure.

In addition to this theoretical difficulty the Kosters approach suffered from an econometric problem known as endogeneity bias. Endogeneity bias may arise because the independent variables used in economic analysis (e.g. in a regression) do not explain all of the variation in the dependent variable. Part of the variation in the dependent variable is thus associated with the error term in the regression. The problem is illustrated in Figure 14.3 where it is assumed a wage rate w is paid for the first AS hours, and that subsequent hours are paid at wp, where p is the overtime premium. In the absence of random error the person would be in equilibrium at E with H_1 hours of work and income of H_1E. The average wage rate would be defined as the slope of the line AE. Because of the random error someone might actually work H_{1+u} hours where his income would be $H_{1+u}D$. The average wage rate would be given by the slope of AD. Our basis theory assumes that wage rates are exogenous. However with random error, the *average* wage rates have become endogenous.

(*ii*) *Type II studies.* The problems with the average wage rate and with non-employment income have led a number of authors to adopt a different approach to measuring price, income and substitution effects. The Type II procedure uses an adjusted non-employment income term or intercept obtained by a linearisation of the budget constraint. The method may be explained by reference to Figure 14.4 which relates to an individual who has non-employment income of OA, starts to pay tax at OC and is paid an overtime premium for hours in excess

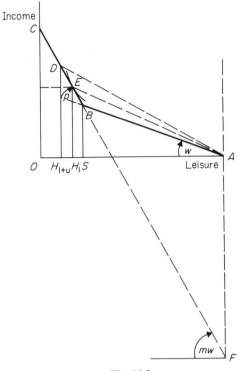

Fig. 14.3

OH_0. The individual will thus have the budget constraint $ABDE$ and will be in equilibrium at point S. Now S would also be the equilibrium *if* the budget constraint had been FE rather than $ABDE$. The new method thus relies on converting a non-linear budget constraint ($ABDE$) into a linear budget constraint (FE). Once this has been done, the price effect is given as the effect of a unit change in the slope of the linearised budget constraint (i.e. in the slope of FE), the income effect from a unit change in adjusted non-employment income (i.e. in OF), and the substitution effect is found in the normal way.

Results from two studies, one American (Dickinson, 1975) and one British (Brown, Levin and Ulph, 1976), that have used this method to study the labour supply of married men are given in Table 14.12. There are a number of differences between the two studies in the way that the wage and adjusted non-employment income variables have been defined and in the treatment of preferences. Nevertheless, the similarity between the two approaches is considerable. For example, it is argued in both studies that the simple model considered in this section (as well as in both of the studies) is more relevant to one-worker households where the worker is free to vary his hours of work.

Given the inconsistency in the signs of the income and substitution effects in some of the earlier studies, it is noteworthy that both studies have found the

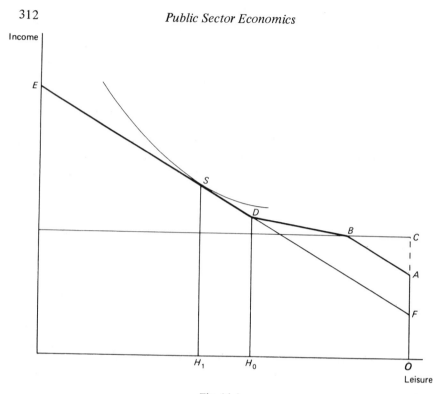

Fig. 14.4

Table 14.12 **Labour supply estimates for American and British married males, wives not working**

	Wage rate	Price elasticity	Income elasticity	Substitution elasticity	Elasticity of substitution
Dickinson[a]	under $3.25 ($\bar{w} = \$2.60$)	−0.12	Negative[d]	+0.14	d
	$3.25–$4.99 ($\bar{w} = \$4.30$)	−0.10	Negative[d]	+0.33	d
	$5.00–$9.99 ($\bar{w} = 6.10$)	−0.11	Negative[d]	+0.38	d
Brown, Levin and Ulph[b]		−0.13	−0.01	+0.22	+0.30
Brown, Levin and Ulph[c]		−0.23	−0.03	+0.26	+0.39

[a] White, no second job, unconstrained.
[b] All.
[c] Unconstrained, not on bonus.
[d] Numerical values cannot be computed from Dickinson's data.
Sources: computed from J. G. Dickinson 'The Estimation of Income – Leisure Structures for Prime Aged Married Males' doctoral dissertation, University of Michigan (1975, Table 5.1) and Brown, Levin and Ulph (1976, Table 1).

positive substitution elasticities predicted by the theory and that both have negative income effects, which are to be expected if income and leisure are normal goods. Both studies find the elasticities are quite low (in this respect they agree with most of the early studies). Type II studies overcome the theoretical problem discussed above. They also overcome the endogeneity problem *for people who remain on the same segment of their budget constraint.* Thus with the linearized budget constraint *CBF* in Figure 14.3 there is the same intercept *AF* and the same marginal wage *mw* at both H_1 and H_{1+y} hours. However if the random error in the model caused someone to work less than *AS* hours both the intercept and the wage rate would be mispredicted (as *A* and *w* respectively).

(*iii*) *Type III models.* Type III models overcome this more limited endogeneity problem by employing the entire budget constraint. When this has been done utility functions are fitted to the budget constraint by a process which allows each individual to reach the highest possible utility on whichever segment of the budget constraint this occurs. Ashworth and Ulph have undertaken such a study on the Stirling data set and their results are shown in Table 14.13 where they are compared with Type II results from the same data set. While there are a number of reasons for the changes (see Table 14.13 note a) it does appear as if the Type II model underestimated the substitution elasticity and the elasticity of substitution. This result is consistent with findings of Wales and Woodland (1979) and of Burtless and Hausman (1978) on US data but not with Ruffell's (1981) work on the Stirling data set. The results in the table refer to married men and it appears that endogeneity bias for married women is larger possibly because many married women work near the tax threshold where random error would be particularly likely to move them around the kink caused by the tax threshold.

Tax avoidance and tax evasion

People naturally take steps to minimise their tax burdens. Some of these measures are perfectly legal. If someone buys a share in a company that pays low dividends and where there is a prospect of the share price rising, he may avoid income tax on the dividend and instead pay capital gains tax at a lower rate. Indeed, tax avoidance measures may be deliberately encouraged because it is thought that, in some instances, the effects of avoidance are beneficial. Thus, taking out a mortgage or a life assurance policy or purchasing capital assets may be thought to be socially desirable ways of avoiding tax. Other ways of reducing one's tax, for example by non-reporting of income, are illegal. These illegal measures, called 'tax evasion', can lead to severe penalties if one gets caught. Clearly there are incentives for both legal avoidance and illegal evasion, and it seems likely that these incentives will rise as marginal tax rates rise.

Table 14.13 Labour supply estimates: comparison of Type II and Type III[a]

	Models	
	Type II[b]	Type III[c]
Price elasticity	−0.11	−0.07
Income elasticity	−0.02	−0.10
Substitution elasticity	0.20	0.50
Elasticity of substitution	0.27	0.58

Notes: [a] All of the differences between the results shown cannot be attributed to the differences between Type II and Type III models. There are also differences in the numbers studied (smaller in the case of the Type III study because of higher data requirements), in functional form, and in the definition of some of the variables.
[b] Note these elasticities differ slightly from those given in Table 14.12 where results from a subsample of the Brown, Levin and Ulph results were selected so as to be as comparable as possible with Dickinson's sample selection criteria.
[c] Using a generalised constant elasticity of substitution indirect utility function.
Source: J. S. Ashworth and D. T. Ulph 'Endogeneity I: Estimating Labour Supply with Piecewise Linear Budget Constraints', in C. V. Brown (ed.) *Taxation and Labour Supply* (Allan and Unwin, 1981).

(1) Tax avoidance

Whenever one activity is taxed more highly than others there is a *ceteris paribus* argument that people will switch to the lightly taxed (or untaxed) activity. An obvious example concerns the choice between paid or market work and home production or non-market work such as decorating one's house or growing vegetables for home consumption. As market work is taxed but non-market work is not taxed, the tax system provides an incentive to substitute non-market work for market work. We have seen that theoretically an increase in income tax may either increase or decrease market work. While this conclusion remains strictly valid, allowing substitution of non-market work adds an additional element which reduces the incentive to undertake market work. However there is a clear-cut prediction that a tax on market work will lead to an increase in non-market work. The argument is illustrated in Figure 14.5, where we show the effects of introducing a tax on market work.

In Figure 14.5, the marginal product of home work is given by the slope of $H_w H_w$ which is curved to reflect diminishing returns to home work. The market wage is given by the slope of the line $W_1 N_1$. In equilibrium the two slopes will be equal. This occurs where $W_1 N_1$ is tangent to $H_w H_w$. The individual devotes HH_1 hours to home work and produces directly an income of YH_1. His overall budget constraint is $W_1 N_1$ and equilibrium is at E_1. The total amount of work done is HT_1 and the amount of market work is HM_1 (i.e. $= HT_1 - HH_1$).

If a tax on market income is introduced, the net market wage rate now falls so that it equals the slope of $W_2 N_2$; the individual will move to E_2, where the market wage is restored to equality with the marginal product of domestic

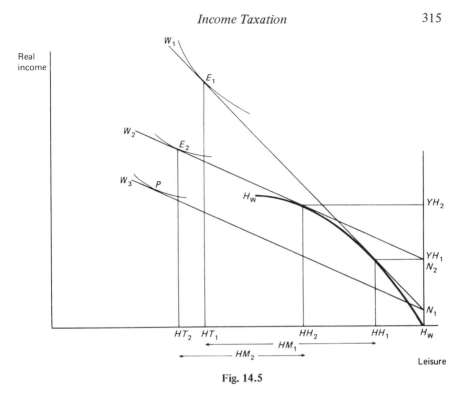

Fig. 14.5

production. The move from E_1 to E_2 involves a number of changes. There is a price effect on *total* hours given by a movement from E_1 to P. The sign of this price effect is unknown: *total* hours may rise or fall. The reduced wage is now below the marginal product of home work. The individual will therefore reduce market work and increase home work until marginal product of home production has fallen to the new lower market wage. In the diagram this occurs at HH_2 hours of home work. As a result of the extra hours of home work the total amount of home production increases – to YH_2 in the diagram. This changes the intercept from N_1 to N_2. The increase in home production is analogous in its effect to an increase in a lump sum hand-out and results in a further fall in market work. Thus within the movement from E_1 to E_2 there are two separate effects reducing hours of market work. Actual hours of market work will thus fall unless there is a negative price effect sufficiently large to offset both the switch to home production and the income effect from the home production. It can be seen that as the diagram is drawn the price effect is negative causing total hours to rise. However, hours of home work increase by more than total hours and this plus the income effect from home work reduces hours of market work. This switch from market work to home work leads to a welfare loss because people will undertake home work when their marginal product is lower than their marginal product in the market. The reason for this is that the individual can equate his marginal rate of substitution to his marginal rate of transformation in the home but not in the market.

Boskin (1975) has estimated that the welfare loss associated with the differential treatment of home and market work in the United States was between $20B and $45B. Boskin made his estimates using the Harberger general equilibrium model that was outlined in Chapter 12. Boskin divided the economy into two sectors: a market sector and home production sector. It will be remembered that it is assumed in the Harberger model that the total supply of labour and capital is fixed. In the explanation of the Harberger model in Chapter 12 we assumed that all elasticities were unity. With similar assumptions Boskin estimated the welfare loss from the tax at $45B. Estimates of welfare losses with this and other elasticity assumptions are given in Table 14.14. It can be seen that within the given ranges the results are much more sensitive to variations in the elasticity of demand than they are to variations in the elasticity of substitution. Boskin thinks the two cases in which it is assumed that the elasticity of substitution in production is unity are more realistic. Table 14.14 also shows that the welfare loss lies between 6 and 13 per cent of government revenue. As we will see in Chapter 18, this is a much larger welfare loss than the loss from corporation tax using the same model.

Table 14.14 Estimated welfare loss from the differential treatment of home and market work, USA, 1972

Compensated price elasticity for market output	Elasticity of substitution in home production	Elasticity of substitution in market production	Welfare loss	
			$b	as % of government revenue
1	1	1	44.5	13
1	$\frac{1}{2}$	1	43.8	13
1	$\frac{1}{2}$	$\frac{1}{2}$	38.6	11
$\frac{1}{2}$	1	1	24.3	7
$\frac{1}{2}$	$\frac{1}{2}$	1	24.2	7
$\frac{1}{2}$	$\frac{1}{2}$	$\frac{1}{2}$	22.2	6

Source: M. J. Boskin, 'Efficiency Aspects of the Differential Tax Treatment of Market and Household Economic Activity', *Journal of Public Economics* (1975), p. 11.

(2) Tax evasion

It is possible to construct a model of tax evasion in which predicted tax evasion depends on the balance between rewards to evasion if less tax paid and the penalties for being caught which would depend both on the probabilities of being caught and on the penalties of being caught.

Clearly, there are incentives to evasion and clearly, tax evasion does exist. What is not known is how prevalent it is. The conventional argument is that it is virtually impossible to measure the extent of evasion because people will not admit to breaking the law. While there is a great deal of force in this argument its significance may be exaggerated. We found a surprisingly large percentage of our sample of weekly paid workers admitted to having income from a second job on which they paid no tax. This proportion was as high as one in eight among single men. We therefore believe that it would be worth the attempt to measure the extent of evasion more systematically.

Indexing income taxes

We have seen that inflation alters the real value of progressive income taxes unless these changes are offset by discretionary acts of budgetary policy. Over a run of years the basic allowances in the UK have been increased roughly in line with inflation but during the 1970s the real value of the single person's allowance was increased sharply and has since fallen back as can be seen from the upper part of Figure 14.6 in comparison with the right-hand side. After a much smaller increase in the early 1970s allowances for a married couple with two children

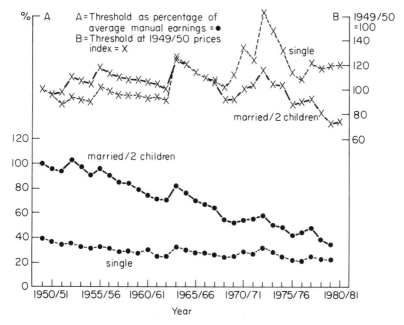

Fig. 14.6

have fallen in real terms. It should be remembered, however, that child allow-ances have been phased out and have been replaced by child benefit. The bottom part of Figure 14.6 shows (with reference to the left-hand scale) that allowances, particularly for married people with children have fallen very sharply relative to average earnings. This is in part due to the change in the real value of the allow-ances shown in the upper part of the figure but much more important has been the increase in real terms in average earnings.

While allowances have come near to increasing at the same rate as prices, the same thing cannot be said of higher rate bands, which have not increased by anything like the amount required to keep pace with inflation. Figure 14.7 shows how the real tax bands shrunk in the period from 1961–62 to 1974–75.

It is not surprising that high rates of inflation have been accompanied by demands to index the tax system. Perhaps the major reason for this demand is the belief that any changes in progressiveness of the real tax system should be made by the conscious decision of Parliament rather than as a side-effect of the rate of inflation.

A number of countries, including Canada, Uruguay, Australia, France, Luxembourg, the Netherlands, Israel and the UK, have some degree of indexa-tion of their tax systems although this is complete only for the first three countries listed. Other countries, including Brazil, Chile, Denmark and Iceland, adjust income tax in response to various measures of changes in earnings.

In the UK the principle of indexation was forced on the government in the late 1970s, but this will not necessarily make any difference to the real tax system (as the 1981 Budget proved) but it will make a difference to the way it is presented. The government is not actually committed to increasing allowances by the full amount required to compensate for inflation. What the Commitment does require is a deliberate act of policy not to put up allowances. Suppose allowances were £1000 in year 1 and inflation 20 per cent between years 1 and 2 and the government wanted to make allowances £1100 in year 2. Prior to the commitment to indexation the chancellor could stand up and say, 'I am reducing taxes by increasing allowances by £100.' After the commitment to indexation he would be forced to admit that he was raising taxes by reducing the real value of the allowance by £100. We think this is an important change of principle which should draw attention to real changes in the tax system, and we hope the same principle will be extended to other taxes wherever this is administratively feasible.

Self-assessment

Britain has a system of collecting income tax which appears to put unusually high collection costs on the tax-collecting agency. The reason for this is that the British pay-as-you-earn (PAYE) system attempts to collect precisely the correct amount of tax *each* pay period (e.g. every week of every month) and it puts the

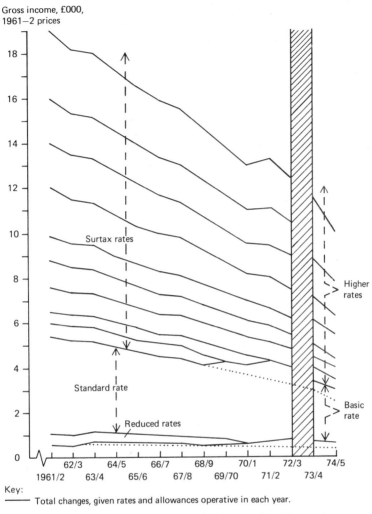

Fig. 14.7 Contraction of the real size of tax brackets, 1961–62 to 1974–75: married couple, two children aged 11 to 16. Source: R. I. G. Allen and D. Savage, 'Inflation and the Personal Income Tax', *National Institute Economic Review*, November 1974, Chart 2.

main burden of calculating the amount of tax due on the Inland Revenue. In other countries no attempt is made to deduct so precisely the correct amount of tax, which means that a much higher proportion of people have an end-of-year assessment in which they receive a tax refund or a demand for a further tax payment. Many other countries also require the taxpayer to compute his own tax liability. This may involve adding up several sources of income, then

Table 14.15 Certain public sector costs of collecting income tax in four countries

Country	Year	Number of employees in revenue ('000)	Population (million)	No. of revenue employees as % of '000 population	Public administration costs as % of tax collected
UK	1973	70.7	56	1.3	1.71
USA	1973	71.8	210	0.3	0.48
Canada	1973	14.6	23	0.7	0.91
Sweden	1973	8.0	8	1.0	1.0

Notes: (1) The number of employees is not strictly comparable, as in each case it refers to total numbers employed in the department responsible for collecting income tax. But in all cases other taxes were collected as well and so there is no obvious bias in the figures.

(2) The approximate number of returns processed was 20 million in UK, 80 million in USA, 11 million in Canada and 5 million in Sweden.

(3) Cf. H.C. 368–iv 1975–76 *op. cit.*, for further discussion.

Source: N. A. Barr, S. R. James and A. R. Prest, *Self Assessment for Income Tax* (London: Heinemann, 1977), p. 150.

deducting various allowances in order to compute taxable income. The tax due is then found by consulting tax tables. The extra costs imposed on the Inland Revenue can be gauged from Table 14.15, where it appears that costs of tax collection are nearly four times as high in Britain as in the United States. These figures are from a study of self-assessment by N. A. Barr, S. R. James and A. R. Prest which on balance favours a change to self-assessment for the UK.

The basic arguments in favour of self-assessment are that it would reduce the public sector costs of tax collection, and that it should lead to a greater understanding of the tax system on the part of taxpayers. It would also make it easier to eliminate the wide basic rate band which many would see as an advantage. The arguments against self-assessment are that it would increase the private sector costs, that it might lead to a decline in standards of tax administration as fewer taxpayers' forms would be checked by the Inland Revenue, and that verification when it did occur might be more obtrusive. Our own view also favours self-assessment, primarily because we hope it would improve the level of understanding of the tax system which as we have seen is now very low.

Conclusion

Clearly, income taxation is controversial and may involve large welfare losses, particularly because of the omission of home production from the tax base. We have seen that in the UK marginal rates of income tax rise very high in comparison with most industrialised countries. We have also seen that evidence that people do adjust their work effort in response to tax changes although the evidence presently available seems more convincing for low-income people than for high-income people. We return to many of these issues in later chapters – particularly in Chapter 19, where we discuss taxes on expenditure as an alternative to taxes on income, and in Chapter 20, where we consider optimal income taxation.

Appendix: Income taxation and employment: an integration of neoclassical and Keynesian approaches

The purpose of this appendix is to show the implications for standard macroeconomic models of incorporating the results from the microeconomic analysis of taxation and labour supply. We will see that the incorporation of these elements alters the Keynesian analysis of the effects of income taxation on the amounts of labour that are actually employed, the full employment level and the levels of unemployment. There are, broadly, three ways in which the neoclassical and Keynesian approaches differ.

First, in the standard microeconomic neoclassical treatment[10] individuals are assumed to maximise their satisfaction given certain preferences, as for example between real consumption goods and leisure, given their budget constraint, which depends among other things on a *net* real wage rate. In the standard Keynesian macroeconomic treatment, equilibrium in the labour market occurs where the aggregate supply curve of labour intersects the aggregate demand curve for labour. While it is typically *not* emphasised, this aggregate supply curve for labour shows the amount of labour that will be supplied at various *gross* wage rates (which are sometimes assumed to be money wages and sometimes real wages – see Branson, 1972).

Another inconsistency between the micro- and macroeconomic treatments of taxation and labour supply is in the assumption(s) about the elasticity of labour supply. Microeconomic treatments consider both the possibility that the individual's supply curve of labour is positively sloped (i.e. that elasticity is greater than zero) and the possibility that the individual supply curve is negatively sloped (elasticity less than zero). Macroeconomic treatments often assume that the aggregate supply of labour has a positive elasticity.[11]

A final difference between the micro- and macro-treatments is that textbook macro-treatments are typically confined to very simple assumptions about the nature of the tax systems (e.g. that there is a proportional income tax). Microeconomic treatments on the other hand consider the effects of more complex tax systems (e.g. ones that are progressive).

In this appendix we show the effects of integrating these three aspects into a static macroeconomic model familiar to readers of standard macroeconomic textbooks. The macroeconomic model that is used is thought to be fairly representative of Keynesian models in standard intermediate textbooks. It is not suggested that such models are especially realistic, but a fully realistic model is not necessary to the argument, which is designed to incorporate some missing elements into a familiar theoretical structure and thereby increase the realism of the models. Section (1) incorporates the effects of assuming that labour supply depends on the net rather than the gross wage assuming a positive elasticity of supply and a proportional income tax. The possibility of a negative elasticity of labour supply is considered in section (2), where the assumption of proportional taxes is retained. In section (3) we look at the macroeconomic implications of non-proportional taxes, and in section (4) the combined results from sections (1), (2) and (3) are summarised.

In order to keep the analysis as simple as possible we assume throughout that:

(1) Individuals' utility depends on net income and leisure.

(2) All variables (except the price level) are measured in real terms. In particular it should be noted that it is assumed that the supply of labour depends on the real net wage.[12]

(3) There is a fixed money wage W_0.[13]

(4) At the initial price level, P_0, the real wage $\bar{W}_0/P_0$ is above the full employment level.

(5) The government has decided to eliminate the resulting unemployment by a cut in income taxation.

(6) The government is able to calculate the required reduction in income taxation accurately[14] and is thus able to eliminate unemployment.

(7) When the demand for labour is less than the supply of labour, it is assumed that the actual level of employment is determined by the demand for labour. It is also assumed that when there is disequilibrium in the labour market goods markets reach a position of (constrained) equilibrium.

(8) There are no other restrictions on labour supply.

(9) The supply of labour is measured in hours.

(10) All individuals have the same preferences and the same wage rate, which means that aggregate labour supply is the supply of a representative individual times the number of individuals.

(11) Unemployment is any excess of hours supplied over hours demanded at the current net wage rate.

(12) Income and leisure are both normal goods (this is consistent with the empirical evidence presented in the body of this chapter).

(1) Incorporation of taxation and labour supply

The purpose of this section is to show how the incorporation of taxation and labour supply can affect a familiar macroeconomic model. It is assumed throughout this section that the tax under consideration is a proportional income tax.

The model is represented graphically in Figure A14.1. Part (a), which has real national income on the vertical axis and the level of prices on the horizontal axis, contains aggregate supply[15] (AS) and demand curves[16] (AD) and shows the equilibrium level of output and prices. Part (b), with output on the vertical axis

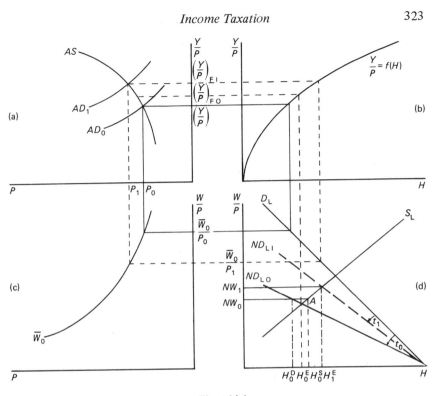

Fig. A14.1

and labour hours on the horizontal axis, shows the short-run production function, which is assumed to exhibit diminishing returns. Part (c), with real wages on the vertical axis and prices on the horizontal axis, shows the relationship between real wages and prices given the fixed money wage.

Part (d) represents the labour market. The horizontal axis shows total hours of labour supplied and *the vertical axis represents both gross and net real-wage rates*. The (derived) demand curve of labour is shown as D_L. This (gross) demand curve for labour shows the amount of labour that employers will wish to hire and the gross wage rate is the cost to the employer of hiring various amounts of labour. When there is tax on income employees do not receive the gross wage, as part of this wage or income is paid in income taxation. With a proportional income tax, the income tax deduction will be a constant proportion of the gross wage irrespective of either the level of the gross wage or the number of hours worked. Thus if the proportional tax rate is t_0, the net of tax demand curve for labour will be ND_{LO}.

We know from standard microeconomics that it is assumed that the supply of labour depends on the net wage rate, which means that the labour market equilibrium would occur where S_L and ND_{LO} intersect at H_0^E hours. Thus, while the demand for labour depends on the gross wage, the supply of labour depends on the net wage. This means that labour market equilibrium occurs where the supply of labour is equal to the net wage rate.

With the current level of wages ($\overline{W}_0$) and of prices (P_0), the real gross wage is $\overline{W}_0/P_0$. At this gross wage the demand for labour is H_0^D and, by assumption, that is the actual level of employment as well. When the gross wage is $\overline{W}_0/P_0$ it can be seen that the net wage is NW_0. With a net wage of NW_0 the supply of labour is H_0^S. This means that with a gross wage of $\overline{W}_0/P_0$ and a net wage NW_0 there will be unemployment amounting to H_0^S less H_0^D. It is assumed that the government decides to eliminate unemployment by reducing the (proportional) income tax. By assumption the reduction in income tax will just eliminate the unemployment. *This cut in the tax rate will have both supply and demand effects.* The cut will increase the net demand curve from ND_{LO} to ND_{LI}. This will raise the equilibrium level of employment from H_0^E to H_1^E. It will also raise the amount of labour supplied from H_0^S to H_1^E. On the demand side, the cut in tax raises disposable incomes, which increases the demand for goods;[17] and with appropriate multiplier effects this will increase the level of aggregate demand from AD_0 to AD_1. It can be seen from part (a) that this increase in aggregate demand will raise the full employment level of income from $(Y/P)_{FO}$ to $(Y/P)_{FI}$ and the equilibrium level of prices from P_0 to P_1. From part (b) it can be seen that the demand for labour will increase. That is to say there will be a movement down the gross demand curve for labour. It can be seen that the increase in the amount of labour demanded is from H_0^D to H_1^E. From part (c) it may be seen that with the money wage fixed at $\overline{W}_0$ the increase in the price level reduces the real wage to $\overline{W}_0/P_1$. This cut in the gross real wage is consistent with the increase in the demand for labour to H_1^E. It may be noted that, while the *gross* real wage *falls*, the *net* real wage *rises*. Thus from the employer's point of view the expansion in employment is associated with a falling wage, while from the employee's point of view the expansion in employment is brought about by an increase in the real wage. It also seems highly probable that real disposable income will rise (the only possible exception is if the labour supply curve bent backwards very sharply).

(2) Negative elasticity of labour supply

The situation is rather different when the labour supply curve is negatively sloped. The position may be analysed with the aid of Figure A14.2, which is identical to A14.1, except for the slope of the labour supply curve. The labour supply curve in Figure A14.2 is constructed so that the initial level of unemployment is the same in A14.1. Thus S_L in Figure A14.2(d) passes through the point A so that in both cases the initial level of unemployment is $H_0^S - H_0^D$. The cut in the tax rate raises the net of tax demand curve from ND_{LO} to ND_{LI} and the (actual) net wage rises from NW_0 to NW_1. This *reduces the equilibrium* supply of labour from H_0^E to H_1^E. It also reduces the amount of labour supplied at the

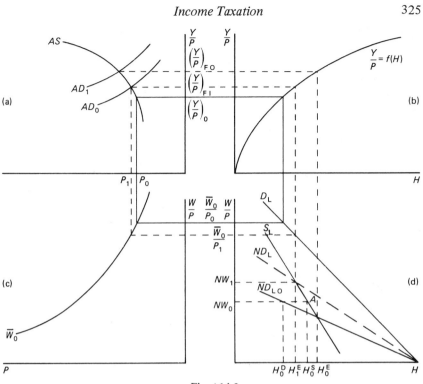

Fig. A14.2

current net wage rate. When, originally, the net wage was NW_0 the amount of labour supplied was H_0^S. When the net wage rises to NW_1 the amount of labour supplied *falls* to H_1^E.

On the demand side, however, the effects are as before. The cut in tax raises aggregate demand, which raises the equilibrium levels of income and of price in Figure A14.2(a). This raises the demand for labour in part (b) and reduces the gross real wage in part (c) so that the demand for labour rises to H_1^E in part (d). Thus, with a negatively sloped supply curve, the supply effects tend to *reduce* unemployment. Thus the actual increase in employment is due entirely to the demand effect.

It has been assumed that the government is able to calculate the required tax cut so that unemployment is eliminated in both cases. However, the effects of the tax cut differ in most other respects. The key to the differences is that, with a positively sloped supply curve, the equilibrium level of employment rises, while with a negatively sloped supply curve the equilibrium level of employment falls. Thus the actual level of employment rises by more with a positively sloped supply curve than it does with a negatively sloped supply curve. A higher level of employment means a higher level of real income when the supply curve is positively sloped. This higher level of real income can be achieved only by a lower gross real wage. With a given money wage a lower gross real wage means higher prices. Thus the achievement of full employment requires a larger rise in prices when the supply curve is positively sloped.

(3) Macroeconomic implications of non-proportional taxes

In this section we consider the macroeconomic effects of non-proportional taxes by examining the implications of changes in allowances and in basic rates in the UK tax structure. The reader will recall from the discussion in Chapter 11 that an increase in allowances will shift the supply curve of labour in the direction of less work, and a cut in the basic tax rate will shift the supply curve in the direction of more work. Non-proportional taxes will also affect the net of tax demand curve for labour. With the non-proportional taxes the net of tax demand curve will no longer be a straight line (as with a proportional tax) but instead will be a curved line of the sort shown in Figures A14.3 and A14.4[18] where for covenience we have assumed that the supply curve of labour is vertical.

An increase in allowances will cause the net demand curve to shift up from ND_{LO} to ND_{LI} in Figure A14.3 and will cause the supply curve to shift to the

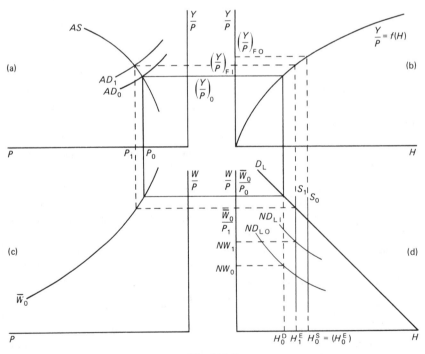

Fig. A14.3

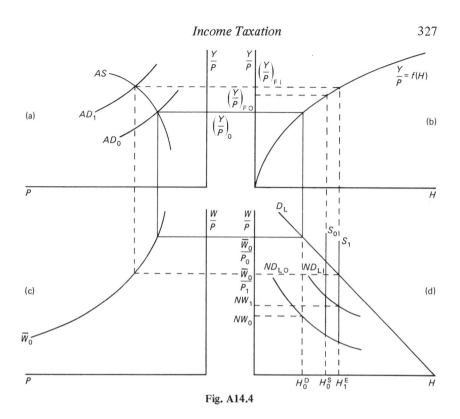

Fig. A14.4

left (the direction of less work) to S_1 (for the reasons explained in Chapter 11). The important consequence in this case is that the leftward shift in the supply curve *reduces* the equilibrium employment level to H_1^E and *reduces* the full employment level of income from $(Y/P)_{FO}$ to $(Y/P)_{FI}$. A cut in the tax rate on the other hand will cause the supply curve to shift to the *right*, to S_1 in Figure A14.4. The shift of the supply curve to S_1 and the shift of the net demand curve to ND_{LI} will *increase* the equilibrium level of employment to H_1^E and will *increase* the full employment level of income from $(Y/P)_{FO}$ to $(Y/P)_{FI}$.

The argument could be easily extended to include supply curves with positive and negative slopes. The essential point is that an increase in the exemption level shifts the supply curve to the left, reducing the full employment level of income relative to the level determined by the original supply curve, while a reduction in the tax rate shifts the supply curve to the right, increasing the full employment level relative to the original supply curve.

(4) Summary

It has been demonstrated that a change in income taxation will change both the actual level of employment and the full employment level. Thus a tax change

Table A14.1   Effect of a tax cut on the full employment level of income

Nature of effect from tax cut	Elasticity of labour supply		
	Positive	Zero	Negative
Positive income effect (e.g. increase in exemption level)	Uncertain	Falls	Falls
Pure price effect (e.g. cut in proportional tax rate)	Rises	No change	Falls
Price effect plus negative income effect (e.g. cut in basic tax rate)	Rises	Rises	Uncertain

designed to bring the economy to a particular full employment target may cause that target to shift. The recognition of this interaction between policy instruments and policy goals is perhaps the most important practical implication of the integration of the neoclassical and Keynesian approaches. A cut in taxation may either increase or decrease the full employment level of income depending on the elasticity of labour supply on the one hand and the nature of the tax cut on the other. These effects are summarised in Table A14.1. If we knew the elasticity of labour supply we could then predict the direction of the effect of different types of tax changes in the level of national income. If all the underlying relationships in the model were fully known it should also be possible to predict the *amount* by which the actual and full employment levels of income would change.

CHAPTER 15

Measures to Reduce Poverty

The purpose of this chapter is to discuss two classes of measures that are designed primarily to raise incomes of the poor. Negative income taxes (NITs) pay a cash sum to persons or households that have income below a specified level. This sum is reduced as income rises towards this level. Means-tested benefits (MTBs) provide benefits frequently, but not always, in kind (e.g. free school meals, reduced rents) to persons or households whose incomes fall below the level specified for that benefit. NITs and MTBs have certain common features:

(1) they raise the net incomes of poor households;
(2) as households raise their own incomes (e.g. by working more), some, or all, of this benefit is lost. The rate at which the benefit is lost is thus the implicit tax rate on the NIT or MTB.

In discussing ways of aiding the poor our focus will be on the effects of programmes on people who are working. We have chosen this focus because it is a controversial area of public concern and because there is a growing body of experimental evidence – particularly from the United States – about the extent to which raising the incomes of poor workers by NITs affects their willingness to work.

We wish to stress at the outset that many of the poor are incapable of work because of mental or physical infirmities including age. For these people the issues are much more straightforward as we do not need to be as concerned with labour supply results. Even among some of the retired, however, the issue remains, for many retired people would like to work and their willingness to provide for themselves will depend in part on the way in which pensions and other incomes are means-tested.

Negative income taxation

One widely discussed means of raising low incomes is for the state to pay out transfers to low-income individuals often using the 'machinery' set up to collect income tax. These schemes are known by a wide and rather confusing set of terms, including 'negative income taxation', 'social dividends', 'income maintenance', 'tax credits', 'guaranteed income', and 'reverse income tax'. The schemes share three common features: (1) they provide some minimum guaranteed level of income; (2) income above this rate is taxed at some rate (or rates); or (3) there is some level of income at which ordinary income tax becomes payable. Indeed, in the simpler schemes with only one tax rate any two of the features listed above determine the third. This can be illustrated in Figure 15.1, which has gross pretax income (GY) on the horizontal axis and net after tax income (NY) on the vertical axis. The $45°$ line shows the equality of gross and net incomes that would occur in the absence of taxation. Suppose that the ordinary income tax system exempts OX gross income from tax, and taxes income above OX at the tax rate t. In these circumstances the tax schedule can be represented by the line OBC, which can be used to find the net income associated with any particular level of gross income. Thus a person with pretax income of GY_M will pay ED in tax receiving an after tax income of NY_M. Suppose further that a negative income tax scheme is introduced that provides a guaranteed minimum income of Y_{min}, at tax rate of t_{nit}, and a break-even level of OX. Thus a person with a pretax income of GY_L will receive a negative tax of FG and will have an after-tax income of NY_L. The complete tax/transfer schedule would then be $Y_{min}BC$. It can easily be seen that the segment $Y_{min}B$ is determined by any two of Y_{min}, t_{nit} and B.

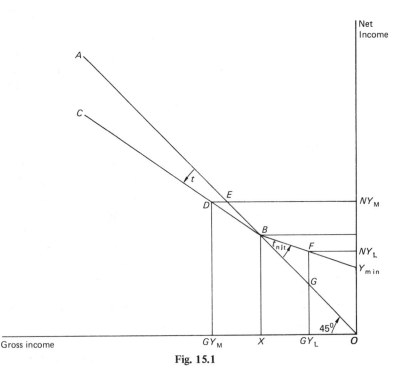

Fig. 15.1

There is a wide variety of negative income tax (NIT) schemes. Perhaps the simplest are those designed to give the *non*-taxpayer the benefit of the exemption level that only benefits taxpayers with an ordinary tax system. Thus if the exemption level were £30 a week and the tax rate one-third, the exemption would be worth £10 a week to taxpayers and nothing to the non-taxpayer. A NIT might provide a minimum income of £10 a week and a tax rate of one-third. The effect would be to convert the tax system to a proportional tax with a lump sum handout.

In practice a guaranteed income arrived at in this manner is unlikely to provide a socially acceptable minimum subsistence income, which means that it would need to be supplemented by other devices to aid the poorest members of the community. Other schemes, which some writers term 'social dividend schemes', are designed to produce a minimum level of income high enough for subsistence and are designed to replace other forms of assistance to the poor. There have been many schemes proposed but it is always convenient for purposes of analysis to reduce them to the common elements of guaranteed income, tax rate(s) and break-even level of incomes. This may be illustrated by three recent British schemes.

Family income supplement (FIS) is for households with at least one child, with (normally) a man in full-time work, and whose family income is below a specified level. From November 1981 FIS provided half the difference between a family's income and the maximum qualifying income, subject to a maximum of £18.50 for a family with one child (the amount increases by £1.50 per child). The qualifying income was £74 a week for one-child families (increased by £8 per child). These requirements can be restated as follows taking a two-child family as an example. The minimum income is £20.00, the tax rate is nil for incomes below £42 and 50 per cent (neglecting income tax) for incomes above £42 up to the break-even level of £82 a week.

In 1972 the government announced plans for the introduction of a NIT which it termed a Tax Credit Scheme. In the Green Paper outlining the proposals illustrative figures were given which were to be updated before the scheme was actually introduced. For example, a married household would receive £6 a week plus an additional £2 a child. These sums, termed tax credits, would be offset against income tax liability and would be paid through the PAYE system to households where the credit exceeded the tax liability. The tax credits were designed to replace the main income tax personal allowances and family allowances. Thus – to take the two-child household as an example – the scheme provided a guaranteed income of £10 a week. If the basic rate was 30 per cent, the break-even level would be £33.33 a week. The tax credit scheme aroused a great deal of opposition – primarily on the grounds that it provided insufficient help to those below the supplementary benefit level – and was never introduced.

In 1979 children's income tax allowances were replaced by Child Benefit. For two-parent families the benefit was £5.25 a week for each child in 1981/82. Thus the minimum income is £10.50 a week for two-child families, the tax rate is nil up to the tax threshold and then becomes the basic rate (30 per cent in 1981/82), so that the breakeven level of income is £35 above the tax threshold.

Britain thus has negative income taxation in substance in the form of FIS and child benefits, although that term has not been officially used.

(1) Comparison of negative taxes and means-tested benefits

While there are many similarities between NITs and MTBs, there is one important distinction. NITs are almost always paid in cash while at least some MTBs are paid in kind (e.g. school meals). Presumably the reason for paying at least some MTBs in kind is to ensure that the money is spent for 'goods' such as housing and children's food and not for 'bads' such as Baccy, Booze and Bingo. That this objective should be achieved can be illustrated with reference to Figure 15.2. In the absence of any MTB the person has a budget constraint of AB and is in equilibrium at E_0 where he purchases G_0 'goods' and B_0 'bads'. If he is then given an additional G_0G_1 of 'goods' by the state the new 'equilibrium' position will be 'E_1'. If instead, a cash payment was made that enabled the person to move to 'E_1', he would in fact choose to move to E_2, which is on a higher indifference curve. At E_2 only G_2 'goods' would be purchased and consumption of 'bads' would rise to B_2. As the discussion of merit goods in Chapter 2 made clear, there

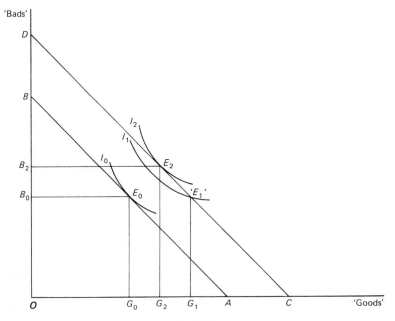

Fig. 15.2

is room for debate about the extent to which it is desirable for the state to take the paternalistic approach of paying benefits in kind, which has the advantage of ensuring that taxpayers' money is not used for socially undesirable purposes, rather than allowing people (though not necessarily their children) to have the additional satisfaction of spending their incomes in the way they think best. In the remainder of this chapter we ignore this distinction between benefits in kind and cash payments and concentrate on the effects of MTBs and NITs on net incomes. We should, however, note that the distinction in this paragraph rests on the assumption that it is not possible for people receiving 'goods' in kind to substitute these for other goods. In practice at least partial substitution may be possible, for example, free school meals may increase children's food consumption but by less than full amount of the dinner.

Analysis of negative taxes and means-tested benefits

Negative taxes and means-tested benefits may have many effects on savings, education, home ownership, family stability, etc., but economists' interest has largely focused on their effects on income distribution and work incentives and we follow this practice.

It is important to recognise that the effects on incentives and income distribution are interrelated, a point that is easily missed if the two issues are studied separately. We have already demonstrated (in Chapter 11) that taxes may increase or decrease work. If an increase in tax increases hours of work for taxpayers it will typically *increase gross* incomes and decrease net income while having no effects on the hours or incomes of non-taxpayers. In these circumstances the tax would increase the inequality of gross income while decreasing inequality of net incomes. Clearly then we must carefully distinguish between effects on gross and net incomes; *and*, as income distribution is about relative positions on the income scale, it will be misleading to confine the analysis to a single person. We have in fact included two persons, as that makes it possible to make many of the most important points with relatively simple graphs. To further simplify the analysis we assume that individuals have the same preferences.

To familiarise the reader with the graphical technique that we will use it is convenient to begin with the now-familiar case of introducing a personal income tax with an exemption. In Figure 15.3(a) the pretax position between gross income (on the horizontal axis) and net income on the vertical axis is represented by the 45° line. Two individuals, Mr Low and Mr Middle, have gross incomes OL_0^G and OM_0^G and net incomes OL_0^N and OM_0^N. In Figure 15.3(b) their respective equilibrium positions are at L_0 and M_0. Mr Low has a wage rate of W_L and he is in equilibrium at L_0 where he has net (and gross) income of $L_0^G = L_0^N$, and he works AH_0^L hours which gives him OH_0^L hours of leisure. Mr Middle with

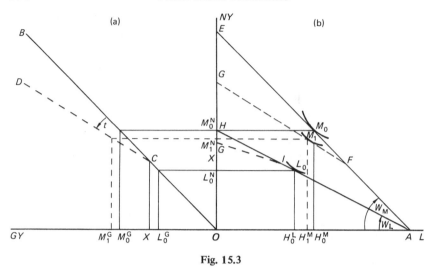

Fig. 15.3

the higher wage of W_M is in equilibrium at M_0 where he has both higher income and greater leisure (i.e. he works less).

A tax is now introduced which exempts the first £OX of income taxing additional income at the rate t. This shifts the line relating gross and net incomes from OB to the broken line OCD. The tax also shifts the budget constraints facing our two representative individuals. Middle's budget constraint shifts from AE to the dashed line AFG. Consequently he moves to a new equilibrium at M_1. The tax could cause him to work either more or less. As the diagram is drawn he has less leisure at M_1 which means that he works more and as a consequence his gross income rises (to M_1^G in Figure 15.3(a)). At the same time his net income has fallen from M_0^N to M_1^N. Low's budget constraint has also shifted from AH to AIG but as his income is below the tax threshold he remains at L_0. The introduction of the tax has not affected Low's absolute position but it has reduced Middle's consumption, leisure and welfare (i.e. he is on a lower indifference curve). The disparity in net income has fallen but the difference in gross income has risen.

We now turn to an analysis of the effects of a simple NIT. It is assumed that before the introduction of the NIT there exists a proportional income tax with an exemption such as the one illustrated in Figure 15.4. The NIT gives non-taxpayers the full value of the exemption level. This shifts the tax schedule in 15.4(a) from OAB to CAB. In Figure 15.4(b) Low's budget constraint shifts from DEF to GEF and Middle's constraint shifts from DHI to GHI. Middle is above the break-even point and as the diagram is drawn (see next paragraph) the NIT has no effect on his behaviour. Low moves from L_0 to L_1. L_1 must necessarily involve more leisure, i.e. less work, than L_0. The reason is that *both* an income effect *and* a substitution effect will reduce Low's work. To see this,

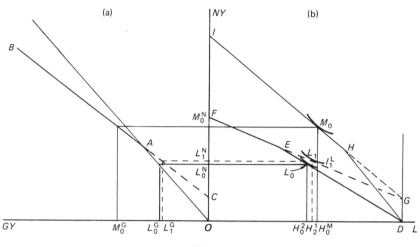

Fig. 15.4

imagine a line parallel to DE and tangent to I_1^L. The movement from L_0 to this new tangency point is a pure income effect and so Low will want more leisure. Likewise, the movement from the new tangency point to L_1, a movement down along I_1^L, is a substitution effect that again increases the consumption of leisure. This unambiguous theoretical prediction coincides with a popular prejudice about state handouts causing people to become workshy and is one reason for the controversy about NIT, particularly in the United States. However, to return to our analysis, Low is on a higher level of welfare with higher income (consumption) and higher leisure. Low's higher consumption is reflected in a higher net income (L_1^N rather than L_0^N in Figure 15.4(a)), which narrows the gap between the two net incomes. Once again, however, the gap in gross income has risen – in this case because Low works less which causes his gross income to fall from L_0^G to L_1^G.

As Figure 15.4 was constructed the introduction of the NIT had no effect on Middle whose income was above the break-even point for the NIT. However, this is not necessarily the case as we illustrate with the aid of Figure 15.5. Low's pre-NIT budget constraint is AB and Middle's is AC. A NIT guaranteeing an income of AD means that their post-NIT budget constraints are DEB, for Low, and DFC for Middle. As before Low has an income effect (L_0 to G) and a substitution effect (G to L_1) both of which reduce work. Middle's initial income at M_0 is above the breakeven level for the NIT (at F). Nevertheless given Middle's preferences he is better off at M_1 and so he reduces his labour supply and ends up at M_1. While Middle is better of at M_1 (i.e. on a higher indifference curve) it may be noted that his net income has fallen (from M_0^N to M_1^N). It may also be noted that the NIT is now much more expensive (the cost has increased by $M_1^N - M_1^G$).

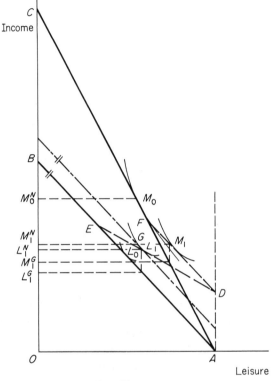

Fig. 15.5

(1) *Means-tested benefits*

We have seen that means-tested benefits (MTBs) have many similarities with NIT and can be analysed in a similar manner. Suppose we start from a position with no MTB (or NIT) but with a proportional tax with an exemption, and that we are considering a benefit for which the entitlement stops below the tax threshold. This would alter the tax/transfer system from *OAB* (in Figure 15.6(a)) to *CDAB* and the budget constraints in 15.6(b) from *EFG* to *HIFG* for Low, and from *EJK* to *HLJK* for Middle. The reader should verify that these effects on labour supply and income distribution are similar to those with the NIT discussed above.

(2) *The poverty trap*

When people are simultaneously liable to income tax and eligible for means-tested benefits they may well face very high marginal rates of tax. This phenomenon is known as the poverty trap because the relatively poor people

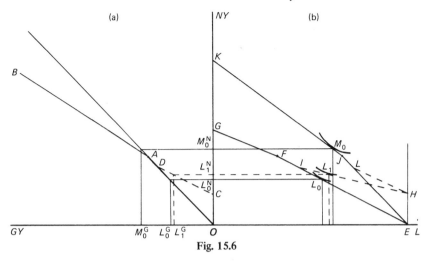

Fig. 15.6

caught in this position can do very little to make themselves better off. For example, if the basic rate of tax is 30 per cent and the implicit tax rate on a MTB is 50 per cent, then the combined marginal rate is 80 per cent. A person in these circumstances would only be 20p better off if he earned an extra £1. Clearly, if there were two MTBs each with a 50 per cent rate as well as income tax, the combined marginal rate would exceed 100 per cent, and the individual would make himself worse off by working more. There are well documented cases where this has happened in Britain (see, for example, Table 15.2), but even when marginal rates remain below 100 per cent disincentive effects may well remain.

The problem of the poverty trap is clearly likely to arise when, as in the UK in the mid-1970s, social security benefits were indexed but income tax exemption levels were not. Thus each year social benefits levels were increased in line with the increase in prices (or in earnings) while tax allowances were usually increased by a smaller percentage. The effect was to cause increasing overlap between the tax and social security systems and hence to exacerbate the poverty trap problem.

This case can be illustrated by reference to Figure 15.7. The solid line $ABCD$ in part (a) (which corresponds to $CDBA$ in Figure 15.6) represents a proportional tax system with an exemption and a means-tested benefit where there is no overlap between the two. If inflation then reduces the real value of the tax allowance (see Chapter 11 above) from OX_0 to OX_1 the new tax transfer line would be $AEFG$ and the segment EF would represent the poverty trap. Middle's budget constraint shifts from $HIJK$ to $HLMN$ but he remains in the basic rate band and so will work harder (see Chapter 11) and will have higher gross income of M_1^G and a lower net income of M_1^N. Low's budget constraint shifts from $HOPQ$ to

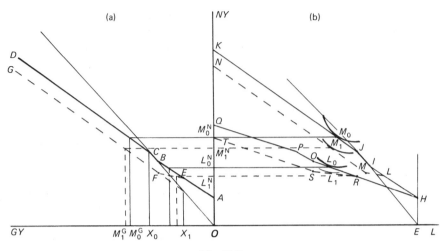

Fig. 15.7

HRST and he is now brought into the poverty trap as he will now have to pay income tax as well as lose part of his MTB if his income rises. His net income will fall. If, as we are assuming, the price elasticity is negative, the price effect associated with the reduction in Low's net wage will make him work more, while the increase in his intercept (not shown) will make him work less. Thus he may work more or less so his gross income may rise, or, as shown, it may fall. Both persons are worse off, both in the sense of having a lower net income and in the sense of being on a lower indifference curve. As Middle's net income falls by more than Low's the gap in their net incomes will fall, but once again the gap in their gross incomes will rise (unless Low works very much more).

Clearly there are many more examples of NITs and MTBs that we could consider, but we hope that the few examples we have examined will enable the reader to construct other examples for himself. A particularly interesting example for the reader to work through is the effect of introducing a NIT where MTBs already exist. Given that MTBs do exist in the UK, this is a very realistic example and the reader should be able to show that the prediction that NIT will reduce work will not, in general, now hold. We also hope that the reader now appreciates that a discussion of measures to redistribute income that does not include a discussion of labour supply will be seriously incomplete. This is a point we plan to return to in Chapter 20.

Before leaving this topic we should reiterate that we have ignored the effects of the various measures we have considered on government revenue and expenditure. Where the change increases revenue the government could finance additional purchases of goods and services or provide additional cash transfers, and either should increase at least some taxpayers' welfare. Where a NIT or additional MTBs are considered the extra expenditure has to be financed in some way. One possibility would be to raise the additional revenue by raising the rate of income tax. This would have further implications for these taxpayers. Some of these implications are considered in Chapter 20 where we discuss optimal taxation.

Effects of means-tested benefits

Little information is available about the actual effects of means-tested benefits on labour supply and on the distribution of income. There is some poor – for our present purpose – information on the effect of MTBs on income distribution and virtually nothing about their effects on labour supply. It is thus impossible in practice to discuss their interaction in the way we have advocated.

Each year the Central Statistical Office publishes in *Economic Trends* estimates of the effects of taxes and government expenditure on household income. These estimates are derived from the *Family Expenditure Survey*, a survey of some 7000 households showing how various household types are affected by certain categories of taxes and expenditure. Income related benefits are shown by the CSO to be about 18 per cent of total cash benefits in 1979. Table 15.1 shows how these were allocated by income range and by household type. As one would expect low income groups receive the largest amounts. By household type one-parent families, receive the most by a substantial margin.

An alternative approach to estimating the effects of MTBs on income distribution is to look at people's entitlements rather than the amounts they

Table 15.1   Income-related cash benefits by household type UK 1979

Household type	Quintile groups of original income within household type					
	Lowest	2nd	3rd	4th	Highest	Average
	£	£	£	£	£	£
1 adult retired	369		255	104	32	226
1 adult non-retired	374	60	11	1	17	92
2 adults retired	325	202	100	66	14	142
2 adults non-retired	210	62	51	9	14	69
2 adults, 1 child	413	21	34	14	28	102
2 adults, 2 children	247	47	12	5	5	63
2 adults, 3 or more children	327	48	48	24	14	92
3 or more adults with no children	527	182	83	96	71	192
3 or more adults with children	503	127	102	80	138	190
1 adult with children	1469	1497	273	123	3	675

Source: *Economic Trends*, January 1981, pp. 124–8.

Table 15.2 Entitlement to benefits. Married couple, 2 children
'The Poverty Trap'

Gross weekly income	Child benefit	Family income supplement	Rent[a] rebate	Rate[a] rebate	Income[b] tax	National[c] insurance contribution	Net income	Implied marginal tax rate
£	£	£	£	£	£	£	£	£
45	10.50	18.50	8.00	4.88	1.12	3.04	82.72	
50	10.50	16.00	8.00	4.58	2.62	3.38	83.08	93
55	10.50	13.50	8.00	4.28	4.12	3.71	83.45	93
65	10.50	3.50	7.63	3.68	7.12	4.39	83.80	96
75	10.50	–	5.13	3.08	10.12	5.06	82.03	117
85	10.50	–	3.32	2.48	13.12	5.74	82.44	96
90	10.50	–	2.47	2.18	14.62	6.08	84.45	60
100	10.50	–	0.77	1.58	17.62	6.75	88.48	60
110	10.50	–	–	0.98	20.62	7.43	93.43	51
120	10.50	–	–	0.38	23.62	8.10	99.16	43
130	10.50	–	–	–	26.62	8.78	105.10	41

Notes: [a] Assumed rent, £8.00 per week; assumed rates, £5.00 per week. Benefits at end 1981 rates.
[b] 30 per cent. Assuming husband only works.
[c] 6.75 per cent of gross earnings up to limit of £165 per week. Assuming not contracted out.

Sources: Department of Health and Social Security leaflets; Inland Revenue.

actually receive. Table 15.2 provides such information for a family of two adults and two children using rates applicable in late 1981. It can be seen that the implied marginal tax rate *falls* from over 90 per cent to 41 per cent as income rises. The very high rates of tax at low income are referred to as the poverty trap. It can be seen that this high rate extends over a substantial range of income. If income doubled from £45 to £90 a week net income would rise by less than £2. This implies marginal tax rate of about 96 per cent over this range. This information has two drawbacks: first, it does not tell us how many people actually exist in the various income classes; second, this information does not tell us if families actually receive their entitlements. It seems likely that a significant number of people do not claim benefits for which they are entitled.

While this information is poor it is better than the information on the effects of MTBs on labour supply. In the theoretical discussion above it was assumed that the recipients of MTBs knew how their budget constraints would be affected. But it became clear from the Stirling study – see Table 15.3 – that only about one-fifth of these incurring MTBs seemed to appreciate that these would be reduced or lost if their income rose. It should be pointed out that some benefits are awarded for a full year so that they would not be lost as a result of a short-run increase in income. Nevertheless the assumption that budget constraints are fully understood could well be wrong. We looked for evidence of differences in behaviour between those knowing that their benefits would fall and those who did not. No evidence of differences has yet emerged, but this means very little given the small numbers involved. It would in our view be wrong to infer that MTBs do not affect labour supply, but more definitive views will have to await further evidence.

Effects of negative income taxes

There was considerable interest in the 1960s in NIT on both sides of the Atlantic. In the United States one of the main obstacles to adopting NIT was a popular fear that the provision of higher incomes might lead to a very large fall in work. In order to study this and other possible effects, NITs were introduced experimentally in at least five places. The first and best known is the Urban Income Maintenance Experiment (UIME) (better known as the 'New Jersey experiment'); and others include the Rural (North Carolina and Iowa) Income Maintenance Experiment (RIME), the Gary (Indiana) Income Maintenance Experiment (GIME), the Seattle (Washington) Income Maintenance Experiment (SIME) and the Denver (Colorado) Income Maintenance Experiment (DIME). We discuss results from all five.

(1) The New Jersey experiment

The New Jersey experiment was carried out at three sites in New Jersey (Trenton, Paterson and Passaic, and Jersey City) and one in Pennsylvania

Table 15.3 Percentage of weekly paid workers with means-tested benefit, and percentage knowing part of the benefit could be lost if earnings rose (1971)

| | (1) Total (= (2) + (3)) | | (2) No means-tested benefit | | One or more means-tested benefits | | | | | |
| | | | | | (3) Total (= (3a) + (3b)) | | (3a) Some or all lost with earnings rise | | (3b) None lost; don't know | |
Marital status	N	%	N	% col. (1)	N	% col. (1)	N	% col. (3)	N	% col. (3)
Single men	341	100	258	76	83	24	7	8	74	89
Married men	954	100	834	87	120	13	24	20	91	76
Single women	195	100	161	83	34	17	3	9	31	91
Married women	523	100	458	88	65	12	15	23	50	77
Widowed; divorced; separated	126	100	98	78	28	22	12	43	15	54
TOTAL	2139	100	1809	85	330	15	61	18	261	79

Source: Stirling study of weekly paid employees.

(Scranton). To be eligible a family had to have an able-bodied male between eighteen and fifty-eight who was not in an institution, the armed forces or full-time education and to have an income not in excess of 150 per cent of the official poverty line. A total of 1374 people were enrolled, 724 as experimental families and 650 as controls. The experimental families were allocated to one of eight separate NIT schemes combining four guarantee levels (at 50 per cent, 75 per cent, 100 per cent and 125 per cent of the poverty line) and three tax rates (30 per cent, 50 per cent and 70 per cent). Table 15.4 shows the eight plans chosen and the number assigned to each plan.

Table 15.4 New Jersey negative income tax experiment: numbers enrolled and average payment for each plan

Guarantee level (per cent of poverty line)	Tax rate		
	30%	50%	70%
125	–	N138 $187	–
100	–	N 81 $124	N80 $66
75	N104 $104	N118 $ 44	N84 $35
50	N 48 $ 46	N 71 $ 22	

Notes: N = Number of families.
$ = Average weekly payment in year 2 of experiment.
Source: C. V. Brown, 'Survey of the Effects of Taxation on Labour Supply of Low Income Groups', in I. F. S. *Fiscal Policy and Labour Supply* (London, 1977).

Some of the weaknesses of the design were evident at the start and probably could not have been overcome within the budget. For example, how could one draw inferences about a permanent NIT from a three-year experiment? (The Seattle/Denver experiments included a longer period.) Other weaknesses have become evident in retrospect. The decision not to require a husband in the household meant that in some households the able-bodied male was not a husband and, because numbers were small, these cases were not analysed. This, plus the breaking up of families and people dropping out of the plan, meant that 41 per cent of the experimental families and 45 per cent of the control families lacked continuous structure and data throughout the experimental period. This high attrition rate was in part the result of New Jersey instituting a welfare programme Aid to Families with Dependent Children (AFDC) that produced higher benefits than several of the NIT programmes. Another unexpected factor was that white, black and Spanish-speaking sub-samples behaved very differently. The relatively small initial numbers combined with high attrition greatly increased the difficulties of simultaneously controlling for site, ethnicity and

NIT. This may explain why little if any evidence was found of the effects of differing tax rates. The truncation of the sample (at 150 per cent of the poverty time) may also have introduced bias. The same amount of data could have provided much more useful information if half the sample had been studied pre-experimentally for half of the total time and the other half of the sample had been studied post-experimentally for half the time.

The size of the payment received (and hence the extent to which poverty is relieved) of course varied between the various experimental groups. Table 15.4 shows the average payment received in each four-week period in the second year of the experiment: 323 families (45 per cent) received more than $25 a week while 321 families (44 per cent) received less than $12 a week. This can be compared with an official poverty line in 1967–68 of $2115 a year ($41 a week) for a two-person family to $5440 a year ($105 a week) for an eight-person family.

The central question of course is what effect these payments, and the accompanying changes in the shape of the budget constraint, had on labour supply. Table 15.5 shows the labour supply results for husbands that were estimated from regressions for the middle two years of the experiment using four measures of labour supply. The first two measures (participation and employment rates) are clearly not comprehensive. Watts and his associates prefer earnings as the best comprehensive measure of labour supply on the grounds that

Table 15.5 New Jersey negative income tax experiment: labour supply results (husband totals: regression estimates of differentials in labour force participation, employment, hours, and earnings for quarters 3 to 10)

	Labour force participation rate	Employment rate	Hours worked per week	Earnings per week
White				
Control group mean	94.3	87.8	34.8	100.4
Absolute differential	−0.3	−2.3	−1.9	0.1
Treatment group mean	94.0	85.5	32.9	100.5
Per cent differential	−0.3	−2.6	−5.6	0.1
Black				
Control group	95.6	85.6	31.9	93.4
Absolute differential	0	0.8	0.7	8.7
Treatment group mean	95.6	86.4	32.6	102.1
Per cent differential	0	0.9	2.3	9.3
Spanish-speaking				
Control group mean	95.2	89.5	34.3	92.2
Absolute differential	1.6	−2.4	−0.2	5.9
Treatment group mean	96.8	87.1	34.1	98.1
Per cent differential	1.6	−2.7	−0.7	6.4

Source: R. H. Haveman and H. W. Watts, 'Social Experimentation as Policy Research: A Review of the Negative Income Tax Experiments' in V. Halberstadt and A. J. Culyer (eds.), *Public Economics and Human Resources* (Editions Cujas, 1977).

it includes all of the three other variables plus any influences the worker may have on his hourly wage rate. The earnings variable, however, may be biased. All families were asked for earnings but it appears that initially some reported net earnings when what the researchers wanted was gross earnings. As experimental families reported income monthly and controls quarterly, Watts *et al.* think it is possible that the experimental families learned what was wanted earlier causing a spurious differential in earnings. They thus put most emphasis on hours. They summarise the results as follows:

> In [Table 15.5] the treatment-control differentials shown for husbands are from regressions in which age, education, number of adults, number and ages of children, sites and pre-program family earnings and labor supply served as control variables. . . .
> The most striking features of the results for husbands are that all of the differentials are quite small in both absolute and relative terms . . . all are statistically insignificant. *There are no findings here to indicate a significant reduction in labour supply. . . . Moreover, many of the differentials, including all those for blacks, are positive. . . .*[1]

These results are so surprising that they deserve comment. The results are from regressions that do not include wage rates as independent variables. Other regressions (not reported) do control 'for normal wages and normal income as a fraction of the poverty level, [and] that permit non-linear wage effects. . . . These regressions do little better than the first set in disclosing significant effects of the treatment.'[2] It is not clear how normal wage and non-linear wage effects were introduced.

Robert Hall has argued that the results for whites do in fact show a significant reduction in hours for white husbands. Hall's data are reported in Table 15.6. Hall compares hours of the experimental group before and during the experiment, which suggests that the experiment reduced work by 2.3 hours per worker per week. A comparison of hours worked by the experimental and control groups during the experiment suggests a reduction in work of 2.6 hours. These measures (plus another two) all show a significant reduction in hours for the experimental group. It is clearly important that someone attempt to account for the differences between Hall's results and those of Watts.

Hall's figures for black and Spanish-speaking families show relatively little change in hours for the experimental families and large reductions in hours for the controls, and the results for blacks seem to confirm the 'wrong' sign found by Watts. However, Hall dismisses the data for non-whites as unreliable on the ground that the attrition rate is so high. Hall gives data, reproduced in Table 15.7, 'on the percentages of families lacking continuous structure and data throughout the experimental period'.

(2) *The Rural Income Maintenance Experiment*

The Rural Income Maintenance Experiment which was jointly administered with the New Jersey experiment was carried out in Iowa and North Carolina.

Table 15.6 Hours worked by husbands in New Jersey experiment

	Experimental group	Control group	Difference
White			
Before experiment	34.1	34.8	
During experiment	31.8	34.4	−2.6
Difference	−2.3	−0.4	
Black			
Before experiment	31.8	31.9	
During experiment	31.2	28.5	+2.7
Difference	−0.6	−3.4	
Spanish-speaking			
Before experiment	32.9	36.7	
During experiment	31.7	32.9	−1.2
Difference	−1.2	−3.8	

Source: R. E. Hall, 'Effects of the Experimental Negative Income Tax on Labour Supply' in J. A. Pechman and P. M. Timpane (eds), *Work Incentives and Income Guarantees* (Washington: Brookings Institution, 1975).

Table 15.7 Percentages of families lacking continuous data and structures

	Experimental group	Control group
	%	%
White	22	34
Black	46	45
Spanish-speaking	56	61
Total	41	45

Source: Hall, *op. cit.*

The experimental design was similar to that used in the New Jersey experiment and we report here results for the 269 husband-and-wife families with wages as the primary source of income. It can be seen from Table 15.8 that the overall reduction in hours was 13 per cent with a much larger reduction from wives than from husbands.

(3) The Seattle and Denver experiments

The jointly administered Seattle and Denver experiments provided for three levels of guaranteed income (in 1971 dollars): $3800, $4800 and $5600, and four tax rates. One of the features of the Seattle and Denver experiments has been to experiment with nonlinear tax rates. Thus, while two of the tax rates employed were constant at 50 and 70 per cent, two of the rates declined by an average of 25 per cent for each $1000 rise in income. The starting tax for these declining programmes were 70 and 80 per cent.

Table 15.8 Weighted experimental responses for selected measures of income and wage work: **Rural experiment**

	Control/Experimental differential as percent of control mean[a]			
	N. Carolina blacks	*N. Carolina whites*	*Iowa*	*Eight-State*[b] *aggregate*
Families				
Total income	−14	−9	−18	−13
Wage income	−14	−8	−17	−12
Wage hours	−10	−18	−5	−13
Number of earners	−6	−16	−8	−11
Husbands				
Wage income	−7	0	−10	−4
Wage hours	−8	+3	−1	−1
If employed	−1	−1	0	−1
Wives				
Wage income	−41	−3	−32	−25
Wage hours	−31	−23	−22	−27
If employed	−25	−28	−38	−28
Dependents				
Wage income	−19	−57	−8	−39
Wage hours	−16	−66	−27	−46

Notes: [a] Responses standardised to a 45 per cent tax/80 per cent basic benefit plan.
[b] Weighted averages of the basic data from which the subsample percentages were derived, using the following weights: NC–B, 0.31788; NC–W, 0.48943; Ia., 0.19269.

Source: Rural Income Maintenance Experiment, (1976), p. 38.

The researchers estimated the effects of the experiment by comparing hours worked in the year prior to the experiment with hours worked in the second year of the experiment. The income effect was estimated as the effect on hours of a change in disposable income at pre-experimental hours and the substitution effect as the effect on hours of a change in the net wage rate as a result of the experiment. The estimates of income and substitution effects at the means of independent variables are given in Table 15.9. It should be noted that these results are the combined results from all of the NIT programmes. The responses for people below the break-even level are quite large as they imply a total reduction in hours of 5.3 per cent for husbands, 22.0 per cent for wives and 11.2 per cent for female heads. A separate analysis for youths (not shown in the table) showed a considerably larger response for 16- to 21-year-old males.

It is particularly interesting that these results are consistent with theoretical predictions, unlike Haveman and Watt's interpretation of the New Jersey results. This lends indirect support to Hall's interpretation of the New Jersey results. It is also of interest, again in contrast to the New Jersey results, that no significant

Table 15.9 Estimated effects of Seattle and Denver NIT treatments on annual hours of work (standard errors in parentheses)

	Husbands	Wives	Single female heads
Below break-even level			
Income effect (per $1000)	−34	−143**	−101**
	(27)	(44)	(39)
Substitution effect (per dollar per hour)	83**	168*	126*
	(37)	(91)	(66)
Above break-even level			
Constant effect	−13	−431*	−345
	(175)	(256)	(291)
Effect of break-even level (per $1000)	−6	8	73
	(21)	(30)	(65)
Effect of earnings above break-even level (per $1000)	12	48	35
	(27)	(42)	(56)
Declining tax rate treatments	−86**	120	22
	(48)	(78)	(73)
Estimated NIT effects for the average working individual in SIME/DIME below the break-even level and not on declining tax rate treatments			
Income effect	−47	−199***	−117**
	(37)	(62)	(46)
Substitution effect	−56**	−64*	−50*
	(25)	(35)	(31)
Total effect	−103***	−263***	−176***
	(33)	(55)	(44)
Percentage effect	−5%	−22%	−11%

$* \ p < 0.10.$
$** \ p < 0.05.$
$*** \ p < 0.01.$

Source: P. K. Robins, 'Labor Supply Response of Family Heads and Implications for a National Program' in P. K. Robins *et al.* (eds) *A Guaranteed Annual Income: Evidence from a Social Experiment* (New York: Academic Press, 1980), p. 62.

differences were found between the labour supply responses of blacks and whites in the Seattle and Denver experiments. It will be remembered (see Figure 15.5) that it is possible for people with incomes above the break-even level to respond to a NIT. There is, however, little evidence of a significant response from people above the break-even level in the Seattle and Denver experiments (see Table 15.9).

One of the problems with the experimental approach is that experiments have a finite time horizon: three years in the case of the New Jersey experiment. This raises the question of whether one can reasonably infer what would happen with permanent NIT from a three-year experiment. In order to test for this time factor at least in part, some of those enrolled in the Seattle and Denver projects were enrolled for three years while others were enrolled for five years or twenty years. There were significant differences in the labour supply responses between the two groups for men which may imply that the figures in Table 15.9 will need to be revised to show a larger effect.

(4) *The Gary Experiment*

The Gary (Indiana) Income Experiment was designed to test the impact of four NIT plans on a black urban sample which contained many families with female heads. The Gary data have been evaluated not only by the researchers but also by Burtless and Hausman using what we have called a Type III model (see Chapter 14). Their results are reported in Table 15.10. It can be seen that what they called wage elasticity (we have used the term price elasticity for the same concept) is for all practical purposes zero. The income elasticity is, however, significantly negative. A zero price elasticity does *not* mean that the experiment will have no effects. The analysis above (see Figures 15.4 and 15.5) still applies. However, with a zero price elasticity some, but not all, people will be unaffected by a change in the tax rate associated with the NIT. Consider Figure 15.8 where the pre-NIT budget constraint is *AB* and where a NIT providing a guaranteed income of *AC* is introduced. With a high tax rate the post-NIT budget constraint becomes *ACDB* for a high tax rate and *ACEB* for a low tax rate. Someone who was at *F*, working H_F hours, with the high tax rate would be at *G*, also working

Table 15.10 Estimates of labour supply and indirect utility function: Gary Experiment

Variable	*Parameter estimates*
Constant	3.75043
	(0.02555)
Primary education	0.01078
	(0.00558)
Adults (N)	0.03300
	(0.01272)
Poor health	−0.02224
	(0.00438)
Age	−0.00869
	(0.01347)
Wage elasticity, $\bar{\alpha}$	0.00003
	(0.01632)
Mean income elasticity, β	−0.04768
	(0.00465)
Variance of β distribution, σ_1^2	0.06751
	(0.00399)
Variance of ϵ_{2i}, σ_2^2	0.00135
	(0.00022)

Note: Observations (N) = 380; log of the likelihood function = − 196.27.

Source: G. Burtless and J. Hausman 'The Effect of Taxation on Labour Supply: Evaluating the Gary Negative Income Tax Experiment', *Journal of Political Economy*, 1978.

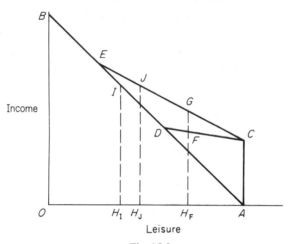

Fig. 15.8
Source: C. V. Brown *Taxation and The Incentive to Work* (Oxford: Oxford University Press, 1980), p. 83.

H_F hours with the low tax rate. On the other hand someone at I, working H_I hours, who would not be affected by the high tax rate, would be at J if the tax rate were low where his hours would be reduced to H_J.

In reporting the results of the NIT experiments we have devoted the most space to the New Jersey experiment partly because it is the first and best-known of the experiments and partly because the initial analysis suggested that the results contradicted a clear theoretical prediction. However, now that results are available from the four other experiments it appears that the results are consistent with theoretical predictions. This tends to lend weight to Hall's criticisms of the initial New Jersey findings.

Conclusion

There is thus growing evidence from the experimental studies reported in this chapter and from the cross-section studies reported in the last chapter that the tax/transfer system does influence labour supply, which means that income redistribution will influence gross incomes as well as net incomes. As a consequence we are faced with an awkward dilemma as we attempt to raise low incomes. If we help only the poorest we keep down costs but we raise the tax rate. (In Figure 15.1 if Y_{min} is fixed this implies reducing B and making BY_{min} flatter.) If we provide the same assistance to the poorest but reduce the tax rate the costs rise dramatically. (In Figure 15.1 this would imply keeping Y_{min} fixed and raising B, thus making BY_{min} steeper.) What this means is that the poverty trap in the broad sense is the automatic and inevitable result of helping the poor. Although it is right to debate the extent of overlap between the systems of state benefits and the income tax systems, we should remember that in part the debate is between means-testing through the system of administering state benefits and means-testing through the income tax system. We should also bear in mind that in this chapter we have largely ignored the costs of raising the incomes of the poor. These costs must of course be met in some way – most likely by higher taxes. We return to these issues in Chapter 20 where we discuss optimal taxation.

CHAPTER 16

The Taxation of Wealth

The taxation of wealth is both complicated and controversial; so much so that a UK House of Commons Select Committee appointed to consider the introduction of an annual wealth tax (AWT) required five reports to express the extent of disagreement among its members. The complications and the controversy arise from a series of issues which we discuss in this chapter: the nature of wealth, the reasons for wishing to tax it, the extent of inequality of, and trends in the inequality of, wealth holdings and the reasons for that inequality, and the present basis of taxing wealth in the United Kingdom.

The nature of wealth

An individual's wealth is the present value of his expected real income. Let us consider the implications of this wide definition of wealth. It clearly includes all of the following (suitably discounted): (1) expected income from working; (2) expected pension; (3) expected real services (e.g. imputed value of owner-occupied housing, the services of owning an old master); (4) expected increase in market value of assets. To use such a definition of wealth as a tax base one would have to be reasonably satisfied that it was possible to answer questions such as the following.

(1) What are the expected real lifetime earnings of an undergraduate reading this textbook?
(2) What should we do about the value of a man's pension when, at the age of fifty, he survives a moderate heart attack?
(3) What is the present value of expected income that is received from living in a mortgaged house?
(4) What is the expected value of the income from owning an old master? A ten-year old carpet?

Ways exist by which all of these questions might be answered, and reasonable people might well disagree about the likely margins of error in actually making the estimates, but clearly none of the questions are both trivially easy and costless to answer.

Because of these difficulties, both actual and proposed wealth taxes almost always use a base that omits certain categories of wealth. Wealth in the form of human capital is always omitted so far as we know. The reason is obvious – unlike most forms of wealth we cannot use the present market value of the wealth as a proxy for the discounted value of the expected income stream because people are not bought and sold. However, there is no uniformity of treatment for such things as pension rights, houses and personal chattels. As we will see both estimates of the existing distribution of wealth and the effects of any wealth tax, whether actual or proposed, depend critically on the actual definition of wealth adopted.

Reasons for taxing wealth

There is a variety of possible reasons for taxing wealth including the following.

(1) Advantages derived from owning wealth

If two people have the same income but one has greater wealth, then the principles of horizontal equity suggest that the latter should pay more tax because he has a greater ability to pay and the wealth may give him greater power and security and reduce his need to save. It is also argued that the income from wealth may be more permanent than earned income and so should be taxed more heavily. Thus earned income ceases on death or retirement of the individual, while the ownership of a consol brings a perpetual income stream to oneself and one's heirs. If wealth itself were taxed, rather than the income from wealth, this would happen automatically because the present value of a perpetual income stream would be higher than the present value of an income stream with a finite life.

(2) More productive use of wealth

A wealth tax is sometimes advocated to encourage the more productive use of wealth. In the UK at present wealth is, as such, not taxed, but the income from wealth is surcharged as investment income. This will encourage people to hold their wealth in the form of unproductive assets such as old masters, or possibly grouse moors, which escape tax because they produce little or no money income. Thus putting a tax on wealth may encourage people to sell assets such as old masters and grouse moors and to invest in productive business. The argument can be illustrated by reference to Table 16.1. A and B both have wealth of £100,000. A owns an asset producing a real return of 5 per cent and B an asset with a real return of 3 per cent. Prior to the introduction of the wealth tax A's wealth yields a real return of 5 per cent all of which is in the form

Table 16.1 Example of combined effects of income and wealth taxes on wealth holdings
with different income yields

	A	B
Wealth	100,000	100,000
Income	5,000	3,000
Income tax at 60 per cent	3,000	1,800
Wealth tax	2,000	2,000
Total tax	5,000	3,800
Tax as a percentage of income	100%	127%

of investment income. B receives a return of 3 per cent in the form of investment income and a further 2 per cent in the form of imputed income (the non-
monetary benefits of owning an old master or a grouse moor), which is untaxed.
Both pay a marginal tax rate of 60 per cent on their investment income. A thus
pays £3000 in income tax and B pays £1800. An annual wealth tax of 2 per cent
is then introduced. Both now pay a marginal rate of income tax of 60 per cent
plus the annual wealth tax of 2 per cent. As can be seen from the table, A's tax
liability is just equal to his income so he could keep his capital intact if his
consumption from his income from wealth were nil. B is liable for tax at 127
per cent of his income and if he wishes to keep his tax rate below 100 per cent
he will have to find a higher return for his assets. The implications of seeking
higher returns are not entirely straightforward. Because a wealth tax might cause
people to try to exchange low-yielding assets for higher-yielding assets the value
of the assets themselves would also be expected to change when a wealth tax
was introduced.

(3) Redistribution of wealth

A wealth tax is sometimes advocated either to promote a more equal distribution of wealth or to remove large holdings of wealth. While removing large
holdings of wealth will produce greater equality, these two objectives are not
identical as may be seen by a simple example. If a man with wealth of £1m pays
all of it in tax and the money is then spent by government to purchase goods
and services, the remaining private wealth will be both smaller and more equal.
But if to escape tax a man with £1m gives £100,000 to each of ten people
private wealth will be the same in total but more equally spread. This distinction
is more important when considering taxes on transfers of wealth. If the aim is to
cause wealth to be more widely distributed it is appropriate to levy lighter taxes
where wealth is being given to many recipients. This may lead to an accession
tax which taxes the recipient of the wealth transfer rather than the donor.

(4) *Discrimination against inherited wealth*

As an important variant on (3) many would wish to distinguish between wealth accumulated by an individual in the course of his own lifetime from his own savings and wealth that is received in the form of an inheritance or gift. Thus it may be thought socially desirable for people to work hard and to save in order to accumulate wealth, and at the same time undesirable for a person to be in a position where he has no need to work or save because he has substantial inherited wealth. As we will see, the best ways of taxing wealth will depend on whether or not we wish to make this distinction.

We should also remember that there are potential conflicts between these objectives. For example, a wealth tax designed to encourage more productive uses of assets and to discriminate against inherited wealth may have other less desirable consequences if people are unwilling to build up a business (or farm) *unless* they can pass it on to their children.

The relationship between wealth and income

We have defined income in any period as potential consumption without reducing wealth and wealth as the present value of expected income. Clearly then the two concepts are related and there are many borderline cases. Taxing investment income (which is taxed at surcharged rates in the UK) is one way of taxing wealth. Capital gains taxes could be thought of as a tax on income or as a tax on gains in wealth. Taxes on the transfer of wealth can be thought of as either income or wealth taxes. For example, an accessions tax might be thought of as a tax on the wealth of the donor or a tax on the income (or the wealth) of the donee. Rates are another example of a borderline tax. Rates in the UK are based in principle on the annual rental value of property. The tax is thus similar to an income tax – here, what the property could rent for. Alternatively the tax base might be the market value of the property in which case one might think of the tax as a wealth tax. In perfect markets the two concepts of rental value and market value would be very closely related.

Economic effects of wealth taxes

In this section we consider the effects of wealth taxes on savings and on work effort. To keep our analysis as simple as possible we confine our attention to the two-period case. We will also assume when we look at the decision to save that the individual wishes to save.[1]

(1) *The incentive to save*

We analyse the effects of each of three ways in which wealth might be taxed on the incentive to save. Case (1) is an income tax where the tax base includes the interest income derived from wealth but not the wealth itself. Case (2) is a wealth tax where the base of the tax is the wealth itself and where income, including income from wealth, is not taxed. Case (3) is an income tax in which the income from non-human wealth or investment income is taxed at a higher rate than the income from human wealth or earned income, which is a simplified version of the present British position.

The analysis is restricted to an examination of the effects on the individual in two periods, which for convenience we can refer to as working period and retirement. It is assumed the individual knows with certainty: his earnings OY_0 during his working life and his state pension OY_1, the date of his death, the rate of interest, i (which is assumed to remain fixed). He also has a stock of (non-human) wealth, OW, at the start of the first period. He is assumed not to wish to make any provision for his heirs and his wealth is assumed to yield no interest in period 1, and to yield the rate of interest i in period 2.

The analysis is conducted with the aid of Figure 16.1, which shows pre-retirement consumption C_0 on the horizontal axis and post-retirement consumption C_1 on the vertical axis. In the absence of tax, consumption in the two periods would be represented by the point WY if the individual during his working life consumed both his earned income OY_0 and his wealth W, and if in retirement he consumed his pension. Thus WY represents the no savings–no borrowing position. His budget constraint, which represents his possibilities for consumption over his working life and retirement, is given by the line AB. $OA(=(W+Y_0)(1+i)+Y_1)$ is the amount he could consume during retirement if, somehow, he managed to have nil pre-retirement consumption. $OB(=W+Y_0+(Y_1/1+i))$ is the amount he could consume in the first period if he borrowed fully against his pension.

(*a*) *Case 1. A tax on both earned and investment income.* Suppose we now introduce a proportional income tax that takes a constant proportion of each period's income. With no borrowing and no savings, the after-tax income position will lie on the line WWY and if the tax rate is FWY/WWY the pivot point for the budget constraint will move from WY to F. The new budget constraint (DE) will be flatter than the old (AB). The maximum amount that could conceivably be consumed in retirement is

$$OD = Y_1(1-t) + Y_0(1-t)[1+i(1-t)] + W[1+i(1-t)]$$

and the maximum pre-retirement consumption is

$$OE = Y_0(1-t) + \frac{Y_1(1-t)}{1+i(1-t)} + W.$$

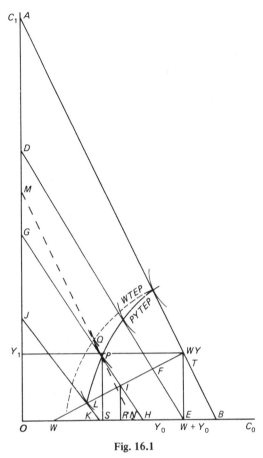

Fig. 16.1

On similar arguments higher tax rates of IWY/WWY and LWY/WWY would produce the budget constraints GH and JK respectively. If our individual has a
preference function represented by the indifference curves in Figure 16.1, then
the combinations of pre- and post-retirement consumption he will choose are
given by the tangency points between his indifference curves and the various
budget constraints. The locus of these tangency points is labelled $PYTEP$ (proportional income tax expansion path) in the figure. As we would expect, higher
tax rates lead to lower consumption and lower savings in both periods.

(*b*) *Case 2. A wealth tax.* We now examine the effects of a wealth tax in place
of an income tax. Non-human wealth is assumed to be taxed but both earned
and investment income are exempted from tax. Thus during the working period
the only tax that is paid is on the individual's wealth holdings. In the retirement

period wealth is again the tax base but wealth holdings will now be larger if there has been any savings. Consequently the new budget constraints such as *MN* will be steeper than *HG*. Thus

$$OM = Y_1 + Y_0[1 + i(1 - t)] + W(1 - t)[1 + i(1 - t)]$$

and

$$ON = Y_0 + \frac{Y_1}{1 + i} + W(1 - t).$$

The locus of equilibrium points is termed the *WTEP* (wealth tax expansion path). An inspection of the figure shows that *WTEP* is to the left of *PYTEP* which means that a wealth tax will lead to higher savings than an income tax of equal yield. To see this suppose we compare the point *P* on *PYTEP* with *Q* on *WTEP*. With the income tax, savings is $RS(= OR - OS)$ or net income less consumption. A wealth tax that raises *PT* in revenue will pass through *P* but will have a steeper slope which leads to a substitution effect resulting in higher savings.

(c) *Case 3. Income tax with investment income surcharge.* We now consider with reference to Figure 16.2 an income tax that taxes investment income (the income from wealth) at higher rate than earned income. The difference between the two tax rates, the investment income surcharge, is, in effect, a reduction in the net interest[2] (but only for savers, unless there is also a surcharged tax relief for borrowers). Thus an income tax with investment income surcharge can be thought of as a combination of an income tax and a fall in the net interest rates. There is a whole family of expansion paths depending on precisely how the surcharge is specified. The investment income surcharge expansion path (*IYSEP*) that is shown is thus not the only possible expansion path but in general such expansion paths will lie to the right of the *PYTEP* expansion path. Not surprisingly, an income tax with an investment income surcharge will lead to less savings than an ordinary income tax that has the same yield. Once again the comparison can be made with the point *P* on *PYTEP*; and, as before, a tax of equal yield will mean the budget constraint passes through *P*. The budget constraint *XZ* passing through *P* is flatter than *EF* as investment income is now more heavily taxed. To keep revenue equal the rate of tax on earned income will now be lower, i.e. it will be reduced from *IWY*/ *WWY* to *VWY*/*WWY*. With this new budget constraint equilibrium will be at *U* on *IYSEP*. Savings at *U* can be seen to be less than at *IP* as *S* lies to the right of *P*.

(2) *Wealth taxes and the incentive to work*

We now turn to the analysis of wealth taxes in a model where the individual does not save but is faced only with a choice between current consumption

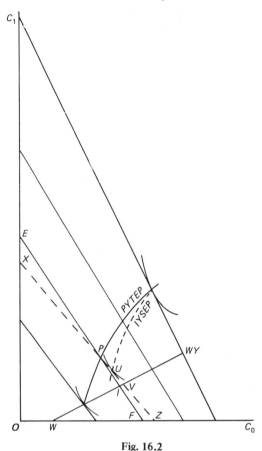

Fig. 16.2

and leisure. In these circumstances a wealth tax will cause a downward shift in the intercept (*OF* in Figure 14.3); it is thus a pure income effect and will cause the person to work longer, i.e. to consume less leisure.

To conclude this discussion of the economic effects of wealth taxes we would like to remind the reader of the restrictive assumptions that have been used in the analysis. In particular, confining the problem to two goods has meant that we have not considered effects on work and on savings simultaneously. We have also assumed that wealth is a homogeneous commodity with a uniform yield which means that we have neglected the possibility that a wealth tax would lead to a rearrangement of assets, e.g. between high- and low-yielding assets and between high- and low-risk assets.

Taxes on wealth holdings and wealth transfers

It is possible to tax wealth holdings, say, by an annual wealth tax, or to tax transfers of wealth. The arguments for taxing the transfer of wealth are as follows.

(1) It makes it possible to tax inherited wealth more heavily than wealth accumulated during one person's lifetime.

(2) It is administratively easier because assets only need to be valued infrequently, perhaps only once a generation, with transfers at death.

(3) The recipients of the transfers may find a tax on money not yet to hand less of a burden than a tax on wealth they already own. Transfer taxes at high rates may require the sale of assets, and this may be less inconvenient when someone has died.

There are several arguments against transfer taxes.

(1) They are more cumbersome to index in inflationary periods, particularly if transfers are taxed at progressive rates.

(2) They provide an incentive to retain wealth to avoid the transfer tax, but this may be partially offset by exemptions for small transfers. If transfers up to a certain limit are exempted annually from the transfer tax, as in the UK, the exemptions may encourage earlier dispersion of wealth.

(3) As the sole bases for wealth taxes, transfer taxes also have the disadvantage that wealth accumulated in one lifetime escapes tax altogether during the individual's lifetime.

(4) It is also more cumbersome, but not impossible, to make transfer taxes progressive when they are levied on the receipt of transfers as in an accessions tax.

(5) If transfer taxes do lead to a retention of wealth holdings this may lead to very thin asset markets.

Annual wealth taxes have the following advantages.

(1) For those who wish to break up concentrations of wealth quickly it is possible to have high rates which will force the break-up of the largest wealth holdings more quickly than could be accomplished with transfer taxes. It may be noted that taxing investment income at over 100 per cent has similar effects, except that it discriminates against high-yielding assets. That is what happens with the present un-indexed investment income surcharge.

(2) Even relatively modest rates, if they are progressive, will encourage people to transfer wealth so as to minimise their tax liability.

(3) Modest rates also help to secure horizontal equity in the tax system.

(4) A tax on wealth should make it possible to abolish the investment income surcharge, which should encourage people to hold their wealth in higher-yielding forms.

The disadvantages of a wealth tax are:

(1) The heavy costs of administration involved in annual valuations, particularly when the exemption level is low;

(2) the fact that, on its own, it cannot discriminate against inherited wealth;

(3) the difficulties, particularly when rates are high, in distinguishing between non-productive estates that one may wish to tax heavily in order to break up and productive estates that one may not want to break up.

As there are disadvantages to taxes on both wealth and the transfer of wealth, and as these disadvantages tend to be more severe when only one is used as the base, many people advocate a tax both on transfers of wealth and on ownership of wealth – both with more modest rates than would be appropriate if either was used as the only base.

The distribution of wealth in the UK

One of the reasons for a wealth tax is to promote a more equal distribution of wealth. This implies that the present distribution is unequal to an undesirable degree and that in turn raises the questions (1) What is the present distribution of wealth? and (2) What causes the observed inequality?

Measuring the actual distribution of wealth is by no means easy because individuals are not required to keep records of, or to disclose the value of their assets – except when they die, when their estates are valued for capital transfer tax or for its predecessor, estate duty. The standard method of estimating the distribution of wealth in the UK is to use the 'estate multiplier method'. The estates of deceased people are regarded as a sample of all estates and these are grossed up using the age of the deceased and the reciprocals of mortality rates to form an estimate of the holdings of wealth. Estimates for 1978 are given in the first of the three columns for 1978 in Table 16.2. It can be seen that the distribution of wealth is very much more unequal than that of income (see Table 13.1). These estimates, made annually by the Inland Revenue, are known to have a number of drawbacks. Estimates for very large estates and the estates of the young are likely to contain errors because of the small sample sizes. Small estates are omitted altogether as they are not liable to tax: the so-called 'omitted population'.

The valuation of assets, particularly of household goods, may be inaccurate. Some assets, e.g. life assurance, are worth more to an estate than to a living person. Other assets, such as pension rights, are valuable to a living person but not to a dead person and hence are not included in this measure of wealth. Finally, it should be remembered that these statistics relate to individuals' wealth and we may be more interested in the wealth of families or households.

These deficiencies were examined by the Royal Commission on the Distribution of Income and Wealth and they made alternative estimates of the distribution

Table 16.2 Personal wealth: Distribution of wealth among adult population. UK 1966–78

	Excluding pensions							Including	
								Occupational pensions	Occupational and state pensions
	1966	1971	1974	1975	1976	1977	1978	1978	1978
	%	%	%	%	%	%	%	%	%
Concentration of wealth among adult population									
Percentage of wealth owned by:									
Most wealthy 1 per cent of adult population	33	31	23	24	24	23	23	19	13
Most wealthy 2 per cent of adult population	42	39	30	31	32	30	30	26	17
Most wealthy 5 per cent of adult population	56	52	43	44	46	44	44	39	25
Most wealthy 10 per cent of adult population	69	65	57	58	61	58	58	52	36
Most wealthy 25 per cent of adult population	87	86	84	83	84	82	83	75–79[a]	57–60[a]
Most wealthy 50 per cent of adult population	97	97	93	93	95	95	95	89–93[a]	79–83[a]
Distribution of adult population by individual net wealth									
Percentage of adult population with wealth value									
Over (£) Not over (£)									
5000	91	85	74	72	72	71	68		
5000 15000	7	12	20	21	20	20	19		
15000 50000	1.7	2.7	5.1	6.0	6.8	7.9	10.7		
50000 100000	{ 0.4	0.4	0.5	0.7	0.9	1.0	1.4		
100000		0.3	0.3	0.3	0.4	0.5	0.6		
Total adult population – thousands	39228	39809	40229	40353	40496	40642	40824	40824	40824
Gini coefficient (Series C)	81	80	74	74	76	74	74	65–71[a]	47–52[a]

Note: [a] See text for explanation of range of estimates.

Source: *Inland Revenue Statistics 1980*, p. 122.

of wealth. These estimates differ in the assumptions made (1) about the wealth owned by people not covered in the estate multiplier method and (2) in the assumptions about pension rights. There are two extreme assumptions about the excluded population. The first is that they had no wealth at all. As a comparison of columns (1) and (2) of Table 16.3 reveals, the assumption that the omitted population has no wealth makes the wealth at the top appear much more highly concentrated. The second assumption derives from the fact that the total amount of wealth estimated by the estate multiplier method falls short of the total wealth in the national balance sheets. There is a variety of reasons for this – related to the deficiencies of the estate multiplier method – one of which is that small estates are not covered. If the whole discrepancy between the balance sheet and the estate multiplier methods is attributed to the population omitted from the estate multiplier method, then the apparent distribution of wealth will be much more nearly equal, as is shown by the rise in the share of the bottom 80 per cent in column (3) of Table 16.3. We have seen that, logically, pension rights belong to the definition of wealth although it must be recognised that, because they may be totally unmarketable or only partially marketable, the advantages of pensions may be less than the advantages of holding marketable securities of equivalent value.

In their estimates of wealth including pension rights the Royal Commission, and the Inland Revenue, have distinguished between occupational and state

Table 16.3 Alternative measures of the distribution of wealth in the UK, 1975: cumulative percentage shares of total wealth and lower limits of individual wealth holdings

				Wealth of persons aged 18 and over		
		(1)		*(2)*	*(3)*	
				Assuming the omitted population have no wealth	*Assuming those omitted own difference between balance sheet wealth and estate multiplier wealth*	
		Estate duty method				
		Minimum individual		*Minimum individual*	*(a) UK*	*(b) GB*
Quantile group	*%*	*wealth (£000)*	*%*	*wealth (£000)*	*%*	*%*
top 1%	17.2	66.0	23.2	46.1	24.3	24.4
2–5%	17.8	26.8	23.3	18.4	21.8	21.7
6–10%	12.3	17.9	15.9	12.0	13.9	13.8
11–20%	16.0	11.7	19.4	6.5	16.2	16.2
21–100%	36.7		18.2		23.8	23.9
Total wealth holders		21.0 million		40.4 million		

Sources: *Royal Commission Report No. 5* (London: HMSO, 1977), Tables 28, 38, 41, pp. 70, 86, 89.
Note: Columns (1) (3a): UK; columns (3b)–(5): Great Britain.

Table 16.4 Trends in the distribution of personal wealth; selected years 1923 to 1966. Percentage shares of personal wealth owned by given quantile groups of the total adult population,[a] for selected years between 1923 and 1966[b] (England and Wales)

Quantile group	1923	1926	1928	1930	1936	1938[d]	1950[c]	1952	1954	1956	1958	1959[d]	1960	1962	1964	1966
	%	%	%	%	%	%	%	%	%	%	%	%	%	%	%	%
Top 1 per cent	60.9	57.3	57.0	57.9	54.2	55.0	47.2	43.0	45.3	44.5	41.4	41.4	33.9	31.4	34.5	30.6
2–5 per cent	21.1	22.6	22.6	21.3	23.2	21.9	27.1	27.2	26.5	26.8	26.4	26.2	25.5	23.4	24.1	24.9
6–10 per cent	7.1	7.5	7.6	7.4	8.3	8.1	–	–	–	–	–	–	12.1	12.5	12.8	13.7
11–20 per cent	5.1	5.8	5.9	6.0	6.3	6.2	–	–	–	–	–	–	11.6	12.9	12.9	14.6
Bottom 80 per cent	5.8	6.8	6.9	7.4	8.0	8.8	–	–	–	–	–	–	16.9	19.8	15.7	16.2
Cumulative basis																
Top 1 per cent	60.9	57.3	57.0	57.9	54.2	55.0	47.2	43.0	45.3	44.5	41.4	41.4	33.9	31.4	34.5	30.6
Top 5 per cent	82.0	79.9	79.6	79.2	77.4	76.9	74.3	70.2	71.8	71.3	67.8	67.6	59.4	54.8	58.6	55.5
Top 10 per cent	89.1	87.4	87.2	86.6	85.7	85.0	–	–	–	–	–	–	71.5	67.3	71.4	69.2
Top 20 per cent	94.2	93.2	93.1	92.6	92.0	91.2	–	–	–	–	–	–	83.1	80.2	84.3	83.8

Notes: [a] In order to give approximate effect to the fall in the age of economic independence, the adult population has been taken to be those aged twenty and over in 1953 and eighteen and over in 1973, linear interpolation between these two years indicating how the adult population should be defined in the intermediate years. For years prior to 1953 extrapolation was used to obtain a definition of the adult population.
 [b] Atkinson's and Harrison's central estimates.
 [c] Estimates of the shares of the top 10 and top 20 per cent quantile groups cannot be obtained for these years in the 1950s as these groups then fell outside the range of the estate duty statistics.
 [d] The extra space between 1938 and 1950 and between 1959 and 1960 indicate breaks in continuity in the series. Since 1960 the estate data have given details of estates below the exemption level which come to the notice of Inland Revenue. In interpreting the figures, therefore, it is particularly important to bear in mind the break in comparability between 1959 and 1960 estimates.

Source: Royal Commission Report No. 7, p. 95.

pensions. If occupational pension rights are included in the definition of total wealth the estimated share of the top 1 per cent fell in 1978 from 23 per cent to 19 per cent and the share of the top decile fell from 58 per cent to 52 per cent as can be seen from Table 16.2. It may be noted that there is a range of estimates for the distributions including occupational pension rights. This reflects alternative assumptions about whether or not people with occupational pensions tend to have above-average amounts of other forms of wealth. (These alternative assumptions make no appreciable difference to the estimates at the top of the distribution). The results are particularly sensitive to the inclusion of state pension schemes because the state pension constitutes part of the wealth of the whole population. As may be expected, the inclusion of state pensions makes the distribution of wealth appear much more equal. If both state and occupational pension rights are included in the estimates the share of the top 1 per cent drops to 13 per cent and that of the top decile to 36 per cent. In Chapter 13 we saw that the estimates of income distribution were rather insensitive to differing definitions of income. However, in the case of wealth we have seen that the distributions are very sensitive to the definition adopted.

So far we have seen that alternative definitions and measurements of wealth can produce very different estimates of the amount of inequality at a point in time. It is also of interest to know what is happening to the distribution of wealth over time. Estimates since 1966 are given in Table 16.2 and for the period before 1966 in Table 16.4. The methods used in constructing the two tables are quite different, so that comparisons between the tables are not justified, but both tables suggest that over time there has been a considerable reduction in the inequality of wealth. The reduction has clearly been most marked at the very top, and the share of total wealth owned by the bottom half of the distribution remains low.

Causes of inequality of wealth

There are many reasons why people may gain large amounts of wealth, including winning the football pools, speculating on exchange markets and marrying someone already wealthy. Not surprisingly, however, the greatest attention has been paid to savings and inheritance as the two most important alternative explanations of inequality of wealth. Life-cycle models of consumption imply that in order to maintain a steady level of consumption expenditure people will accumulate savings (wealth) which will peak at retirement age. Calculations made on the assumption that all individuals have equal earnings and save in order to equalise consumption over their lifetime show some degree of wealth concentration as is shown in column (1) of Table 16.5, but this concentration is far less than the actual concentration of wealth. However, it has been suggested by Atkinson that this assumption of equality of earnings makes no allowance for

Table 16.5 Predicted distributions of wealth from life cycle models and the UK distribution of wealth

| | Predicted wealth (accumulated savings) | | | | | Distribution of total wealth GB, 1975 | | | |
| | *(1)* Identical individuals' equal earnings | *(2)* Unequal earnings savings at 7% | *(3)* As (2) but with propensity to save rising with income | | *(4)* Omitting pension rights | | *(5)* Including pensions | |
Quantile shares	(a)	(a)	(a)	(b)	(a)	(b)	(a)	(b)
top 1%	2.0	3.8	10.3		24.4		21.0	
2–5%	7.8	12.4	17.9	28.2	21.7	46.1	20.3	41.3
6–10%	9.3	12.9	14.7	42.9	13.8	59.9	13.7	55.0
11–20%	(not available)	21.6	20.7	63.6	16.2	76.1	16.9	71.9
21–100%	(not available)	49.3	36.4	100	23.9	100	28.1	100

Notes: (a) Share of total wealth, (b) Cumulative share of total wealth.

Source: *Royal Commission Report No. 1* (London: HMSO, 1975), paras 254–255; *Report No. 5* (London: HMSO, 1977), Table K2, p. 292, Table 15.2.

housewives. If it is assumed that half of women are housewives with no earnings, savings or wealth, the predicted distribution becomes more unequal as column (2) of Table 16.5 shows.

More sophisticated estimates have been made by the Royal Commission. These predictions are based on a steady state population that has many of the characteristics of the 1973 British population. For example, women and persons in higher social classes live longer than men and persons in lower social classes and the assumed population reflects this. The proportion of persons of working age actually in employment varies by sex and marital status and this has been allowed for. Earnings vary by social class (occupation), and this has been allowed for in a crude manner. Using these assumptions a distribution of earnings is produced showing earnings at various ages. Persons were then assumed to save an average of 7 per cent of income (somewhat less than UK recent experience would suggest) until retirement, when they were assumed to start consuming capital at the rate of 2 per cent a year, which implies that not all capital would be consumed before death. The resulting prediction for wealth-holding is shown in column (2) of Table 16.5. This prediction is made on the assumption that the average propensity to save is the same at all income levels. As there is reason to suppose that the propensity to save rises with income, an alternative projection was made with the same overall level of savings but in which savings were assumed to rise in steps from nil for incomes below £1000 to 16 per cent for incomes above £7000. The resulting distribution is shown in column (3) of Table 16.5. These predicted distributions may be compared with actual distributions of wealth for 1975 shown in columns (4) and (5). It can be seen that the life-cycle models that make allowances for unequal earnings account reasonably well for observed inequality for the groups in the quantile ranges between 6 and 20 per cent but do less well in the top 5 per cent and, in particular, within the top 1 per cent. There is disagreement about the validity of the life-cycle pre-dictions – it is only an arithmetical exercise and its prediction that wealth, including pension rights, will peak at the time of retirement does not conform with estate duty figures which show wealth continuing to increase past retire-ment. However, it must be remembered that the estate duty figures exclude pension rights.

If we tentatively conclude that life-cycle factors may account for a substantial proportion of observed inequality of wealth except in the top 1 per cent, then we naturally wish to see if inheritance can account for the inequality at the very top. Several studies by Harbury have examined the relationships between the estates of fathers and the estates of sons. These studies lend support to the hypothesis that inheritance is an important source of wealth. Table 16.6 summarises the results at constant 1956-57 prices. It can be seen that in 1956-57 51 per cent of sons with estates over £100,000 had fathers who also had estates over £100,000. The relationships appear particularly strong for peers, the landed gentry and those listed in *Who's Who* and for rich sons in agriculture, public administration, food, drink and tobacco, and distribution.

Table 16.6 Estates of fathers and sons, 1956–57, 1965 and 1973 (valuation at constant prices – 1956–7 average)

Size of sons' estate	Year	Size of fathers' estates: cumulative percentages										Sample size
		Over £1,000,000	Over £500,000	Over £250,000	Over £100,000	Over £50,000	Over £25,000	Over £10,000	Over £5000	Over £1000	All	
		%	%	%	%	%	%	%	%	%	%	
£500,000 and over	1956–57	35	42	46	62	77	77	81	81	85	100	26
	1965	17	17	50	50	50	50	50	50	67	100	6
	1973	25	25	50	63	63	63	88	88	88	100	8
£300,000 and under £500,000	1956–57	22	32	46	56	63	66	68	71	83	100	41
	1965	14	43	57	57	100	100	100	100	100	100	7
	1973	17	33	33	67	83	83	83	83	83	100	6
£200,000 and under £300,000	1956–57	12	23	35	55	66	68	73	81	85	100	72
	1965	0	18	46	73	91	100	100	100	100	100	11
	1973	11	22	22	44	61	72	78	89	89	100	18
£100,000 and under £200,000	1956–57	5	15	29	48	59	67	75	78	85	100	391
	1965	3	7	18	38	49	60	74	79	82	100	68
	1973	3	7	15[a]	27[a]	41[a]	51[a]	66	68	76	100	74
All sons £100,000 and over	1956–57	9	19	33	51	57	68	75	78	85	100	530
	1965	4	12	26	45	58	67[a]	77	82	85	100	92
	1973	7	12	20[a]	35[a]	48	58[a]	71	74	79	100	106

Note: [a] Statistically significant differences between 1973 and 1956/7 at the 5 per cent level. No individual difference in proportions between 1965 and 1973 is statistically significant at this level.

Source: C. S. Harbury and D. M. Hitchens, 'The Inheritances of Tax Wealth Leavers' *Economic Journal* 86 (June 1976), pp. 321–6.

While inheritance remains an important source of wealth there are signs that its importance is declining. Thus while in 1956–57 51 per cent of sons with wealth over £100,000 had fathers with wealth over £100,000 this proportion had dropped significantly to 35 per cent by 1973.

Two studies by the Royal Commission shed further light on the role of inheritance. One is based on a sample of 238 estates receiving probate in 1973. The estates were selected (by over-sampling the largest estates) to give roughly equal numbers of estates in each of four ranges of size of estate. The Royal Commission then examined the beneficiaries of each estate to see the extent to which the largest estates tended to remain intact between generations. Some of the results from this exercise are given in Table 16.7, when it can be seen that on average the number of beneficiaries rose with the size of estate. It can also be seen that proportion of the estate given to the immediate family declined as the size of the estate rose. This suggests that the largest estates are dispersed more widely than smaller estates which should lead to a reduction in the concentration of wealth over time (see below and Table 16.4). However, this conclusion needs to be treated with caution for a number of reasons. The analysis is historical in the sense that it is based in a 1973 sample. At that time capital transfer tax (CTT) had not come into existence and thus the pattern of bequests will reflect the impact of the old estate duty rather than CTT. Gifts made more than seven years before death were free of estate duty and hence are not reflected in the sample. If people with large estates were more likely to give their money away before death, and if these gifts were to their children, then the figures could overstate the extent to which estates were dispersed. It should also be remembered that, while the large estates have been more widely dispersed than small ones, the proportion given to relations as a whole has remained high. Nevertheless, this information is consistent with the falling inequality of wealth shown in Table 16.4, where the share of the top 1 per cent has dropped from 33 to 23 per cent between 1966 and 1978, and the share of the bottom 90 per cent has risen from 31 to 42 per cent.

In another exercise the Royal Commission used what they termed the 'perpetual investing method' to estimate the effects of inheritance in the

Table 16.7 Analysis of a sample of 238 bequests

Size of estate (£000)	Average bequests on estates	Percentage of disposable estate bequeathed to:		
		spouses and children	other relations	others
	N	%	%	%
over 500	24	36.9	38.6	24.5
100–500	13	55.8	31.4	12.8
50–100	7	63.8	21.1	15.1
15–50	5	66.0	24.6	9.4

Source: *Royal Commission Report No. 5* (London: HMSO, 1977), Tables 82 and 83, pp. 170–1.

distribution of wealth. This method estimates the stock of inherited wealth from the flow of bequests. In this exercise it was assumed that men died at age seventy-one (the average male age of death in England and Wales) and left 68 per cent of their wealth to their wives who were then aged sixty-eight. The remaining wealth was distributed to younger persons (e.g. children in their forties) and charity. Women were assumed to die at age seventy-seven (again the average age) and to leave two-thirds of their wealth to the next generation, then in their early fifties, with the remainder of their wealth divided among slightly younger women, charities and persons in their early twenties. These factors were derived from the sample of estates referred to earlier. The resulting estimate of the stock of inherited wealth is given in column (1) of Table 16.8. A comparison of this estimated stock of inheritances with the actual stock of wealth suggests that inheritance might account for 20 per cent of the stock of wealth. If a further 5 per cent is added for gifts *inter vivos* this suggests that transmitted wealth might account for one-quarter of the total wealth.

While none of this evidence is conclusive, it does suggest roles for both life cycle and inheritance factors in explaining the inequality of wealth although the importance of inheritance may be declining.

Our views about wealth taxation may well also depend on the actual amount of wealth people own and on the form in which it is held. It may be seen from Table 16.2 that in 1978 it was estimated that 87 per cent of the adult population owned less than £15,000 in wealth and only just over half of 1 per cent owned more than £100,000. Table 16.9 shows the distribution of wealth by class of asset, excluding pension rights, in 1976. It can be seen that the asset

Table 16.8 Inheritances and total wealth subdivided by sex and marital status of women

	(1) *Estimated inheritances 1973*	(2) *Total wealth (estate duty method) 1973*	(3) *(1) as percentage of (2)*
	£b	£b	%
Men	10.6	99.3	10.7
Married women	8.5	31.7	26.8 ⎤
Unmarried women	14.0	32.9	42.6 ⎦ 34.8
Total	33.1	163.9	20.2
	%	%	
Proportion owned by:			
Married women	25.7	19.3	
Unmarried women	42.3	20.1	
All women	68.0	39.4	

Source: *Royal Commission Report No. 5* (London: HMSO, 1977), Table 90, p. 194.

Table 16.9 Asset composition of personal wealth by range of net wealth; 1976[a] (UK)

Asset/liability	Range of net wealth (lower limit)							Total
	Nil	£5,000	£10,000	£20,000	£50,000	£100,000	£200,000	
	%	%	%	%	%	%	%	%
Physical assets:								
Dwellings[b]	28.7	50.2	56.7	41.5	30.4	21.2	13.1	41.0
Land	0.2	0.5	1.0	3.1	5.2	7.1	20.0	3.8
Other buildings	0.2	0.4	0.8	1.3	2.2	2.6	1.3	1.1
Household goods	7.3	4.5	3.5	3.3	3.3	3.7	4.5	4.0
Trade assets	0.7	1.3	1.3	3.9	5.1	4.9	2.8	2.6
Financial assets:								
Listed ordinary shares[c]	1.1	0.9	1.5	5.8	15.3	21.7	21.8	6.9
Other company securities	0.4	0.2	0.6	2.4	8.1	11.8	14.3	3.6
Life policies	26.9	20.4	17.6	15.7	7.2	4.3	2.7	15.1
Building Society deposits	11.7	9.2	9.0	11.5	8.2	4.8	1.2	8.9
Listed UK government securities	1.2	0.5	0.4	1.5	2.7	4.4	6.4	1.8
Cash and bank deposits	12.0	6.1	4.9	5.9	7.9	10.0	8.5	6.9
National savings	10.3	5.0	3.7	2.7	1.5	0.8	0.3	3.5
Other financial assets	21.3	14.4	9.1	9.8	8.4	8.2	8.6	10.9
Liabilities:								
Personal debts	−8.7	−3.2	−2.5	−3.6	−3.8	−4.7	−4.9	−3.9
Property debts	−13.3	−10.4	−7.6	−4.8	−1.7	−0.8	−0.6	−6.2
Net wealth	100.0	100.0	100.0	100.0	100.0	100.0	100.0	100.0

Notes: [a] This table relates only to the population and types of wealth covered by the unadjusted estate multiplier estimates, that is all those individuals whose estates would require probate, or be liable to Capital Transfer Tax (formerly estate duty) in the event of their deaths. In previous reports (see for example Table 29 of Report No. 5, which corresponds to this table) we referred to such estimates as 'Series A'.
[b] Gross.
[c] Including unit trusts.

Source: *Royal Commission Report No. 7*, p. 99.

composition changes markedly as the size of wealth holding increases. With relatively small amounts of wealth, say up to £20,000, housing, life policies and building society deposits are particularly important. The ownership of shares and other securities becomes important for the larger estates.

Existing British taxes on wealth

As income can be thought of as the expected return on wealth and wealth as the present value of expected income, the dividing line between the two is somewhat arbitrary and consequently so is the dividing line between income taxes and wealth taxes. Nevertheless, we will consider the following as wealth taxes: capital transfer tax, capital gains tax, stamp duties and the investment income surcharge.

(1) *Capital transfer tax*

Capital transfer tax (CTT) was introduced in 1974 and replaced estate duty. CTT is a tax on transfers of wealth both at death and during a person's lifetime: transfers *inter vivos*. The tax is levied on the person making the transfer and the tax rates are heavier for transfers at death (or within three years of death) than for transfers made during a person's lifetime. Until 1981 the rate on transfers made during a person's lifetime depended on the cumulative total over the donor's life. Since 1981 the period of cumulation is restricted to ten years. From 1980 the exemption level is nominally (see below) £50,000. Marginal tax rates rise from 30 to 75 per cent for transfers at death and from 15 to 50 per cent for lifetime transfers. The highest rates both for transfers at death and transfer *inter vivos* start at just over £2m. Average rates are of course much less than marginal rates. Sutherland has calculated, for example, that a married couple paying standard rate of CTT in 1981 would pay nothing on an amount of £200,000, 23 per cent on £300,000, 41 per cent on £1m and 69 per cent on £10m. Lower rates apply to businesses, agricultural landlords and working farmers. These lower rates could reduce the liability on a £10m transfer to 12 per cent. In addition a variety of special exemptions are made for gifts. The most important is that transfers between spouses are exempted. Also exempted are gifts not exceeding £3000 in any one year, other gifts not exceeding £250 to any one person, gifts counting as normal expenditures out of income and certain gifts on marriage.

CTT, like most other British taxes, is expressed in nominal terms. Unless the bands are adjusted for inflation, this means that the tax would become more progressive in real terms over time. In fact, however, nominal amounts have been increased faster than inflation. When the tax was introduced the exemption was £15,000 and from 1980 it was £50,000. Sutherland has calculated that in order to maintain its 1974 value it would have needed to be £34,000 in 1980. The effective exemption level was further increased in 1981 by the decision only to accumulate lifetime gifts for ten years. In eleven years an individual can transfer £133,000 tax free (twice £50,000, plus £3000 a year for eleven years, plus unlimited amounts from normal expenditures from income). Couples can transfer twice as much. Sutherland in an article entitled 'Capital Transfer Tax, an Obituary' concluded that 99 per cent of wealth owners will no longer have to pay CTT even without resort to sophisticated tax avoidance schemes and the remaining 1 per cent will pay much less.

(2) Capital gains tax

Capital gains tax (CGT) is levied on realised money gains of many assets, excluding an owner-occupier's main residence, at a rate of 30 per cent or less. It may be noted that 30 per cent is very much less than the top rates of income tax, which rise to 75 per cent including the investment income surcharge. This naturally creates an incentive to receive one's income in a form that is liable to CGT tax rather than income tax. Thus a shareholder may prefer to purchase shares in companies that retain most of their profits (so putting up share prices) even if the profitability of the company is lower. While such a distortion is clearly to the taxpayers' advantage it is likely to be to society's disadvantage. CGT is levied on *realised* capital gains. Thus a person can postpone tax by holding on to an asset and there is a tendency to become 'locked in' to particular assets, particularly as no CGT is payable on death.

There are complicated interactions between CGT, corporation tax and income tax which depend on whether or not a firm is incorporated or unincorporated, whether it raises capital by issuing shares or by borrowing, and whether or not capital allowances are payable. These relationships have been studied by the Meade Committee. They have produced an example showing that after-tax rates of return to savings can vary between 0.1 and 58.8 per cent when the pretax rate of return is constant at 10 per cent. The results of this example are summarised in Table 19.5.

As CGT is levied on money gains it can be in effect, although not in intention, a tax on capital losses, as the example makes clear. A person buys 100 of shares in year 1 and sells them in year 5 for 150. He is thus liable for tax of 15 ($=0.3 \times 50$). If prices in year 5 are twice as high as in year 1 he has actually made a loss of 25 but he still has to pay 15 in tax.

(3) Stamp duties

Like CGT, stamp duties are taxes on the transfer of assets. The most important are *ad valorem* duties on sales of houses, land and shares. As usual, *ad valorem* taxes remain fixed in real terms when the prices of assets change.

(4) The investment income surcharge

The investment income surcharge is a tax on investment or unearned income above a certain amount. In 1981–82 the surcharge was 15 per cent for investment incomes above £5500. Where it is payable the investment income surcharge is paid in addition to income tax.

The real rate of 'tax' on unearned income can very easily exceed 100 per cent in an inflationary period, as the example in Table 16.10 makes clear. Because inflation hits both the income and wealth the real value of the wealth holding will fall whenever the rate of inflation exceeds the net return on capital.

Table 16.10 Example of tax rates on investment incomes

| | | Marginal tax rate | |
		0	*50%*
Start of year	Deposit £1000		
	Interest at 10%	£100	£100
	Tax	0	50
	After-tax income	£100	£50
End of year	Deposit plus net interest	£1100	£1050
	Real value of deposit plus net interest if 15% inflation	£935	£892
	Implied 'tax' rate on income of 100	165%	208%

Revenue from wealth taxes in the UK

The yield from UK wealth taxes is shown in Table 16.11 where it can be seen that the combined yield is small and of declining importance. The reduction of CTT in the 1981 budget is likely to cause this decline to continue. Revenue from the investment-income surcharge is only available on a financial year basis and is shown separately in the table.

Incidence of wealth taxes

Very little is known about the incidence of taxes on wealth. One estimate has been made by O'Higgins and Ruggles for 1971 based on FES data and is given in Table 17.11. Wealth (capital) taxes are assumed to be proportional to the income from capital.

Table 16.11 Revenue from UK wealth taxes (£m)

Calendar year	(1) Capital gains tax	(2) Death duties	(3) Capital transfer tax	(4) Stamp duties	(5) Total[a]	(6) Column (5) as % of total receipts of central government	(7) Column (5) as % of GDP	Fiscal year	(8) Investment income surcharge
1966	4.0	306.0	—	77.3	387.3	3.49	1.17		
1967	13.5	314.6	—	71.6	419.7	3.39	1.20		
1968	33.8	371.0	—	117.3	522.1	3.72	1.39		
1969	102.5	367.7	—	121.8	592.0	3.74	1.50		
1970	151.9	374.6	—	123.1	649.9	3.62	1.49		
1971	145.2	401.0	—	139.4	685.6	3.61	1.40		
1972	174.4	478.9	—	223.4	876.7	4.40	1.59		
1973	293.8	415.7	—	203.8	913.3	4.11	1.44	1973–74	136
1974	380.8	378.8	—	178.9	938.5	3.40	1.28	1974–75	202
1975	383.5	238.8	68.3	266.4	956.9	2.68	1.03		
1976	335.8	147.1	243.0	275.8	1001.7	2.37	0.93		
1977	330.9	94.2	298.8	340.6	1064.5	2.17	0.84		
1978	332.1	53.6	328.0	433.8	1147.5	2.11	0.80		
1979	412.7	33.5	384.6	564.2	1395.0	2.14	0.85		
1980	491.5	29.1	418.0	630.5	1569.1	1.98	0.82		

Note: [a] Excluding investment income surcharge.

Source: *Financial Statistics*, (various years) and *National Income and Expenditure 1980*.

International comparison of wealth taxes

Table 16.12 shows taxes on wealth as a percentage of total tax revenue in OECD countries. Included in this definition of wealth taxes are recurrent taxes on net wealth (OECD code 4200); estate inheritance, and gift taxes (4300); taxes on financial and capital transactions (4400); and non-recurrent and other taxes on net wealth and property (4500 and 4600). Britain's reliance on wealth taxes can be seen to have dropped both absolutely and relative to other OECD countries.

Table 16.12 Taxes on wealth (OECD codes[a] 4200 to 4600) as a percentage of total tax revenue

	1965	1970	1975	1979
Australia	4.89	5.50	4.10	3.62
Austria	2.48	2.61	2.17	2.21
Belgium	3.74	3.05	2.36	2.78
Canada	2.37	2.18	1.05	1.01
Denmark	3.11	1.85	1.91	2.65
Finland	4.08	2.29	2.05	2.20
France	2.32	2.03	2.02	1.88
Germany	3.39	2.99	1.96	1.62
Greece	N.A.	9.30	9.66	7.47
Ireland	2.86	2.07	2.38	2.14
Italy	5.90	5.36	3.44	4.25
Japan	3.00	3.20	3.28	3.14
Luxembourg	5.04	5.58	4.42	5.19
Netherlands	3.34	2.35	1.82	2.56
New Zealand	3.21	2.70	2.29	1.29
Norway	2.52	1.79	1.90	1.41
Portugal	5.10	4.22	2.52	1.53
Spain	5.92	6.03	5.93	4.84
Sweden	1.74	1.43	1.10	0.90
Switzerland	8.17	8.22	6.55	6.80
Turkey	5.42	5.81	5.27	4.72
United Kingdom	3.32	2.79	1.53	1.57
United States	2.08	1.78	1.48	1.18

Note: [a] See Table 10.1.

Source: *Revenue Statistics of OECD Member Countries 1965-1980* (Paris: OECD, 1981), pp. 94-143.

Proposals for reform

The present taxation of wealth is unsatisfactory from almost everyone's point of view, so it is not surprising that proposals for reform are both widespread and lacking in unanimity. (The Select Committee on the Wealth Tax produced five different reports but the Committee failed to agree on any of them.)

The diversity of opinion about wealth tax reform is not hard to understand, for as we have seen it is possible for reasonable people to differ on each of the following:

(1) the present degree of inequality of distribution of wealth;

(2) whether or not the trend towards greater equality has gone far enough or too far;

(3) the causes of inequality;

(4) whether inequality through inheritance should be treated differently from inequality resulting from hard work and savings;

(5) whether the primary object of wealth taxation is horizontal equity or vertical equity;

(6) whether special provision should be made either (a) to prevent businesses, including farms, being broken up or (b) to prevent total tax rates exceeding 100 per cent (or some other figure);

(7) whether owner-occupied housing and pensions should be included in the wealth tax base;

(8) what taxes, if any, should be abolished when wealth taxes are introduced.

Given this diversity of views it is hardly surprising to find proposals as wide ranging as:

(1) an exemption of about £20,000 with rates starting at $1\frac{1}{2}$ per cent and rising to 20 per cent on the largest estates. This proposal by Fleming and Little includes the abolition of the investment income surcharge and of capital gains tax and of all taxes on the transfers of wealth. As the authors estimate that the yield from the largest estates is about 4 per cent, the rate of tax on the largest estates would amount to about 500 per cent of income and is deliberately designed to break up large holdings of wealth;

(2) an exemption of £30,000 with a constant rate of $\frac{1}{2}$ to 1 per cent and a tax ceiling of 70 per cent of income. This proposal by the Conservative members of the Select Committee was designed for horizontal equity. It would be introduced only after problems of administering the tax had been solved.

The distribution of wealth has become a great deal more equal during this century (see Tables 16.2 and 16.4) and this must reduce the need for a wealth tax in order to secure still more equality. In the first edition of this book we said, 'in our view vertical equity now becomes of secondary importance except for the largest estates, say those over £250,000. Even here the case for vertical equity needs to be balanced against the possible damage to efficient businesses'. However, the case for a tax on wealth holdings is increased by the very large reductions in CTT made in the 1981 budget. There is certainly a strong case for having either an annual wealth tax *or* an effective capital transfer tax. Other important reasons for introducing wealth taxes are the need for horizontal equity and in order to reduce other taxes, particularly the highest rates of income tax and the investment income surcharge. A wealth tax with low rates could be justified on ability-to-pay grounds and seems likely to have less harmful effects on the incentives to work and save than the highest rates of tax on income, including the investment income surcharge which can exceed 100 per cent in real terms during an inflationary period. As the Meade Committee have made clear, sensible proposals for a wealth tax depend not only on the objectives of the wealth tax but also on other taxes.

CHAPTER 17

Taxes on Goods and Services

Taxes on goods and services, or indirect taxes as they are sometimes called, account for a large proportion of government revenue in the UK as well as in all other OECD countries. The share of revenue from these taxes fell sharply in most countries during the early 1970s but by 1980 the UK had put its proportion of taxes on goods and services back up to its mid-1960s levels partly as the result of the introduction of the National Insurance Surcharge and North Sea Oil taxes. Fairly radical changes in these taxes on goods were made in Britain in the 1970s as part of the process of joining the European Economic Community (EEC). In this chapter we look at the changes that have taken place and put the changes in an international context. We then look at the evidence on the incidence of these taxes.

Taxes on goods and services in the UK

(1) Unit taxes

In the UK the Customs and Excise Department collects 75 per cent of taxes on expenditure. The most important Customs and Excise duties are shown in Table 17.1. The table shows the rates of duty payable and estimated receipts in 1980-81. Until VAT was introduced in 1973 (see below) oil, tobacco and alcoholic drink were taxed exclusively by unit taxes in which the duty was shillings per gallon, per pound etc. These goods are now taxed by both unit taxes and *ad valorem* taxes. Entry to the EEC has had a number of effects on these taxes. Some of these changes only involve the adoption of new units. Thus the duty on wine (before 1976) and spirits (before 1979) was expressed in terms of alcoholic strength measured by the imperial proof system (where originally 100 proof – 'proof spirits' – corresponded to the minimum alcoholic strength that would burn when mixed with gunpowder). A more prosaic system is now used which simply relies on the percentage of alcohol. Other changes are of greater significance, with perhaps the most important being the method of taxing cigarettes. Prior to 1973 the tax was a unit tax with the tax liability *depending on the weight of tobacco*. After two transitional phases the present EEC system was adopted in 1978. This new system has an *ad valorem* element based on the recommended retail price including taxes and the unit element in the tax is now

Table 17.1 Selected UK Customs and Excise rates, 1980–81

Predominate type of tax	Commodity	Rate 1980–81	Estimated revenue[a] 1980–81 (£m)	Percentage[a] total customs and excise (%)
Unit[b]	Cigarettes	21% of retail price plus £13.42 per thousand	2775[c]	11.6
	Spirits	£11.87 per litre of alcohol	1270	5.3
	Beer	£13.05 per hectolitre[d] at 1030° plus 0.435 per additional degree	1130	4.7
	Wine	£81.42 per hectolitre[d] not exceeding 15% alcohol £93.93 per hectolitre[d] over 15% and up to 18% £110.59 per hectolitre[d] over 18% and up to 22%	363	1.5
	Petrol	£0.4546 per gallon	3650	15.2
Ad valorem VAT		0% or 15% (see Table 17.2)	12450	51.9
Car Tax		10% of wholesale price	575	2.4
Total Customs and Excise Revenue			24000	100.0

Notes: [a] About 93 per cent of revenue is accounted for by the selected items.
[b] These goods are all subject to VAT at 15 per cent in addition.
[c] For all tobacco products.
[d] A hectolitre is 100 litres.

Source: *71st Report of the Commissioners of Her Majesty's Customs and Excise for the Year ended 31 March 1980.* Cmnd 8099 (London: HMSO, 1980), various tables.

based on the number of cigarettes rather than the amount of tobacco. Under the old system small cigarettes attracted less duty than large cigarettes because a smaller weight of tobacco was needed for their manufacture. While the *ad valorem* element will continue to benefit small cigarettes the unit element will no longer give an advantage to them. One would expect this to narrow the price differential between large and small cigarettes and to lead to a change in consumption to larger cigarettes, and this is what has happened. Whether one favours this change or not it provides an excellent example of the way in which taxes can influence the behaviour of manufacturers and customers.

(2) Ad valorem *taxes*

The two most important *ad valorem* taxes are the car tax, which is set at 10 per cent of the wholesale price of cars, and value added tax (VAT). Prior to April

1973 the most important *ad valorem* tax on goods was purchase tax, which was levied at relatively high rates on a relatively narrow range of goods. The tax was a single-stage tax levied at the wholesale stage.

VAT. In April 1973 purchase tax was replaced by VAT, which is a multi-stage tax. At each stage of manufacturing and distribution firms are liable to pay VAT if they supply more than £15,000 (in 1981–82) of taxable goods a year. The system works as follows. When a firm buys raw materials or other goods it will be charged VAT by the supplying firm. This is called input tax. When the firm subsequently sells these or other goods it charges VAT to its customers. This is output tax. In general input tax is deductable which means that firms have to pay to Customs and Excise the difference between the input and output taxes. The difference between the value of a firm's output and the value of its inputs is the firm's value added, which is the origin of the term 'value added tax'.

There are now two rates of VAT, the standard rate (15 per cent in 1981–82) and the zero rate (until 1978/1979 there was a higher rate of $12\frac{1}{2}$ per cent with the standard rate then 8 per cent). There are also certain goods that are exempt. Having both a zero-rated class and an exempt class may sound confusing but the distinction is as follows. Zero-rated goods are technically taxable which means they can claim back tax paid on their inputs but they do not have to charge tax on their output. Exempt goods are not taxable and for this reason are not permitted to reclaim tax on inputs. Table 17.2 shows the main groups of goods in each class.

(3) Other

There are two new important sources of revenue in the UK that are classified as taxes on expenditure in the UK National Income Accounts. One is the quaintly named royalties and taxes on 'seaward activities' which are taxes on oil and gas production. They accounted for 1.4 per cent of central government revenue (slightly more than beer duties) in 1980 (see Table 17.4). The other is the national insurance surcharge first introduced at a rate of 2 per cent in 1977 and increased to $3\frac{1}{2}$ per cent the following year. It raised £3.5b in 1980 or 4.4 per cent of central government revenue (see Table 17.4). It is a curious feature of the accounts that the basic National Insurance contributions are not treated as expenditure tax while the surcharge (which is levied on the same basis) is treated as an expenditure tax. (The OECD treats the surcharge as a payroll tax.) A possible implication of the differences in treatment could be that there is an expectation that the incidence of the taxes will be different although it is hard to see any reason why this should be so. The CSO assume in their studies of incidence (see Table 13.6) that employ*ees*' national insurance contribution falls on labour income and that employ*ers*' contributions including the surcharge are passed forward 100 per cent into prices. (See section on incidence below.)

Table 17.2   Goods and services liable to and exempted from VAT in 1980–81

Group	Zero-rated	Standard rate	Exempted
1	Food and drink, except (a) when supplied in the course of catering and (b) certain less essential foods, alcoholic and soft drinks and pet food	All goods and services not noted elsewhere	Land
2	Sewerage services and water		Insurance
3	Books and newspapers		Postal services
4	Talking books for the blind and handicapped and wireless sets for the blind		Betting, gaming and lotteries
5	Newspaper advertisements		Finance
6	News services		Education
7	Fuel and power (but not road fuel)		Health
8	Construction of buildings		Burial and cremation
9	International services		
10	Transport		
11	Caravans and houseboats		
12	Gold		
13	Bank notes		
14	Drugs, medicines and appliances supplied on prescription		
15	Certain import transactions prior to customs entry of the goods; transfer of goods or provisions of services by a United Kingdom or Isle of Man business to its address abroad; supplies to fulfil contracts relating to international defence collaboration projects		
16	Charities		
17	Young children's clothing and footwear		
	Suppliers of goods are also zero-rated if the goods are exported or shipped as stores on a voyage or flight to a destination outside the UK		

Source: *71st Report of the Commissioners of Her Majesty's Customs and Excise for the Year ended 31 March 1980.*

Revenue from taxes on goods and services

In money terms revenue from taxes on goods and services has risen rapidly, as can be seen from Table 17.3. For example, in 1966 total Customs and Excise receipts were £3.6b while in 1980 they were £20.1b. The table also shows total taxes on expenditure according to the UK National Income and Expenditure definition. It can be seen that this definition includes motor vehicle taxes, stamp duty and the short-lived Selective Employment Tax, as well as the National Insurance Surcharge and the taxes on seaward activities.

Table 17.3 UK taxes on expenditure (£ million)

	1966	1968	1970	1972	1974	1976	1978	1980
Customs and Excise duties								
Beer	361	395	460	492	427	773	907	1006
Wines and spirits	314	382	459	570	681	1116	1328	1514
Tobacco	1029	1084	1150	1171	1283	1808	2153	2696
Hydrocarbon oils	856	1081	1368	1517	1556	1941	2465	3424
Protective duties	182	224	250	352	533	659	740	869
Temporary charge on imports	133	−2	–	–	–	–	–	–
EC Agricultural Levy	–	–	–	–	–	–	225	252
Purchase tax	686	971	1304	1389	–	–	–	–
Value added tax	–	–	–	–	2721	3982	5215	11395
Car tax	–	–	–	–	135	224	380	456
Betting and gaming	43	96	124	166	226	285	345	455
Total[a]	3617	4244	5129	5670	7571	10802	13769	22081
Motor vehicle duties (gross)	270	385	455	489	524	820	1125	1322
Selective employment tax	141	531	850	449	–	–	–	–
Stamp duties	78	118	124	224	179	276	433	630
National Insurance Surcharge	–	–	–	–	–	–	1746	3500
Royalties and taxes from seaward activities	–	–	–	–	–	–	286	1156
Total[a]	4047	5261	6588	6885	8378	12120	17565	28987

Note: [a] The totals are greater than the sum of the detail because minor items have been omitted.
Source: *National Income and Expenditure* 1980 edition and earlier years.

Table 17.4 Share of UK central government revenue raised by taxes on expenditure

Predominant base of tax	Commodity	Percentage of central government revenue				
		1965	*1970*	*1973*	*1976*	*1980*
		%	%	%	%	%
Unit	Beer	3.3	2.6	1.7	1.8	1.3
	Wines and spirits	2.8	2.6	2.6	2.6	1.9
	Tobacco	9.9	6.4	4.8	4.2	3.4
	Oil	7.6	7.6	7.2	4.6	4.3
	Total of above	23.6	19.2	16.3	13.2	10.9
Ad valorem	Purchase tax	6.3	7.3	1.6		
	VAT			7.7	9.4	14.4
	Car tax			0.5	0.5	0.6
	Total of above	6.3	7.4	9.8	10.1	15.0
	Total Customs and Excise[a]	33.8	28.5	29.0	25.4	27.8
	Vehicle duty	2.4	2.5	2.3	1.9	1.7
	National Insurance Surcharge					4.4
	Royalties and taxes from seaward activities	0.0	0.0	0.1	0.2	1.4
	Total expenditure taxes[b]	36.8	36.7	33.1	28.5	36.5

Notes: [a] Totals exceed detail because some minor items are omitted.
[b] *National Income and Expenditure* definition which includes stamp duties, selective employment tax and National Insurance Surcharge.
Source: Calculated from *National Income and Expenditure* 1981 and earlier years.

While there has been a rapid growth in the amounts of money collected by taxes on goods and services, their importance in terms of their share in government expenditure declined sharply during the early 1970s as can be seen in Table 17.4. Between 1965 and 1976 Customs and Excise receipts fell from one-third to one-quarter of central government revenue. Part of the reason for this decline can be seen from the division of the table into sections. The top section shows the major Customs and Excise duties that were exclusively unit taxes before the introduction of VAT and that still have a substantial unit-based component. The bottom section shows the major *ad valorem*-based taxes (purchase tax before 1973 and VAT and car tax since 1973). It can be seen that the unit-based taxes' share of central government revenue fell by 10 per cent between 1965 and 1976. The share of *ad valorem* taxes increased by 4 per cent during the same period. Part of the reason for this pattern is that, as we saw in Chapter 11 inflation decreases the real value of unit taxes if there are no discretionary tax changes, while the real value of *ad valorem* taxes is not affected by inflation. For much of the period there was no change in the nominal rates of many unit taxes. For example, from November 1968 to early 1974 (April 1976 in the case of oil) there were only minor changes in the main Customs and Excise rates although the retail price index increased by 66 per cent between 1968 and 1974.

Table 17.5 Duty as a percentage of retail prices selected goods, UK

Commodity	Year	Unit	Retail price	Duty	Duty as % of retail price	Duty as % of retail price less duty
Scotch whisky	1968[a]	Bottle	£2.35[b]	£2.20	94	1467
	1977	Bottle[b]	4.45[b]	3.16	71	245
	1980	Bottle[b]	5.50	3.56	65	184
Beer	1967[a]	Pint	0.0958[c]	0.0425	44	80
	1977	Pint	0.30[c]	0.075	25	33
	1980	Pint[c]	0.44	0.091	21	26
Cigarettes	1966[a]	20 standard tipped	0.2292	0.1583	69	224
	1977	20 standard tipped	0.55	0.345	63	168
	1980	20 standard tipped	0.73	0.516	71	241

Notes: [a] In each case the earliest year shown in the source.
[b] Minimum retail price.
[c] Typical public bar price.
Source: *68th Report of the Commissioners of Her Majesty's Customs and Excise for the Year ended 31 March 1977*, and *71st Report of the Commissioners of Her Majesty's Customs and Excise for the Year ended 31st March 1980*. Various tables.

By 1980 the share of revenue from commodities with a predominance of unit taxes had fallen still further and was less than half the share 15 years earlier. However, there was a sharp increase in the share of *ad valorem* taxes following the increase in the basic rate of VAT from 8 per cent to 15 per cent in 1979. The new National Insurance Surcharge and the seaward activities taxes boosted the overall share of taxes classified as taxes in expenditure back to its mid-60s share.

The revenue from tobacco tax has continued to decline in relative importance. This is due in part to a fall in tobacco consumption, which may be associated with a growing awareness of the health risks from tobacco even more than to the change in duty. The continued decline in the importance of revenue from the oil tax reflects in part the fact that the duty was not raised until April 1976, and in part the fall in the consumption of oil as a result of the very large increases in the price of crude oil. Table 17.5 shows a similar effect in more concrete terms for three commodities. It can be seen that in each case the nominal amount of duty was higher in 1980 than it was in 1968 or 1977. However, duty as a percentage of the estimated retail price had fallen in 1977 and this fall appeared even larger when the retail price less duty was used as the base. The fall in tax as a proportion of price was reversed by 1980 in the case of cigarettes but continued in the case of the other two goods. While it is instructive that the revenue share of unit taxes has fallen so rapidly, this in itself does not explain why Chancellors have failed to use their discretion to maintain the real values of these taxes. It may, however, be that this is in line with voters preferences. In 1980 (after the 1979 switch from income tax to VAT) a sample of people (from households where at least one person could vary their income by varying their labour supply) were asked if they would prefer to have a cut in income tax or cut in taxes such as VAT. A cut in income tax was preferred by 53 per cent and a cut in VAT by 43 per cent (Stirling Study).

A full explanation of the reasons for the decline in the importance of goods and service taxes is perhaps more a matter for the political scientist than the economist but two possible reasons may be mentioned. Raising taxes on goods clearly raises the prices of these goods (not necessarily by the exact amount of the tax) and the resulting increase in the retail price index may be difficult to defend when a major objective of policy is to reduce the rate of inflation. Unit taxes are levied on a very narrow range of goods, and failure to raise these duties may have been motivated by a desire not to damage the industries concerned – perhaps in particular the Scotch whisky industry which is a major export-earner.

International comparison of taxes on goods and services

Every other country in the OECD, like the United Kingdom, had a fall in the share of government revenue raised by taxes on goods and services in the period from 1965 to 1975, as can be seen from Table 17.6. However, a rather different picture emerges if one takes tax receipts on goods and services as a proportion of GDP at market prices. In just over half the countries including the UK these taxes fell as a proportion of GDP, but in eleven countries the tax-to-GDP ratio rose. Part of the reason for these trends is again attributable to the unit tax – *ad valorem* tax division. The ratio of unit tax receipts to GDP rose in only five countries: Australia, Canada, Luxembourg, Norway and Turkey (as is given in an OECD table we have not reproduced). Since 1975 nine OECD countries including the UK have increased the share of revenue from taxes on goods and services and seventeen have increased the share of GDP taken in these taxes. It would appear that many countries came to realise about the same time the effects of inflation on unit-based taxes.

The incidence of taxes on goods and services

The incidence of taxes may be studied using either the partial equilibrium approach outlined in Chapter 11 or a general equilibrium approach such as was outlined in Chapter 12. The partial equilibrium method is far easier but is inappropriate for major changes such as the 1973 UK reform which involved the replacement of purchase tax by VAT. In this section we look at some US evidence from partial equilibrium studies, at a general equilibrium study of the 1973 UK reforms and at studies that examine how taxes on goods influence the distribution of incomes between rich and poor households. This last group of

Table 17.6   **Taxes on goods and services in OECD countries**

Taxes on goods and services (OECD code 500)

	as a percentage of GDP at market prices			as a percentage of total taxation		
	1965	*1975*	*1980*[a]	*1965*	*1975*	*1980*[a]
Australia	8.27	8.50	9.45[b]	34.78	29.16	31.71[b]
Austria	12.86	13.31	12.98	37.14	34.54	31.25
Belgium	11.61	10.81	10.16	37.20	26.32	23.92
Canada	10.70	10.58	10.71	41.23	32.12	32.63
Denmark	12.21	13.81	16.94	40.62	33.64	37.52
Finland	13.11	12.56	14.10	43.52	34.76	40.92
France	13.44	12.30	12.81	38.42	32.85	30.14
Germany	10.42	9.54	10.05	32.97	26.75	26.99
Greece	10.74	11.91	12.48[b]	52.19	48.34	45.07[b]
Ireland	13.70	15.12	16.40	52.66	46.53	43.70
Italy	10.67	8.41	8.58	39.05	29.03	27.49[b]
Japan	4.89	3.63	4.19	27.10	17.21	16.21
Luxembourg	7.60	9.10	9.37	24.67	20.89	19.71
Netherlands	10.10	10.94	11.46	28.48	23.89	24.82
New Zealand	6.86	7.28	7.15[b]	28.19	24.22	22.94[b]
Norway	13.62	16.96	16.76	41.01	37.83	35.39
Portugal	7.66	9.34	12.01	41.25	37.62	40.33
Spain	6.02	4.74	5.33	40.84	24.16	23.03
Sweden	11.33	10.92	12.12	31.83	24.69	24.31
Switzerland	6.31	5.88	6.29	30.48	19.87	20.45
Turkey	8.07	8.56	6.91[b]	54.05	41.43	33.18[b]
United Kingdom	10.16	9.16	10.31	33.00	25.38	28.72
United States	5.72	5.46	5.10	21.59	18.11	16.62

Notes: [a] 1980 figures are provisional.
　　　　[b] 1979 figure.
Source: *Revenue Statistics of OECD Member Countries 1965-1980* (Paris: OECD, 1981), pp. 86, 87, 174, 175.

studies typically assumes that prices fully and exactly reflect taxes, i.e. that the incidence of the tax is on the consumer.

(1) Partial equilibrium studies

The partial equilibrium studies have concentrated on the effects of taxes on the prices of goods in the industries concerned. The basic technique is to compare the tax change with prices before and after the tax change. The key assumption is thus that any changes in prices that occur result from the change in taxes. But this may not be correct. Suppose manufacturer A is planning a price rise and B is planning no price rise. When a tax increase is announced A puts up his price by the full amount of the tax and B's price rises by half the amount of the tax. Any study would have difficulty in distinguishing between these cases. In any event

Table 17.7 Behaviour of price indices of items on which US excise taxes were reduced on April 1 1954

Commodity	1953				1954			
	March	June	Sept.	Dec.	March	June	Sept.	Dec.
All items in index	92.6	93.3	93.9	93.6	93.6	93.8	93.5	93.2
Water heaters	96.6	97.2	97.7	97.7	98.1	96.3	96.3	96.3
Telephone service	95.0	96.9	98.6	98.6	98.6	93.9	93.9	94.0
Refrigerators	149.6	146.6	146.7	144.4	142.1	135.6	135.3	132.4
Ranges	101.8	103.7	103.6	104.6	104.8	101.2	100.2	98.2
Toasters	134.7	135.1	136.3	136.1	134.6	129.1	129.1	128.3
Fur coats	–	–	123.9	118.6	–	–	101.0	98.9
Face cream	86.6	86.7	86.9	86.9	87.5	80.1	80.2	79.7
Sporting goods	103.3	103.3	102.3	101.2	101.7	97.5	97.8	97.8

Source: US Department of Labor, Bureau of Labor Statistics, *Consumer Price Index* (*1957-59 = 100*), *Price Indexes for Selected Items and Groups, 1947- 61*. Quoted in J. F. Due and A. F. Friedlander, *Government Finance* (Homewood, Ill.: Richard D. Irwin, 1973), p. 375.

the long-run effects of the tax change may differ from these short-run effects if for example the tax increase caused some firms to leave an industry.

In the United States the rate of excise tax on electrical appliances and a few other goods was reduced from 10 to 5 per cent in the second quarter of 1954. It can be seen from Table 17.7 that the general price index rose slightly between March and June 1954 while special price indices for the affected goods all fell. Due and Johnson have studied the same tax cuts. Due found that prices were cut in 94 per cent of cases with a median price cut of 4.8 per cent of the retail price, whereas the tax only amounted to 2.5 per cent of the price. Johnson found prices cut in a smaller proportion of cases with a somewhat lower fall in prices in industries with low concentration ratios. The apparent reason for this result, which is contrary to the theoretical predictions in a profit-maximising model, is to be found in the extent of mark-up pricing, which as we saw in Chapter 11 can lead to price changes in excess of the underlying tax changes.

US federal excise taxes were also cut in 1965 and the effects of these cuts have been analysed by Woodward and Siegelman and by Brownlee and Perry. Woodward and Siegelman examined the effects on the prices of automotive replacement parts. They found that regularly replaced parts such as spark plugs fell in price, while there was little change in the prices of irregularly replaced parts, probably because the demand for these parts is very inelastic. Brownlee and Perry studied the full range of reductions and found that in most, but not all, cases prices fell by the full amount of the tax. The group of commodities for which the price decline was less than the amount of the tax reduction consisted mainly of lower valued items and also admissions to cinemas and club subscriptions. After the price decreases it was observed that prices rose again as total demand in the economy rose sharply. The price increases were observed not to be confined to those commodities on which the taxes had been reduced. The increase in prices could have been accounted for by the increase in the federal budget deficit, which followed the tax reduction.

Hamovitch analysed the effects of changes in retail sales tax rates on taxable retail sales in the city of New York and in the State of Alabama over the period 1948-65. Over the period the sales taxes in the two areas did not undergo changes in coverage but the rates varied. The city of New York was surrounded by a sales tax-free shopping area whereas Alabama was not. Hamovitch estimated the effect on sales of changes in the sales tax rate. For New York City a 1 per cent rise in the sales tax rate resulted in a 6 per cent decline in taxable sales without subsequent recovery. In Alabama there was no statistically discernible sales loss owing to the sales tax increase. This suggests that shopping patterns are influenced by geographically varied tax rates.

(2) A general equilibrium study of the 1973 UK tax changes

Whalley has estimated the general equilibrium effects of the various tax changes made in 1973. The changes Whalley considers include changes in income tax and corporation tax as well as taxes on goods and services. Whalley used the general equilibrium approach described briefly in Chapter 12. He employed twenty commodities: nine domestic outputs, six foreign outputs, two domestic inputs (capital and labour), two foreign inputs, public corporation output; and seven groups of individuals who were assumed to own the factors. The model assumed constant returns to scale, and competitive equilibria were computed that equated demand and supply for each commodity.

The effects of the changes on efficiency as measured by the change in domestic output were strikingly small whether measured at pre- or post-reform prices. Most noteworthy of Whalley's findings is that the replacement of selective employment tax (SET) and purchase tax (PT) by a 10 per cent value added tax (VAT) and a 10 per cent car tax resulted in an efficiency loss that exceeded the efficiency loss from the whole package. Whalley concluded

(1) The welfare gain accruing from the 1973 UK tax changes is at best small and for plausible elasticities of substitution may be negative.
(2) The replacement of purchase tax and SET by VAT seems to account for a negative welfare effect whereas the change in the income tax system seems to yield some gain. The changes in personal allowances given in the 1972 budget seem to be more important than the April 1973 change in the income tax system.
(3) An explanation of the loss in the replacement of SET and purchase tax by VAT is that taxed industries under SET coincide with the heavily capital taxed industries owing to the effect of the rating system. The removal of SET more heavily distorts relative factor prices across industries.
(4) The change in the corporation tax has little effect. ... The distributional impact of the tax reform appears small.[1]

(3) Incidence between high- and low-income households

We now look at work that has attempted to analyse the incidence of taxes on goods and services to see whether the taxes are progressive or regressive. These studies typically start by assuming that the taxes in question are fully shifted forward, i.e. that prices rise by just the amount of the tax. We saw in Chapter 11 that on theoretical grounds we would expect this to happen only in certain rather special circumstances. However, the limited information available from partial equilibrium studies reviewed above suggests that in practice full forward shifting may be a reasonable approximation, at least in the short run. One might try to reconcile the theoretical and empirical evidence with a mark-up model where competitive forces prevented the mark-up on the tax from exceeding one.

(a) The incidence of 'indirect taxes' in the UK. In Britain the major work done on incidence of taxes in goods and services is the annual exercise undertaken by the CSO using *FES* data that we referred to in Chapter 13. The CSO use the term 'indirect taxes' and include within that term not only customs and excise duties but also a variety of other items including television licences, stamp duties, motor vehicle duties, employers' national insurance contributions, domestic and commercial rates, etc. (see Table 13.6 for the complete list). The CSO definition of indirect taxes thus conforms to neither the OECD definition of taxes on goods and services (in UK terms, roughly Customs and Excise receipts plus vehicle duties) nor to the UK definition of expenditure taxes (roughly, Customs and Excise plus vehicle duty plus stamp duty).

Table 17.8 shows the average amount of indirect taxes (excluding rates) and of net rates by decile of original income for 1979. In Table 13.7 indirect taxes were shown as very roughly proportional first rising and then falling as a percentage of income. This result follows because the CSO showed the degree of progression with reference to disposable income which, it will be remembered is original income plus cash transfers and less direct taxes. It is thus shown after a great deal of redistribution has taken place. With other definitions of income as the base other results follow as can be seen from Table 17.9 where indirect taxes appear highly regressive if original income is used as the base. Original income is perhaps what occurs to one as the natural base but it can nevertheless be misleading. The reason for this is that indirect (and other) taxes are used to finance cash transfers which go predominantly to low-income households. How progressive cash transfers are can be seen from Table 17.10, where once again various income definitions are used as the base. Some information on the composition of cash transfers is given in Table 17.8.

The CSO treats employees National Insurance contributions as a direct tax but employers National Insurance and the National Insurance Surcharge as indirect taxes. This difference in treatment is arbitrary and there is no particular reason why the economic incidence should follow the legal incidence (see Chapter 11). The estimated incidence naturally depends on which assumption

Table 17.8 Average incomes, taxes and benefits, UK 1979 by deciles of original income

£ per year

	1st	2nd	3rd	4th	5th	6th	7th	8th	9th	10th	Average over all decile groups
Decile groups of original income											
All households											
Deciles	46	608	2413	3780	4923	5941	7004	8398	10602		
Number of households in the sample	678	677	678	678	677	678	678	678	677	678	6777
Original income											
Earned income	—	36	668	2623	4016	5102	6081	7342	8951	13221	4804
Other income	6	234	726	537	362	329	375	329	413	818	413
Total	6	270	1394	3160	4378	5431	6456	7671	9364	14038	5217
Direct benefits in cash											
Age-related	957	1231	978	363	186	125	109	84	103	112	425
Child-related	55	26	61	157	201	242	204	198	187	165	150
Income-related	527	263	209	146	73	66	52	35	42	56	147
Other	181	113	186	150	68	64	63	54	45	48	97
Gross income	1726	1903	2828	3976	4906	5927	6884	8042	9742	14418	6036
Direct taxes	1	17	167	548	853	1080	1328	1570	1987	3246	1080
Disposable income	1725	1886	2661	3428	4053	4847	5556	6472	7755	11172	4956
Domestic rates (net of rebates)	117	103	139	153	159	173	182	197	210	249	168
Other indirect taxes	265	336	533	723	901	1024	1153	1357	1557	2073	992
Benefits in kind											
Education	137	76	209	309	393	414	446	449	451	438	332
National Health Service	437	477	391	378	381	400	355	339	353	381	389
Welfare foods	21	10	16	32	26	33	32	31	28	23	25
Housing subsidy	179	116	115	126	127	98	92	86	74	76	109
Other allocated benefits	4	6	10	23	34	35	38	55	62	95	36
Final income	2122	2132	2731	3420	3953	4630	5185	5876	6955	9864	4687

Source: *Economic Trends* January 1981, p. 123.

Table 17.9   Indirect taxes including rates as a percentage of income UK 1978/79

Quintile	Original income	Gross income	Disposable income	Final income
Bottom	293	23	23	19
Next	34	23	25	25
Middle	23	21	25	26
Next	20	19	24	26
Top	17	17	22	24

Source: Calculated from *Economic Trends*, January 1981, p. 113.

Table 17.10   Cash benefits as a percentage of income UK 1978/79

Quintile	Original income	Gross income	Disposable income	Final income
Bottom	1200	92	93	79
Next	49	33	37	36
Middle	10	9	11	12
Next	6	5	7	7
Top	3	3	4	5

Source: Calculated from *Economic Trends*, January 1981, p. 113.

is used as can be seen from Table 17.11 in which O'Higgins and Ruggles treat the 1971 employers contribution first as an indirect tax and assume it falls on consumption and second as a direct tax and assume it falls on earnings. In the former case it is regressive relative to original income throughout. In the latter it is progressive over the first four deciles.

The figures in the tables are all estimates of the incidence of the actual amounts of tax paid. However there are in addition, costs of collecting the tax. These costs comprise the public-sector costs of collecting the money and the private-sector costs of paying it. Sandford, Godwin, Hardwick and Butterworth have estimated these costs for VAT in a careful study. They estimate that total compliance costs amounted to about 11 per cent of VAT revenue in 1977/78 and that the incidence of the tax was highly regressive by size of firm paying the tax. Indeed they suggest that the high costs of compliance is one of the reasons for the decline in the number of retail outlets.

Indirect *taxes* are payments to the government and subsidies paid by the government are conceptually similar with the sign reversed. There are few indirect subsidies *per se* in the UK but it is nevertheless convenient to consider here the benefits in kind included in the CSO redistribution exercise. The major items are included in Table 17.8. The item requiring most comment for our purposes is the housing subsidy. This definition is clearly a narrow one as, for example, it excludes the subsidy on mortgage interest payments. Not surprisingly, given this definition, the monetary value of housing subsidies declines with income from £179 in the lowest decile to £74 in the next to highest decile. Benefits in kind are progressive even when final income is used as the base (Table 17.8).

(*b*) *The incidence of sales and excise taxes in the US*. Pechman and Okner have studied the allocation of US taxes (this study is also discussed in the next chapter). They assume that sales and excise taxes are borne fully by consumers, which is the same as the CSO's assumption for the UK. They justify this assumption as follows:

> A *general sales tax* would be borne by consumers in proportion to their total expenditures, because the tax does not change relative prices and hence does not alter consumption patterns. Excise taxes do change relative prices, thus burdening those who consume the commodities that are subject to tax. There is no burden on the sources-of-income side, however, because any labor or capital that may shift from the taxed industries ultimately receives approximately the same income when it is reemployed in the untaxed industries.[2]

As they recognise, the statement about general sales taxes depends on the assumption that there is no savings. Their conclusions about there being no burden on the income of labour and capital clearly depend on mobile factors and competitive markets, as they point out. Their findings about the incidence of sales and excise taxes are shown in Table 18.6 below where it can be seen that the taxes are very clearly regressive. As a proportion of income, the tax falls from over 9 per cent of adjusted family income at the lowest income levels to 1 per cent of adjusted family income at the highest income levels. These rates cannot be directly compared with the CSO figures in Table 13.7. The CSO definition of indirect taxes is very much wider than Pechman and Okner's excise and sales taxes and there are also differences in the definition of income. The CSO uses disposable income whereas Pechman and Okner use adjusted family income from a special distribution of income called the MERGE File, which is available only for 1966. Adjusted family income is a fairly complicated concept designed to be consistent with net national product at *market prices*. Total family income is national income, plus transfers and capital gains less income not received by households (e.g. income of persons in institutions). Total adjusted family income is family income plus indirect business taxes. This concept of income corresponds quite closely to the definition of income given in Chapter 14: the amount that could be consumed in a period without reducing the stock of wealth. It is a more comprehensive concept than the CSO's original income but is nearer to that original income than to their disposable income. The apparent difference in the degree of progressivity of taxes on goods and services between the UK and US may thus be largely due to differences in methodology.

Browning has argued that most studies of tax incidence, including Pechman and Okner (and by implication those of the CSO) are in error in concluding that indirect taxes are not progressive. The conventional argument is as follows: indirect taxes raise prices; if indirect taxes (which always exclude savings from the tax base) are levied on things which the poor tend to buy, and if indirect

Table 17.11 The distribution of taxes by decile of original income, UK 1971

Decile	Lowest	2nd	3rd	4th	5th	6th	7th	8th	9th	Highest	All households
Income tax	1	15	68	119	176	230	287	328	460	918	260
	(4.0)	(5.7)	(8.8)	(10.0)	(11.5)	(12.6)	(13.6)	(13.3)	(15.3)	(19.1)	(14.5)
	(0.0)	(0.6)	(2.6)	(4.6)	(6.8)	(8.8)	(11.0)	(12.6)	(17.7)	(35.3)	(100)
Employees National Insurance contributions	0	3	31	60	73	84	92	100	115	132	69
	(0.8)	(1.2)	(4.0)	(5.0)	(4.8)	(4.6)	(4.3)	(4.1)	(3.8)	(2.8)	(3.8)
	(0.0)	(0.4)	(4.5)	(8.6)	(10.5)	(12.2)	(13.3)	(14.6)	(16.6)	(19.2)	(100)
Employers National Insurance (consumption)	16	26	36	42	48	52	58	65	78	122	54
	(70.8)	(10.0)	(4.6)	(3.5)	(3.1)	(2.8)	(2.8)	(2.6)	(2.6)	(2.5)	(3.0)
	(3.0)	(4.7)	(6.6)	(7.7)	(8.8)	(9.6)	(10.8)	(12.0)	(14.4)	(22.4)	(100)
Employers National Insurance (earnings)	0	2	27	54	67	79	87	97	113	125	65
	(0)	(0.7)	(3.5)	(4.5)	(4.4)	(4.3)	(4.1)	(3.9)	(3.7)	(2.6)	(3.6)
	(0.0)	(0.3)	(4.1)	(8.3)	(10.4)	(12.1)	(13.3)	(14.9)	(17.3)	(19.3)	(100)
Domestic rates	31	35	40	39	44	46	48	52	58	73	47
	(135.1)	(13.7)	(5.2)	(3.3)	(2.9)	(2.5)	(2.3)	(2.1)	(1.9)	(1.5)	(2.6)
	(6.6)	(7.5)	(8.6)	(8.4)	(9.4)	(9.9)	(10.4)	(11.1)	(12.4)	(15.7)	(100)

	1	2	3	4	5	6	7	8	9	10	
Direct expenditure taxes	47 (205.4) *(2.1)*	76 (29.4) *(3.4)*	126 (16.3) *(5.7)*	172 (14.4) *(7.7)*	212 (13.9) *(9.5)*	233 (12.8) *(10.5)*	256 (12.1) *(11.5)*	286 (11.6) *(12.9)*	351 (11.6) *(15.8)*	465 (9.7) *(20.9)*	222 (12.3) *(100)*
Corporation tax	13 (55.6) *(2.6)*	32 (12.6) *(6.7)*	43 (5.6) *(8.9)*	36 (3.0) *(7.4)*	40 (2.6) *(8.3)*	40 (2.2) *(8.3)*	47 (2.2) *(9.8)*	50 (2.0) *(10.3)*	62 (2.1) *(12.8)*	121 (2.5) *(25.0)*	49 (2.7) *(100)*
Capital taxes	1 (6.2) *(1.0)*	15 (5.7) *(9.8)*	20 (2.5) *(13.2)*	9 (0.8) *(6.3)*	10 (0.7) *(6.8)*	8 (0.4) *(5.1)*	11 (0.5) *(7.5)*	10 (0.4) *(6.4)*	15 (0.5) *(9.9)*	51 (1.1) *(34.0)*	15 (0.8) *(100)*
All taxes	148 (643.4) *(1.8)*	263 (102.2) *(3.1)*	449 (57.8) *(5.3)*	575 (48.1) *(6.8)*	715 (46.7) *(8.5)*	816 (44.7) *(9.7)*	936 (44.3) *(11.1)*	1042 (42.1) *(12.4)*	1319 (43.7) *(15.7)*	2161 (44.9) *(25.7)*	842 (46.7) *(100)*

Notes:
(1) The first entry in each cell is the average tax paid in pounds per year in each decile; the bracketed entry expresses this figure as a percentage of average original income in each decile; and the italicised figure indicates the percentage of the tax paid by each decile.

(2) For a discussion of the two assumptions about the employers national insurance contribution see Appendix. The consumption assumption is used in calculating total taxes. If the earnings assumption were to be generally used, original income figures would be increased by the value of employers national insurance; strictly speaking, therefore, the values of employers contributions as a percentage of original income are slightly overestimated in the table.

(3) Direct expenditure taxes include those parts of customs and excise duties, purchase tax, motor vehicle and stamp duties, and of various licensing charges which are assumed to fall directly on the consumer.

Source: M. O'Higgins and P. Ruggles 'The Distribution of Public Expenditure and Taxes among Households in the United Kingdom', *The Review of Income and Wealth*, 1981, p. 310.

Table 17.12 Comparison of Pechman and Okner, and of Browning. Estimated effective rates of tax

Decile	Pechman and Okner		Browning	
	Sales and Excise	All taxes	Sales and Excise	All taxes
1	8.9	16.8	2.2	10.1
2	7.8	18.9	2.2	13.3
3	7.1	21.7	4.5	19.1
4	6.7	22.6	4.5	20.4
5	6.4	22.8	5.1	21.5
6	6.1	22.7	5.1	21.7
7	5.7	22.7	5.4	22.4
8	5.5	23.1	5.4	23.0
9	5.0	23.3	5.7	24.0
10	3.2	30.1	5.7	32.6
All	5.1	25.2	5.1	25.2

Source: Edgar K. Browning 'The Burden of Taxation', *Journal of Political Economy*, 1978, pp. 660-1.

taxes put up prices the poor will suffer disproportionately. Browning argues that this neglects the importance of state transfer payments. In particular if state transfers are increased in line with inflation then the recipients of the transfers are protected from the effects of the tax increases on that proportion of their income represented by transfers. As transfer income is a much higher proportion of the income of the poor they are - to a large extent - insulated from the effects of the indirect tax increases. Table 17.12 compares Browning's results with those of Pechman and Okner (the Pechman and Okner results differ slightly from those given in Table 18.6 as different assumptions are employed). It can be seen that Browning estimates that the sales and excise taxes are progressive while Pechman and Okner estimate they are regressive. This change makes the tax system as a whole much more progressive as the comparison of the 'All taxes' columns show.

(4) Stipulated versus estimated approximations to the incidence of indirect taxes. While there are many differences in assumption between the CSO study in the UK and the Pechman-Okner study in the US they are similar in that both assume or stipulate the incidence of taxes. These assumptions may of course be wrong. Devarajan, Fullerton and Musgrave have tried to assess this by comparing the assumed or stipulated results such as those of Pechman and Okner with estimated results from a general equilibrium model. The general equilibrium model they use is the one developed by Fullerton, King, Shoven and Whalley and is broadly similar in principle to the Whalley model briefly summarised above. The results of the general equilibrium approach differ from the stipulated studies except for the case of the income tax. Deverajan *et al.* are, however,

cautious in interpreting the results pointing out that even the general equilibrium model is not fully general as inelastic factor supplies are assumed. Nevertheless their results do add weight to the view that assuming the incidence of taxes may well be misleading.

The reader may have noted that we have not considered the question of whether taxes on goods and services should be progressive or regressive. This issue is considered briefly in Chapter 20.

CHAPTER 18

Corporation Tax

The corporation tax, which is levied on the profits of incorporated, but not unincorporated, businesses, has produced a great deal of controversy. This controversy has focused on a number of issues. For example, is there any theoretical or other justification for imposing a tax on corporate profits? What are profits? What are the likely, *a priori*, effects of the tax on the allocation of resources and what are the effects in practice? After an examination of the general features and characteristics of the tax we will look at the incidence of the tax, both in the short run and in the long run, and the effects of the tax on savings, on investment, and upon the financial structure of the firm. The chapter concludes with a consideration of the taxation of corporate profits during periods of inflation.

The reader should note that this chapter is concerned with only one of the ways in which governments may affect the activities of companies. Companies are required from time to time to follow government directives about prices and wages; they are required to pay capital gains taxes, valued added tax, excise tax, social security contributions and to act as tax collectors for income tax. Some activities may be specially rewarded – by special subsidies to capital and/or labour in special areas or by regulations permitting accelerated depreciation of certain assets. The items we have just listed will also have allocative and distributive effects and many will affect profitability and hence will interact with the effects of corporation tax. Our object in this chapter is thus a limited one.

Reasons for corporation tax

A very powerful argument for any existing tax is that we have it, that people are more or less used to it, and that a switch to any alternative source of revenue could have high costs associated with change. Corporation tax has also been defended on a variety of other grounds. Incorporation carries the important legal advantage of limiting the legal liability of the owners of the company, and this limited liability may create taxable capacity. The presence of a corporation tax may make it easier for governments to regulate the affairs of companies (for example by encouraging or discouraging the retention of profits in the company).

Perhaps the most important arguments for a separate tax on corporate income arises from the fact that corporations usually do not pay out all of their income in the form of dividends. If all profits were paid out in dividends, corporate profits could be straightforwardly taxed as part of the income of shareholders. However, the no-corporation-tax solution creates problems when some profits are retained in the corporation. These profits are usually retained because corporate managers or shareholders or both think they will be useful to the company and will probably increase the future profitability of the company. Higher future profitability, or its prospect, is likely to increase the market value of the companies' shares. For the shareholder, the increase in share prices is a realisable capital gain (whether or not it is actually realised) and is thus in effect income. If capital gains are not taxed, or if they are taxed at lower rates than income, this creates problems of horizontal equity between taxpayers.

The nature and measurement of corporate profits

As corporation tax is a tax on corporate profits there are a number of issues that arise concerning corporate profits and we discuss some of these in this section.

It is fairly clear that wages are the return to labour and rent the return to land, but what are profits the return to? If they are simply the return to capital, then what is interest? There are a variety of views on this subject. Profits could be thought of as the return to equity capital or as the return to entrepreneurs for undertaking risk in introducing inventions and/or innovations, or profits may be thought of as rents that accrue to scarce factors of production.

It is not easy to decide which of these views is correct, and indeed profits may include all of these elements. While we cannot demonstrate the superiority of any one of these views we can point to the importance of the issue. For example if profits are simply economic rents, taxing them will have no allocative effects if the tax is not shifted, while if profits are a return to risk and entrepreneurship taxing profits may reduce the basic dynamism of the economy.

Another point to note is that the tax base for corporation tax is rarely if ever real business profit. Business profits may be defined as the amount that a company could pay in dividends in a year without becoming worse off. The differences between real business profits and taxable profit can be seen from the following classification originally devised by E. D. Edwards and P. W. Bell:

A Current operating profit
B Realisable capital gains
  1 Real
  2 Money
C Capital gains realised through the sale of an asset
  1 Real
  2 Money

D Capital gains realised through the use (e.g. of inputs)
  1 Real
  2 Money

Tax law typically levies tax on sales less current operating expenses such as wages, raw materials and interest. This is current operating profit (A) and to this we need to add capital gains (and subtract losses) arising from changes in the value of machinery and stocks of raw materials and finished goods. The economist would include these gains as they accrued whether or not they were actually realised. Thus business profit is $A + B_1$. Taxable profits on the other hand tend to be defined to include only realised gains and losses and both real and money gains. Thus taxable profits are $A + C_1 + C_2 + D_1 + D_2$. The distinction between real and money gains arises because, in general, tax legislation in the UK and in many other countries insists that assets be valued at their historical costs. We return to these issues in the section on inflation accounting where we also discuss certain practical provisions in the UK tax code that may have the effect of mitigating some of the harmful effects of the historical cost basis for computing corporate profits.

Classification of corporation tax systems

Corporation income tax systems can be classified according to the extent to which corporation income tax and personal income taxes on shareholders are integrated. There are four major categories in the classification:

  (1) separate entity system;
  (2) full integration system;
  (3) split rate system;
  (4) imputation system.

With the separate entity or classical system as it is sometimes called, the corporation is viewed as a separate entity, distinct from its shareholders and therefore taxed in its own capacity. The tax on corporate income and the tax on the personal income of the shareholders are levied independently of each other. Thus personal incomes, which originate as distributed corporate income to shareholders (i.e. dividends), will be taxed twice. In the first instance corporate income will be taxed and in the second place distributed incomes will be liable to the personal income tax. Examples of tax systems that conform to this type are to be found in the United States, the Netherlands, Luxembourg, and Switzerland (federal corporate tax). In Denmark, Iceland and Sweden they use a slightly modified variant of the pure system. The UK had a separate entity system from 1965 to 1973.

The full integration system is the polar opposite of the above. The corporation is not seen as a separate entity but is instead viewed as being made up of shareholders. The corporate tax is treated as a withholding tax, which is then credited in full to shareholders. This credit is used against the personal income tax, which is due on their imputed share of the corporate profits. Another functional form of this system is that the corporation tax is abolished completely and shareholders are taxed under the personal income tax on their share of imputed corporate incomes. A full integration system has never been used in practice. The Canadian Royal Commission on Taxation, 1967, did however propose it.

The split rate system lies between these two extremes. Provision is made for this relief of corporate distributions by a lower tax rate on corporate distributions than on retained profits. This is called the 'split rate system' and is used in the Federal Republic of Germany.

The imputation system is designed to avoid the double taxation of dividends in a different manner by imputing part of corporate profit tax to the personal tax liability of shareholders. This is the system used in the UK and it is described more fully in the next section.

UK corporation tax

In 1973 the imputation system of corporation tax was introduced to remove the discrimination against distributed profits that had existed under the separate entity system. In 1981–82 the rate of corporation tax was 52 per cent with a reduced rate of 40 per cent for companies with profits of less than £80,000 and with an intermediate rate on profits under £200,000.

With the UK imputation system the company pays corporation tax at a single rate of 52 per cent on all profits, whether distributed or undistributed.

Income tax is not deducted from dividends. When the company distributes dividends to its shareholders it makes an advance payment of corporation tax to the Inland Revenue, at a rate of three-sevenths of the dividend paid to the shareholder. Advanced payments of corporation tax are then set off against the firm's corporation tax bill. The recipient of a distribution on which advanced corporation tax (ACT) has been paid is entitled to a tax credit.

A simple numerical example given in Table 18.1 will illustrate the points, assuming that a company's pretax profits are 100 and that it wants to pay out all of its after-tax income in the form of dividends (using 1982 tax rates for corporation tax of 52 per cent and basic rate income tax of 30 per cent). As shown in the table, the shareholder receives an actual cash dividend of 48 but he also has an imputed income of 20.57, being his tax credit, giving him a total income of 68.57. The shareholder is liable for income tax on this income of 68.57. If he is a basic-rate taxpayer the tax credit of 20.57 (which is 30 per cent of 68.57) exactly covers his liability. People who pay no tax are entitled to a refund and higher-rate payers have to pay additional tax. The company pays this 20.57 to the Inland Revenue when it declares its dividend. This payment is the advance corporation tax (ACT) and is offset against the companies' eventual

Table 18.1 Example of imputation system for UK
corporation tax

All profits distributed		
Pretax profits	100	
Corporation tax	52	
After tax profits or dividend	48	
Tax credit of $\frac{3}{7}$ imputed on dividend		20.57
Dividend plus tax credit		68.57

liability for corporation tax of 52. The net effect is that the shareholder is paid a gross dividend of 68.57 out of the profits of 100, which means that the rate of *corporation tax* amounts to 31.43 per cent (= 100 − 68.57) on distributed profits. The total tax on both retained and distributive profits is thus 52 per cent for basic-rate payers. The imputation system eliminates the double taxation of dividends that would occur with the separate entity system where the tax would be 64.4 [= 52 + (48 × 0.3)] for the basic-rate taxpayer if all after-tax profits were distributed.

Revenue from corporation tax

Revenue from corporation tax (and related company taxes) is shown in Table 18.2. Total receipts (in column 3) have grown fairly modestly in money terms and consequently as it can be seen from columns 6 and 7 total taxes on company income (defined in note d of Table 18.2) have fallen sharply as a proportion of central government tax receipts. Excluding the North Sea the proportion had fallen by about two-thirds between 1967/68 and estimates for 1981/82. Table 18.3 shows that one reason for this is the share of profits in GDP which have fallen from about 11 per cent of GDP in 1968 to about 2 per cent in 1980. The relative importance of taxes on corporate income in the UK compared with other countries may be gauged from Table 18.4 where it can be seen that the UK taxes on corporate income are in the middle third of OECD countries whether the measure is proportion of tax revenue or proportion of GDP.

Economic effects of corporation tax

The imposition of any tax other than a lump sum tax will produce distortionary effects in the economy. Moreover, when considering the distributional conse-quences of the corporation tax we need to distinguish between the formal and actual incidence of the tax. Asking who pays the corporation tax upon the allocation of capital resources it is necessary to distinguish between effects in the short run and in the long run.

Table 18.2 Yield of company taxation, 1966-67 to 1981-82

	Corporation tax[a]	Schedule F	(1) + (2)	Taxes on company income[d] including North Sea oil and gas	Taxes on company income[d] excluding North Sea oil and gas	Percent of total Central Government tax receipts including North Sea oil and gas	Percent of total Central Government tax receipts excluding North Sea oil and gas
	(1)	(2)	(3)	(4)	(5)		
	£m	£m	£m	£m	£m	£m	£m
1966-67	1050	300	1350	1320	1320	14.8	14.8
1967-68	1210	640	1850	1810	1810	13.4	13.4
1968-69	1340	640	1980	1900	1900	13.7	13.7
1969-70	1700	670	2370	2190	2190	12.3	12.3
1970-71	1580	700	2280	2160	2160	12.0	12.0
1971-72	1550	750	2300	2230	2230	11.1	11.1
1972-73	1530	740	2270	2160	2160	11.1	11.1
	Mainstream corporation tax[ab]	Advance corporation tax[bc]					
1973-74	1860	620	2480	2240	2240	10.1	10.1
1974-75	1730	1130	2860	2670	2670	9.3	9.3
1975-76	1120	880	2000	1920	1920	5.4	5.4
1976-77	1640	1010	2650	2610	2610	6.2	6.2
1977-78	2140	1200	3340	3400	3400	7.2	7.2
1978-79	2560	1380	3940	4080	3850	7.7	7.3
1979-80	2820	1830	4650	5980	4380	9.1	6.6
1980-81	2830	1820	4650	6730	4080	8.7	5.3
1981-82							
(Budget estimate)	2840	1760	4600	8630	4270	9.6	4.8

Notes: [a] Before deducting overspill relief.
[b] Net of repayments.
[c] Including ACT addition: 1974/75, £374m; 1975/76, £8m.
[d] Mainstream corporation tax (excluding CT on capital gains and excluding public corporations), ACT, ACT addition, Schedule F, income tax deducted at source from investment income received by companies, petroleum revenue tax, supplementary petroleum duty.

Source: *Corporation Tax* (London: HMSO, 1982), pp. 130, 131.

Table 18.3 Net trading profits[a] and rent of companies as a percentage of net domestic product

	All companies	Excluding North Sea
	%	%
Average 1960–70	11.8	11.8
1968	10.8	10.8
1969	10.6	10.6
1970	9.4	9.4
1971	10.0	10.0
1972	10.1	10.1
1973	9.9	9.9
1974	5.9	6.1
1975	4.6	4.9
1976	5.5	5.4
1977	8.1	7.2
1978	8.4	7.4
1979	7.4	5.1
1980	5.2	2.1

Note: [a] After providing for stock appreciation and capital consumption at replacement cost.
Source: *Corporation Tax* (London: HMSO, 1982), p. 131.

(a) *Short run.* Who pays the corporation tax in the short run? If the tax is viewed as a tax on the return to equity capital invested in the corporate sector, and if it is assumed that the equity capital is efficiently and fully employed before the introduction of the tax, then in the short run the owners of equity capital must pay the tax. This follows from the definition of the Marshallian short run, in which the capital stock and the capital structure of the firm are fixed. In the short run the owners of equity capital cannot leave the firm.

Moreover, there is no shifting of the tax: neither forward on to consumers by increasing prices, nor backwards on to the factors of production by reducing factor prices. If the firm is maximising its profits prior to the imposition of the tax, then because the tax is a tax on profit and does not affect demand or costs, it will not influence price or output (see Figure 11.6 above and the accompanying analysis).

However, different results are obtained if we drop the assumption of profit maximisation. For example, when we examined the effects of a tax on a sales-maximising firm in Chapter 11 (see Figure 11.5 and the accompanying analysis) we found that when there is a minimum profits constraint a tax on profits would lead the firm to reduce output from Q_0 to Q_1 and increase price from P_0 to P_1. The reduction in output means that part of the burden of the tax is shifted back to the suppliers of inputs as fewer inputs are now needed. The increase in price means that part of the tax is shifted forward to consumers. Thus the short run effects on the distribution of income and the allocation of resources depend on whether or not firms are profit-maximisers.

Table 18.4 Taxes on corporate income in OECD countries

	Taxes on Corporate Income at % of GDP				Taxes on Corporate Income as % of total taxation			
	1965	1970	1975	1980[a]	1965	1970	1975	1980[a]
Australia	3.82	4.25	3.82	3.08	16.08	16.66	12.27	10.32
Austria	1.87	1.57	1.68	1.43	5.39	4.40	4.35	3.44
Belgium	1.93	2.45	3.04	2.50	6.17	6.81	7.41	5.89
Canada	3.93	3.60	4.50	3.53	15.14	11.26	13.66	10.74
Denmark	1.36	1.06	1.28	1.46	4.54	2.64	3.12	3.24
Finland	2.51	1.77	1.53	1.49	8.32	5.50	4.23	4.32
France	1.84	2.24	1.98	2.30	5.27	6.30	5.29	5.41
Germany	2.47	1.86	1.58	2.05	7.83	5.67	4.43	5.51
Greece	0.40	0.41	0.86	0.97[b]	1.92	1.70	3.48	3.49[b]
Ireland	2.36	2.75	1.57	1.71	9.06	8.80	4.83	4.57
Italy	1.88	1.83	1.83	0.00	6.89	6.55	6.31[b]	8.40[b]
Japan	3.22	3.97	3.38	0.00	17.83	20.13	16.02	16.92
Luxembourg	3.39	6.06	6.76	8.00	11.00	18.96	15.51	16.83
Netherlands	2.85	2.66	3.54	3.08	8.03	6.67	7.72	6.68
New Zealand	5.07	4.86	4.06	3.52	20.86	18.41	13.50	11.29[b]
Norway	1.27	1.29	1.28	6.32	3.81	3.28	2.85	13.34
Portugal	–	–	–	–	–	–	–	–
Spain	1.50	1.50	1.48	1.39	10.21	8.73	7.54	6.02
Sweden	2.16	1.80	1.92	1.20	6.08	4.40	4.34	2.41
Switzerland	1.47	1.80	2.29	1.81	7.08	7.55	7.73	5.88
Turkey	0.72	1.13	1.06	0.94[b]	4.81	6.43	5.15	4.51[b]
United Kingdom	2.15	3.44	2.24	3.05	6.97	9.17	6.20	8.49
United States	4.19	3.83	3.26	3.09	15.81	12.71	10.79	10.06

Notes: [a] Estimates.
[b] 1979 figures.

Source: *Revenue Statistics of OECD member countries 1965-1980* (Paris: OECD, 1981), pp. 82, 172, 175.

(*b*) *Long run.* What are the effects of the corporation tax when the assumptions of the short run are relaxed? In the long run it is possible for capital to leave the corporate sector where it is taxed and to move to the non-corporate sector.

(*c*) *The Harberger model.* Perhaps the best-known model for analysing the long-run effects of the corporate income tax is the Harberger model, which we outlined in Chapter 12. It will be remembered that Harberger assumes two sectors, a corporate sector and an unincorporated sector, and two factors of production, both of which are in inelastic supply. The introduction of a tax on corporate profits reduces the after-tax return to capital in the corporate sector (from P_0^k to NP_1^k in Figure 12.2), which causes capital to leave the taxed corporate sector (termed the clothing industry in Chapter 12's example), so as to equalise the net of tax return between the two sectors. Thus in the long run the tax leads to a reduction in the return to equity capital throughout the economy while in the short run this happens only in the corporate sector. As we saw, the full effects of the tax involve a fall in output and an increase in price in the taxed sector and a rise in output and a fall in price in the untaxed sector. There are also effects on the distribution of income and the final distribution of consumption goods as between the owners of equity capital and the owners of labour. As we emphasised, the precise results depend on the elasticities of substitution. Harberger has provided estimates which are reproduced in Table 18.5 of the total flow of capital (ΔK_x) from the corporate to unincorporated sector under various elasticity estimates. It can be seen that the estimated flow varies from £2.4b to £6.9b out of a total capital stock estimated by Harberger at £20b and he concluded 'that the present pattern of taxes on income from capital in the United States probably has reduced the capital stock in the corporate sector by between $\frac{1}{6}$ and $\frac{1}{3}$'. Table 18.5 also estimates the efficiency cost of the tax. This cost is estimated as one-half the tax on capital times the change in the capital stock $(\frac{1}{2}T_x\Delta K_x)$, which may be thought of as an approximation to the area *ABC* in Figure 12.2(a). This efficiency cost was about 1 per cent of US GNP in order of magnitude.

This overall efficiency loss for the whole economy is unevenly distributed. The reduction in the capital stock of the corporate sector means that output of that sector will fall and so the market price of the output will rise. Consumers,

Table 18.5 Estimates of efficiency cost of existing taxes on income from capital in the United States

(1) S_x	(2) S_y	(3) V	(4) ΔK_x (billions of units)	(5) $-\frac{1}{2}T_x\Delta K_x$ (billions)
−1	−1	−1	−6.9	$2.9
−0.5	−0.5	−0.5	−3.5	1.5
−1	−1	−0.5	−5.3	2.3
−1	−0.5	−1	−5.9	2.5
−0.5	−1	−1	−5.2	2.2
−1	−0.5	−0.5	−4.2	1.8
−0.5	−1	−0.5	−4.1	1.7
−0.5	−0.5	−1	−4.8	2.0
−1	0	−1	−4.7	2.0
−0.5	0	−0.5	−2.4	1.0
−1	0	−0.5	−5.0	2.1
−0.5	0	−1	−3.9	1.7

Notes: S_x = elasticity of substitution between labour and capital in the corporate sector (defined as a negative number)
S_y = elasticity of substitution between labour and capital in the non-incorporated sector (defined as a negative number)
V = elasticity of substitution between the products of the incorporated and un-incorporated sectors (defined as a negative number)
ΔK_x = change in the units of capital employed in the corporate sector
T_x = amount of tax per unit of capital in the corporate sector

Source: A. C. Harberger, *Taxation and Welfare* (Boston: Little, Brown, 1974), p. 169.

for whom corporate output features prominently in their basket of goods, will suffer a welfare loss. On the other hand the increase in the capital stock and therefore the increase in output of the non-corporate sector means that the prices of that sector's output will fall. Consumers of non-corporate output will therefore enjoy an income gain.

Moreover, since the average price of capital falls, the incomes of the owners of capital will also fall so that the macroeconomic distribution of income between capital and labour will be shifted. If we assume that the marginal propensity to save out of the income of capital exceeds that of labour, then the imposition of the corporation tax will affect the rate of saving in the economy.

(*d*) *Critique of Harberger's analysis.* Harberger's analysis has not passed without criticisms. J. E. Stiglitz and M. A. King take a different view of whether or not the corporate profits tax distorts the firms' investment decision. Their main thesis rests upon the treatment, *in practice*, of tax allowances. According to King,

> the question of the distortionary effects and the incidence of the corporation tax is not well defined until the special provisions relating to depreciation allowances and the treatment of interest payments are known.

and Stiglitz:

> To analyse the effect of the corporation profits tax on the financial structure and the cost of capital of firms, one must include a full analysis of all the relevant provisions of the personal as well as the corporate tax code.

Since actual behaviour is likely to be sensitive to the provision made for allowances against the tax, an understanding of *a priori* effects of these allowances is crucial to the judgement of the tax. Stiglitz's criticism of the Harberger model is that Harberger has confused the average and the marginal cost of capital. If the firm can raise debt finance and if the interest payments are tax deductable, then the required gross return is just the interest rate, as is also the case in the non-corporate sector. For Stiglitz firms will invest up to the point where the marginal return on investment equals the rate of interest. Thus, under conditions of certainty and given the provisions of the tax system,

> the cost of capital, and hence the firms' optimal investment policy, is independent of the corporate profits tax. The cost of capital is thus simply the rate of interest and investment is simply continued up to the point where the marginal pre-tax rate of return net of depreciation is equal to the rate of interest.

This is seen as follows.

$$(\Delta\pi - r - \delta) \equiv \text{increase in pretax company income}$$

where $\Delta\pi$ = change in profits that would result from an investment;
    r = interest payments; and
    δ = economic depreciation value.

The investment is profitable if $\Delta\pi - \delta \geqslant r$, i.e. the firm invests up to the point where the pretax rate of return, net of depreciation, is equal to the rate of interest. If depreciation and interest payments are deductable for tax purposes then the after-corporation tax (τ) income is

$$(1 - \tau)(\Delta\pi - r - \delta).$$

Under these assumptions the corporation tax is, from an efficiency point of view, like a lump sum tax on corporations, and the firms' optimal investment policy is independent of the rate of corporate profits tax.

In comparing the Harberger and the Stiglitz–King views it should be pointed out that Harberger assumed all investment is equity-financed whereas Stiglitz and King assume all investment is debt-financed; thus in their model a change in the corporation tax does not affect the rate of interest. The outcome of the Harberger, Stiglitz–King debate would, therefore, appear to be that both models stand on their own assumptions of the method of financing corporate investment. This conclusion is instructive since it demonstrates the importance of the assumptions made. However, given that interest payments and depreciation are deductable in real corporation tax systems, the Stiglitz–King model is of more immediate relevance when judging the efficiency of actual tax systems.

There are other criticisms of the Harberger model which should be borne in mind. First, there is the assumption of perfectly competitive markets upon which his model is based. While the purely static profit-maximising monopoly model also implies that the tax is borne by capital, this is not generally true of non-competitive markets. However, as was demonstrated in the short-run model, both the sales-maximising and the marketing models result in the prediction that much or all of the tax is passed forward to consumers. Second, the results of the Harberger model depend upon the assumption that factors are mobile. This ensures that capital will leave the corporate sector and migrate to the non-corporate sector in response to the tax. However, this is unlikely to be the case in practice. Labour has specific skills that cannot be easily transferred and capital is also process-specific (consider the case of vintage capital models). In the case of low mobility of capital a greater proportion of the tax may be borne by the shareholders. Finally, the Harberger model assumes complete certainty, only two goods, and is based upon marginalist analysis. If the tax change is large (as in the case when the tax is introduced initially) and if other marginal conditions do not hold in the rest of the economy, then the analysis becomes much more complex and, indeed, such analysis as yet remains to be done.

(*e*) *The Shoven and Whalley model.* Brief mention may also be made of the study by Shoven and Whalley. They have studied the same data that Harberger studied but with much more powerful mathematical techniques, which have made it possible for them to introduce a number of sectors, to consider a variety of taxes simultaneously, and to make (somewhat crude) allowances for the distribution of income and for the labour/leisure choice. They have made their estimates under a variety of assumptions about the elasticities of substitution (both production and consumption). Their results in general support Harberger in that they have found that capital bears close to 100 per cent of the burden of the tax.

Where these results are most comparable with the Harberger results they show a slightly smaller movement of capital out of the taxed sectors. Shoven and Whalley provide upper and lower bound estimates of the efficiency cost of the tax on the income from capital. There are two cases where it is possible to compare Shoven and Whalley's results with Harberger. Where the elasticity of substitution is one in both industries (which is the case we explained in Chapter 12), Shoven and Whalley estimate the burden at between $2.0b and $4.8b while Harberger's figure is $2.9b. The other case where comparison is possible is when the elasticity of substitution is one in the sectors bearing the tax and 0.5 in the untaxed sectors. The Shoven and Whalley estimates are $1.4b and $4.6b with the Harberger figure $2.5b. These early results from an interesting new approach clearly support the Harberger results, but it must be remembered that this must in part be because of similarity of assumption; for example, that there are no long-run barriers to the movement of capital.

(2) *Distortion between future consumption and present consumption*

It was seen in the earlier discussion of the effects of the corporation tax that the rate of return to capital in both the corporate and the non-corporate sectors of the economy falls. Thus the return to savings in the economy will fall also. This will raise the cost of retirement and will distort households' choices in favour of current consumption.

(3) *Distortion between dividends and retained earnings*

A corporation tax system, which taxes dividends more heavily relative to retained earnings, gives an incentive to the firm to increase its retained earnings. This generates funds for the purpose of investment. However, it helps existing firms but discourages new firms that must go to the market for funds. There is, therefore, a distortion against external finance. Also, investment projects that appear to be worth while when financed from retained earnings might not be worth while if financed from external funds. Thus inefficient firms that retain earnings will continue to invest them in inefficient projects. Retained earnings, however, might not be used for increase in X-inefficiency or an increase in the liquidity of the company. If firms do not have an immediately available set of investment opportunities, then they could invest their savings in financial assets, thereby lending to those firms or other sectors of the economy that can use them efficiently.

Empirical research on this question has shown quite clearly that discriminatory taxation of dividends has decreased the proportion of profits that is distributed as dividends. This fall in dividends also reduces personal savings by shareholders. Second, are the retained earnings inefficiently used? Unfortunately the evidence on the quality of investment of retained earnings is not clear. For excellent summaries of the analysis of these questions see works by G. Whittington and M. Sumner.

(4) Distortion between equity finance and debt finance

The firm has two principal financial instruments: debt finance, on which interest is paid to investors, and equity finance, on which dividends are paid out to shareholders. In a world of uncertainty in which bankruptcy is possible, the firm is obliged to meet its commitments to debt-holders before it meets those of equity-holders.

In 1958, Modigliani and Miller, in their celebrated article, demonstrated the indeterminancy of the firms debt–equity ratio (D/E). The crucial assumption of their model was that there were no taxes. What difference, therefore, does taxation make to the firms' D/E ratio?

If debt interest is deductable for calculating the profits tax then such tax laws provide an incentive to firms to expand their debt finance relative to their equity finance, thereby encouraging an increase in the D/E ratio. As the D/E ratio rises, however, this increases the perceived uncertainty of the firm's interest and equity payments (i.e., there is an increased risk of bankruptcy). This increased risk raises the cost of debt and equity capital to the firm. But firms wish to minimise their cost of capital.

There are, therefore, costs and benefits associated with each value of the D/E ratio. An equilibrium value for the D/E ratio is established when the tax advantage of expanding debt is balanced by the cost induced by the increased riskiness of the higher leverage.

The answer, however, does not stop here, since the effects of the whole tax system on the choice of the D/E ratio must be considered. The absence of any personal tax on retained earnings and the relatively low rate of tax on capital gains (as in the US) gives favour to equity finance and could explain why firms have not relied more on debt finance. Thus the costs and benefits of debt finance versus equity finance are complicated in a multi-tax system. However, any observed D/E ratio can be explained only by weighing up these costs and benefits in relation to the risk effects of a change in the D/E ratio.

(5) Effects of corporation tax on the income of households

This far we have been concerned with the incidence of taxes by class of income: wages, profits, etc. But we are also interested in the incidence of taxes by income range. An American study by J. A. Pechman and B. A. Okner has shown that sharply ranging incidence estimates are implied by using different assumptions. The study includes a total of eight sets of assumptions which are set out in Table 18.6. All eight assume that income taxes are not shifted and that sales and excise taxes are shifted fully to consumers, but there are differing assumptions about the incidence of corporate taxes, property taxes and payroll taxes.

The most widely divergent results were produced by assumptions 1c and 3b. In 1c the incidence of corporate taxes is assumed to be half on dividends and half on property income generally, while in 3b half remains on general property income with the other half shifted forward to prices and consumption. There are also different assumptions about the incidence of property taxes and the payroll

Table 18.6 Tax incidence assumptions used by Pechman and Okner

Tax and basis of allocation	Variant 1			Variant 2		Variant 3		
	a	*b*	*c*	*a*	*b*	*a*	*b*	*c*
Individual income tax								
To taxpayers	X	X	X	X	X	X	X	X
Sales and excise taxes								
To consumption of taxed commodities	X	X	X	X	X	X	X	X
Corporation income tax								
To dividends	—	—	—	X	X	—	—	—
To property income in general	X	X	—	—	—	—	—	—
Half to dividends; half to property income in general	—	—	X	—	—	—	—	X
Half to dividends; one-fourth to consumption; one-fourth to employee compensation	—	—	—	—	—	X	—	—
Half to property income in general; half to consumption	—	—	—	—	—	—	X	—
Property tax on land								
To landowners	X	—	—	X	X	X	X	X
To property income in general	—	X	X	—	—	—	—	—
Property tax on improvements								
To shelter and consumption	—	—	—	X	X	X	X	—
To property income in general	X	X	X	—	—	—	—	—
Half to shelter and consumption; half to property income in general	—	—	—	—	—	—	—	X
Payroll tax on employees								
To employee compensation	X	X	X	X	X	X	X	X
Payroll tax on employers								
To employee compensation	X	X	X	X	—	X	—	X
Half to employee compensation; half to consumption	—	—	—	—	X	—	X	—

Source: J. A. Pechman and B. A. Okner, *Who Bears the Tax Burden?* (Washington: Brookings Institution, 1974), p. 38.

tax on employers which are given in Table 18.6. It can be seen that the two sets of assumptions have very different implications for the progressivity of the corporate taxation and of taxation generally. With assumption 1c the corporation tax appears to be very progressive except at the low income levels, as is shown in Table 18.7, while with assumption 3b the apparent degree of progressivity is

Table 18.7 Effective rates of federal, state, and local taxes, by type of tax, variants 1c and 3b, by adjusted family income class, 1966

Adjusted family income	Indi- vidual income tax	Corpo- ration income tax	Property tax	Sales and excise taxes	Payroll taxes	Personal property and motor vehicle taxes	Total taxes
			Variant 1c				
$000	%	%	%	%	%	%	%
0–3	1.4	2.1	2.5	9.4	2.9	0.4	18.7
3–5	3.1	2.2	2.7	7.4	4.6	0.4	20.6
5–10	5.8	1.8	2.0	6.5	6.1	0.4	22.6
10–15	7.6	1.6	1.7	5.8	5.8	0.3	22.8
15–20	8.7	2.0	2.0	5.2	5.0	0.3	23.2
20–25	9.2	3.0	2.6	4.6	4.3	0.2	24.0
25–30	9.3	4.6	3.7	4.0	3.3	0.2	25.1
30–50	10.4	5.8	4.5	3.4	2.2	0.1	26.4
50–100	13.4	8.8	6.2	2.4	0.7	0.1	31.5
100–500	15.3	16.5	8.2	1.5	0.3	0.1	41.8
500–1000	14.1	23.0	9.6	1.1	0.1	0.2	48.0
1000 and over	12.4	25.7	10.1	1.0	[a]	0.1	49.3
All classes[b]	8.5	3.9	3.0	5.1	4.4	0.3	25.2
			Variant 3b				
0–3	1.2	6.1	6.5	9.2	4.6	0.4	28.1
3–5	2.8	5.3	4.8	7.1	4.9	0.4	25.3
5–10	5.5	4.3	3.6	6.4	5.7	0.3	25.9
10–15	7.2	3.8	3.2	5.6	5.3	0.3	25.5
15–20	8.2	3.8	3.2	5.1	4.7	0.3	25.3
20–25	9.1	4.0	3.1	4.6	4.1	0.2	25.1
25–30	9.1	4.3	3.1	4.0	3.6	0.2	24.3
30–50	10.5	4.7	3.0	3.5	2.6	0.2	24.4
50–100	14.1	5.6	2.8	2.4	1.3	0.1	26.4
100–500	18.0	7.4	2.4	1.7	0.7	0.1	30.3
500–1000	17.7	9.0	1.7	1.4	0.4	0.2	30.3
1000 and over	16.6	9.8	0.8	1.3	0.3	0.2	29.0
All classes[b]	8.4	4.4	3.4	5.0	4.4	0.3	25.9

Notes: Variant 1c is the most progressive and 3b the least progressive set of incidence assumptions examined in this study.
   [a] Less than 0.05 per cent.
   [b] Includes negative incomes not shown separately.

Source: Pechman and Okner, *op. cit.*, p. 49.

much less. It may also be noted that even where there is no change in the incidence assumption, as in the case of the income tax, there is a change in the apparent progressivity of the tax system. The reason for this is that changing incidence assumptions means changing assumed income. For example, if employers' payroll tax is assumed to be paid by employees then it must be added to employee income in the first instance.

In the UK the CSO does not include corporation tax in their studies of incidence but O'Higgins and Ruggles did include corporation tax in their study based on 1971 FES data (see also Chapter 14 for a fuller discussion of their study). They allocated half of corporation tax in proportion to the income from capital and half to household expenditure. Their results are given in Table 17.11 where incidence is regressive relative to original income over the bottom eight deciles. These incidence assumptions are similar to Pechman and Okner's assumptions in variant 3b in Table 18.6. Pechman and Okner also found corporation tax to be regressive (relative to adjusted family income) in variant 3b. However, when Pechman and Okner assumed that half of corporation tax fell on dividend income and half on property income (variant 1c) the tax incidence was progressive particularly over the upper ranges of income. Clearly then the issue of the incidence of the corporate income tax is far from finally settled.

Corporation tax in an inflationary period

We have had occasion to point out at various places that inflation can change effective tax rates, and corporation tax is no exception. The root of the problem is that the law provides that corporate profits, on which corporation tax is assessed, are computed using historical costs. When prices are changing rapidly, costs incurred, perhaps many years ago in the case of machines or even a few weeks ago in the case of stocks, may be out of date. As profits are basically sales minus costs, then any understatement of costs results in an automatic and equal overstatement of profits. Corporation tax may thus be levied on money profits, which can overstate – possibly grossly overstate – the company's real profitability. An official estimate of the effective rate of corporation tax – taken from the 1982 Green Paper *Corporation Tax* is given in Table 18.8. Rates

Table 18.8 **Effective rate of UK tax on company income: average 1976–80. (Home industrial and commercial companies.)**

	Historical cost basis	*Current cost basis*
	%	%
Total corporation tax	25	65
Excluding ACT	15	40

Source: *Corporation Tax* (London: HMSO, 1982), p. 138.

are calculated on net profits, that is after subtracting the losses of companies trading at a loss. Clearly the effective rates would have been higher had loss-making companies been excluded. On an historical cost basis the effective rate is estimated at 25 per cent but that rate jumps to 65 per cent once allowance has been made for inflation (using the principles of SSAP16 which are explained below). Given both that 65 per cent is an average and that it includes losses, it would be surprising if some companies do not pay over 100 per cent of their true profits.

In the UK a committee chaired by F. E. P. Sandilands considered three alternatives to the valuation of assets at historic cost. Present value (PV) accounting bases the value of an asset on the present (discounted) value of the stream of future earnings. This forward-looking concept is thus a subjective measure of the profits that a firm could earn from the ownership of an asset. Net realisable value (NRV) is what a firm could sell an asset for, as such, is particularly interesting measure for a firm's creditors. Replacement cost (RC) is what it would now cost to replace an asset and is the concept most favoured by Sandilands (for a criticism of this view see Kay).

Whatever method of valuing assets is elected, in principle some practical method of measuring price changes has to be adopted. The possibilities can be grouped under three broad headings: (1) the use of some general measure of the rate of inflation such as the retail price index; (2) the use of a general index of the prices of capital goods and/or of stocks; and (3) the construction of specific indices for various subsets of assets. If all prices are not rising at the same rate these various indices will naturally produce different figures for profits and hence different tax liabilities. The use of a general index has been termed current purchasing power (CPP) accounting and has the important merit of simplicity. Methods (2) and especially (3) will approximate more closely the changes in the prices of particular assets but are more difficult to administer. After the Sandilands report there were several years of debate and in 1980 the accountancy profession produced *The Statement of Standard Accounting Practice* on CCA (SSAP16). SSAP16 recommended that profits measured on an historical cost basis should be adjusted in two stages which are explained in Table 18.9. In the first stage allowance is made for changes in the prices of fixed assets, stocks and working capital. If prices are rising and if a firm is a net supplier of trade credit the adjustments will reduce historical profits. In the second stage allowance is made for the falling value of debt. The purpose of SSAP16 is to produce accurate accounts for firms, and not necessarily to provide a basis for calculating tax liabilities. Much of the 1982 Green Paper on *Corporation Tax* is devoted to a discussion of the problems that could arise in applying SSAP16 in calculating tax liability. Space does not permit a full discussion of the problems but two issues will serve to illustrate the practical difficulties. First, the use of very specific price indices may make the depreciation adjustment and the cost of sales adjustment more accurate for specific firms but this is more difficult for the tax authorities to administer than more general indices. Second if the changes

Table 18.9   SSAP16

Historical profits	
+ or −	
The depreciation adjustment	The difference between historical cost depreciation and replacement cost depreciation
+ or −	
The cost of sales adjustment (COSA)	The difference between historical and replacement cost of business stocks
+ or −	
The monetary working capital adjustment (MWCA)	Allows for the effects of price changes on the value of trade debtors and creditors (working capital)
=	
Current cost operating profit	
+	
Gearing adjustment	Reduces the other three adjustments to allow for the benefit of nominal debt. After this adjustment interest, taxation and extraordinary items are deducted
=	
Current cost profit attributable to share holders	

Source: Derived from *Corporation Tax* (London: HMSO, 1982), pp. 45–6.

were made on a revenue neutral basis (which the government may insist on) some (largely manufacturing) firms will pay more tax while other (largely financial) firms will pay less.

These issues are unlikely to be resolved very quickly and in the meantime there are two measures that have the effect of moving the actual UK tax system towards an inflation-adjusted basis at least in very crude terms. First firms are allowed to write off 100 per cent of the cost of their plant and machinery in the year in which it was purchased. This has the effect of postponing, perhaps indefinitely, its liability to tax on some or all of its profits. Suppose a firm towards the end of the year estimates that it will make profits of 100 in that year. If on the last day of the year it buys a machine for 100 its taxable profits will in fact be nil for that year so it will not have to pay corporation tax of 52. In that year it will have purchased 100 worth of machinery for 48. In later years if the machine increases profitability extra tax may become payable, but if new machines are purchased every year, tax may be continually postponed.

The motive for introducing 100 per cent write-off in the first year appears to have been to increase investment and not to approximate to inflation accounting. Nevertheless, like inflation accounting, it will reduce reported profits and in this sense can be thought of as a very crude approximation to inflation accounting.

Another innovation is a government decision allowing firms tax relief on increases in their stocks. In 1975 the government decided that 15 per cent of taxable profits could be deducted from any increase in stocks and the remaining increase in stock is set against corporation profits for tax purposes. Table 18.10 contains an example. Company A starts the year with stocks valued at 100. At

Table 18.10 Example of UK corporation tax relief on increases in stocks

	Company A		Company B	
(1) Opening stocks	100		1000	
(2) Closing stocks	180		1345	
(3) Increase in stocks ((2)–(1))		80		345
(4) Unadjusted taxable profits	300		300	
(5) 15% of profits		45		45
(6) Stocks adjustment factor ((3)–(5))		35		300
(7) Adjusted taxable profits ((4)–(6))			265	0

the end of the year its stocks are valued at 180. Taxable profits are 300. Fifteen per cent of these profits or 45 is deducted from the increase in stocks of 80. The difference of 35 (= 80 − 45) is then deducted from profits so that company is in fact taxed on 265 (= 300 − 35). It should be noted that when increases in stocks are large relative to profits, as with Company B in Table 18.10, no corporation tax may be payable. Clearly this relief made it less likely that firms would have to pay corporation tax on purely paper profits; however, this solution was rough and ready at best. The particular amount of relief was clearly arbitrary, and perhaps worse it encouraged companies to hold unnecessarily large stocks, for the law applies to increases in the value of stocks without distinguishing between quantity changes and price changes.

Table 18.11 Number of companies paying corporation tax (as in 1977)

	Companies paying:		
	Mainstream CT	ACT	All live companies
Manufacturing	50,000	8,000	140,000
Distribution	40,000	5,000	110,000
Other HIC[a]	130,000	10,000	320,000
Total HIC[a]	220,000	23,000	570,000
Financial	10,000	2,000	30,000
All companies	230,000	25,000	600,000

Notes: [a] Home industrial and commercial companies.
1. Figures are to nearest 10,000. There are also some 1000 (out of 3000) overseas companies and some 150 (out of 350) North Sea companies paying mainstream CT. In addition there are about 50 principal public corporations or groups of public corporations (e.g. Passenger Transport Executives), of which only a few pay mainstream CT.
2. 'Other Home Industrial and Commercial Companies' comprises agriculture, forestry and fishing, mining, construction, water, transport, services, property and holding companies.

Source: *Corporation Tax* (London: HMSO, 1982), p. 133.

This adjustment applied to decreases in stocks as well as to increases. When the depression caused firms to reduce their stocks sharply in 1980, they suddenly became liable for substantial amounts of tax that they could not afford to pay. In 1981 a new, more sensible method of adjustment was announced. All stocks (except the first £2000) are adjusted using a general index of the prices of stocks and the adjustment is not clawed back if profits fall.

The combination of the low level of company profits (Table 18.2) and the large reliefs arising from capital allowances and stock relief have meant first that less than half of companies paid any corporation tax in 1977, as can be seen from Table 18.11, and second that large tax losses have accumulated. These were estimated in *Corporation Tax* to have reached £30b by 1982. These losses are referred to as the 'overhang' and can be offset against future profits for up to six years. As a result many companies are unlikely to pay corporation tax for several years.

Unless the government can find a satisfactory way of dealing with inflation in the treatment of company profits we think it should scrap corporation tax. It will be remembered that in 1980 to 1982 it raised only about 5 per cent of government revenue outside the North Sea. Some of this revenue was almost certainly raised at effective rates of tax in excess of 100 per cent of real profits. We believe that if corporation tax is retained that it should be put on a rational basis and that one rational basis would be SSAP16.

CHAPTER 19

Expenditure Taxation

Interest in expenditure taxation has been reawakened by several recent reports (see Further Reading p. 488) including the 1978 report of the Meade Committee: *The Structure and Reform of Direct Taxation* (commonly known as the *Meade Report*). This chapter draws heavily on that report. What is meant by expenditure taxation is rather more than simply taxes on goods and services. The distinguishing feature of taxes on goods and services is that one's tax liability depends on the goods and services that one buys, while a distinguishing feature of an expenditure tax is that one's liability may depend on one's personal circumstances. In this respect it is like an income tax. The major difference between an income tax and an expenditure tax is in the treatment of savings, which is included in the base of an income tax but not in the base of an expenditure tax. Thus in the basic accounting identity $Y \equiv C + S$, Y is the base for the income tax while C is the base for the expenditure tax. An expenditure tax is sometimes justified by reference to the fact that liability to an expenditure tax depends on how much one takes out of the economy, while liability to an income tax depends on how much one puts into the economy.

Treatment of savings and investment

With an expenditure tax the post-tax rate of return to savings is equal to the rate of return on investment that can be financed by that savings. As we saw in Chapter 16, an income tax reduces the net rate of return to savings (see Figure 16.2) and hence causes a welfare loss because the marginal rate of time preference does not equal the marginal productivity of capital. An expenditure tax avoids this loss as the example in Table 19.1 makes clear. Part A shows the same tax liability for the expenditure tax (column (2)) as for an income tax in column (1), when all income is spent. There is, however, an important difference when income is saved. This is illustrated in part B of the table, where it is assumed that the return to investment is 10 per cent in perpetuity. With income tax of $33\frac{1}{3}$ per cent savings of 100 are invested. This yields gross income of 10 and makes it possible to finance consumption of 6.67 in perpetuity. The net return to the consumption forgone is thus 6.67 per cent compared with the 10 per cent return on investment. With an expenditure tax, savings of 150 are invested

Table 19.1 Examples of tax treatment of savings and investment

	(1) Income tax	(2) Expenditure tax	(3) Income tax with exemption for investment income	(4) Income tax with deduction for savings	(5) Income tax with capital allowance
A Income spent					
Income	150	150	150	150	150
Income tax	(50)		(50)	(50)	(50)
Expenditure tax		(50)			
Consumption	100	100	100	100	100
B Income saved					
Income	150	150	150	150	150
Income tax	(50)		(50)	nil	(50)
Savings	100	150	100	150	100
Investment	100	150	100	150	100
Tax remission					(50)
Investment with tax remission					150
Gross return to investment	10	15	10	15	15
Income tax	(3.33)		nil	5	5
Expenditure tax		5			
Annual consumption	6.67	10	10	10	10

Source: Similar to Table 8.2 of the *Meade Report*.

which yields a gross return of 15, which means that, after tax, 10 is available for consumption. The net return to forgone consumption and the return to investment are thus both 10 per cent. The equality avoids the welfare loss associated with income tax, and is the most basic characteristic of an expenditure tax. An income tax could be altered so as to equate the return to investment with the net return to savings. If this were done an income tax would, in effect, be converted into an expenditure tax. This could be done in various ways. Perhaps the most straightforward way to do it in principle would be to exempt the yield from savings from the tax base, as can be seen from column (3) of Table 19.1, where there is no deduction for income tax and the net return to savings would equal the return on investment. The same effect could be achieved by giving tax relief for savings as can be seen from column (4). It may be noted that this makes the tax identical to an expenditure tax except in name, as a comparison of columns (2) and (4) indicates. Another way of achieving the same effect would be to give full tax allowances for capital goods purchased as is illustrated in column (5). Without the income tax remission we have investment of 100. However if there were full tax remission for investment then savings of 100 could finance investment of 150. This would give a gross annual yield of 15. Income tax of 5 would be payable which means that 10 would be available for consumption. Once again the return to savings and the return to investment would be equal.

Returns to savings and investment in the UK

While the UK has a tax called an income tax, the returns to savings and investment are *not* as suggested in column (1) of Table 19.1. (See also the section below 'The UK income tax as an expenditure tax'.) Perhaps the greatest service that the Meade Committee did was to point to the very large number of ways in which the return to savings is *not* equal to the return to investment. It should be remembered that – at least in simple competitive models – distortions will arise if the return to savings is not equal to the return to investment. If in various alternative uses of savings the MRS is not the same for all savers and if in various alternative uses of investment the MRT is not the same for all investors and if the various MRSs are not equal to the MRTs a serious loss of efficiency may arise.

We start with looking at the ways in which tax and inflation can interact in the UK to distort the savings choice. In the example in Table 19.2 it is assumed that £100 is saved and that the nominal rate of interest is 15 per cent. The £15 of interest is shown in row (1). In row (2) the tax liability is shown for two tax rates (33.3 per cent and 66.7 per cent). Row (3) gives after tax interest and row (4) gives the original deposit plus net interest. Row (5) shows the real value of this deposit plus net interest by deflating the nominal sum by three assumed rates of inflation: 5 per cent, 10 per cent and 15 per cent. Row (6) shows the

Table 19.2 **Examples of real after tax returns to savings**

Marginal rate of tax %	33.3	66.7	33.3	66.7	33.3	66.7
Rate of inflation %	5	5	10	10	15	15
Deposit £100	£	£	£	£	£	£
(1) Interest at 15%	15.00	15.00	15.00	15.00	15.00	15.00
(2) Tax	5.00	10.00	5.00	10.00	5.00	10.00
(3) After tax interest	10.00	5.00	10.00	5.00	10.00	5.00
(4) Deposit plus net interest	110.00	105.00	110.00	105.00	110.00	105.00
(5) Real value of deposit plus net interest	104.76	100.00	100.00	95.45	95.62	91.30
(6) Real net return to savings	4.76%	0%	0%	−4.55%	−4.38%	−8.7%
(7) Implied real 'tax' rate on £15	68%	100%	100%	130%	129%	158%

real returns to savings. It can be seen for example that if nominal interest rates are 15 per cent with inflation at 10 per cent (giving a real interest rate of 5 per cent) the real return to someone paying tax at 33.3 per cent is zero. If real rates of interest are lower or tax rates higher the real return is negative. When real returns are negative because of the interaction of tax and inflation the result is equivalent to the effect of a tax rate in excess of 100 per cent in the absence of inflation. The final row of Table 19.2 shows the implied tax rates in the example. It can be seen that if the nominal *tax* rate of interest is 15 per cent and inflation 10 per cent then the real tax rate would be 130 per cent for someone facing a nominal tax rate of 66.7 per cent.

We now look at how tax affects the return to savings and investment in the case of unincorporated businesses. We assume

(1) The market rate of interest is 15 per cent.
(2) That firms can borrow as much as they wish at this rate and that they will choose to borrow to the point where *at the margin* their net return is nil.
(3) That the investment attracts 100 per cent capital allowances.
(4) Initially, that there is no inflation.

Table 19.3 provides an example which shows the returns to investment and savings of £100 being borrowed. The £100 borrowed is shown in row (1). Because of the 100 per cent capital allowance the borrower can invest more than £100 for each £100 borrowed if he is a taxpayer. For example if he pays tax at 33.3 per cent he will save tax of £50 on an investment of £150. Tax remission for marginal tax rates of 0, 33.3 per cent and 66.7 per cent are given in rows (2) and (3) the investment possible from a marginal borrowing of £100 is shown. By assumption this investment will yield £15 (row 4) which is just sufficient to repay the interest of £15 leaving net profit of zero (row 5). It can be seen from row (6) that the tax system has induced people to invest at

Table 19.3 Example distortions to returns to savings and investment caused by taxation

Borrower		£	£	£
(1) Marginal amount borrowed		100	100	100
(2) Remission of tax for borrower	0	0		
whose marginal tax rate on	33.3		50	
earned income is	66.7			200
(3) Investment		100	150	300
(4) Required yield		15	15	15
(4) Less interest paid of £15				
equals taxable income		0	0	0
(6) Yield on investment (= 4 ÷ 3)		15%	10%	5%
Lender		£	£	£
(1) Marginal amount lent		100	100	100
(2) Interest received		15	15	15
(3) Net interest after tax at	0	15	15	15
lender's rate of	33.3	10	10	10
	66.7	5	5	5
		%	%	%
(4) Net return to savings for	0	15	15	15
lender with marginal	33.3	10	10	10
tax rate of	66.7	5	5	5

Source: Modified from C. V. Brown 'Some Defects of the UK Tax System', in C. V. Brown, P. Bird and D. N. King (eds), *Tax Reform in the UK*, Table 5. That table was based on a private communication from J. E. Meade and is an alternative and more realistic version of Table 4.6 of the *Meade Report*.

three very different real rates of return. The bottom of the table shows the position of the lender. For lending £100 he received £15 in interest on which he is liable to pay tax. His net interest after deducting tax is shown in row (3) and the corresponding real rates of return are shown in row (4). The net return to savings varies from 5 to 15 per cent. If a zero marginal-rate lender lends to a 66.7 per cent marginal-rate borrower the return to savings is 15 per cent and the return to investment is 5 per cent. On the other hand if a 66.7 per cent rate lender lends to a zero rate borrower the return to savings is 5 per cent and the return in investment 15 per cent. Only when borrowers and lenders have the same marginal tax rate are the returns equalised.

Finally, we relax the assumption of the previous paragraph that there is no inflation and assume instead that there is 10 per cent inflation. To keep the example as simple as possible it is assumed that the nominal yield is received at the end of the year when the principal plus interest is repaid to the lender. We first look at the position of the borrower in Table 19.4 where the first six rows are repeated from Table 19.3. In row (7) the real value of the £15 yield is given and in row (8) the gain is shown from the repayment of the principal in deflated currency. Row (9) shows the yield on the investment after allowing for inflation. This is the sum of row (7) plus row (8) expressed as a percentage of the original investment in row (3). The position of the lender is shown in the bottom half of Table 19.4 where rows (1)–(4) are repeated from Table 19.3. With inflation the

Table 19.4 Example of distortions to returns to savings and investment caused by taxation and inflation

		£	£	£
Borrower				
(1) Marginal amount borrowed		100	100	100
(2) Remission of tax for borrower	0	0		
whose marginal tax rate on	33.3		50	
earned income is	66.7			200
(3) Investment		100	150	300
(4) Required yield		15	15	15
(5) Less interest paid of £15 equals taxable				
income		0	0	0
(6) Nominal yield on investment (= 4 ÷ 3)		15%	10%	5%
		£	£	£
(7) Real value of 4 (= £15/1.10)		13.64	13.64	13.64
(8) Gain from repayment of principal in				
deflated currency (= £100 − [£100/1.10])		9.09	9.09	9.09
(9) Yield on investment after inflation				
(= (7) + (8)/(3))		22.73%	15.15%	7.58%
Lender		£	£	£
(1) Marginal amount lent		100	100	100
(2) Interest received		15	15	15
(3) Net interest after tax at lender's	0	15	15	15
marginal tax rate of	33.3	10	10	10
	66.7	5	5	5
		%	%	%
(4) Nominal net return to savings	0	15	15	15
for lender with	33.3	10	10	10
marginal tax rate of	66.7	5	5	5
(5) Loss from repayment of principal and				
interest in deflated currency				
(= £115 − [£115/1.10])		£10.46	£10.46	£10.46
		%	%	%
(6) Real net return to savings for	0	4.54	4.54	4.54
lender with marginal tax rate of	33.3	−0.46	−0.46	−0.46
(= (3)−(5)/(1))	66.7	−5.46	−5.46	−5.46

Source: Borrower rows (1)–(6) and lender rows (1)–(4) from Table 19.3.

lender is worse off because his loan (both principal *and* interest) is repaid in deflated currency. In the example his real return to savings is about 5 per cent if the saver pays no tax, approximately nil if he pays tax at 33.3 per cent and about −5 per cent if he pays tax at 66.7 per cent. Unlike the previous example without inflation there is now no case where the returns to savings and investment are equal. In every case the return to investment exceeds the return to savings. (The reader should resist jumping to the conclusion that this is 'a good thing' if investment is thought to be too low. There are many reasons for this including the incentive to the lender to find some other use for his money where – because of other distorting effects of the tax system – his return will be higher.)

We have given a detailed exposition of unincorporated businesses where investment is financed from borrowed funds. Space constraints prohibit our

Table 19.5   Meade Committee estimates of post-tax returns to investment in incorporated businessses

	Saver's or lender's marginal rate of tax			
Incorporated business	0%	33%	48%	98%
Equity finance				
(a) Profits distributed				
(i) 100% capital allowances	14.9	10.0	7.7	0.3
(ii) true economic depreciation	7.2	4.8	3.7	0.1
(b) Profits undistributed				
(i) 100% capital allowances	10.0	8.3	7.6	7.0
(ii) true economic depreciation	4.8	4.0	3.6	3.4
Debt finance				
(i) 100% capital allowances	20.8	13.9	10.8	0.4
(ii) true economic depreciation	10.0	6.7	5.2	0.2

Source: *Meade Report*, p. 69.

repeating the exercise for other incorporated businesses but the *Meade Report* showed that similar problems exist. Table 19.5 which is from the *Meade Report* shows the percentage returns to savings from an investment giving a real return of 10 per cent. It can be seen that when the return to investment is held constant at 10 per cent the return to savers may vary between 0.1 per cent and 20.8 per cent depending on the method of finance, whether profits are distributed, the method of depreciation and the savers' marginal tax rates. While it is perhaps not surprising that returns are lower for savers with high tax rates (i.e. that the percentages fall moving from left to right along any row), it is surprising that the return varies so much for other reasons (see the variation up and down any column). For example a tax exempt institution might earn anything from less than half to more than double the real rates of return on investment.

We believe that these distorting effects of the tax system are very serious. The combination of tax base which is *both* illogical in nominal terms (see next section) *and* unindexed can produce gross distortions. While we have no evidence about actual misallocation of resources resulting from this morass, it would not surprise us if this were shown to be an important part of the explanation for Britain's poor economic performance. We believe that the distortions of this sort have received far too little attention in the discussion of economic policy and in the discussion of the costs of inflation. Providing a coherent indexed tax base would not cause inflation to disappear but it might greatly diminish its harmful allocative effects.

The UK income tax as an expenditure tax

The United Kingdom has a tax called the 'income tax' but in fact the base of that tax may be nearer an expenditure base than an income base. As we have seen, taxable income is the sum of taxable receipts less certain allowances and certain deductions. However some of these allowances and deductions move the tax base towards – if not beyond – an expenditure base. The clearest example is the tax relief on certain forms of savings. Full tax relief for savings would convert an income tax into an expenditure tax as a comparison of columns (2) and (4) of Table 19.1 showed. In the UK individuals can deduct payments to approved pension funds from their income. People are also relieved from half the basic rate of tax for most life assurance premiums. Tax relief for these approved forms of savings moves the tax base towards an expenditure base. With an expenditure tax the sale of a registered asset to finance additional consumption would give rise to a tax liability. With a pension fund the pension paid to a retired person is taxed as earned income. If the pensioner spends his pension the result is the same as with an expenditure tax. However the tax relief to pension funds may exceed the relief that would occur with an expenditure tax. The reason is that part of a pension may be taken in the form of a tax-free lump sum. This lump sum is provided from tax free savings so that in this case the relief with the present UK income tax exceeds the relief that would arise with an expenditure tax.

Another way in which the present income tax system is moving towards an expenditure tax is in the treatment of capital allowances. With an expenditure tax the purchase of a registered asset means the postponement of tax – perhaps indefinitely. With the present income tax (and corporation tax) most, but not all, purchases of investment goods attract full tax relief in the first year. If all capital attracted full allowances we would again have an expenditure tax in principle – see column (5) of Table 19.1. Once again the relief with the present UK income tax can exceed the relief with an expenditure tax because in some instances there may be relief for both savings and investment. As we have seen there is tax relief for contributions to pension funds. If these funds are subsequently used to finance investment they may attract relief for a second time.

We now turn to an examination of some of the questions that arise in implementing an expenditure tax.

Assessment of liability for an expenditure tax

Liability for an expenditure tax could be computed in a variety of ways. As we saw in Table 19.1, we could use the mechanism of the income tax if we modified income tax in any of the ways that would convert an income tax into the equivalent of an expenditure tax. Or, if we wanted an expenditure tax that was proportional to expenditure this could be simply achieved by a uniform rate of VAT on all expenditure. Some degree of progression could be built into the system in a variety of ways. Goods that form large proportions of the expenditure of the poor (e.g. food) could be zero-rated. Goods that account for large proportions of the expenditure of the rich could be taxed at higher rates. These measures would of course be very rough-and-ready, and tax liability would depend on what goods were purchased rather than on the total amounts of expenditure *per se*. An expenditure tax could be more directly tailored to the needs of different-sized households by combining it with a lump sum payment which could be set according to household composition. Within limits these grants could be more closely tailored to needs by for example having higher rates for retired and disabled persons.

However, most proposals for an expenditure tax envisage a different procedure for calculating the liability for the tax. In principle expenditure or consumption is defined as a residual. In the simplest case $C \equiv Y - S$. The taxpayer fills in a return showing his income and his savings and is liable for tax on the difference. Having found the taxpayer's total expenditure in this manner it is then a straight-forward matter to apply a progressive structure of tax rates so that the tax-consumption ratio would rise with consumption.

If the tax base is equal to $Y - S$ then the definition of both Y and S become critical. Table 19.6 from the *Meade Report* shows a typical scheme. It may be noted that the definition of income in (1) and (3) corresponds quite closely to Simon's comprehensive definition of income. To this income one must add receipts from the sale of assets, borrowings etc. because such capital receipts make it possible for consumption expenditure to exceed income. From the total of these receipts one deducts outgoings, which are forms of savings recognised for tax purposes, and would include increases in bank balances and the purchase of registered assets.

Clearly there are a number of problems in the detailed definition of the tax and we now turn to a discussion of some of these.

(1) Gifts

How should we treat gifts? If we wish to tax the receipt of gifts from outside the tax unit, and in principle we believe this is correct, then gifts should be included among receipts. But whether to allow gifts to be subtracted as part of non-taxed outgoings is less straightforward. One view is that if gifts are counted as income of the recipient they should be subtracted from the income of the giver on the grounds that the gift is simply a transfer of a constant amount of purchasing power from one person to another. Another view is that the giver of the gift has simply chosen to use his income in this particular way and therefore there should be no deduction from income for the giver but there should nevertheless be an addition to the income of the recipient. Yet another course would be to ignore gifts altogether in which case they would be taken out of both sections (3) and (4) of the table.

(2) Expenditure taxes paid

Table 19.6 has a query against deduction of taxes paid. If the tax is deducted under (4) consumption expenditure in (5) will be on the exclusive basis, whereas

Table 19.6 Debits and credits for the assessment of liability to a comprehensive expenditure tax

Add								
(1)	*Personal incomes*							
	Wages	X	X	X				
	Salaries	X	X	X				
	Dividends	X	X	X				
	Interest	X	X	X				
	Rent	X	X	X				
	Profits	X	X	X				
	Royalties	X	X	X		X	X	X
(2)	*Capital receipts*							
	Realisation of capital assets	X	X	X				
	Amount borrowed	X	X	X				
	Receipt of repayment of past loans	X	X	X				
	Reduction in money balances	X	X	X		X	X	X
(3)	*Windfall incomings*							
	Inheritances	X	X	X				
	Gifts received	X	X	X		X	X	X
	Total chargeable debits					X	X	X
Deduct credits								
(4)	*Non-consumption outgoing*							
	Acquisition of assets	X	X	X				
	Amount lent	X	X	X				
	Repayment of past borrowings	X	X	X				
	Increase in money balances	X	X	X				
	(? Gifts made)	X	X	X				
	(? Direct taxes paid)	X	X	X		(X	X	X)
	Total allowable credits					(X	X	X)
(5)	*Balance of chargeable debits*							
	(Representing expenditure on consumption)					X	X	X

Source: *Meade Report*, Table 8.1.

if it is not deducted in (4) then in (5) consumption expenditure will be on a tax-inclusive basis. To see the distinction between the inclusive and exclusive basis suppose income is 150, savings nil, consumption 100 and tax 50. Tax could be expressed as a proportion of income, i.e. 50/150, which is the tax-inclusive basis, or as a proportion of expenditure i.e. 50/100, which is the tax-exclusive basis.

(3) Acquisition of registered assets

If an individual buys a registered asset he postpones his tax liability so long as he holds that asset. When the registered asset is sold there is a corresponding rise in receipts. If this receipt is spent tax will be due. Purchase of an unregistered asset would on the other hand count as ordinary expenditure and sale of an unregistered asset would not add to income. The decision as to which assets will count as registered assets is thus a critical one. Generally of course a person will prefer to purchase registered assets because he is better off by the interest he can earn on the deferred tax. However if a person plans to buy an expensive item such as a car this could push him into a higher tax bracket in the year in which this happened. To avoid this extra tax liability he might choose to purchase an unregistered asset in the preceding year.

(4) Capital gains

As the proceeds from the sales of registered assets will attract expenditure tax unless they are switched into one of the other exempted categories, capital gains are automatically included and there is therefore no need for a separate capital gains tax. It is however important to ensure that the definition of registered assets is wide enough so that people cannot avoid tax by the acquisition of unregistered assets which could then be held for untaxed capital gains. To avoid changes in the real tax system, indexing would be required, particularly for registered assets.

(5) Housing

Administrative simplicity clearly requires that most personal possessions are treated as unregistered assets. If they were not the tax authorities would have to concern themselves with the acquisition and disposal of clothes, furniture, etc. However for reasons that were given above exceptionally valuable personal assets should probably be registered. For most people the most obvious candidate for inclusion is housing. If houses are a registered asset then the purchase of a house would not count as expenditure. The sale of a house would add to taxable receipts unless the money were used to purchase another house. If houses were treated as registered assets, mortgages would count as registered liabilities, and mortgage interest would be offset against imputed income from owner occupation. The Meade Committee suggest that the simplest way of assessing imputed income would be to assess the market value of the house (as has been suggested by the Layfield Committee on local government finance) and then to assume arbitrarily that the imputed rent amounted to some modest real rate of return on this market value – perhaps 3 per cent.

A two-tier expenditure tax

A change to an expenditure tax should involve less upheaval than would be the case if we now had a true income tax. Indeed, the Meade Committee recommend that the move to an expenditure base might be continued for most taxpayers and a two tier expenditure tax (TTET) introduced. With TTET the great bulk of taxpayers might continue to pay something called income tax and those with unusually high expenditure would pay TTET in addition. Higher rates of income tax would be abolished but rates of TTET could be designed to give approximately the same incidence. As the Meade Committee admit, this situation would be potentially confusing. Everyone would be paying an expenditure tax: those with low and middle expenditures would pay something called income tax but with something approximating expenditure rather than income as the base. Those with high expenditure would pay the expenditure tax. To avoid confusion income tax might be replaced by VAT which sounds more like an expenditure tax. The rates of VAT would have to be high if it were to replace income tax. In addition the base should logically be widened to include food, books and other exempted goods which might be politically unacceptable. If TTET were adopted the liability to tax would be calculated as in Table 19.7 The exemption level might be set say two-thirds of the way up the basic rate band.

Table 19.7 Calculation of taxpayer's liability to expenditure surcharge

(1)	Income			X X X
(2)	Expenditure tax adjustments:			
	Add Disposals of registered assets	X X X		
	Receipt of gifts and other windfalls	X X X		
	Deduct Acquisitions of registered assets	(X X X)		
	Gifts made during the year[a]	(X X X)		
	IT paid during the year	(X X X)		
	ET paid during the year	(X X X)	X X X	
(3)	Expenditure during the year			X X X
(4)	*Less* personal allowance for ET			(X X X)
(5)	Balance liable to ET			X X X

Note: [a] Gifts made are excluded from the tax base for the upper tier of expenditure tax in this calculation, on the assumption that they would be separately taxed under some form of tax on capital transfer. If, however, it were desired to submit gifts made, like other forms of consumption, to ET instead of to a separate transfer tax (as in the case discussed for UET) this could be done by charging on gifts as they were made both the basic rate of tax on income or on value added and also, where relevant, the expenditure surcharge.

Source: *Meade Report*, Table 10.1, p. 205.

Transitional problems

On thinking about tax reform it is all too easy to consider whether or not a proposed reform is better than the present system. However the costs of change can be very high and one therefore needs to ask if the discounted benefits exceed the costs. This is a question that is easier to ask than it is to answer but what is clear is that the costs of change will include not only the straightforward administrative upheaval but also the costs of trying to ensure that the changeover is fair. This is not the place to consider the full complexity of these transitional problems, but something of their nature can be seen from the following example. Suppose a man who is about to retire has saved a great deal out of his taxed income over his working life. If an expenditure tax is introduced and the man discovers that all his assets are registered assets, he will then be taxed again when he disposes of his assets. Clearly arrangements would have to be made to ensure that such people were treated equitably.

Administrative problems

Would there be administrative problems in addition to the transitional administrative problems discussed above? To answer this question we look first at a universal expenditure tax (UET) and then at a TTET.

With a UET, liability to tax would be assessed as shown in Table 19.5. Year-end adjustments would become the norm rather than the exception. It is hard to see how the cumulative basis of the present PAYE system could be retained and the case for self-assessment would be much stronger (see section on self-assessment in Chapter 14). Procedures for the verification of the acquisition and disposal of registered assets would be required. On the other hand a capital gains tax would no longer be needed; close company legislation would be unnecessary as liability to tax would depend on expenditure, and the number of shareholders in a company would be irrelevant. The present complicated rules for life assurance could be simplified.

With a TTET many of the administrative advantages of an expenditure tax could be retained and there would be fewer cases which would require year-end adjustments. On the other hand, procedures would have to be found for discovering who was liable for TTET. One possiblity would be to continue piecemeal adjustments until the income tax system corresponds even more closely to an expenditure tax. This approach has the considerable advantage of avoiding large-scale upheavals. Perhaps the main drawback of this approach is that it would leave most people confused if an expenditure tax were called an income tax.

How would one explain that the rich paid an expenditure tax called an expenditure tax and the poor paid an expenditure tax called an income tax? If a TTET were adopted we would favour replacing income tax with a much more broadly based VAT.

CHAPTER 20

Optimal Income Taxation

Optimal taxation is the term used to describe a new approach to an old concern: the design of tax systems to minimise excess burdens while achieving a socially desirable redistribution of income. The problem is to strike the correct balance between equity and efficiency. We know from our earlier discussion that to avoid the excess burden of income tax we should have a zero marginal rate. The problem is to reconcile this efficiency requirement with some means of making those with high incomes pay more tax on equity grounds. One possibility would be to have lump sum taxes that varied with ability. Those with great ability who had the capacity to earn large incomes would be faced with a high lump sum tax. Any income earned over and above this lump sum would be free of tax, which would provide the highest possible incentive to extra work. Those with lower ability would be required to pay a smaller lump sum tax and those with the lowest incomes would receive a lump sum transfer from the government. The variation in the lump sum would cause the average rate of tax to rise with earnings capacity but the marginal rate would always be zero.

There are two obvious drawbacks to this proposal: first, it would require the collection of an enormous amount of information about people's potential earnings capacity; and second, there would be a very strong incentive for people to try to underestimate their earnings capacity. As this direct approach to the problem is 'not on', the optimal tax approach tries to solve the problem in the absence of knowledge of what *individuals'* levels of skills are. As we will see it is assumed that, although the government is not able to assign abilities to particular individuals, it does know the distribution of ability in society. Given this, and certain other information, e.g. about the elasticity of the supply of labour and views about the desirable degree of inequality, it is then possible to recommend a schedule of tax rates that provides the optimal balance between equity and efficiency.

This approach, which is interesting, difficult, and important, has its origin in a paper of F. P. Ramsay and has recently been revived in seminal papers by J. A. Mirrlees, and by P. A. Diamond and J. A. Mirrlees both published in 1971. Much of the literature is of a highly technical mathematical character, and our object is to give a non-technical account of the basic issues underlying the design of schedules of rates of income taxes. It may be noted that this is the same concern that underlies the discussion of the benefit and ability to pay principles of taxation (see the appendix to Chapter 3). The subject of optimal taxation is much wider than concern with income tax rates alone, and at the end of the chapter we mention briefly some of the results of optimal taxation as they affect other taxes; in Chapter 20 we consider the effects of government expenditure on income distribution.

Much earlier work in public finance (including for example some of the material summarised in Chapter 11) has proceeded by analysing the behaviour of a representative individual. An example can serve to illustrate why this can be misleading. Much of the empirical evidence on labour supply, including evidence from our own study, suggests that the price elasticity is negative. This means that as the wage rate is raised a 'representative' individual works less. Changes in the net wage rate caused by taxation would be expected to have similar effects. Thus an increase in a proportional income tax would cause a fall in the net wage rate which would lead to an increase in work effort by the individual. Given this line of thinking it is perhaps not surprising that some people appear to conclude that the implication of a negative price elasticity of labour supply is that there is no limit to the amount of redistributive taxation that is either possible or desirable. As we will see, this apparently plausible result can be shown to be wrong as soon as we include more than one individual. Another apparent article of faith is that if we wish to redistribute income we require a schedule of marginal tax rates that rise with income. We will see that in general this is not true and, what is perhaps more surprising, that except in special cases the marginal rate of tax on the highest incomes should be zero.

As we have said we will focus on the question of the optimal schedule of rates of income taxes. The question can conveniently be subdivided into two questions. First: What would be the optimum rate of income tax in the special case where there is a single marginal rate of income tax? Second: What would be the optimum schedule of marginal taxes rates if we are not restricted to a single marginal rate? The answers to these questions can be referred to as the optimal linear income tax and the optimal (nonlinear) income tax, and they are discussed in turn below.

Before embarking on this discussion we would like to draw attention to the fact that we will confine our attention to the case when there are only two goods: a composite consumption good, which we call net income, and leisure. As there is a single consumption good it is possible to assume away the complexities that arise when we consider taxing different consumption goods at different rates. We may, however, note that as we are not allowing for the possibility of savings, the discussion that follows applies equally to income and to expenditure as the tax base.

Optimal linear income tax

We begin with a discussion of the optimal linear income tax, which is a special case of optimal taxation in which there is only one marginal rate of income tax.

Part of the tax revenue raised from this tax is used to finance government expenditure on goods and services and part is used to finance redistributive lump-sum transfers. The optimal level of government expenditure on goods and services is discussed in the next chapter. To keep the discussion as simple as possible, we assume that:

(1) the only type of government expenditure is on a lump sum transfer (*LST*) to households. We are thus assuming there is no government expenditure on goods and services. The reader should be able to modify the argument for himself to allow for the case where there is a fixed revenue requirement for expenditure in goods and services;

(2) the government must balance its budget, and the only form of taxation is an income tax with a constant, i.e. linear marginal rate (*t*).

(3) there are only two individuals, Mr Low and Mr High;

(4) there are two goods, a generalised current consumption good called net income (*NY*) and leisure (*L*);

(5) both individuals have the same preferences between *NY* and *L*;

(6) Mr High has more ability than Mr Low and as a consequence Mr High's wage rate exceeds Mr Low's wage rate;

(7) the individuals maximise their welfare subject to their budget constraint;

(8) the government knows the preference function of both individuals.

Each individual's gross income (*GY*) is his gross wage (*W*) times the number of hours (*H*) that he works ($GY = WH$). Net income is gross income *less* the income tax paid *plus* the lump sum transfer: $NY = [(1 - t) GY + LST]$. *GDP* is the sum of Low's gross income (GY^L) and High's gross income (GY^H) and total government revenue (*T*) is *GDP* times the marginal tax rate ($T = tGDP$). As the budget is balanced, tax revenue equals the sum of lump transfers ($T = LST = LST^L + LST^H$). (It should be noted that LST^L must equal LST^H.)

Our two-person society is illustrated in Figure 20.1. The left-hand panel in the diagram refers to Mr Low and the right-hand panel to Mr High. If there were no government, each budget constraint, shown by the lines *AB*, would be determined entirely by the wage rates, and equilibrium would be at E_0^L and E_0^H. If a tax were imposed at a constant rate *without* a lump sum transfer, the two individuals would move down their labour supply curves or price consumption curves, so that if a tax at the rate of *t* were imposed equilibrium would be at E_{t1}^L and E_{t1}^H. As the figure is drawn the hours worked increase as the net wage falls. There is of course no theoretical reason why this should be so (see Chapter 11), but it appears to be consistent with empirical evidence for men (see Chapter 14). An increase in the lump-sum transfer with a given net wage rate will have a pure income effect causing a movement up an income consumption curve. If, as the empirical evidence suggests, income and leisure are both normal goods, an increase in the *LST* will result in an increase in leisure, that is to say a decrease in work. Higher tax rates cause a movement down the *PCC* that

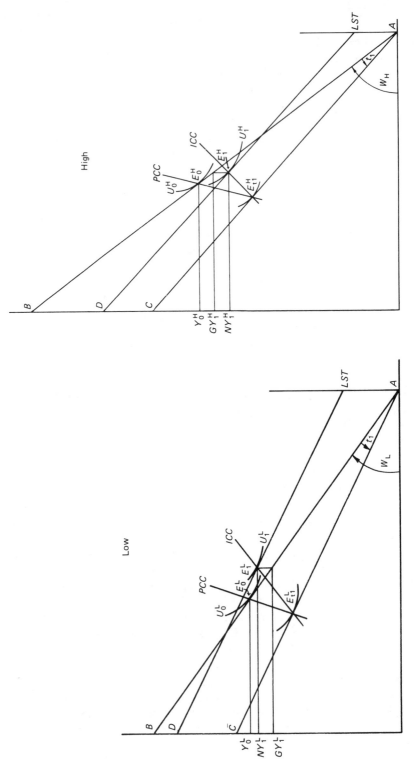

Fig. 20.1

increases work (as the diagram is drawn) and higher LSTs financed by these taxes cause a movement up an *ICC* decreasing work.

Figure 20.1 shows the effect of introducing a tax transfer system with a tax rate of t_1, which is sufficient to finance a transfer of *LST*. The after-tax budget constraints are thus *DLST*. The outcome for Low is in principle the same as the outcome of introducing a NIT (see Chapter 15), as there is an income effect and a substitution effect both of which decrease work. Low's gross income falls from Y_0^L to GY_1^L as he works less but his net income is now higher than his gross income. Low's welfare has increased and his net income might either rise or fall. The net effect on High's work and his gross income is less certain. He is subjected to a price effect which as the figure is drawn will increase work and an income effect that will reduce work. In Figure 20.1 the net effect is a reduction in work and in gross income. With only two people in our society the balanced budget condition amounts to requiring that High's net tax paid $(GY_1^H - NY_1^H)$ must just equal Low's net handout $(NY_1^L - GY_1^L)$.

There are several effects of introducing this linear income tax that we should note. *As the figure is drawn* both High and Low reduce their work (despite both having a negative price elasticity of demand) so that both have a fall in gross income. As the figure is drawn High's gross income falls by more than Low's so that gross incomes become somewhat more equal and net incomes considerably more equal as Low's net income rises and High's falls. There is also greater equality of welfare. Low's welfare has risen from U_0^L to U_1^L and High's has fallen from U_0^H to U_1^H. We wish to stress that the detailed results shown depend on the labour supply responses implicit in the indifference curves that we have drawn. Nevertheless it is instructive to note that our views on the desirability of the tax introduced will depend on the criteria that we employ and even in this simple example these criteria give us differing results. If the criteria were to maximise GDP the introduction of the tax would not be beneficial as GDP has fallen. On the other hand if the criteria were the equality of gross and net incomes the change would be regarded as beneficial. These measures all share the defect of giving no weight to leisure.

This suggests that indifference curves that do include leisure are a better measure of welfare. Has welfare increased? Once again the answer depends on the criteria, and once again there are several possibilities. We discuss three: Pareto's criterion, Rawls's criterion, and total welfare. By Pareto's criterion the tax change is not an improvement as High is worse off. (This neglects the possibility that High's own preferences includes Low's welfare.) Another criterion, suggested by Rawls, is that anything that improves the welfare of the least well off person is an improvement. The new tax system is clearly an improvement by this criterion as Low moves into a higher indifference curve. If we use total welfare as the criterion the answer turns on whether High's loss of welfare is greater or less than Low's gain in welfare.

We have thus far asked whether the tax/transfer system represents an improvement on the no-tax system. If instead we ask if the tax transfer shown in Figure 20.1 is optimal we are asking if some higher or lower tax rate than t_1 would be superior to t_1. As we increase tax rates we increase work (as we have drawn the figure) and hence tax revenue, but as we use this revenue to finance higher lump sum transfers we decrease work which decreases tax revenue. This suggests that as we raise tax rates revenue rises at first but that there comes a point where tax receipts start to fall. When this occurs we have reached the Rawls's point – the maximum welfare for Low. Simulation studies discussed in more detail below suggest that total welfare is maximised with lower tax rates than are required by the Rawls's criterion. This means that the optimal rate depends on society's view of the desirable amount of redistribution.

To conclude our theoretical discussion we have seen that in this simple example the optimum linear tax thus depends on two factors: the shapes of the individuals' preference maps for net income and leisure and society's views about redistribution. The shapes of the preference maps are important because they determine how responsive people are to changes in their budget constraints, and society's views about redistribution are important because it determines how far redistribution should go.

The distribution of wage rates is also important. We return to this point in our discussion of optimal nonlinear income taxes.

(1) *Estimates of optimal tax rates and the UK tax/transfer system*

We now look at a study in which N. H. Stern has calculated the optimal linear income tax rate under a variety of assumptions. Stern assumes that all people have the same preferences between income and labour and that these preferences exhibit the same elasticity of substitution throughout.[1] He then calculates the optimum linear tax rate for values for the elasticity of substitution varying between 0 and 1. Stern's results are summarised in Figure 20.2 for the case when all tax revenue is used for redistributive purposes (i.e. there is no government expenditure on goods and services), which is the case we have examined. The The graph has the tax rate on the vertical axis and the elasticity of substitution on the horizontal axis. It can be seen that there are four optimum tax schedules in the figure corresponding to various values of v: v is used by Stern to represent preferences for equality. If there is no preference for equality $v = 1$, and it can be seen that the optimum linear tax rate falls quite sharply as the elasticity of substitution rises. With Rawlsian preferences, that is if we wish to maximise the welfare of the poorest person, $v = -\infty$ and it can be seen that the optimum tax rate declines much less rapidly.

It can be seen from Figure 20.2 that the optimum tax rate is quite sensitive to the elasticity of substitution and to views about equality. Other calculations (see Table 20.2) show that the optimum rate is also fairly sensitive to the government's revenue requirement for expenditures on goods and services. Despite the sensitivity of Stern's estimates to these factors, very high tax rates emerge only when the elasticity of substitution is very low. This means that very high

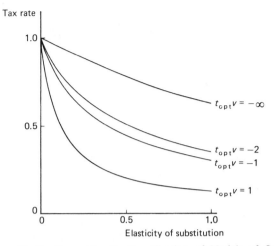

Fig. 20.2 Source: N. H. Stern, 'On the Specification of Models of Optimum Income Taxation', *Journal of Public Economics* 1976.

marginal tax rates are not justified either by extremely egalitarian views or by very high government expenditure on goods and services. Stern concluded:

> we should emphasise that the study of optimum income taxation is in its infancy, there is much work, empirical and conceptual as well as theoretical to do, and therefore all our estimates and calculations must be viewed with circumspection and as attempts to understand the best model currently available rather than prescriptions for policy.[2]

Mirrlees has compared the actual British tax system with Stern's calculations. Mirrlees begins by dividing taxes and expenditure into items that vary with income and those that do not. His calculations, which are admitted to be rough and ready, are reproduced by Table 20.1. These actual rates of tax and expenditure are then compared with the optimum rates as calculated by Stern. A sample of Stern's results are given in Table 20.2 for the case where $v = -1$ (which implies that the elasticity of marginal utility with respect to income is 2).

It can be seen from Table 20.1 that Mirrlees calculated R/Y, the proportion of expenditure on social goods, as rising from 11 per cent of NNP in 1966 to 12 per cent in 1976. This is slightly higher than the 10 per cent R/Y ratio shown in the middle row of Table 20.2. If the elasticity of substitution were unity that would imply that the amount of redistribution was about optimal in 1966 and was too high in 1976. On the other hand if the elasticity of substitution were 0.5 the amount of redistribution would have been too little in 1966 and about right in 1976. Mirrlees concludes:

> Believing that the elasticity of substitution is probably rather greater than a half, I would take the view, from this calculation, that the actual degree of redistribution [in 1976] is a little too large, but a reasonable man could well

Table 20.1 Mirrlees's estimates of UK tax and expenditure

| | (£000 million) | | | |
	1966	1974	1975	1976
Net national product at market prices, Y	35.2	75.0	93.4	109.9
Taxes,[a] T	12.1	32.3	41.3	49.3
$t = T/Y$	0.34	0.43	0.44	0.45
Subsidies,[b] B	7.3	25.0	32.4	38.5
B/Y	0.21	0.33	0.35	0.35
Expenditure on social goods,[c] R	3.9	8.8	11.2	13.4
R/Y	0.11	0.12	0.12	0.12
Government deficit, $R + B - T = D$	−0.9	1.5	2.3	2.6
D/Y	−0.03	0.02	0.03	0.02

Notes: [a] Taxes and subsidies related to income and expenditure
[b] Subsidies not related to income and expenditure
[c] Government expenditure excluding roads and social services.

Source: J. A. Mirrlees, 'Arguments for Public Expenditure', in M. Artis and A. R. Nobay, *Contemporary Contributions to Economic Analysis* (Oxford: Basil Blackwell, 1978).

Table 20.2 Optimal rates of income tax and subsidies

| $\dfrac{R}{Y}$ | Elasticity of substitution | |
	0.5	1
0	$t = 0.43$, $B/Y = 0.43$	$t = 0.29$, $B/Y = 0.29$
0.1	$t = 0.46$, $B/Y = 0.36$	$t = 0.32$, $B/Y = 0.21$
0.2	$t = 0.49$, $B/Y = 0.29$	$t = 0.34$, $B/Y = 0.14$

Source: Mirrlees, *op. cit.*

believe that it is just right, or perhaps too little.... On the other hand, it does seem very likely that the degree of redistribution was too low in 1966....[3]

Optimal (nonlinear) income tax

We now examine the arguments for optimal income tax in the more general case where there can be a number of different marginal rates of income tax and where we wish to find the best marginal rate schedule. Once again we start with a society of two persons, then go on to three persons and finally indicate in general terms what happens with large numbers.

(1) A two-person society

It is instructive to proceed by posing the question, Is the present income tax system optimal? We undertake the analysis for a hypothetical two-person economy with the aid of Figure 20.3. The two people are assumed to have the same preferences for income (consumption) and leisure. These preferences are assumed to be fully revealed to the authorities. However, as a result of differences in ability Mr High has a relatively high wage rate while the other person, Mr Low, has a relatively low wage rate. In each case their gross wage is given by the slope of the line AB. It is assumed that there is a progressive income tax structure which has low marginal tax rates on low incomes and steadily rising marginal tax rates as incomes rise so that with very high incomes the marginal tax rate is approaching 100 per cent. Because of this progressive tax structure both individuals face an after-tax budget constraint, AC, which curves away from AB as hours and income increase, i.e. as we move to the left from A. Given their budget constraints and their preferences, they are in equilibrium at E_0^L and E_0^H. Several features of this initial equilibrium are worth noting. The distribution of gross and net incomes is given by GY_0^L and GY_0^H and by NY_0^L and NY_0^H respectively. The total income of society is

$$GDP = GY_0^L + GY_0^H.$$

It may be noted that GDP is determined entirely by the supply of labour in this model. Disposable income of society is

$$DY = GDP - T = NY_0^L + NY_0^H.$$

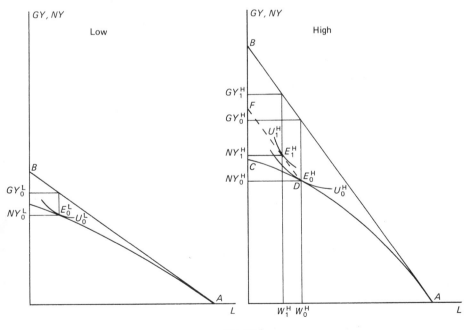

Fig. 20.3

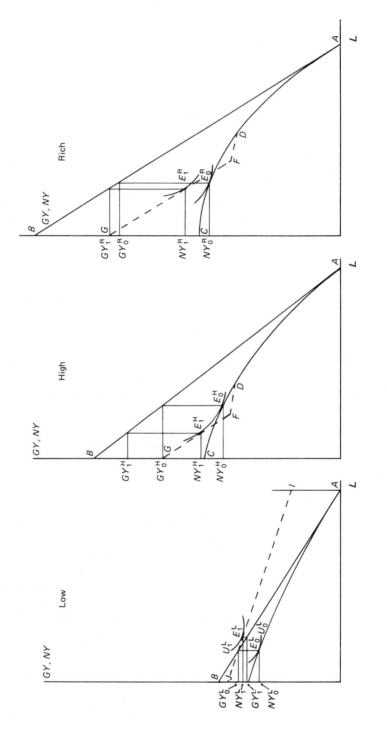

Fig. 20.4

Total tax revenue of the government is

$$T = T^L + T^H = GY_0^L - NY_0^L + GY_0^H - NY_0^H = GDP - DY.$$

If we give equal weight to High's and Low's welfare, total welfare of society is

$$U = U_0^H + U_0^L$$

and the distribution of welfare is given the relative position of U_0^L and U_0^H. Alternatively, society's welfare might be a weighted average of the welfare of its members if, for example, we wished to put more emphasis on the welfare of those who, like Low, are least well off.

One of the most robust findings of the work in optimal taxation is that marginal tax rates on the highest income should be zero. We can explain the reasoning behind this surprising conclusion by setting Mr High's marginal tax rate equal to zero for any increases in his income beyond his present income level of GY_0^H. High's post-tax budget constraint now becomes ADF with the new segment DF shown as a broken line. It should be noted that with a zero marginal tax rate the new segment DF is parallel to AB; i.e. the gross and net marginal wage rates are equal. It should also be noted High's total tax liability will be the same at any point on DF as it is at E_0^H. However, with the new budget constraint ADF, High's equilibrium will be at E_1^H rather than at E_0^H. High's gross income has increased at E_1^H and GDP has risen to $GY_0^L + GY_1^H$. Disposable income has risen to $NY_0^L + NY_1^H$. Tax receipts are unchanged. Total welfare has risen to $U_0^L + U_1^H$. Using Pareto's criteria we have a clear improvement in welfare. However, only High's welfare has increased and the distribution of gross income, of net income, and of welfare have all become more unequal. Whether society would regard this as an improved position would depend on society's views about the distribution of income and of welfare. If society places no weight or negative weight on High's welfare and great weight on Low's welfare then it would not be attracted to a Pareto improvement that increased inequality.

Lowering High's marginal tax rate to zero would be more attractive to most people if it were accompanied by more rather than less equality. It emerges that this is possible as we now illustrate with reference to Figure 20.4. The reader should ignore the right-hand panel of this figure for the time being. Suppose that we adopt the tax schedule that gives High the budget constraint $ADFG$. This new tax schedule also has a zero rate tax band, and it has been carefully constructed so as to leave High on his original indifference curve but to move him along this indifference curve to E_1^H. High's welfare is unaffected but he is now being induced to work more and as a result both his gross and his net income have risen. It is worth observing that at this stage in the process total welfare and its distribution are unaffected, but the distribution of both gross and net income is less equal. However, it is most unlikely that society would stop at this stage because one of the results of the new tax schedule has been to raise tax receipts. Part of High's extra gross income has been taken by the government. The extra tax revenue can be seen on the diagram as

$$(GY_1^H - NY_1^H) > (GY_0^H - NY_0^H).$$

This higher tax revenue could be used in a variety of ways to increase welfare. For example it could be used to finance a higher level of expenditure on public goods. Another way the extra tax revenue could be used is to finance a new means-tested benefit that Low could qualify for. We have seen (in Chapter 15) that a means-tested benefit for Low may raise his net income and his welfare, but will reduce his hours of work. Suppose a NIT is chosen such that Low's budget constraint becomes the broken line IJ (High's budget constraint would also change, but in a part that would not affect his equilibrium, and to keep the diagram simple this change is not shown). Low moves to E_1^L where he will pay no positive tax and will receive negative tax (a handout) of $NY_1^L - GY_1^L$. If the NIT has been calculated in a revenue-neutral way the changes in the net tax positions of High and Low will just cancel out. On Pareto's criterion welfare has again increased as Low is better off and High is no worse off. However, if society wishes a more equal distribution of welfare this second alternative will be preferred to the first. Let us look at what happens to the other variables as the figure is drawn. GDP will increase as the increase in High's gross income exceeds the decrease in Low's gross income. The distribution of gross income will become less equal in the example because High's gross income will rise as he works more and Low's gross income will fall as he works less. Both High and Low have a rise in disposable income (consumption), but without more information we cannot say what would happen to the distribution of net income (as the diagram is drawn percentile shares remain about the same).

This second alternative tax schedule has a higher total welfare than the original schedule and a more equal distribution as well. Using total welfare as a criteria we can recommend this new schedule over the original schedule, and with a more equal distribution of welfare we can recommend the new schedule over the first alternative schedule. Welfare has clearly increased, and yet the field is littered with sacred cows that have been slaughtered. The highest marginal tax rate has been cut to zero. The distribution of gross incomes is less equal and we do not know what has happened to the distribution of net income. As we will see below, life becomes more complex when we bring in more people. However, provided that there is a finite upper limit to the highest wage rate, the conclusion about the zero marginal tax rate remains. We return to the policy implications of this statement later. Before introducing further complications we would like to reiterate the importance of society's views about the distribution of welfare. If an equal distribution is unimportant then our first alternative might be preferable to our second and might result in a larger increase in total welfare.

We should also look at the significance of the elasticity of labour supply. This is perhaps most easily shown with our second alternative shown in Figure 20.4. If the substitution effect and, in particular, the elasticity of substitution is large, the indifference curve will be quite flat. In this case the change in High's budget constraint will cause him to increase work by a large amount which will increase both his gross and net incomes by large amounts and will also provide a lot more revenue for the government to use for redistribution (or some other purpose). On the other hand, if the elasticity of substitution is small the indifference curve would be much more sharply curved and the change in the budget constraint would have less effect. In the extreme case, if the elasticities of substitution were zero the indifference curve would be L-shaped and an alteration in the slope of the budget constraint would have no effect on High's behaviour. Thus the strength of the argument for low marginal tax rates rises as the elasticity of substitution rises.

(2) A three-person society

With our two-person society we were able to assume away a problem that we must now face up to. The problem is that reducing marginal rate of tax on moderately high-income people may cause even richer people to pay too little tax. We can illustrate how this problem may arise by introducing a third person into our society. This third person is assumed to have a wage rate even higher than Mr High's and we will call this man Mr Rich; and we illustrate his budget constraint in the right panel of Figure 20.4. With the original unimproved tax system, Rich's budget constraint is AC and Rich is in equilibrium at E_0^R (with High and Low at E_0^H and E_0^L). As in the two-person society we can induce High to work more and pay more tax by altering the tax system so that High's budget constraint becomes $ADFG$. So far nothing has changed. However, if we alter High's tax schedule we must alter Rich's tax schedule as well. Rich's budget constraint now becomes $ADFG$ and he moves to a new equilibrium at E_1^R.

The new zero rate band starts considerably below Rich's original income level. The reason for this is that Rich's original income level (E_0^R) is considerably higher than High's original income (E_0^H). When Rich moves to his new equilibrium at E_1^R he will pay less tax than previously $(GY_1^R - NY_1^R) < (GY_0^R - NY_0^R)$. Rich has moved to a higher indifference curve but he pays less tax. There are now two conflicting forces operating on government revenue. High pays more tax and Rich pays less tax, so that total tax receipts might either rise or fall. Even if they rise, however, the net increase in the three-person case will be less than in the two-person case, so that the amount available for redistribution will be less.

(3) Multi-person societies

We now consider the effects of introducing more people. If there were several people like High and only one like Rich it is more likely that total tax receipts would rise which would make greater redistribution possible. More generally the underlying principle is that the distribution of wage rates is important. If at any point in the distribution there are only a few people with higher wage rates, then reducing marginal tax rates is more likely to increase revenue.

While there is a risk of loss of tax revenue from reducing marginal tax rates except for the very highest income levels, J. K. Seade has shown that careful reconstruction of a tax schedule can increase everyone's welfare, induce them to earn more and preserve government tax revenue if the current tax schedule has a positive marginal rate at the top. We illustrate Seade's argument with the aid of Figure 20.5. Our exposition of the argument is confined to High and Rich but the principle applies to any number of persons throughout the income (wage rate) range.

The existing tax schedule results in the budget constraints AC and High and Rich are in equilibrium at E_0^H and E_0^R. It is important to the argument to note that if High and Rich are induced to move out along the lines FD they will (1) continue to pay the same amount of tax, as FD is parallel to AB; (2) work more; and (3) have higher welfare. If we permitted High and Rich to move to their preferred positions along the line FD, High would choose E_1^H and Rich would choose E_*^R. It should be apparent from our earlier discussion that if we permit High to go to E_1^R Rich will pay too little tax. We must therefore proceed in a

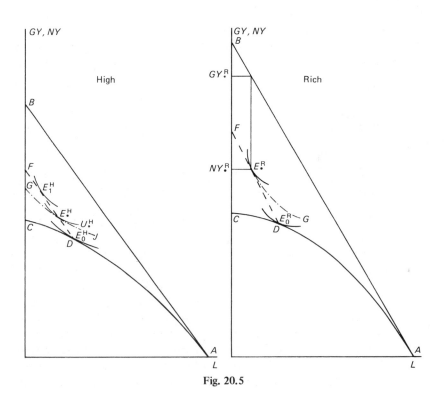

Fig. 20.5

different manner. We can permit Rich to reach E_*^R by starting the zero marginal rate band at a gross income of GY_*^R. A tax schedule that shifted the upper part of Rich's budget constraint to FG would achieve this. Now turning our attention to High, it is clear that he will have to face a positive marginal rate of tax as his income is below the starting point of the zero marginal rate band. If we move High to E_*^H, which lies on FD, he will be better off, work more, and pay the same tax. To move High to E_*^H we require a tax schedule that will give High a budget constraint that is tangent to U_*^H at E_*^H. The line GJ shows a segment of such a budget constraint. In the multi-person case we can use the same principle to construct complete tax schedules that make everyone better off. This represents a considerable extension of the principle that marginal taxes should fall for high incomes. The earlier argument strictly requires only that one single person (with the highest wage rate) pays a zero marginal rate of tax, which could imply very high marginal rates for all but one person. It should now be clear that marginal tax rates should be falling over a rather wider range.

The arguments just presented suggest that marginal rates of tax should fall towards zero at high income levels and similar arguments have been advanced, e.g. by Seade, to suggest that marginal tax rates should also fall towards zero at the bottom. These arguments are consistent with results obtained by Mirrlees and Stern. While there are exceptions,[4] it appears that if one were to draw a graph with marginal tax rates on the vertical axis and incomes on the horizontal axis, the graph of optimal marginal rates would look something like an upside-down U. Mirrlees has summarised the conclusion from the literature about the shape of this schedule as follows:

(1) Marginal tax rates are greater, the less elastic is labour supply. (The effect of migration propensities is, of course, similar.) . . .
(2) Marginal tax rates are greater, the more unequal is the distribution of income-earning capacity within the population.
(3) Marginal tax rates are greater, but chiefly in the middle- and lower-income ranges, the more weight is given to the utility of low-utility households relative to others.
(4) Marginal tax rates are greater, but chiefly in the middle- and low-income ranges, the greater is the government revenue to be raised from the population.
(5) In many, but not all, cases, marginal tax rates should be higher for the middle-income groups.[5, 6]

If it is indeed correct that an optimum schedule of marginal income tax rates would look like an upside-down U, this is in sharp contrast to the current UK schedule. As we saw in Chapter 14 British marginal income tax rates start at zero and rise to 60 per cent for earned income. However, for low incomes the tax/transfer system as a whole includes means-tested benefits and negative income taxes. It was pointed out in Chapter 15 that the implicit tax rates on these transfers are very high for low incomes (the poverty trap) (see Table 15.4). Taking the tax/transfer system as a whole a graph of marginal tax rates would start, for low incomes, with high rates; drop to the basic rate of tax plus social security contribution for middle incomes then drop again to the basic rate of tax (above the upper limit for social security contribution) before rising again when higher rates of tax are paid. Thus, crudely, the present UK marginal rate schedule could be described as U-shaped. There may therefore be very dramatic differences between the optimal tax schedule and the current British tax schedule.

Should we radically reorder our tax schedule in the light of this evidence from the optimal tax literature? On the side of complacency, one could point to the special cases that may justify high marginal rates; one can point out that while zero marginal tax rates may well be required for the highest incomes, we are not in a position to say whether this band should start at £10,000 or £100,000 or £1,000,000 a year. One could also point to the omissions from the version of optimum taxation presented here. (Some but by no means all have been taken account of in the literature.) There is an underlying assumption of perfect markets. If markets are not perfect gross wage rates may not reflect marginal products, and unemployment may arise. Even with perfect markets a variety of issues are neglected. If taxes change the supply of labour to various occupations, because of narrowing of differentials, there may be changes in competitive wage rates. The analysis as usually presented assumes away problems caused by (1) uncertainty about future earnings and taxes, (2) variation in incomes over the life cycle, (3) households' (as opposed to individual) labour supply, (4) other countries' tax schedules, which may cause substantial variations in labour supply if people leave highly taxed countries, (5) payment systems that do not have a constant gross hourly wage rate (e.g. overtime payments, bonus payment, salaries), (6) variations in work effort not captured by hours (e.g. the intensity of work, the length of vacations, age of retirement). We can then add uncertainty about the precise value of the marginal rate of substitution between income and leisure – particularly among top-income people, and lack of consensus about the desirable amount of redistribution.

There are thus ample reasons why we may not wish to immediately propose tipping the present U-shaped schedule upside-down. Nevertheless, we believe that the findings from the optimal taxation approach strengthens the case for trying to reduce the very high marginal tax rates on both the lowest and the highest incomes. A constant marginal tax rate has many attractive features. It would reduce any harmful incentives at both ends of the present schedule, and it would have enormous advantages in terms of administration simplicity.

The optimal balance between taxes on goods and taxes on income

We end by briefly summarising the conclusions on the optimal balance of taxes as between taxes on goods and services and taxes on incomes as reported in recent survey papers by A. B. Atkinson and A. Sandmo.

Atkinson first considers the case where all individuals have identical preferences *and* identical wage rates. In these circumstances there is no problem of redistribution and so concern can be restricted to the efficiency aspects of taxes. When considering a choice between a uniform rate of tax on all goods and differing rates of taxes on different goods, the uniform tax rate is superior if labour supply is totally inelastic. However, if labour supply is elastic this conclusion does not hold and minimising excess burden may require differing tax rates on differing goods. This is consistent with the view expressed in Chapter 11 on the superiority of generalised taxes in the two-good case and reinforces the caveat about the dangers of generalising to the multi-good case.

If the choice of taxes is changed to a linear income tax and differentiated taxes on goods, only the linear income tax will be used and the marginal income tax rate will be set equal to zero. This converts the linear income tax into a lump sum tax or poll tax. The reason for the superiority of the poll tax is that it has no excess burden and by assumption there is no redistributive problem.

We now relax the assumption that all individuals have the same wage rate while retaining the assumption of identical preferences. This reintroduces the problem of distribution that we considered earlier in this chapter but with the complication that there is no longer a single consumption good. If the choice is between a linear income tax and differentiated sales taxes, we have the result that the linear income tax is again set as a lump sum tax with a zero marginal rate and taxes on goods and services are set with higher rates on luxuries so as to provide redistribution and to permit the revenue requirement to be met with a lower lump sum tax.

If the choice is between a nonlinear income tax and taxes on goods and services, the optimal solution is typically to rely exclusively on the income tax. Taxes on goods and services are set at zero (if positive rates are used a uniform rate on all goods and services is employed). This result depends on marginal rates of substitution between any pair of goods being independent of the amount of labour supplied. If this condition does not hold for a subset of goods, as it presumably would not in the case of goods complementary to leisure (e.g. golf clubs), then this subset of goods should be taxed at a positive uniform rate.

The conclusion from this analysis is that nonlinear income taxes are preferred on both equity and efficiency grounds to differentiated taxes on goods and services, except where there is an interaction between the supply of labour and the marginal rates of substitution between goods. However, as Atkinson points out the analysis neglects problems of administration, evasion, horizontal equity and taxpayers' preferences between taxes. Thus far we have ignored the effects on the distribution of income of government expenditure on goods and services. Work on this topic is summarised in the next chapter.

CHAPTER 21

Public Expenditures and Income Distribution

The Anglo-Saxon tradition in public finance concentrated upon the analysis of taxation until Samuelson's seminal contribution to the theory of public goods (public expenditures). This was, of course, in contrast to the Italian and the Scandinavian approaches to the subject; these schools had already developed theories of public expenditure by the late nineteenth and early twentieth centuries. One of the notable contributions to that tradition is found in the writings of Wicksell. In his discussions of budgetary reform, Wicksell recognised the necessity of discussing taxation along with public expenditures. For Wicksell, an exclusive concentration of the normative principles of taxation without recourse to expenditure considerations would result in an indeterminacy. Completeness in the discussion of the distributive justice of alternative budgets required knowledge of who benefited from public expenditures in addition to who paid taxes.

In this chapter we will take a closer look at the distribution of benefits from public expenditures and the effects of public expenditures on the distribution of income. Previous chapters have examined the incidence of the tax side of the budget. We will begin by asking the question, Why is the expenditure side of the budget important to income distribution? This will be followed up by an explicit treatment of the accounting framework used to study fiscal incidence in which we will clearly identify public expenditures. The remainder of the chapter will review alternative approaches, both theoretical and empirical, to the study of public expenditure incidence.

The reader should realise at the outset that the topic we are dealing with is in its infancy. This means that the chapter will take the form of a review of the 'current state of the art', pointing out the nature of the problems and the pitfalls involved when studying this part of the subject, rather than providing firm conclusions.

Why is the problem important?

Despite Wicksell's earlier discussions, the distribution of benefits from public expenditures has, until recently, received relatively scant attention when compared with the volume of tax incidence studies. There are many good reasons why this is the case. First, there is a lack of information on the distribution of public expenditure benefits. Second, the theory of public expenditure benefit incidence is relatively underdeveloped. Third, there has been a general lack of regard by fiscal economists that public expenditure benefits matter to the income distribution; and finally, many of the other problems arise because public outputs are difficult to measure.

We are now in a period of transition. Interest in the distribution of public expenditure benefits is now gathering momentum. Many economists are coming to the view that there is a limit to the amount of redistribution that can take place through the tax system. Bird and De Wulf put the case this way:

> Taxes cannot, of course, make poor people rich. If our main concern is with poverty as such, with the waste and misuse of human resources, and the stunted opportunities of those whose incomes fall below some minimum decent standard, remedies must come primarily through the expenditure side of the budget, either by direct public provision of such services as housing, medical care, and education, or by simple transfers of income, or through employment-creating policies. If the principal aim of redistributive policy is to level up – to make the poor better off – the main role the tax system has to play is thus the limited and essentially negative one of not making them poorer.[1]

From this rather long quotation it is readily seen that public expenditures, both exhaustive expenditures and transfer expenditures, play an important role in terms of their effects on income distribution.

Almost all government policies will have distributional consequences even if that is not their primary objective. Indeed, the distribution of the benefits of particular policies is an integral part of government's redistributive role. Thus, government will influence the size distribution of incomes through its tax policies, through subsidies on goods, means-tested benefits, transfer payments such as old age pensions, and through direct expenditures on goods and services.

The use of direct (or exhaustive) expenditures on goods and services, such as publicly provided housing, education or health services, as part of government's distribution policy was identified in Chapter 1. There it was seen that Musgrave had identified many such goods as 'merit goods', i.e. 'private' goods for individual consumption which are publicly supplied because of their high consumption externalities and also because it is important that the individual consumes an appropriate quantity of such goods. Government, therefore, takes a 'paternalistic' role in the provision of merit goods because individuals are thought to be poorly informed and hence likely to make poor consumption decisions.[2]

Public expenditures on benefits-in-kind (including merit goods) and transfer payments have become an important part of the 'social wage'.[3] Increases in the social wage, brought about by increases in public expenditures, have been used to justify the holding down of 'private wages' in the UK during the succession of incomes policies of the 1970s. Thus the benefits of public expenditures have come to play a prominent political role between the government of the day and the leaders of organised labour.

There is also a growing awareness that public expenditures do not appear to be equally distributed. They seem to depend upon where you are born and where you live. Thus, some regions of the UK economy have high *per capita* expenditures on education and health services, etc., whereas in other regions they are very much lower. This regional distribution of public expenditures raises a number of interesting questions; for example, Does the unevenness in the regional distribution of public expenditures correspond to the regional distribution of incomes? Are these areas that are in receipt of large amounts of public expenditure also regions of high social need and deprivation? Regardless of the answers to these questions, the point to note is the growing awareness of people to the distribution of public expenditures.

The relatively faster growth in transfer payments in the UK budget compared with the growth in direct public expenditures on goods and services has also caused economists to think more about the distributional impact of public expenditures. Thus it was seen in Chapter 6 (Table 6.7) that current grants had increased from 6.5 per cent of GNP in 1955 to 12.3 per cent in 1976; subsidies had risen from 2.1 per cent in 1955 to 3.1 per cent in 1976 and had reached 4.1 per cent in 1975; whereas direct expenditures on goods and services had risen from 22.9 to 28.2 per cent.

Finally, a good deal of the 'complaints' voiced about the recent rapid growth in the public sector are frequently expressed in terms of 'Who does, in fact, benefit from all of this increase in public spending?' Thus, individuals weigh up their tax costs and the benefits they perceive that they receive from public expenditures and ask if they are getting their money's worth. Now, put like that, the question is extremely crude and is ambiguous, but it is distributional questions like this that are asked and that must, therefore, be carefully sorted out if we are to answer them. Individuals may incorrectly perceive the costs and benefits of the fiscal system as they affect them. Also, the result of a redistribution of incomes will make some people worse off while it makes others better off. Some of these questions have already been discussed in Chapter 15 in the context of the negative income tax experiments in the United States.

At the end of the day, we want to know more about the *net* incidence of the budget, i.e. the effect of the budget on different classes of individuals once taxes and benefits have been accounted for and allocated. These are the questions that are increasingly being asked. In Chapter 13 it was seen that the allocation of the benefits of public expenditures, as currently carried out in the UK by the Central Statistical Office, is an extremely arbitrary process (see Table 13.7). This was shown in Chapters 14 and 15. The current state of the art of distributing the benefits of public expenditures is still in its infancy with regards to both theory and empirical research. What the remainder of this chapter will do is to consider the framework within which these questions might be asked and then present a balance sheet account of where current research in this area lies and where it is going. In this respect the present chapter should be read keeping in mind the points made about optimal public expenditure in Chapter 19.

Throughout the chapter we will make reference to the incidence of the effects of taxes and public expenditures. We will also talk about the distribution of these effects. Clearly there are problems involved in defining the relevant group over which the distribution is considered; e.g., is it the distribution of benefits over individuals or over households, and is it the distribution of benefits over income classes, regions, the age of the individual etc.? These problems of definition and identification have already been examined in earlier chapters. For present purposes, the incidence, or the distribution of public expenditure benefits, will be loosely regarded as relating to a distribution over individual incomes.

A budget incidence accounting framework

Accounting for and measuring the distribution of the benefits of public expenditures is an exercise in fiscal incidence. That is, we can imagine that there was a pre-budget distribution of personal incomes over income groups (individuals or households). The taxes and the public expenditures are then allocated to income groups and the pre-budget and post-budget income distributions are compared.

This is the kind of exercise that the CSO publishes each year (see Chapter 13 above, especially Table 13.7). The analysis used in such an exercise is partial and static. That is, it does not consider all the repercussions of the budget changes in terms of the redistribution of income resulting from changes in relative factor rewards and relative product prices. For example, VAT is allocated to income classes on the assumption that it is paid by firms. The immediate questions that arise, therefore, are what is the appropriate methodology or process that should be used when allocating taxes and public expenditures, and what methods should be used when comparing the pre- and post-budget distributions?

The distribution and incidence of taxes has already been considered in earlier chapters along with an examination of statistical measures such as the Gini coefficient which enable a comparison to be made between pre- and post-budget distributions.[4] The immediate problem is to consider the difficulties that public expenditures produce. The problem can be defined in the following way:

$$\Delta Y = Y^1 + G^1 - Y^0$$

where:

ΔY = change in real income;

Y^1 = private real income given the existence of government;

G^1 = the real income equivalent of the benefits of public expenditures;

Y^0 = real income in the absence of government.

What fiscal incidence studies attempt to measure, therefore, is ΔY. A finer breakdown of public expenditures and taxes would be useful in order to identify the elements of the problem. Thus,

$$\sum_{i=1}^{m} y_i^0 + \sum_1^m (g_i^1 + g_i^c) - \sum_1^m (t_i^d + t_i^e) \equiv \sum_1^m y_i^p$$

where:

m = number of income groups
y_i^0 = original pre-budget income;
y^p = post budget income;
g_i^1 = transfer payments
g^c = expenditures on goods and services $g_i^c = g_i^s + g_i^p$;
    i.e. g_i^s = specific services, e.g. health, and g_i^p = indivisible services,
    e.g. defence;
t_i^d = taxes on incomes;
t_i^e = taxes on goods and services (less subsidies).

That is, g_i^s can be thought of as 'merit goods' or private goods which are publicly supplied and g_i^p are public goods.

The budget is assumed to balance, i.e.

$$\sum (g_i^1 + g_i^c) - \sum (t_i^d + t_i^e) = 0.$$

These accounting identities, therefore, summarise the formal budget incidence studies that are normally carried out. In performing such calculations the following problems emerge: What levels of government are to be covered? Should we treat government capital expenditure as a benefit to individuals in the year in which it occurs? How do we evaluate pure public goods? Can we find a distribution of expenditure that will reflect the distribution of benefits of publicly provided goods? and How can we convert these benefits into income equivalents?

In attempting to come to grips with some of these questions it is useful to separate out two different approaches. We will call the first 'public expenditure incidence' and the second 'benefit incidence'. These two approaches as we will see deal with different aspects of the problem and, therefore, help to keep separate the many issues that are involved.

Public expenditure incidence

The CSO budget incidence studies are static and partial. They therefore fail to account for the repercussions of the budget throughout the rest of the economy. A wider general equilibrium approach, like that of the Harberger model which was discussed in relation to tax incidence in Chapter 11, is also appropriate when examining the incidence of public expenditures.

If public and private sector expenditure patterns differ, then if purchasing power is transmitted from the private sector to the public sector following a budget change, relative prices in the economy are likely to change. That is to say, the relative prices of factors of production and the relative prices of final consumption and production goods will change. Changes in these relative prices will affect individuals directly through changes in factor incomes and indirectly through changes in the prices of consumption goods. Thus the public expenditure side of the budget will have an effect upon the distribution of incomes.[5]

Since the Harberger model was set out in considerable detail in Chapter 11 it is only necessary to summarise the essential features of the analysis that are of particular relevance to the treatment of the incidence of public expenditures. As in tax incidence analysis, the key determinants of public expenditure incidence are:

(1) the mobility of factors of production between industries;
(2) the ease of factor substitution in each industry;
(3) the price and income elasticities of demand for goods;
(4) the elasticity of substitution in production;
(5) the relative factor intensities in the industries;
(6) the degree of complementarity or substitutability; between publicly and privately provided goods;
(7) differences in the propensities of different households to consume various goods;
(8) differences in the factor endowments of households;
(9) the supply elasticity of products.

A simple example can be used to illustrate how a complete general equilibrium model might analyse the incidence following a change in public expenditures. Take first of all an increase in public sector transfers to the elderly in society. The incomes of the elderly increase following the receipt of the transfer, whereas there is a fall in the incomes of those who pay the taxes to finance the transfers. The formal incidence study of the CSO would record these changes as in Table 13.7 and stop there. But the average (or the marginal) propensity to consume of those who paid the tax is unlikely to be the same as those who receive the benefit of the public expenditure transfer. This change in consumption patterns in the economy will then change relative prices and hence the income distribution will be further changed as a result of the budget. The extent of the change in income distribution depends upon the change in relative prices, which in turn depends upon the values of the parameters of the system as outlined above.

Thus it can be seen from the above example that the post-budget changes in income distribution that are calculated by the CSO give only a part of the picture. The secondary effects of the budget are not shown. This is of course not to be interpreted as a criticism of CSO practice. It is an attempt to show the limitations of such statistics and therefore the constraints that must be placed on inferences drawn from the data. To attempt to compute the full general equilibrium effects of the public expenditure side of the budget would almost be an impossible task at this moment in time. Our knowledge of the values of many of the key parameters of the system is scant as too is our knowledge of many of the economic relationships between parts of the system.

Public expenditures can be thought to influence income distribution not so much through changes in relative prices but through employment creation. This is, of course, the standard Keynesian notion of the employment multiplier effect of public works programmes. For a balanced budget to have employment-creating effects it is necessary to assume the existence of unemployment prior to the introduction of the budget. The effects of such employment-creating public expenditure programmes on income distribution would require us to know something about pre- and post-unemployment incomes. Since unemployment is unevenly spread over regions of an economy, employment creation will also affect the regional distribution of incomes.

It is generally assumed in all budget incidence studies that the government's budget is balanced. In practice, however, we know that this is seldom the case. Chapter 6 showed that the public sector borrowing requirement for the UK was in excess of 10 per cent of GNP for part of the 1970s. Unbalanced budgets can have a number of possible effects, e.g. increased inflation, deterioration in the balance of payments, and even an increase in unemployment. Obviously effects such as inflation will affect different groups in different ways. However, to attribute these effects to an unbalanced budget, let alone measure their consequences for income distribution, would be a Herculean task! Nevertheless, it is certainly worth while bearing such points in mind.

(1) Public expenditure incidence and cost–benefit analysis

At this stage it is convenient to relate the discussion of public expenditure incidence to cost-benefit analysis. It will be recalled from our discussions in Chapter 8 that the objective of cost–benefit analysis was to ensure that the public sector allocated scarce resources efficiently to competing public sector projects. In the concluding section to Chapter 8 attention was drawn to the possibility of there being objectives other than the efficiency one. For example, some public sector investment programmes might be considered to serve distributional objectives rather than efficiency objectives. In other instances the decision-maker would have to make a choice as to where the project lay on the efficiency/distribution trade-off. Thus, Eckstein wrote in 1961,

> One of the criteria on which a project must be judged and which benefit cost analysis disregards altogether, is the redistribution of income which a project brings about.[6]

Haveman[7] examined the decision criteria used on a number of water resource projects. During the year 1960 150 projects were authorised; 29 received appropriations and of the 29, 11 had lower benefit–cost ratios than would have been considered to be efficient. He concluded that these projects were chosen on distributional criteria and because they were likely to create employment and generate incomes in specific regions.

Not all economists, however, would agree that distribution criteria should be taken into account when making public expenditure decisions. Thus Harberger, in a recent essay, pointed out,

> any programme or project that is subjected to applied welfare economic analysis is likely to have characteristics upon which the economist is not professionally qualified to check out the opinion of another. These elements which surely include the income distribution ... aspects ... may be exceedingly important ... but they are not a part of expertise that distinguishes the professional economist from the rest of humanity ... economists should probably participate more rather than less in the public discussion of such matters, but hopefully in a context that recognises the extra-professional nature of their intervention.[8]

Mishan[9] also holds similar views to Harberger's. However, we must take care how we interpret such positions. The economist's views on where society should lie on the equity – efficiency trade-off should not be regarded as having any more weight than any other individual's. However, the economist does have a rational framework within which to discuss and to measure the income distribution effects of public expenditures and other aspects of public policies, and that should not be ignored. If a decision-maker wants to know the distributional effects of any particular piece of policy or any specific public sector investment project, then who should he turn to to answer such a question? The social philosopher may advise him on how best to formulate his question, but the economist has probably the best framework within which to answer it.

The distributional considerations that are of interest to CBA are, therefore, the effects of the public expenditure programme on the relative prices of factors and final outputs. This is, it is interested to know the primary and the secondary incidence of public expenditures. It will also be recalled from Chapter 8 that pecuniary externalities were excluded from the efficiency calculation. Clearly, a discussion of the incidence of the public expenditures of a project must take pecuniary externalities into account because pecuniary externalities are, by their nature, redistributive.

Discussions of the distributional effects of public policies take a much wider view than that originally suggested by Prest and Turvey in their discussion of the scope of CBA.[10] Moreover, this widening of the scope of CBA moves it from the sphere of partial equilibrium analysis into that of general equilibrium analysis.

The distributional effects of public expenditure programmes rather than efficiency considerations may on occasions weigh heavily in the objective function of the political decision-maker.

This is especially true in the case of Downsian vote-maximising politicians. Thus, short-term distributional objectives may come into conflict with longer-term efficiency and distributional objectives. For example, decisions by the UK government to continue to subsidise inefficient plants in the British Steel Corporation and to give support to British Leyland depend, to a great extent, upon whether or not it can accept the political damage (in terms of votes lost) that will follow if withdrawing aid to these industries results in massive unemployment. The problem is particularly acute if the unemployment increases in those regions that coincide with the constituency boundaries of senior politicians in the Cabinet.

Benefit incidence

The public expenditure incidence studies looked at the consequences for relative prices and the distribution of incomes following a change in public expenditures. However, the usual means of approaching the questions of the impact of public expenditures on income distribution would be to ask what is the distribution of the benefits of public programmes/services? Which groups in society gain most from the benefits of public services and how does this distribution vary gross and net of tax payments?

It might be possible (if all conceptual and measurement problems were overcome) to make such a calculation for *total* public expenditures. However, from the point of view of policy analysis and decision-making, it would be preferable to know the distributional implications of specific public services/programmes.

Public expenditures, in the accounting framework set out above, were divided between (g^1) transfer payments and (g^c) expenditures on goods and services. Expenditures on goods and services were then subdivided between (g^s) specific services such as education or health services and (g^p) indivisible services, i.e. 'merit goods' such as pure public goods or near public goods like defence. In this section we will consider, in turn, the problems of valuing and allocating to income classes the benefits obtained from these different categories of public expenditures.

First, however, we must consider in more detail how we get from a change in the benefits of public expenditures to a change in personal incomes and thus to a change in the distribution of incomes. It will be recalled that fiscal incidence analysis examines the following problem:

$$\Delta Y = Y^1 + G^1 - Y^0$$

(see above for a definition of the symbols used).

In this simple accounting framework the change in real incomes (ΔY) is a function of the change in the real *income equivalent* (G^1) of the benefits of public expenditures. What is required, therefore, is to spell out the nature of the transformation relationship between the benefits of the service and its income equivalent.

Each individual (i) has a utility function in private goods (X) and publicly provided goods (G). i.e.:

$$U^i = \Phi^i(X, G).$$

An increase in the volume of G results in an increase in utility (i.e. benefits). Thus the problem can be stated as:

$$\Delta U = \lambda \times \text{income equivalent}$$

where λ = marginal utility of income. Thus to obtain a measure of the income equivalent of the benefits of the change in G we need to have a measure of ΔU and λ. Moreover, we need to know the value of λ for different groups of individuals. Introspective beliefs generally assume that λ for lower-income groups is greater than for higher-income groups. We will discuss empirical estimates of λ later in the chapter.

The change in utility can be thought of as being equivalent to a change in the area under the individual's demand curve.

Thus, using consumer surplus analysis, the change in utility due to a change in the price of the kth good (*ceteris paribus*) can be written as:[11]

$$dU = (-x^k \, dp^k).$$

This is the change in the area under the demand curve and could be measured if price changes were sufficiently small and if the *ceteris paribus* assumptions of this partial equilibrium approach were assumed to occur in practice. In the event of a breakdown in these assumptions, a general equilibrium approach would be necessary. This is reviewed below. Another important point to note about this model is that, since the demand curve depends upon incomes, then the change in utility measured by $(-x^k \, dp^k)$ is not independent of the initial distribution of income.

There are a number of problems in applying this framework. The majority of public sector goods and services are not sold; therefore, there are no market prices to observe. Also, public sector outputs are illusive magnitudes and therefore difficult to measure. This means, once again, that the only data that the analyst has readily available at his disposal are public expenditure data, i.e. the costs of providing public services. The CSO study, along with those carried out by Cartter[12] and Gillespie,[13] therefore, allocate the benefits from public services on the basis of costs or expenditures using *ad hoc* assumptions. For example, expenditures may be apportioned between socioeconomic groupings of the population on the basis of *per capita* expenditures or in proportion to incomes. In some studies the per student cost of education, for example, would be allocated to families depending on the number of children in the family. In this case the assumed benefits of specific services are allocated to users.

Clearly, allocation of benefits in this *ad hoc* way does not accord with the framework of income equivalence. Public expenditures or costs do not measure benefits. The reasons for this are now explained.

(1) Transfer payments (g^1) and benefit incidence

Generally in the empirical studies of benefit incidence the full value of transfer payments have been apportioned to those in receipt of them. Transfer payments are a source of income, and so this means of allocation would appear to be correct; however, it ignores the effects that the transfer payment has upon the individual's behaviour. As we saw in Chapter 14, an increase in transfer payments may result in a reduction in the amount of labour supplied; therefore, the benefit of the transfer should be calculated as the value of the transfer payment plus the value of any increased leisure time and the value of the income that would have been earned in the absence of the transfer. Given the problem of making this calculation, transfer payments are allocated to their recipients on an expenditure basis. Money transfers to individuals are negative direct taxes and subsidies are negative indirect taxes.

(2) Public expenditures on goods and services (g^c) and benefit incidence

In the case of expenditures on goods and services, individuals may not measure the benefits of these services as being worth the value of the inputs (i.e. costs). There are a number of reasons why this may arise.

The production function used to produce the service may be non-convex, displaying decreasing costs; i.e., average cost lies above marginal cost. The price that the marginal consumer would be willing to pay for the output is reflected in marginal cost rather than average cost, which implies that using public expenditures or costs will not be a true reflection of the value of the benefits of the service to the consumer. The consumer's valuation of benefits will lie somewhere below the costs of provision. Likewise, there may be an element of X-inefficiency in the production of the good. Once again, the consumer's valuation of the benefits will lie below the costs of provision.

The public service may also possess high consumption externalities. If the consumer values such external economies, the value of the benefits received would exceed the costs of provision as reflected in public expenditures. Reversing the argument, for external diseconomies, implies that in other instances the valuation placed on the benefits is less than the costs of provision.

It is certainly the case that market prices do not necessarily reflect the benefits of consumption externalities and so by insisting upon including them in the valuation of public services may be regarded by some as going too far. But surely this is more a revelation of a shortcoming in our treatment of private sector benefits in income distribution studies. A correct valuation procedure for both public and private goods is required rather than ignoring the problem for both classes of goods.

The valuation of the benefits for one particular set of direct expenditures on goods and services that causes problems is that of public goods and publicly provided indivisible goods, e.g. defence, law and order, etc. Gillespie *et al.* deal with these goods by distributing expenditures as follows:

(1) per family;
(2) by income;
(3) by capital income; and
(4) by disposable income.

Allocating public expenditures for police services on a *per capita* basis assumes that all individuals benefit equally from the service. But as we saw in Chapter 3, this statement would be true only if all individuals had identical demand curves for these services (i.e., for example, identical utility functions and identical incomes). In so far as individuals have different demand curves, then as 'quantity-takers' each individual has a 'personalised price' that he is willing to pay for the quantity provided.

Thus in order to calculate the benefits received from the consumption of public goods or indivisible publicly provided goods, we would need to know much more about individual utility functions. This would seem to be an impossible task and to be regarded as an impasse for empirical analysis. However, Aaron and McGuire[14] have made an interesting attempt to overcome some of these difficulties.

(3) Aaron and McGuire's analysis

In contrast to the earlier studies outlined briefly in the previous section, which allocated the benefits of direct public expenditures on goods and services in an *ad hoc* fashion, Aaron and McGuire (A–McG) have developed an approach based upon an explicit formation of the utility function. Their approach, which shows that the benefit incidence results depend upon the specific assumptions made about the values of the individual's utility function, can be stated as follows: The benefits of pure public goods should be allocated in proportion to the reciprocal of the household's marginal utility of income. Thus those studies that allocate the benefits of public services on a *per capita* cost of service basis implicitly assume that the marginal utility of income is constant across all income classes.

The Aaron and McGuire allocation rule is, therefore, formally stated as

$$Y_i^p = \frac{Y^p}{\lambda_i} \text{ such that } \lambda_i = \frac{1}{(Y_i^d + Y_i^s)^\Phi}$$

where $Y_i^p \equiv$ pure public good income of household i; $Y^p \equiv$ total public good income;

$\lambda_i \equiv$ marginal utility of income of household i; $Y_i^d \equiv$ disposable income (i.e. net cash income including transfers) of household i; $Y_i^s \equiv$ non-cash income provided by public sector via specific or 'merit goods' such as health, education etc.

In other words, once the benefits of public expenditures on transfer payments and specific goods are allocated, this gives a post-budget income equivalent of $(Y_i^d + Y_i^s)$. The remaining public expenditures represent expenditures on public goods and indivisible services. The total income equivalent of these public expenditures is Y_p, which is allocated to households in proportion to the inverse of the household's marginal utility of income.

The derivation of the A–McG allocation rule would be too complex. The logical foundations of the rule will, instead, be outlined so that its assumptions and limitations may be fully appreciated. Then the A–McG results will be demonstrated by means of an arithmetic example.

In deriving their rule, A–McG make the following assumptions.

(1) The population is divided into income classes. The utility functions for each individual in income class k are all assumed to be identical, so that the marginal utility function for all members of that class are identical.

(2) Each individual's utility function is additively separable in private goods and public goods; i.e. public goods and private goods are independent, there are no complementarities of substitutions between the two broad categories of goods; i.e.,

$$U_i = U_i^p(P) + U_i^G(G)$$

where $P \equiv$ vector of private goods; $G \equiv$ vector of public goods and
$\qquad U_i \equiv$ utility function of ith individual.

(3) the allocation of public goods is assumed to be Pareto-efficient and $AC = MC$; hence $\Sigma MRS_i = MC$.

Having set out the assumptions on which the rule is based, we will now examine its properties by means of a simple example.[15] Assume a two-person economy made up of individuals A and B, who have respectively incomes equal to £1000 and £2000. Both individuals have the same separable utility function for public and private goods and G_1 units of the public good are provided.

Both A and B will, by definition, consume the same volume of the public good. However, because their incomes differ, their valuations, or willingness to pay, for the same amount of the public good will be different. (The reader who is unfamiliar with this result should refer back to Chapter 3).

Let the marginal rates of substitution between public and private goods for A and B be given as MRS^A and MRS^B respectively. It will be recalled from assumption (3) above that public goods are allocated Pareto-efficiently, which means that

$$(MRS^A)(G_1) + (MRS^B)(G_1) = E \qquad\qquad (21.1)$$

where E is the public expenditure on G_1 units of the public good. That is, the marginal rates of substitution are used as 'prices' to evaluate the public good; since $AC = MC$ the left-hand side of the equation represents total willingness to pay by A and B and that equals the total cost or expenditure (E) of providing G_1 units of the public good.

If the individual utility functions are additive and identical, then;

$$\frac{\delta U^A}{\delta G_1} = \frac{\delta U^B}{\delta G_1} = C \qquad \text{where } C = \text{a constant.} \qquad (21.2)$$

$$\frac{MRS^A}{MRS^B} = \frac{\delta U^A/\delta G_1}{\lambda^A} \div \frac{\delta U^B/\delta G_1}{\lambda^B} \qquad (21.3)$$

(recall that λ^A and λ^B are the marginal utilities of incomes of A and B respectively). Hence, after rearranging equation (21.3),

$$\lambda^A \cdot MRS^A = \lambda^B \cdot MRS^B = C. \qquad (21.4)$$

Therefore

$$MRS^A = \frac{C}{\lambda^A} \qquad (21.5)$$

and

$$MRS^B = \frac{C}{\lambda^B}. \qquad (21.6)$$

Substituting equations (21.5) and (21.6) back into equation (21.1) gives;

$$C\left(\frac{G_1}{\lambda^A} + \frac{G_1}{\lambda^B}\right) = E. \qquad (21.7)$$

What equation (21.7) says is that the money values (or benefits) of the public good are allocated to individuals in inverse proportion to their marginal utility of income. Thus if we know the individual utility functions and the total money outlay on the public good (E), then its money value can be allocated to individuals by income class.

Consider now the following example. Let public expenditure on a public or indivisibly publicly supplied good equal £500. There are two individuals consuming the food with incomes of £1000 and £2000 respectively. Each individual, furthermore, has an identical utility function, which is separable in public and private goods. As we have shown, the individual valuations of the public good depend upon the precise nature of the utility functions. In order to see what happens with different assumption of the utility functions, assume three different utility functions with the following implicit marginal utilities of income:

(1) $\lambda = K$
(2) $\lambda = K/Y$
(3) $\lambda = K/Y^2$
(where $Y \equiv$ income and $K \equiv$ a constant)

By substituting these values of λ into equation (21.7) the value of the £500 spent on the public good can be calculated for the two individuals. These are shown in Table 21.1. It can be seen that under assumption (1), i.e. that the marginal utility of income is constant, the benefits are equal for the two individuals. Under assumption (2) the marginal utility of income falls directly in proportion with income and the marginal utility of income for the person with income of £2000 is half that for the person with £1000 income. Thus, in that case the money value of the benefits for the person with £2000 income is twice that for the person with £1000 income. Under assumption (3) the money value of the benefits from the public good is four times greater for the person with income of £2000 compared with the person with £1000.

Table 21.1 Allocation of benefits from public goods under different assumptions of the utility function

	Benefits		
Income of individuals	Assumption (a) $\lambda = K$	Assumption (b) $\lambda = K/Y$	Assumption (c) $\lambda = K/Y^2$
£	£	£	£
1000	250.00	166.67	100.00
2000	250.00	333.34	400.00

From this simple numerical example it can be seen, as A–McG demonstrated, that the allocation of benefits from public goods across income classes is very sensitive to the form of the utility function that is implicitly (as in the case of the CSO and Gillespie type studies) or explicitly chosen.[16]

The consequences of the allocation rules used in these exercises for imputing the values of the benefits from public goods can be quite startling in terms of our interpretation of whether or not the budget is pro-poor across income classes.

Consider once again Table 13.7 above. The benefits of public expenditures have been allocated in such a way that it is implicitly assumed that the marginal utility of income is identical for all individuals. Thus it follows (as in Table 21.1) that this assumption allocates larger money values to lower income groups than would be the case under alternative assumptions of the utility function. The total incidence of the budget will appear more 'pro-poor' under assumptions of a constant marginal utility of income than it would otherwise using different assumptions.

Aaron and McGuire applied their methodology to the distribution of income in the United States for 1961 and compared their results with those of the 'orthodox' study carried out by the Tax Foundation for the same year, which allocated indivisible expenditures on a per family basis. The flavour of the A-McG results in comparison with those of the Tax Foundation are presented in Table 21.2.

Table 21.2   Net income distribution, 1961

	Net gain or loss (−) per family		
Money income class	*Under $2000*	*$5000 to $5999*	*$15000 and over*
I Allocation NE[a]	$	$	$
1 Tax foundation	1493	125	−10,632
2 $(U = A \log Y)^a$	968	113	−8682
3 $(U = E − C/Y)^c$	691	−359	1790
II Allocation E[b]			
1 Tax foundation	1427	115	−10,048
2 $(U = A \log Y)$	640	100	−7019
3 $(U = E − C/Y)$	313	−567	8373

Notes: [a] Allocation NE includes no allowances for external benefits of specific goods.
          [b] Allocation E assumes the following proportions of the cost of specific goods are allocatable as public goods: elementary and secondary education (0.7), higher education (0.5), public assistance and other welfare expenditures (0.3), labour (0.3), veterans' benefits (0.3), streets and highways (0.5), agriculture (0.5), net interest (0), social insurance (0.3).
          [c] In the utility functions, income (Y) is 'product received' income, and A, E and C are arbitrary constants whose values do not affect the results.

Source: A. Aaron and M. McGuire 'Benefits and Burdens of Government Expenditure' *Econometrica* 38, 6 (November 1970), table III, p. 919.

Thus, the Aaron and McGuire study of the US fiscal incidence shows that there is a great deal of doubt that taking account of public expenditure results in a noticeable redistribution of income from higher to lower income groups. Instead, A-McG concluded that redistribution had taken place from middle-income families to both rich and poor families!

Clearly, however, the Aaron and McGuire results firmly depend upon the utility function chosen and also the amount of indivisible expenditure identified in the total budget. Thus it would be rather nice to know more precisely the value of the marginal utility of income rather than assume alternative forms of the utility function and simulate the results. Maital[17] has looked at this problem and has made attempts at estimating the value of the marginal utility of income.

Maital used a general functional form to estimate the marginal utility of income, i.e.:

$$\lambda = KY^{-\Phi} \qquad (21.8)$$

where $K \equiv$ constant; $Y \equiv$ income and $\Phi \equiv$ the elasticity of marginal utility with respect to income and is, moreover, also under the assumption of separability in the utility function, the inverse of the elasticity of substitution between goods (σ).[18]

Maital, therefore, estimates Φ from estimated value of (σ). He finds from international estimates that σ lies in the range from 1.04 for the UK to 3.84 for the Netherlands (USA = 1.50). If Φ is greater than one then this implies that the marginal utility of income declines more than proportionately with income.

Thus, Maital's evidence on the value of λ re-inforces the A–McG result that, contrary to popular opinion when public expenditures are included government budgets do not significantly redistribute incomes, but may instead even be regressively pro-rich. Thus, the tax-transfer system would have to be substantially progressive.

Aaron and McGuire's results are, therefore, provocative. It would be a grave mistake to infer from this that the matter is resolved. This is very far from the truth. The Aaron and McGuire analysis has been a first attempt to deal with an extremely difficult problem in fiscal incidence analysis. Thanks to their efforts we are now in a very much clearer position to know what parameters of the system the results of public expenditure benefit incidence are sensitive to and where future empirical work has to be directed in order to get more accurate results.

Their results have not gone without criticism. Brennan[19] has looked more closely at the theoretical foundations of the A–McG model, and Gillespie[20] and Dodge,[21] examining Canadian data, found that the A–McG approach produced almost identical results to the traditional studies, indicating redistribution of incomes from rich to poor families.

Moreover, future empirical developments may lie in using questionnaires in an attempt to get people to reveal their preferences for public goods and services. But this approach runs into many problems of preference revelation.[22] There may also be some scope for integrating analysis of the expression of preferences via the political system.

Empirical studies of public expenditure distribution

In 1970 Stigler enunciated 'Director's Law' which essentially stated that it was the middle and upper income groups which were the main beneficiaries of public expenditure programmes. Since then a number of studies have been carried out to test the validity or otherwise of this proposition. In the UK most of this work has been carried out by LeGrand (1982). A sample of this analysis which gives the flavour of its approach is taken from LeGrand's study of education. The approach is straight forward; ask the question: 'Who uses public services?' The groups are, therefore, the principal beneficiaries of public expenditure programmes. Table 21.3 presents data on public expenditures on education allocated to each socio-economic group. It is readily seen that the upper and lower income groups are the main recipients thereby confirming Director's Law. Le Grand produces similar conclusions for other public services such as transport, housing and the health services. Readers should also consult O'Higgins (1980) and O'Higgins and Ruggles (1981). Consider now the following question; given the empirical findings of Le Grand and O'Higgins and Ruggles, what can be said about the overall amount of progressivity in the total UK fiscal system?

Table 21.3 Public expenditure on education by socio-economic group

All persons						*England and Wales 1973*
			Expenditure per person in client population: [a] *percentage of mean*			
Socio-economic group	*Primary*	*Secondary pupils under 16*	*Secondary pupils over 16*	*Further education*	*University*	*Total* [b]
Professional, employers and managers	90	88	165	149	272	128
Intermediate and junior non-manual	102	99	134	133	172	121
Skilled manual	103	105	65	99	37	89
Semi- and unskilled manual	103	103	91	43	50	84
Mean (£) = 100	139.7	206.0	65.3	17.2	16.3	70.7

Notes: [a] Client population: population in age range whence sector draws most of its pupils/students.
[b] Includes nursery education and evening institutes.

Source: Le Grand, (1982), p. 58.

Concluding remarks

Public sector economics is an exciting and rapidly developing area of inquiry. It is one of the more challenging areas of our subject presenting extremely complex questions for theoretical analysis and some of the most difficult problems for empirical solution. As the last two chapters of this book have attempted to show, many problems remain to be solved. The agenda of on-going and future theoretical and empirical work is long and is continually being added to. The subject matter that we are dealing with is such that what seems to be true about the tax system or public expenditures may or may not conform to original impressions. At the end of the day, the reliability of our knowledge about the fiscal system matters because social and economic welfare will be affected by policies that are based on either good analysis or bad analysis. Whether or not the fiscal economist has any influence on policy is not at issue. All policy-makers have a belief in some theory of the world. What we have to ensure is that good theories drive out bad, rather than bad theories driving out the good.

Notes

Chapter 1

1. This gives a very simplified account of what amounts to a major area in political theory and the reader should be aware of this. After reading Chapters 2 and 4 the reader should reconsider some of these questions: Where does the social contract originate? What purpose does it serve? Why should individuals who are by chance born into a particular society observe a social contract that they did not discuss when it was formulated? How can we change the social contract? An associated set of questions focus on individual freedom and liberty: Why should individuals surrender some of their freedom when they join a group? What particular freedoms do they surrender? What would society look like if no single person surrendered his freedom?

For the reader who is interested in pursuing these questions more deeply, an excellent introduction is to be found in the writings of James Buchanan who, as an economist, has spent a great deal of his professional career explaining the links which lie between political theory and economics: see especially, J. M. Buchanan, *The Limits of Liberty: Between Anarchy and Leviathan* (Chicago: University Press, 1975).

2. This section draws heavily from J. M. Buchanan, 'Public Finance and Public Choice', *National Tax Journal*, 28, no. 4 (December 1975).

3. For an extremely interesting and scholarly review of Adam Smith's treatment of public finance see A. T. Peacock, 'The Treatment of the Principles of Public Finance in The Wealth of Nations', in A. S. Skinner and T. Wilson (eds), *Essays on Adam Smith* (Oxford: Clarendon Press, 1976).

4. Adam Smith, *The Wealth of Nations*, IV ix. 51 (5th) Cannan edn (reprinted by Methuen and Co., 1961).

5. Having read through this passage the reader should now be able to start answering the questions in note 1 above.

6. A. Marshall, *Principles of Economics*, 8th edn (London: Macmillan, 1930), p. 413. Marshall's Principles also contained an early discussion of local government finance.

7. Buchanan, *op. cit.*, p. 384, n. (2).

8. A. C. Pigou, *A Study in Public Finance* (London: Macmillan, 1928); Pigou assumed interpersonal comparisons were possible and allocated the tax burden according to 'equi-marginal sacrifice'.

9. For English translations of these economists see R. A. Musgrave and A. T. Peacock, *Classics in the Theory of Public Finance* (London: Macmillan, 1958).

10. See Musgrave and Peacock, *op. cit.*

11. *ibid.*

12. R. A. Musgrave, 'The Voluntary Exchange Theory of Public Economy', *Quarterly Journal of Economics*, 53 (February 1938), pp. 213–37.

13. H. R. Bowen, 'The Interpretation of Voting in the Allocation of Resources', *Quarterly Journal of Economics*, 58 (November 1943), pp. 27–48.

14. J. M. Buchanan, 'The Pure Theory of Government Finance: A Suggested Approach', *Journal of Political Economy*, 57 (December 1949), pp. 496–505.

15. P. A. Samuelson, 'The Pure Theory of Public Expenditure', *Review of Economics and Statistics* (November 1954), pp. 387–9.

16. D. Black, 'On the Rationale of Group Decision-making', *Journal of Political Economy*, 7 (February 1948), pp. 23–34.

17. K. J. Arrow, 'A difficulty in the Concept of Social Welfare', *Journal of Political Economy*, 58 (August 1950), pp. 328–46.

18. J. M. Buchanan and G. Tullock, *The Calculus of Consent* (Ann Arbor: University of Michigan Press, 1962).

19. A. Downs, *An Economic Theory of Democracy* (New York: Harper, 1957).

20. J. M. Buchanan and G. Tullock, *The Calculus of Consent* (Ann Arbor Paperbacks, The University of Michigan Press, 1971).

21. W. A. Niskanen, *Bureaucracy and Representative Government* (Chicago: Aldine, 1974).

22. This section can do nothing other than give a set of summary notes. The reader who is weak on basic microeconomics should consult J. Hirschliefer, *Price Theory and Applications* (Englewood Cliffs, N.J.: Prentice-Hall).

23. For a useful discussion of when it's appropriate to use partial equilibrium analysis and when not, see J. Whalley, 'How Reliable is Partial Equilibrium Analysis?', *Review of Economics and Statistics*, 57 (1975), pp. 299–310.

24. J. Rawls, *A Theory of Justice* (Cambridge, Mass.: Harvard University Press, 1971).

Chapter 2

1. D. Hume, *Treatise on Human Nature* (1740).

2. P. A. Samuelson, 'The Pure Theory of Public Expenditure', *Review of Economics and Statistics*, 36 (November 1954).

3. G. Tullock, *Private Wants, Public Means: An Economic Analysis of the Desirable Scope of Government* (New York: Basic Books, 1970), p. vi.

4. G. J. Stigler, *The Citizen and the State* (Chicago: University Press, 1975).

5. M. Friedman, *Capitalism and Freedom* (Chicago: University Press, 1962), Chapter 2.

Chapter 3

1. A. C. Pigou, *A Study in Public Finance* (London: Macmillan, 1928).

2. The methodological problems involved in using this 'organic theory of the state' are explored in Chapter 4 – see 'The public interest approach'.

3. The reader should try the following simple exercise. Reconstruct Figure 3.2, this time assuming that for *one* individual the public commodity is a public bad whereas for the other individual it is a public good. Defence to a pacifist may be considered as a public bad. Repeat the analysis carried out in the text using these new assumptions and derive the optimal pricing rule for a commodity like defence. Then repeat the defence example assuming that the pacifist can evade consumption of defence by moving to another region.

4. R. A. Musgrave, 'The Voluntary Exchange Theory of Public Economy', *Quarterly Journal of Economics*, 53 (February 1938), pp. 213–37; R. A. Musgrave, *The Theory of Public Finance* (New York: McGraw-Hill, 1958); and R. A. Musgrave in J. Margolis and H. Guitton (eds), *Public Economics* (New York: St Martins, 1969).

5. H. R. Bowen, 'The Interpretation of Voting in the Allocation of Resources', *Quarterly Journal of Economics*, 58 (November 1943), pp. 27–48.

6. P. A. Samuelson, 'The Pure Theory of Public Expenditure', *Review of Economics and Statistics*, 36 (November 1954), pp. 387–9.

7. J. M. Buchanan, *The Demand and Supply of Public Goods* (Chicago: Rand McNally, 1968), pp. 41–3.

8. Samuelson, *op. cit.*

9. F. M. Bator, 'The Simple Analytics of Welfare Maximization', *American Economic Review*, 47 (March 1957).

10. K. Wicksell, *Finanztheoretische Untersuchungen* (Jena: Gustar Fisher, 1896). A substantial part is translated in R. A. Musgrave and A. T. Peacock, *Classics in The Theory of Public Finance* (London: Macmillan, 1958).

11. Erik Lindahl, *Die Gerechtigkeit der Besteurung* (Lund, 1919). The main part of this is translated in Musgrave and Peacock, *op. cit.*

12. The form of the Lindahl model presented in this chapter owes a great deal to Lief

Johansen, who formalised Lindahl's earlier work; see L. Johansen, 'Some Notes on Lindahl's Theory of Determination of Public Expenditures', *International Economic Review*, 4 (September 1963), pp. 346-56. See also J. G. Head, 'Lindahl's Theory of the Budget', *Finanzarciv*, 23 (October 1964), pp. 421-54.

13. D. K. Foley, 'Lindahl's Solution and the Core of An Economy with Public Goods', *Econometrica*, 38 (January 1970), pp. 66-72.

14. J. Milleron, 'Theory of Value with Public Goods: A Survey Article', *Journal of Economic Theory*, 5 (December 1972), pp. 419-77.

15. D. J. Roberts, 'The Lindahl Solution for Economies with Public Goods, *Journal of Public Economics*, 3 (February 1974), pp. 23-42.

16. See Johansen, *op. cit.*

17. C. M. Tiebout, 'A Pure Theory of Local Expenditures', *Journal of Political Economy*, 64 (October 1956), pp. 416-26.

18. See especially W. Oates, *Fiscal Federalism* (New York: Harcourt Brace Janovitch 1972); J. M. Buchanan and C. J. Goetz, 'Efficiency Limits of Fiscal Mobility: An Assessment of the Tiebout Model', *Journal of Public Economics*, 2 (1972), pp. 25-43. For an excellent critique and extension of Tiebout's model see J. E. Stiglitz, *The Theory of Local Public Goods* in M. S. Feldstein and R. P. Inman (eds), *The Economics of Public Services* (London: Macmillan, 1977).

19. Adam Smith, *The Wealth of Nations*, E. Cannan edition reprinted in Modern Library Series, Volume II, p. 310.

20. *ibid.*, Volume 5, ii e 6.

21. John Stuart Mill, *Principles of Political Economy*, Book 5, Ch. 2.

22. *ibid.*

23. Lord Robbins 'Interpersonal Comparisons of Utility', *Economic Journal*, 48 (December 1938).

Chapter 4

1. K. Arrow, *Social Choice and Individual Values* (New Haven, Conn.: Yale University Press, 1963), p. 59.

2. See especially I. M. D. Little, 'Social Choice and Individual Values' *Journal of Political Economy*, 60 (1952).

3. See A. K. Sen, *Collective Choice and Social Welfare* (Edinburgh: Oliver & Boyd, 1970).

4. D. Black, *Theory of Committees and Elections* (Cambridge: University Press, 1958).

5. F. De Meyer and C. R. Plott, 'The Probability of a Cyclical Majority', *Econometrica*, 38 (March 1970), pp. 345-54.

6. G. Tullock and R. Campbell, 'Computer Simulation of a Small Voting System', *Economic Journal* 28 (1970), pp. 97-104.

7. G. Tullock, 'The General Irrelevance of the General Possibility Theorem', *Quarterly Journal of Economics*, 81 (1967).

8. This example has used 'strong preference' and 'indifference' as the basis of the exchange of votes. Indifference is sufficient but not necessary for the exchange to take place. The reader should work out the necessary conditions.

9. In other words, politics is a non-zero sum repeatable co-operative game. The way in which such a game can go is so variable, depending on the sequence in which incentives are played, that predicting its outcome is extremely difficult.

10. J. M. Buchanan and G. Tullock, 'Gains from Trade', *Ethics*, 76 (July 1966).

11. That is, in the absence of side payments.

12. Wicksell recognised this and relaxed his requirement of unanimity to one of proximate unanimity.

13. W. J. Baumol, *Welfare Economics and the Theory of the State*, 2nd edn (London: LSE G. Bell and Sons, 1965), pp. 43-4.

14. A. Downs, *An Economic Theory of Democracy* (New York: Harper, 1957), p. 178.

15. As in the sales revenue maximisation model of the firm, we could modify the Downsian model from voter maximisation to the achievement of a 'satisfactory' number of

es necessary to get elected. However, this is a minor point since politicians are generally
...ays keen to increase the size of their majority.

16. If the costs of holding political office exceed the benefits derived, why do inviduals run for election?

17. The reader should try this for five voters.

18. A useful comprehensive introduction to this subject is found in A. Breton, *The Economic Theory of Representative Government* (London: Macmillan, 1974).

19. See R. D. Tollison and T. D. Willett, 'Some Simple Economics of Voting and Not Voting', *Public Choice* (Fall, 1973), pp. 59–71; and W. H. Ricker and P. C. Ordeshook, 'A Theory of the Calculus of Voting', *American Political Science Review*, 62 (1968), pp. 24–42.

Chapter 5

1. Statistical definitions of public expenditure are given in Chapter 6. In the meantime we simply take public expenditure to represent the costs of undertaking public sector activities including transfer payments.

2. In distinguishing between the two classes of public expenditure models a useful analogy may be drawn between public expenditure and consumer expenditure. Aggregate macroeconomic consumption functions relate the total decisions of consumers to total personal disposable income etc. Underlying the aggregate consumption function there is a well-developed microeconomic theory of consumer demand.

3. R. A. Musgrave, 'Expenditure Policy for Development', in D. T. Geithman (ed.), *Fiscal Policy for Industrialization and Development in Latin America* (Gainesville: University of Florida Press, 1974) and R. A. Musgrave, *Fiscal Systems* (New Haven: Yale University Press, 1969).

4. W. W. Rostow, *Politics and the Stages of Growth* (Cambridge: University Press, 1971).

5. See R. M. Bird, 'Wagner's Law of Expanding State Activity', *Public Finance*, 26 (1971). Bird gives an excellent account of the background and interpretations of Wagner's original contribution which appeared in German.

6. Musgrave, *Fiscal Systems, op. cit.*, p. 72 n. 1.

7. The reader will recall the problems of this approach which were discussed in Chapter 3.

8. A. T. Peacock and J. Wiseman, *The Growth of Public Expenditure in the United Kingdom* (Princeton: University Press, 1961).

9. C. Clark, 'Public Finance and Changes in the Value of Money', *Economic Journal* (December 1945). For a recent statement see C. Clark, *Taxmanship: Principles and Proposals for the Reform of Taxation* (London: Institute for Economic Affairs, 1970). Clark believed that there was a limit to the level of taxation that any mature economy could absorb, he put it at about 25 per cent of GNP. If that level were exceeded then Clark believed that a decline in the state of the economy and indeed perhaps even of the social and political fabric of society itself would result. Incentives to work and to save would be destroyed at such high levels of taxation. Clearly Clark's view is open to criticism. The reader should consider providing his own critique.

10. See especially Musgrave, *Fiscal Systems, op. cit.* and R. M. Bird, *The Growth of Government Spending in Canada* (Toronto: Canadian Tax Foundation, 1970). The critique of Peacock and Wiseman presented in this chapter is drawn from Musgrave and Bird.

11. Other studies were prompted by Peacock and Wiseman's. For a survey of these subsequent studies see the Preface to the second edition of Peacock and Wiseman, *op. cit.* and Ved P. Gandhi, 'Trends in Public Consumption and Investment: A Review of Issues and Evidence' (paper read at International Institute of Public Finance meeting, Edinburgh, 1976; to be published in conference proceedings).

12. For further details see Table 6.7 in Chapter 6.

13. Recall that publicly provided goods need not be produced in the public sector. It is, however, useful to talk about public production, especially since a very large proportion of public outputs are produced in the public sector.

14. Modifications and developments to the simple model have been made by Jackson from whom further details are available.

15. Incorporating a set of private collective activities into the domain of the public sector will obviously result in an absolute increase in the size of the public sector and an

increase in its size relative to the private sector. Increases in the scope and sphere of government activity must, therefore, account for some of its relative growth.

16. The reader should take a service such as 'the health service' and consider the objectives and demands that such a service provides. Repeat the exercise for a number of services. Do any two services serve the same objective (consider library services and education)?

17. What does the car enthusiast demand?

18. The reader should consider other examples? Are there instances when intermediate public sector consumption goods are produced?

19. Patrick J. Lucey, in *Public Administration Review* No. 6 (1972).

20. See Peacock and Wiseman, *op cit.*

21. The reader should consider other changes in the demand variables and check that changes in these variables correspond to how he would expect public expenditures to move following the change.

22. R. A. Carr-Hill and N. H. Stern, 'Theory and Estimation in Models of Crime and its Social Control and their Relations to Concepts of Social Output in M. S. Feldstein and R. P. Inman (eds.), *The Economics of Public Services* (London: Macmillan, 1977).

23. See J. Buchanan, 'The Economic Theory of Clubs', *Economica* (February 1965) pp. 1–14, and F. Hirsch, *The Social Limits to Growth* (London: Routledge & Kegan Paul, 1977).

24. W. J. Baumol, 'The Macro-economics of Unbalanced Growth', *American Economic Review*, 57 (June 1967), pp. 415–26.

25. *ibid.*, p. 416.

26. A. T. Peacock, 'Welfare Economics and Public Subsidies to the Arts', *Manchester School of Economics and Social Studies*, 37 (December, 1969).

27. W. J. Baumol and W. E. Oates, 'The Cost Disease of the Personal Social Services and the Quality of Life', *Skandinavska Enskilda Banken Quarterly Review*, 2 (1972).

28. P. M. Jackson and D. T. Ulph, *The Relative Prices of Public Sector and Private Sector Goods*, University of Stirling Discussion Papers in Economics, Finance and Investment No. 15 (March 1973).

29. The change in demand from D_0 to D_1 following the change in real incomes depends upon the income elasticity of demand for G_k. The actual shift chosen in this example is for diagrammatic simplicity.

30. See H.M. Treasury, *Public Expenditure White Papers: Handbook on Methodology* (HMSO 1972).

31. See S. Brittan, *The Economic Consequences of Democracy* (London: Temple Smith, 1977) especially Part IV and Ch. 23 in particular.

32. A. Downs, 'Why the Government Budget is too Small', *World Politics*, July 1960.

Chapter 6

1. When reading this chapter the reader should keep in mind the discussion of the theoretical determinants of the growth of public expenditure which were presented in Chapter 5.

2. A representation of this kind of discussion is found in the OECD document, *Expenditure Trends in OECD Countries 1960-80* (July 1972). See especially pp. 12–13 and R. W. Bacon and W. A. Eltis, *Britain's Economic Problem: Too Few Producers* (London: Macmillan, 1976).

3. This is obviously an oversimplified picture of a very complex set of events; for an extremely useful discussion of these topics see A. Cairncross *et al.*, *Midlands Bank Review* (1977).

Chapter 7

1. This was seen in Chapter 4 when we considered log-rolling. For an interesting, if perhaps biased, account of Cabinet decision-making the reader is referred to the published *Diaries* of Richard Crossman, an ex-Labour MP and sometime Cabinet member (London: Hamish Hamilton/Jonathan Cape, 1975-7).

2. The *Report of the Royal Commission on the Constitution*, Cmnd 5460 (London: HMSO, 1973) was very much concerned with questions of this kind. From the evidence that was presented to the Commission it was agreed that the political power of individuals and their elected representatives in Parliament had declined, while that of the central administration (i.e. bureaucrats) and *ad hoc* bodies appointed on its recommendation had increased.

3. C. Schultze, *The Politics and Economics of Public Spending* (Washington: Brookings Institution, 1968), pp. 2–3.

4. The terminology is due to Leibenstein. For an interesting discussion in the context of the public sector see Rowley.

5. We have already come across these notions when considering the problems involved in enforcing property rights for non-excludable goods such as pure public goods; see Chapter 2.

6. See R. McKean, 'The Unseen Hand in Government', *American Economic Review* (1965).

7. See O. E. Williamson, *The Economics of Discretionary Behavior: Managerial Objectives in a Theory of the Firm* (Englewood Cliffs, NJ: Prentice Hall, 1964).

8. A. Wildavsky, *The Politics of the Budgetary Process* (Boston: Little, Brown, 1964), p. 13.

9. Herbert Simon refers to this as 'bounded rationality'.

10. The costs of change are clear to those who experienced the reorganisation of the health services and of local government in the UK during the 1970s.

11. The problem of the 'second-best' refers to the problem that a sub-optimisation of a total system can take the whole system further away from its optimum, rather than closer to it, if the marginal conditions for an optimum are not satisfied in other parts of the system.

12. R. Nield and T. S. Ward, University of Cambridge lecture presented to a meeting at the Institute for Fiscal Studies (1977).

Chapter 8

1. A. R. Prest and R. Turvey, 'Cost Benefit Analysis, a Survey', *Economic Journal*, 65 (December 1955), p. 155.

2. For those who are unfamiliar with this terminology, the MRTP is defined as an individual's marginal rate of substitution between present and future consumption. Since there are a large number of investors and savers in the capital market, equality between individual MRTPs is established. The market rate of interest, therefore, represents the price individuals are willing to pay to give up current consumption on the expectation of receiving, *with certainty*, a positive amount from the investment in the future.

3. The marginal product of capital (see also the marginal efficiency of capital) is the rate of transformation of investment opportunity, i.e. the marginal rate of transforming present for future consumption in production.

4. Such advantages of scale are enjoyed by all large organisations but the public sector is many times larger than the largest private sector organisation. Moreover, the public sector has access to the printing press and tax revenues.

5. The source of the information required to calculate a probability density function might come from previous experiences, in which case the events have occurred with sufficient regularity in the past to enable the decision-maker to calculate relative frequencies. These are generally referred to as 'empirical probabilities'. On the other hand, the event might have occurred so seldom or, in the limit, never at all, so that empirical probabilities are not available. The decision-maker might nevertheless make a judgement and assign 'subjective probabilities' to the future events.

6. The distinction between uncertainty and risk used to be fashionable and is generally attributed to Knight. However, probability theorists such as Savage tend to dispense with the distinction and talk only about risk.

7. See G. Menges *Economic Decision Making: Basic Concepts and Models* (London: Longman 1974).

Chapter 11

1. In 1978 the British ceased to tax cigarettes by the weight of tobacco. Instead tax liability depends on the number and value of cigarettes. What should have happened to the average size of cigarettes as a result? Has it happened? Petrol is subject to a VAT as well as a unit tax in Britain.

2. This proposal is particularly associated with the name of the American economist Henry George, who proposed (at a time when government budgets were tiny) that all taxes other than a tax on land be scrapped.

The Development Land Tax does not fit the model in the text because, while it is reasonable to assume that the total supply of land is approximately fixed, the supply for one purpose such as building houses is not fixed.

3. Maximisation of revenue from a unit tax given linear supply and demand schedules will occur when the tax rate is equal to half the difference between horizontal and the vertical axis intercepts of the supply and demand curves.

Proof:

Let the demand curve before tax be

$$P_G = a - bQ \tag{1}$$

and the supply curve be

$$S = c + dQ. \tag{2}$$

The demand curve after the imposition of a unit tax of t is

$$P_N = a - bQ - t \tag{3}$$

Output is

$$Q = \frac{a - c - t}{b + d}$$

and the total tax revenue T is

$$T = tQ = \frac{t(a - c - t)}{b + d}$$

differentiating,

$$\frac{dT}{dt} = \frac{a - c - 2t}{b + d}.$$

To maximise T, we set

$$\frac{dT}{dt} = 0$$

giving

$$t = \frac{a - c}{2}.$$

4. The reader should verify that if marginal cost is rising with output, price will rise less and quantity fall less than with constant marginal price. If marginal cost falls as output rises, then price will rise more and output fall more than in the constant cost case.

5. The italicised phrase in the text is important. If someone's indifference curve was tangent to the kink at B they might well move to F increasing their work.

Chapter 12

1. The present *graphical* exposition of the Harberger model relies heavily on a *numerical* exposition of the Harberger model by C. E. McClure and W. R. Thirsk, 'A Simplified Exposition of the Harberger Model, I: Tax Incidence', *National Tax Journal*, 28 (March 1975), pp. 1–27. The reader is referred to this article or to standard works on production functions

for proofs of the proposition about the characteristics of the Cobb–Douglas production and consumption functions.

Chapter 14

1. Attorney-General *v.* London County Council (1900), 4.T.C. at p. 293. Quoted in the Memorandum of Dissent to the *Royal Commission on the Taxation of Profit and Incomes.* 9474 HMSO, 1955 (In R. W. Houghton, *Public Finance* (Harmondsworth: 1970), p. 50.

2. Whitney *v.* C.I.R. (1925), 10.T.C. at p. 133. In Memorandum of Dissent, *ibid.*

3. Quoted in Houghton, *op. cit.*, p. 39.

4. The very interesting Canadian *Report of the Royal Commission on Taxation* (Ottawa 1966) explicitly starts from Simons's definition and makes recommendations for reform of the Canadian tax system using a comprehensive tax system as a basis.

5. In the US experiments designed to discover the effects of negative income taxes on labour supply have also been employed – see Chapter 15.

6. Royal Commission, 1954, para. 1091.

7. *ibid.*, para. 112.

8. C. V. Brown and E. Levin, 'The Effects of Income Taxation on Overtime: The Results of a National Survey', *Economic Journal* (December 1974), pp. 846–7.

9. For all sources cited below, see 'Further Reading', pp. 486–7.

10. As the microeconomic treatment of taxation and labour supply is in the neoclassical tradition, the terms neoclassical and microeconomic are used more or less interchangeably and similarly the 'macroeconomic' and 'Keynesian' are used as near synonyms for the present purpose.

11. This neglect of negative supply elasticities at the macro-level is perhaps even more surprising given the increasing evidence that individual price elasticities are negative. However, in defence of the standard assumption it should be pointed out both that elasticity estimates for married women are typically positive and that the simple extrapolation from the micro- to the macro-level is complicated when labour supply decisions are made on a household rather than an individual basis.

12. The reader is referred to Branson (1972) for a discussion of the implications of assuming that labour supply depends on the money wage rather than the real wage.

13. For alternative assumptions the reader is again referred to Branson (1972).

14. If it cannot, then of course there may be over-full employment or unemployment after the tax cut.

15. The aggregate supply curve is derived from the production function in part B, the demand for labour in part D, and the fixed money wage is part C.

16. The aggregate demand curve is assumed to be derived from a standard *IS/LM* curve.

17. Changes in tax receipts (and government expenditure) shift the *IS* curve and as a consequence the *AD* curve.

18. With a straightline demand curve, total expenditure on wages, and hence labour income, will reach its maximum at the mid-point of the demand curve. It is at this point that the maximum divergence between the gross and net demand will occur.

Chapter 15

1. R. H. Haveman and H. W. Watts, 'Social Experimentation as Policy Research: A Review of the Negative Income Tax Experiments' in V. Halberstadt and A. J. Culyer (eds.), *Public Economics and Human Resources* (Editions Cujas, 1977), italics added.

2. A. Rees and H. W. Watts, 'An Overview of the Labor Supply Results' in J. A. Pechman and P. M. Timpane, *Work Incentives and Income Guarantees: The New Jersey Income Tax Experiment* (Washington: Brookings Institution, 1975).

Chapter 16

1. To extend the argument to cover more than two goods is complicated and the interested reader is referred to Williams. However, the extension to cover dis-savers (borrowers)

as well as savers (lenders) is straightforward and the reader may wish to undertake this extension as an exercise.

2. A change in the net interest rate on its own would cause the budget constraint to pivot about *WY*. The locus of tangency points, which might be termed an interest rate expansion path, is a pure price effect and hence the line (not shown) could also be called a price consumption curve.

Chapter 17

1. J. Whalley, 'A General Equilibrium Assessment of the 1973 United Kingdom Tax Reform', *Economica* (1975), pp. 159–61.

2. J. A. Pechman and B. A. Okner, *Who Bears The Burden?* (Washington: Brookings Institution, 1974), p. 31.

Chapter 20

1. 'This utility function is not totally absurd, and may fit available empirical studies quite well; but it predicts an unrealistically low labour supply at high wage rates. This means that the community offer curves have too great a backward slope in their upper reaches. One would guess that the calculated optimum tax rates are biased upwards as a result, since the labour-encouraging effects of high tax rates are exaggerated; but guessing is probably rather unreliable in this area' (J. A. Mirrlees, 'Arguments for Government Expenditure', in M. Artis and A. R. Nobay *Contemporary Contributions to Economic Analysis*, Oxford: Basil Blackwell, 1978).

2. N. H. Stern, 'On the Specification of Models of Optimum Income Taxation', *Journal of Public Economics* (1976), pp. 161–2.

3. Mirrlees, *op. cit.*

4. Perhaps the most important exception is that marginal tax rates do not tend to zero when it is assumed that incomes can increase without limit.

5. J. A. Mirrlees, 'Labour Supply Behaviour and Optimal Taxes' in *Fiscal Policy and Labour Supply* (IFS, 1977), p. 14.

6. See n. 4 above.

Chapter 21

1. R. M. Bird and L. De Wulf, 'Taxation and Income Distribution in Latin America', a paper presented at a Conference on Equity and Income Distribution in Latin America, Georgetown University, November 17 1972.

2. Is there any reason to believe that government can make any better informed decisions about the optimal level and the quality of merit goods to provide?

3. The 'social wage' is a somewhat ill-defined concept and so it is difficult to measure it statistically before it is defined. However, broadly it refers to the lump sum income, or more precisely income equivalent, of certain benefits received from government, e.g. housing subsidies, food subsidies, rate rebates, fuel price subsidies, benefits from education and health services, etc.

4. See also A. K. Sen, *On Economic Inequality* (Oxford: University Press, 1973), especially Chapter 2.

5. This general equilibrium approach is similar to that adopted by Samuelson. Musgrave, who followed in the Wicksellian tradition, assumed that if the pretax income distribution was Pareto-optimal, then, if the government provided an optimal output of public goods, the post-budget distribution of incomes would remain unchanged. Samuelson disputed this proposition, pointing out that relative factor prices and final consumption good prices could change following the introduction of the budget which would result in a change in the income distribution. The discussion between Samuelson and Musgrave on this is found in M. Margolis and H. Guitton, *Public Economics* (International Economic Association Publication, 1967).

6. O. Eckstein, *Water Resource Development: The Economics of Project Evaluation* (Cambridge, Mass.: Harvard University Press), p. 17.

7. R. Haveman, *Water Resource Investment and the Public Interest* (Vanderbilt University Press, 1965).

8. A. C. Harberger, 'Three Basic Postulates for Applied Welfare Economists', *Journal of Economic Literature*, 9 (September 1971), pp. 785-6.

9. E. J. Mishan, 'Cost Benefit Rules for Poorer Countries', *Canadian Journal of Economics* (February 1971), pp. 86-98.

10. See B. A. Weisbrod, 'Income Redistribution, Effects and Benefit Cost Analysis', in S. B. Chase (ed.), *Problems in Public Expenditure Analysis* (Washington: Brookings Institution, 1968). Weisbrod proposes an empirical framework within which the problem can be studied. Another interesting and extremely valuable contribution to the debate has been provided by M. S. Feldstein, 'Distributional Preferences in Public Expenditure Analysis', in H. M. Hochman and G. E. Peterson (eds.), *Redistribution Through Public Choice* (New York: Urban Institute Columbia University Press, 1974). Feldstein's essay extends beyond a consideration of income distribution and CBA.

11. See M. E. Burns, 'A Note on the Concept and Measure of Consumers Surplus', *American Economic Review*, 63 (June 1973), pp. 335-44.

12. A. Cartter, *The Redistribution of Income in Post War Britain*, Cambridge University Press (1955).

13. W. I. Gillespie, 'Effects of Public Expenditure on the Distribution of Income', in R. A. Musgrave (ed.), *Essays in Fiscal Federalism* (Washington: Brookings Institution, 1965), and W. I. Gillespie, 'The Incidence of Taxes and Public Expenditures', in *The Canadian Economy* (a study prepared for the Royal Commission on Taxation, Ottawa, 1965).

14. A. Aaron and M. C. McGuire, 'Benefits and Burdens of Government Expenditure', *Econometrica*, 38 (November 1970).

15. This example is adapted from K. V. Greene, W. B. Neenan and C. D. Scott, *Fiscal Interactions in a Metropolitan Area* (Farnborough, Hants.: Heath, Lexington Books, 1974). Since that example is clearly presented in Greene, Neenan and Scott we have not tried to improve on it.

16. The reader should return to the CSO study of the allocation of the benefits from public goods and consider the implicit utility function that has been assumed in making the allocations.

17. S. Maital, 'Public Goods and Income Distribution: Some Further Results', *Econometrica*, 41 (1973), pp. 561-8.

18. This depends on the assumption that utility functions are separable so that as the consumption of one class of good changes the marginal utility of the other remains unchanged. Thus any decrease in the value of the inverse of the marginal rate of substitution between the two goods reduces the marginal utility of additional real incomes.

If the two goods are substitutes or complements then clearly the assumption of separability in the utility function will not hold:

(1) if the goods are complements, then as the marginal utility of one good increases, the marginal utility of the other increases also;
(2) if the goods are substitutes, then as the marginal utility of one of the goods increases, the marginal utility of the other decreases.

Thus, any change in the inverse of the marginal rate of substitution is not an unambiguous measure of the change in the marginal utility of real income.

19. G. Brennan, 'The Distributional Implication of Public Goods', *Econometrica*, 44 (1976), pp. 391-6, and the exchange between Brennan and Aaron and McGuire that followed; H. Aaron and M. McGuire, 'Reply to Geoffrey Brennan', *Econometrica*, 44 (1976), pp. 401-4 and G. Brennan, 'Public Goods and Income Distribution: A Rejoinder to the Aaron-McGuire Reply', *Econometrica*, 44 (1976), pp. 405-7. An interesting extension to and critique of the Aaron-McGuire-Brennan debate is found in D. T. Ulph, 'Income Distribution and Public Goods' (mimeo – paper presented to the Econometric Society European Meeting, 1977).

20. W. I. Gillespie, 'On the Redistribution of Income in Canada', *Canadian Tax Journal*, 24 (July-August 1976), pp. 419-50.

21. D. A. Dodge, 'Impact of Tax, Transfer and Expenditure Policies of Government on the Distribution of Personal Incomes in Canada', *Review of Income and Wealth*, 21 (March 1975), pp. 1–52.

22. J. A. Mirrlees, 'Arguments for Public Expenditure', in M. Artis and A. R. Nobay, *Contemporary Contributions to Economic Analysis* (Oxford: Basil Blackwell, 1978).

Further Reading

Chapter 1

The following reading list is intended to provide a wide set of general sources and useful collections of essays and reprints of articles etc.

General public finance
(i)   Two classics which are comprehensive and encyclopaedic in their treatment of the subject and to which all teachers of public sector economics owe a great debt are:
R. A. Musgrave, *The Theory of Public Finance* (New York: McGraw-Hill, 1959).
C. S. Shoup, *Public Finance* (Chicago: Aldine, 1970).
(ii) A useful guide to the background of public sector studies is found in *Public Expenditure and Taxation: Economic Research Retrospect and Prospect: Fiftieth Anniversary Colloquium IV* (Washington: National Bureau of Economic Research, 1972).
(iii) A. B. Atkinson and J. E. Stiglitz, *Lectures on Public Economics* (New York: McGraw-Hill, 1981).
(vi) G. A. Hughes and G. M. Heal (eds.), *Public Policy and The Tax System* (London: George Allen and Unwin, 1980). A collection of essays presented to James Meade. Each essay is a clear statement of an application of taxation theory to an area of policy analysis.
(vii) H. J. Aaron and M. J. Boskin (eds.), *The Economics of Taxation* (Washington: The Brookings Institution, 1980). A collection of original essays on tax burdens and tax reform.

Readings and collected essays, in public finance
(i)   R. A. Musgrave and C. S. Shoup, *Readings in the Economics of Taxation* (London: Allen & Unwin, 1959). This collection contains many of the classic and seminal contributions to tax analysis.
(ii) R. W. Houghton (ed.), *Public Finance* (Harmondsworth: Penguin, 1970), a useful collection of articles which are frequently referred to in subsequent chapters.
(iii) J. Margolis and H. Guitton, *Public Economics* (London: Macmillan, 1969). This contains the proceedings of the International Economics Association Biarritz conference. Many of the papers represent major contributions and resulted in stimulating many of the developments in 1970s. The articles are generally difficult to read but are rewarding.
(iv) M. S. Feldstein and R. P. Inman, *The Economics of Public Services* (London: Macmillan, 1977). The proceedings of the International Economics Association Turin conference. The papers contained in this volume represent a statement of the current state of some parts of the subject. Most of the papers are highly abstract.
(v)   A. S. Blinder *et al.*, *The Economics of Public Finance* (Washington: Brookings Institution, 1974). Contains two very useful survey articles which are of relevance in the chapters that follow; G. F. Break, 'The Incidence and Economic Effects of Taxation', and P. O. Steiner, 'Public Expenditure Budgeting'.

478

Chapter 2

General

K. J. Arrow, 'The Organisation of Economic Activity: Issues Pertinent to the Choice of Market vs Non Market Allocation', in R. H. Haveman and J. Margolis (eds.), *Public Expenditures and Policy Analysis* (Chicago: Markham, 1970).

P. O. Steiner, 'Public Expenditure and Budgeting', in A. S. Blinder *et al.*, *The Economics of Public Finance* (Washington: Brookings Institution, 1974).

M. Olson, *The Logic of Collective Actions* (Cambridge, Mass.: Harvard University Press, 1965).

Externalities

R. H. Coase, 'The Problem of Social Costs', *Journal of Law and Economics*, 3 (1960), pp. 1–44.

O. A. Davis and M. I. Kamien, 'Externalities Information and Alternative Collective Action', in Haveman and Margolis (eds.) *Public Expenditure Analysis* (Chicago: Markham 2c 1977).

J. E. Meade, 'External Economics and Diseconomies in a Competitive Situation', *Economic Journal*, 62 (1952), pp. 54–67.

E. J. Mishan, 'The Relationship between Joint Products, Collective Goods, and External Effects', *Journal of Political Economy* (May/June 1969), pp. 329–48. This is a useful survey article in addition to providing a means of organising the debate. The reader should follow up the discussion that this article generated between Mishan and his commentators in subsequent issues of the *Journal of Political Economy*.

Property rights and transactions costs

H. Demsetz, 'Towards a Theory of Property Rights', *American Economic Review* (Papers and Proceedings) (May 1967), pp. 347–59.

H. Demsetz, 'The Costs of Transacting', *Quarterly Journal of Economics*, 82 (1968), pp. 33–53.

E. Furubotn and S. Pejovich, 'Property Rights and Economic Theory: A Survey of the Recent Literature', *Journal of Economic Literature*, 10 (December 1972).

Decreasing costs and regulation

W. J. Baumol and A. K. Klevorick, 'Input Choices and the Rate of Return Regulation: An Overview of the Discussion', *Bell Journal of Economics and Management Science*, 1 (Autumn 1970), pp. 162–90. This provides an excellent review of the literature.

R. Rees, *Public Enterprise Economics* (London: Weidenfeld & Nicolson, 1976). A useful account of the economics of nationalised industries.

G. J. Stigler, 'The Theory of Economic Regulation', *Bell Journal of Economics and Management Science*, 2 (1971), pp. 3–21.

Redistribution role of government

A great deal has been written on this subject – a useful introduction is found in

B. A. Weisbrod, 'Collective Action and the Distribution of Income, a Conceptual Approach, in Haveman and Margolis (eds.), *op. cit.*

Government and uncertainty

R. Zeckhauser, 'Uncertainty and The Need for Collective Action', in Haveman and Margolis, *op cit.*

Chapter 3

J. M. Buchanan, *The Demand and Supply of Public Goods* (Chicago: Rand McNally, 1968).

R. Dorfman, 'General Equilibrium with Public Goods', in J. Margolis and H. Guitton, *Public Economics* (London: Macmillan, 1969), pp. 98–123.

R. Musgrave, 'Provision for Social Goods', in Margolis and Guitton, *op. cit.*

P. A. Samuelson, 'The Pure Theory of Public Expenditures', *Review of Economics and Statistics* (November 1954), pp. 387–9.

P. A. Samuelson, 'Diagrammatic Exposition of a Theory of Public Expenditures', *Review of Economics and Statistics* (November 1955), pp. 360–6.

P. A. Samuelson, 'Pitfalls in the Analysis of Public Goods', *Journal of Law and Economics* (1967), pp. 199–204.

P. A. Samuelson, 'Contrast between Welfare Conditions for Joint Supply and for Public Goods', *Review of Economics and Statistics* (February 1969), pp. 26–30.

P. A. Samuelson, 'Pure Theory of Public Expenditure and Taxation', in Margolis and Guitton, *op. cit.*

C. L. Schultze, *The Politics and Economics of Public Spending* (Washington: Brookings Institution, 1968).

Chapter 4

K. J. Arrow, *Social Choice and Individual Values*, revised edn (New Haven, Conn.: Yale University Press, 1963); see also Arrow's essays in S. Hook (ed.), *Human Values and Economic Policy* (New York: University Press, 1967) and in P. Laslett and W. C. Runciman (eds), *Philosophy Politics and Society* (New York: Cambridge University Press, 1967).

B. Barry, *Sociologists, Economists and Democracy* (London: Collier-MacMillan, 1970).

J. M. Buchanan, *The Demand and Supply of Public Goods* (Chicago: Rand McNally, 1968).

K. A. Chrystal and J. E. Alt, 'Some Problems in Formulating and Testing a Politico-Economic Model of the United Kingdom', *Economic Journal*, 91 (September 1981).

R. A. Dahl and C. E. Lindblom, *Politics Economics and Welfare* (New York: Harper and Row, 1953).

A. Downs, *An Economic Theory of Democracy* (New York: Harper and Row, 1957).

R. Farquharson, *Theory of Voting* (New Haven, Conn: Yale University Press, 1969).

B. S. Frey, 'Politico Economic Models of the Business Cycle', *Journal of Public Economics*, 9 (1978), pp. 203–20.

B. S. Frey and F. Schneider, 'A model of Politico-Economic Behaviour in the U.K.', *Economic Journal*, 88 (1978), pp. 243–53.

N. Frohlich and J. A. Oppenheimer, *Modern Political Economy* (Prentice Hall Foundations of Modern Political Science Series; Prentice-Hall, Inc., Englewood Cliffs, New Jersey, 1978).

A. Lindbeck, 'Stabilization Policy in Open Economies with Endogenous Politicians', *American Economic Review*, 66 (May 1976), pp. 1–19.

D. Mayston, *The Idea of Social Choice* (London: Macmillan, 1974).

D. C. Mueller, 'Public Choice: A Survey', *Journal of Economic Literature* (1976), pp. 395–433.

D. C. Mueller, *Public Choice* (Cambridge University Press, 1980).

W. D. Nordhaus, 'The Political Business Cycle', *Review of Economic Studies*, 42 (1975), pp. 169–90.

P. K. Pattanaik, *Voting and Collective Choice* (Cambridge: University Press, 1971).

W. H. Rickett and P. C. Ordeshook, *An Introduction to Positive Political Theory* (Englewood Cliffs: Prentice Hall, 1973).

P. A. Samuelson, 'Arrow's Mathematical Politics', in S. Hook (ed.), *Human Values and Economic Policy* (New York: University Press, 1967).

A. K. Sen, *Collective Choice and Social Welfare* (Edinburgh: Oliver and Boyd, 1970).

E. Tufte, *Political Control of the Economy* (Princeton: Princeton University Press, 1978).

G. Tullock, *Towards a Mathematics of Politics* (Ann Arbor: University of Michigan Press, 1967).

Chapter 5

A. D. Bain, *The Economics of the Financial System* (Oxford: Martin Robertson, 1981).

T. E. Borcherding (ed.), *Budgets and Bureaucrats: The Sources of Government Growth* (Duke University Press, 1977).

J. Gough, *The Political Economy of the Welfare State* (London: Macmillan, 1979).

F. Gould and B. Roweth, 'Public Spending and Social Policy in the United Kingdom 1950–77', *Journal of Social Policy*, 9, 3 (July 1980).

E. M. Gramlich, 'Excessive Government Spending in the U.S.: Facts and Theories', paper presented to International Institute for Public Finance Conference, Jerusalem 1980, to be published in Conference Proceedings.

P. M. Jackson, 'The Growth of the Relative Size of the Public Sector', in D. A. Currie and W. Peters (eds.), *Contemporary Economic Analysis*, Vol. 2 (London: Croom Helm, 1980).

P. D. Larkey, C. Stolp, and M. Winer, 'Theorising about the growth of government: a research assessment', *Journal of Public Policy*, 1, 2 (May 1981), pp. 157–220 (this article contains the most comprehensive bibliography available on the subject).

Chapter 6

Information relating to the growth of public expenditure in the UK

(i) A. E. Holmans, 'The Growth of Public Expenditure in the U.K. Since 1950', *Manchester School* (1969), pp. 313–27.

(ii) A. T. Peacock and J. Wiseman, *The Growth of Public Expenditure in the United Kingdom*, 2nd edn (London: Allen & Unwin, 1967).

(iii) T. S. Ward, 'The Prospects for Public Expenditure and Taxation' in *Growth and Control of Public Expenditure* (London: Institute of Fiscal Studies, 1976).

(iv) P. M. Jackson, 'Trends in Local Government expenditure' in *Growth and Control of Public Expenditure* (London: Institute for Fiscal Studies, 1976).

(v) R. Klein (ed.), *Inflation and Priorities* (London: Centre for Studies in Social Policy, 1975). This volume contains an excellent examination of trends in the public expenditures of special groups of public services.

Information relating to Canada

(i) R. M. Bird, *The Growth of Government Spending in Canada* (Ottawa: Canadian Tax Foundation, 1970).

(ii) D. A. Curtis and H. M. Kitchen, 'Some Quantitative Aspects of Canadian Budgetary Policy, 1953–71', *Public Finance* (1975), pp. 108–26.

Information on US public expenditures

(i) F. M. Bator, *The Question of Government Spending* (New York: Collier Books, 1962).

(ii) R. A. Musgrave and J. M. Culbertson, 'The Growth of Public Expenditures in the U.S. 1890–1948', in *National Tax Journal*, 6 (June 1953).

(iii) S. Fabricant, *The Trend of Government Activity in The United States Since 1900* (Washington: National Bureau of Economic Research, 1952).

(iv) J. E. Pluta, 'Growth and Patterns in U.S. Government Expenditures 1956–1972', *National Tax Journal*, 27 (1974).

Information on Australian public expenditures

J. D. Stanford and P. M. Jackson, *The Growth and Composition of Australian Public Expenditures*, Public Sector Economics Research Centre, Occasional Paper Series (Leicester: University Press, 1978).

Useful collection of data relating to the public expenditures of developing countries

(i) R. A. Musgrave, *Fiscal Systems* (New Haven, Conn.: Yale University Press, 1969).

(ii) C. Enweze, 'Structure of Public Expenditures in Selected Developing Countries: A Time Series Study', *Manchester School* (1974), pp. 430–63.

International comparisons of taxation: national income accounting: miscellaneous

K. Messere, *Recent and Prospective Trends in Tax Levels and Tax Structures*, Institute for Fiscal Studies Lecture Series No. 2 (1975).

K. Messere, *Tax Levels and Structures: Inter-temporal and International Comparisons*, paper presented to International Public Finance Association Meeting in Edinburgh, September 1976 (to be published).

J. Veverka, 'The Growth of Government Expenditure in the United Kingdom since 1790', *Scottish Journal of Political Economy* (1963).

National income accounting concepts and conventions
A. R. Prest, 'Government revenue, the national income, and all that', in R. Bird and J. Head (eds) *Modern Fiscal Issues* (Toronto: University Press, 1972).
R. Maurice (ed.), *National Accounts Statistics: Sources and Methods* (London: HMSO, 1968).
HM Treasury, *Public Expenditure White Papers: Handbook on Methodology* London: HMSO, 1972).

Chapter 7

Sir Richard Clarke, *Public Expenditure Management and Control* (London: Macmillan, 1978).
O. A. Davis, M. A. H. Dempster and A. Wildavsky, 'A Theory of the Budgetary Process', *American Political Science Review* (September 1966), pp. 529–47.
P. K. Else and G. P. Marshall, 'The Unplanning of Public Expenditure: Recent Problems in Expenditure Planning and The Consequences of Cash Limits', *Public Administration*, 59 (Autumn 1981), pp. 253–78.
K. Hartley, 'The Economics of Bureaucracy and Local Government', in *Town Hall Power or Whitehall Pawn* (London: Institute of Economic Affairs, Readings 25, 1980).
H. Helco and A. Wildavsky, *The Private Government of Public Money* (London: Macmillan, 1974). This provides an account of the institutions of public expenditure control in the UK.
P. M. Jackson, *Planning and Control of Public Expenditure in the U.K.* (Milton Keynes: Open University Press, 1979).
P. M. Jackson, 'The Public Expenditure Cuts: Rationale and Consequences', *Fiscal Studies*, 1, 2 (March 1980), pp. 66–82.
P. M. Jackson, 'Fiscal Crisis and Parliamentary Democracy', in *British Politics in Perspective*, R. Borthwick and J. E. Spence (eds) (Leicester: Leicester University Press, 1982).
P. M. Jackson, *The Political Economy of Bureaucracy* (Oxford: Philip Allen, 1982).
H. Leibenstein, 'Allocative Efficiency vs *X*-Efficiency', *American Economic Review*, 56 (1966).
F. J. Lyden and E. G. Miller (eds), *Programme Planning and Budgeting: A Systems Approach to Management* (Chicago: Markham, 1968). An interesting collection of essays, many of which show the political aspects of budgeting.
J. P. Mackintosh, 'The House of Commons and Taxation', in B. Crick and W. A. Robson (eds), *Taxation Policy* (Harmondsworth: Penguin, 1972).
R. McKean, 'The Unseen Hand in Government', *American Economic Review* (June 1965).
W. A. Niskanen, *Bureaucracy: Servant or Master?* (London: Institute of Economic Affairs 1973). Introduces Niskanen's analysis of bureaucracy.
W. E. Oates, *Fiscal Federalism* (New York: Harcourt Brace Jovanovich, 1972).
C. Rowley, 'Efficiency in The Public Sector', Chapter 2 in E. Bowe (ed.), *Industrial Efficiency and the Role of Government* (London: Department of Industry HMSO, 1977).
C. Schultze, *The Politics and Economics of Public Spending* (Washington: The Brookings Institution, 1968).
H. Simon, *Administrative Behaviour* 2nd edn (New York: Free Press Collier Macmillan, 1965).
O. E. Williamson, *The Economics of Discretionary Behaviour: Managerial Objectives in a Theory of the Firm* (Englewood Cliffs, NJ: Prentice Hall, 1964).
M. Wright, 'Public Expenditure in Britain: The Crisis of Control', *Public Administration*, 55 (Summer 1977).
M. Wright, 'From Planning to Control: PESC in the 1970s' in M. Wright (ed.) *Public Spending Decisions: Growth and Restraint in the 1970s* (London: George Allen and Unwin, 1980).

Chapter 8

Cost Benefit Analysis is nowadays frequently taught as a separate course in universities and colleges. This Chapter has only managed to introduce the reader to the problems. The further reading will enable the reader to follow up many of the issues which have been raised.

General texts on CBA and government efficiency
E. Mishan, *Cost Benefit Analysis* (London: Unwin University Books, 1971).
D. W. Pearce, *Cost Benefit Analysis* (London: Macmillan, 1971).
A. Williams and R. Anderson, *Efficiency in the Social Services* (Oxford/London: Basil Blackwell/Martin Robertson, 1975).

CBA and project appraisal in economic development
Many of the foundations of CBA have been set out in the context of developing countries

A. C. Harberger, *Project Evaluation* (London: Macmillan, 1972).
I. M. D. Little and J. A. Mirrlees, *Project Appraisal and Planning for Developing Countries* (London: Heinemann, 1974).
L. Squire and H. G. van der Tak, *Economic Analysis of Projects* (Baltimore: World Bank Johns Hopkins University Press, 1975).
United Nations Industrial Development Organisation, *Guidelines for Project Evaluation* (New York: United Nations, 1972).

Readings, surveys and more advanced texts
R. Layard, *Cost Benefit Analysis* (Harmondsworth: Penguin 1972) provides an extremely interesting collection of readings from journal articles, etc. The introduction by Layard gives a useful summary and the questions at the end of the book are worth while trying.
R. A. Musgrave, 'Cost Benefit Analysis and The Theory of Public Finance', *Journal of Economic Literature* (September 1969).
A. R. Prest and R. Turvey, 'Cost Benefit Analysis a Survey', *Economic Journal* (December 1965).
K. J. Arrow and M. Kurz, *Public Investment The Rate of Return and Optimal Fiscal Policy* (Baltimore: Johns Hopkins Press, 1970).

Rate of interest
A useful discussion of the choice of rate of interest for discounting is found in two papers by Feldstein: see M. S. Feldstein, 'Financing in the Evaluations of Public Expenditure', in W. A. Smith and W. Culbertson (eds), *Essays in Honour of R. A. Musgrave* (Amsterdam: North Holland, 1976); also M. S. Feldstein, 'The Social Time Preference Discount Rate in Cost Benefit Analysis', *Economic Journal*, 74 (1964), pp. 360–79.

W. J. Baumol, 'On the Social Rate of Discount', *American Economic Review*, 58 (1968), pp. 788–802.
A. K. Sen, 'Isolation, Assurance and the Social Rate of Discount', *Quarterly Journal of Economics*, 81 (1967), pp. 112–24.

CBA uncertainty and risk
K. J. Arrow, 'Alternative Approaches to the Theory of Choice in Risk Taking Situations', *Econometrica* (October 1951).
K. J. Arrow, 'Uncertainty and the Welfare Economics of Medical Care', *American Economic Review*, 53 (December 1963), pp. 941–73.
K. J. Arrow and R. C. Lind, 'Uncertainty and The Evaluation of Public Investment Decisions', *American Economic Review*, 60 (1970), pp. 364–78.
F. Knight, *Risk, Uncertainty and Profit* (Boston/New York: Little Brown, 1921).
R. D. Luce and H. Raiffa, *Games and Decisions* (New York: Wiley, 1967).

Programme budgeting in the UK
HMSO, *Output Budgeting for the Department of Education and Science*, Education Planning Paper No. 1 (1970).

PPBS, ZBB, PAR and all that
T. H. Hammond and J. H. Knott, *A Zero Based Look at Zero Based Budgeting* (London: Transaction Books, 1980).

K. Hartley, 'Programme Budgeting and the Economics of Defence', *Public Administration* (Spring 1974), pp. 55-72.
G. J. Wasserman, 'Planning, Programming, Budgeting in the Police Service in England and Wales', *O and M Bulletin* (November 1970), pp. 27-37.
A. Williams, *Output Budgeting and the Contribution of Micro-economics to Efficiency in Government*, CAS Occasional Papers No. 4 (London: HMSO, 1967).

Critique and Counter-critique of the Rational Model
P. Self, 'Nonsense on Stilts: The Futility of Roskill', *New Society* (July 1970), also published in *Political Quarterly* (July 1970).
A. Wildavsky, 'Rescuing Policy Analysis from PPBS', *Public Administration Review*, XXIX, (March/April 1969).
A. Wildavsky, 'Does Planning Work?', *Public Interest* (1973).
A. Williams, 'Cost Benefit Analysis: Bastard Science? And/or Insidious Poison in the Body Politick?', in J. N. Wolfe (ed.) *Cost Benefit Analysis and Cost Effectiveness* (London: George Allen and Unwin, 1973).

Chapter 9

General Reading on Fiscal Federalism
(i)   W. E. Oates, *Fiscal Federalism* (New York: Harcourt Brace Jovanovich, 1972) (now a standard text on the subject).
(ii) J. Buchanan, 'Federalism and Fiscal Equity', *American Economic Review*, 40 (1950), pp. 583-99.
(iii) W. E. Oates (ed.), *Financing the New Federalism: Review Sharing Conditional Grants and Taxation* (Baltimore: Johns Hopkins Press, 1975) (this book contains an excellent treatment of the theoretical issues).
(iv) W. E. Oates (ed.), *The Political Economy of Fiscal Federalism* (Toronto: D. C. Heath & Co. Lexington Books, 1977) (an interesting mixture of theory and applied material drawn from a wide set of international perspectives).
(v)   N. Topham, 'Local Government Economics' in R. Millward, M. Sumner and G. Zis (eds), *Surveys in Economics*, The Public Sector (London: Longman, forthcoming).

Tiebout and decentralisation etc.
(i)   C. Tiebout, 'A Pure Theory of Local Expenditures', *Journal of Political Economy*, 64 (1956), pp. 416-24.
(ii)   J. Buchanan and C. Goetz, 'Efficiency Limits of Fiscal Mobility: An Assessment of the Tiebout Model', *Journal of Public Economics*, 1 (1972), pp. 25-44.
(iii) W. E. Oates, 'The Effects of Property Taxes and Local Public Spending on Property Values: An Empirical Study of Tax Capitalization and the Tiebout Hypothesis', *Journal of Political Economy*, 77, 6 (November/December 1969), pp. 957-71.
(iv)   W. E. Oates, 'The Effects of Property Taxes and Local Public Spending on Property Values: A Reply and Yet Further Results', *Journal of Political Economy*, 81, 4 (July/August, 1973), pp. 1004-8.
(v)   B. W. Hamilton, 'The Effects of Property Taxes and Local Public Spending on Property Values: A Theoretical Comment', *Journal of Political Economy*, 84, 3 (June 1976), pp. 647-50.
(vi)   P. Linneman, 'The Capitalization of Local Taxes: A Note on Specification', *Journal of Political Economy*, 86, 3 (June 1978), pp. 535-8.
(vii) R. M. Reinhard, 'Estimating Property Tax Capitalization a Further Comment', *Journal of Political Economy*, 89, 6 (December 1981), pp. 1251-60.
(viii) J. M. Buchanan and R. E. Wagner, 'An Efficiency Basis for Federal Fiscal Equalization', in J. Margolis (ed.), *The Analysis of Public Output* (Columbia University Press for the National Bureau of Economic Research, 1970).
(ix)   M. Edel and E. Sclar, 'Taxes, Spending and Property Values: Supply Adjustment in a Tiebout-Oates Model', *Journal of Political Economy*, 82 (1974), pp. 941-54.

Property tax
(i) H. J. Aaron, *Who Pays the Property Tax* (Washington: The Brookings Institution, 1975).
(ii) P. Mieszkowski, 'The Property Tax: An Excise Tax or a Profits Tax?' *Journal of Public Economics*, 1 (1972), pp. 73–96.
(iii) R. A. Musgrave, 'Is a Property Tax on Housing Regressive?' *American Economic Review*, 64 (1974), pp. 222–9.

Grants in Aid
In addition to Oates (1972, 1975, 1977) see also:

(i) J. A. Wilde, 'Grants-in-Aid: The Analysis of Design and Response', *National Tax Journal*, 24 (1971), pp. 143–56 (gives an excellent exposition of the theory).
(ii) E. M. Gramlich and H. Galper, 'State and Local Fiscal Behaviour and Federal Grant Policy', in *Brookings Papers on Economic Activity* (1973), pp. 15–58.
(iii) T. F. Pogue and L. G. Sgontz, 'The Effect of Grants-in-Aid on State Local Spending', *National Tax Journal* (June 1968).
(iv) R. P. Inman, 'Grants in a Metropolitan Economy – A Framework for Policy', in Oates (1975).
(v) J. Jackson, 'Politics and the Budgetary Process', *Social Science Research* (April 1972), pp. 35–60.

United Kingdom analysis
(i) C. D. Foster, R. A. Jackman and M. Perlman, *Local Government Finance in a Unitary System* (London: Allen and Unwin 1980) (a compendium of facts and analysis pertaining to the UK).
(ii) A. R. Prest, *Intergovernmental Financial Relations in the United Kingdom* (Centre for Federal Financial Relations: The Australian National University: Research Monograph, No. 23, 1978).
(iii) Layfield Report, *Local Government Finance*, Cmnd 6453 (London: HMSO, 1976) (an official enquiry into the workings of local government finance in the UK).
(iv) J. Le Grand 'Fiscal Equity and Central Government Grants to Local Authorities', *Economic Journal*, 85 (1976), pp. 531–47.
(v) Green Paper on *Alternatives to Domestic Rates*, Cmnd 8449 (London, HMSO, 1981) (provides useful information).

Chapter 10

Revenue Statistics of OECD Member Countries 1965-1980 (Paris: OECD, 1981).
D. Walker, 'The Direct/Indirect Tax Problem: Fifteen Years of Controversy', *Public Finance* (1955), pp. 153–76.

Chapter 11

C. V. Brown, *Taxation and the Incentive to Work* (Oxford: Oxford University Press, 1980).
C. V. Brown, E. Levin and D. T. Ulph, 'Inflation, Taxation and Income Distribution' in V. Halberstadt and A. J. Culyer (eds), *Public Economics and Human Resources* (Editions Cujas, 1977).
R. A. Musgrave, *The Theory of Public Finance* (New York: McGraw-Hill, 1959), especially Part Three.

Chapter 12

A. C. Harberger, 'The Incidence of the Corporation Income Tax', *Journal of Political Economy* (June 1962), pp. 215–40. The basic statement of the Harberger model. This paper, and several others both expounding the model and discussing its incidence, are reproduced in Harberger's *Taxation and Welfare* (Boston: Little, Brown, 1974). This collection of essays also includes the critique of Harberger's empirical work by Krzyaniak and Musgrave.

C. E. McClure and W. R. Thirsk, 'A Simplified Exposition of the Harberger model, I: Tax Incidence', *National Tax Journal* (March 1975), pp. 1–27. Contains an elaborate numerical example of the Harberger example which is based on Cobb–Douglas assumptions.

J. Shoven and J. Whalley, 'General Equilibrium with Taxes: A Computational Procedure and an Existence Proof', *Review of Economic Studies* (1973), pp. 465–89. A difficult technical paper that provides the theoretical background and explains the computational procedure.

Chapter 13

A. B. Atkinson, 'On the Measurement of Inequality', in A. B. Atkinson (ed.) *Wealth, Income and Inequality* 2nd edn (Oxford: Oxford University Press, 1980). Much of this paper is very mathematical but there is a 'Non-mathematical Summary' only four pages long.

D. T. Ulph, 'Labour Supply, Taxation and the Measurement of Inequality', in C. V. Brown (ed.) *Taxation and Labour Supply* (London: Allen & Unwin, 1981).

Chapter 14

R. I. G. Allen and D. Savage, 'Inflation and the Personal Income Tax', *National Institute Economic Review* (November, 1974), pp. 61–74.

J. S. Ashworth and D. T. Ulph, 'Endogeneity I: Estimating Labour Supply with Piecewise Linear Budget Constraints', in Brown (ed.) *op cit.* 1981.

N. A. Barr, S. R. James and A. R. Prest, *Self Assessment for Income Tax* (London: Heinemann, 1977).

M. J. Boskin, 'Efficiency Aspects of the Differential Tax Treatment of Market and Household Economic Activity', *Journal of Public Economics* (1975), pp. 1–25.

G. F. Break, 'Income Taxes and Incentives to Work: An Empirical Study', *American Economic Review* (September 1957).

C. V. Brown, *Taxation and Incentive to Work* (Oxford: Oxford University Press, 1980). A survey of the US and UK literature on taxation and labour supply originally written for the Commission of European Communities.

C. V. Brown (ed.), *Taxation and Labour Supply* (London: Allen & Unwin, 1981). A technical account of the Stirling study of taxation and labour supply of weekly paid workers in the UK.

C. V. Brown and E. Levin. 'The Effects of Income Taxation on Overtime: The Results of a National Survey', *Economic Journal* (December 1974).

C. V. Brown, E. Levin and D. T. Ulph, 'Estimates of Labour Hours Supplied by Married Male Workers in Great Britain', *Scottish Journal of Political Economy* (November 1976).

G. Burtless and J. Hausman, 'The Effect of Taxation on Labour Supply – Evaluating the Gary Negative Income Tax Experiment', *Journal of Political Economy* (1978).

G. G. Cain and H. W. Watts, *Income Maintenance and Labor Supply* (Chicago: Markham, 1973).

J. G. Dickinson, 'The Estimation of Income–Leisure Structures for Prime Aged Married Males', doctoral dissertation, University of Michigan, 1975.

M. S. Feldstein, 'Tax Incidence in a Growing Economy with Variable Factor Supply', *Quarterly Journal of Economics*, 88 (1974).

G. C. Fiegehen with W. B. Reddaway, *Companies, Incentives and Senior Managers* (London: Oxford University Press for Institute for Fiscal Studies, 1981).

D. B. Fields and W. T. Stanbury, 'Incentives, Disincentives and the Income Tax – Further Empirical Evidence', *Public Finance*, 3 (1970).

D. B. Fields and W. T. Stanbury, 'Income Taxes and Incentives to Work: Some Additional Empirical Evidence', *American Economic Review* (June 1971).

D. H. Holland, 'The Effect of Taxation on Effort: Some Results for Business Executives' in *The Proceedings of the Sixty-Second National Tax Conference* (September 1969).

D. H. Holland, 'The Effect of Taxation on Incentives in Higher Income Groups', in *Fiscal Policy and Labour Supply* (IFS, 1977).

M. R. Killinsworth, 'Neo-Classical Labor Supply Models: A Survey of Recent Literature on

Determinants of Labor Supply at the Micro Level', Fisk University, Nashville, Tenn., Mimeograph (1973).

M. H. Kosters, 'Effects of an Income Tax on Labor Supply', in A. C. Harberger and M. J. Bailey (eds), *The Taxation of Income from Capital* (Washington: Brookings Institution, 1969).

J. E. Meade (report of a Committee chaired by), *The Structure and Reform of Direct Taxation* (IFS, 1978).

P. K. Robins *et al.* (eds), *A Guaranteed Annual Income: Evidence from a Social Experiment* (New York: Academic Press, 1980).

Royal Commission on the Taxation of Profits and Income, *Second Report*, Cmnd 9105 (London: HMSO, 1954), Appendix 1.

R. J. Ruffell, 'Endogeneity II: Direct Estimation of Labour Supply Functions with Piecewise Linear Budget Constraints', in Brown (ed.) *op cit.* 1981.

H. C. Simons, 'The Comprehensive Definition of Income' (excerpt from H. C. Simons Personal Income Taxation) in R. W. Houghton (ed.), *Public Finance* (Harmondsworth: Penguin, 1970).

Appendix

Either W. H. Branson, *Macroeconomic Theory and Policy* (New York: Harper and Row, 1972) *or* W. H. Branson and J. M. Litvack, *Macroeconomics* (New York: Harper and Row, 1976).

These two books, which have nearly identical chapters on the labour market, contain the most satisfactory treatment of labour markets in macroeconomic textbooks.

Chapter 15

Brown *op cit.* 1980.

R. E. Hall, 'Effects of the Experimental Negative Income Tax on Labor Supply' in Pechman and Timpane (see below).

R. H. Haveman and H. W. Watts, 'Social Experimentation as Policy Research: A Review of Negative Income Tax Experiments' in V. Halberstadt and A. J. Culyer, *Public Economics and Human Resources* (Editions Cujas, 1977).

M. C. Keeley *et al.*, *The Labor Supply Effects of Alternative Negative Income Tax Programs: Evidence from the Seattle and Denver Income Maintenance Experiments Part I The Labour Supply Response Function* (Centre for the Study of Welfare Policy Stanford Research Institute. Research Memorandum 38 (1977)).

J. A. Pechman and P. M. Timpane (eds), *Work Incentives and Income Guarantees: The New Jersey Negative Income Tax Experiment* (Washington: Brookings Institution, 1975).

Chapter 16

A. B. Atkinson, *Unequal Shares* (London: Allen Lane, 1972).

J. S. Flemming and I. M. D. Little, *Why We Need a Wealth Tax* (London: Methuen, 1974).

C. D. Harbury and D. M. W. N. Hitchens, *Inheritance and Wealth Inequality in Britain* (London: George Allen & Unwin, 1979).

J. E. Meade (chairman), *The Structure and Reform of Direct Taxation* (IFS, 1978).

M. O'Higgins and P. Ruggles, 'The Distribution of Public Expenditure and Taxes among Households in the United Kingdom', *The Review of Income and Wealth*, Series 27, Number 3, September (1981).

Royal Commission on Distribution of Income and Wealth, *Report No. 5*, Cmnd 6999 (London: HMSO, 1977) and *No. 7*, Cmnd 7595 (London: HMSO, 1979).

C. T. Sandford, J. R. M. Willis, and D. J. Ironside, *An Annual Wealth Tax* (London: IFS Heinemann, 1975).

A. Sutherland, 'Capital Transfer Tax: an Obituary', *Fiscal Studies* (1981).

A. Williams, *Public Finance and Budgetary Policy* (London: Allen and Unwin, 1963).

Chapter 17

E. K. Browning, 'The Burden of Taxation', *Journal of Political Economy* (1978).
O. Brownlee and G. L. Perry, 'The Effects of the 1965 Federal Excise Tax Reductions on Prices', *National Tax Journal* (1967).
CSO, 'Effects of Taxes and Benefits on Household Income 1975', *Economic Trends* (December 1976). This is one of an annual series of articles of this subject.
S. Deverajan *et al.*, 'Estimating the Distribution of Tax Burdens', *Journal of Public Economics* (1980).
J. F. Due, 'The Effects of the 1954 Reduction of Federal Excise Taxes upon the First Prices of Electrical Appliances', *National Tax Journal* (1954).
M. Hamovitch, 'Tax Subsidy Policies for Regional Development', *National Tax Journal* (1966).
H. L. Johnson, 'Tax Pyramiding and the Manufacturers Excise Tax Reduction of 1954', *National Tax Journal* (1964).
P. Mieszkowski, 'Tax Incidence Theory', *Journal of Economic Literature* (1972).
O'Higgins and Ruggles, *op cit.*
J. A. Pechman and B. A. Okner, *Who Bears the Tax Burden?* (Washington: Brookings Institution, 1974).
C. Sandford *et al.*, *Costs and Benefits of VAT* (London: Heinemann Educational Books, 1981).
J. Whalley, 'A General Equilibrium Assessment of the 1973 United Kingdom Tax Reform', *Economica* (1975).
F. O. Woodward and H. Siegelman, 'Effects of the 1965 Federal Tax Reduction on the Prices of Automotive Replacement Parts', *National Tax Journal* (1967).

Chapter 18

G. F. Break, 'The Incidence and Economic Effects of Taxation' in A. S. Blinder *et al.*, *The Economics of Public Finance* (Washington: Brookings Institution, 1974).
E. D. Edwards and P. W. Bell, *The Theory and Measurement of Business Income* (Berkeley: University of California Press, 1967).
A. C. Harberger, *Taxation and Welfare* (Boston: Little, Brown, 1974).
J. A. Kay, 'Inflation Accounting – A Review Article', *Economic Journal* (June 1977).
G. A. Lee, *Modern Financial Accounting* 2nd edn (London: Thomas Nelson, 1975).
M. A. King, 'Taxation and the Cost of Capital', *Review of Economic Studies*, 41 (1974), pp. 21–35.
J. A. Pechman and B. A. Okner, *Who Bears the Tax Burden?* (Washington: Brookings Institution, 1974).
J. B. Shoven and J. Whalley, 'A General Equilibrium Calculation of the Effects of Differential Taxation of Income from Capital', in the US *Journal of Public Economics* (1972), pp. 281–321.
J. E. Stiglitz, 'Taxation, Corporate Financial Policy, and the Cost of Capital', *Journal of Public Economics* 2 (1973), pp. 1–34.
M. Summer, 'The Effect of Taxation on Corporate Saving and Investment' IFS Lecture Series No. 4, Institute of Fiscal Studies, 1976.
G. Whittington, 'Company Taxation and Dividends' IFS Lecture Series No. 1 Institute for Fiscal Studies, 1974.

Chapter 19

N. Kaldor, *An Expenditure Tax* (London: Allen & Unwin, 1955).
J. E. Meade (chairman), *The Structure and Reform of Direct Taxation* (London, IFS, 1978).
J. A. Pechman (ed.), *What Should be Taxed: Income or Expenditure?* (Washington: The Brookings Institution, 1980).
US Department of the Treasury, *Blue Prints for Basic Tax Reform* (Washington: Department of The Treasury, 1977).

Chapter 20

A. B. Atkinson, 'Optimal Taxation and the Direct versus Indirect Tax Controversy', *Canadian Journal of Economics* (November 1977), pp. 590–606. A useful, relatively non-technical survey of the optimal balance between taxes on goods and taxes on incomes.

A. B. Atkinson and J. E. Stiglitz, *Lectures on Public Economics* (London: McGraw-Hill, 1980). Chapters 12–14 contain an excellent, but technical, discussion of optimal taxation.

P. A. Diamond and J. A. Mirrlees, 'Optimal Taxation and Public Production' I–II. *American Economic Review* (1971), pp. 8–27, 261–78. One of two seminal papers published in 1971.

J. E. Meade (chairman), *The Structure and Reform of Direct Taxation* (London: IFS, 1978). Chapter 14 contains a non-technical discussion of the principles of optimum income taxation and their policy implications.

J. A. Mirrlees, 'An Exploration in the Theory of Optimum Income Taxation', *Review of Economic Studies* (1971), pp. 175–208. A seminal paper on optimum taxation.

J. A. Mirrlees, 'Labour Supply Behaviour and Optimal Taxes', in *Fiscal Policy and Labour Supply* (London: IFS, 1977).

F. P. Ramsay, 'A Contribution to the Theory of Taxation', *Economic Journal* (1927), pp. 47–61. A precurser of what is now termed optimal taxation.

A. Sandmo, 'Optimal Taxation: An Introduction to the Literature', *Journal of Public Economics* (1976), pp. 37–54. Despite some mathematics, this paper is largely accessible to the non-mathematician. Concerned primarily with commodity taxation.

J. K. Seade, 'On the Shape of Optimal Tax Schedules', *Journal of Public Economics* (1976), pp. 203–35. Perhaps the clearest non-technical account of the reasons for optimal tax structures having an upside-down U shape.

N. H. Stern, 'On the Specification of Models of Optimum Income Taxation', *Journal of Public Economics* (1976), pp. 123–62.

Chapter 21

A. Culyer, *The Economics of Social Policy* (London: Martin Robertson, 1973); see Chapter 3.

J. Le Grand, 'The Distribution of Public Expenditure: The Case of Health Care', *Economica* (1978).

J. Le Grand, *The Strategy of Equality: Redistribution and the Social Services* (London: George Allen and Unwin, 1982).

C. E. McLure, 'The Theory of Expenditure Incidence', *Finanzarchiv* (1972), pp. 432–53.

C. E. McLure, W. R. Thirsk and R. Klein, 'A Simplified Exposition of the Harberger Model II: Expenditure Incidence', *National Tax Journal*, 28 (1975), pp. 195–207.

R. A. Musgrave, 'Adam Smith on Public Finance and Distribution', in T. Wilson and A. S. Skinner (eds), *The Market and the State: Essays in Honour of Adam Smith* (Oxford: University Press, 1976). See also the comments by A. R. Prest and A. B. Atkinson in the same volume.

M. O'Higgins, 'The Distributive Effects of Public Expenditure and Taxation: An Agnostic View of the CSO Analysis' in C. Sandford, C. Pond and R. Waler (eds), *Taxation and Social Policy* (London: Heinemann, 1980).

A. T. Peacock, 'Government Expenditure in Studies of Income Distribution', in W. L. Smith and J. M. Culbertson (eds), *Public Finance and Stabilization Policy: Essays in Honour of R. Musgrave* (Amsterdam: North Holland, 1974).

A. T. Peacock and R. Shannon, 'The Welfare State and the Redistribution of Income', *Westminster Bank Review* (August 1968).

P. Ruggles and M. O'Higgins, 'The Distribution of Government Expenditures Among Households in the United Kingdom', *Review of Income and Wealth* (1981).

P. Willmott, *Sharing Inflation? Poverty Report 1976* (London: Billing and Sons, 1976).

Index of Names

491

Index of Subjects

495